THE ANALOGY OF RELIGION,

NATURAL AND REVEALED

TO THE

CONSTITUTION AND COURSE OF NATURE.

TO WHICH ARE ADDED,

TWO BRIEF DISSERTATIONS:

I. ON PERSONAL IDENTITY.—II. ON THE NATURE OF VIRTUE.

BY

JOSEPH BUTLER, D.C.L.

LATE LORD BISHOP OF DURHAM.

Ejus [Analogiæ] hæc vis est, ut id quod dubium est ad aliquid simile, de quo non quæritur, referat ut incerta certis probet.—Quintil. l. i. c. 6.

WITH

AN ACCOUNT OF THE CHARACTER AND WRITINGS OF THE AUTHOR,

BY SAMUEL HALIFAX, D.D.

LATE LORD BISHOP OF GLOUCESTER.

NEW YORK:

ROBERT CARTER & BROTHERS,

No. 530 BROADWAY.

TO

THE REVEREND

DR THOMAS BALGUY,

ARCHDEACON AND PREBENDARY OF WINCHESTER, &c.

Dear Sir,

I trust you will excuse the liberty I have taken of prefixing your name to the following sheets; the latter part of which, I am confident, will not be thought undeserving of your approbation; and of the former part you will commend the intention at least, if not the execution. In vindicating the character of Bishop Butler from the aspersions thrown upon it since his death, I have but discharged a common duty of humanity, which survivors owe to those who have deserved well of mankind by their lives or writings, when they are past the power of appearing in their own defence. And if what I have added, by way of opening the general design of the Works of this great Prelate, be of use in exciting the younger class of Students in our Universities to read, and so to read as to understand, the Two Volumes prepared and published by the Author himself; I flatter myself I shall have done no inconsiderable service to Morality and Religion. Your time and studies have been long successfully devoted to the support of the same great cause: and in what you have lately given to the world, both as an Author and an Editor, you have largely contributed to the defence of our common Christianity, and of what was esteemed by One, who was perfectly competent to judge, its best Establishment, the Church of England. In the present publication I consider myself

CONTENTS.

PART I.

OF NATURAL RELIGION.

PART II.

OF REVEALED RELIGION.

CONTENTS.

ADVERTISEMENT

PREFIXED TO THE FIRST EDITION.

If the reader should meet here with any thing which he had not before attended to, it will not be in the observations upon the constitution and course of nature, these being all obvious; but in the application of them: in which, though there is nothing but what appears to me of some real weight, and therefore of great importance; yet he will observe several things, which will appear to him of very little, if he can think things to be of little importance, which are of any real weight at all, upon such a subject as religion. However, the proper force of the following Treatise lies in the whole general analogy considered together.

It is come, I know not how, to be taken for granted, by many persons, that Christianity is not so much as a subject of inquiry; but that it is, now at length, discovered to be fictitious. And accordingly they treat it, as if, in the present age, this were an agreed point among all people of discernment; and nothing remained, but to set it up as a principal subject of mirth and ridicule, as it were by way of reprisals, for its having so long interrupted the pleasures of the world. On the contrary, thus much, at least, will be here found, not taken for granted, but proved, that any reasonable man, who will thoroughly consider the matter, may be as much assured, as he is of his own being, that it is not, however, so clear a case, that there is nothing in it. There is, I think, strong evidence of its truth; but it is certain no one can, upon principles of reason, be satisfied of the contrary. And the practical consequence to be drawn from this is not attended to by every one who is concerned in it.

May, 1736.

as a fellow labourer with you in the same design, and tracing the path you have trod before, but at great distance, and with unequal paces. When, by His Majesty's goodness, I was raised to that station of eminence in the Church, to which you had been first named, and which, on account of the infirmity of your health, you had desired to decline; it was honour enough for me on such an occasion to have been thought of next to you: and I know of no better rule by which to govern my conduct, so as not to discredit the Royal Hand which conferred on me so signal and unmerited a favour, than in cases of difficulty to put the question to myself, How you would probably have acted in the same situation. You see, Sir, I still look up to you, as I have been wont, both as my Superior and my Example. That I may long reap the benefit of your advice and friendship; and that such a measure of health and strength may be continued to you, as may enable you to pass the evening of your days with comfort, and enjoy the blessings of the life you love; is the cordial wish of,

Dear Sir,

Your very affectionate

and faithful Servant,

S. GLOUCESTER

Dartmouth Street, Westminster

12th May, 1780

PREFACE BY THE EDITOR

"When I consider how light a matter very often subjects the best established characters to the suspicions of posterity, posterity often as malignant to virtue as the age that saw it was envious of its glory; and how ready a remote age is to catch at a low revived slander, which the times that brought it forth saw despised and forgotten almost in its birth; I cannot but think it a matter that deserves attention."—*Letter to the Editor of the Letters on the Spirit of Patriotism*, &c., by Bishop Warburton. See his Works, vol. vii. p. 547.

The Charge to the Clergy of the Diocese of Durham was printed and published in the year 1751, by the learned Prelate whose name it bears; and, together with the Sermons and Analogy of the same writer, both too well known to need a more particular description, completes the collection of his Works. It has long been considered as a matter of curiosity, on account of its scarceness; and it is equally curious on other accounts—its subject, and the calumny to which it gave occasion, of representing the Author as *addicted to superstition*, as *inclined to popery*, and as *dying in the communion of the Church of Rome*. The improved edition of the *Biographia Britannica*, published under the care of Dr Kippis, having unavoidably brought this calumny again into notice, it may not be unseasonable to offer a few reflections in this place, by way of obviating any impressions that may hence arise to the disadvantage of so great a character as that of the late Bishop Butler; referring those who desire a more particular account of his life, to the third volume of the same entertaining work, printed in 1784, art. Butler (Josepn).*

I. The principal design of the Bishop in his Charge is, to exhort his Clergy to "do their part towards reviving a practical sense of religion amongst the people committed to their care;" and, as one way of effecting this, to "instruct them in the *Importance of External Religion*," or the usefulness of outward observances in promoting inward piety. Now, from the compound

* The account here alluded to is subjoined to this Preface.

nature of man, consisting of two parts, the body and the mind, together with the influence which these are found to have on one another, it follows, that the religious regards of such a creature ought to be so framed, as to be in some way properly accommodated to both. A religion which is purely spiritual, stripped of every thing that may affect the senses, and considered only as a divine philosophy of the mind, if it do not mount up into enthusiasm, as has frequently been the case, often sinks, after a few short fervours, into indifference: an abstracted invisible object, like that which natural religion offers, ceases to move or interest the heart; and something further is wanting to bring it nearer, and render it more present to our view, than merely an intellectual contemplation. On the other hand, when, in order to remedy this inconvenience, recourse is had to instituted forms and ritual injunctions, there is always danger lest men be tempted to rest entirely on these, and persuade themselves that a painful attention to such observances will atone for the want of genuine piety and virtue. Yet surely there is a way of steering safely between these two extremes; of so consulting both the parts of our constitution, that the body and the mind may concur in rendering our religious services acceptable to God, and at the same time useful to ourselves. And what way can this be, but precisely that which is recommended in the Charge; such a cultivation of outward as well as inward religion, that from both may result, what is the point chiefly to be laboured, and at all events to be secured, a correspondent temper and behaviour; or, in other words, such an application of the forms of godliness, as may be subservient in promoting the power and spirit of it? No man, who believes the Scriptures of the Old and New Testament, and understands what he believes, but must know, that external religion is as much enjoined, and constitutes as real a part of revelation, as that which is internal. The many ceremonies in use among the Jews, in consequence of a divine command; the baptism of water, as an emblem of moral purity; the eating and drinking of bread and wine, as symbols and representations of the body and blood of Christ, required of Christians, are proofs of this. On comparing these two parts of religion together, one, it is immediately seen, is of much greater importance than the other; and, whenever they happen to interfere, is always to be preferred: but does it follow from hence, that therefore that other is of little or no importance, and, in cases where there is no competition, may entirely be neglected? Or rather is not the legitimate conclusion directly the reverse, that nothing is to be looked upon as of little importance, which is of any use at all in preserving upon our minds a sense of the Divine authority, which recalls to our remembrance the obligations we are under, and helps to keep us, as the Scripture expresses it, "in the fear of the Lord all the day long?"* If, to adopt the instance mentioned in the Charge, the sight of a church should remind a man of some sentiment of piety; if, from the view of a material building dedicated to the service of God, he should be led to regard himself, his own body, as a living "temple of the Holy Ghost,"† and therefore no more than the other to be profaned or desecrated by any thing that defileth or is impure; could it be truly said of such a one, that he was superstitious, or mistook the means of religion for the end? If, to use another, and what has been thought a more obnoxious instance, taken from the Bishop's practice, a cross, erected in a place of public worship,‡ should cause us to reflect on Him who died on a cross for our salvation, and on the necessity of our "own dying to sin,"§ and of "crucifying the flesh with its affection and lusts;"‖ would any worse consequences follow from such sentiments so excited, than if the same sentiments had been excited by the view of a picture, of the crucifixion suppose, such as is commonly placed, and with this very design, in foreign churches, and indeed in many of our own? Both the instances here adduced, it is very possible, may be

* Prov. xxiii. 17. † 1 Cor. vi. 19.

‡ Dr Butler, when Bishop of Bristol, put up a cross, a plain piece of marble inlaid, in the chapel of his episcopal house. This, which was intended by the blameless Prelate merely as a sign or memorial, that true Christians are to bear their cross, and not to be ashamed of following a crucified Master, was considered as affording a presumption that he was secretly inclined to Popish forms and ceremonies, and had no great dislike to Popery itself. And, on account of the offence it occasioned, both at the time and since, it were to be wished, in prudence, it had not been done.

§ Rom. vi. 11. ‖ Gal. v. 24.

far from being approved, even by those who are under the most sincere convictions of the importance of true religion: and it is easy to conceive how open to scorn and censure they must be from others, who think they have a talent for ridicule, and have accustomed themselves to regard all pretensions to piety as hypocritical or superstitious. But "Wisdom is justified of her children."* Religion is what it is, "whether men will hear, or whether they will forbear;"† and whatever in the smallest degree promotes its interests, and assists us in performing its commands, whether that assistance be derived from the medium of the body or the mind, ought to be esteemed of great weight, and deserving of our most serious attention.

However, be the danger of superstition what it may, no one was more sensible of that danger, or more in earnest in maintaining, that external acts of themselves are nothing, and that moral holiness, as distinguished from bodily observances of every kind, is that which constitutes the essence of religion, than Bishop Butler. Not only the Charge itself, the whole intention of which is plainly nothing more than to enforce the necessity of *practical religion*, the reality as well as form, is a demonstration of this, but many passages besides to the same purpose, selected from his other writings. Take the two following as specimens. In his Analogy he observes thus: "Though mankind have, in all ages, been greatly prone to place their religion in peculiar positive rites, by way of equivalent for obedience to moral precepts; yet, without making any comparison at all between them, and consequently without determining which is to have the preference, the nature of the thing abundantly shows all notions of that kind to be utterly subversive of true religion: as they are, moreover, contrary to the whole tenor of Scripture; and likewise to the most express particular declarations of it, that nothing can render us accepted of God, without moral virtue."‡ And to the same purpose in his Sermon, preached before the Society for the Propagation of the Gospel, in February, 1738–9. "Indeed, amongst crea-

* Matt. xi 19. † Ezek. ii. 5 ‡ Analogy, Part II. Chap. i

tures naturally formed for religion, yet so much under the power of imagination as men are, superstition is an evil, which can never be out of sight. But even against this, true religion is a great security, and the only one. True religion takes up that place in the mind, which superstition would usurp, and so leaves little room for it; and likewise lays us under the strongest obligations to oppose it. On the contrary, the danger of superstition cannot but be increased by the prevalence of irreligion; and, by its general prevalence, the evil will be unavoidable. For the common people, wanting a religion, will of course take up with almost any superstition which is thrown in their way: and in process of time, amidst the infinite vicissitudes of the political world, the leaders of parties will certainly be able to serve themselves of that superstition, whatever it be, which is getting ground; and will not fail to carry it to the utmost length their occasions require. The general nature of the thing shows this; and history and fact confirm it. It is therefore wonderful, those people who seem to think there is but one evil in life, that of superstition, should not see that atheism and profaneness must be the introduction of it."*

He who can think and write in such a manner, can never be said to mistake the nature of real religion: and he, who, after such proofs to the contrary, can persist in asserting of so discreet and learned a person, that he was *addicted to superstition,* must himself be much a stranger both to truth and charity.

And here it may be worth our while to observe, that the same excellent Prelate, who by one set of men was suspected of *superstition,* on account of his Charge, has by another been represented as leaning to the opposite extreme of *enthusiasm,* on account of his two discourses *On the Love of God.* But both opinions are equally without foundation. He was neither superstitious, nor an enthusiast: his mind was much too strong, and his habits of thinking and reasoning much too strict and severe, to suffer him to descend to the weaknesses of either character. His piety was at once fervent and rational.

* Ser. xvi.

When impressed with a generous concern for the declining cause of religion, he laboured to revive its dying interests; nothing he judged would be more effectual to that end, among creatures so much engaged with bodily things, and so apt to be affected with whatever strongly solicits the senses, as men are, than a religion of such a frame as should in its exercise require the joint exertions of the body and the mind. On the other hand, when penetrated with the dignity and importance of "the first and great commandment,"* love to God, he set himself to inquire, what those movements of the heart are, which are due to Him, the Author and Cause of all things; he found, in the coolest way of consideration, that God is the natural object of the *same* affections of gratitude, reverence, fear, desire of approbation, trust, and dependence, the same affections in *kind*, though doubtless in a very disproportionate *degree*, which any one would feel from contemplating a perfect character in a creature, in which goodness, with wisdom and power, are supposed to be the predominant qualities, with the further circumstance, that this creature was also his governor and friend. This subject is manifestly a real one; there is nothing in it fanciful or unreasonable: this way of being affected towards God is piety, in the strictest sense: this is religion, considered as a habit of mind; a religion, suited to the nature and condition of man.†

II. From superstition to *Popery*, the transition is easy: no wonder then, that, in the progress of detraction, the simple imputation of the former of these, with which the attack on the character of our Author was opened, should be followed by the more aggravated imputation of the latter. Nothing, I think, can fairly be gathered in support of such a suggestion from the Charge, in which Popery is barely mentioned, and occasionally

* Matt. xxii. 38.

† Many of the sentiments, in these Two Discourses of Bishop Butler, containing the sovereign good of man; the impossibility of procuring it in the present life; the unsatisfactoriness of earthly enjoyments; together with the somewhat beyond and above them all, which once attained, there will rest nothing further to be wished or hoped; and which is then only to be expected, when we shall have put off this mortal body, and our union with God shall be complete; occur in *Hooker's Ecclesiastical Polity*. Book I. §. 11.

only, and in a sentence or two; yet even there, it should be remarked, the Bishop takes care to describe the peculiar observances required by it, "some as in themselves wrong and superstitious, and others of them as being made subservient to the purposes of superstition." With respect to his other writings, any one at all conversant with them needs not to be told, that the matters treated of both in his Sermons and his Analogy did none of them directly lead him to consider, and much less to combat, the opinions, whether relating to faith or worship, which are peculiar to the Church of Rome: it might therefore have happened, yet without any just conclusion arising from thence, of being himself inclined to favour those opinions, that he had never mentioned, so much as incidentally, the subject of Popery at all. But fortunately for the reputation of the Bishop, and to the eternal disgrace of his calumniators, even this poor resource is wanting to support their malevolence. In his Sermon at St Bride's before the Lord Mayor in 1740, after having said that "our laws and whole constitution go more upon supposition of an equality amongst mankind, than the constitution and laws of other countries;" he goes on to observe, that "this plainly requires, that more particular regard should be had to the education of the lower people here, than in places where they are born slaves of power, and to be made *slaves of superstition:** meaning evidently in this place, by the general term superstition, the particular errors of the Romanists. This is something: but we have a still plainer indication what his sentiments concerning Popery really were, from another of his additional Sermons, I mean that before the House of Lords on June the 11th, 1747, the anniversary of his late Majesty's accession. The passage alluded to is as follows; and my readers will not be displeased that I give it them at length. "The value of our religious Establishment ought to be very much heightened in our esteem, by considering what it is a security from; I mean that great corruption of Christianity, Popery, which is ever hard at work to bring us again under its yoke. Whoever will consider the Po-

* Serm. xvii.

pish claims, to the disposal of the whole earth, as of divine right, to dispense with the most sacred engagements, the claims to supreme absolute authority in religion; in short, the general claims which the Canonists express by the words, *plenitude of power*—whoever, I say, will consider Popery as it is professed at Rome, may see, that it is manifest, open usurpation of all human and divine authority. But even in those Roman Catholic countries where these monstrous claims are not admitted, and the civil power does, in many respects, restrain the papal; yet persecution is professed, as it is absolutely enjoined by what is acknowledged to be their highest authority, a general council, so called, with the Pope at the head of it; and is practised in all of them, I think, without exception, where it can be done safely. Thus they go on to substitute force instead of argument; and external profession made by force, instead of reasonable conviction. And thus corruptions of the grossest sort have been in vogue, for many generations, in many parts of Christendom; and are so still, even where Popery obtains in its least absurd form: and their antiquity and wide extent are insisted upon as proofs of their truth; a kind of proof, which at best can only be presumptive, but which loses all its little weight, in proportion as the long and large prevalence of such corruptions have been obtained by force."* In another part of the same Sermon, where he is again speaking of our ecclesiastical constitution, he reminds his audience that it is to be valued, "not because it leaves us at liberty to have as little religion as we please, without being accountable to human judicatories; but because it exhibits to our view, and enforces upon our consciences, genuine Christianity, free from the superstitions with which it is defiled in other countries; which superstitions, he observes, "naturally tend to abate its force." The date of this Sermon should here be attended to. It was preached in June, 1747; that is, four years before the delivery and publication of the Charge, which was in the year 1751; and exactly five years before the Author died, which was in June, 1752. We

* Serm. xx.

have then, in the passages now laid before the reader, a clear and unequivocal proof, brought down to within a few years of Bishop Butler's death, that Popery was held by him in the utmost abhorrence, and that he regarded it in no other light, than as *the great corruption of Christianity*, and a *manifest, open usurpation of all human and divine authority*. The argument is decisive; nor will any thing be of force to invalidate it, unless from some *after-act* during the short remainder of the Bishop's life, *besides* that of delivering and printing his Charge (which, after what I have said here, and in the Notes added to this Preface and to the Charge I must have leave to consider as affording no evidence at all of his inclination to Papistical doctrines or ceremonies), the contrary shall incontrovertibly appear.

III. One such after-act, however, has been alleged, which would effectually demolish all that we have urged in behalf of our Prelate, were it true, as is pretended, that he *died in the communion of the Church of Rome*. Had a story of this sort been invented and propagated by Papists, the wonder might have been less:

Hoc Ithacus velit, et magno mercentur Atridæ.

But to the reproach of Protestantism, the fabrication of this calumny, for such we shall find it, originated from among ourselves. It is pretty remarkable, that a circumstance so extraordinary should never have been divulged till the year 1767, fifteen years after the Bishop's decease. At that time Dr Thomas Secker was Archbishop of Canterbury; who of all others was the most likely to know the truth or falsehood of the fact asserted, having been educated with our Author in his early youth, and having lived in a constant habit of intimacy with him to the very time of his death. The good Archbishop was not silent on this occasion: with a virtuous indignation he stood forth to protect the posthumous character of his friend; and in a public newspaper, under the signature of *Misopseudes*, called upon his accuser to support what he had advanced, by whatever proofs he could. No proof, however, nor any thing like a proof, appeared in reply; and every man of sense and candour at that time was perfectly convinced the assertion was entirely groundless.* As a further confirmation of the rectitude

* When the first edition of this Preface was published, I had in vain endeavoured to procure a sight of the papers, in which Bishop Butler was accused of having died a Papist, and Archbishop Secker's replies to them; though I well remembered to have read both, when they first appeared in the public prints. But a learned Professor in the University of Oxford has furnished me with the whole controversy in its original form; a brief history of which it may not be unacceptable to offer here to the curious reader.

The attack was opened in the year 1767, in an anonymous pamphlet, entitled, "The Root of Protestant Errors examined;" in which the author asserted, that, "by an anecdote lately given him, that same Prelate" (who at the bottom of the page is called B—p of D—m) "is said to have died in the communion of a Church, that makes much use of saints, saints' days, and all the trumpery of saint worship." When this remarkable fact, now first divulged, came to be generally known, it occasioned, as might be expected, no little alarm; and intelligence of it was no sooner conveyed to Archbishop Secker, than in a short letter, signed *Misopseudes*, and printed in the St James's Chronicle of May 9, he called upon the writer to produce his authority for publishing "so gross and scandalous a falsehood." To this challenge an immediate answer was returned by the author of the pamphlet, who, now assuming the name of *Phileleutheros*, informed *Misopseudes*, through the channel of the same paper, that "such anecdote had been given him; and that he was yet of opinion, that there was nothing improbable in it, when it is considered that the same Prelate put up the Popish *insignia* of the *cross* in his chapel, when at Bristol; and in his last Episcopal Charge has squinted very much towards that superstition." Here we find the accusation not only repeated, but supported by reasons, such as they are, of which it seemed necessary that some notice should be taken: nor did the Archbishop conceive it unbecoming his own dignity to stand up on this occasion, as the vindicator of innocence against the calumniator of the helpless dead. Accordingly, in a second letter in the same newspaper of May 23, and subscribed *Misopseudes* as before; after reciting from Bishop Butler's Sermon before the Lords the very passage here printed in the Preface, and observing, that "there are, in the same Sermon, declarations as strong as can be made against temporal punishments for heresy, schism, or even for idolatry;" his Grace expresses himself thus: "Now he (Bishop Butler) was universally esteemed throughout his life, a man of strict piety and honesty, as well as uncommon abilities. He gave all the proofs, public and private, which his station led him to give, and they were decisive and daily, of his continuing to the last a sincere member of the Church of England. Nor had ever any of his acquaintance, or most intimate friends, nor have they to this day, the least doubt of it." As to putting up a *cross* in his chapel, the Archbishop frankly owns, that for himself he wishes he had not; and thinks that in so doing the Bishop did amiss. But then he asks, "Can that be opposed, as any proof of Popery, to all the evidence on the other side; or even to the single evidence of the above-mentioned Sermon? Most of our churches have crosses upon them: are they therefore Popish churches? The Lutherans have more than crosses in theirs: are the Lutherans therefore Papists?" And as to the Charge, no Papist, his Grace remarks, would have spoken as Bishop Butler there does, of the observances peculiar to Roman Catholics, some of which he expressly censures as wrong and superstitious, and others, as made subservient to the purposes of superstition, and, on these accounts, abolished at the Reformation. After the publication of this letter *Phileleutheros* replied in a short defence of his own conduct, but without producing any thing new in confirmation of what he had advanced. And here the controversy, so far as the two principals were concerned, seems to have ended.

But the dispute was not suffered to die away quite so soon. For in the same year and in the same newspaper of July 21, another letter appeared; in which the author not only contended that the cross in the Episcopal chapel at Bristol, and the Charge to the Clergy of Durham in 1751, amount to full proof of a strong attachment to the idolatrous communion of the Church of Rome, but, with the reader's leave, he would fain account for the Bishop's "tendency this way." And this he attempted to do, "from the natural melancholy and gloominess of Dr Butler's disposition; from his great fondness for the lives of Romish saints, and their books of mystic piety; from his drawing his notions of teaching men religion, not from the New Testament, but

of this judgment, it may not be amiss to mention, there is yet in existence a strong *presumptive* argument at least in its favour, drawn from the testimony of those who attended our Author in the sickness of which he died. The last days of this excellent Prelate were passed at Bath; Dr Nathanael Forster, his chaplain, being continually with him; and for one day, and at the very end of his illness, Dr Martin Benson also, the then Bishop of Gloucester, who shortened his own life in his pious haste to visit his dying friend. Both these persons constantly wrote letters to Dr Secker, then Bishop of Oxford, containing accounts of Bishop Butler's declining health, and of the symptoms and progress of his disorder, which, as was conjectured, soon terminated in his death.

from philosophical and political opinions of his own; and above all, from his transition from a strict Dissenter amongst the Presbyterians to a rigid Churchman, and his sudden and unexpected elevation to great wealth and dignity in the Church." The attack, thus renewed, excited the Archbishop's attention a second time, and drew from him a fresh answer, subscribed also *Misopseudes*, in the St James's Chronicle of August 4. In this letter, our excellent Metropolitan, first of all obliquely hinting at the unfairness of sitting in judgment on the character of a man who had been dead fifteen years; and then reminding his correspondent, that "full proof had been already published, that Bishop Butler abhorred Popery as a vile corruption of Christianity, and that it might be proved, if needful, that he held the Pope to be Antichrist;" (to which decisive testimonies of undoubted aversion from the Romish Church, another is also added in the Postscript, his taking, when promoted to the see of Durham, for his domestic Chaplain, Dr Nath. Forster, who had published, not four years before, a Sermon, entitled, Popery destructive of the Evidence of Christianity;) proceeds to observe, "that the natural melancholy of the Bishop's temper would rather have fixed him amongst his first friends, than prompted him to the change he made: that he read books of all sorts, as well as books of mystic piety, and knew how to pick the good that was in them out of the bad: that his opinions were exposed without reserve in his Analogy and his Sermons, and if the doctrine of either be Popish or unscriptural, the learned world hath mistaken strangely in admiring both: that, instead of being a strict Dissenter, he never was a communicant in any Dissenting assembly; on the contrary, that he went occasionally, from his early years, to the established worship, and became a constant conformist to it when he was barely of age, and entered himself, in 1714, of Oriel College: that his elevation to great dignity in the Church, far from being sudden and unexpected, was a gradual and natural rise, through a variety of preferments, and a period of thirty-two years: that, as Bishop of Durham, he had very little authority beyond his brethren, and in ecclesiastical matters, had none beyond them; a larger income than most of them he had; but this he employed, not, as was insinuated, in augmenting the pomp of worship in his cathedral, where indeed it is no greater than in others, but for the purposes of charity, and in the repairing of his houses." After these remarks, the letter closes with the following words: "Upon the whole, few accusations, so entirely groundless, have been so pertinaciously, I am unwilling to say maliciously, carried on, as the present: and surely it is high time for the authors and abettors of it, in mere common prudence, to show some regard, if not to truth, at least to shame."

It only remains to be mentioned, that the above letters of Archbishop Secker had such an effect on a writer, who signed himself in the St James's Chronicle of August 25, *A Dissenting Minister*, that he declared it as his opinion, that "the author of the pamphlet, called, 'The Root of Protestant Errors examined,' and his friends, were obliged in candour, in justice, and in honour to retract their charge, unless they could establish it on much better grounds than had hitherto appeared:" and he ex

These letters, which are still preserved in the Lambeth library,* I have read; and not the slenderest argument can be collected from them, in justification of the ridiculous slander we are here considering. If at that awful season the Bishop was not known to have expressed any opinion tending to show his *dislike* to Popery, neither was he known to have said any thing, that could at all be construed in *approbation* of it; and the natural presumption is that whatever sentiments he had formerly entertained concerning that corrupt system of religion, he continued to entertain them to the last. The truth is, neither the word nor the idea of Popery seems once to have occurred either to the Bishop himself, or to those who watched his parting moments: their thoughts were otherwise engaged. His disorder had reduced him to such debility, as to render him incapable of speaking much or long on any subject: the few bright intervals that occurred were passed in a state of the utmost tranquillity and composure; and in that composure he expired. "Mark the perfect man, and behold the upright: for the end of that man is peace."† "Let me die the death of the righteous, and let my last end be like his!"‡

Out of pure respect for the virtues of a man, whom I

pressed his "hopes, that it would be understood that the Dissenters in general had no hand in the accusation, and that it had only been the act of two or three mistaken men." Another person also, "a foreigner by birth," as he says of himself, who had been long an admirer of Bishop Butler, and had perused with great attention all that had been written on both sides in the present controversy, confesses he had been "wonderfully pleased with observing, with what candour and temper, as well as clearness and solidity, he was vindicated from the aspersions laid against him." All the adversaries of our Prelate, however, had not the virtue or sense to be thus convinced; some of whom still continued, under the signatures of *Old Martin*, *Latimer*, *An Impartial Protestant*, *Paulinus*, *Misonothos*, to repeat their confuted falsehoods in the public prints; as if the curse of calumniators had fallen upon them, and their memory, by being long a traitor to truth, had taken at last a severe revenge, and compelled them to credit their own lie. The first of these gentlemen, *Old Martin*, who dates from Newcastle, May 29, from the rancour and malignity with which his letter abounds, and from the particular virulence he discovers towards the characters of Bishop Butler and his defender, I conjecture to be no other than the very person who had already figured in this dispute, so early as the year 1752; of whose work, entitled, "A Serious Inquiry into the Use and Importance of External Religion," the reader will find some account in the notes subjoined to the Bishop's Charge in the volume of Sermons.

* The letters, with a sight of which I was indulged by the favour of our present most worthy Metropolitan, are all, as I remember, wrapped together under one cover; on the back of which is written, in Archbishop Secker's own hand, the following words, or words to this effect: "Presumptive Arguments that Bishop Butler did not die a Papist."

† Psalm xxxvii. 37. ‡ Numb. xxiii. 10.

had never the happiness of knowing, or even of seeing, but from whose writings I have received the greatest benefit and illumination, and which I have reason to be thankful to Providence for having early thrown in my way, I have adventured, in what I have now offered to the public, to step forth in his defence, and to vindicate his honest fame from the attacks of those, who, with the vain hope of bringing down superior characters to their own level, are for ever at work in detracting from their just praise. For the literary reputation of Bishop Butler, it stands too high in the opinion of the world, to incur the danger of any diminution: but this in truth is the least of his excellences. He was more than a good writer, he was a good man; and what is an addition even to this eulogy, he was a sincere Christian. His whole study was directed to the knowledge and practice of sound morality and true religion: these he adorned by his life, and has recommended to future ages in his writings; in which, if my judgment be of any avail, he has done essential service to both, as much, perhaps, as any single person, since the extraordinary gifts of "the word of wisdom and the word of knowledge"* have been withdrawn.

In what follows I propose to give a short account of the Bishop's *moral and religious systems,* as these are collected from his Works.

I. His way of treating the subject of *morals* is to be gathered from the volume of his Sermons, and particularly from the three first, and from the preface to that volume.

"There is," as our Author with singular sagacity has observed, "a much more exact correspondence between the natural and moral world, than we are apt to take notice of."† The inward frame of man answers to his outward condition; the several propensities, passions, and affections, implanted in our hearts by the Author of nature, are in a peculiar manner adapted to the circumstances of life in which he hath placed us. This general observation, properly pursued, leads to several im-

* 1 Cor. xii. 8. † Serm. vi.

portant conclusions. The original internal constitution of man, compared with his external condition, enables us to discern what course of action and behaviour that constitution leads to, what is our duty respecting that condition, and furnishes us besides with the most powerful arguments to the practice of it.

What the inward frame and constitution of man is, is a question of fact; to be determined, as other facts are, from experience, from our internal feelings and external senses, and from the testimony of others. Whether human nature, and the circumstances in which it is placed, might not have been ordered otherwise, is foreign to our inquiry, and none of our concern: our province is, taking both of these as they are, and viewing the connexion between them, from that connexion to discover if we can, what course of action is fitted to that nature and those circumstances. From contemplating the bodily senses, and the organs or instruments adapted to them, we learn that the eye was given to see with, the ear to hear with. In like manner, from considering our inward perceptions and the final causes of them, we collect that the feeling of shame, for instance, was given to prevent the doing of things shameful; compassion, to carry us to relieve others in distress; anger, to resist sudden violence offered to ourselves. If, continuing our inquiries in this way, it should at length appear, that the nature, the whole nature, of man leads him to and is fitted for that particular course of behaviour which we usually distinguish by the name of virtue, we are authorized to conclude, that virtue is the law we are born under, that it was so intended by the Author of our being; and we are bound by the most intimate of all obligations, a regard to our own highest interest and happiness, to conform to it in all situations and events.

Human nature is not simple and uniform, but made up of several parts; and we can have no just idea of it as a system or constitution, unless we take into our view the respects and relations which these parts have to each other. As the body is not one member, but many; so our inward structure consists of various instincts, appetites, and propensions. Thus far there is no difference between human creatures and brutes. But besides these common passions and affections, there is another principle, peculiar to mankind, that of conscience, moral sense, reflection, call it what you please, by which they are enabled to review their whole conduct, to approve of some actions in themselves, and to disapprove of others. That this principle will of course have *some* influence on our behaviour, at least at times, will hardly be disputed: but the particular influence which it *ought* to have, the precise degree of power in the regulating of our internal frame that is assigned it by Him who placed it there, is a point of the utmost consequence in itself, and on the determination of which the very hinge of our Author's Moral System turns. If the faculty here spoken of be, indeed, what it is asserted to be, in nature and kind *superior* to every other passion and affection; if it be given, not merely that it may exert its force occasionally, or as our present humour or fancy may dispose us, but that it may at all times exercise an uncontrollable authority and government over all the rest; it will then follow, that, in order to complete the idea of human nature, as a system, we must not only take in each particular bias, propension, instinct, which are seen to belong to it, but we must add besides the principle of conscience, together with the subjection that is due to it from all the other appetites and passions: just as the idea of a civil constitution is formed, not barely from enumerating the several members and ranks of which it is composed, but from these considered as acting in various degrees of subordination to each other, and all under the direction of the same supreme authority, whether that authority be vested in one person or more.

The view here given of the internal constitution of man, and of the supremacy of conscience, agreeably to the conceptions of Bishop Butler, enables us to comprehend the force of that expression, common to him and the ancient moralists, that virtue consists in *following nature.* The meaning cannot be, that it consists in acting agreeably to that propensity of our nature which happens to be the strongest; or which propels us towards certain objects, without any regard to the methods by which they are to be obtained: but the meaning must be, that virtue consists in the due regulation and subjection of all the other appetites and affections to the superior faculty of conscience; from a conformity to which alone our actions are properly *natural*, or correspondent to the nature, to the whole nature, of such an agent as man. From hence too it appears, that the author of our frame is by no means indifferent to virtue and vice, or has left us at liberty to act at random, as humour or appetite may prompt us; but that every man has the rule of right within him; a rule attended in the very notion of it with authority, and such as has the force of a direction and a command from Him who made us what we are, what course of behaviour is suited to our nature, and which he expects that we should follow. This moral faculty implies also a presentiment and apprehension, that the judgment which it passes on our actions, considered as of good or ill desert, will hereafter be confirmed by the unerring judgment of God; when virtue and happiness, vice and misery, whose ideas are now so closely connected, shall be indissolubly united, and the divine government be found to correspond in the most exact proportion to the nature he has given us. Lastly, this just prerogative or supremacy of conscience it is, which Mr Pope has described in his *Universal Prayer*, though perhaps he may have expressed it rather *too* strongly where he says,

> "What conscience dictates to be done,
> Or warns me not to do,
> This teach me *more than* hell to shun,
> That *more than* heaven pursue."

The reader will observe, that this way of treating the subject of morals, by an appeal to *facts*, does not at all interfere with that other way, adopted by Dr Samuel Clarke and others, which begins with inquiring into the *relations* and *fitnesses of things*, but rather illustrates and confirms it. That there are essential differences in the qualities of human actions, established by nature, and that this *natural* difference of things, prior to and independent of all *will*, creates a natural *fitness* in the agent to act agreeably to it, seems as little to be denied, as that there is the moral difference before explained, from which we approve and feel a pleasure in what is right, and conceive a distaste to what is wrong. Still, however, when we are endeavouring to establish either this moral or that natural difference, it ought never to be forgotten, or rather it will require to be distinctly shown, that both of these, when traced up to their source, suppose an intelligent Author of nature and moral Ruler of the world; who originally appointed these differences, and by such an appointment has signified his *will* that we should conform to them, as the only effectual method of securing our *happiness* on the whole under his government.* And of this consideration our Prelate himself was not unmindful; as may be collected from many expressions in different parts of his writings, and particularly from the following passages in his eleventh Sermon. "It may be allowed, without any prejudice to the cause of virtue and religion, that our ideas of happiness and misery are of all our ideas the nearest and most important to us; that they will, nay if you please, they ought to prevail over those of order, and beauty, and harmony, and proportion, if there should ever be, as it is impossible there ever should be, any inconsistence between them." And again, "Though virtue or moral rectitude does indeed consist in affection to and pursuit of what is right and good, as such; yet, when we sit down in a cool hour, we can neither justify to ourselves this or any other pursuit, till we are convinced that it will be for our happiness, or at least not contrary to it."†

Besides the general system of morality opened above, our Author in his volume of Sermons has stated with accuracy the difference between self-love and benevolence;

* "Far be it from me," says the excellent Dr T. Balguy (Discourse ix.) "to dispute the reality of a *moral* principle in the human heart. I *feel* its existence: I clearly discern its use and importance. But in no respect is it *more* important, than as it suggests the idea of a *moral Governor*. Let this idea be once effaced, and the principle of conscience will soon be found weak and ineffectual. Its influence on men's conduct has, indeed, been *too much* undervalued by some philosophical inquirers. But be that influence, while it lasts, more or less, it is not a *steady* and *permanent* principle of action. Unhappily we always have it in our power to lay it *asleep.—Neglect* alone will suppress and stifle it, and bring it almost into a state of stupefaction. Nor can any thing, less than the *terrors* of religion, awaken our minds from this dangerous and deadly sleep. It can never be a matter of indifference to a *thinking* man, whether he is to be happy or miserable beyond the grave."

† Serm. xi.

in opposition to those who, on the one hand, make the whole of virtue to consist in benevolence,* and to those who, on the other, assert that every particular affection and action is resolvable into self-love. In combating these opinions, he has shown, I think unanswerably, that there are the same kind of indications in human nature, that we were made to promote the happiness of others, as that we were made to promote our own: that it is no just objection to this, that we have dispositions to do *evil* to *others* as well as good; for we have also dispositions to do *evil* as well as good to *ourselves*, to our own most important interests even in this life, for the sake of gratifying a present passion: that the thing to be lamented is, not that men have too great a regard to their own real good, but that they have not enough: that benevolence is not more at variance with or unfriendly to self-love, than any other particular affection is: and that by consulting the happiness of others a man is so far from *lessening* his own, that the very endeavour to do so, though he should fail in the accomplishment, is a source of the highest satisfaction and peace of mind.† He has also, in passing, animadverted on the philosopher of Malmsbury, who, in his book "Of Human Nature," has advanced, as discoveries in moral science, that benevolence is only the love of power, and compassion the fear of future calamity to ourselves. And this our Author has done, not so much with the design of exposing the false reasoning of Mr Hobbes, but because on so perverse an account of human nature he has raised a system, subversive of all justice and honesty.‡

II. The religious system of Bishop Butler is chiefly to be collected from the treatise, entitled, "The Analogy of Religion, Natural and Revealed, to the Constitution and Course of Nature."

"All things are double one against another, and God hath made nothing imperfect."§ On this single observation of the son of Sirach, the whole fabric of our Prelate's defence of religion, in his Analogy, is raised. Instead

* See the second Dissertation "On the Nature of Virtue, at the end of the Analogy.

† See Serm. i. and xi. and the preface to the volume of Sermons.

‡ See the Notes to Serm. i. and v

§ Eccles. xlii. 24.

of indulging in idle speculations, how the world might possibly have been better than it is; or, forgetful of the difference between hypothesis and fact, attempting to explain the divine economy with respect to intelligent creatures, from preconceived notions of his own; he first inquires what the constitution of nature, as made known to us in the way of experiment, actually is; and from this, now seen and acknowledged, he endeavours to form a judgment of that larger constitution, which religion discovers to us. If the dispensation of Providence we are now under, considered as inhabitants of this world, and having a temporal interest to secure in it, be found, on examination, to be analogous to, and of a piece with, that further dispensation, which relates to us as designed for another world, in which we have an eternal interest, depending on our behaviour here; if both may be traced up to the same general laws, and appear to be carried on according to the same plan of administration; the fair presumption is, that both proceed from one and the same Author. And if the principal parts objected to in this latter dispensation be similar to and of the same kind with what we certainly experience under the former; the objections, being clearly inconclusive in one case, because contradicted by plain fact, must, in all reason, be allowed to be inconclusive also in the other.

This way of arguing from what is acknowledged to what is disputed, from things known to other things that resemble them, from that part of the divine establishment which is exposed to our view to that more important one which lies beyond it, is on all hands confessed to be just. By this method Sir Isaac Newton has unfolded the system of nature; by the same method Bishop Butler has explained the system of grace; and thus, to use the words of a writer, whom I quote with pleasure, "has formed and concluded a happy alliance between faith and philosophy."*

And although the argument from analogy be allowed to be imperfect, and by no means sufficient to solve all difficulties respecting the government of God, and the designs of his Providence with regard to mankind (

* Mr Mainwaring's Dissertation, prefixed to his volume of Sermons.

degree of knowledge, which we are not furnished with faculties for attaining, at least in the present state); yet surely it is of importance to learn from it, that the natural and moral world are intimately connected, and parts of one stupendous whole or system; and that the chief objections which are brought against religion may be urged with equal force against the constitution and course of nature, where they are certainly false in fact. And this information we may derive from the work before us; the proper design of which, it may be of use to observe, is not to prove the truth of religion, either natural or revealed, but to confirm that proof, already known, by considerations from analogy.

After this account of the method of reasoning employed by our Author, let us now advert to his manner of applying it, first to the subject of Natural Religion, and secondly to that of Revealed.

1. The foundation of all our hopes and fears is a future life; and with this the treatise begins. Neither the reason of the thing, nor the analogy of nature, according to Bishop Butler, give ground for imagining, that the unknown event, death, will be our destruction. The states in which we have formerly existed, in the womb and in infancy, are not more different from each other than from that of mature age in which we now exist: therefore, that we shall continue to exist hereafter, in a state as different from the present as the present is from those through which we have passed already, is a presumption favoured by the analogy of nature. All that we know from reason concerning death, is the effects it has upon animal bodies: and the frequent instances among men of the intellectual powers continuing in high health and vigour, at the very time when a mortal disease is on the point of putting an end to all the powers of sensation, induce us to hope that it may have no effect at all on the human soul, not even so much as to suspend the exercise of its faculties; though, if it have, the suspension of a power by no means implies its extinction, as sleep or a swoon may convince us.*

The probability of a future state once granted, an im-

* Part I. chap. i.

portant question arises, How best to secure our interest in that state. We find from what passes daily before us, that the constitution of nature admits of misery as well as happiness; that both of these are the consequences of our own actions; and these consequences we are enabled to foresee. Therefore, that our happiness or misery in a future world may depend on our own actions also, and that rewards or punishments hereafter may follow our good or ill behaviour here, is but an appointment of the same sort with what we experience under the divine government, according to the regular course of nature.*

This supposition is confirmed from another circumstance, that the natural government of God, under which we now live, is also moral; in which rewards and punishments are the consequences of actions, considered as virtuous and vicious. Not that every man is rewarded or punished here in exact proportion to his desert; for the essential tendencies of virtue and vice, to produce happiness and the contrary, are often hindered from taking effect from accidental causes. However, there are plainly the rudiments and beginnings of a righteous administration to be discerned in the constitution of nature: from whence we are led to expect, that these accidental hindrances will one day be removed, and the rule of distributive justice obtain completely in a more perfect state.†

The moral government of God, thus established, implies in the notion of it some sort of trial, or a moral possibility of acting wrong as well as right, in those who are the subjects of it. And the doctrine of religion, that the present life is in fact a state of probation for a future one, is rendered credible, from its being analogous throughout to the general conduct of Providence towards us with respect to this world; in which prudence is necessary to secure our temporal interest, just as we are taught that virtue is necessary to secure our eternal interest; and both are trusted to ourselves.‡

But the present life is not merely a state of probation, implying in it difficulties and danger; it is also a state of discipline and improvement; and that both in our tem-

* Chap. ii. † Chap. iii. ‡ Chap. iv.

poral and religious capacity. Thus childhood is a state of discipline for youth; youth for manhood; and that for old age. Strength of body, and maturity of understanding, are acquired by degrees; and neither of them without continual exercise and attention on our part, not only in the beginning of life, but through the whole course of it. So again with respect to our religious concerns, the present world is fitted to be, and to good men is in event, a state of discipline and improvement for a future one. The several passions and propensions implanted in our hearts incline us, in a multitude of instances, to forbidden pleasures: this inward infirmity is increased by various snares and temptations, perpetually occurring from without: hence arises the necessity of recollection and self-government; of withstanding the calls of appetite, and forming our minds to habits of piety and virtue; habits, of which we are capable, and which, to creatures in a state of moral imperfection, and fallen from their original integrity, must be of the greatest use, as an additional security, over and above the principle of conscience, from the dangers to which we are exposed.*

Nor is the credibility here given, by the analogy of nature, to the general doctrine of religion, destroyed or weakened by any notions concerning necessity. Of itself it is a mere word, the sign of an abstract idea; and as much requires an agent, that is, a necessary agent, in order to effect any thing, as freedom requires a free agent. Admitting it to be speculatively true, if considered as influencing practice, it is the same as false: for it is matter of experience, that, with regard to our present interest, and as inhabitants of this world, we are treated as if we were free; and therefore the analogy of nature leads us to conclude, that, with regard to our future interest, and as designed for another world, we shall be treated as free also. Nor does the opinion of necessity, supposing it possible, at all affect either the general proof of religion, or its external evidence.†

Still objections may be made against the wisdom and goodness of the divine government, to which analogy, which can only show the truth or credibility of facts,

* Part I. chap. 7. † Chap. vi.

affords no answer. Yet even here analogy is of use, if it suggest that the divine government is a scheme or system, and not a number of unconnected acts, and that this system is also above our comprehension. Now the government of the natural world appears to be a system of this kind; with parts, related to each other, and together composing a whole: in which system ends are brought about by the use of means, many of which means, before experience, would have been suspected to have had a quite contrary tendency; which is carried on by general laws, similar causes uniformly producing similar effects: the utility of which general laws, and the inconveniences which would probably arise from the occasional or even secret suspension of them, we are in some sort enabled to discern;* but of the whole we are incompetent judges, because of the small part which comes within our view. Reasoning then from what we know, it is highly credible, that the government of the moral world is a system also, carried on by general laws, and in which ends are accomplished by the intervention of means; and that both constitutions, the natural and the moral, are so connected, as to form together but one scheme. But of this scheme, as of that of the natural world taken alone, we are not qualified to judge, on account of the mutual respect of the several parts to each other and to the whole, and our own incapacity to survey the whole, or, with accuracy, any single part. All objections therefore to the wisdom and goodness of the divine government may be founded merely on our ignorance;† and to such objections our ignorance is the proper, and a satisfactory answer.‡

2. The chief difficulties concerning Natural Religion being now removed, our Author proceeds, in the next place, to that which is Revealed; and as an Introduction to an inquiry into the Credibility of Christianity, begins with the consideration of its Importance.

* See a treatise on Divine Benevolence, by Dr Thomas Balguy, part ii.

† *The ignorance of man*, is a favourite doctrine with Bishop Butler. It occurs in the Second Part of the Analogy; it makes the subject of his Fifteenth Sermon; and we meet with it again in his Charge. Whether sometimes it be not carried to a length which is excessive, may admit of doubt.

‡ Part I. chap. vii.

The importance of Christianity appears in two respects. First, in its being a republication of Natural Religion, in its native simplicity, with authority, and with circumstances of advantage; ascertaining in many instances of moment, what before was only probable, and particularly confirming the doctrine of a future state of rewards and punishments.* Secondly, as revealing a new dispensation of Providence, originating from the pure love and mercy of God, and conducted by the mediation of his Son, and the guidance of his Spirit for the recovery and salvation of mankind, represented in a state of apostasy and ruin. This account of Christianity being admitted to be just, and the distinct offices of these three divine Persons being once discovered to us, we are as much obliged in point of duty to acknowledge the relations we stand in to the Son and Holy Ghost, as our Mediator and Sanctifier, as we are obliged in point of duty to acknowledge the relation we stand in to God the Father; although the two former of these relations be learnt from Revelation only, and in the last we are instructed by the light of nature; the obligation in either case arising from the offices themselves, and not at all depending on the manner in which they are made known to us.†

The presumptions against Revelation in general are, that it is not discoverable by reason, that it is unlike to what is so discovered, and that it was introduced and supported by miracles. But in a scheme so large as

* Admirable to this purpose are the words of Dr T. Balguy, in the Ninth of his Discourses already referred to, p. xxv. "The doctrine of a *life to come*, some persons will say, is a doctrine of *natural* religion; and can never therefore be properly alleged to show the importance of revelation. They judge perhaps from the frame of the world, that the present system is *imperfect;* they see designs in it, not yet *completed;* and they think they have grounds for expecting *another* state, in which these designs shall be *farther* carried on, and brought to a conclusion, worthy of infinite wisdom. I am not concerned to dispute the *justness* of this reasoning; nor do I wish to dispute it. But how far will it reach? Will it lead us to the *Christian* doctrine of a judgment to come? Will it give us the prospect of an *eternity* of happiness? Nothing of all this. It shows us only, that *death* is not the end of our being; that we are likely to pass hereafter into other systems, more favourable than the present to the great ends of God's providence, the *virtue* and the *happiness* of his intelligent creatures. But into *what* systems we are to be removed; what new scenes are to be presented to us, either of pleasure or pain; what new parts we shall have to act, and to what trials and temptations we may yet be exposed; on all these subjects we know just nothing. That our happiness *for ever* depends on our conduct *here*, is a most important proposition, which we learn *only* from *revelation*."

† Part II. chap i.

that of the universe, unbounded in extent and everlasting in duration, there must of necessity be numberless circumstances which are beyond the reach of our faculties to discern, and which can only be known by divine illumination. And both in the natural and moral government of the world, under which we live, we find many things unlike one to another, and therefore ought not to wonder if the same unlikeness obtain between things visible and invisible; although it be far from true, that revealed religion is entirely unlike the constitution of nature, as analogy may teach us. Nor is there any thing incredible in Revelation, considered as miraculous; whether miracles be supposed to have been performed at the beginning of the world, or after a course of nature has been established. Not *at the beginning of the world;* for then there was either no course of nature at all, or a power must have been exerted totally different from what that course is at present: all men and animals cannot have been born, as they are now; but a pair of each sort must have been produced at first, in a way altogether unlike to that in which they have been since produced; unless we affirm, that men and animals have existed from eternity in an endless succession; one miracle therefore at least there must have been at the beginning of the world, or at the time of man's creation. Not *after the settlement of a course of nature,* on account of miracles being contrary to that course, or, in other words, contrary to experience; for, in order to know whether miracles, worked in attestation of a divine religion, be contrary to experience or not, we ought to be acquainted with other cases, similar or parallel to those, in which miracles are alleged to have been wrought. But where shall we find such similar or parallel cases? The world which we inhabit affords none: we know of no extraordinary revelations from God to man, but those recorded in the Old and New Testament; all of which were established by miracles; it cannot therefore be said, that miracles are incredible, because contrary to experience, when all the experience we have is in favour of miracles, and on the side of religion.* Besides, in reasoning con-

* "In the common affairs of life, common *experience* is sufficient to direct us. But

cerning miracles, they ought not to be compared with common natural events, but with uncommon appearances, such as comets, magnetism, electricity; which, to one acquainted only with the usual phenomena of nature, and the common powers of matter, must, before proof of their actual existence, be thought incredible.*

The presumption against Revelation in general being dispatched, objections against the Christian Revelation in particular, against the scheme of it, as distinguished from objections against its evidence, are considered next. Now supposing a revelation to be really given, it is highly probable beforehand, that it must contain many things appearing to us liable to objections. The acknowledged dispensation of nature is very different from what we should have expected: reasoning then from analogy, the revealed dispensation, it is credible, would be also different. Nor are we in any sort judges at what time, or in what degree, or manner, it is fit or expedient for God to instruct us, in things confessedly of the greatest use, either by natural reason, or by supernatural information. Thus, arguing on speculation only, and without experience, it would seem very unlikely that so important a remedy as that provided by Christianity, for the recovery of mankind from ruin, should have been for so many ages withheld; and, when at last vouchsafed, should be imparted to so few; and, after it has been imparted, should be attended with obscurity and doubt. And just so we might have argued, before experience, concerning the remedies provided in nature for bodily diseases, to which by nature we are exposed: for many of these were unknown to mankind for a number of ages;

will common experience serve to guide our judgment concerning the *fall* and *redemption* of mankind? From what we see every day, can we explain the *commencement*, or foretell the *dissolution* of the world? To judge of events like these, we should be conversant in the history of other planets; should be distinctly informed of God's various dispensations to all the different orders of rational beings. Instead then of grounding our religious opinions on what *we* call *experience*, let us apply to a more certain guide, let us hearken to the *testimony* of God himself. The credibility of *human testimony*, and the conduct of *human agents*, are subjects perfectly within the reach of our natural faculties; and we ought to desire no firmer foundation for our belief of religion, than for the judgments we form in the common affairs of life: where we see a little plain testimony easily outweighs the most specious conjectures, and not seldom even strong probabilities." Dr Balguy's Fourth Charge. See also an excellent pamphlet, entitled, "Remarks on Mr Hume's Essay on the Natural History of Religion," sect. 5; and the Sixth of Dr Powell's Discourses.

* Chap. ii.

are known but to few now; some important ones probably not discovered yet; and those which are, neither certain in their application, nor universal in their use: and the same mode of reasoning that would lead us to expect they should have been so, would lead us to expect that the necessity of them should have been superseded, by there being no diseases; as the necessity of the Christian scheme, it may be thought, might also have been superseded, by preventing the fall of man, so that he should not have stood in need of a Redeemer at all.*

As to objections against the wisdom and goodness of Christianity, the same answer may be applied to them as was to the like objections against the constitution of nature. For here also, Christianity is a scheme or economy, composed of various parts, forming a whole; in which scheme means are used for the accomplishing of ends; and which is conducted by general laws, of all of which we know as little as we do of the constitution of nature. And the seeming want of wisdom or goodness in this system is to be ascribed to the same cause, as the like appearances of defects in the natural system; our inability to discern the whole scheme, and our ignorance of the relation of those parts which are discernible to others beyond our view.

The objections against Christianity as a matter of fact, and against the wisdom and goodness of it, having been obviated together, the chief of them are now to be considered distinctly. One of these, which is levelled against the entire system itself, is of this sort: the restoration of mankind, represented in Scripture as the great design of the Gospel, is described as requiring a long series of means, and persons, and dispensations, before it can be brought to its completion; whereas the whole ought to have been effected at once. Now every thing we see in the course of nature shows the folly of this objection. For in the natural course of Providence, ends are brought about by means, not operating immediately and at once, but deliberately, and in a way of progression; one thing being subservient to another, this to somewhat further. The change of seasons, the ripening

* Chap. iii.

of fruits, the growth of vegetable and animal bodies, are instances of this. And therefore, that the same progressive method should be followed in the dispensation of Christianity, as is observed in the common dispensation of Providence, is a reasonable expectation, justified by the analogy of nature.*

Another circumstance objected to in the Christian scheme is the appointment of a Mediator, and the saving of the world through him. But the visible government of God being actually administered in this way, or by the mediation and instrumentality of others, there can be no general presumption against an appointment of this kind, against his invisible government being exercised in the same manner. We have seen already, that with regard to ourselves this visible government is carried on by rewards and punishments; for happiness and misery are the consequences of our own actions, considered as virtuous and vicious; and these consequences we are enabled to foresee. It might have been imagined, before consulting experience, that after we had rendered ourselves liable to misery by our own ill conduct, sorrow for what was past, and behaving well for the future, would, alone and of themselves, have exempted us from deserved punishment, and restored us to the divine favour. But the fact is otherwise; and real reformation is often found to be of no avail, so as to secure the criminal from poverty, sickness, infamy, and death, the never-failing attendants on vice and extravagance, exceeding a certain degree. By the course of nature then it appears, God does not always pardon a sinner on his repentance. Yet there is provision made, even in nature, that the miseries, which men bring on themselves by unlawful indulgences, may in many cases be mitigated, and in some removed; partly by extraordinary exertions of the offender himself, but more especially and frequently by the intervention of others, who voluntarily, and from motives of compassion, submit to labour and sorrow, such as produce long and lasting inconveniences to themselves, as the means of rescuing another from the wretched effects of former imprudences.

* Chap. iv.

Vicarious punishment, therefore, or one person's sufferings contributing to the relief of another, is a providential disposition in the economy of nature:* and it ought not to be matter of surprise, if by a method analogous to this we be redeemed from sin and misery, in the economy of grace. That mankind at present are in a state of degradation, different from that in which they were originally created, is the very ground of the Christian revelation, as contained in the Scriptures. Whether we acquiesce in the account, that our being placed in such a state is owing to the crime of our first parents, or choose to ascribe it to any other cause, it makes no difference as to our condition: the vice and unhappiness of the world are still there, notwithstanding all our suppositions: nor is it Christianity that hath put us into this state. We learn also from the same Scriptures, what experience and the use of expiatory sacrifices from the most early times might have taught us, that repentance alone is not sufficient to prevent the fatal consequences of past transgressions: but that still there is room for mercy, and that repentance shall be available, though not of itself, yet through the mediation of a divine Person, the Messiah; who, from the sublimest principles of compassion, when we were *dead in trespasses and sins*,† suffered and died, the innocent for the guilty, *the just for the unjust*,‡ that *we might have redemption through his blood, even the forgiveness of sins.*§ In what way the death of Christ was of that efficacy it is said to be, in procuring the reconciliation of sinners, the Scriptures have not explained; it is enough that the doctrine is revealed; that it is not contrary to any truths which reason and experience teach us; and that it accords in

* Dr Arthur Ashley Sykes, from whose writings some good may be collected out of a multitude of things of a contrary tendency, in what he is pleased to call "The Scripture Doctrine of Redemption," (see the observations on the texts cited in his first chapter, and also in chapters the fifth and sixth,) opposes what is here advanced by Bishop Butler; quoting his words, but without mentioning his name. If what is said above be not thought a sufficient answer to the objections of this author, the reader may do well to consult a Charge "On the Use and Abuse of Philosophy in the Study of Religion," by the late Dr Powell; who seems to me to have had the observations of Dr Sykes in his view, where he is confuting the reasonings of certain philosophizing Divines against the doctrine of the Atonement. Powell's Discourses. Charge III. p. 342—348.

† Ephes ii. 1. ‡ 1 Pet. iii. 18. § Colos. i. 14.

perfect harmony with the usual method of the divine conduct in the government of the world.*

Again, it hath been said, that if the Christian revelation were true, it must have been universal, and could not have been left upon doubtful evidence. But God, in his natural providence, dispenses his gifts in great variety, not only among creatures of the same species, but to the same individuals also at different times. Had the Christian revelation been universal at first, yet, from the diversity of men's abilities, both of mind and body, their various means of improvement, and other external advantages, some persons must soon have been in a situation, with respect to religious knowledge, much superior to that of others, as much perhaps as they are at present: and all men will be equitably dealt with at last; and to whom little is given, of him little will be required. Then as to the evidence for religion being left doubtful, difficulties of this sort, like difficulties in practice, afford scope and opportunity for a virtuous exercise of the understanding, and dispose the mind to acquiesce and rest satisfied with any evidence that is real. In the daily commerce of life, men are obliged to act upon great uncertainties, with regard to success in their temporal pursuits: and the case with regard to religion is parallel. However, though religion be not intuitively true, the proofs of it which we have are amply sufficient in reason to induce us to embrace it; and dissatisfaction with those proofs may possibly be men's own fault.†

Nothing remains but to attend to the positive evidence there is for the truth of Christianity. Now, besides its direct and fundamental proofs, which are miracles and prophecies, there are many collateral circumstances, which may be united into one view, and all together may be considered as making up one argument. In this way of treating the subject, the revelation, whether real or otherwise, may be supposed to be wholly historical: the design of which appears to be, to give an account of the condition of religion, and its professors, with a concise narration of the political state of things, as far as religion is affected by it, during a great length of time, near six

* Chap. v.

† Chap. vi.

thousand years of which are already past. More particularly it comprehends an account of God's entering into covenant with one nation, the Jews, that he would be their God, and that they should be his people; of his often interposing in their affairs; giving them the promise, and afterwards the possession, of a flourishing country; assuring them of the greatest national prosperity, in case of their obedience, and threatening the severest national punishment, in case they forsook him, and joined in the idolatry of their Pagan neighbours. It contains also a prediction of a particular person to appear in the fulness of time, in whom all the promises of God to the Jews were to be fulfilled: and it relates, that, at the time expected, a person did actually appear, assuming to be the Saviour foretold; that he worked various miracles among them, in confirmation of his divine authority; and, as was foretold also, was rejected and put to death by the very people who had long desired and waited for his coming; but that his religion, in spite of all opposition, was established in the world by his disciples, invested with supernatural powers for that purpose; of the fate and fortunes of which religion there is a prophetical description, carried down to the end of time. Let any one now, after reading the above history, and not knowing whether the whole were not a fiction, be supposed to ask, Whether all that is here related be true? and instead of a direct answer, let him be informed of the several acknowledged facts, which are found to correspond to it in real life; and then let him compare the history and facts together, and observe the astonishing coincidence of both: such a joint review must appear to him of very great weight, and to amount to evidence somewhat more than human. And unless the whole series, and every particular circumstance contained in it, can be thought to have arisen from accident, the truth of Christianity is proved.*

The view here given of the moral and religious sys-

* Chap. vii. To the Analogy are subjoined two Dissertations, both originally inserted in the body of the work. One on *Personal Identity*, in which are contained some strictures on Mr Locke, who asserts that consciousness makes or constitutes personal identity; whereas, as our Author observes, consciousness makes only personality, or is necessary to the idea of a person, *i. e.* a thinking intelligent being, but

tems of Bishop Butler, it will immediately be perceived, is chiefly intended for younger students, especially for students in Divinity; to whom it is hoped it may be of use, so as to encourage them to peruse, with proper diligence, the original works of the Author himself. For it may be necessary to observe, that neither of the volumes of this excellent Prelate are addressed to those who read for amusement, or curiosity, or to get rid of time. All subjects are not to be comprehended with the same ease; and morality and religion, when treated as sciences, each accompanied with difficulties of its own, can neither of them be understood as they ought without a very peculiar attention. But morality and religion are not merely to be studied as sciences, or as being speculatively true; they are to be regarded in another and higher light, as the rule of life and manners, as containing authoritative directions by which to regulate our faith and practice. And in this view, the infinite importance of them, considered, it can never be an indifferent matter whether they be received or rejected. For both claim to be the voice of God; and whether they be so or not, cannot be known, till their claims be impartially examined. If they indeed come from Him, we are bound to conform to them at our peril; nor is it left to our choice, whether we will submit to the obligations they impose upon us or not; for submit to them we must, in such a sense, as to incur the punishments denounced by both against wilful disobedience to their injunctions.

presupposes, and therefore cannot constitute, personal identity: just as knowledge presupposes truth, but does not constitute it. Consciousness of past actions does indeed show us the identity of ourselves, or gives us a certain assurance that we are the same persons or living agents now, which we were at the time to which our remembrance can look back: but still we should be the same persons as we were, though this consciousness of what is past were wanting, though all that had been done by us formerly were forgotten; unless it be true, that no person has existed a single moment beyond what he can remember. The other Dissertation is *On the Nature of Virtue*, which properly belongs to the moral system of our Author already explained.

THE

LIFE OF DR BUTLER.

Dr Joseph Butler, a Prelate of the most distinguished character and abilities, was born at Wantage, in Berkshire, in the year 1692. His father, Mr Thomas Butler, who was a substantial and reputable shopkeeper in that town, observing in his son Joseph* an excellent genius and inclination for learning, determined to educate him for the ministry, among the Protestant Dissenters of the Presbyterian denomination. For this purpose, after he had gone through a proper course of grammatical literature, at the free grammar school of his native place, under the care of the Rev. Mr Philip Barton, a Clergyman of the Church of England, he was sent to a Dissenting academy, then kept at Gloucester, but which was soon afterwards removed to Tewkesbury. The principal tutor of this academy was Mr Jones, a man of uncommon abilities and knowledge, who had the honour of training up several scholars, who became of great eminence, both in the Established Church and among the Dissenters. At Tewkesbury Mr Butler made an extraordinary progress in the study of Divinity; of which he gave a remarkable proof, in the letters addressed by him, while he resided at Tewkesbury, to Dr Samuel Clarke, laying before him the doubts that had arisen in his mind, concerning the conclusiveness of some arguments in the Doctor's demonstration of the being and attributes of God. The first of these letters was dated the 4th of November, 1713; and the sagacity and depth of thought displayed in it, immediately excited Dr Clarke's particular notice. This condescension encouraged Mr Butler to address the Doctor again upon the same subject, which likewise was answered by him; and the correspondence being carried on in three other

* He was the youngest of eight children.

letters, the whole was annexed to the celebrated treatise before mentioned, and the collection has been retained in all the subsequent editions of that work. The management of this correspondence was entrusted by Mr Butler to his friend and fellow-pupil, Mr Secker, who, in order to conceal the affair, undertook to convey the letters to the post-office at Gloucester, and to bring back Dr Clarke's answers. When Mr Butler's name was discovered to the Doctor, the candour, modesty, and good sense, with which he had written, immediately procured him the friendship of that eminent and excellent man. Our young student was not, however, during his continuance at Tewkesbury, solely employed in metaphysical speculations and inquiries. Another subject of his serious consideration was, the propriety of his becoming a Dissenting minister. Accordingly, he entered into an examination of the principles of non-conformity; the result of which was, such a dissatisfaction with them, as determined him to conform to the Established Church. This intention was, at first, disagreeable to his father, who endeavoured to divert him from his purpose; and, with that view, called in the assistance of some eminent Presbyterian Divines; but finding his son's resolution to be fixed, he at length suffered him to be removed to Oxford, where he was admitted a commoner of Oriel College, on the 17th of March, 1714. At what time he took Orders doth not appear, nor who the Bishop was by whom he was ordained; but it is certain that he entered into the Church soon after his admission at Oxford, if it be true, as is asserted, that he sometimes assisted Mr Edward Talbot in the divine service, at his living of Hendred, near Wantage. With this gentleman, who was the second son of Dr William Talbot, successively Bishop of Oxford, Salisbury, and Durham, Mr Butler formed an intimate friendship at Oriel College; which friendship laid the foundation of all his subsequent preferments, and procured for him a very honourable situation, when he was only twenty-six years of age. For it was in 1718 that, at the recommendation of Mr Talbot, in conjunction with that of Dr Clarke, he was appointed by Sir Joseph Jekyll to be preacher at the Rolls. This was three years before he had taken any degree at the University, where he did not go out Bachelor of Law till the 10th of June, 1721, which, however, was as soon as that degree could suitably be conferred upon him. Mr Butler continued at the Rolls till 1726; in the beginning of which year he published, in one volume, octavo, "Fifteen Sermons preached at that Chapel." In the mean while, by the patronage of Dr Talbot, Bishop of Durham, to whose notice he had been recommended (together with Mr Benson and Mr Secker) by Mr Edward Talbot, on his death-bed, our Author had been presented first to the rectory of Haughton, near Darlington, and afterwards to that of Stanhope, in the same diocese. The benefice of Haughton was given to him in 1722, and that of Stanhope in 1725. At Haughton there was a necessity for rebuilding a great part of the parsonage-house, and Mr Butler had neither money nor talents for that work. Mr Secker, therefore, who had always the interest of his friends at heart, and had acquired a very considerable influence with Bishop Talbot, persuaded that Prelate to give Mr Butler, in exchange for Haughton, the rectory of Stanhope, which was not only free from any such incumbrance, but was likewise of much superior value, being indeed one of the richest parsonages in England. Whilst our Author continued preacher at the Rolls Chapel, he divided his time between his duty in town and country; but when he quitted the Rolls, he resided during seven years, wholly at Stanhope, in the conscientious discharge of every obligation appertaining to a good parish priest. This retirement, however, was too solitary for his disposition, which had in it a natural cast of gloominess. And though his recluse hours were by no means lost, either to private improvement or public utility, yet he felt at times, very painfully, the want of that select society of friends to which he had been accustomed, and which could inspire him with the greatest cheerfulness. Mr Secker, therefore, who knew this, was extremely anxious to draw him out into a more active and conspicuous scene, and omitted no opportunity of expressing this desire to such as he thought capable of promoting it. Having himself been appointed King's

Chaplain in 1732, he took occasion, in a conversation which he had the honour of holding with Queen Caroline, to mention to her his friend Mr Butler. The Queen said she thought he had been dead. Mr Secker assured her he was not. Yet her Majesty afterwards asked Archbishop Blackburn, if he was not dead: his answer was, "No, madam; but he is buried." Mr Secker continuing his purpose of endeavouring to bring his friend out of his retirement, found means, upon Mr Charles Talbot's being made Lord Chancellor, to have Mr Butler recommended to him for his Chaplain. His Lordship accepted, and sent for him; and this promotion calling him to Town, he took Oxford in his way, and was admitted there to the degree of Doctor of Law, on the 8th of December, 1733. The Lord Chancellor, who gave him also a prebend in the church of Rochester, had consented that he should reside at his parish of Stanhope one half of the year.

Dr Butler being thus brought back into the world, his merit and his talents soon introduced him to particular notice, and paved the way for his rising to those high dignities which he afterwards enjoyed. In 1736 he was appointed Clerk of the Closet to Queen Caroline; and, in the same year, he presented to her Majesty a copy of his excellent Treatise, entitled, "The Analogy of Religion, Natural and Revealed, to the Constitution and Course of Nature." His attendance upon his Royal Mistress, by her especial command, was from seven to nine in the evening every day: and though this particular relation to that excellent and learned Queen was soon determined by her death, in 1737, yet he had been so effectually recommended by her, as well as by the late Lord Chancellor Talbot, to his Majesty's favour, that in the next year he was raised to the highest order of the Church, by a nomination to the bishopric of Bristol; to which see he was consecrated on the 3d of December 1738. King George II. not being satisfied with this proof of his regard to Dr Butler, promoted him, in 1740, to the Deanery of St Paul's, London, into which he was installed on the 24th of May in that year. Finding the demands of this dignity to be incompatible with his parish duty at Stanhope, he immediately resigned that rich benefice. Besides our Prelate's unremitted attention to his peculiar obligations, he was called upon to preach several discourses on public occasions, which were afterwards separately printed, and have since been annexed to the latter editions of the Sermons at the Rolls Chapel. In 1746, upon the death of Dr Egerton, Bishop of Hereford, Dr Butler was made Clerk of the Closet to the King; and, on the 16th of October 1750, he received another distinguished mark of his Majesty's favour, by being translated to the see of Durham. This was on the 16th of October in that year, upon the decease of Dr Edward Chandler. Our Prelate being thus appointed to preside over a diocese with which he had long been connected, delivered his first, and indeed his last Charge to his Clergy, at his primary visitation in 1751. The principal object of it was "External Religion." The Bishop having observed, with deep concern, the great and growing neglect of serious piety in the kingdom, insisted strongly on the usefulness of outward forms and institutions, in fixing and preserving a sense of devotion and duty in the minds of men. In doing this, he was thought by several persons to speak too favourably of Pagan and Popish ceremonies, and to countenance, in a certain degree, the cause of superstition. Under that apprehension, an able and spirited writer, who was understood to be a Clergyman of the Church of England, published, in 1752, a pamphlet, entitled, "A Serious Inquiry into the Use and Importance of External Religion; occasioned by some Passages in the Right Rev. the Lord Bishop of Durham's Charge to the Clergy of that Diocese;—Humbly addressed to his Lordship." Many persons, however, and we believe the greater part of the Clergy of the diocese, did not think our Prelate's Charge so exceptionable as it appeared to this author. The Charge, being printed at Durham, and having never been annexed to any of Dr Butler's other works, is now become extremely scarce; and it is observable, that it is the only one of his publications which ever produced him a direct literary antagonist.

By this promotion, our worthy Bishop was furnished

with ample means of exerting the virtue of charity; a virtue which eminently abounded in him, and the exercise of which was his highest delight. But this gratification he did not long enjoy. He had been but a short time seated in his new bishopric, when his health began visibly to decline; and having been complimented, during his indisposition, upon account of his great resignation to the Divine will, he is said to have expressed some regret, that he should be taken from the present world so soon after he had been rendered capable of becoming much more useful in it. In his illness he was carried to Bristol, to try the waters of that place; but these proving ineffectual, he removed to Bath, where, being past recovery, he died on the 16th of June, 1752. His corpse was conveyed to Bristol, and interred in the cathedral there, where a monument, with an inscription, is erected to his memory.

On the greatness of Bishop Butler's character we need not enlarge; for his profound knowledge, and the prodigious strength of his mind, are amply displayed in his incomparable writings. His piety was of the most serious and fervent, and, perhaps, somewhat of the ascetic kind. His benevolence was warm, generous, and diffusive. Whilst he was Bishop of Bristol, he expended, in repairing and improving the episcopal palace, four thousand pounds, which is said to have been more than the whole revenues of the bishopric amounted to, during his continuance in that see. Besides his private benefactions, he was a contributor to the infirmary at Bristol, and a subscriber to three of the hospitals at London. He was likewise a principal promoter, though not the first founder, of the infirmary at Newcastle, in Northumberland. In supporting the hospitality and dignity of the rich and powerful diocese of Durham, he was desirous of imitating the spirit of his patron, Bishop Talbot. In this spirit he set apart three days every week for the reception and entertainment of the principal gentry of the country. Nor were even the Clergy who had the poorest benefices neglected by him. He not only occasionally invited them to dine with him, but condescended to visit them at their respective parishes. By his will he left five hundred pounds to the Society for propagating the Gospel in Foreign Parts, and some legacies to his friends and domestics. His executor and residuary legatee was his chaplain, the Rev. Dr Nathanael Forster, a divine of distinguished literature. Bishop Butler was never married. Soon after his decease, the following lines, by way of epitaph, were written concerning him; and were printed first, if we recollect aright, in the London Magazine.

Beneath this marble Butler lies entomb'd,
  Who, with a soul inflamed by love divine,
His life in presence of his God consumed,
  Like the bright lamps before the holy shrine.
His aspect pleasing, mind with learning fraught
  His eloquence was like a chain of gold,
  That the wild passions of mankind controll'd ;
Merit, wherever to be found, he sought.
Desire of transient riches he had none ;
  These he, with bounteous hand, did well dispense ;
  Bent to fulfill the ends of Providence ;
His heart still fix'd on an immortal crown.
  His heart a mirror was, of purest kind,
  Where the bright image of his Maker shined ;
Reflecting faithful to the throne above,
Th' irradiant glories of the Mystic Dove.

THE following Epitaph, said to be written by Dr Nathanael Forster, is inscribed on a flat marble stone, in the cathedral church of Bristol, placed over the spot where the remains of Bishop Butler are deposited; and which, as it is now almost obliterated, it may be worth while here to preserve.

H. S.
Reverendus admodum in Christo Pater
JOSEPHUS BUTLER, LL.D.
Hujusce primo Diœceseos
Deinde Dunelmensis Episcopus.
Qualis quantusque Vir erat
Sua libentissime agnovit ætas:
Et si quid Præsuli aut Scriptori ad famam valent
Mens altissima,
Ingenii perspicacis et subacti Vis,
Animusque pius, simplex, candidus, liberalis,
Mortui haud facile evanescet memoria.
Obiit Bathoniæ 16 Kalend. Julii,
A. D. 1752.
Annos natus 60

INTRODUCTION.

PROBABLE evidence is essentially distinguished from demonstrative by this, that it admits of degrees; and of all variety of them, from the highest moral certainty, to the very lowest presumption. We cannot indeed say a thing is probably true upon one very slight presumption for it; because, as there may be probabilities on both sides of a question, there may be some against it; and though there be not, yet a slight presumption does not beget that degree of conviction, which is implied in saying a thing is probably true. But that the slightest possible presumption is of the nature of a probability, appears from hence; that such low presumption often repeated, will amount even to moral certainty. Thus a man's having observed the ebb and flow of the tide to-day, affords some sort of presumption, though the lowest imaginable, that it may happen again to-morrow: but the observation of this event for so many days, and months, and ages together, as it has been observed by mankind, gives us a full assurance that it will.

That which chiefly constitutes Probability is expressed in the word Likely, *i. e.* like some truth,* or true event; like it, in itself, in its evidence, in some more or fewer of its circumstances. For when we determine a thing to be probably true, suppose that an event has or will come to pass, it is from the mind's remarking in it a likeness to some other event, which we have observed has come to pass. And this observation forms, in numberless daily instances, a presumption, opinion, or full conviction, that such event has or will come to pass; according as the observation is, that the like event has sometimes, most commonly, or always, so far as our observation reaches, come to pass at like distances of time, or place, or upon like occasions. Hence arises the belief, that a child, if it lives twenty years, will grow up to

* Verisimile.

the stature and strength of a man; that food will contribute to the preservation of its life, and the want of it for such a number of days, be its certain destruction. So likewise the rule and measure of our hopes and fears concerning the success of our pursuits; our expectations that others will act so and so in such circumstances; and our judgment that such actions proceed from such principles; all these rely upon our having observed the like to what we hope, fear, expect, judge; I say, upon our having observed the like, either with respect to others or ourselves. And thus, whereas the prince* who had always lived in a warm climate, naturally concluded in the way of analogy, that there was no such thing as water's becoming hard, because he had always observed it to be fluid and yielding: we, on the contrary, from analogy conclude, that there is no presumption at all against this: that it is supposable there may be frost in England any given day in January next; probable that there will on some day of the month; and that there is a moral certainty, *i. e.* ground for an expectation without any doubt of it, in some part or other of the winter.

Probable evidence, in its very nature, affords but an imperfect kind of information; and is to be considered as relative only to beings of limited capacities. For nothing which is the possible object of knowledge, whether past, present, or future, can be probable to an infinite Intelligence; since it cannot but be discerned absolutely as it is in itself, certainly true, or certainly false. But to us, probability is the very guide of life.

From these things it follows, that in questions of difficulty, or such as are thought so, where more satisfactory evidence cannot be had, or is not seen; if the result of examination be, that there appears upon the whole, any the lowest presumption on one side, and none on the other, or a greater presumption on one side, though in the lowest degree greater; this determines the question, even in matters of speculation; and in matters of practice, will lay us under an absolute and formal obligation, in point of prudence and of interest, to act upon that presumption or low probability, though it be so low

* The story is told by Mr Locke in the Chapter of Probability.

as to leave the mind in very great doubt which is the truth. For surely a man is as really bound in prudence to do what upon the whole appears, according to the best of his judgment, to be for his happiness, as what he certainly knows to be so. Nay further, in questions of great consequence, a reasonable man will think it concerns him to remark lower probabilities and presumptions than these; such as amount to no more than showing one side of a question to be as supposable and credible as the other: nay, such as but amount to much less even than this. For numberless instances might be mentioned respecting the common pursuits of life, where a man would be thought, in a literal sense, distracted, who would not act, and with great application too, not only upon an even chance, but upon much less, and where the probability or chance was greatly against his succeeding.*

It is not my design to inquire further into the nature, the foundation, and measure of probability; or whence it proceeds that *likeness* should beget that presumption, opinion, and full conviction, which the human mind is formed to receive from it, and which it does necessarily produce in every one; or to guard against the errors, to which reasoning from analogy is liable. This belongs to the subject of Logic; and is a part of that subject which has not yet been thoroughly considered. Indeed I shall not take upon me to say, how far the extent, compass, and force, of analogical reasoning, can be reduced to general heads and rules; and the whole be formed into a system. But though so little in this way has been attempted by those who have treated of our intellectual powers, and the exercise of them; this does not hinder but that we may be, as we unquestionably are, assured, that analogy is of weight, in various degrees, towards determining our judgment and our practice. Nor does it in any wise cease to be of weight in those cases, because persons, either given to dispute, or who require things to be stated with greater exactness than our faculties appear to admit of in practical matters, may find other cases in which it is not easy to say, whether it be, or be

* See Part II. Chap. vi.

not, of any weight; or instances of seeming analogies, which are really of none. It is enough to the present purpose to observe, that this general way of arguing is evidently natural, just, and conclusive. For there is no man can make a question but that the sun will rise to-morrow and be seen, where it is seen at all, in the figure of a circle, and not in that of a square.

Hence, namely from analogical reasoning, Origen* has with singular sagacity observed, that *he who believes the Scripture to have proceeded from him who is the Author of Nature, may well expect to find the same sort of difficulties in it, as are found in the constitution of Nature.* And in a like way of reflection it may be added, that he who denies the Scripture to have been from God upon account of these difficulties, may, for the very same reason, deny the world to have been formed by him. On the other hand, if there be an analogy or likeness between that system of things and dispensation of Providence, which Revelation informs us of, and that system of things and dispensation of Providence, which Experience together with Reason informs us of, *i. e.* the known course of Nature; this is a presumption, that they have both the same author and cause; at least so far as to answer objections against the former's being from God, drawn from any thing which is analogical or similar to what is in the latter, which is acknowledged to be from him; for an Author of Nature is here supposed.

Forming our notions of the constitution and government of the world upon reasoning, without foundation for the principles which we assume, whether from the attributes of God, or any thing else, is building a world upon hypothesis, like Des Cartes. Forming our notions upon reasoning from principles which are certain, but applied to cases to which we have no ground to apply them (like those who explain the structure of the human body, and the nature of diseases and medicines from mere mathematics without sufficient *data.*) is an error much akin to the former: since what is assumed in order to make the

* Χρὴ μέν τοί γε τὸν ἅπαξ παραδεξάμενον τοῦ κτίσαντος τὸν κόσμον εἶναι ταύτας τὰς γραφὰς πεπεῖσθαι, ὅτι ὅσα περὶ τῆς κτίσεως ἀπαντᾷ τοῖς ζητοῦσι τὸν περὶ αὐτῆς λόγον, ταῦτα καὶ περὶ τῶν γραφῶν. Philocal. p. 23. Ed. Cant.

reasoning applicable, is Hypothesis. But it must be allowed just, to join abstract reasonings with the observation of facts, and argue from such facts as are known, to others that are like them; from that part of the Divine government over intelligent creatures which comes under our view, to that larger and more general government over them which is beyond it; and from what is present, to collect what is likely, credible, or not incredible, will be hereafter.

This method then of concluding and determining being practical, and what, if we will act at all, we cannot but act upon in the common pursuits of life; being evidently conclusive, in various degrees, proportionable to the degree and exactness of the whole analogy or likeness; and having so great authority for its introduction into the subject of religion, even revealed religion; my design is to apply it to that subject in general, both natural and revealed: taking for proved, that there is an intelligent Author of Nature, and natural Governor of the world. For as there is no presumption against this prior to the proof of it: so it has been often proved with accumulated evidence; from this argument of analogy and final causes; from abstract reasonings; from the most ancient tradition and testimony; and from the general consent of mankind. Nor does it appear, so far as I can find, to be denied by the generality of those who profess themselves dissatisfied with the evidence of religion.

As there are some, who, instead of thus attending to what is in fact the constitution of Nature, form their notions of God's government upon hypothesis: so there are others, who indulge themselves in vain and idle speculations, how the world might possibly have been framed otherwise than it is; and upon supposition that things might, in imagining that they should, have been disposed and carried on after a better model, than what appears in the present disposition and conduct of them. Suppose now a person of such a turn of mind, to go on with his reveries, till he had at length fixed upon some particular plan of Nature, as appearing to him the best — One shall scarce be thought guilty of detraction against human understanding, if one should say, even beforehand, that the plan which this speculative person would fix upon, though he were the wisest of the sons of men, probably would not be the very best, even according to his own notions of *best;* whether he thought that to be so, which afforded occasions and motives for the exercise of the greatest virtue, or which was productive of the greatest happiness, or that these two were necessarily connected, and run up into one and the same plan. However, it may not be amiss, once for all, to see what would be the amount of these emendations and imaginary improvements upon the system of nature, or how far they would mislead us. And it seems there could be no stopping, till we came to some such conclusions as these: that all creatures should at first be made as perfect and as happy as they were capable of ever being: that nothing, to be sure, of hazard or danger should be put upon them to do; some indolent persons would perhaps think nothing at all: or certainly, that effectual care should be taken, that they should, whether necessarily or not, yet eventually and in fact, always do what was right and most conducive to happiness, which would be thought easy for infinite power to effect; either by not giving them any principles which would endanger their going wrong; or by laying the right motive of action in every instance before their minds continually in so strong a manner, as would never fail of inducing them to act conformably to it: and that the whole method of government by punishments should be rejected as absurd; as an awkward round-about method of carrying things on; nay, as contrary to a principal purpose, for which it would be supposed creatures were made, namely, happiness.

Now, without considering what is to be said in particular to the several parts of this train of folly and extravagance; what has been above intimated, is a full direct general answer to it, namely, that we may see beforehand that we have not faculties for this kind of speculation. For though it be admitted that, from the first principles of our nature, we unavoidably judge or determine some ends to be absolutely in themselves preferable to others, and that the ends now mentioned, or if they run up into one, that this one is absolutely the best; and consequently that we must conclude the ultimate end designed, in the constitution of Nature and conduct of Providence, is the most virtue and happiness possible; yet we are far from being able to judge what particular disposition of things would be most friendly and assistant to virtue; or what means might be absolutely necessary to produce the most happiness in a system of such extent as our own world may be, taking in all that is past and to come, though we should suppose it detached from the whole of things. Indeed we are so far from being able to judge of this, that we are not judges what may be the necessary means of raising and conducting one person to the highest perfection and happiness of his nature. Nay, even in the little affairs of the present life, we find men of different educations and ranks are not competent judges of the conduct of each other. Our whole nature leads us to ascribe all moral perfection to God, and to deny all imperfection of him. And this will for ever be a practical proof of his moral character, to such as will consider what a practical proof is; because it is the voice of God speaking in us. And from hence we conclude, that virtue must be the happiness, and vice the misery, of every creature; and that regularity and order and right cannot but prevail finally in a universe under his government. But we are in no sort judges, what are the necessary means of accomplishing this end.

Let us then, instead of that idle and not very innocent employment of forming imaginary models of a world, and schemes of governing it, turn our thoughts to what we experience to be the conduct of Nature with respect to intelligent creatures; which may be resolved into general laws or rules of administration, in the same way as many of the laws of Nature respecting inanimate matter may be collected from experiments. And let us compare the known constitution and course of things with what is said to be the moral system of Nature; the acknowledged dispensations of Providence, or that government which we find ourselves under, with what religion teaches us to believe and expect; and see whether they are not analogous and of a piece. And upon such a comparison it will, I think, be found that they are very much so: that both may be traced up to the same general laws, and resolved into the same principles of divine conduct.

The analogy here proposed to be considered is of pretty large extent, and consists of several parts; in some more, in others less exact. In some few instances perhaps it may amount to a real practical proof; in others not so. Yet in these it is a confirmation of what is proved otherwise. It will undeniably show, what too many want to have shown them, that the system of Religion, both natural and revealed, considered only as a system, and prior to the proof of it, is not a subject of ridicule, unless that of Nature be so too. And it will afford an answer to almost all objections against the system both of natural and revealed Religion; though not perhaps an answer in so great a degree, yet in a very considerable degree an answer to the objections against the evidence of it: for objections against a proof, and objections against what is said to be proved, the reader will observe are different things.

Now the divine government of the world, implied in the notion of religion in general and of Christianity, contains in it; that mankind is appointed to live in a future state;* that there every one shall be rewarded or punished;† rewarded or punished respectively for all tha behaviour here, which we comprehend under the words, virtuous or vicious, morally good or evil:‡ that our present life is a probation, a state of trial,§ and of discipline,‖ for that future one; notwithstanding the objections, which men may fancy they have, from notions of Necessity, against there being any such moral plan as this at all;¶ and whatever objections may appear to lie against the wisdom and goodness of it, as it stands so imperfectly made known to us at present:** that this world being in a state of apostasy and wickedness, and consequently of ruin, and the sense both of their condition and duty being greatly corrupted amongst men, this gave occasion for an additional dispensation of Providence; of the utmost importance;†† proved by miracles;‡‡

* Ch. i. † Ch. ii ‡ Ch. iii. § Ch. iv. ‖ Ch. v. ¶ Ch. vi. ** Ch. vii. †† Part II. ch. i. ‡‡ Ch. ii.

but containing in it many things appearing to us strange, and not to have been expected;* a dispensation of Providence, which is a scheme or system of things;† carried on by the mediation of a divine person, the Messiah, in order to the recovery of the world;‡ yet not revealed to all men, nor proved with the strongest possible evidence to all those to whom it is revealed; but only to such a part of mankind, and with such particular evidence, as the wisdom of God thought fit.§ The design then of the following Treatise will be to show, that the several parts principally objected against in this moral and Christian dispensation, including its scheme, its publication, and the proof which God has afforded us of its truth; that the particular parts principally objected against in this whole dispensation, are analogous to what is experienced in the constitution and course of Nature, or Providence; that the chief objections themselves which are alleged against the former, are no other than what may be alleged with like justness against the latter, where they are found in fact to be inconclusive; and that this argument from analogy is in general unanswerable, and undoubtedly of weight on the side of religion,‖ notwithstanding the objections which may seem to lie against it, and the real ground which there may be for difference of opinion, as to the particular degree of weight which is to be laid upon it. This is a general account of what may be looked for in the following Treatise. And I shall begin it with that which is the foundation of all our hopes and of all our fears; all our hopes and fears, which are of any consideration; I mean a Future Life.

* Ch. iii. † Ch. iv. ‡ Ch. v. § Ch. vi. vii. ‖ Ch. viii.

THE

ANALOGY OF RELIGION.

PART I.

OF NATURAL RELIGION.

CHAP. I.

OF A FUTURE LIFE.

Strange difficulties have been raised by some concerning personal identity, or the sameness of living agents, implied in the notion of our existing now and hereafter, or in any two successive moments; which whoever thinks it worth while, may see considered in the first Dissertation at the end of this Treatise. But without regard to any of them here, let us consider what the analogy of nature, and the several changes which we have undergone, and those which we know we may undergo without being destroyed, suggest, as to the effect which death may, or may not, have upon us; and whether it be not from thence probable, that we may survive this change, and exist in a future state of life and perception.

I. From our being born into the present world in the helpless imperfect state of infancy, and having arrived from thence to mature age, we find it to be a general law of nature in our own species, that the same creatures, the same individuals, should exist in degrees of life and perception, with capacities of action, of enjoyment and suffering, in one period of their being, greatly different from those appointed them in another period of it. And in other creatures the same law holds. For the difference of their capacities and states of life at their birth (to go no higher) and in maturity; the change of worms into flies, and the vast enlargement of their locomotive powers by such change: and birds and insects bursting the shell of their habitation, and by this means entering into a new world, furnished with new accommodations for them, and finding a new sphere of action assigned them; these are instances of this general law of nature. Thus all the various and wonderful transformations of animals are to be taken into consideration here. But the states of life in which we ourselves existed formerly in the womb and in our infancy, are almost as different from our present in mature age, as it is possible to conceive any two states or degrees of life can be. Therefore that we are to exist hereafter, in a state as different (suppose) from our present, as this is from our former, is but according to the analogy of nature; according to a natural order or appointment of the very same kind, with what we have already experienced.

II. We know we are endued with capacities of action, of happiness and misery: for we are conscious of acting, of enjoying pleasure and suffering pain. Now that we have these powers and capacities before death, is a presumption that we shall retain them through and after death; indeed a probability of it abundantly sufficient to act upon, unless there be some positive reason to think that death is the destruction of those living powers: because there is in every case a probability, that all things will continue as we experience they are, in all respects, except those in which we have some reason to think they will be altered. This is that *kind** of presumption or probability from analogy, expressed in the very word *continuance*, which seems our only natural reason for believing the course of the world will continue to-morrow, as it has done so far as our experience or knowledge of history can carry us back. Nay it seems our only reason for believing, that any one substance now existing will continue to exist a moment longer; the self-existent substance only excepted. Thus if men were assured that the unknown event, death, was not the destruction of our faculties of perception and of action, there would be no apprehension, that any other power or event, unconnected with this of death, would destroy these

* I say *kind* of presumption or probability; for I do not mean to affirm that there is the same *degree* of conviction, that our living powers will continue after death, as there is, that our substances will.

faculties just at the instant of each creature's death; and therefore no doubt but that they would remain after it; which shows the high probability that our living powers will continue after death, unless there be some ground to think that death is their destruction.* For, if it would be in a manner certain that we should survive death, provided it were certain that death would not be our destruction, it must be highly probable we shall survive it, if there be no ground to think death will be our destruction.

Now, though I think it must be acknowledged, that prior to the natural and moral proofs of a future life commonly insisted upon, there would arise a general confused suspicion, that in the great shock and alteration which we shall undergo by death, we, *i. e.* our living powers, might be wholly destroyed; yet even prior to those proofs, there is really no particular distinct ground or reason for this apprehension at all, so far as I can find. If there be, it must arise either from *the reason of the thing*, or from *the analogy of nature.*

But we cannot argue from *the reason of the thing*, that death is the destruction of living agents, because we know not at all what death is in itself; but only some of its effects, such as the dissolution of flesh, skin, and bones. And these effects do in no wise appear to imply the destruction of a living agent. And besides, as we are greatly in the dark, upon what the exercise of our living powers depends, so we are wholly ignorant what the powers themselves depend upon; the powers themselves as distinguished, not only from their actual exercise, but also from the present capacity of exercising them; and as opposed to their destruction: for sleep, or however a swoon, shows us, not only that these powers exist when they are not exercised, as the passive power of motion does in inanimate matter; but shows

* *Destruction of living powers*, is a manner of expression unavoidably ambiguous; and may signify either *the destruction of a living being, so as that the same living being shall be uncapable of ever perceiving or acting again at all*; or *the destruction of those means and instruments by which it is capable of its present life, of its present state of perception and of action.* It is here used in the former sense. When it is used in the latter, the epithet *present* is added. The loss of a man's eye is a destruction of living powers in the latter sense. But we have no reason to think the destruction of living powers, in the former sense, to be possible. We have no more reason to think a being endued with living powers, ever loses them during its whole existence, than to believe that a stone ever acquires them.

also that they exist, when there is no present capacity of exercising them: or that the capacities of exercising them for the present, as well as the actual exercise of them, may be suspended, and yet the powers themselves remain undestroyed. Since then we know not at all upon what the existence of our living powers depends, this shows further, there can no probability be collected from the reason of the thing, that death will be their destruction: because their existence may depend upon somewhat in no degree affected by death; upon somewhat quite out of the reach of this king of terrors. So that there is nothing more certain, than that *the reason of the thing* shows us no connexion between death and the destruction of living agents. Nor can we find any thing throughout the whole *analogy of nature*, to afford us even the slightest presumption, that animals ever lose their living powers; much less if it were possible, that they lose them by death: for we have no faculties wherewith to trace any beyond or through it, so as to see what becomes of them. This event removes them from our view. It destroys the *sensible* proof, which we had before their death, of their being possessed of living powers, but does not appear to afford the least reason to believe that they are, then, or by that event, deprived of them.

And our knowing, that they were possessed of these powers, up to the very period to which we have faculties capable of tracing them, is itself a probability of their retaining them beyond it. And this is confirmed, and a sensible credibility is given to it, by observing the very great and astonishing changes which we have experienced; so great, that our existence in another state of life, of perception and of action, will be but according to a method of providential conduct, the like to which has been already exercised even with regard to ourselves; according to a course of nature, the like to which we have already gone through.

However, as one cannot but be greatly sensible, how difficult it is to silence imagination enough to make the voice of reason even distinctly heard in this case; as we are accustomed, from our youth up, to indulge that forward, delusive faculty, ever obtruding beyond its sphere; of some assistance indeed to apprehension, but the author of all error: as we plainly lose ourselves in gross and crude conceptions of things, taking for granted that we are acquainted with what indeed we are wholly ignorant of: it may be proper to consider the imaginary presumptions, that death will be our destruction, arising from these kinds of early and lasting prejudices; and to show how little they can really amount to, even though we cannot wholly divest ourselves of them. And,

I. All presumption of death's being the destruction of living beings, must go upon supposition that they are compounded; and so, discerptible. But since consciousness is a single and indivisible power, it should seem that the subject in which it resides must be so too. For were the motion of any particle of matter absolutely one and indivisible, so as that it should imply a contradiction to suppose part of this motion to exist, and part not to exist, *i. e.* part of this matter to move, and part to be at rest; then its power of motion would be indivisible; and so also would the subject in which the power inheres, namely, the particle of matter: for if this could be devided into two, one part might be moved and the other at rest, which is contrary to the supposition. In like manner it has been argued,* and, for any thing appearing to the contrary, justly, that since the perception or consciousness, which we have of our own existence, is indivisible, so as that it is a contradiction to suppose one part of it should be here and the other there; the perceptive power, or the power of consciousness, is indivisible too: and consequently the subject in which it resides; *i. e.* the conscious Being. Now upon supposition that living agent each man calls himself, is thus a single being, which there is at least no more difficulty in conceiving than in conceiving it to be a compound, and of which there is the proof now mentioned; it follows, that our organized bodies are no more ourselves or part of ourselves, than any other matter around us. And it is as easy to conceive, how matter, which is no part of ourselves, may be appropriated to us in the

* See Dr Clarke's Letter to Mr Dodwell, and the defences of it.

manner which our present bodies are; as how we can receive impressions from, and have power over, any matter. It is as easy to conceive, that we may exist out of bodies, as in them; that we might have animated bodies of any other organs and senses wholly different from these now given us, and that we may hereafter animate these same or new bodies variously modified and organized; as to conceive how we can animate such bodies as our present. And lastly, the dissolution of all these several organized bodies, supposing ourselves to have successively animated them, would have no more conceivable tendency to destroy the living beings ourselves, or deprive us of living faculties, the faculties of perception and of action, than the dissolution of any foreign matter, which we are capable of receiving impressions from, and making use of, for the common occasions of life.

II. The simplicity and absolute oneness of a living agent cannot indeed, from the nature of the thing, be properly proved by experimental observations. But as these *fall in* with the supposition of its unity, so they plainly lead us to *conclude* certainly, that our gross organized bodies, with which we perceive the objects of sense, and with which we act, are no part of ourselves; and therefore show us, that we have no reason to believe their destruction to be ours: even without determining whether our living substances be material or immaterial. For we see by experience, that men may lose their limbs, their organs of sense, and even the greatest part of these bodies, and yet remain the same living agents. And persons can trace up the existence of themselves to a time, when the bulk of their bodies was extremely small, in comparison of what it is in mature age: and we cannot but think, that they might then have lost a considerable part of that small body, and yet have remained the same living agents; as they may now lose great part of their present body, and remain so. And it is certain, that the bodies of all animals are in a constant flux, from that never-ceasing attrition, which there is in every part of them. Now things of this kind unavoidably teach us to distinguish, between these living agents ourselves, and large quantities of matter, in which we are very nearly interested: since these may be alienated, and actually are in a daily course of succession, and changing their owners; whilst we are assured, that each living agent remains one and the same permanent being.* And this general observation leads us on to the following ones.

First, That we have no way of determining by experience, what is the certain bulk of the living being each man calls himself: and yet, till it be determined that it is larger in bulk than the solid elementary particles of matter, which there is no ground to think any natural power can dissolve, there is no sort of reason to think death to be the dissolution of it, of the living being, even though it should not be absolutely indiscerptible.

Secondly, From our being so nearly related to and interested in certain systems of matter, suppose our flesh and bones, and afterwards ceasing to be at all related to them, the living agents ourselves remaining all this while undestroyed notwithstanding such alienation; and consequently these systems of matter not being ourselves: it follows further, that we have no ground to conclude any other, suppose *internal systems* of matter, to be the living agents ourselves; because we can have no ground to conclude this, but from our relation to and interest in such other systems of matter: and therefore we can have no reason to conclude, what befalls those systems of matter at death, to be the destruction of the living agents. We have already several times over lost a great part or perhaps the whole of our body, according to certain common established laws of nature; yet we remain the same living agents: when we shall lose as great a part, or the whole, by another common established law of nature, death; why may we not also remain the same? That the alienation has been gradual in one case, and in the other will be more at once, does not prove any thing to the contrary. We have passed undestroyed through those many and great revolutions of matter, so peculiarly appropriated to us ourselves; why should we imagine death will be so

* See Dissertation I.

fatal to us? Nor can it be objected, that what is thus alienated or lost, is no part of our original solid body, but only adventitious matter; because we may lose entire limbs, which must have contained many solid parts and vessels of the original body; or if this be not admitted, we have no proof, that any of these solid parts are dissolved or alienated by death. Though, by the way, we are very nearly related to that extraneous or adventitious matter, whilst it continues united to and distending the several parts of our solid body. But after all; the relation a person bears to those parts of his body, to which he is the most nearly related; what does it appear to amount to but this, that the living agent, and those parts of the body, mutually affect each other? And the same thing, the same thing in kind though not in degree, may be said of *all foreign* matter, which gives us ideas, and which we have any power over. From these observations the whole ground of the imagination is removed, that the dissolution of any matter, is the destruction of a living agent, from the interest he once had in such matter.

Thirdly, If we consider our body somewhat more distinctly, as made up of organs and instruments of perception and of motion, it will bring us to the same conclusion. Thus the common optical experiments show, and even the observation how sight is assisted by glasses shows, that we see with our eyes in the same sense as we see with glasses. Nor is there any reason to believe, that we see with them in any other sense; any other, I mean, which would lead us to think the eye itself a percipient. The like is to be said of hearing: and our feeling distant solid matter by means of somewhat in our hand seems an instance of the like kind, as to the subject we are considering. All these are instances of foreign matter, or such as is no part of our body, being instrumental in preparing objects for, and conveying them to, the perceiving power, in a manner similar or like to the manner in which our organs of sense prepare and convey them. Both are in a like way instruments of our receiving such ideas from external objects, as the Author of nature appointed those external objects to be the occasions of exciting in us. However, glasses are evidently instances of this; namely of matter which is no part of our body, preparing objects for and conveying them towards the perceiving power, in like manner as our bodily organs do. And if we see with our eyes only in the same manner as we do with glasses, the like may justly be concluded, from analogy, of all our other senses. It is not intended, by any thing here said, to affirm, that the whole apparatus of vision, or of perception by any other of our senses, can be traced through all its steps, quite up to the living power of seeing, or perceiving: but that so far as it can be traced by experimental observations, so far it appears, that our organs of sense prepare and convey on objects, in order to their being perceived, in like manner as foreign matter does, without affording any shadow of appearance, that they themselves perceive. And that we have no reason to think our organs of sense percipients, is confirmed by instances of persons losing some of them, the living beings themselves, their former occupiers, remaining unimpaired. It is confirmed also by the experience of dreams; by which we find we are at present possessed of a latent, and what would otherwise be, an unimagined unknown power of perceiving sensible objects, in as strong and lively a manner without our external organs of sense as with them.

So also with regard to our power of moving, or directing motion by will and choice; upon the destruction of a limb, this active power remains, as it evidently seems, unlessened; so as that the living being, who has suffered this loss, would be capable of moving as before, if it had another limb to move with. It can walk by the help of an artificial leg; just as it can make use of a pole or a lever, to reach towards itself and to move things, beyond the length and the power of its natural arm; and this last it does in the same manner as it reaches and moves, with its natural arm, things nearer and of less weight. Nor is there so much as any appearance of our limbs being endued with a power of moving or directing themselves; though they are adapted, like the several parts of a machine, to be the instruments of motion to each other; and some parts of the same limb, to be instruments of motion to other parts of it.

Thus a man determines, that he will look at such an object through a microscope; or being lame suppose, that he will walk to such a place with a staff a week hence. His eyes and his feet no more determine in these cases, than the microscope and the staff. Nor is there any ground to think they any more put the determination in practice; or that his eyes are the seers or his feet the movers, in any other sense than as the microscope and the staff are. Upon the whole then, our organs of sense and our limbs are certainly instruments, which the living persons ourselves make use of to perceive and move with: there is not any probability, that they are any more; nor consequently, that we have any other kind of relation to them, than what we have to any other foreign matter formed into instruments of perception and motion, suppose into a microscope or a staff (I say any other kind of relation, for I am not speaking of the degree of it); nor consequently is there any probability, that the alienation or dissolution of these instruments is the destruction of the perceiving and moving agent.

And thus our finding, that the dissolution of matter, in which living beings were most nearly interested, is not their dissolution; and that the destruction of several of the organs and instruments of perception and of motion belonging to them, is not their destruction; shows demonstratively, that there is no ground to think that the dissolution of any other matter, or destruction of any other organs and instruments, will be the dissolution or destruction of living agents, from the like kind of relation. And we have no reason to think we stand in any other kind of relation to any thing which we find dissolved by death.

But it is said these observations are equally applicable to brutes: and it is thought an insuperable difficulty, that they should be immortal, and by consequence capable of everlasting happiness. Now this manner of expression is both invidious and weak: but the thing intended by it, is really no difficulty at all, either in the way of natural or moral consideration. For 1st, Suppose the invidious thing, designed in such a manner of expression, were really implied, as it is not in the least, in the natural immortality of brutes: namely, that they must arrive at great attainments, and become rational and moral agents; even this would be no difficulty: since we know not what latent powers and capacities they may be endued with. There was once, prior to experience, as great presumption against human creatures as there is against the brute creatures, arriving at that degree of understanding, which we have in mature age. For we can trace up our own existence to the same original with the[illegible]s. And we find it to be a general law of nature, that creatures endued with capacities of virtue and religion should be placed in a condition of being, in which they are altogether without the use of them, for a considerable length of their duration; as in infancy and childhood. And great part of the human species go out of the present world, before they come to the exercise of these capacities in any degree at all. But then, 2dly, the natural immortality of brutes does not in the least imply, that they are endued with any latent capacities of a rational or moral nature. And the economy of the universe might require, that there should be living creatures without any capacities of this kind. And all difficulties as to the manner how they are to be disposed of are so apparently and wholly founded in our ignorance, that it is wonderful they should be insisted upon by any, but such as are weak enough to think they are acquainted with the whole system of things. There is then absolutely nothing at all in this objection, which is so rhetorically urged, against the greatest part of the natural proofs or presumptions of the immortality of human minds; I say the greatest part; for it is less applicable to the following observation, which is more peculiar to mankind:

III. That as it is evident our *present* powers and capacities of reason, memory, and affection, do not depend upon our gross body in the manner in which perception by our organs of sense does; so they do not appear to depend upon it at all in any such manner, as to gi ground to think, that the dissolution of this body will be the destruction of these our *present* powers of reflection, as it will of our powers of sensation; or to give ground to conclude, even that it will be so much as a suspension of the former.

Human creatures exist at present in two states of life and perception, greatly different from each other; each of which has its own peculiar laws and its own peculiar enjoyments and sufferings. When any of our senses are affected or appetites gratified with the objects of them, we may be said to exist or live in a state of sensation. When none of our senses are affected or appetites gratified, and yet we perceive, and reason, and act; we may be said to exist or live in a state of reflection. Now it is by no means certain, that any thing which is dissolved by death, is any way necessary to the living being in this its state of reflection, after ideas are gained. For, though, from our present constitution and condition of being, our external organs of sense are necessary for conveying in ideas to our reflecting powers, as carriages, and levers, and scaffolds are in architecture: yet when these ideas are brought in, we are capable of reflecting in the most intense degree, and of enjoying the greatest pleasure, and feeling the greatest pain, by means of that reflection, without any assistance from our senses; and without any at all, which we know of, from that body which will be dissolved by death. It does not appear then, that the relation of this gross body to the reflecting being is, in any degree, necessary to thinking; to our intellectual enjoyments or sufferings: nor, consequently, that the dissolution or alienation of the former by death, will be the destruction of those present powers, which render us capable of this state of reflection. Further, there are instances of mortal diseases, which do not at all affect our present intellectual powers; and this affords a presumption, that those diseases will not destroy these present powers. Indeed, from the observations made above, * it appears, that there is no presumption, from their mutually affecting each other, that the dissolution of the body is the destruction of the liv-

* Pp. 64, 65.

ing agent. And by the same reasoning, it must appear too, that there is no presumption, from their mutually affecting each other, that the dissolution of the body is the destruction of our present reflecting powers: but instances of their not affecting each other, afford a presumption of the contrary. Instances of mortal diseases not impairing our present reflecting powers, evidently turn our thoughts even from imagining such diseases to be the destruction of them. Several things indeed greatly affect all our living powers, and at length suspend the exercise of them; as for instance drowsiness, increasing till it ends in sound sleep: and from hence we might have imagined it would destroy them, till we found by experience the weakness of this way of judging. But in the diseases now mentioned, there is not so much as this shadow of probability, to lead us to any such conclusion, as to the reflecting powers which we have at present. For in those diseases, persons the moment before death appear to be in the highest vigour of life. They discover apprehension, memory, reason, all entire; with the utmost force of affection; sense of a character, of shame and honour; and the highest mental enjoyments and sufferings, even to the last gasp: and these surely prove even greater vigour of life than bodily strength does. Now what pretence is there for thinking, that a progressive disease when arrived to such a degree, I mean that degree which is mortal, will destroy those powers, which were not impaired, which were not affected by it, during its whole progress quite up to that degree? And if death by diseases of this kind is not the destruction of our present reflecting powers, it will scarce be thought that death by any other means is.

It is obvious that this general observation may be carried on further: and there appears so little connexion between our bodily powers of sensation, and our present powers of reflection, that there is no reason to conclude, that death, which destroys the former, does so much as suspend the exercise of the latter, or interrupt our *continuing* to exist in the like state of reflection which we do now. For suspension of reason, memory, and the affections which they excite, is no part of the idea of death, nor is implied in our notion of it. And our daily experiencing these powers to be exercised, without any assistance, that we know of, from those bodies, which will be dissolved by death; and our finding often, that the exercise of them is so lively to the last; these things afford a sensible apprehension, that death may not perhaps be so much as a discontinuance of the exercise of these powers, nor of the enjoyments and sufferings which it implies.* So that our posthumous life, whatever there may be in it additional to our present, yet may not be entirely beginning anew; but going on. Death may, in some sort, and in some respects, answer to our birth; which is not a suspension of the faculties which we had before it, or a total change of the state of life in which we existed when in the womb; but a continuation of both, with such and such great alterations.

Nay, for ought we know of ourselves, of our present life and of death; death may immediately, in the natural course of things, put us into a higher and more enlarged state of life, as our birth does;† a state in which our capacities, and sphere of perception and of action, may be much greater than at present. For as our relation to our external organs of sense, renders us capable of existing in our present state of sensation; so it may be the only natural hinderance to our existing, immediately, and of course, in a higher state of reflection. The truth is, reason does not at all show us, in what state death naturally leaves us. But were we sure, that it would suspend all our perceptive and active powers; yet the suspension of a power and the destruction of it, are effects

* There are three distinct questions, relating to a future life, here considered: Whether death be the destruction of living agents; if not, Whether it be the destruction of their *present* powers of reflection, as it certainly is the destruction of their present powers of sensation; and if not, Whether it be the suspension, or discontinuance of the exercise of these present reflecting powers. Now, if there be no reason to believe the last, there will be, if that were possible, less for the next, and less still for the first.

† This, according to Strabo, was the opinion of the Brachmans, νομίζειν μὲν γὰρ δὴ τὸν μὲν ἐνθάδε βίον, ὡς ἂν ἀκμὴν κυομένων εἶναι· τὸν δὲ θάνατον, γένεσιν εἰς τὸν ὄντως βίον, καὶ τὸν εὐδαίμονα τοῖς φιλοσοφήσασι· Lib. xv. p. 1039, Ed. Amst. 1707. To which opinion perhaps Antoninus may allude in these words, ὡς νῦν περιμένεις, πότε ἔμβρυον ἐκ τῆς γαστρὸς τῆς γυναικός σου ἐξέλθῃ. οὕτως ἐκδέχεσθαι, τὴν ὥραν ἐν ᾗ τὸ ψυχάριόν σου τοῦ ἐλύτρου τούτου ἐκπεσεῖται. Lib. ix. c. 3.

so totally different in kind, as we experience from sleep and a swoon, that we cannot in any wise argue from one to the other; or conclude even to the lowest degree of probability, that the same kind of force which is sufficient to suspend our faculties, though it be increased ever so much, will be sufficient to destroy them.

These observations together may be sufficient to show, how little presumption there is, that death is the destruction of human creatures. However, there is the shadow of an analogy, which may lead us to imagine it is the supposed likeness which is observed between the decay of vegetables, and of living creatures. And this likeness is indeed sufficient to afford the poets very apt allusions to the flowers of the field, in their pictures of the frailty of our present life. But in reason, the analogy is so far from holding, that there appears no ground even for the comparison, as to the present question; because one of the two subjects compared is wholly void of that, which is the principal and chief thing in the other, the power of perception and of action; and which is the only thing we are inquiring about the continuance of. So that the destruction of a vegetable, is an event not similar or analogous to the destruction of a living agent.

But if, as was above intimated, leaving off the delusive custom of substituting imagination in the room of experience, we would confine ourselves to what we do know and understand; if we would argue only from that, and from that form our expectations; it would appear at first sight, that as no probability of living beings ever ceasing to be so, can be concluded from the reason of the thing; so none can be collected from the analogy of Nature; because we cannot trace any living beings beyond death. But as we are conscious that we are endued with capacities of perception and of action, and are living persons; what we are to go upon is, that we shall continue so, till we foresee some accident or event, which will endanger those capacities, or be likely to destroy us: which death does in no wise appear to be.

And thus, when we go out of this world, we may pass into new scenes, and a new state of life and action, just as naturally as we came into the present. And this new state may naturally be a social one. And the advantages of it, advantages of every kind, may naturally be bestowed, according to some fixed general laws of wisdom, upon every one in proportion to the degrees of his virtue. And though the advantages of that future natural state should not be bestowed, as these of the present in some measure are, by the will of the society; but entirely by his more immediate action, upon whom the whole frame of nature depends: yet this distribution may be just as natural, as their being distributed here by the instrumentality of men. And indeed, though one were to allow any confused undetermined sense, which people please to put upon the word *natural*, it would be a shortness of thought scarce credible, to imagine, that no system or course of things can be so, but only what we see at present:* especially whilst the probability of a future life, or the natural immortality of the soul, is admitted upon the evidence of reason; because this is really both admitting and denying at once, a state of being different from the present to be natural. But the only distinct meaning of that word is, *stated*, *fixed*, or *settled:* since what is natural as much requires and presupposes an intelligent agent to render it so, *i. e.* to effect it continually, or at stated times; as what is supernatural or miraculous does to effect it for once. And from hence it must follow, that persons' notion of what is natural, will be enlarged in proportion to their greater knowledge of the works of God, and the dispensations of his Providence. Nor is there any absurdity in supposing, that there may be beings in the universe, whose capacities, and knowledge, and views, may be so extensive, as that the whole Christian dispensation may to them appear natural, *i. e.* analogous or conformable to God's dealings with other parts of his creation; as natural as the visible known course of things appears to us. For there seems scarce any other possible sense to be put upon the word, but that only in which it is here used; similar, stated, or uniform.

This credibility of a future life, which has been here insisted upon, how little soever it may satisfy our curiosity,

* See Part II. Chap. ii. and Part II. Chap. iv.

seems to answer all the purposes of religion, in like manner as a demonstrative proof would. Indeed a proof, even a demonstrative one, of a future life, would not be a proof of religion. For, that we are to live hereafter, is just as reconcilable with the scheme of atheism, and as well to be accounted for by it, as that we are now alive is: and therefore nothing can be more absurd than to argue from that scheme, that there can be no future state. But as religion implies a future state, any presumption against such a state, is a presumption against religion. And the foregoing observations remove all presumptions of that sort, and prove, to a very considerable degree of probability, one fundamental doctrine of religion; which, if believed, would greatly open and dispose the mind seriously to attend to the general evidence of the whole.

CHAP. II.

OF THE GOVERNMENT OF GOD BY REWARDS AND PUNISHMENTS; AND PARTICULARLY OF THE LATTER.

THAT which makes the question concerning a future life to be of so great importance to us, is our capacity of happiness and misery. And that which makes the consideration of it to be of so great importance to us, is the supposition of our happiness and misery hereafter depending upon our actions here. Without this indeed, curiosity could not but sometimes bring a subject, in which we may be so highly interested, to our thoughts; especially upon the mortality of others, or the near prospect of our own. But reasonable men would not take any further thought about hereafter, than what should happen thus occasionally to rise in their minds, if it were certain that our future interest no way depended upon our present behaviour; whereas, on the contrary, if there be ground, either from analogy or any thing else, to think it does; then there is reason also for the most active thought and solicitude, to secure that interest; to behave so as that we may escape that misery, and obtain that happiness, in another life, which we not only suppose ourselves capable of, but which we apprehend also is put in our own power. And whether there be ground for this last apprehension, certainly would deserve to be most seriously considered, were there no other proof of a future life and interest, than that presumptive one, which the foregoing observations amount to.

Now in the present state, all which we enjoy, and a great part of what we suffer, *is put in our own power.* For pleasure and pain are the consequences of our actions; and we are endued by the Author of our nature with capacities of foreseeing these consequences. We find by experience he does not so much as preserve our lives, exclusively of our own care and attention, to provide ourselves with, and to make use of, that sustenance, by which he has appointed our lives shall be preserved; and without which, he has appointed, they shall not be preserved at all. And in general we foresee, that the external things, which are the objects of our various passions, can neither be obtained nor enjoyed, without exerting ourselves in such and such manners: but by thus exerting ourselves, we obtain and enjoy these objects, in which our natural good consists; or by this means God gives us the possession and enjoyment of them. I know not, that we have any one kind or degree of enjoyment, but by the means of our own actions. And by prudence and care, we may, for the most part, pass our days in tolerable ease and quiet: or, on the contrary, we may, by rashness, ungoverned passion, wilfulness, or even by negligence, make ourselves as miserable as ever we please. And many do please to make themselves extremely miserable, *i. e.* to do what they know beforehand will render them so. They follow those ways, the fruit of which they know, by instruction, example, experience, will be disgrace, and poverty, and sickness, and untimely death. This every one observes to be the general course of things; though it is to be allowed, we cannot find by experience, that all our sufferings are owing to our own follies.

Why the Author of Nature does not give his creatures promiscuously such and such perceptions, without regard to their behaviour; why he does not make them happy without the instrumentality of their own actions, and prevent their bringing any sufferings upon themselves; is another matter. Perhaps there may be some impossibilities in the nature of things, which we are unacquainted with.* Or less happiness, it may be, would upon the whole be produced by such a method of conduct, than is by the present. Or perhaps divine goodness, with which, if I mistake not, we make very free in our speculations, may not be a bare single disposition to produce happiness; but a disposition to make the good, the faithful, the honest man happy. Perhaps an infinitely perfect Mind may be pleased with seeing his creatures behave suitably to the nature which he has given them; to the relations which he has placed them in to each other; and to that which they stand in to himself: that relation to himself, which, during their existence, is even necessary, and which is the most important one of all: perhaps, I say, an infinitely perfect Mind may be pleased with this moral piety of moral agents, in and for itself; as well as upon account of its being essentially conducive to the happiness of his creation. Or the whole end, for which God made, and thus governs the world, may be utterly beyond the reach of our faculties: there may be somewhat in it as impossible for us to have any conception of, as for a blind man to have a conception of colours. But however this be, it is certain matter of universal experience, that the general method of divine administration is, forewarning us, or giving us capacities to foresee, with more or less clearness, that if we act so and so, we shall have such enjoyments, if so and so, such sufferings; and giving us those enjoyments, and making us feel those sufferings, in consequence of our actions.

"But all this is to be ascribed to the general course of nature." True. This is the very thing which I am observing. It is to be ascribed to the general course of nature: *i. e.* not surely to the words or ideas, *course of nature;* but to him who appointed it, and put things into it: or to a course of operation, from its uniformity or constancy, called natural;† and which necessarily implies an operating agent. For when men find them-

* Part I. Chap. vii. † P. 72.

selves necessitated to confess an Author of Nature, or that God is the natural governor of the world; they must not deny this again, because his government is uniform; they must not deny that he does things at all, because he does them constantly; because the effects of his acting are permanent, whether his acting be so or not; though there is no reason to think it is not. In short, every man, in every thing he does, naturally acts upon the forethought and apprehension of avoiding evil or obtaining good: and if the natural course of things be the appointment of God, and our natural faculties of knowledge and experience are given us by him; then the good and bad consequences which follow our actions, are his appointment, and our foresight of those consequences, is a warning given us by him, how we are to act.

"Is the pleasure then, naturally accompanying every particular gratification of passion, intended to put us upon gratifying ourselves in every such particular instance, and as a reward to us for so doing?" No certainly. Nor is it to be said, that our eyes were naturally intended to give us the sight of each particular object, to which they do or can extend; objects which are destructive of them, or which, for any other reason, it may become us to turn our eyes from. Yet there is no doubt, but that our eyes were intended for us to see with. So neither is there any doubt, but that the foreseen pleasures and pains belonging to the passions, were intended, in general, to induce mankind to act in such and such manners.

Now from this general observation, obvious to every one, that God has given us to understand, he has appointed satisfaction and delight to be the consequence of our acting in one manner, and pain and uneasiness of our acting in another, and of our not acting at all; and that we find the consequences, which we were beforehand informed of, uniformly to follow; we may learn, that we are at present actually under his government in the strictest and most proper sense; in such a sense, as that he rewards and punishes us for our actions An Author of nature being supposed, it is not so much a deduction of reason, as a matter of experience, that we are thus under his government; under his government, in the same sense, as we are under the government of civil magistrates. Because the annexing pleasure to some actions, and pain to others, in our power to do or forbear, and giving notice of this appointment beforehand to those whom it concerns; is the proper formal notion of government. Whether the pleasure or pain which thus follows upon our behaviour, be owing to the Author of Nature's acting upon us every moment which we feel it; or to his having at once contrived and executed his own part in the plan of the world; makes no alteration as to the matter before us. For if civil magistrates could make the sanctions of their laws take place, without interposing at all, after they had passed them; without a trial, and the formalities of an execution: if they were able to make their laws execute themselves, or every offender to execute them upon himself; we should be just in the same sense under their government then, as we are now; but in a much higher degree, and more perfect manner. Vain is the ridicule, with which one foresees some persons will divert themselves, upon finding lesser pains considered as instances of divine punishment. There is no possibility of answering or evading the general thing here intended, without denying all final causes. For final causes being admitted, the pleasures and pains now mentioned must be admitted too as instances of them. And if they are; if God annexes delight to some actions, and uneasiness to others, with an apparent design to induce us to act so and so: then he not only dispenses happiness and misery, but also rewards and punishes actions. If, for example, the pain which we feel, upon doing what tends to the destruction of our bodies, suppose upon too near approaches to fire, or upon wounding ourselves, be appointed by the Author of Nature to prevent our doing what thus tends to our destruction; this is altogether as much an instance of his punishing our actions, and consequently of our being under his government, as declaring by a voice from heaven, that if we acted so, he would inflict such pain upon us, and inflicting it, whether it be greater or less.

Thus we find, that the true notion or conception of

the Author of Nature, is that of a master or governor, prior to the consideration of his moral attributes. The fact of our case, which we find by experience, is, that he actually exercises dominion or government over us at present, by rewarding and punishing us for our actions, in as strict and proper a sense of these words, and even in the same sense, as children, servants, subjects, are rewarded and punished by those who govern them.

And thus the whole analogy of Nature, the whole present course of things, most fully shows, that there is nothing incredible in the general doctrine of religion, that God will reward and punish men for their actions hereafter: nothing incredible, I mean, arising out of the notion of rewarding and punishing. For the whole course of nature is a present instance of his exercising that government over us, which implies in it rewarding and punishing.

But as divine punishment is what men chiefly object against, and are most unwilling to allow; it may be proper to mention some circumstances in the natural course of punishments at present, which are analogous to what religion teaches us concerning a future state of punishment; indeed so analogous, that as they add a further credibility to it, so they cannot but raise a most serious apprehension of it in those who will attend to them.

It has been now observed, that such and such miseries naturally follow such and such actions of imprudence and wilfulness, as well as actions more commonly and more distinctly considered as vicious; and that these consequences, when they may be foreseen, are properly natural punishments annexed to such actions. For the general thing here insisted upon, is, not that we see a great deal of misery in the world, but a great deal which men bring upon themselves by their own behaviour, which they might have foreseen and avoided. Now the circumstances of these natural punishments, particularly deserving our attention, are such as these; That oftentimes they follow, or are inflicted in consequence of, actions which procure many present advantages, and are accompanied with much present pleasure; for instance, sickness and untimely death are the consequence of intemperance, though accompanied with the highest mirth and jollity: that these punishments are often much greater, than the advantages or pleasures obtained by the actions, of which they are the punishments or consequences: that though we may imagine a constitution of nature, in which these natural punishments, which are in fact to follow, would follow, immediately upon such actions being done, or very soon after; we find on the contrary in our world, that they are often delayed a great while, sometimes even till long after the actions occasioning them are forgot; so that the constitution of nature is such, that delay of punishment is no sort nor degree of presumption of final impunity: that after such delay, these natural punishments or miseries often come, not by degrees, but suddenly, with violence, and at once; however, the chief misery often does: that as certainty of such distant misery following such actions, is never afforded persons; so perhaps during the actions, they have seldom a distinct, full expectation of its following:* and many times the case is only thus, that they see in general, or may see, the credibility, that intemperance, suppose, will bring after it diseases; civil crimes, civil punishments; when yet the real probability often is, that they shall escape; but things notwithstanding take their destined course, and the misery inevitably follows at its appointed time, in very many of these cases. Thus also though youth may be alleged as an excuse for rashness and folly, as being naturally thoughtless, and not clearly foreseeing all the consequences of being untractable and profligate; this does not hinder, but that these consequences follow; and are grievously felt, throughout the whole course of mature life. Habits contracted even in that age, are often utter ruin: and men's success in the world, not only in the common sense of worldly success, but their real happiness and misery, depends, in a great degree, and in various ways, upon the manner in which they pass their youth which consequences they for the most part ne-

* See Part II. Chap. vi.

glect to consider, and perhaps seldom can properly be said to believe, beforehand. It requires also to be mentioned, that, in numberless cases, the natural course of things affords us opportunities for procuring advantages to ourselves at certain times, which we cannot procure when we will; nor ever recall the opportunities, if we have neglected them. Indeed the general course of nature is an example of this. If, during the opportunity of youth, persons are indocile and self-willed; they inevitably suffer in their future life, for want of those acquirements, which they neglected the natural season of attaining. If the husbandman lets his seedtime pass without sowing, the whole year is lost to him beyond recovery. In like manner, though after men have been guilty of folly and extravagance *up to a certain degree*, it is often in their power, for instance, to retrieve their affairs, to recover their health and character; at least in good measure, yet real reformation is in many cases, of no avail at all towards preventing the miseries, poverty, sickness, infamy, naturally annexed to folly and extravagance *exceeding that degree.* There is a certain bound to imprudence and misbehaviour, which being transgressed, there remains no place for repentance in the natural course of things. It is further very much to be remarked, that neglects from inconsiderateness, want of attention,* not looking about us to see what we have to do, are often attended with consequences altogether as dreadful, as any active misbehaviour, from the most extravagant passion. And lastly, civil government being natural, the punishments of it are so too: and some of these punishments are capital; as the effects of a dissolute course of pleasure are often mortal. So that many natural punishments are final † to him who incurs them, if considered only in his

* Part II. Chap. vi.

† The general consideration of a future state of punishment, most evidently belongs to the subject of natural Religion. But if any of these reflections should be thought to relate more peculiarly to this doctrine, as taught in Scripture; the reader is desired to observe, that Gentile writers, both moralists and poets, speak of the future punishment of the wicked, both as to the duration and degree of it, in a like manner of expression and of description, as the Scripture does. So that all which can positively be asserted to be matter of mere Revelation, with regard to this doctrine, seems to be, that the great distinction between the righteous and the wicked shall be made at the end of this world; that each shall *then* receive according to

temporal capacity: and seem inflicted by natural appointment, either to remove the offender out of the way of being further mischievous; or as an example, though frequently a disregarded one, to those who are left behind.

These things are not what we call accidental, or to be met with only now and then; but they are things of every day's experience: they proceed from general laws, very general ones, by which God governs the world, in the natural course of his providence. And they are so analogous, to what Religion teaches us concerning the future punishment of the wicked, so much of a piece with it, that both would naturally be expressed in the very same words, and manner of description. In the book of *Proverbs*,* for instance, Wisdom is introduced, as frequenting the most public places of resort, and as rejected when she offers herself as the natural appointed guide of human life. *How long*, speaking to those who are passing through it, *how long, ye simple ones, will ye love folly, and the scorners delight in their scorning, and fools hate knowledge? Turn ye at my reproof. Behold, I will pour out my spirit upon you, I will make known my words unto you.* But upon being neglected, *Because I have called, and ye refused, I have stretched out my hand, and no man regarded; but ye have set at nought all my counsel, and would none of my reproof: I also will laugh at your calamity, I will mock when your fear cometh; when your fear cometh as desolation, and your destruction cometh as a whirlwind; when distress and anguish cometh upon you. Then shall they call upon me, but I will not answer; they shall seek me early, but they shall not find me.* This passage, every one sees, is poetical, and some parts of it are highly figurative; but their meaning is obvious. And

deserts. Reason did, as it well might, conclude that it should, finally and upon the whole, be well with the righteous, and ill with the wicked: but it could not be determined upon any principles of reason, whether human creatures might not have been appointed to pass through other states of life and being, before that distributive justice should finally and effectually take place. Revelation teaches us, that the next state of things after the present is appointed for the execution of this justice; that it shall be no longer delayed; but *the mystery of God*, the great mystery of his suffering vice and confusion to prevail, *shall then be finished; and he will take to him his great power and will reign* by rendering to every one according to his works.

* Chap. i.

the thing intended is expressed more literally in the following words; *For that they hated knowledge, and did not choose the fear of the Lord——therefore shall they eat of the fruit of their own way, and be filled with their own devices. For the security of the simple shall slay them, and the prosperity of fools shall destroy them.* And the whole passage is so equally applicable to what we experience in the present world, concerning the consequences of men's actions, and to what Religion teaches us is to be expected in another, that it may be questioned which of the two was principally intended.

Indeed when one has been recollecting the proper proofs of a future state of rewards and punishments, nothing methinks can give one so sensible an apprehension of the latter, or representation of it to the mind; as observing, that after the many disregarded checks, admonitions, and warnings, which people meet with in the ways of vice and folly and extravagance: warnings from their very nature; from the examples of others; from the lesser inconveniences which they bring upon themselves; from the instructions of wise and virtuous men: after these have been long despised, scorned, ridiculed: after the chief bad consequences, temporal consequences, of their follies, have been delayed for a great while; at length they break in irresistibly, like an armed force: repentance is too late to relieve, and can serve only to aggravate their distress, the case is become desperate: and poverty and sickness, remorse and anguish, infamy and death, the effects of their own doings, overwhelm them beyond possibility of remedy or escape. This is an account of what is in fact the general constitution of nature.

It is not in any sort meant, that, according to what appears at present of the natural course of things, men are always uniformly punished in proportion to their misbehaviour: but that there are very many instances of misbehaviour punished in the several ways now mentioned, and very dreadful instances too; sufficient to show what the laws of the universe may admit; and, if thoroughly considered, sufficient fully to answer all objections against the credibility of a future state of punishments, from any imaginations, that the frailty of our nature and external temptations, almost annihilate the guilt of human vices: as well as objections of another sort; from necessity; from suppositions, that the will of an infinite Being cannot be contradicted; or that he must be incapable of offence and provocation.*

Reflections of this kind are not without their terrors to serious persons, the most free from enthusiasm, and of the greatest strength of mind; but it is fit things be stated and considered as they really are. And there is, in the present age, a certain fearlessness, with regard to what may be hereafter under the government of God, which nothing but an universally acknowledged demonstration on the side of atheism can justify; and which makes it quite necessary, that men be reminded, and if possible made to feel, that there is no sort of ground for being thus presumptuous, even upon the most sceptical principles. For, may it not be said of any person upon his being born into the world, he may behave so, as to be of no service to it, but by being made an example of the woeful effects of vice and folly? That he may, as any one may, if he will, incur an infamous execution, from the hands of civil justice; or in some other course of extravagance shorten his days; or bring upon himself infamy and diseases worse than death? So that it had been better for him, even with regard to the present world, that he had never been born. And is there any pretence of reason, for people to think themselves secure, and talk as if they had certain proof, that, let them act as licentiously as they will, there can be nothing analogous to this, with regard to a future and more general interest, under the providence and government of the same God?

CHAP. III.

OF THE MORAL GOVERNMENT OF GOD.

As the manifold appearances of design and of **final causes,** in the constitution of the world, prove it to be the

* See Chap. iv. and vi.

work of an intelligent Mind; so the particular final causes of pleasure and pain distributed amongst his creatures, prove that they are under his government; what may be called his natural government of creatures endued with sense and reason. This, however, implies somewhat more than seems usually attended to, when we speak of God's natural government of the world. It implies government of the very same kind with that which a master exercises over his servants, or a civil magistrate over his subjects. These latter instances of final causes, as really prove an intelligent *Governor* of the world, in the sense now mentioned, and before* distinctly treated of; as any other instances of final causes prove an intelligent *Maker* of it.

But this alone does not appear at first sight to determine any thing certainly, concerning the moral character of the Author of Nature, considered in this relation of governor; does not ascertain his government to be moral, or prove that he is the righteous judge of the world. Moral government consists, not barely in rewarding and punishing men for their actions, which the most tyrannical person may do: but in rewarding the righteous, and punishing the wicked: in rendering to men according to their actions, considered as good or evil. And the perfection of moral government consists in doing this, with regard to all intelligent creatures, in an exact proportion to their personal merits or demerits.

Some men seem to think the only character of the Author of Nature to be that of simple absolute benevolence. This, considered as a principle of action and infinite in degree, is a disposition to produce the greatest possible happiness, without regard to persons' behaviour, otherwise than as such regard would produce higher degrees of it. And supposing this to be the only character of God, veracity and justice in him would be nothing but benevolence conducted by wisdom. Now surely this ought not to be asserted, unless it can be proved; for we should speak with cautious reverence upon such a subject. And whether it can be proved or no, is not the thing here to be inquired into; but whether in the constitution

* Chap. ii.

and conduct of the world, a righteous government be not discernibly planned out: which necessarily implies a righteous governor. There may possibly be in the creation beings, to whom the Author of Nature manifests himself under this most amiable of all characters, this of infinite absolute benevolence; for it is the most amiable, supposing it not, as perhaps it is not, incompatible with justice; but he manifests himself to us under the character of a righteous governor. He may, consistently with this, be simply and absolutely benevolent, in the sense now explained: but he is (for he has given us a proof in the constitution and conduct of the world that he is) a governor over servants, as he rewards and punishes us for our actions. And in the constitution and conduct of it, he may also have given, besides the reason of the thing, and the natural presages of conscience, clear and distinct intimations, that his government is righteous or moral: clear to such as think the nature of it deserving their attention; and yet not to every careless person, who casts a transient reflection upon the subject.*

But it is particularly to be observed, that the divine government, which we experience ourselves under in the present state, taken alone, is allowed not to be the perfection of moral government. And yet this by no means hinders, but that there may be somewhat, be it more or less, truly moral in it. A righteous government may plainly appear to be carried on to some degree: enough to give us the apprehension that it shall be completed, or carried on to that degree of perfection which religion teaches us it shall; but which cannot appear, till much more of the divine administration be seen, than can in the present life. And the design of this Chapter is to inquire how far this is the case: how far, over and above the moral nature† which God has given us, and our natural notion

* The objections against religion, from the evidence of it not being universal, nor so strong as might possibly have been, may be urged against natural religion, as well as against revealed. And therefore the consideration of them belongs to the first part of this Treatise, as well as the second. But as these objections are chiefly urged against revealed religion, I choose to consider them in the second part. And the answer to them there, Ch. vi., as urged against Christianity, being almost equally applicable to them as urged against the Religion of Nature; to avoid repetition, the reader is referred to that chapter.

† Dissertation II.

of him as righteous governor of those his creatures, to whom he has given this nature;* I say how far besides this, the principles and beginnings of a moral government over the world may be discerned, notwithstanding and amidst all the confusion and disorder of it.

Now one might mention here, what has been often urged with great force, that, in general, less uneasiness and more satisfaction, are the natural consequences† of a virtuous than of a vicious course of life, in the present state, as an instance of a moral government established in nature; an instance of it collected from experience and present matter of fact. But it must be owned a thing of difficulty to weigh and balance pleasures and uneasinesses, each amongst themselves, and also against each other, so as to make an estimate with any exactness, of the overplus of happiness on the side of virtue. And it is not impossible, that, amidst the infinite disorders of the world, there may be exceptions to the happiness of virtue; even with regard to those persons, whose course of life from their youth up has been blameless: and more with regard to those who have gone on for some time in the ways of vice, and have afterwards reformed. For suppose an instance of the latter case; a person with his passions inflamed, his natural faculty of self-government impaired by habits of indulgence, and with all his vices about him, like so many harpies, craving for their accustomed gratification: who can say how long it might be, before such a person would find more satisfaction in the reasonableness and present good consequences of virtue, than difficulties and self-denial in the restraints of it? Experience also shows, that men can to a great degree, get over their sense of shame, so as that by professing themselves to be without principle, and avowing even direct villany, they can support themselves against the infamy of it. But as the ill actions of any one will probably be more talked of, and oftener thrown in his way, upon his reformation; so the infamy of them will be much more felt, after the natural sense of virtue and of honour is recovered. Uneasinesses of this kind

* Chap. vi.

† See Lord Shaftesbury's Inquiry concerning Virtue, Part II.

ought indeed to be put to the account of former vices: yet it will be said they are in part the consequences of reformation. Still I am far from allowing it doubtful, whether virtue, upon the whole, be happier than vice in the present world. But if it were, yet the beginnings of a righteous administration may, beyond all question, be found in nature, if we will attentively inquire after them. And,

I. In whatever manner the notion of God's moral government over the world might be treated, if it did not appear, whether he were in a proper sense our governor at all; yet when it is certain matter of experience, that he does manifest himself to us under the character of a governor in the sense explained;* it must deserve to be considered, whether there be not reason to apprehend, that he may be a righteous or moral governor. Since it appears to be fact, that God does govern mankind by the method of rewards and punishments, according to some settled rules of distribution; it is surely a question to be asked, what presumption is there against his finally rewarding and punishing them according to this particular rule, namely, as they act reasonably, or unreasonably, virtuously or viciously? since rendering men happy or miserable by this rule, certainly falls in, much more falls in, with our natural apprehensions and sense of things, than doing so by any other rule whatever; since rewarding and punishing actions by any other rule, would appear much harder to be accounted for, by minds formed as he has formed ours. Be the evidence of religion then more or less clear, the expectation which it raises in us, that the righteous shall, upon the whole, be happy, and the wicked miserable, cannot however possibly be considered as absurd or chimerical; because it is no more than an expectation, that a method of government already begun, shall be carried on, the method of rewarding and punishing actions; and shall be carried on by a particular rule, which unavoidably appears to us at first sight more natural than any other, the rule which we call distributive justice. Nor,

II. Ought it to be entirely passed over, that tranquillity

* Chap. ii.

satisfaction, and external advantages, being the natural consequences of prudent management of ourselves, and our affairs; and rashness, profligate negligence, and wilful folly, bringing after them many inconveniences and sufferings; these afford instances of a right constitution of nature: as the correction of children, for their own sakes, and by way of example, when they run into danger or hurt themselves, is a part of right education? And thus, that God governs the world by general fixed laws, that he has endued us with capacities of reflecting upon this constitution of things, and foreseeing the good and bad consequences of our behaviour; plainly implies some sort of moral government; since from such a constitution of things it cannot but follow, that prudence and imprudence, which are of the nature of virtue and vice,* must be, as they are, respectively rewarded and punished.

III. From the natural course of things, vicious actions are, to a great degree, actually punished as mischievous to society; and besides punishment actually inflicted upon this account, there is also the fear and apprehension of it in those persons, whose crimes have rendered them obnoxious to it, in case of a discovery; this state of fear being itself often a very considerable punishment. The natural fear and apprehension of it too, which restrains from such crimes, is a declaration of nature against them. It is necessary to the very being of society, that vices, destructive of it, should be punished *as being so;* the vices of falsehood, injustice, cruelty: which punishment therefore is as natural as society; and so is an instance of a kind of moral government, naturally established, and actually taking place. And, since the certain natural course of things is the conduct of Providence or the government of God, though carried on by the instrumentality of men; the observation here made amounts to this, that mankind find themselves placed by him in such circumstances, as that they are unavoidably accountable for their behaviour, and are often punished, and sometimes rewarded under his government, in the view of their being mischievous, or eminently beneficial to society.

If it be objected that good actions and such as are bene-

* See Dissert. II.

ficial to society, are often punished, as in the case of persecution and in other cases; and that ill and mischievous actions are often rewarded: it may be answered distinctly; first, that this is in no sort necessary, and consequently not natural, in the sense in which it is necessary, and therefore natural, that ill or mischievous actions should be punished: and in the next place, that good actions are never punished, considered as beneficial to society, nor ill actions rewarded, under the view of their being hurtful to it. So that it stands good, without any thing on the side of vice to be set over against it, that the Author of Nature has as truly directed, that vicious actions, considered as mischievous to society, should be punished, and put mankind under a necessity of thus punishing them; as he has directed and necessitated us to preserve our lives by food.

IV. In the natural course of things, virtue *as such* is actually rewarded, and vice *as such* punished: which seems to afford an instance or example, not only of government, but of moral government begun and established; moral in the strictest sense; though not in that perfection of degree, which religion teaches us to expect. In order to see this more clearly, we must distinguish between actions themselves, and that quality ascribed to them, which we call virtuous or vicious. The gratification itself of every natural passion, must be attended with delight: and acquisitions of fortune, however made, are acquisitions of the means or materials of enjoyment. An action then, by which any natural passion is gratified or fortune acquired, procures delight or advantage; abstracted from all consideration of the morality of such action. Consequently, the pleasure or advantage in this case, is gained by the action itself, not by the morality, the virtuousness or viciousness of it; though it be, perhaps, virtuous or vicious. Thus, to say such an action or course of behaviour, procured such pleasure or advantage, or brought on such inconvenience and pain, is quite a different thing from saying, that such good or bad effect was owing to the virtue or vice of such action or behaviour. In one case, an action abstracted from all moral consideration, produced its effect: in the other case, for it will appear that there are such cases, the morality of the action under a moral consideration, *i. e.* the virtuousness or viciousness of it, produced the effect. Now I say virtue as such, naturally procures considerable advantages to the virtuous, and vice as such, naturally occasions great inconvenience and even misery to the vicious, in very many instances. The immediate effects of virtue and vice upon the mind and temper, are to be mentioned as instances of it. Vice as such is naturally attended with some sort of uneasiness, and, not uncommonly, with great disturbance and apprehension. That inward feeling, which, respecting lesser matters, and in familiar speech, we call being vexed with oneself, and in matters of importance and in more serious language, remorse; is an uneasiness naturally arising from an action of a man's own, reflected upon by himself as wrong, unreasonable, faulty, *i. e.* vicious in greater or less degrees: and this manifestly is a different feeling from that uneasiness, which arises from a sense of mere loss or harm. What is more common, than to hear a man lamenting an accident or event, and adding——but however he has the satisfaction that he cannot blame himself for it; or on the contrary, that he has the uneasiness of being sensible it was his own doing? Thus also the disturbance and fear, which often follow upon a man's having done an injury, arise from a sense of his being blame-worthy; otherwise there would, in many cases, be no ground of disturbance, nor any reason to fear resentment or shame. On the other hand, inward security and peace, and a mind open to the several gratifications of life, are the natural attendants of innocence and virtue. To which must be added the complacency, satisfaction, and even joy of heart, which accompany the exercise, the real exercise of gratitude, friendship, benevolence.

And here, I think, ought to be mentioned, the fears of future punishment, and peaceful hopes of a better life, in those who fully believe, or have any serious apprehension of religion: because these hopes and fears are present uneasiness and satisfaction to the mind; and cannot be got rid of by great part of the world, even by men who have thought most thoroughly upon that subject of religion.

And no one can say, how considerable this uneasiness and satisfaction may be, or what upon the whole it may amount to.

In the next place comes in the consideration, that all honest and good men are disposed to befriend honest good men as such, and to discountenance the vicious as such, and do so in some degree; indeed in a considerable degree: from which favour and discouragement cannot but arise considerable advantage and inconvenience. And though the generality of the world have little regard to the morality of their own actions, and may be supposed to have less to that of others, when they themselves are not concerned; yet let any one be known to be a man of virtue, some how or other he will be favoured and good offices will be done him, from regard to his character, without remote views, occasionally, and in some low degree, I think, by the generality of the world, as it happens to come in their way. Public honours too and advantages are the natural consequences, are sometimes at least the consequences in fact, of virtuous actions; of eminent justice, fidelity, charity, love to our country, considered in the view of being virtuous. And sometimes even death itself, often infamy and external inconveniences, are the public consequences of vice as vice. For instance, the sense which mankind have of tyranny, injustice, oppression, additional to the mere feeling or fear of misery, has doubtless been instrumental in bringing about revolutions, which make a figure even in the history of the world. For it is plain, men resent injuries as implying faultiness, and retaliate, not merely under the notion of having received harm, but of having received wrong; and they have this resentment in behalf of others, as well as of themselves. So likewise even the generality are, in some degree, grateful and disposed to return good offices, not merely because such a one has been the occasion of good to them, but under the view, that such good offices implied kind intention and good desert in the doer. To all this may be added two or three particular things, which many persons will think frivolous; but to me nothing appears so, which at all comes in towards determining a question of such importance, as, whether there be, or be not, a moral institution of government, in the strictest sense moral, *visibly* established and begun in nature. The particular things are these: That in domestic government, which is doubtless natural, children and others also are very generally punished for falsehood and injustice and ill-behaviour, as such, and rewarded for the contrary: which are instances where veracity and justice and right behaviour, as such, are naturally enforced by rewards and punishments, whether more or less considerable in degree: that, though civil government be supposed to take cognizance of actions in no other view than as prejudicial to society, without respect to the immorality of them; yet as such actions are immoral, so the sense which men have of the immorality of them, very greatly contributes, in different ways, to bring offenders to justice: and that entire absence of all crime and guilt in the moral sense, when plainly appearing, will almost of course procure, and circumstances of aggravated guilt prevent, a remission of the penalties annexed to civil crimes, in many cases, though by no means in all.

Upon the whole then, besides the good and bad effects of virtue and vice upon men's own minds, the course of the world does, in some measure, turn upon the approbation and disapprobation of them as such in others. The sense of well and ill doing, the presages of conscience, the love of good characters and dislike of bad ones, honour, shame, resentment, gratitude; all these, considered in themselves, and in their effects, do afford manifest real instances of virtue as such naturally favoured, and of vice as such discountenanced, more or less, in the daily course of human life; in every age, in every relation, in every general circumstance of it. That God has given us a moral nature,* may most justly be urged as a proof of our being under his moral government: but that he has placed us in a condition, which gives this nature, as one may speak, scope to operate, and in which it does unavoidably operate; *i. e.* influence mankind to act, so as thus to favour and reward virtue, and discountenance and punish vice; this is not the same, but

* See Dissert. II.

a further, additional proof of his moral government: for it is an instance of it. The first is a proof, that he will finally favour and support virtue effectually: the second is an example of his favouring and supporting it at present, in some degree.

If a more distinct inquiry be made, whence it arises, that virtue as such is often rewarded, and vice as such is punished, and this rule never inverted: it will be found to proceed, in part, immediately from the moral nature itself, which God has given us; and also in part, from his having given us, together with this nature, so great a power over each other's happiness and misery. For, *first*, it is certain, that peace and delight, in some degree and upon some occasions, is the necessary and present effect of virtuous practice; an effect arising immediately from that constitution of our nature. We are so made, that well-doing as such gives us satisfaction, at least, in some instances; ill-doing as such, in none. And, *secondly*, from our moral nature, joined with God's having put our happiness and misery in many respects in each other's power, it cannot but be, that vice as such, some kinds and instances of it at least, will be infamous, and men will be disposed to punish it as in itself detestable; and the villain will by no means be able always to avoid feeling that infamy, any more than he will be able to escape this further punishment, which mankind will be disposed to inflict upon him, under the notion of his deserving it. But there can be nothing on the side of vice, to answer this; because there is nothing in the human mind contradictory, as the logicians speak, to virtue. For virtue consists in a regard to what is right and reasonable, as being so; in a regard to veracity, justice, charity, in themselves: and there is surely no such thing, as a like natural regard to falsehood, injustice, cruelty. If it be thought, that there are instances of an approbation of vice, as such, in itself, and for its own sake (though it does not appear to me, that there is any such thing at all; but supposing there be), it is evidently monstrous: as much so, as the most acknowledged perversion of any passion whatever. Such instances of perversion then being left out, as merely imaginary, or, however, unnatural; it must follow, from the frame of our nature, and from our condition, in the respects now described, that vice cannot at all be, and virtue cannot but be, favoured as such by others, upon some occasions, and happy in itself, in some degree. For what is here insisted upon, is not the degree in which virtue and vice are thus distinguished, but only the thing itself, that they are so in some degree; though the whole good and bad effect of virtue and vice as such, is not inconsiderable in degree. But that they must be thus distinguished in some degree, is in a manner necessary: it is matter of fact of daily experience, even in the greatest confusion of human affairs.

It is not pretended but that, in the natural course of things, happiness and misery appear to be distributed by other rules, than only the personal merit and demerit of characters. They may sometimes be distributed by way of mere discipline. There may be the wisest and best reasons, why the world should be governed by general laws, from whence such promiscuous distribution perhaps must follow; and also why our happiness and misery should be put in each other's power, in the degree which they are. And these things, as in general they contribute to the rewarding virtue and punishing vice, as such: so they often contribute also, not to the inversion of this, which is impossible; but to the rendering persons prosperous, though wicked; afflicted, though righteous; and, which is worse, to the *rewarding some actions*, though vicious, and *punishing other actions*, though virtuous. But all this cannot drown the voice of Nature in the conduct of Providence, plainly declaring itself for virtue, by way of distinction from vice, and preference to it. For our being so constituted as that virtue and vice are thus naturally favoured and discountenanced, rewarded and punished, respectively as such, is an intuitive proof of the intent of Nature, that it should be so; otherwise the constitution of our mind, from which it thus immediately and directly proceeds, would be absurd. But it cannot be said, because virtuous actions are sometimes punished, and vicious actions rewarded, that Nature intended it. For, though this great disorder is brought about, as all actions are done, by means of some natural passion; yet *this may be*, as it undoubtedly is, brought about by the perversion of such passion, implanted in us for other, and those very good purposes. And indeed these other and good purposes, even of every passion, may be clearly seen.

We have then a declaration, in some degree of present effect, from Him who is supreme in Nature, which side he is of, or what part he takes; a declaration for virtue, and against vice. So far therefore as a man is true to virtue, to veracity and justice, to equity and charity, and the right of the case, in whatever he is concerned; so far he is on the side of the divine administration, and co-operates with it: and from hence, to such a man, arises naturally a secret satisfaction and sense of security, and implicit hope of somewhat further. And,

V. This hope is confirmed by the necessary tendencies of virtue, which, though not of present effect, yet are at present discernible in nature; and so afford an instance of somewhat moral in the essential constitution of it. There is, in the nature of things, a tendency in virtue and vice to produce the good and bad effects now mentioned, in a greater degree than they do in fact produce them. For instance; good and bad men would be much more rewarded and punished as such, were it not, that justice is often artificially eluded, that characters are not known, and many, who would thus favour virtue and discourage vice, are hindered from doing so by accidental causes. These tendencies of virtue and vice are obvious with regard to *individuals*. But it may require more particularly to be considered, that power in a *society*, by being under the direction of virtue, naturally increases, and has a necessary tendency to prevail over opposite power, not under the direction of it; in like manner, as power, by being under the direction of reason, increases, and has a tendency to prevail over brute force. There are several brute creatures of equal, and several of superior strength, to that of men; and possibly the sum of the whole strength of brutes may be greater than that of mankind; but reason gives us the advantage and superiority over them; and thus man is the acknowledged governing animal upon the earth. Nor is this superiority considered by any as accidental; but as what reason has a tendency, in the nature of the thing, to obtain. And yet perhaps difficulties may be raised about the meaning, as well as the truth, of the assertion, that virtue has the like tendency.

To obviate these difficulties, let us see more distinctly, how the case stands with regard to reason; which is so readily acknowledged to have this advantageous tendency. Suppose then two or three men, of the best and most improved understanding, in a desolate open plain, attacked by ten times the number of beasts of prey: would their reason secure them the victory in this unequal combat? Power then, though joined with reason, and under its direction, cannot be expected to prevail over opposite power, though merely brutal, unless the one bears some proportion to the other. Again: put the imaginary case, that rational and irrational creatures were of like external shape and manner: it is certain, before there were opportunities for the first to distinguish each other, to separate from their adversaries, and to form a union among themselves, they might be upon a level, or in several respects upon great disadvantage; though united they might be vastly superior; since union is of such efficacy, that ten men united, might be able to accomplish, what ten thousand of the same natural strength and understanding wholly ununited, could not. In this case then, brute force might more than maintain its ground against reason, for want of union among the rational creatures. Or suppose a number of men to land upon an island inhabited only by wild beasts; a number of men who, by the regulations of civil government, the inventions of art, and the experience of some years, could they be preserved so long, would be really sufficient to subdue the wild beasts, and to preserve themselves in security from them: yet a conjuncture of accidents might give such advantage to the irrational animals as that they might at once overpower, and even extirpate, the whole species of rational ones. Length of time then, proper scope and opportunities, for reason to exert itself, may be absolutely necessary to its prevailing over brute force. Further still: there are many instances of brutes succeeding in attempts, which they could not have undertaken, had not their irrational nature rendered them incapable of foreseeing the danger of such attempt, or the fury of passion hindered their attending to it: and there are instances of reason and real prudence preventing men's undertaking what, it hath appeared afterwards, they might have succeeded in by a lucky rashness. And in certain conjunctures, ignorance and folly, weakness and discord, may have their advantages. So that rational animals have not necessarily the superiority over irrational ones; but, how improbable soever it may be, it is evidently possible, that in some globes the latter may be superior. And were the former wholly at variance and disunited, by false self-interest and envy, by treachery and injustice, and consequent rage and malice against each other, whilst the latter were firmly united among themselves by instinct; this might greatly contribute to the introducing such an inverted order of things. For every one would consider it as inverted: since reason has, in the nature of it, a tendency to prevail over brute force; notwithstanding the possibility it may not prevail, and the necessity, which there is, of many concurring circumstances to render it prevalent.

Now I say, virtue in a society has a like tendency to procure superiority and additional power: whether this power be considered as the means of security from opposite power, or of obtaining other advantages. And it has this tendency, by rendering public good, an object and end, to every member of the society; by putting every one upon consideration and diligence, recollection and self-government, both in order to see what is the most effectual method, and also in order to perform their proper part, for obtaining and preserving it; by uniting a society within itself, and so increasing its strength; and, which is particularly to be mentioned, uniting it by means of veracity and justice. For as these last are principal bonds of union, so benevolence or public spirit, undirected, unrestrained by them, is, nobody knows what.

And suppose the invisible world, and the invisible

dispensations of Providence, to be, in any sort, analogous to what appears: or that both together make up one uniform scheme, the two parts of which, the part which we see, and that which is beyond our observation, are analogous to each other: then, there must be a like natural tendency in the derived power, throughout the universe, under the direction of virtue, to prevail in general over that which is not under its direction; as there is in reason, derived reason in the universe, to prevail over brute force. But then, in order to the prevalence of virtue, or that it may actually produce, what it has a tendency to produce; the like concurrences are necessary, as are, to the prevalence of reason. There must be some proportion, between the natural power or force which is, and that which is not, under the direction of virtue: there must be sufficient length of time; for the complete success of virtue, as of reason, cannot, from the nature of the thing, be otherwise than gradual: there must be, as one may speak, a fair field of trial, a stage large and extensive enough, proper occasions and opportunities, for the virtuous to join together, to exert themselves against lawless force, and to reap the fruit of their united labours. Now indeed it is to be hoped, that the disproportion between the good and bad, even here on earth, is not so great, but that the former have natural power sufficient to their prevailing to a considerable degree, if circumstances would permit this power to be united. For, much less, very much less, power under the direction of virtue, would prevail over much greater not under the direction of it. However, good men over the face of the earth cannot unite; as for other reasons, so because they cannot be sufficiently ascertained of each other's characters. And the known course of human things, the scene we are now passing through, particularly the shortness of life, denies to virtue its full scope in several other respects. The natural tendency which we have been considering, though real, is *hindered* from being carried into effect in the present state: but these hinderances may be removed in a future one. Virtue, to borrow the Christian allusion, is militant here; and various untoward accidents contribute to its being often overborne: but it may combat with greater advantage hereafter, and prevail completely, and enjoy its consequent rewards, in some future states. Neglected as it is, perhaps unknown, perhaps despised and oppressed here; there may be scenes in eternity, lasting enough, and in every other way adapted, to afford it a sufficient sphere of action; and a sufficient sphere for the natural consequences of it to follow in fact. If the soul be naturally immortal, and this state be a progress towards a future one, as childhood is towards mature age; good men may naturally unite, not only amongst themselves, but also with other orders of virtuous creatures, in that future state. For virtue, from the very nature of it, is a principle and bond of union, in some degree, amongst all who are endued with it, and known to each other; so as that by it, a good man cannot but recommend himself to the favour and protection of all virtuous beings, throughout the whole universe, who can be acquainted with his character, and can any way interpose in his behalf in any part of his duration. And one might add, that suppose all this advantageous tendency of virtue to become effect, amongst one or more orders of creatures, in any distant scenes and periods, and to be seen by any orders of vicious creatures, throughout the universal kingdom of God; this happy effect of virtue would have a tendency, by way of example, and possibly in other ways, to amend those of them who are capable of amendment, and being recovered to a just sense of virtue. If our notions of the plan of Providence were enlarged in any sort proportionable to what late discoveries have enlarged our views with respect to the material world; representations of this kind would not appear absurd or extravagant. However, they are not to be taken as intended for a literal delineation of what is in fact the particular scheme of the universe, which cannot be known without revelation: for suppositions are not to be looked on as true, because not incredible: but they are mentioned to show, that our finding virtue to be hindered from procuring to itself such superiority and advantages, is no objection against its having, in the essential nature of the thing, a tendency to procure them. And the suppositions now mentioned do plainly show this: for they show, that these hinderances are so far from being necessary, that we ourselves can easily conceive, how they may be removed in future states, and full scope be granted to virtue. And all these advantageous tendencies of it are to be considered as declarations of God in its favour. This however is taking a pretty large compass: though it is certain, that, as the material world appears to be, in a manner, boundless and immense; there must be *some* scheme of Providence vast in proportion to it.

But let us return to the earth our habitation; and we shall see this happy tendency of virtue, by imagining an instance not so vast and remote: by supposing a kingdom or society of men upon it, perfectly virtuous, for a succession of many ages; to which, if you please, may be given a situation advantageous for universal monarchy. In such a state, there would be no such thing as faction: but men of the greatest capacity would of course, all along, have the chief direction of affairs willingly yielded to them; and they would share it among themselves without envy. Each of these would have the part assigned him, to which his genius was peculiarly adapted: and others, who had not any distinguished genius, would be safe, and think themselves very happy, by being under the protection and guidance of those who had. Public determinations would really be the result of the united wisdom of the community: and they would faithfully be executed, by the united strength of it. Some would in a higher way contribute, but all would in some way contribute, to the public prosperity: and in it, each would enjoy the fruits of his own virtue. And as injustice, whether by fraud or force, would be unknown among themselves; so they would be sufficiently secured from it in their neighbours. For cunning and false self-interest, confederacies in injustice, ever slight, and accompanied with faction and intestine treachery; these on one hand would be found mere childish folly and weakness, when set in opposition against wisdom, public spirit, union inviolable, and fidelity on the other: allowing both a sufficient length of years to try their force. Add the general influence, which such a kingdom would have over the face of the earth, by way of example particularly, and the reverence which would be paid it. It would plainly be superior to all others, and the world must gradually come under its empire; not by means of lawless violence; but partly by what must be allowed to be just conquest; and partly by other kingdoms submitting themselves voluntarily to it, throughout a course of ages, and claiming its protection, one after another, in successive exigencies. The head of it would be an universal monarch, in another sense than any mortal has yet been; and the eastern style would be literally applicable to him, *that all people, nations, and languages should serve him.* And though indeed our knowledge of human nature, and the whole history of mankind, show the impossibility, without some miraculous interposition, that a number of men, here on earth, should unite in one society or government, in the fear of God and universal practice of virtue; and that such a government should continue so united for a succession of ages: yet admitting or supposing this, the effect would be as now drawn out. And thus for instance, the wonderful power and prosperity promised to the Jewish nation in the Scripture, would be, in a great measure, the consequence of what is predicted of them; that the *people should be all righteous, and inherit the land for ever;** were we to understand the latter phrase of a long continuance only, sufficient to give things time to work. The predictions of this kind, for there are many of them, cannot come to pass, in the present known course of nature; but suppose them come to pass, and then, the dominion and pre-eminence promised must naturally follow, to a very considerable degree.

Consider now the general system of religion; that the government of the world is uniform, and one, and moral; that virtue and right shall finally have the advantage, and prevail over fraud and lawless force, over the deceits as well as the violence of wickedness, under the conduct of one supreme governor: and from the observations above made, it will appear, that God has, by our reason, given us to see a peculiar connexion in the several parts of this scheme, and a tendency towards the completion of it,

* Isa. lx. 21.

arising out of the very nature of virtue: which tendency is to be considered as somewhat moral in the essential constitution of things. If any one should think all this to be of little importance; I desire him to consider, what he would think, if vice had, essentially and in its nature, these advantageous tendencies; or if virtue had essentially the direct contrary ones.

But it may be objected, that notwithstanding all these natural effects and these natural tendencies of virtue; yet things may be now going on throughout the universe, and may go on hereafter, in the same mixed way as here at present upon earth: virtue sometimes prosperous, sometimes depressed; vice sometimes punished, sometimes successful. The answer to which is, that it is not the purpose of this chapter, nor of this treatise, properly to prove God's perfect moral government over the world, or the truth of Religion; but to observe what there is in the constitution and course of nature, to confirm the proper proof of it, supposed to be known: and that the weight of the foregoing observations to this purpose may be thus distinctly proved. Pleasure and pain are indeed to a certain degree, say to a very high degree, distributed amongst us without any apparent regard to the merit or demerit of characters. And were there nothing else concerning this matter discernible in the constitution and course of nature; there would be no ground from the constitution and course of nature to hope or to fear, that men would be rewarded or punished hereafter according to their deserts: which, however, it is to be remarked, implies, that even then there would be no ground from appearances to think, that vice upon the whole would have the advantage, rather than that virtue would. And thus the proof of a future state of retribution would rest upon the usual known arguments for it: which are I think plainly unanswerable; and would be so, though there were no additional confirmation of them from the things above insisted on. But these things are a very strong confirmation of them. For,

First, They show that the Author of Nature is not indifferent to virtue and vice. They amount to a declaration, from him, determinate and not to be evaded, in favour of one, and against the other; such a declaration, as there is nothing to be set over against or answer, on the part of vice. So that were a man, laying aside the proper proof of Religion, to determine from the course of nature only, whether it were most probable, that the righteous or the wicked would have the advantage in a future life; there can be no doubt, but that he would determine the probability to be, that the former would. The course of nature then, in the view of it now given furnishes us with a real practical proof of the obligations of Religion.

Secondly, When, conformably to what Religion teaches us, God shall reward and punish virtue and vice as such, so as that every one shall, upon the whole, have his deserts; this distributive justice will not be a thing different in *kind*, but only in *degree*, from what we experience in his present government. It will be that in *effect*, toward which we now see a *tendency*. It will be no more than the *completion* of that moral government, the *principles and beginning* of which have been shown, beyond all dispute, discernible in the present constitution and course of nature. And from hence it follows,

Thirdly, That, as under the natural government of God, our experience of those kinds and degrees of happiness and misery, which we do experience at present, gives just ground to hope for, and to fear, higher degrees and other kinds of both in a future state, supposing a future state admitted: so under his moral government our experience, that virtue and vice are, in the manners above mentioned, actually rewarded and punished at present, in a certain degree, gives just ground to hope and to fear, that they *may be* rewarded and punished in a higher degree hereafter. It is acknowledged indeed that this alone is not sufficient ground to think, that they *actually will be* rewarded and punished in a higher degree, rather than in a lower: but then,

Lastly, There is sufficient ground to think so, from the good and bad tendencies of virtue and vice. For these tendencies are essential, and founded in the nature of things: whereas the hinderances to their becoming effect are, in numberless cases, not necessary, but artificial only. Now it may be much more strongly argued, that these tendencies, as well as the actual rewards and punishments, of virtue and vice, which arise directly out of the nature of things, will remain hereafter, than that the accidental hinderances of them will. And if these hinderances do not remain; those rewards and punishments cannot but be carried on much farther towards the perfection of moral government: *i. e.* the tendencies of virtue and vice will become effect; but when, or where, or in what particular way, cannot be known at all, but by revelation.

Upon the whole: there is a kind of moral government implied in God's natural government:* virtue and vice are naturally rewarded and punished as beneficial and mischievous to society;† and rewarded and punished directly as virtue and vice.‡ The notion then of a moral scheme of government is not fictitious, but natural; for it is suggested to our thoughts by the constitution and course of nature: and the execution of this scheme is actually begun, in the instances here mentioned. And these things are to be considered as a declaration of the Author of Nature, for virtue, and against vice: they give a credibility to the supposition of their being rewarded and punished hereafter; and also ground to hope and to fear, that they may be rewarded and punished in higher degrees than they are here. And as all this is confirmed, so the argument for Religion, from the constitution and course of nature, is carried on farther, by observing, that there are natural tendencies, and, in innumerable cases, only artificial hinderances, to this moral scheme's being carried on much farther towards perfection, than it is at present.§ The notion then of a moral scheme of government, much more perfect than what is seen, is not a fictitious, but a natural notion; for it is suggested to our thoughts, by the essential tendencies of virtue and vice. And these tendencies are to be considered as intimations, as implicit promises and threatenings, from the Author of Nature, of much greater rewards and punishments to follow virtue and vice, than do at present. And

* P. 87. † P. 88. ‡ P. 89, &c. § P. 95, &c.

indeed, every *natural* tendency, which is to continue, but which is hindered from becoming effect by only *accidental* causes, affords a presumption, that such tendency will, some time or other, become effect: a presumption in degree proportionable to the length of the duration, through which such tendency will continue. And from these things together, arises a real presumption, that the moral scheme of government established in nature, shall be carried on much farther towards perfection hereafter; and, I think, a presumption that it will be absolutely completed. But from these things, joined with the moral nature which God has given us, considered as given us by him, arises a practical proof* that it will be completed: a proof from fact; and therefore a distinct one from that which is deduced from the eternal and unalterable relations, the fitness and unfitness of actions.

CHAP. IV.

OF A STATE OF PROBATION, AS IMPLYING TRIAL, DIFFICULTIES, AND DANGER.

THE general doctrine of Religion, that our present life is a state of probation for a future one, comprehends under it several particular things, distinct from each other. But the first and most common meaning of it seems to be, that our future interest is now depending, and depending upon ourselves; that we have scope and opportunities here, for that good and bad behaviour, which God will reward and punish hereafter; together with temptations to one, as well as inducements of reason to the other. And this is, in a great measure, the same with saying, that we are under the moral government of God, and to give an account of our actions to him. For the notion of a future account and general righteous judgment, implies some sort of temptations to what is wrong: otherwise there would be no moral possibility of doing wrong, nor ground for judgment, or discrimination. But there is this difference, that the word *probation* is

* See this proof drawn out briefly, Ch. vi.

more distinctly and particularly expressive of allurements to wrong, or difficulties in adhering uniformly to what is right, and of the danger of miscarrying by such temptations, than the words *moral government.* A state of probation then, as thus particularly implying in it trial, difficulties, and danger, may require to be considered distinctly by itself.

And as the moral government of God, which Religion teaches us, implies, that we are in a state of trial with regard to a future world: so also his natural government over us implies, that we are in a state of trial, in the like sense, with regard to the present world. Natural government by rewards and punishments, as much implies natural trial, as moral government does moral trial. The natural government of God here meant* consists in his annexing pleasure to some actions, and pain to others, which are in our power to do or forbear, and in giving us notice of such appointment beforehand. This necessarily implies, that he has made our happiness and misery, or our interest, to depend in part upon ourselves. And so far as men have temptations to any course of action, which will probably occasion them greater temporal inconvenience and uneasiness, than satisfaction; so far their temporal interest is in danger from themselves, or they are in a state of trial with respect to it. Now people often blame others, and even themselves, for their misconduct in their temporal concerns. And we find many are greatly wanting to themselves, and miss of that natural happiness, which they might have obtained in the present life: perhaps every one does in some degree. But many run themselves into great inconvenience, and into extreme distress and misery: not through incapacity of knowing better, and doing better, for themselves, which would be nothing to the present purpose; but through their own fault. And these things necessarily imply temptation, and danger of miscarrying, in a greater or less degree with respect to our worldly interest or happiness. Every one too, without having Religion in his thoughts, speaks of the hazards which young people run, upon their setting out in the

* Ch. ii.

world: hazards from other causes, than merely their ignorance, and unavoidable accidents. And some courses of vice, at least, being contrary to men's worldly interest or good; temptations to these must at the same time be temptations to forego our present and our future interest. Thus in our natural or temporal capacity, we are in a state of trial, *i. e.* of difficulty and danger, analogous, or like to our moral and religious trial.

This will more distinctly appear to any one, who thinks it worth while, more distinctly, to consider, what it is which constitutes our trial in both capacities, and to observe, how mankind behave under it.

And that which constitutes this our trial, in both these capacities, must be somewhat either in our external circumstances, or in our nature. For, on the one hand, persons may be betrayed into wrong behaviour upon surprise, or overcome upon any other very singular and extraordinary external occasions; who would, otherwise, have preserved their character of prudence and of virtue: in which cases, every one, in speaking of the wrong behaviour of these persons, would impute it to such particular external circumstances. And on the other hand, men who have contracted habits of vice and folly of any kind, or have some particular passions in excess, will seek opportunities, and, as it were, go out of their way, to gratify themselves in these respects, at the expense of their wisdom and their virtue; led to it, as every one would say, not by external temptations, but by such habits and passions. And the account of this last case is, that particular passions are no more coincident with prudence, or that reasonable self-love, the end of which is our worldly interest, than they are with the principle of virtue and religion; but often draw contrary ways to one, as well as to the other: and so such particular passions are as much temptations, to act imprudently with regard to our worldly interest, as to act viciously.* However, as when we say, men are misled by external circumstances of temptation; it cannot but be understood, that there is somewhat within themselves, to render those

* See Sermons preached at the *Rolls*, 1726. 2d ed. p. 205, &c. Pref. p. 25. &c Serm. p. 21, &c.

circumstances temptations, or to render them susceptible of impressions from them; so when we say, they are misled by passions; it is always supposed, that there are occasions, circumstances, and objects, exciting these passions, and affording means for gratifying them. And therefore, temptations from within, and from without, coincide, and mutually imply each other. Now the several external objects of the appetites, passions, and affections, being present to the senses, or offering themselves to the mind, and so exciting emotions suitable to their nature; not only in cases where they can be gratified consistently with innocence and prudence, but also in cases where they cannot, and yet can be gratified imprudently and viciously: this as really puts them in danger of voluntarily foregoing their present interest or good, as their future; and as really renders self-denial necessary to secure one, as the other: *i. e.* we are in a like state of trial with respect to both, by the very same passions, excited by the very same means. Thus mankind having a temporal interest depending upon themselves, and a prudent course of behaviour being necessary to secure it; passions inordinately excited, whether by means of example, or by any other external circumstance, towards such objects, at such times, or in such degrees, as that they cannot be gratified consistently with worldly prudence; are temptations, dangerous, and too often successful temptations, to forego a greater temporal good for a less; *i. e.* to forego what is, upon the whole, our temporal interest, for the sake of a present gratification. This is a description of our state of trial in our temporal capacity. Substitute now the word *future* for *temporal*, and *virtue* for *prudence;* and it will be just as proper a description of our state of trial in our religious capacity; so analogous are they to each other.

If, from consideration of this our like state of trial in both capacities, we go on to observe farther, how mankind behave under it; we shall find there are some, who have so little sense of it, that they scarce look beyond the passing day: they are so taken up with present gratifications, as to have, in a manner, no feeling of consequences, no regard to their future case or fortune in this life; any more than to their happiness in another. Some appear to be blinded and deceived by inordinate passion, in their worldly concerns, as much as in Religion. Others are, not deceived, but, as it were, forcibly carried away by the like passions, against their better judgment, and feeble resolutions too of acting better. And there are men, and truly they are not a few, who shamelessly avow, not their interest, but their mere will and pleasure, to be their law of life: and who, in open defiance of every thing that is reasonable, will go on in a course of vicious extravagance, foreseeing, with no remorse and little fear, that it will be their temporal ruin; and some of them, under the apprehension of the consequences of wickedness in another state. And to speak in the most moderate way, human creatures are not only continually liable to go wrong voluntarily, but we see likewise that they often actually do so, with respect to their temporal interests, as well as with respect to Religion.

Thus our difficulties and dangers, or our trials, in our temporal and our religious capacity, as they proceed from the same causes, and have the same effect upon men's behaviour, are evidently analogous, and of the same kind.

It may be added, that as the difficulties and dangers of miscarrying in our religious state of trial, are greatly increased, and one is ready to think, in a manner wholly *made*, by the ill behaviour of others; by a wrong education, wrong in a moral sense, sometimes positively vicious; by general bad example; by the dishonest artifices which are got into business of all kinds; and, in very many parts of the world, by religion's being corrupted into superstitions, which indulge men in their vices: so in like manner, the difficulties of conducting ourselves prudently in respect to our present interest, and our danger of being led aside from pursuing it, are greatly increased, by a foolish education; and, after we come to mature age, by the extravagance and carelessness of others, whom we have intercourse with: and by mistaken notions, very generally prevalent, and taken up from common opinion, concerning temporal happiness, and wherein it consists. And persons, by their own negligence and folly in their temporal affairs, no less than by a course of vice, bring themselves into new difficulties; and, by habits of indulgence, become less qualified to go through them: and one irregularity after another, embarrasses things to such a degree, that they know not whereabout they are; and often makes the path of conduct so intricate and perplexed, that it is difficult to trace it out; difficult even to determine what is the prudent or the moral part. Thus, for instance, wrong behaviour in one stage of life, youth; wrong, I mean, considering ourselves only in our temporal capacity, without taking in religion; this, in several ways, increases the difficulties of right behaviour in mature age; *i. e.* puts us into a more disadvantageous state of trial in our temporal capacity.

We are an inferior part of the creation of God. There are natural appearances of our being in a state of degradation.* And we certainly are in a condition, which *does not seem*, by any means, the most advantageous we could imagine or desire, either in our natural or moral capacity, for securing either our present or future interest. However, this condition, low and careful and uncertain as it is, does not afford any just ground of complaint. For, as men may manage their temporal affairs with prudence, and so pass their days here on earth in tolerable ease and satisfaction, by a moderate degree of care: so likewise with regard to religion, there is no more required than what they are well able to do, and what they must be greatly wanting to themselves, if they neglect. And for persons to have that put upon them, which they are well able to go through, and no more, we naturally consider as an equitable thing; supposing it done by proper authority. Nor have we any more reason to complain of it, with regard to the Author of Nature, than of his not having given us other advantages, belonging to other orders of creatures.

But the thing here insisted upon is, that the state of trial, which Religion teaches us we are in, is rendered credible, by its being throughout uniform and of a piece with the general conduct of Providence towards us, in all other respects within the compass of our knowledge.

* Part II. Chap. v.

Indeed if mankind, considered in their natural capacity, as inhabitants of this world only, found themselves, from their birth to their death, in a settled state of security and happiness, without any solicitude or thought of their own: or if they were in no danger of being brought into inconveniences and distress, by carelessness, or the folly of passion, through bad example, the treachery of others, or the deceitful appearances of things: were this our natural condition, then it might seem strange, and be some presumption against the truth of Religion, that it represents our future and more general interest, as not secure of course, but as depending upon our behaviour, and requiring recollection and self-government to obtain it. For it might be alleged, "What you say is our condition, in one respect, is not in any wise of a sort with what we find, by experience, our condition is in another. Our whole present interest is secured to our hands, without any solicitude of ours; and why should not our future interest, if we have any such, be so too?" But since, on the contrary, thought and consideration, the voluntary denying ourselves many things which we desire, and a course of behaviour, far from being always agreeable to us; are absolutely necessary to our acting even a common decent, and common prudent part, so as to pass with any satisfaction through the present world, and be received upon any tolerable good terms in it: since this is the case, all presumption against self-denial and attention being necessary to secure our higher interest, is removed. Had we not experience, it might, perhaps speciously, be urged, that it is improbable any thing of hazard and danger should be put upon us by an infinite Being; when every thing which is hazard and danger in our manner of conception, and will end in error, confusion, and misery, is now already certain in his foreknowledge. And indeed, why any thing of hazard and danger should be put upon such frail creatures as we are, may well be thought a difficulty in speculation; and cannot but be so, till we know the whole, or, however, much more of the case. But still the constitution of nature is as it is. Our happiness and misery are trusted to our conduct, and made to depend upon it. Somewhat, and, in many circumstances, a great deal too, is put upon us, either to do, or to suffer, as we choose. And all the various miseries of life, which people bring upon themselves by negligence and folly, and might have avoided by proper care, are instances of this: which miseries are beforehand, just as contingent and undetermined as their conduct, and left to be determined by it.

These observations are an answer to the objections against the credibility of a state of trial, as implying temptations, and real danger of miscarrying with regard to our general interest, under the moral government of God: and they show, that, if we are at all to be considered in such a capacity, and as having such an interest; the general analogy of Providence must lead us to apprehend ourselves in danger of miscarrying, in different degrees, as to this interest, by our neglecting to act the proper part belonging to us in that capacity. For we have a present interest under the government of God, which we experience here upon earth. And this interest, as it is not forced upon us, so neither is it offered to our acceptance, but to our acquisition; in such sort, as that we are in danger of missing it, by means of temptations to neglect, or act contrary to it; and without attention and self-denial, must and do miss of it. It is then perfectly credible, that this may be our case, with respect to that chief and final good, which Religion proposes to us.

CHAP. V.

OF A STATE OF PROBATION, AS INTENDED FOR MORAL DISCIPLINE AND IMPROVEMENT.

FROM the consideration of our being in a probation-state, of so much difficulty and hazard, naturally arises the question, how we came to be placed in it? But such a general inquiry as this would be found involved in insuperable difficulties. For, though some of these difficulties would be lessened by observing, that all wickedness is voluntary, as is implied in its very notion; and that many of the miseries of life have apparent good, effects: yet, when we consider other circumstances belonging to both, and what must be the consequence of the former in a life to come; it cannot but be acknowledged plain folly and presumption, to pretend to give an account of the whole reasons of this matter: the whole reasons of our being allotted a condition, out of which so much wickedness and misery, so circumstanced, would in fact arise. Whether it be not beyond our faculties, not only to find out, but even to understand, the whole account of this; or, though we should be supposed capable of understanding it, yet, whether it would be of service or prejudice to us to be informed of it, is impossible to say. But as our present condition can in no wise be shown inconsistent with the perfect moral government of God: so Religion teaches us we were placed in it, that we might qualify ourselves, by the practice of virtue, for another state which is to follow it. And this, though but a partial answer, a very partial one indeed, to the inquiry now mentioned; yet, is a more satisfactory answer to another, which is of real, and of the utmost importance to us to have answered: the inquiry, What is our business here? The known end then, why we are placed in a state of so much affliction, hazard, and difficulty, is, our improvement in virtue and piety, as the requisite qualification for a future state of security and happiness.

Now the beginning of life, considered as an education for mature age in the present world, appears plainly, at first sight, analogous to this our trial for a future one: the former being in our temporal capacity, what the latter is in our religious capacity. But some observations common to both of them, and a more distinct consideration of each, will more distinctly show the extent and force of the analogy between them; and the credibility, which arises from hence, as well as from the nature of the thing, that the present life was intended to be a state of discipline for a future one.

I. Every species of creatures is, we see, designed for a particular way of life; to which, the nature, the capacities, temper, and qualifications of each species, are as necessary, as their external circumstances. Both come into the notion of such state, or particular way of life, and are constituent parts of it. Change a man's capacities or character to the degree in which it is conceivable they may be changed; and he would be altogether incapable of a human course of life, and human happiness; as incapable, as if, his nature continuing unchanged, he were placed in a world, where he had no sphere of action, nor any objects to answer his appetites, passions, and affections of any sort. One thing is set over against another, as an ancient writer expresses it. Our nature corresponds to our external condition. Without this correspondence, there would be no possibility of any such thing as human life and human happiness: which life and happiness are, therefore, a *result* from our nature and condition jointly: meaning by human life, not living in the literal sense, but the whole complex notion commonly understood by those words. So that, without determining what will be the employment and happiness, the particular life, of good men hereafter; there must be some determinate capacities, some necessary character and qualifications, without which persons cannot but be utterly incapable of it: in like manner, as there must be some, without which men would be incapable of their present state of life. Now,

II. The constitution of human creatures, and indeed of all creatures which come under our notice, is such, as that they are capable of naturally becoming qualified for states of life, for which they were once wholly unqualified. In imagination we may indeed conceive of creatures, as incapable of having any of their faculties naturally enlarged, or as being unable naturally to acquire any new qualifications: but the faculties of every species known to us are made for enlargement; for acquirements of experience and habits. We find ourselves in particular endued with capacities, not only of perceiving ideas, and of knowledge or perceiving truth, but also of storing up our ideas and knowledge by memory. We are capable, not only of acting, and of having different momentary impressions made upon us; but of getting a new facility in any kind of action, and of settled alterations in our temper or character. The power of the two last is the power of habits. But neither the perception of ideas, nor knowledge of any sort, are habits; though absolutely necessary to the forming of them. However, apprehension, reason, memory, which are the capacities of acquiring knowledge, are greatly improved by exercise. Whether the word habit is applicable to all these improvements, and in particular how far the powers of memory and of habits may be powers of the same nature, I shall not inquire. But that perceptions come into our minds readily and of course, by means of their having been there before, seems a thing of the same sort, as readiness in any particular kind of action, proceeding from being accustomed to it. And aptness to recollect practical observations of service in our conduct, is plainly habit in many cases. There are habits of perception, and habits of action. An instance of the former, is our constant and even involuntary readiness, in correcting the impressions of our sight concerning magnitudes and distances, so as to substitute judgment in the room of sensation imperceptibly to ourselves. And it seems as if all other associations of ideas not naturally connected might be called passive habits; as properly as our readiness in understanding languages upon sight, or hearing of words. And our readiness in speaking and writing them is an instance of the latter, of active habits. For distinctness, we may consider habits, as belonging to the body, or the mind: and the latter will be explained by the former. Under the former are comprehended all bodily activities or motions, whether graceful or unbecoming, which are owing to use: under the latter, general habits of life and conduct; such as those of obedience and submission to authority, or to any particular person; those of veracity, justice, and charity; those of attention, industry, self-government, envy, revenge. And habits of this latter kind seem produced by repeated acts, as well as the former. And in like manner as habits belonging to the body are produced by external acts: so habits of the mind are produced by the exertion of inward practical principles; *i. e.* by carrying them into act, or acting upon them; the principles of obedience, of veracity, justice, and charity. Nor can those habits be formed by any external course of action, otherwise than as it proceeds from these principles: because it is only these inward principles exerted, which are strictly acts of obedience, of veracity, of justice, and of charity. So likewise habits of attention, industry, self-government, are in the same manner acquired by exercise; and habits of envy and revenge by indulgence, whether in outward act, or in thought and intention; *i. e.* inward act: for such intention is an act. Resolutions also to do well are properly acts. And endeavouring to enforce upon our own minds a practical sense of virtue, or to beget in others that practical sense of it, which a man really has himself, is a virtuous act. All these, therefore, may and will contribute towards forming good habits. But going over the theory of virtue in one's thoughts, talking well, and drawing fine pictures, of it; this is so far from necessarily or certainly conducing to form a habit of it, in him who thus employs himself, that it may harden the mind in a contrary course, and render it gradually more insensible; *i. e.* form a habit of insensibility to all moral considerations. For, from our very faculty of habits, passive impressions, by being repeated, grow weaker. Thoughts, by often passing through the mind, are felt less sensibly: being accustomed to danger, begets intrepidity, *i. e.* lessens fear; to distress, lessens the passion of pity; to instances of others' mortality, lessens the sensible apprehension of our own. And from these two observations together; that practical habits are formed and strengthened by repeated acts, and that passive impressions grow weaker by being repeated upon us; it must follow, that active habits may be gradually forming and strengthening, by a course of acting upon such and such motives and excitements, whilst these motives and excitements themselves are, by proportionable degrees, growing less sensible; *i. e.* are continually less and less sensibly felt, even as the active habits strengthen. And experience confirms this: for active principles, at the very time that they are less lively in perception than they were, are found to be, somehow, wrought more thoroughly into the temper and character, and become more effectual in influencing our practice. The three things just mentioned may afford instances of it. Perception of danger is a natural excitement of passive fear, and active caution: and by being inured to danger, habits of the latter are gradually wrought, at the same time that the former gradually lessens. Perception of distress in others is a natural excitement, passively to pity, and actively to relieve it: but let a man set himself to attend to, inquire out, and relieve distressed persons, and he cannot but grow less and less sensibly affected with the various miseries of life, with which he must become acquainted; when yet, at the same time, benevolence, considered not as a passion, but as a practical principle of action, will strengthen: and whilst he passively compassionates the distressed less, he will acquire a greater aptitude actively to assist and befriend them. So also at the same time that the daily instances of men's dying around us give us daily a less sensible passive feeling or apprehension of our own mortality, such instances greatly contribute to the strengthening a practical regard to it in serious men; *i. e.* to forming a habit of acting with a constant view to it. And this seems again further to show, that passive impressions made upon our minds by admonition, experience, example, though they may have a remote efficacy, and a very great one, towards forming active habits, yet can have this efficacy no otherwise than by inducing us to such a course of action: and that it is not being affected so and so, but acting, which forms those habits: only it must be always remembered, that real endeavours to enforce good impressions upon ourselves are a species of virtuous action. Nor do we know how far it is possible, in the nature of things, that effects should be wrought in us at once, equivalent to habits; *i. e.* what is wrought by use and exercise. However, the thing insisted upon is, not what may be possible, but what is in fact the appointment of nature: which is, that active habits are to be formed by exercise. Their progress may be so gradual, as to be imperceptible in its steps: it may be hard to explain the faculty, by which we are capable of habits, throughout its several parts; and to trace it up to its original, so as to distinguish it from all others in our mind: and it seems as if contrary effects were to be ascribed to it. But the thing in general, that our nature is formed to yield, in some such manner as this, to use and exercise, is matter of certain experience.

Thus, by accustoming ourselves to any course of action, we get an aptness to go on, a facility, readiness, and often pleasure, in it. The inclinations which rendered us averse to it grow weaker: the difficulties in it, not only the imaginary but the real ones, lessen: the reasons for it offer themselves of course to our thoughts upon all occasions: and the least glimpse of them is sufficient to make us go on, in a course of action, to which we have been accustomed. And practical principles appear to grow stronger, absolutely in themselves, by exercise; as well as relatively, with regard to contrary principles, which, by being accustomed to submit, do so habitually, and of course. And thus a new character, in several respects, may be formed; and many habitudes of life, not given by nature, but which nature directs us to acquire.

III. Indeed we may be assured, that we should never have had these capacities of improving by experience, acquired knowledge, and habits, had they not been necessary, and intended to be made use of. And accordingly we find them so necessary, and so much intended, that without them we should be utterly incapable of that which was the end for which we were made, considered in our temporal capacity only: the employments and satisfactions of our mature state of life.

Nature does in nowise qualify us wholly, much less at once, for this mature state of life. Even maturity of understanding, and bodily strength, are not only arrived to gradually, but are also very much owing to the continued exercise of our powers of body and mind from infancy. But if we suppose a person brought into the world with both these in maturity, as far as this is conceivable; he would plainly at first be as unqualified for the human life of mature age, as an idiot. He would be in a manner distracted, with astonishment, and apprehension, and curiosity, and suspense: nor can one guess, how long it would be, before he would be familiarized to himself and the objects about him enough, even to set himself to any thing. It may be questioned too, whether the natural information of his sight and hearing would be of any manner of use at all to him in acting, before experience. And it seems, that men would be strangely headstrong and self-willed, and disposed to exert themselves with an impetuosity, which would render society insupportable, and the living in it impracticable; were it not for some acquired moderation and self-government, some aptitude and readiness in restraining themselves, and concealing their sense of things. Want of every thing of this kind which is learnt would render a man as uncapable of society, as want of language would; or as his natural ignorance of any of the particular employments of life would render him uncapable of providing himself with the common conveniences, or supplying the necessary wants of it. In these respects, and probably in many more of which we have no particular notion, mankind is left, by nature, an unformed, unfinished creature; utterly deficient and unqualified, before the acquirement of knowledge, experience, and habits, for that mature state of life, which was the end of his creation, considering him as related only to this world.

But then, as nature has endued us with a power of supplying those deficiencies, by acquired knowledge, experience, and habits: so likewise we are placed in a condition, in infancy, childhood, and youth, fitted for it; fitted for our acquiring those qualifications of all sorts, which we stand in need of in mature age. Hence children, from their very birth, are daily growing acquainted with the objects about them, with the scene in which they are placed, and to have a future part; and learning somewhat or other, necessary to the performance of it. The subordinations, to which they are accustomed in domestic life, teach them self-government in common behaviour abroad, and prepare them for subjection and obedience to civil authority. What passes before their eyes, and daily happens to them, gives them experience, caution against treachery and deceit, together with numberless little rules of action and conduct, which we could not live without; and which are learnt so insensibly and so perfectly, as to be mistaken perhaps for instinct:

though they are the effect of long experience and exercise; as much so as language, or knowledge in particular business, or the qualifications and behaviour belonging to the several ranks and professions. Thus the beginning of our days is adapted to be, and is, a state of education in the theory and practice of mature life. We are much assisted in it by example, instruction, and the care of others; but a great deal is left to ourselves to do. And of this, as part is done easily and of course; so part requires diligence and care, the voluntary foregoing many things which we desire, and setting ourselves to what we should have no inclination to, but for the necessity or expedience of it. For that labour and industry, which the station of so many absolutely requires, they would be greatly unqualified for, in maturity, as those in other stations would be for any other sorts of application; if both were not accustomed to them in their youth. And, according as persons behave themselves, in the general education which all go through, and in the particular ones adapted to particular employments; their character is formed, and made appear; they recommend themselves more or less; and are capable of, and placed in, different stations in the society of mankind.

The former part of life, then, is to be considered as an important opportunity, which nature puts into our hands; and which, when lost is not to be recovered. And our being placed in a state of discipline throughout this life, for another world, is a providential disposition of things, exactly of the same kind, as our being placed in a state of discipline during childhood, for mature age. Our condition in both respects is uniform and of a-piece, and comprehended under one and the same general law of nature.

And if we were not able at all to discern, how or in what way the present life could be our preparation for another; this would be no objection against the credibility of its being so. For we do not discern, how food and sleep contribute to the growth of the body; nor could have any thought that they would, before we had experience. Nor do children at all think, on the one hand, that the sports and exercises, to which they are so much addicted, contribute to their health and growth; nor, on the other, of the necessity which there is for their being restrained in them: nor are they capable of understanding the use of many parts of discipline, which nevertheless they must be made to go through, in order to qualify them for the business of mature age. Were we not able then to discover, in what respects the present life could form us for a future one; yet nothing would be more supposable than that it might, in some respects or other, from the general analogy of Providence. And this, for ought I see, might reasonably be said even though we should not take in the consideration of God's moral government over the world. But,

IV. Take in this consideration, and consequently, that the character of virtue and piety is a necessary qualification for the future state; and then we may distinctly see, how, and in what respects, the present life may be a preparation for it: since we *want, and are capable of, improvement in that character, by moral and religious habits;* and *the present life is fit to be a state of discipline for such improvement:* in like manner as we have already observed, how, and in what respects, infancy, childhood, and youth, are a necessary preparation, and a natural state of discipline, for mature age.

Nothing which we at present see would lead us to the thought of a solitary unactive state hereafter: but, if we judge at all from the analogy of nature, we must suppose, according to the Scripture account of it, that it will be a community. And there is no shadow of any thing unreasonable in conceiving, though there be no analogy for it, that this community will be, as the Scripture represents it, under the more immediate, or, if such an expression may be used, the more sensible government of God. Nor is our ignorance, what will be the employments of this happy community, nor our consequent ignorance, what particular scope or occasion there will be for the exercise of veracity, justice, and charity, amongst the members of it with regard to each other; any proof, that there will be no sphere of exercise for those virtues. Much less, if that were possible, is our ignorance any proof, that there will be no occasion for that frame of mind, or character, which is formed by the daily practice of those particular virtues here, and which is a result from it. This at least must be owned in general, that, as the government established in the universe is moral, the character of virtue and piety must, in some way or other, be the condition of our happiness or the qualification for it.

Now from what is above observed, concerning our natural power of habits, it is easy to see, that we are *capable* of moral improvement by discipline. And how greatly we *want* it, need not be proved to any one who is acquainted with the great wickedness of mankind; or even with those imperfections, which the best are conscious of. But it is not perhaps distinctly attended to by every one, that the occasion which human creatures have for discipline, to improve in them this character of virtue and piety, is to be traced up higher than to excess in the passions, by indulgence and habits of vice. Mankind, and perhaps all finite creatures, from the very constitution of their nature, before habits of virtue, are deficient, and in danger of deviating from what is right; and therefore stand in need of virtuous habits, for a security against this danger. For, together with the general principle of moral understanding, we have in our inward frame various affections towards particular external objects. These affections are naturally, and of right, subject to the government of the moral principle, as to the occasions upon which they may be gratified; as to the times, degrees, and manner, in which the objects of them may be pursued: but then the principle of virtue can neither excite them, nor prevent their being excited. On the contrary, they are naturally felt, when the objects of them are present to the mind, not only before all consideration whether they can be obtained by lawful means, but after it is found they cannot. For the natural objects of affection continue so; the necessaries, conveniences, and pleasures of life, remain naturally desirable; though they cannot be obtained innocently: nay, though they cannot possibly be obtained at all. And when the objects of any affection whatever cannot be obtained without unlawful means; but may be obtained by them: such affection, though its being excited, and its continuing some time in the mind, be as innocent as it is natural and necessary; yet cannot but be conceived to have a tendency to incline persons to venture upon such unlawful means: and therefore must be conceived as putting them in some danger of it. Now what is the general security against this danger, against their actually deviating from right? As the danger is, so also must the security be, from within: from the practical principle of virtue.* And the strengthening or improving this principle, considered as practical, or as a principle of action, will lessen the danger, or increase the security against it. And this moral principle is capable of improvement, by proper discipline and exercise: by recollecting the practical impressions which example and experience have made upon us: and, instead of following humour and mere inclination, by continually attending to the equity and right of the case, in whatever we are engaged, be it in greater or less matters; and accustoming ourselves always to act upon it; as being itself the just and natural motive of action; and as this moral course of behaviour must necessarily, under the divine government, be our final interest. *Thus the principle of virtue, improved into a habit, of which improvement we are thus capable, will plainly be, in proportion to the strength of it, a security against the danger which finite creatures are in, from the very nature of propension, or particular affections.* This way of putting the matter, supposes particular affections to remain in a future state; which it is scarce possible to avoid supposing. And if they do; we clearly see, that

* It may be thought, that a sense of interest would as effectually restrain creatures from doing wrong. But if by a *sense of interest* is meant a speculative conviction or belief, that such and such indulgence would occasion them greater uneasiness, upon the whole, than satisfaction; it is contrary to present experience to say, that this sense of interest is sufficient to restrain them from thus indulging themselves. And if by a *sense of interest* is meant a practical regard to what is upon the whole our happiness; this is not only coincident with the principle of virtue or moral rectitude, but is a part of the idea itself. And it is evident this reasonable self-love wants to be improved, as really as any principle in our nature. For we daily see it overmatched, not only by the more boisterous passions, but by curiosity, shame, love of imitation, by any thing, even indolence: especially if the interest, the temporal interest, suppose, which is the end of such self-love, be at a distance. So greatly are profligate men mistaken, when they affirm they are wholly governed by interestedness and self-love; and so little cause is there for moralists to disclaim this principle.—See p. 108.

acquired habits of virtue and self-government may be necessary for the regulation of them. However, though we were not distinctly to take in this supposition, but to speak only in general; the thing really comes to the same. For habits of virtue, thus acquired by discipline, are improvement in virtue: and improvement in virtue must be advancement in happiness, if the government of the universe be moral

From these things we may observe, and it will further show this our natural and original need of being improved by discipline, how it comes to pass, that creatures made upright fall; and that those who preserve their uprightness, by so doing, raise themselves to a more secure state of virtue. To say that the former is accounted for by the nature of liberty, is to say no more, than that an event's actually happening is accounted for by a mere possibility of its happening. But it seems distinctly conceivable from the very nature of particular affections or propensions. For, suppose creatures intended for such a particular state of life, for which such propensions were necessary: suppose them endued with such propensions, together with moral understanding, as well including a practical sense of virtue as a speculative perception of it; and that all these several principles, both natural and moral, forming an inward constitution of mind, were in the most exact proportion possible; *i. e.* in a proportion the most exactly adapted to their intended state of life; such creatures would be made upright, or finitely perfect. Now particular propensions, from their very nature, must be felt, the objects of them being present; though they cannot be gratified at all, or not with the allowance of the moral principle. But if they can be gratified without its allowance, or by contradicting it; then they must be conceived to have some tendency, in how low a degree soever, yet some tendency, to induce persons to such forbidden gratification. This tendency, in some one particular propension, may be increased, by the greater frequency of occasions naturally exciting it, than of occasions exciting others. The least voluntary indulgence in forbidden circumstances, though but in thought, will increase this wrong tendency; and may increase it further, till, peculiar conjunctures perhaps conspiring, it becomes effect; and danger of deviating from right, ends in actual deviation from it; a danger necessarily arising from the very nature of propension; and which therefore could not have been prevented, though it might have been escaped, or got innocently through. The case would be, as if we were to suppose a straight path marked out for a person, in which such a degree of attention would keep him steady: but if he would not attend in this degree, any one of a thousand objects, catching his eye, might lead him out of it. Now it is impossible to say, how much even the first full overt act of irregularity might disorder the inward constitution; unsettle the adjustments, and alter the proportions, which formed it, and in which the uprightness of its make consisted: but repetition of irregularities would produce habits. And thus the constitution would be spoiled; and creatures made upright, become corrupt and depraved in their settled character, proportionably to their repeated irregularities in occasional acts. But, on the contrary, these creatures might have improved and raised themselves, to a higher and more secure state of virtue, by the contrary behaviour: by steadily following the moral principle, supposed to be one part of their nature: and thus withstanding that unavoidable danger of defection, which necessarily arose from propension, the other part of it. For, by thus preserving their integrity for some time, their danger would lessen; since propensions, by being inured to submit, would do it more easily and of course: and their security against this lessening danger would increase; since the moral principle would gain additional strength by exercise: both which things are implied in the notion of virtuous habits. Thus then vicious indulgence is not only criminal in itself, but also depraves the inward constitution and character. And virtuous self-government is not only right in itself, but also improves the inward constitution or character: and may improve it to such a degree, that though we should suppose it impossible for particular affections to be absolutely coincident with the moral principle; and consequently should allow, that such creatures as have been above supposed, would for ever remain defectible; yet their danger of actually deviating from right may be almost infinitely lessened, and they fully fortified against what remains of it; if that may be called danger, against which there is an adequate, effectual security. But still, this their higher perfection may continue to consist in habits of virtue formed in a state of discipline, and this their more complete security remain to proceed from them. And thus it is plainly conceivable, that creatures without blemish, as they came out of the hands of God, may be in danger of going wrong; and so may stand in need of the security of virtuous habits, additional to the moral principle wrought into their natures by him. That which is the ground of their danger, or their want of security, may be considered as a deficiency in them, to which virtuous habits are the natural supply. And as they are naturally capable of being raised and improved by discipline, it may be a thing fit and requisite, that they should be placed in circumstances with an eye to it: in circumstances peculiarly fitted to be to them a state of discipline for their improvement in virtue.

But how much more strongly must this hold with respect to those who have corrupted their natures, are fallen from their original rectitude, and whose passions are become excessive by repeated violations of their inward constitution? Upright creatures may want to be improved: depraved creatures want to be renewed. Education and discipline, which may be in all degrees and sorts of gentleness and of severity, are expedient for those: but must be absolutely necessary for these. For these, discipline of the severer sort too, and in the higher degrees of it, must be necessary, in order to wear out vicious habits; to recover their primitive strength of self-government, which indulgence must have weakened; to repair, as well as raise into a habit, the moral principle, in order to their arriving at a secure state of virtuous happiness.

Now, whoever will consider the thing may clearly see, that the present world is *peculiarly fit* to be a state of discipline for this purpose, to such as will set themselves to mend and improve. For, the various temptations with which we are surrounded; our experience of the deceits of wickedness; having been in many instances led wrong ourselves; the great viciousness of the world; the infinite disorders consequent upon it; our being made acquainted with pain and sorrow, either from our own feeling of it, or from the sight of it in others; these things, though some of them may indeed produce wrong effects upon our minds, yet when duly reflected upon, have, all of them, a direct tendency to bring us to a settled moderation and reasonableness of temper: the contrary both to thoughtless levity, and also to that unrestrained self-will, and violent bent to follow present inclination, which may be observed in undisciplined minds. Such experience, as the present state affords, of the frailty of our nature; of the boundless extravagance of ungoverned passion; of the power which an infinite Being has over us, by the various capacities of misery which he has given us; in short, that kind and degree of experience, which the present state affords us, that the constitution of nature is such as to admit the possibility, the danger, and the actual event, of creatures losing their innocence and happiness, and becoming vicious and wretched; hath a tendency to give us a practical sense of things very different from a mere speculative knowledge, that we are liable to vice, and capable of misery. And who knows, whether the security of creatures in the highest and most settled state of perfection, may not in part arise, from their having had such a sense of things as this, formed, and habitually fixed within them, in some state of probation. And passing through the present world with that moral attention, which is necessary to the acting a right part in it, may leave everlasting impressions of this sort upon our minds. But to be a little more distinct: allurements to what is wrong; difficulties in the discharge of our duty; our not being able to act a uniform right part without some thought and care; and the opportunities which we have, or imagine we have, of avoiding what we dislike, or obtaining what we desire, by unlawful means, when we either cannot do it at all, or at least not so easily, by lawful ones; these things, *i. e.* the snares and temptations of vice, are what render the present world peculiarly fit to be a state of discipline, to those who will preserve their integrity: because they render being upon our guard, resolution, and the denial of our passions, necessary in order to that end. And the exercise of such particular recollection, intention of mind, and self-government, in the practice of virtue, has, from the make of our nature, a peculiar tendency to form habits of virtue; as implying, not only a real, but also a more continued, and a more intense exercise of the virtuous principle; or a more constant and a stronger effort of virtue exerted into act. Thus suppose a person to know himself to be in particular danger, for some time, of doing any thing wrong, which yet he fully resolves not to do: continued recollection, and keeping upon his guard, in order to make good his resolution, is a *continued* exerting of that act of virtue in a *high degree*, which need have been, and perhaps would have been, only *instantaneous* and *weak*, had the temptation been so. It is indeed ridiculous to assert, that self-denial is essential to virtue and piety: but it would have been nearer the truth, though not strictly the truth itself, to have said, that it is essential to discipline and improvement. For though actions materially virtuous, which have no sort of difficulty, but are perfectly agreeable to our particular inclinations, may possibly be done only from these particular inclinations, and so may not be any exercise of the principle of virtue, *i. e.* not be virtuous actions at all; yet, on the contrary, they may be an exercise of that principle: and when they are, they have a tendency to form and fix the habit of virtue. But when the exercise of the virtuous principle is more continued, oftener repeated, and more intense; as it must be in circumstances of danger, temptation, and difficulty, of any kind and in any degree; this tendency is increased proportionably, and a more confirmed habit is the consequence.

This undoubtedly holds to a certain length: but how far it may hold, I know not. Neither our intellectual powers, nor our bodily strength can be improved beyond such a degree: and both may be over-wrought. Possibly there may be somewhat analogous to this, with respect to the moral character; which is scarce worth considering. And I mention it only, lest it should come into some persons' thoughts, not as an exception to the foregoing observations, which perhaps it is; but as a confutation of them, which it is not. And there may be several other exceptions. Observations of this kind cannot be supposed to hold minutely, and in every case. It is enough that they hold in general. And these plainly hold so far, as that from them may be seen distinctly, which is all that is intended by them, that *the present world is peculiarly fit to be a state of discipline, for our improvement in virtue and piety:* in the same sense as some sciences, by requiring and engaging the attention, not to be sure of such persons as will not, but of such as will, set themselves to them; are fit to form the mind to habits of attention.

Indeed the present state is so far from proving, in event, a discipline of virtue to the generality of men, that, on the contrary, they seem to make it a discipline of vice. And the viciousness of the world is, in different ways, the great temptation which renders it a state of virtuous discipline, in the degree it is, to good men. The whole end, and the whole occasion, of mankind's being placed in such a state as the present, is not pretended to be accounted for. That which appears amidst the general corruption, is, that there are some persons, who, having within them the principle of amendment and recovery, attend to and follow the notices of virtue and religion, be they more clear or more obscure which are afforded them; and that the present world is, not only an exercise of virtue in these persons, but an exercise of it in ways and degrees, peculiarly apt to improve it: apt to improve it, in some respects, even beyond what would be, by the exercise of it, required in a perfectly virtuous society, or in a society of equally imperfect virtue with themselves. But that the present world does not actually become a state of moral discipline to many, even to the generality, *i. e.* that they do not improve or grow better in it, cannot be urged as a proof, that it was not intended for moral discipline, by any who at all observe the analogy of nature. For, of the numerous seeds of vegetables and bodies of animals, which are adapted and put in the way, to improve to such a point or state of natural maturity and perfection, we do not see perhaps that one in a million actually does. Far the greatest part of them decay before they are improved to it; and appear to be absolutely destroyed. Yet no one, who does not deny all final causes, will deny, that those seeds and bodies, which do attain to that point of maturity and perfection, answer the end for which they were really designed by nature; and therefore that nature designed them for such perfection. And I cannot forbear adding, though it is not to the present purpose, that the *appearance* of such an amazing *waste* in nature, with respect to these seeds and bodies, by foreign causes, is to us as unaccountable, as, what is much more terrible, the present and future ruin of so many moral agents by themselves, *i. e.* by vice.

Against this whole notion of moral discipline, it may be objected, in another way; that so far as a course of behaviour, materially virtuous, proceeds from hope and fear, so far it is only a discipline and strengthening of self-love. But doing what God commands, because he commands it, is obedience, though it proceeds from hope or fear. And a course of such obedience will form habits of it. And a constant regard to veracity, justice, and charity, may form distinct habits of these particular virtues; and will certainly form habits of self-government, and of denying our inclinations, whenever veracity, justice, or charity requires it. Nor is there any foundation for this great nicety, with which some affect to distinguish in this case, in order to depreciate all Religion proceeding from hope or fear. For, veracity, justice, and charity, regard to God's authority, and to our own chief interest, are not only all three coincident; but each of them is, in itself, a just and natural motive or principle of action. And he who begins a good life from any one of them, and perseveres in it, as he is already in some degree, so he cannot fail of becoming more and more, of that character which is correspondent to the constitution of nature as moral; and to the relation which God stands in to us as moral governor of it: nor consequently can he fail of obtaining that happiness, which this constitution and relation necessarily suppose connected with that character.

These several observations, concerning the active principle of virtue and obedience to God's commands, are applicable to passive submission or resignation to his will: which is another essential part of a right character, connected with the former, and very much in our power to form ourselves to. It may be imagined, that nothing but afflictions can give occasion for or require this virtue; that it can have no respect to, nor be any way necessary to qualify for, a state of perfect happiness: but it is not experience which can make us think thus. Prosperity itself, whilst any thing supposed desirable is not ours, it gets extravagant and unbounded thoughts. Imagination is altogether as much a source of discontent, as any thing in our external condition. It is indeed true, that there can be no scope for patience, when sorrow shall be no more; but there may be need of a temper of mind, which shall have been formed by patience. For, though self-love, considered merely as an active principle leading us to pursue our chief interest, cannot but be uniformly coincident with the principle of obedience to God's commands, our interest being rightly understood; because this obedience, and the pursuit of our own chief interest, must be in every case one and the same thing: yet it may be questioned, whether self-love, considered merely as the desire of our own interest or happiness, can, from its nature, be thus absolutely and uniformly coincident with the will of God; any more than particular affections can:* coincident in such sort, as not to be liable to be excited upon occasions and in degrees, impossible to be gratified consistently with the constitution of things, or the divine appointments. So that *habits* of resignation may, upon this account, be requisite for all creatures: habits, I say; which signify what is formed by use. However, in general it is obvious that both self-love and particular affection in human creatures considered only as passive feelings, distort and rend the mind; and therefore stand in need of discipline. Now denial of those particular affections, in a course of active

* P. 122.

virtue and obedience to God's will, has a tendency to moderate them; and seems also to have a tendency to habituate the mind, to be easy and satisfied with that degree of happiness which is allotted us, *i. e.* to moderate self-love. But the proper discipline for resignation is affliction. For a right behaviour under that trial; recollecting ourselves so as to consider it in the view, in which Religion teaches us to consider it, as from the hand of God; receiving it as what he appoints, or thinks proper to permit, in his world and under his government; this will habituate the mind to a dutiful submission. And such submission, together with the active principle of obedience, make up the temper and character in us, which answers to his sovereignty; and which absolutely belongs to the condition of our being, as dependent creatures. Nor can it be said, that this is only breaking the mind to a submission to mere power; for mere power may be accidental, and precarious, and usurped: but it is forming within ourselves the temper of resignation to his rightful authority, who is, by nature, supreme over all.

Upon the whole: such a character, and such qualifications, are necessary for a mature state of life in the present world, as nature alone does in no wise bestow; but has put it upon us, in great part, to acquire, in our progress from one stage of life to another, from childhood to mature age; put it upon us to acquire them, by giving us capacities of doing it, and by placing us, in the beginning of life, in a condition fit for it. And this is a general analogy to our condition in the present world, as in a state of moral discipline for another. It is in vain then to object against the credibility of the present life's being intended for this purpose, that all the trouble and the danger unavoidably accompanying such discipline, might have been saved us, by our being made at once the creatures and the characters, *which we were to be.* For we experience, that *what we were to be,* was to be the effect of *what we would do:* and that the general conduct of nature is, not to save us trouble or danger, but to make us capable of going through them, and to put it upon us to do so. Acquirements of our own, experience and habits, are the *natural* supply to our deficiencies, and security against our dangers: since it is as plainly natural to set ourselves to acquire the qualifications, as the external things, which we stand in need of. In particular, it is as plainly a general law of nature, that we should with regard to our temporal interest, form and cultivate practical principles within us, by attention, use, and discipline, as any thing whatever is a natural law; chiefly in the beginning of life, but also throughout the whole course of it. And the alternative is left to our choice: either to improve ourselves, and better our condition; or, in default of such improvement, to remain deficient and wretched. It is therefore perfectly credible, from the analogy of nature, that the same may be our case, with respect to the happiness of a future state, and the qualifications necessary for it.

There is a third thing, which may seem implied in the present world's being a state of probation; that it is a theatre of action, for the manifestation of persons' characters, with respect to a future one: not, to be sure, to an all-knowing Being, but to his creation or part of it. This may, perhaps, be only a consequence of our being in a state of probation in the other senses. However, it is not impossible, that men's showing and making manifest, what is in their heart, what their real character is, may have respect to a future life, in ways and manners which we are not acquainted with: particularly it may be a means, for the Author of Nature does not appear to do any thing without means, of their being disposed of suitably to their characters; and of its being known to the creation, by way of example, that they are thus disposed of. But not to enter upon any conjectural account of this; one may just mention, that the manifestation of persons' characters contributes very much, in various ways, to the carrying on a great part of that general course of nature, respecting mankind, which comes under our observation at present. I shall only add, that probation, in both these senses, as well as in that treated of in the foregoing chapter, is implied in moral government; since by persons' behaviour under it, their characters cannot but be manifested, and if they behave well, improved.

CHAP. VI.

OF THE OPINION OF NECESSITY, CONSIDERED AS INFLUENCING PRACTICE.

THROUGHOUT the foregoing Treatise it appears, that the condition of mankind, considered as inhabitants of this world only, and under the government of God which we experience, is greatly analogous to our condition, as designed for another world, or under that farther government, which Religion teaches us. If therefore any assert, as a Fatalist must, that the opinion of universal Necessity is reconcilable with the former; there immediately arises a question in the way of analogy, whether he must not also own it to be reconcilable with the latter, *i. e.* with the system of Religion itself, and the proof of it. The reader then will observe, that the question now before us is not absolute. Whether the opinion of Fate be reconcilable with Religion; but hypothetical, whether, upon supposition of its being reconcilable with the constitution of Nature, it be not reconcilable with Religion also: or, what pretence a Fatalist, not other persons, but a Fatalist, has to conclude from his opinion, that there can be no such thing as Religion. And as the puzzle and obscurity, which must unavoidably arise from arguing upon so absurd a supposition as that of universal Necessity, will, I fear, easily be seen; it will, I hope, as easily be excused.

But since it has been all along taken for granted, as a thing proved, that there is an intelligent Author of Nature, or natural Governor of the world; and since an objection may be made against the proof of this, from the opinion of universal Necessity, as it may be supposed, that such Necessity will itself account for the origin and preservation of all things: it is requisite, that this objection be distinctly answered; or that it be shown, that a Fatality supposed consistent with what we certainly experience, does not destroy the proof of an intelligent Author and Governor of Nature; before we proceed to consider, whether it destroys the proof of a moral Governor of it, or of our being in a state of Religion.

Now, when it is said by a Fatalist, that the whole constitution of Nature, and the actions of men, that every thing, and every mode and circumstance of every thing, is necessary, and could not possibly have been otherwise; it is to be observed, that this Necessity does not exclude deliberation, choice, preference, and acting from certain principles, and to certain ends: because all this is matter of undoubted experience, acknowledged by all, and what every man may, every moment, be conscious of. And from hence it follows, that Necessity, alone and of itself, is in no sort an account of the constitution of Nature, and how things came *to be* and *to continue* as they are; but only an account of this *circumstance* relating to their origin and continuance, that they could not have been otherwise, than they are and have been. The assertion, that every thing is by Necessity of Nature, is not an answer to the question; Whether the world came into being as it is, by an intelligent Agent forming it thus, or not: but to quite another question; Whether it came into being as it is, in that way and manner which we call *necessarily*, or in that way and manner which we call *freely*. For suppose farther, that one who was a Fatalist, and one who kept to his natural sense of things, and believed himself a Free Agent, were disputing together, and vindicating their respective opinions; and they should happen to instance in a house: they would agree that it was built by an architect. Their difference concerning Necessity and Freedom would occasion no difference of judgment concerning this; but only concerning another matter; whether the architect built it necessarily or freely. Suppose then they should proceed to inquire concerning the constitution of nature: in a lax way of speaking, one of them might say, it was by Necessity; and the other, by Freedom: but if they had any meaning to their words, as the latter must mean a Free Agent, so the former must at length be reduced to mean an Agent, whether he would say one or more, acting by Necessity: for abstract notions can do nothing. Indeed we ascribe to God a necessary existence, uncaused by any agent. For we find within ourselves the idea of infinity, *i. e.* immensity and eternity, impossible, even in imagination, to be removed out of being. We seem to discern intuitively, that there must, and cannot but be, somewhat, external to ourselves, answering this idea, or the archetype of it. And from hence (for *this abstract*, as much as any other, implies a *concrete*) we conclude, that there is, and cannot but be, an infinite and immense eternal Being existing, prior to all design contributing to his existence, and exclusive of it. And from the scantiness of language, a manner of speaking has been introduced; that Necessity is the foundation, the reason, the account of the existence of God. But it is not alleged, nor can it be at all intended, that *every thing* exists as it does, by this kind of Necessity; a Necessity antecedent in nature to design: it cannot, I say, be meant that every thing exists as it does, by this kind of Necessity, upon several accounts; and particularly because it is admitted, that design, in the actions of men, contributes to many alterations in nature. For if any deny this, I shall not pretend to reason with them.

From these things it follows; *First*, That when a Fatalist asserts, that every thing is *by Necessity*, he must mean, *by an Agent acting necessarily;* he must, I say, mean this, for I am very sensible he would not choose to mean it: and *Secondly*, That the Necessity, by which such an Agent is supposed to act, does not exclude intelligence and design. So that, were the system of Fatality admitted, it would just as much account for the formation of the world, as for the structure of a house, and no more. Necessity as much requires and supposes a Necessary Agent, as Freedom requires and supposes a Free Agent, to be the former of the world. And the appearances of *design* and of *final causes* in the constitution of nature as really prove this acting Agent to be an *intelligent designer*, or to act from choice; upon the scheme of Necessity, supposed possible, as upon that of Freedom.

It appearing thus, that the notion of Necessity does not destroy the proof, that there is an intelligent Author of Nature and natural Governor of the world; the present question, which the analogy before mentioned suggests,* and which, I think, it will answer, is this: Whether the opinion of Necessity, supposed consistent with possibility, with the constitution of the world, and the natural government which we experience exercised over it, destroys all reasonable ground of belief, that we are in a state of Religion: or whether that opinion be reconcilable with Religion; with the system, and the proof of it.

Suppose then a Fatalist to educate any one, from his youth up, in his own principles; that the child should reason upon them, and conclude, that since he cannot possibly behave otherwise than he does, he is not a subject of blame or commendation, nor can deserve to be rewarded or punished: imagine him to eradicate the very perceptions of blame and commendation out of his mind, by means of this system; to form his temper, and character, and behaviour to it; and from it to judge of the treatment he was to expect, say, from reasonable men, upon his coming abroad into the world: as the Fatalist judges from this system, what he is to expect from the Author of Nature, and with regard to a future state. I cannot forbear stopping here to ask, whether any one of common sense would think fit, that a child should be put upon these speculations, and be left to apply them to practice. And a man has little pretence to reason, who is not sensible, that we are all children in speculations of this kind. However, the child would doubtless be highly delighted to find himself freed from the restraints of fear and shame, with which his play-fellows were fettered and embarrassed; and highly conceited in his superior knowledge, so far beyond his years. But conceit and vanity would be the least bad part of the influence, which these principles must have, when thus reasoned and acted upon, during the course of his education. He must either be allowed to go on and be the plague of all about him, and himself too, even to his own destruction: or else correction must be continually made use of, to supply the want of those natural perceptions of blame and commendation, which we have supposed to be removed; and to give him a practical impression, of what he had reasoned himself out of the belief of, that he was

* P. 134.

in fact an accountable child, and to be punished for doing what he was forbid. It is therefore in reality impossible, but that the correction which he must meet with, in the course of his education, must convince him, that if the scheme he was instructed in were not false; yet that he reasoned inconclusively upon it, and somehow or other misapplied it to practice and common life; as what the Fatalist experiences of the conduct of Providence at present, ought in all reason to convince him, that this scheme is misapplied, when applied to the subject of Religion.* But supposing the child's temper could remain still formed to the system, and his expectation of the treatment he was to have in the world be regulated by it; so as to expect that no reasonable man would blame or punish him, for any thing which he should do, because he could not help doing it: upon this supposition it is manifest he would, upon his coming abroad into the world, be insupportable to society, and the treatment which he would receive from it would render it so to him; and he could not fail of doing somewhat, very soon, for which he would be delivered over into the hands of civil justice. And thus, in the end, he would be convinced of the obligations he was under to his wise instructor. Or suppose this scheme of Fatality in any other way, applied to practice, such practical application of it will be found equally absurd; equally fallacious in a practical sense: for instance, that if a man be destined to live such a time, he shall live to it, though he take no care of his own preservation; or if he be destined to die before that time, no care can prevent it: therefore all care about preserving one's life is to be neglected: which is the fallacy instanced in by the ancients. But now, on the contrary, none of these practical absurdities can be drawn from reasoning, upon the supposition that we are free; but all such reasoning with regard to the common affairs of life is justified by experience. And therefore, though it were admitted that this opinion of Necessity were speculatively true; yet, with regard to practice, it is as if it were false, so far as our experience reaches: that is, to the whole of our present

* P. 135.

life. For, the constitution of the present world, and the condition in which we are actually placed, is, as if we were free. And it may perhaps justly be concluded, that since the whole process of action, through every step of it, suspense, deliberation, inclining one way, determining, and at last doing as we determine, is as if we were free, therefore we are so. But the thing here insisted upon is, that under the present natural government of the world, we find we are treated and dealt with, as if we were free, prior to all consideration whether we are or not. Were this opinion therefore of Necessity admitted to be ever so true; yet such is in fact our condition and the natural course of things, that whenever we apply it to life and practice, this application of it always misleads us, and cannot but mislead us, in a most dreadful manner, with regard to our present interest. And how can people think themselves so very secure then, that the same application of the same opinion may not mislead them also, in some analogous manner, with respect to a future, a more general, and more important interest? For, Religion being a practical subject; and the analogy of nature showing us, that we have not faculties to apply this opinion, were it a true one, to practical subjects; whenever we do apply it to the subject of Religion, and thence conclude, that we are free from its obligations, it is plain this conclusion cannot be depended upon. There will still remain just reason to think, whatever appearances are, that we deceive ourselves; in somewhat of a like manner, as when people fancy they can draw contradictory conclusions from the idea of infinity.

From these things together, the attentive reader will see it follows, that if upon supposition of Freedom the evidence of Religion be conclusive, it remains so, upon supposition of Necessity, because the notion of Necessity is not applicable to practical subjects: *i. e.* with respect to them, is as if it were not true. Nor does this contain any reflection upon reason, but only upon what is unreasonable. For to pretend to act upon reason, in opposition to practical principles, which the Author of our nature gave us to act upon; and to pretend to apply our reason to subjects, with regard to which, our own short views, and even our experience, will show us, it cannot be depended upon; and such, at best, the subject of Necessity must be; this is vanity, conceit, and unreasonableness.

But this is not all. For we find within ourselves a will, and are conscious of a character. Now if this, in us, be reconcilable with Fate, it is reconcilable with it, in the Author of Nature. And besides, natural government and final causes imply a character and a will in the Governor and Designer;* a will concerning the creatures whom he governs. The Author of Nature then being certainly of some character or other, notwithstanding Necessity; it is evident this Necessity is as reconcilable with the particular character of benevolence, veracity, and justice, in him, which attributes are the foundation of Religion, as with any other character: since we find this Necessity no more hinders *men* from being benevolent, than cruel; true, than faithless; just, than unjust; or, if the Fatalist pleases, what we call unjust. For it is said indeed, that what, upon supposition of Freedom, would be just punishment; upon supposition of Necessity, becomes manifestly unjust: because it is punishment inflicted for doing that which persons could not avoid doing. As if the Necessity, which is supposed to destroy the injustice of murder, for instance, would not also destroy the injustice of punishing it. However, as little to the purpose as this objection is in itself, it is very much to the purpose to observe from it, how the notions of justice and injustice remain, even whilst we endeavour to suppose them removed; how they force themselves upon the mind, even whilst we are making suppositions destructive of them: for there is not, perhaps, a man in the world, but would be ready to make this objection at first thought.

But though it is most evident, that universal Necessity, if it be reconcilable with any thing, is reconcilable with that character in the Author of Nature, which is the foundation of Religion; "Yet, does it not plainly destroy the proof, that he is of that character, and consequently

* By *will* and *character* is meant that which, in speaking of men, we should express, not only by these words, but also by the words *temper, taste, dispositions, practical principles: that whole frame of mind, from whence we act in one manner rather than another.*

the proof of Religion?" By no means. For we find, that happiness and misery are not our fate, in any such sense as not to be the consequences of our behaviour; but that they are the consequences of it.* We find God exercises the same kind of government over us, with that which a father exercises over his children, and a civil magistrate over his subjects. Now, whatever becomes of abstract questions concerning Liberty and Necessity, it evidently appears to us, that veracity and justice must be the natural rule and measure of exercising this authority or government, to a Being who can have no competitions, or interfering of interests, with his creatures and his subjects.

But as the doctrine of Liberty, though we experience its truth, may be perplexed with difficulties, which run up into the most abstruse of all speculations; and as the opinion of Necessity seems to be the very basis upon which infidelity grounds itself; it may be of some use to offer a more particular proof of the obligations of Religion, which may distinctly be shown not to be destroyed by this opinion.

The proof from final causes of an intelligent Author of Nature is not affected by the opinion of Necessity; supposing Necessity a thing possible in itself, and reconcilable with the constitution of things.† And it is a matter of fact, independent on this or any other speculation, that he governs the world by the method of rewards and punishments:‡ and also that he hath given us a moral faculty, by which we distinguish between actions, and approve some as virtuous and of good desert, and disapprove others as vicious and of ill desert.§ Now this moral discernment implies, in the notion of it, a rule of action, and a rule of a very peculiar kind: for it carries in it authority and a right of direction; authority in such a sense, as that we cannot depart from it without being self-condemned.‖ And that the dictates of this moral faculty, which are by nature a rule to us, are moreover the laws of God, laws in a sense including sanctions; may be thus proved. Consciousness of a rule or guide of

* Chap. ii. † P. 134, &c. ‡ Chap. ii.
§ Dissert. II. ‖ Serm. 2. at the *Rolls*

action, in creatures who are capable of considering it as given them by their Maker, not only raises immediately a sense of duty, but also a sense of security in following it, and of danger in deviating from it. A direction of the Author of Nature, given to creatures capable of looking upon it as such, is plainly a command from him: and a command from him necessarily includes in it, at least, an implicit promise in case of obedience, or threatening in case of disobedience. But then the sense or perception of good and ill desert,* which is contained in the moral discernment, renders the sanction explicit, and makes it appear, as one may say, expressed. For since his method of government is to reward and punish actions, his having annexed to some actions an inseparable sense of good desert, and to others of ill, this surely amounts to declaring, upon whom his punishments shall be inflicted, and his rewards be bestowed. For he must have given us this discernment and sense of things, as a presentiment of what is to be hereafter: that is, by way of information beforehand, what we are finally to expect in this world. There is then most evident ground to think, that the government of God, upon the whole, will be found to correspond to the nature which he has given us: and that, in the upshot and issue of things, happiness and misery shall, in fact and event, be made to follow virtue and vice respectively; as he has already, in so peculiar a manner, associated the ideas of them in our minds. And from hence might easily be deduced the obligations of religious worship, were it only to be considered as a means of preserving upon our minds a sense of this moral government of God, and securing our obedience to it: which yet is an extremely imperfect view of that most important duty.

Now, I say, no objection from Necessity can lie against this general proof of Religion. None against the proposition reasoned upon, that we have such a moral faculty and discernment; because this is a mere matter of fact, a thing of experience, that human kind is thus constituted: none against the conclusion; because it is immediate and wholly from this fact. For the conclusion, that

* Dissert. II.

God will finally reward the righteous and punish the wicked, is not here drawn, from its appearing to us fit* that *he should;* but from its appearing, that he has told us, *he will.* And this he hath certainly told us, in the promise and threatening, which it hath been observed the notion of a command implies, and the sense of good and ill desert which he has given us, more distinctly expresses. And this reasoning from fact is confirmed, and in some degree even verified, by other facts; by the natural tendencies of virtue and of vice;† and by this, that God, in the natural course of his providence, punishes vicious actions as mischievous to society; and also vicious actions as such in the strictest sense.‡ So that the general proof of Religion is unanswerably real, even upon the wild supposition which we are arguing upon.

It must likewise be observed further, that natural Religion hath, besides this, an external evidence; which the doctrine of Necessity, if it could be true, would not affect. For suppose a person, by the observations and reasoning above, or by any other, convinced of the truth of Religion; that there is a God, who made the world, who is the moral Governor and Judge of mankind, and will upon the whole deal with every one according to his works: I say, suppose a person convinced of this by reason; but to know nothing at all of antiquity, or the present state of mankind: it would be natural for such a one to be inquisitive, what was the history of this system of doctrine; at what time, and in what manner, it came first into the world; and whether it were believed by any considerable part of it. And were he upon inquiry to find, that a parti-

* However, I am far from intending to deny, that the will of God is determined, by what is fit, by the right and reason of the case; though one chooses to decline matters of such abstract speculation, and to speak with caution when one does speak of them. But if it be intelligible to say, that *it is fit and reasonable for every one to consult his own happiness*, then *fitness of action, or the right and reason of the case*, is an intelligible manner of speaking. And it seems as inconceivable, to suppose God to approve one course of action, or one end, preferably to another, which yet his acting at all from design implies that he does, without supposing somewhat prior in that end, to be the ground of the preference; as to suppose him to discern an abstract proposition to be true, without supposing somewhat prior in it, to be the ground of the discernment. It doth not therefore appear, that moral right is any more relative to perception, than abstract truth is; or that it is any more improper, to speak of the fitness and rightness of actions and ends, as founded in the nature of things, than to speak of abstract truth, as thus founded.

† P. 95. ‡ P. 88, &c.

cular person, in a late age, first of all proposed it, as a deduction of reason, and that mankind were before wholly ignorant of it; then, though its evidence from reason would remain, there would be no additional probability of its truth, from the account of its discovery. But instead of this being the fact of the case, on the contrary, he would find, what could not but afford him a very strong confirmation of its truth: *First*, That somewhat of this system, with more or fewer additions and alterations, hath been professed in all ages and countries, of which we have any certain information relating to this matter. *Secondly*, That it is certain historical fact, so far as we can trace things up, that this whole system of belief, that there is one God, the Creator and moral Governor of the world, and that mankind is in a state of Religion, was received in the first ages. And *Thirdly*, That as there is no hint or intimation in history, that this system was first reasoned out; so there is express historical or traditional evidence, as ancient as history, that it was taught first by revelation. Now these things must be allowed to be of great weight. The first of them, general consent, shows this system to be conformable to the common sense of mankind. The second, namely, that Religion was believed in the first ages of the world, especially as it does not appear that there were then any superstitious or false additions to it, cannot but be a further confirmation of its truth. For it is a proof of this alternative: either that it came into the world by revelation; or that it is natural, obvious, and forces itself upon the mind. The former of these is the conclusion of learned men. And whoever will consider, how unapt for speculation rude and uncultivated minds are, will, perhaps from hence alone, be strongly inclined to believe it the truth. And as it is shown in the Second Part* of this Treatise, that there is nothing of such peculiar presumption against a revelation in the beginning of the world, as there is supposed to be against subsequent ones: a sceptic could not, I think, give any account, which would appear more probable even to himself, of the early pretences to revelation, than by

* Chap. ii.

supposing some real original one, from whence they were copied. And the third thing above mentioned, that there is express historical or traditional evidence as ancient as history, of the system of Religion being taught mankind by revelation; this must be admitted as some degree of real proof, that it was so taught. For why should not the most ancient tradition be admitted as some additional proof of a fact, against which there is no presumption? And this proof is mentioned here, because it has its weight to show, that Religion came into the world by revelation, prior to all consideration of the proper authority of any book supposed to contain it; and even prior to all consideration, whether the revelation itself be uncorruptly handed down, and related, or mixed and darkened with fables. Thus the historical account, which we have of the origin of Religion, taking in all circumstances, is a real confirmation of its truth, no way affected by the opinion of Necessity. And the *external* evidence, even of natural Religion, is by no means inconsiderable.

But it is carefully to be observed, and ought to be recollected after all proofs of virtue and religion, which are only general; that as speculative reason may be neglected, prejudiced, and deceived, so also may our moral understanding be impaired and perverted, and the dictates of it not impartially attended to. This indeed proves nothing against the reality of our speculative or practical faculties of perception; against their being intended by nature, to inform us in the theory of things, and instruct us how we are to behave, and what we are to expect in consequence of our behaviour. Yet our liableness, in the degree we are liable, to prejudice and perversion, is a most serious admonition to us to be upon our guard, with respect to what is of such consequence, as our determinations concerning virtue and religion; and particularly not to take custom, and fashion, and slight notions of honour, or imaginations of present ease, use, and convenience to mankind, for the only moral rule.*

The foregoing observations, drawn from the nature of

* Dissert. II.

the thing, and the history of Religion, amount, when taken together, to a real practical proof of it, not to be confuted: such a proof as, considering the infinite importance of the thing, I apprehend, would be admitted fully sufficient, in reason, to influence the actions of men, who act upon thought and reflection; if it were admitted that there is no proof of the contrary. But it may be said; "There are many probabilities, which cannot indeed be confuted, *i. e.* shown to be no probabilities, and yet may be overbalanced by greater probabilities on the other side; much more by demonstration. And there is no occasion to object against particular arguments alleged for an opinion, when the opinion itself may be clearly shown to be false, without meddling with such arguments at all, but leaving them just as they are.* Now the method of government by rewards and punishments, and especially rewarding and punishing good and ill desert as such respectively, must go upon supposition, that we are Free and not Necessary Agents. And it is incredible, that the Author of Nature should govern us upon a supposition as true, which he knows to be false; and therefore absurd to think, he will reward or punish us for our actions hereafter; especially that he will do it under the notion, that they are of good or ill desert." Here then the matter is brought to a point. And the answer to all this is full, and not to be evaded; that the whole constitution and course of things, the whole analogy of providence, shows beyond possibility of doubt, that the conclusion from this reasoning is false; wherever the fallacy lies. The doctrine of freedom indeed clearly shows where: in supposing ourselves Necessary, when in truth we are Free Agents. But, upon the supposition of Necessity, the fallacy lies in taking for granted, that it is incredible Necessary Agents should be rewarded and punished. But that, somehow or other, the conclusion now mentioned is false, is most certain. For it is fact, that God does govern even brute creatures by the method of rewards and punishments, in the natural course of things. And men are rewarded and punished for their actions, punished for actions

* P. 49, 52.

mischievous to society as being so, punished for vicious actions as such; by the natural instrumentality of each other, under the present conduct of Providence. Nay even the affection of gratitude, and the passion of resentment, and the rewards and punishments following from them, which in general are to be considered as natural, *i. e.* from the Author of Nature; these rewards and punishments, being naturally* annexed to actions considered as implying good intention and good desert, ill intention and ill desert; these natural rewards and punishments, I say, are as much a contradiction to the conclusion above, and show its falsehood, as a more exact and complete rewarding and punishing of good and ill desert as such. So that if it be incredible, that Necessary Agents should be thus rewarded and punished; then, men are not necessary but free; since it is matter of fact, that they are thus rewarded and punished. But if, on the contrary, which is the supposition we have been arguing upon, it be insisted, that men are Necessary Agents; then, there is nothing incredible in the further supposition of Necessary Agents being thus rewarded and punished: since we ourselves are thus dealt with.

From the whole therefore it must follow, that a Necessity supposed possible, and reconcilable with the constitution of things, does in no sort prove that the Author of Nature will not, nor destroy the proof that he will, finally and upon the whole, in his eternal government, render his creatures happy or miserable, by some means or other, as they behave well or ill. Or, to express this conclusion in words conformable to the title of the Chapter, the analogy of nature shows us, that the opinion of Necessity, considered as practical, is false. And if Necessity, upon the supposition above mentioned, doth not destroy the proof of natural Religion, it evidently makes no alteration in the proof of revealed.

From these things likewise we may learn, in what sense to understand that general assertion, that the opinion of Necessity is essentially destructive of all religion. First, in a practical sense; that by this notion,

* Serm. 8th, at the *Rolls.*

atheistical men pretend to satisfy and encourage themselves in vice, and justify to others their disregard to all religion. And secondly, in the strictest sense; that it is a contradiction to the whole constitution of nature, and to what we may every moment experience in ourselves, and so overturns every thing. But by no means is this assertion to be understood, as if Necessity, supposing it could possibly be reconciled with the constitution of things and with what we experience, were not also reconcilable with Religion: for upon this supposition, it demonstrably is so.

CHAP. VII.

OF THE GOVERNMENT OF GOD, CONSIDERED AS A SCHEME OR CONSTITUTION, IMPERFECTLY COMPREHENDED.

THOUGH it be, as it cannot but be, acknowledged, that the analogy of nature gives a strong credibility to the general doctrine of Religion, and to the several particular things contained in it, considered as so many matters of fact; and likewise that it shows this credibility not to be destroyed by any notions of Necessity: yet still, objections may be insisted upon, against the wisdom, equity, and goodness of the divine government implied in the notion of Religion, and against the method by which this government is conducted; to which objections analogy can be no direct answer. For the credibility, or the certain truth, of a matter of fact, does not immediately prove any thing concerning the wisdom or goodness of it: and analogy can do no more, immediately or directly, than show such and such things to be true or credible, considered only as matters of fact. But still, if, upon supposition of a moral constitution of nature and a moral government over it, analogy suggests and makes it credible, that this government must be a scheme, system, or constitution of government, as distinguished from a number of single unconnected acts of distributive justice and goodness; and likewise, that it must be a scheme, so imperfectly comprehended, and of such a sort in other respects, as to afford a direct general answer to all objections against the justice and goodness of it: then analogy is, remotely, of great service in answering those objections; both by suggesting the answer, and showing it to be a credible one.

Now this, upon inquiry, will be found to be the case. For, *First,* Upon supposition that God exercises a moral government over the world, the analogy of his natural government suggests and makes it credible, that his moral government must be a scheme, quite beyond our comprehension: and this affords a general answer to all objections against the justice and goodness of it. And, *Secondly,* A more distinct observation of some particular things contained in God's scheme of natural government, the like things being supposed, by analogy, to be contained in his moral government, will further show, how little weight is to be laid upon these objections.

I. Upon supposition that God exercises a moral government over the world, the analogy of his natural government suggests and makes it credible, that his moral government must be a scheme, quite beyond our comprehension; and this affords a general answer to all objections against the justice and goodness of it. It is most obvious, analogy renders it highly credible, that, upon supposition of a moral government, it must be a scheme: for the world, and the whole natural government of it, appears to be so: to be a scheme, system, or constitution, whose parts correspond to each other, and to a whole; as really as any work of art, or as any particular model of a civil constitution and government. In this great scheme of the natural world, individuals have various peculiar relations to other individuals of their own species. And whole species are, we find, variously related to other species, upon this earth. Nor do we know, how much further these kinds of relations may extend. And, as there is not any action or natural event, which we are acquainted with, so single and unconnected, as not to have a respect to some other actions and events; so possibly each of them, when it has not an immediate, may yet have a remote, natural relation to other actions and events, much beyond the compass of this present world. There seems indeed nothing, from whence we can so much as make a conjecture, whether all creatures, actions, and events, throughout the whole of nature, have relations to each other. But, as it is obvious, that all events have future unknown consequences; so if we trace any, as far as we can go, into what is connected with it, we shall find, that if such event were not connected with somewhat further in nature unknown to us, somewhat both past and present, such event could not possibly have been at all. Nor can we give the whole account of any one thing whatever; of all its causes, ends, and necessary adjuncts; those adjuncts, I mean, without which it could not have been. By this most astonishing connexion, these reciprocal correspondences and mutual relations, every thing which we see in the course of nature is actually brought about. And things seemingly the most insignificant imaginable are perpetually observed to be necessary conditions to other things of the greatest importance; so that any one thing whatever may, for ought we know to the contrary, be a necessary condition to any other. The natural world then, and natural government of it, being such an incomprehensible scheme; so incomprehensible, that a man must, really in the literal sense, know nothing at all, who is not sensible of his ignorance in it; this immediately suggests, and strongly shows the credibility, that the moral world and government of it may be so too. Indeed the natural and moral constitution and government of the world are so connected, as to make up together but one scheme: and it is highly probable, that the first is formed and carried on merely in subserviency to the latter; as the vegetable world is for the animal, and organized bodies for minds. But the thing intended here is, without inquiring how far the administration of the natural world is subordinate to that of the moral, only to observe the credibility, that one should be analogous or similar to the other: that therefore every act of divine justice and goodness may be supposed to look much beyond itself, and its immediate object; may have some reference to other parts of God's moral administration, and to a general moral plan; and that every circumstance of this his moral government may be adjusted beforehand with a view to the whole of it. Thus for example: the determined length of time, and the degrees and ways, in which virtue is to remain in a state of warfare and discipline, and in which wickedness is permitted to have its progress; the times appointed for the execution of justice; the appointed instruments of it; the kinds. of rewards and punishments, and the manners of their distribution; all particular instances of divine justice and goodness, and every circumstance of them, may have such respects to each other, as to make up altogether a whole, connected and related in all its parts; a scheme or system, which is as properly one as the natural world is, and of the like kind. And supposing this to be the case; it is most evident, that we are not competent judges of this scheme, from the small parts of it which come within our view in the present life: and therefore no objections against any of these parts can be insisted upon by reasonable men.

This our ignorance, and the consequence here drawn from it, are universally acknowledged upon other occasions; and though scarce denied, yet are universally forgot, when persons come to argue against Religion. And it is not perhaps easy, even for the most reasonable men, always to bear in mind the degree of our ignorance, and make due allowances for it. Upon these accounts, it may not be useless to go on a little further, in order to show more distinctly, how just an answer our ignorance is, to objections against the scheme of Providence. Suppose then a person boldly to assert, that the things complained of, the origin and continuance of evil, might easily have been prevented by repeated interpositions;* interpositions so guarded and circumstanced, as would preclude all mischief arising from them; or, if this were impracticable, that a *scheme* of government is itself an imperfection; since more good might have been produced, without any scheme, system, or constitution at all, by continued single unrelated acts of distributive justice and goodness; because these would have occasioned no

* P. 154, 155.

irregularities. And farther than this, it is presumed, the objections will not be carried. Yet the answer is obvious: that were these assertions true, still the observations above, concerning our ignorance in the scheme of divine government and the consequence drawn from it, would hold, in great measure; enough to vindicate Religion, against all objections from the disorders of the present state. Were these assertions true, yet the government of the world might be just and good notwithstanding; for, at the most, they would infer nothing more than that it might have been better. But indeed they are mere arbitrary assertions; no man being sufficiently acquainted with the possibilities of things, to bring any proof of them to the lowest degree of probability. For however possible what is asserted may seem; yet many instances may be alleged, in things much less out of our reach, of suppositions absolutely impossible, and reducible to the most palpable self-contradictions, which, not every one by any means would perceive to be such, nor perhaps any one at first sight suspect. From these things, it is easy to see distinctly, how our ignorance, as it is the common, is really a satisfactory answer to all objections against the justice and goodness of Providence. If a man, contemplating any one providential dispensation, which had no relation to any others, should object, that he discerned in it a disregard to justice, or a deficiency of goodness; nothing would be less an answer to such objection, than our ignorance in other parts of providence, or in the Possibilities of things, no way related to what he was contemplating. But when we know not but the parts objected against may be relative to other parts unknown to us; and when we are unacquainted with what is, in the nature of the thing, practicable in the case before us; then our ignorance is a satisfactory answer; because, some unknown relation, or some unknown impossibility, may render what is objected against, just and good; nay good in the highest practicable degree.

II. And how little weight is to be laid upon such objections, will further appear, by a more distinct observation of some particular things contained in the natural government of God, the like to which may be supposed, from analogy, to be contained in his moral government.

First, As in the scheme of the natural world, no ends appear to be accomplished without means: so we find that means very undesirable, often conduce to bring about ends in such a measure desirable, as greatly to overbalance the disagreeableness of the means. And in cases where such means are conducive to such ends, it is not reason, but experience, which shows us, that they are thus conducive. Experience also shows many means to be conducive and necessary to accomplish ends, which means, before experience, we should have thought, would have had even a contrary tendency. Now from these observations relating to the natural scheme of the world, the moral being supposed analogous to it, arises a great credibility, that the putting our misery in each other's power to the degree it is, and making men liable to vice to the degree we are; and in general, that those things which are objected against the moral scheme of Providence, may be, upon the whole, friendly and assistant to virtue, and productive of an overbalance of happiness: *i. e.* the things objected against may be means, by which an overbalance of good will, in the end, be found produced. And from the same observations, it appears to be no presumption against this, that we do not, if indeed we do not, see those means to have any such tendency, or that they seem to us to have a contrary one. Thus those things, which we call irregularities, may not be so at all: because they may be means of accomplishing wise and good ends more considerable. And it may be added, as above, that they may also be the only means, by which these wise and good ends are capable of being accomplished.

After these observations it may be proper to add, in order to obviate an absurd and wicked conclusion from any of them, that though the constitution of our nature, from whence we are capable of vice and misery, may, as it undoubtedly does, contribute to the perfection and happiness of the world; and though the actual permission of evil may be beneficial to it: (*i. e.* it would have been more mischievous, not that a wicked person had himself abstained from his own wickedness, but that any one had forcibly prevented it, than that it was permitted:) yet notwithstanding, it might have been much better for the world, if this very evil had never been done. Nay it is most clearly conceivable, that the very commission of wickedness may be beneficial to the world, and yet, that it would be infinitely more beneficial for men to refrain from it. For thus, in the wise and good constitution of the natural world, there are disorders which bring their own cures; diseases, which are themselves remedies. Many a man would have died, had it not been for the gout or a fever; yet it would be thought madness to assert, that sickness is a better or more perfect state than health; though the like, with regard to the moral world, has been asserted. But,

Secondly, The natural government of the world is carried on by general laws. For this there may be wise and good reasons: the wisest and best, for ought we know to the contrary. And that there are such reasons, is suggested to our thoughts by the analogy of nature: by our being made to experience good ends to be accomplished, as indeed all the good which we enjoy is accomplished, by this means, that the laws, by which the world is governed, are general. For we have scarce any kind of enjoyments, but what we are, in some way or other, instrumental in procuring ourselves, by acting in a manner which we foresee likely to procure them: now this foresight could not be at all, were not the government of the world carried on by general laws. And though, for ought we know to the contrary, every single case may be, at length, found to have been provided for even by these: yet to prevent all irregularities, or remedy them as they arise, by the wisest and best general laws, may be impossible in the nature of things; as we see it is absolutely impossible in civil government. But then we are ready to think, that, the constitution of nature remaining as it is, and the course of things being permitted to go on, in other respects, as it does, there might be interpositions to prevent irregularities; though they could not have been prevented, or remedied by any general laws. And there would indeed be reason to wish, which, by the way, is very different from a right to claim, that all irregularities were prevented or remedied by present interpositions, if these interpositions would have no other effect than this. But it is plain they would have some visible and immediate bad effects: for instance, they would encourage idleness and negligence; and they would render doubtful the natural rule of life, which is ascertained by this very thing, that the course of the world is carried on by general laws. And further, it is certain they would have distant effects, and very great ones too; by means of the wonderful connexions before mentioned.* So that we cannot so much as guess, what would be the whole result of the interpositions desired. It may be said, any bad result might be prevented by further interpositions, whenever there was occasion for them: but this again is talking quite at random, and in the dark.† Upon the whole then, we see wise reasons, why the course of the world should be carried on by general laws, and good ends accomplished by this means: and for ought we know, there may be the wisest reasons for it, and the best ends accomplished by it. We have no ground to believe, that all irregularities could be remedied as they arise, or could have been precluded, by general laws. We find that interpositions would produce evil, and prevent good: and, for ought we know, they would produce greater evil than they would prevent; and prevent greater good than they would produce. And if this be the case, then the not interposing is so far from being a ground of complaint, that it is an instance of goodness. This is intelligible and sufficient: and going further, seems beyond the utmost reach of our faculties.

But it may be said, that "after all, these supposed impossibilities and relations are what we are unacquainted with; and we must judge of Religion, as of other things, by what we do know, and look upon the rest as nothing: or however, that the answers here given to what is objected against Religion, may equally be made use of to invalidate the proof of it; since their stress lies so very much upon our ignorance." But,

* P. 150, &c. † P. 152.

First, Though total ignorance in any matter does indeed equally destroy, or rather preclude, all proof concerning it, and objections against it; yet partial ignorance does not. For we may in any degree be convinced, that a person is of such a character, and consequently will pursue such ends; though we are greatly ignorant, what is the proper way of acting, in order the most effectually to obtain those ends: and in this case, objections against his manner of acting, as seemingly not conducive to obtain them, might be answered by our ignorance; though the proof that such ends were intended, might not at all be invalidated by it. Thus, the proof of Religion is a proof of the moral character of God, and consequently that his government is moral, and that every one upon the whole shall receive according to his deserts; a proof that this is the designed end of his government. But we are not competent judges, what is the proper way of acting, in order the most effectually to accomplish this end.* Therefore our ignorance is an answer to objections against the conduct of Providence, in permitting irregularities, as seeming contradictory to this end. Now, since it is so obvious, that our ignorance may be a satisfactory answer to objections against a thing, and yet not affect the proof of it; till it can be shown, it is frivolous to assert, that our ignorance invalidates the proof of Religion, as it does the objections against it.

Secondly, Suppose unknown impossibilities, and unknown relations, might justly be urged to invalidate the proof of Religion, as well as to answer objections against it: and that, in consequence of this, the proof of it were doubtful. Yet still, let the assertion be despised, or let it be ridiculed, it is undeniably true, that moral obligations would remain certain, though it were not certain what would, upon the whole, be the consequences of observing or violating them. For, these obligations arise immediately and necessarily from the judgment of our own mind, unless perverted, which we cannot violate without being self-condemned. And they would be certain too, from considerations of interest.

* Pp. 53, 54.

For though it were doubtful, what will be the future consequences of virtue and vice; yet it is, however, credible, that they may have those consequences, which Religion teaches us they will: and this credibility is a certain * obligation in point of prudence, to abstain from all wickedness, and to live in the conscientious practice of all that is good. But,

Thirdly, The answers above given to the objections against Religion cannot equally be made use of to invalidate the proof of it. For, upon suspicion that God exercises a moral government over the world, analogy does most strongly lead us to conclude, that this moral government must be a scheme, or constitution, beyond our comprehension. And a thousand particular analogies show us, that parts of such a scheme, from their relation to other parts, may conduce to accomplish ends, which we should have thought they had no tendency at all to accomplish: nay ends, which before experience, we should have thought such parts were contradictory to, and had a tendency to prevent. And therefore all these analogies show, that the way of arguing made use of in objecting against Religion is delusive: because they show it is not at all incredible, that, could we comprehend the whole, we should find the permission of the disorders objected against to be consistent with justice and goodness; and even to be instances of them. Now this is not applicable to the proof of Religion, as it is to the objections against it;† and therefore cannot invalidate that proof, as it does these objections.

Lastly, From the observation now made, it is easy to see, that the answers above given to the objections against Providence, though, in a general way of speaking, they may be said to be taken from our ignorance; yet are by no means taken merely from that, but from somewhat which analogy shows us concerning it. For analogy shows us positively, that our ignorance in the possibilities of things, and the various relations in nature, renders us incompetent judges, and leads us to false conclusions, in cases similar to this, in which we pretend to judge and to object. So that the things above insisted

* P. 49, and Part II. Chap. vi. † Serm. at the *Rolls* p. 312. 2d. ed.

upon are not mere suppositions of unknown impossibilities and relations: but they are suggested to our thoughts, and even forced upon the observation of serious men, and rendered credible too, by the analogy of nature. And therefore to take these things into the account, is to judge by experience and what we do know: and it is not judging so, to take no notice of them.

CONCLUSION.

THE observations of the last Chapter lead us to consider this little scene of human life, in which we are so busily engaged, as having a reference, of some sort or other, to a much larger plan of things. Whether we are, any way, related to the more distant parts of the boundless universe, into which we are brought, is altogether uncertain. But it is evident, that the course of things, which comes within our view, is connected with somewhat, past, present, and future, beyond it.* So that we are placed, as one may speak, in the middle of a scheme, not a fixed but a progressive one, every way, incomprehensible: incomprehensible, in a manner equally, with respect to what has been, what now is, and what shall be hereafter. And this scheme cannot but contain in it somewhat as wonderful, and as much beyond our thought and conception,† as any thing in that of Religion. For, will any man in his senses say, that it is less difficult to conceive, how the world came to be and to continue as it is, without, than with, an intelligent Author and Governor of it? or, admitting an intelligent Governor of it, that there is some other rule of government more natural, and of easier conception, than that which we call moral? Indeed, without an intelligent Author and Governor of Nature, no account at all can be given, how this universe, or the part of it particularly in which we are concerned, came to be, and the course of it to be carried on, as it is: nor any, of its general end and design, without a moral Governor of it. That there is an intelligent Author of Nature, and natural Governor of

* P. 149, &c.

† See Part II. Ch. ii.

the world, is a principle gone upon in the foregoing treatise; as proved, and generally known and confessed to be proved. And the very notion of an intelligent Author of Nature, proved by particular final causes, implies a will and a character.* Now, as our whole nature, the nature which he has given us, leads us to conclude his will and character to be moral, just, and good: so we can scarce in imagination conceive, what it can be otherwise. However, in consequence of this his will and character, whatever it be, he formed the universe as it is, and carries on the course of it as he does, rather than in any other manner; and has assigned to us, and to all living creatures, a part and a lot in it. Irrational creatures act this their part, and enjoy and undergo the pleasures and the pains allotted them, without any reflection. But one would think it impossible, that creatures endued with reason could avoid reflecting sometimes upon all this; reflecting, if not from whence we came, yet, at least, whither we are going; and what the mysterious scheme, in the midst of which we find ourselves, will, at length, come out and produce: a scheme in which it is certain we are highly interested, and in which we may be interested even beyond conception. For many things prove it palpably absurd to conclude, that we shall cease to be, at death. Particular analogies do most sensibly show us, that there is nothing to be thought strange, in our being to exist in another state of life. And that we are now living beings, affords a strong probability that we shall *continue* so; unless there be some positive ground, and there is none from reason or analogy, to think death will destroy us. Were a persuasion of this kind ever so well grounded, there would, surely, be little reason to take pleasure in it. But indeed it can have no other ground, than some such imagination, as that of our gross bodies being ourselves; which is contrary to experience. Experience too most clearly shows us the folly of concluding, from the body and the living agent affecting each other mutually, that the dissolution of the former is the destruction of the latter. And there are remarkable instances of their not affecting each other,

* P. 140.

which lead us to a contrary conclusion. The supposition, then, which in all reason we are to go upon, is, that our living nature will *continue* after death. And it is infinitely unreasonable to form an institution of life, or to act upon any other supposition. Now all expectation of immortality, whether more or less certain, opens an unbounded prospect to our hopes and our fears: since we see the constitution of nature is such, as to admit of misery, as well as to be productive of happiness, and experience ourselves to partake of both in some degree; and since we cannot but know, what higher degrees of both we are capable of. And there is no presumption against believing further, that our future interest depends upon our present behaviour: for we see our present interest doth; and that the happiness and misery, which are naturally annexed to our actions, very frequently do not follow, till long after the actions are done, to which they are respectively annexed. So that were speculation to leave us uncertain, whether it were likely, that the Author of Nature, in giving happiness and misery to his creatures, hath regard to their actions or not: yet, since we find by experience that he hath such regard, the whole sense of things which he has given us, plainly leads us, at once and without any elaborate inquiries, to think, that it may, indeed must, be to good actions chiefly that he hath annexed happiness, and to bad actions misery; or that he will, upon the whole, reward those who do well, and punish those who do evil. To confirm this from the constitution of the world, it has been observed, that some sort of moral government is necessarily implied in that natural government of God, which we experience ourselves under; that good and bad actions, at present, are naturally rewarded and punished, not only as beneficial and mischievous to society, but also as virtuous and vicious: and that there is, in the very nature of the thing, a tendency to their being rewarded and punished in a much higher degree than they are at present. And though this higher degree of distributive justice, which nature thus points out and leads towards, is prevented for a time from taking place; it is by obstacles, which the state of this world unhappily throws in its way, and which therefore are in their nature temporary. Now, as these things in the natural conduct of Providence are observable on the side of virtue; so there is nothing to be set against them on the side of vice. A moral scheme of government then is visibly established, and, in some degree, carried into execution: and this, together with the essential tendencies of virtue and vice duly considered, naturally raise in us an apprehension, that it will be carried on further towards perfection in a future state, and that every one shall there receive according to his deserts. And if this be so, then our future and general interest, under the moral government of God, is appointed to depend upon our behaviour; notwithstanding the difficulty, which this may occasion, of securing it, and the danger of losing it: just in the same manner as our temporal interest, under his natural government, is appointed to depend upon our behaviour; notwithstanding the like difficulty and danger. For, from our original constitution, and that of the world which we inhabit, we are naturally trusted with ourselves; with our own conduct and our own interest. And from the same constitution of nature, especially joined with that course of things which is owing to men, we have temptations to be unfaithful in this trust; to forfeit this interest, to neglect it, and run ourselves into misery and ruin. From these temptations arise the difficulties of behaving so as to secure our temporal interest, and the hazard of behaving so as to miscarry in it. There is therefore nothing incredible in supposing there may be the like difficulty and hazard with regard to that chief and final good, which Religion lays before us. Indeed the whole account, how it came to pass that we were placed in such a condition as this, must be beyond our comprehension. But it is in part accounted for by what Religion teaches us, that the character of virtue and piety must be a necessary qualification for a future state of security and happiness, under the moral government of God; in like manner, as some certain qualifications or other are necessary for every particular condition of life, under his natural government: and that the present state was intended to be a school of discipline, for improving in ourselves that character. Now this intention of nature is rendered highly credible by observing; that we are plainly made for improvement of all kinds: that it is a general appointment of Providence, that we cultivate practical principles, and form within ourselves habits of action, in order to become fit for what we were wholly unfit for before: that in particular, childhood and youth is naturally appointed to be a state of discipline for mature age: and that the present world is peculiarly fitted for a state of moral discipline. And, whereas objections are urged against the whole notion of moral government and a probationary state, from the opinion of Necessity; it has been shown, that God has given us the evidence, as it were, of experience, that all objections against Religion, on this head, are vain and delusive. He has also, in his natural government, suggested an answer to all our short-sighted objections, against the equity and goodness of his moral government; and in general he has exemplified to us the latter by the former.

These things, which it is to be remembered, are matters of fact, ought, in all common sense, to awaken mankind; to induce them to consider in earnest their condition, and what they have to do. It is absurd, absurd to the degree of being ridiculous, if the subject were not of so serious a kind, for men to think themselves secure in a vicious life; or even in that immoral thoughtlessness, which far the greatest part of them are fallen into. And the credibility of Religion, arising from experience and facts here considered, is fully sufficient, in reason, to engage them to live in the general practice of all virtue and piety; under the serious apprehension, though it should be mixed with some doubt,* of a righteous administration established in nature, and a future judgment in consequence of it: especially when we consider, how very questionable it is, whether any thing at all can be gained by vice;† how unquestionably little as well as precarious, the pleasures and profits of it are at the best, and how soon they must be parted with at the longest. For, in the deliberations of reason, concerning what we

* Part II. Ch. vi. † P. 86.

are to pursue and what to avoid, as temptations to any thing from mere passion are supposed out of the case: so inducements to vice, from cool expectations of pleasure and interest so small and uncertain and short, are really so insignificant, as, in the view of reason to be almost nothing in themselves; and in comparison with the importance of Religion they quite disappear and are lost. Mere passion indeed may be alleged, though not as a reason, yet as an excuse, for a vicious course of life. And how sorry an excuse it is, will be manifest by observing, that we are placed in a condition in which we are unavoidably inured to govern our passions, by being necessitated to govern them: and to lay ourselves under the same kind of restraints, and as great ones too, from temporal regards, as virtue and piety, in the ordinary course of things, require. The plea of ungovernable passion then, on the side of vice, is the poorest of all things; for it is no reason, and but a poor excuse. But the proper motives to religion are the proper proofs of it, from our moral nature, from the presages of conscience, and our natural apprehension of God under the character of a righteous Governor and Judge: a nature, and conscience, and apprehension, given us by him; and from the confirmation of the dictates of reason, by *life and immortality brought to light by the Gospel; and the wrath of God revealed from heaven against all ungodliness and unrighteousness of men.*

END OF THE FIRST PART.

THE

ANALOGY OF RELIGION.

PART II.

OF REVEALED RELIGION.

CHAP I.

OF THE IMPORTANCE OF CHRISTIANITY.

Some persons, upon pretence of the sufficiency of the light of nature, avowedly reject all revelation, as, in its very notion, incredible, and what must be fictitious. And indeed it is certain, no revelation would have been given, had the light of nature been sufficient in such a sense, as to render one not wanting and useless. But no man, in seriousness and simplicity of mind, can possibly think it so, who considers the state of Religion in the heathen world before revelation, and its present state in those places which have borrowed no light from it: particularly the doubtfulness of some of the greatest men, concerning things of the utmost importance, as well as the natural inattention and ignorance of mankind in general. It is impossible to say, who would have been able to have reasoned out that whole system, which we call natural Religion, in its genuine simplicity, clear of superstition: but there is certainly no ground to affirm that the generality could. If they could, there is no sort of probability that they would. Admitting there were, they would highly want a standing admonition to remind them of it, and inculcate it upon them.

And further still, were they as much disposed to attend to Religion, as the better sort of men are; yet even upon this supposition, there would be various occasions for supernatural instruction and assistance, and the greatest advantages might be afforded by them. So that to say revelation is a thing superfluous, what there was no need of, and what can be of no service, is, I think, to talk quite wildly and at random. Nor would it be more extravagant to affirm, that mankind is so entirely at ease in the present state, and life so completely happy, that it is a contradiction to suppose our condition capable of being, in any respect, better.

There are other persons, not to be ranked with these, who seem to be getting into a way of neglecting, and, as it were, overlooking revelation, as of small importance, provided natural Religion be kept to. With little regard either to the evidence of the former, or to the objections against it, and even upon supposition of its truth; "the only design of it," say they, "must be, to establish a belief of the moral system of nature, and to enforce the practice of natural piety and virtue. The belief and practice of these things were, perhaps, much promoted by the first publication of Christianity: but whether they are believed and practised, upon the evidence and motives of nature or of revelation, is no great matter."* This way of considering revelation, though it is not the same with the former, yet borders nearly upon it, and very much, at length, runs up into it: and requires to be particularly considered, with regard to the persons who seem to be getting into this way. The consideration of it will likewise further show the extravagance of the former opinion, and the truth of the observations in answer to it, just mentioned. And an inquiry into the Importance of Christianity, cannot be an improper introduction to a treatise concerning the credibility of it.

Now if God has given a revelation to mankind, and commanded those things which are commanded in Christianity; it is evident, at first sight, that it cannot in any wise be an indifferent matter, whether we obey or disobey those commands: unless we are certainly assured,

* Invenis multos ——— propterea nolle fieri Christianos, quia quasi sufficiunt sibi de bona vita sua. Bene vivere opus est, ait. Quid mihi præcepturus est Christus? Ut bene vivam? Jam bene vivo. Quid mihi necessarius est Christus; nullum homicidium, nullum furtum, nullam rapinam facio, res alienas non concupisco, nullo adulterio contaminor? Nam inveniatur in vita mea aliquid quod reprehendatur, et qui reprehenderit faciat Christianum. *Aug. in Psal.* xxxi.

that we know all the reasons for them, and that all those reasons are now ceased, with regard to mankind in general, or to ourselves in particular. And it is absolutely impossible we can be assured of this. For our ignorance of these reasons proves nothing in the case: since the whole analogy of nature shows, what is indeed in itself evident, that there may be infinite reasons for things, with which we are not acquainted.

But the importance of Christianity will more distinctly appear, by considering it more distinctly: *First*, as a republication, and external institution, of natural or essential Religion, adapted to the present circumstances of mankind, and intended to promote natural piety and virtue: and *Secondly*, as containing an account of a dispensation of things, not discoverable by reason, in consequence of which several distinct precepts are enjoined us. For though natural Religion is the foundation and principal part of Christianity, it is not in any sense the whole of it.

I. Christianity is a republication of natural Religion. It instructs mankind in the moral system of the world: that it is the work of an infinitely perfect Being, and under his government; that virtue is his law; and that he will finally judge mankind in righteousness, and render to all according to their works, in a future state. And, which is very material, it teaches natural Religion in its genuine simplicity; free from those superstitions, with which it was totally corrupted, and under which it was in a manner lost.

Revelation is, further, an authoritative publication of natural Religion, and so affords the evidence of testimony for the truth of it. Indeed the miracles and prophecies recorded in Scripture, were intended to prove a particular dispensation of Providence, the redemption of the world by the Messiah: but this does not hinder, but that they may also prove God's general providence over the world, as our moral Governor and Judge. And they evidently do prove it; because this character of the Author of Nature, is necessarily connected with and implied in that particular revealed dispensation of things: it is likewise continually taught expressly, and insisted upon, by those persons who wrought the miracles and delivered the prophecies. So that indeed natural Religion seems as much proved by the Scripture revelation, as it would have been, had the design of revelation been nothing else than to prove it.

But it may possibly be disputed, how far miracles can prove natural Religion; and notable objections may be urged against this proof of it, considered as a matter of speculation: but considered as a practical thing, there can be none. For suppose a person to teach natural Religion to a nation, who had lived in total ignorance or forgetfulness of it; and to declare he was commissioned by God so to do: suppose him, in proof of his commission, to foretell things future, which no human foresight could have guessed at; to divide the sea with a word; feed great multitudes with bread from heaven; cure all manner of diseases; and raise the dead, even himself, to life; would not this give additional credibility to his teaching, a credibility beyond what that of a common man would have; and be an authoritative publication of the law of nature, *i. e.* a new proof of it? It would be a practical one, of the strongest kind, perhaps, which human creatures are capable of having given them. The Law of Moses then, and the Gospel of Christ, are authoritative publications of the religion of nature; they afford a proof of God's general providence, as moral Governor of the world, as well as of his particular dispensations of providence towards sinful creatures, revealed in the Law and the Gospel. As they are the only evidence of the latter, so they are an additional evidence of the former.

To show this further, let us suppose a man of the greatest and most improved capacity, who had never heard of revelation, convinced upon the whole, notwithstanding the disorders of the world, that it was under the direction and moral government of an infinitely perfect Being; but ready to question, whether he were not got beyond the reach of his faculties: suppose him brought, by this suspicion, into great danger of being carried away by the universal bad example of almost every one around him, who appeared to have no sense, no practical sense at least, of these things: and this, perhaps, would be as advantageous a situation with regard to Religion, as nature alone ever placed any man in. What a confirmation now must it be to such a person, all at once, to find, that this moral system of things was revealed to mankind, in the name of that infinite Being, whom he had from principles of reason believed in: and that the publishers of the revelation proved their commission from him, by making it appear, that he had entrusted them with a power of suspending and changing the general laws of nature.

Nor must it by any means be omitted, for it is a thing of the utmost importance, that life and immortality are eminently brought to light by the Gospel. The great doctrines of a future state, the danger of a course of wickedness, and the efficacy of repentance, are not only confirmed in the Gospel, but are taught, especially the last is, with a degree of light, to which that of nature is but darkness.

Further: As Christianity served these ends and purposes, when it was first published, by the miraculous publication itself; so it was intended to serve the same purposes in future ages, by means of the settlement of a visible church: of a society, distinguished from common ones, and from the rest of the world, by peculiar religious institutions; by an instituted method of instruction, and an instituted form of external Religion. Miraculous powers were given to the first preachers of Christianity, in order to their introducing it into the world: a visible church was established, in order to continue it, and carry it on successively throughout all ages. Had Moses and the Prophets, Christ and his Apostles, only taught, and by miracles proved, Religion to their contemporaries; the benefits of their instructions would have reached but to a small part of mankind. Christianity must have been, in a great degree, sunk and forgot in a very few ages. To prevent this, appears to have been one reason why a visible church was instituted: to be, like a city upon a hill, a standing memorial to the world of the duty which we owe our Maker: to call men continually, both by example and instruction, to attend to it, and, by the form of Religion, ever before their eyes, remind them of the reality: to be the repository of the oracles of God: to hold up the light of revelation in aid to that of nature, and propagate it throughout all generations to the end of the world—the light of revelation, considered here in no other view, than as designed to enforce natural Religion. And in proportion as Christianity is professed and taught in the world, Religion, natural or essential Religion, is thus distinctly and advantageously laid before mankind, and brought again and again to their thoughts, as a matter of infinite importance. A visible church has also a further tendency to promote natural Religion, as being an instituted method of education, originally intended to be of more peculiar advantage to those who conform to it. For one end of the institution was, that, by admonition and reproof, as well as instruction; by a general regular discipline, and public exercises of Religion; *the body of Christ*, as the Scripture speaks, should be *edified;* *i. e.* trained up in piety and virtue for a higher and better state. This settlement, then, appearing thus beneficial; tending in the nature of the thing to answer, and, in some degree, actually answering, those ends; it is to be remembered, that the very notion of it implies positive institutions; for the visibility of the church consists in them. Take away every thing of this kind, and you lose the very notion itself. So that if the things now mentioned are advantages, the reason and importance of positive institutions in general is most obvious; since without them these advantages could not be secured to the world. And it is mere idle wantonness, to insist upon knowing the reasons, why such particular ones were fixed upon rather than others.

The benefit arising from this supernatural assistance, which Christianity affords to natural Religion, is what some persons are very slow in apprehending. And yet it is a thing distinct in itself, and a very plain obvious one. For will any in good earnest really say, that the bulk of mankind in the heathen world were in as advantageous a situation with regard to natural Religion, as they are now amongst us: that it was laid before them, and enforced upon them, in a manner as distinct, and as much tending to influence their practice?

The objections against all this, from the perversion of Christianity, and from the supposition of its having had but little good influence, however innocently they may be proposed, yet cannot be insisted upon as conclusive, upon any principles, but such as lead to downright Atheism; because the manifestation of the law of nature by reason, which, upon all principles of Theism, must have been from God, has been perverted and rendered ineffectual in the same manner. It may indeed, I think, truly be said, that the good effects of Christianity have not been small; nor its supposed ill effects, any effects at all of it, properly speaking. Perhaps, too, the things themselves done have been aggravated; and if not, Christianity hath been often only a pretence; and the same evils in the main would have been done upon some other pretence. However, great and shocking as the corruptions and abuses of it have really been, they cannot be insisted upon as arguments against it, upon principles of Theism. For one cannot proceed one step in reasoning upon natural Religion, any more than upon Christianity, without laying it down as a first principle, that the dispensations of Providence are not to be judged of by their perversions, but by their genuine tendencies: not by what they do actually seem to effect, but by what they would effect if mankind did their part; that part which is justly put and left upon them. It is altogether as much the language of one as of the other: *He that is unjust, let him be unjust still: and he that is holy, let him be holy still.** The light of reason does not, any more than that of revelation, force men to submit to its authority; both admonish them of what they ought to do and avoid, together with the consequences of each; and after this, leave them at full liberty to act just as they please, till the appointed time of judgment. Every moment's experience shows, that this is God's general rule of government.

To return then: Christianity being a promulgation of the law of nature; being moreover an authoritative promulgation of it; with new light, and other circumstances of peculiar advantage, adapted to the wants of mankind;

* Rev. xxii. 11.

these things fully show its importance. And it is to be observed further, that as the nature of the case requires, so all Christians are commanded to contribute, by their profession of Christianity, to preserve it in the world, and render it such a promulgation and enforcement of Religion. For it is the very scheme of the Gospel, that each Christian should, in his degree, contribute towards continuing and carrying it on: all by uniting in the public profession and external practice of Christianity; some by instructing, by having the oversight and taking care of this religious community, the Church of God. Now this further shows the importance of Christianity; and, which is what I chiefly intend, its importance in a practical sense: or the high obligations we are under, to take it into our most serious consideration; and the danger there must necessarily be, not only in treating it despitefully, which I am not now speaking of, but in disregarding and neglecting it. For this is neglecting to do what is expressly enjoined us, for continuing those benefits to the world, and transmitting them down to future times. And all this holds, even though the only thing to be considered in Christianity, were its subserviency to natural Religion. But,

II. Christianity is to be considered in a further view; as containing an account of a dispensation of things, not at all discoverable by reason, in consequence of which several distinct precepts are enjoined us. Christianity is not only an external institution of natural Religion, and a new promulgation of God's general providence, as righteous Governor and Judge of the world; but it contains also a revelation of a particular dispensation of Providence, carrying on by his Son and Spirit, for the recovery and salvation of mankind, who are represented in Scripture to be in a state of ruin. And in consequence of this revelation being made, we are commanded *to be baptized*, not only *in the name of the Father*, but also, *of the Son, and of the Holy Ghost:* and other obligations of duty, unknown before, to the Son and the Holy Ghost, are revealed. Now the importance of these duties may be judged of, by observing that they arise, not from positive command merely, but also from the offices, which appear, from Scripture, to belong to those divine persons in the Gospel dispensation; or from the relations, which, we are there informed, they stand in to us. By reason is revealed the relation, which God the Father stands in to us. Hence arises the obligation of duty which we are under to him. In Scripture are revealed the relations, which the Son and Holy Spirit stand in to us. Hence arise the obligations of duty, which we are under to them. The truth of the case, as one may speak, in each of these three respects being admitted: that God is the governor of the world, upon the evidence of reason; that Christ is the mediator between God and man, and the Holy Ghost our guide and sanctifier, upon the evidence of revelation: the truth of the case, I say, in each of these respects being admitted; it is no more a question, why it should be commanded, that we be baptized in the name of the Son and of the Holy Ghost, than that we be baptized in the name of the Father. This matter seems to require to be more fully stated.*

Let it be remembered, then, that Religion comes under the twofold consideration of internal and external: for the latter is as real a part of Religion, of true Religion, as the former. Now when Religion is considered under the first notion, as an inward principle, to be exerted in such and such inward acts of the mind and heart; the essence of natural Religion may be said to consist in religious regards to *God the Father Almighty:* and the essence of revealed Religion, as distinguished from natural, to consist in religious regards to *the Son,* and to *the Holy Ghost.* And the obligation we are under, of paying these religious regards to each of these divine persons respectively, arises from the respective relations which they each stand in to us. How these relations are made known, whether by reason or revelation, makes no alteration in the case: because the duties arise out of the relations themselves, not out of the manner in which we are informed of them. The Son and Spirit have each his proper office in that great dispensation of

* See The Nature, Obligation, and Efficacy, of the Christian Sacraments, &c., and Colliber of revealed Religion as there quoted.

Providence, the redemption of the world; the one our mediator, the other our sanctifier. Does not then the duty of religious regards to both these divine persons, as immediately arise to the view of reason, out of the very nature of these offices and relations; as the inward good-will and kind intention, which we owe to our fellow creatures, arises out of the common relations between us and them? But it will be asked, "What are the inward religious regards, appearing thus obviously due to the Son and Holy Spirit; as arising, not merely from command in Scripture, but from the very nature of the revealed relations, which they stand in to us?" I answer, the religious regards of reverence, honour, love, trust, gratitude, fear, hope. In what external manner this inward worship is to be expressed, is a matter of pure revealed command; as perhaps the external manner, in which God the Father is to be worshipped, may be more so, than we are ready to think: but the worship, the internal worship itself, to the Son and Holy Ghost, is no further matter of pure revealed command, than as the relations they stand in to us are matter of pure revelation: for the relations being known, the obligations to such internal worship are obligations of reason, arising out of those relations themselves. In short, the history of the Gospel as immediately shows us the reason of these obligations, as it shows us the meaning of the words, Son and Holy Ghost.

If this account of the Christian Religion be just; those persons who can speak lightly of it, as of little consequence, provided natural Religion be kept to, plainly forget, that Christianity, even what is peculiarly so called, as distinguished from natural Religion, has yet somewhat very important, even of a moral nature. For the office of our Lord being made known, and the relation he stands in to us, the obligation of religious regards to him is plainly moral, as much as charity to mankind is; since this obligation arises, before external command, immediately out of that his office and relation itself. Those persons appear to forget, that revelation is to be considered, as informing us of somewhat new in the state of mankind, and in the government of the world: as acquainting us with some relations we stand in, which could not otherwise have been known. And these relations being real (though before revelation we could be under no obligations from them, yet upon their being revealed), there is no reason to think, but that neglect of behaving suitably to them will be attended with the same kind of consequences under God's government, as neglecting to behave suitably to any other relations made known to us by reason. And ignorance, whether unavoidable or voluntary, so far as we can possibly see, will just as much, and just as little, excuse in one case as in the other: the ignorance being supposed equally unavoidable, or equally voluntary, in both cases.

If therefore Christ be indeed the mediator between God and man, *i. e.* if Christianity be true; if he be indeed our Lord, our Saviour, and our God; no one can say, what may follow, not only the obstinate, but the careless disregard to him, in those high relations. Nay no one can say, what may follow such disregard, even in the way of natural consequence.* For, as the natural consequences of vice in this life are doubtless to be considered as judicial punishments inflicted by God; so likewise, for aught we know, the judicial punishments of the future life may be, in a like way or a like sense, the natural consequence of vice:† of men's violating or disregarding the relations which God has placed them in here, and made known to them.

Again: If mankind are corrupted and depraved in their moral character, and so are unfit for that state, which Christ is gone to prepare for his disciples; and if the assistance of God's Spirit be necessary to renew their nature, in the degree requisite to their being qualified for that state; all which is implied in the express, though figurative declaration, *Except a man be born of the Spirit, he cannot enter into the kingdom of God*:‡ supposing this, is it possible any serious person can think it a slight matter, whether or no he makes use of the means, expressly commanded by God, for obtaining this divine assistance? especially since the whole analogy of nature shows, that we are not to expect any benefits, without

* P. 72. 73. † Ch. v. ‡ John iii. v.

making use of the appointed means for obtaining or enjoying them. Now reason shows us nothing, of the particular immediate means of obtaining either temporal or spiritual benefits. This therefore we must learn, either from experience or revelation. And experience, the present case does not admit of.

The conclusion from all this evidently is, that, Christianity being supposed either true or credible, it is unspeakable irreverence, and really the most presumptuous rashness, to treat it as a light matter. It can never justly be esteemed of little consequence, till it be positively supposed false. Nor do I know a higher and more important obligation which we are under, than that of examining most seriously into the evidence of it, supposing its credibility; and of embracing it, upon supposition of its truth.

The two following deductions may be proper to be added, in order to illustrate the foregoing observations, and to prevent their being mistaken.

First, Hence we may clearly see, where lies the distinction between what is positive and what is moral in Religion. Moral *precepts* are precepts, the reasons of which we see: positive *precepts* are precepts, the reasons of which we do not see.* Moral *duties* arise out of the nature of the case itself, prior to external command. Positive *duties* do not arise out of the nature of the case, but from external command; nor would they be duties at all, were it not for such command, received from him whose creatures and subjects we are. But the manner in which the nature of the case, or the fact of the relation, is made known, this doth not denominate any duty either positive or moral. That we be baptized in the name of the Father is as much a positive duty, as that we be baptized in the name of the Son; because both arise equally from revealed command: though the relation which we stand in to God the Father is made known to us by reason; the relation we stand in to Christ, by revelation only.

* This is the distinction between moral and positive precepts considered respectively as such. But yet, since the latter have somewhat of a moral nature, we may see the reason of them, considered in this view. Moral and positive precepts are in some respects alike, in other respects different. So far as they are alike, we discern the reasons of both; so far as they are different, we discern the reasons of the former, but not of the latter. See p. 168, &c., and p. 177.

On the other hand, the dispensation of the Gospel admitted, gratitude as immediately becomes due to Christ, from his being the voluntary minister of this dispensation, as it is due to God the Father, from his being the fountain of all good; though the first is made known to us by revelation only, the second by reason. Hence also we may see, and, for distinctness' sake, it may be worth mentioning, that positive institutions come under a twofold consideration. They are either institutions founded on natural Religion, as baptism in the name of the Father; though this has also a particular reference to the Gospel dispensation, for it is in the name of God, as the Father of our Lord Jesus Christ: or they are external institutions founded on revealed Religion; as baptism in the name of the Son, and of the Holy Ghost.

Secondly, From the distinction between what is moral and what is positive in Religion, appears the ground of that peculiar preference, which the Scripture teaches us to be due to the former.

The reason of positive institutions in general is very obvious; though we should not see the reason, why such particular ones are pitched upon rather than others. Whoever therefore, instead of cavilling at words, will attend to the thing itself, may clearly see, that positive institutions in general, as distinguished from this or that particular one, have the nature of moral commands; since the reasons of them appear. Thus, for instance, the *external* worship of God is a moral duty, though no particular mode of it be so. Care then is to be taken, when a comparison is made between positive and moral duties, that they be compared no further than as they are different; no further than as the former are positive, or arise out of mere external command, the reasons of which we are not acquainted with; and as the latter are moral, or arise out of the apparent reason of the case, without such external command. Unless this caution be observed, we shall run into endless confusion.

Now this being premised, suppose two standing precepts enjoined by the same authority; that, in certain conjunctures, it is impossible to obey both; that the former is moral *i. e.* a precept of which we see the reasons, and that they hold in the particular case before us; but that the latter is positive, *i. e.* a precept of which we do not see the reasons: it is indisputable that our obligations are to obey the former; because there is an apparent reason for this preference, and none against it. Further, positive institutions, I suppose all those which Christianity enjoins, are means to a moral end: and the end must be acknowledged more excellent than the means. Nor is observance of these institutions any religious obedience at all, or of any value, otherwise than as it proceeds from a moral principle. This seems to be the strict logical way of stating and determining this matter; but will, perhaps, be found less applicable to practice, than may be thought at first sight.

And therefore, in a more practical, though more lax way of consideration, and taking the words, *moral law* and *positive institutions*, in the popular sense; I add, that the whole moral law is as much matter of revealed command, as positive institutions are: for the Scripture enjoins every moral virtue. In this respect then they are both upon a level. But the moral law is, moreover, written upon our hearts; interwoven into our very nature. And this is a plain intimation of the Author of it, which is to be preferred, when they interfere.

But there is not altogether so much necessity for the determination of this question, as some persons seem to think. Nor are we left to reason alone to determine it. For, *First*, Though mankind have, in all ages, been greatly prone to place their religion in peculiar positive rites, by way of equivalent for obedience to moral precepts; yet, without making any comparison at all between them, and consequently without determining which is to have the preference, the nature of the thing abundantly shows all notions of that kind to be utterly subversive of true Religion as they are, moreover, contrary to the whole general tenor of Scripture; and likewise to the most express particular declarations of it, that nothing can render us accepted of God, without moral virtue. *Secondly*, Upon the occasion of mentioning together positive and moral duties, the Scripture always puts the stress of Religion upon the latter, and never upon the former: which, though no sort of allowance to neglect the former, when they do not interfere with the latter, yet is a plain intimation, that when they do, the latter are to be preferred. And further, as mankind are for placing the stress of their religion any where, rather than upon virtue; lest both the reason of the thing, and the general spirit of Christianity, appearing in the intimation now mentioned, should be ineffectual against this prevalent folly: our Lord himself, from whose command alone the obligation of positive institutions arises, has taken occasion to make the comparison between them and moral precepts; when the Pharisees censured him, for *eating with publicans and sinners;* and also when they censured his disciples, for *plucking the ears of corn on the Sabbath day.* Upon this comparison, he has determined expressly, and in form, which shall have the preference when they interfere. And by delivering his authoritative determination in a proverbial manner of expression, he has made it general: *I will have mercy, and not sacrifice.** The propriety of the word *proverbial,* is not the thing insisted upon: though I think the manner of speaking is to be called so. But that the manner of speaking very remarkably renders the determination general, is surely indisputable. For, had it, in the latter case, been said only, that God preferred mercy to the rigid observance of the Sabbath; even then, by parity of reason, most justly might we have argued, that he preferred mercy likewise, to the observance of other ritual institutions; and in general, moral duties, to positive ones. And thus the determination would have been general; though its being so were inferred and not expressed. But as the passage really stands in the Gospel, it is much stronger. For the sense and the very literal words of our Lord's answer are as applicable to any other instance of a comparison, between positive and moral duties, as to this upon which they were spoken. And if, in case of competition, mercy is to be preferred to positive institutions, it will scarce be thought, that

* Matth. ix. 13, and xii. 7.

justice is to give place to them. It is remarkable too, that, as the words are a quotation from the Old Testament, they are introduced, on both the forementioned occasions, with a declaration, that the Pharisees did not understand the meaning of them. This, I say, is very remarkable. For, since it is scarce possible, for the most ignorant person, not to understand the literal sense of the passage, in the Prophet;* and since understanding the literal sense would not have prevented their *condemning the guiltless*,† it can hardly be doubted, that the thing which our Lord really intended in that declaration was, that the Pharisees had not learned from it, as they might, wherein the *general* spirit of Religion consists: that it consists in moral piety and virtue, as distinguished from forms, and ritual observances. However, it is certain we may learn this from his divine application of the passage, in the Gospel.

But, as it is one of the peculiar weaknesses of human nature, when, upon a comparison of two things, one is found to be of greater importance than the other, to consider this other as of scarce any importance at all: it is highly necessary that we remind ourselves, how great presumption it is, to make light of any institutions of divine appointment; that our obligations to obey all God's commands whatever are absolute and indispensable; and that commands merely positive, admitted to be from him, lay us under a moral obligation to obey them: an obligation moral in the strictest and most proper sense.

To these things I cannot forbear adding, that the account now given of Christianity most strongly shows and enforces upon us the obligation of searching the Scriptures, in order to see, what the scheme of revelation really is; instead of determining beforehand, from reason, what the scheme of it must be.‡ Indeed if in Revelation there be found any passages, the seeming meaning of which is contrary to natural Religion; we may most certainly conclude, such seeming meaning not to be the real one. But it is not any degree of a presumption against an interpretation of Scripture, that

* Hos. vi. † See Matth. xii. vii. ‡ See Chap. iii.

such interpretation contains a doctrine, which the light of nature cannot discover;* or a precept, which the la of nature does not oblige to.

CHAP. II.

OF THE SUPPOSED PRESUMPTION AGAINST A REVELATION CONSIDERED AS MIRACULOUS.

HAVING shown the importance of the Christian revelation, and the obligations which we are under seriously to attend to it, upon supposition of its truth, or its credibility: the next thing in order, is to consider the supposed presumptions against revelation in general; which shall be the subject of this Chapter: and the objections against the Christian in particular; which shall be the subject of some following ones.† For it seems the most natural method, to remove the prejudices against Christianity, before we proceed to the consideration of the positive evidence for it, and the objections against that evidence.‡

It is, I think, commonly supposed, that there is some peculiar presumption, from the analogy of nature, against the Christian scheme of things; at least against miracles; so as that stronger evidence is necessary to prove the truth and reality of them, than would be sufficient to convince us of other events, or matters of fact. Indeed the consideration of this supposed presumption cannot but be thought very insignificant, by many persons. Yet, as it belongs to the subject of this Treatise; so it may tend to open the mind, and remove some prejudices: however needless the consideration of it be, upon its own account.

I. I find no appearance of a presumption, from the analogy of nature, against the general scheme of Christianity, that God created and invisibly governs the world by Jesus Christ; and by him also will hereafter judge it in righteousness, *i. e.* render to every one according to his works; and that good men are under the secret

* P. 181, 182. † Ch. iii. iv. v. vi. ‡ Ch. vii.

influence of his Spirit. Whether these things are, or are not, to be called miraculous, is, perhaps, only a question about words; or however, is of no moment in the case. If the analogy of nature raises any presumption against this general scheme of Christianity, it must be, either because it is not discoverable by reason or experience; or else, because it is unlike that course of nature, which is. But analogy raises no presumption against the truth of this scheme, upon either of these accounts.

First, There is no presumption, from analogy, against the truth of it, upon account of its not being discoverable by reason or experience. For suppose one who never heard of revelation, of the most improved understanding, and acquainted with our whole system of natural philosophy and natural religion; such a one could not but be sensible, that it was but a very small part of the natural and moral system of the universe, which he was acquainted with. He could not but be sensible, that there must be innumerable things, in the dispensations of Providence past, in the invisible government over the world at present carrying on, and in what is to come; of which he was wholly ignorant,* and which could not be discovered without revelation. Whether the scheme of nature be, in the strictest sense, infinite or not; it is evidently vast, even beyond all possible imagination. And doubtless that part of it, which is opened to our view, is but as a point, in comparison of the whole plan of Providence, reaching throughout eternity past and future; in comparison of what is even now going on in the remote parts of the boundless universe; nay, in comparison of the whole scheme of this world. And therefore, that things lie beyond the natural reach of our faculties, is no sort of presumption against the truth and reality of them: because it is certain, there are innumerable things, in the constitution and government of the universe, which are thus beyond the natural reach of our faculties. *Secondly,* Analogy raises no presumption against any of the things contained in this general doctrine of Scripture now mentioned, upon account of their being unlike the known

* P. 149.

course of nature. For there is no presumption at all from analogy, that the *whole* course of things, or divine government, naturally unknown to us, and *every thing* in it, is like to any thing in that which is known; and therefore no peculiar presumption against any thing in the former, upon account of its being unlike to any thing in the latter. And in the constitution and natural government of the world, as well as in the moral government of it, we see things, in a great degree, unlike one another: and therefore ought not to wonder at such unlikeness between things visible and invisible. However, the scheme of Christianity is by no means entirely unlike the scheme of nature; as will appear in the following part of this Treatise.

The notion of a miracle, considered as a proof of a divine mission, has been stated with great exactness by divines; and is, I think, sufficiently understood by every one. There are also invisible miracles, the Incarnation of Christ, for instance, which, being secret, cannot be alleged as a proof of such a mission; but require themselves to be proved by visible miracles. Revelation itself too is miraculous; and miracles are the proof of it; and the supposed presumption against these shall presently be considered. All which I have been observing here is, that, whether we choose to call every thing in the dispensations of Providence, not discoverable without revelation, nor like the known course of things, miraculous; and whether the general Christian dispensation now mentioned is to be called so, or not; the foregoing observations seem certainly to show, that there is no presumption against it from the analogy of nature.

II. There is no presumption, from analogy, against some operations, which we should now call miraculous; particularly none against a revelation at the beginning of the world: nothing of such presumption against it, as is supposed to be implied or expressed in the word, *miraculous*. For a miracle, in its very notion, is relative to a course of nature; and implies somewhat different from it, considered as being so. Now, either there was no course of nature at the time which we are speaking of; or if there were, we are not acquainted what the course of nature is, upon the first peopling of worlds. And therefore the question, whether mankind had a revelation made to them at that time, is to be considered, not as a question concerning a miracle, but as a common question of fact. And we have the like reason, be it more or less, to admit the report of tradition, concerning this question, and concerning common matters of fact of the same antiquity; for instance, what part of the earth was first peopled.

Or thus: When mankind was first placed in this state, there was a power exerted, totally different from the present course of nature. Now, whether this power, thus wholly different from the present course of nature, for we cannot properly apply to it the word *miraculous;* whether this power stopped immediately after it had made man, or went on, and exerted itself further in giving him a revelation, is a question of the same kind, as whether an ordinary power exerted itself in such a particular degree and manner, or not.

Or suppose the power exerted in the formation of the world be considered as miraculous, or rather, be called by that name; the case will not be different: since it must be acknowledged, that such a power was exerted. For supposing it acknowledged, that our Saviour spent some years in a course of working miracles: there is no more presumption, worth mentioning, against his having exerted this miraculous power, in a certain degree greater, than in a certain degree less; in one or two more instances, than in one or two fewer; in this, than in another manner.

It is evident then, that there can be no peculiar presumption, from the analogy of nature, against supposing a revelation, when man was first placed upon earth.

Add, that there does not appear the least intimation in history or tradition, that Religion was first reasoned out: but the whole of history and tradition makes for the other side, that it came into the world by revelation. Indeed the state of Religion in the first ages, of which we have any account, seems to suppose and imply, that this was the original of it amongst mankind. And these reflections together, without taking in the peculiar authority of Scripture, amount to real and a very material degree of evidence, that there was a revelation at the beginning of the world. Now this, as it is a confirmation of natural Religion, and therefore mentioned in the former part of this Treatise;* so likewise it has a tendency to remove any prejudices against a subsequent revelation.

III. But still it may be objected, that there is some peculiar presumption, from analogy, against miracles; particularly against revelation, after the settlement and during the continuance of a course of nature.

Now with regard to this supposed presumption, it is to be observed in general, that before we can have ground for raising what can, with any propriety, be called an *argument* from analogy, for or against revelation considered as somewhat miraculous, we must be acquainted with a similar or parallel case. But the history of some other world, seemingly in like circumstances with our own, is no more than a parallel case: and therefore nothing short of this can be so. Yet, could we come at a presumptive proof, for or against a revelation, from being informed, whether such world had one, or not; such a proof, being drawn from one single instance only, must be infinitely precarious. More particularly: *First* of all; There is a very strong presumption against common speculative truths, and against the most ordinary facts, before the proof of them; which yet is overcome by almost any proof. There is a presumption of millions to one, against the story of Cæsar, or of any other man. For suppose a number of common facts so and so circumstanced, of which one had no kind of proof, should happen to come into one's thoughts; every one would, without any possible doubt, conclude them to be false. And the like may be said of a single common fact. And from hence it appears, that the question of importance, as to the matter before us, is, concerning the degree of the peculiar presumption supposed against miracles; not whether there be any peculiar presumption at all against them. For, if there be the presumption of millions to one, against the most common facts; what can a small

* P. 143, &c.

presumption, additional to this, amount to, though it be peculiar? It cannot be estimated, and is as nothing. The only material question is, whether there be any such presumption against miracles, as to render them in any sort incredible. *Secondly,* If we leave out the consideration of Religion, we are in such total darkness, upon what causes, occasions, reasons, or circumstances, the present course of nature depends; that there does not appear any improbability for or against supposing, that five or six thousand years may have given scope for causes, occasions, reasons, or circumstances, from whence miraculous interpositions may have arisen. And from this, joined with the foregoing observation, it will follow, that there must be a presumption, beyond all comparison, greater, against the *particular* common facts just now instanced in, than against miracles *in general;* before any evidence of either. But, *Thirdly,* Take in the consideration of Religion, or the moral system of the world, and then we see distinct particular reasons for miracles: to afford mankind instruction additional to that of nature, and to attest the truth of it. And this gives a real credibility to the supposition, that it might be part of the original plan of things, that there should be miraculous interpositions. Then, *Lastly,* Miracles must not be compared to common natural events; or to events which, though uncommon, are similar to what we daily experience: but to the extraordinary phenomena of nature. And then the comparison will be between the presumption against miracles, and the presumption against such uncommon appearances, suppose, as comets, and against there being any such powers in nature as magnetism and electricity, so contrary to the properties of other bodies not endued with these powers. And before any one can determine, whether there be any peculiar presumption against miracles, more than against other extraordinary things; he must consider, what, upon first hearing, would be the presumption against the last mentioned appearances and powers, to a person acquainted only with the daily, monthly, and annual course of nature respecting this earth, and with those common powers of matter which we every day see.

Upon all this I conclude; that there certainly is no such presumption against miracles, as to render them in any wise incredible: that, on the contrary, our being able to discern reasons for them, gives a positive credibility to the history of them, in cases where those reasons hold: and that it is by no means certain, that there is any peculiar presumption at all, from analogy, even in the lowest degree, against miracles, as distinguished from other extraordinary phenomena: though it is not worth while to perplex the reader with inquiries into the abstract nature of evidence, in order to determine a question, which, without such inquiries, we see* is of no importance

CHAP. III.

OF OUR INCAPACITY OF JUDGING, WHAT WERE TO BE EXPECTED IN A REVELATION; AND THE CREDIBILITY, FROM ANALOGY, THAT IT MUST CONTAIN THINGS APPEARING LIABLE TO OBJECTIONS.

BESIDES the objections against the evidence for Christianity, many are alleged against the scheme of it; against the whole manner in which it is put and left with the world; as well as against several particular relations in Scripture: objections drawn from the deficiencies of revelation: from things in it appearing to men *foolishness*;† from its containing matters of offence, which have led, and it must have been foreseen would lead, into strange enthusiasm and superstition, and be made to serve the purposes of tyranny and wickedness; from its not being universal; and, which is a thing of the same kind, from its evidence not being so convincing and satisfactory as it might have been: for this last is sometimes turned into a positive argument against its truth.‡ It would be tedious, indeed impossible, to enumerate the several particulars comprehended under the objections here referred to; they being so various, according to the different fancies of men. There are persons who think it a strong objection against the

* P. 185. † 1 Cor. i. 28. ‡ See Ch. vi.

authority of Scripture, that it is not composed by rules of art, agreed upon by critics, for polite and correct writing. And the scorn is inexpressible, with which some of the prophetic parts of Scripture are treated: partly through the rashness of interpreters; but very much also, on account of the hieroglyphical and figurative language, in which they are left us. Some of the principal things of this sort shall be particularly considered in the following Chapters. But my design at present is to observe in general, with respect to this whole way of arguing, that, upon supposition of a revelation, it is highly credible beforehand, we should be incompetent judges of it to a great degree: and that it would contain many things appearing to us liable to great objections; in case we judge of it otherwise, than by the analogy of nature. And therefore, though objections against the evidence of Christianity are most seriously to be considered; yet objections against Christianity itself are, in a great measure, frivolous: almost all objections against it, excepting those which are alleged against the particular proofs of its coming from God. I express myself with caution, lest I should be mistaken to vilify reason; which is indeed the only faculty we have wherewith to judge concerning any thing, even revelation itself: or be misunderstood to assert, that a supposed revelation cannot be proved false, from internal characters. For, it may contain clear immoralities or contradictions; and either of these would prove it false. Nor will I take upon me to affirm, that nothing else can possibly render any supposed revelation incredible. Yet still the observation above, is, I think, true beyond doubt; that objections against Christianity, as distinguished from objections against its evidence, are frivolous. To make out this, is the general design of the present Chapter. And with regard to the whole of it, I cannot but particularly wish, that the proofs might be attended to; rather than the assertions cavilled at, upon account of any unacceptable consequences, whether real or supposed, which may be drawn from them. For, after all, that which is true, must be admitted, though it should show us the shortness of our faculties; and that we are in no wise judges of many things, of which we are apt to think ourselves very competent ones. Nor will this be any objection with reasonable men, at least upon second thought it will not be any objection with such, against the justness of the following observations.

As God governs the world and instructs his creatures, according to certain laws or rules, in the known course of nature; known by reason together with experience: so the Scripture informs us of a scheme of divine Providence, additional to this. It relates, that God has, by revelation, instructed men in things concerning his government, which they could not otherwise have known; and reminded them of things, which they might otherwise know; and attested the truth of the whole by miracles. Now if the natural and the revealed dispensation of things are both from God, if they coincide with each other, and together make up one scheme of Providence; our being incompetent judges of one, must render it credible, that we may be incompetent judges also of the other. Since, upon experience, the acknowledged constitution and course of nature is found to be greatly different from what, before experience, would have been expected; and such as, men fancy, there lie great objections against: this renders it beforehand highly credible, that they may find the revealed dispensation likewise, if they judge of it as they do of the constitution of nature, very different from expectations formed beforehand; and liable, in appearance, to great objections: objections against the scheme itself, and against the degrees and manners of the miraculous interpositions, by which it was attested and carried on. Thus, suppose a prince to govern his dominions in the wisest manner possible, by common known laws; and that upon some exigencies he should suspend these laws; and govern, in several instances, in a different manner; if one of his subjects were not a competent judge beforehand, by what common rules the government should or would be carried on; it could not be expected, that the same person would be a competent judge, in what exigencies, or in what manner, or to what degree, those laws commonly observed would be suspended or deviated from. If he were not a judge of the wisdom of the ordinary administration, there is no reason to think he would be a judge of the wisdom of the extraordinary. If he thought he had objections against the former; doubtless, it is highly supposable, he might think also, that he had objections against the latter. And thus, as we fall into infinite follies and mistakes, whenever we pretend, otherwise than from experience and analogy, to judge of the constitution and course of nature; it is evidently supposable beforehand, that we should fall into as great, in pretending to judge, in like manner, concerning revelation. Nor is there any more ground to expect that this latter should appear to us clear of objections, than that the former should.

These observations, relating to the whole of Christianity, are applicable to inspiration in particular. As we are in no sort judges beforehand, by what laws or rules, in what degree, or by what means, it were to have been expected, that God would naturally instruct us; so upon supposition of his affording us light and instruction by revelation, additional to what he has afforded us by reason and experience, we are in no sort judges, by what methods, and in what proportion, it were to be expected that this supernatural light and instruction would be afforded us. We know not beforehand, what degree or kind of natural information it were to be expected God would afford men, each by his own reason and experience: nor how far he would enable and effectually dispose them to communicate it, whatever it should be, to each other; nor whether the evidence of it would be certain, highly probable, or doubtful; nor whether it would be given with equal clearness and conviction to all. Nor could we guess, upon any good ground I mean, whether natural knowledge, or even the faculty itself, by which we are capable of attaining it, reason, would be given us at once, or gradually. In like manner, we are wholly ignorant, what degree of new knowledge, it were to be expected God would give mankind by revelation, upon supposition of his affording one: or how far, or in what way he would interpose miraculously, to qualify them, to whom he should originally make the revelation, for communicating the knowledge given by it; and to secure their doing it to the age in which they should live; and to secure its being transmitted to posterity. We are equally ignorant, whether the evidence of it would be certain or highly probable, or doubtful:* or whether all who should have any degree of instruction from it, and any degree of evidence of its truth, would have the same: or whether the scheme would be revealed at once, or unfolded gradually. Nay we are not in any sort able to judge, whether it were to have been expected, that the revelation should have been committed to writing; or left to be handed down, and consequently corrupted, by verbal tradition, and at length sunk under it, if mankind so pleased, and during such time as they are permitted, in the degree they evidently are, to act as they will.

But it may be said, "that a revelation in some of the above mentioned circumstances, one, for instance, which was not committed to writing, and thus secured against danger of corruption, would not have answered its purpose." I ask, what purpose? It would not have answered all the purposes, which it has now answered, and in the same degree: but it would have answered others, or the same in different degrees. And which of these were the purposes of God, and best fell in with his general government, we could not at all have determined beforehand.

Now since it has been shown, that we have no principles of reason, upon which to judge beforehand, how it were to be expected revelation should have been left, or what was most suitable to the divine plan of government, in any of the forementioned respects; it must be quite frivolous to object afterward as to any of them, against its being left in one way, rather than another: for this would be to object against things, upon account of their being different from expectations, which have been shown to be without reason. And thus we see, that the only question concerning the truth of Christianity is, whether it be a real revelation; not whether it be attended with every circumstance which we should have looked for:

* See Chap. vi.

and concerning the authority of Scripture, whether it be what it claims to be; not whether it be a book of such sort, and so promulged, as weak men are apt to fancy a book containing a divine revelation should. And therefore, neither obscurity, nor seeming inaccuracy of style, nor various readings, nor early disputes about the authors of particular parts; nor any other things of the like kind, though they had been much more considerable in degree than they are, could overthrow the authority of the Scripture: unless the Prophets, Apostles, or our Lord, had promised, that the book containing the divine revelation should be secure from those things. Nor indeed can any objections overthrow such a kind of revelation as the Christian claims to be, since there are no objections against the morality of it,* but such as can show, that there is no proof of miracles wrought originally in attestation of it; no appearance of any thing miraculous in its obtaining in the world; nor any of prophecy, that is, of events foretold, which human sagacity could not foresee. If it can be shown, that the proof alleged for all these is absolutely none at all, then is revelation overturned. But were it allowed, that the proof of any one or all of them is lower than is allowed; yet, whilst any proof of them remains, revelation will stand upon much the same foot it does at present, as to all the purposes of life and practice, and ought to have the like influence upon our behaviour.

From the foregoing observations too, it will follow, and those who will thoroughly examine into revelation will find it worth remarking; that there are several ways of arguing, which, though just with regard to other writings, are not applicable to Scripture: at least not to the prophetic parts of it. We cannot argue, for instance, that this cannot be the sense or intent of such a passage of Scripture; for, if it had, it would have been expressed more plainly, or have been represented under a more apt figure or hieroglyphic: yet we may justly argue thus, with respect to common books. And the reason of this difference is very evident; that in Scripture we are not competent judges, as we are in common books, how

* P. 198.

plainly it were to have been expected, what is the true sense should have been expressed, or under how apt an image figured. The only question is, what appearance there is, that this is the sense; and scarce at all, how much more determinately or accurately it might have been expressed or figured.

"But is it not self-evident, that internal improbabilities of all kinds weaken external probable proof?" Doubtless. But to what practical purpose can this be alleged here, when it has been proved before,* that real internal improbabilities, which rise even to moral certainty, are overcome by the most ordinary testimony; and when it now has been made appear, that we scarce know what are improbabilities, as to the matter we are here considering: as it will further appear from what follows.

For though from the observations above made it is manifest, that we are not in any sort competent judges, what supernatural instruction were to have been expected; and though it is self-evident, that the objections of an incompetent judgment must be frivolous; yet it may be proper to go one step further, and observe; that if men will be regardless of these things, and pretend to judge of the Scripture by preconceived expectations; the analogy of nature shows beforehand, not only that it is highly credible they may, but also probable that they will, imagine they have strong objections against it, however really unexceptionable: for so, prior to experience, they would think they had, against the circumstances, and degrees, and the whole manner of that instruction, which is afforded by the ordinary course of nature. Were the instruction which God affords to brute creatures by instincts and mere propensions, and to mankind by these together with reason, matter of probable proof, and not of certain observation; it would be rejected as incredible, in many instances of it, only upon account of the means by which this instruction is given, the seeming disproportions, the limitations, necessary conditions, and circumstances of it. For instance: would it not have been thought highly improbable, that men should have been so much more capable of discovering, even to certainty

* P. 184.

the general laws of matter, and the magnitudes, paths, and revolutions, of heavenly bodies; than the occasions and cures of distempers, and many other things, in which human life seems so much more nearly concerned, than in astronomy? How capricious and irregular a way of information would it be said, is that of *invention*, by means of which nature instructs us in matters of science, and in many things, upon which the affairs of the world greatly depend: that a man should, by this faculty, be made acquainted with a thing in an instant, when perhaps he is thinking of somewhat else, which he has in vain been searching after, it may be, for years. So likewise the imperfections attending the only method, by which nature enables and directs us to communicate our thoughts to each other, are innumerable. Language is, in its very nature, inadequate, ambiguous, liable to infinite abuse, even from negligence; and so liable to it from design, that every man can deceive and betray by it. And, to mention but one instance more; that brutes, without reason, should act, in many respects, with a sagacity and foresight vastly greater than what men have in those respects, would be thought impossible. Yet it is certain they do act with such superior foresight: whether it be their own, indeed, is another question. From these things, it is highly credible beforehand, that upon supposition God should afford men some additional instruction by revelation, it would be with circumstances, in manners, degrees, and respects, which we should be apt to fancy we had great objections against the credibility of. Nor are the objections against the Scripture, nor against Christianity in general, at all more or greater, than the analogy of nature would beforehand—not perhaps give ground to expect; for this analogy may not be sufficient, in some cases, to ground an expectation upon; but no more nor greater, than analogy would show it, beforehand, to be supposable and credible, that there might seem to lie against revelation.

By applying these general observations to a particular objection, it will be more distinctly seen, how they are applicable to others of the like kind: and indeed to almost all objections against Christianity, as distinguish from objections against its evidence. It appears from Scripture, that, as it was not unusual in the apostolic age, for persons, upon their conversion to Christianity, to be endued with miraculous gifts; so, some of those persons exercised these gifts in a strangely irregular and disorderly manner; and this is made an objection against their being really miraculous. Now the foregoing observations quite remove this objection, how considerable soever it may appear at first sight. For, consider a person endued with any of these gifts; for instance, that of tongues: it is to be supposed, that he had the same power over this miraculous gift, as he would have had over it, had it been the effect of habit, of study and use, as it ordinarily is; or the same power over it, as he had over any other natural endowment. Consequently, he would use it in the same manner he did any other; either regularly, and upon proper occasions only, or irregularly, and upon improper ones: according to his sense of decency, and his character of prudence. Where then is the objection? Why, if this miraculous power was indeed given to the world to propagate Christianity, and attest the truth of it, we might, it seems, have expected, that other sort of persons should have been chosen to be invested with it; or that these should, at the same time, have been endued with prudence; or that they should have been continually restrained and directed in the exercise of it: *i. e.* that God should have miraculously interposed, if at all, in a different manner, or higher degree. But, from the observations made above, it is undeniably evident, that we are not judges in what degrees and manners it were to have been expected he should miraculously interpose; upon supposition of his doing it in some degree and manner. Nor, in the natural course of Providence, are superior gifts of memory, eloquence, knowledge, and other talents of great influence, conferred only on persons of prudence and decency, or such as are disposed to make the properest use of them. Nor is the instruction and admonition naturally afforded us for the conduct of life, particularly in our education, commonly given in a manner the most suited to recommend it; but often with circumstances apt to prejudice us against such instruction.

One might go on to add, that there is a great resemblance between the light of nature and of revelation, in several other respects. Practical Christianity, or that faith and behaviour which renders a man a Christian, is a plain and obvious thing: like the common rules of conduct, with respect to our ordinary temporal affairs. The more distinct and particular knowledge of those things, the study of which the Apostle calls *going on unto perfection*,* and of the prophetic parts of revelation, like many parts of natural and even civil knowledge, may require very exact thought, and careful consideration. The hinderances too, of natural, and of supernatural light and knowledge, have been of the same kind. And as it is owned the whole scheme of Scripture is not yet understood; so, if it ever comes to be understood, before the *restitution of all things*,† and without miraculous interpositions; it must be in the same way as natural knowledge is come at: by the continuance and progress of learning and of liberty; and by particular persons attending to, comparing, and pursuing, intimations scattered up and down it, which are overlooked and disregarded by the generality of the world. For this is the way, in which all improvements are made; by thoughtful men's tracing on obscure hints, as it were, dropped us by nature accidentally, or which seem to come into our minds by chance. Nor is it at all incredible, that a book, which has been so long in the possession of mankind, should contain many truths as yet undiscovered. For, all the same phenomena, and the same faculties of investigation, from which such great discoveries in natural knowledge have been made in the present and last age, were equally in the possession of mankind, several thousand years before. And possibly it might be intended, that events, as they come to pass, should open and ascertain the meaning of several parts of Scripture.

It may be objected, that this analogy fails in a material respect: for that natural knowledge is of little or no consequence. But I have been speaking of the general instruction which nature does or does not afford us.

* Heb. vi. 1. † Acts iii. 21.

And besides, some parts of natural knowledge, in the more common restrained sense of the words, are of the greatest consequence to the ease and convenience of life. But suppose the analogy did, as it does not, fail in this respect; yet it might be abundantly supplied, from the whole constitution and course of nature: which shows, that God does not dispense his gifts according to our notions of the advantage and consequence they would be of to us. And this in general, with his method of dispensing knowledge in particular, would together make out an analogy full to the point before us.

But it may be objected still further and more generally; "The Scripture represents the world as in a state of ruin, and Christianity as an expedient to recover it, to help in these respects where nature fails: in particular, to supply the deficiencies of natural light. Is it credible then, that so many ages should have been let pass, before a matter of such a sort, of so great and so general importance, was made known to mankind; and then that it should be made known to so small a part of them? Is it conceivable, that this supply should be so very deficient, should have the like obscurity and doubtfulness, be liable to the like perversions, in short, lie open to all the like objections, as the light of nature itself?* Without determining how far this, in fact, is so, I answer; it is by no means incredible, that it might be so, if the light of nature and of revelation be from the same hand. Men are naturally liable to diseases: for which God, in his good providence, has provided natural remedies.† But remedies existing in nature have been unknown to mankind for many ages: are known but to few now: probably many valuable ones are not known yet. Great has been and is the obscurity and difficulty, in the nature and application of them. Circumstances seem often to make them very improper, where they are absolutely necessary. It is after long labour and study, and many unsuccessful endeavours, that they are brought to be as useful as they are; after high contempt and absolute rejection of the most useful we have; and after disputes and doubts, which have

* Ch. vi. † Ch. v.

seemed to be endless. The best remedies too, when unskilfully, much more if dishonestly applied, may produce new diseases; and with the rightest application the success of them is often doubtful. In many cases they are not at all effectual: where they are, it is often very slowly: and the application of them, and the necessary regimen accompanying it, is, not uncommonly, so disagreeable, that some will not submit to them; and satisfy themselves with the excuse, that, if they would, it is not certain whether it would be successful. And many persons, who labour under diseases, for which there are known natural remedies, are not so happy as to be always, if ever, in the way of them. In a word, the remedies which nature has provided for diseases are neither certain, perfect, nor universal. And indeed the same principles of arguing, which would lead us to conclude, that they must be so, would lead us likewise to conclude, that there could be no occasion for them; *i. e.* that there could be no diseases at all. And therefore our experience that there are diseases shows, that it is credible beforehand, upon supposition nature has provided remedies for them, that these remedies may be, as by experience we find they are, not certain, nor perfect, nor universal; because it shows, that the principles upon which we should expect the contrary are fallacious.

And now, what is the just consequence from all these things? Not that reason is no judge of what is offered to us as being of divine revelation. For this would be to infer that we are unable to judge of any thing, because we are unable to judge of all things. Reason can, and it ought to judge, not only of the meaning, but also of the morality and the evidence of revelation. *First,* It is the province of reason to judge of the morality of the Scripture; *i. e.* not whether it contains things different from what we should have expected from a wise, just, and good Being; for objections from hence have been now obviated: but whether it contains things plainly contradictory to wisdom, justice, or goodness; to what the light of nature teaches us of God. And I know nothing of this sort objected against Scripture, excepting such objections as are formed upon suppositions, which would equally conclude, that the constitution of nature is contradictory to wisdom, justice or goodness; which most certainly it is not. Indeed there are some particular precepts in Scripture, given to particular persons, requiring actions, which would be immoral and vicious, were it not for such precepts. But it is easy to see, that all these are of such a kind, as that the precept changes the whole nature of the case and of the action; and both constitutes and shows that not to be unjust or immoral, which, prior to the precept, must have appeared and really have been so: which may well be, since none of these precepts are contrary to immutable morality. If it were commanded, to cultivate the principles, and act from the spirit of treachery, ingratitude, cruelty; the command would not alter the nature of the case or of the action, in any of these instances. But it is quite otherwise in precepts, which require only the doing an external action: for instance, taking away the property, or life of any. For men have no right to either life or property, but what arises solely from the grant of God: when this grant is revoked, they cease to have any right at all in either: and when this revocation is made known, as surely it is possible it may be, it must cease to be unjust to deprive them of either. And though a course of external acts, which without command would be immoral, must make an immoral habit; yet a few detached commands have no such natural tendency. I thought proper to say thus much of the few Scripture precepts, which require, not vicious actions, but actions which would have been vicious, had it not been for such precepts; because they are sometimes weakly urged as immoral, and great weight is laid upon objections drawn from them. But to me there seems no difficulty at all in these precepts, but what arises from their being offences: *i. e.* from their being liable to be perverted, as indeed they are, by wicked designing men, to serve the most horrid purposes; and, perhaps, to mislead the weak and enthusiastic. And objections from this head are not objections against revelation; but against the whole notion of religion, as a trial: and against the general constitution of nature. *Secondly*, Reason is able to judge, and must, of the evidence of revelation, and of the objections urged against that evidence: which shall be the subject of a following Chapter.*

But the consequence of the foregoing observations is, that the question upon which the truth of Christianity depends is scarce at all, what objections there are against its scheme, since there are none against the morality of it; but *what objections there are against its evidence;* or, *what proof there remains of it, after due allowances made for the objections against that proof:* because it has been shown, that the *objections against Christianity, as distinguished from objections against its evidence, are frivolous.* For surely very little weight, if any at all, is to be laid upon a way of arguing and objecting, which, when applied to the general constitution of nature, experience shows not to be conclusive: and such, I think, is the whole way of objecting treated of throughout this Chapter. It is resolvable into principles, and goes upon suppositions, which mislead us to think, that the Author of Nature would not act, as we experience he does; or would act, in such and such cases, as we experience he does not in like cases. But the unreasonableness of this way of objecting will appear yet more evidently from hence, that the chief things thus objected against are justified, as shall be further shown,† by distinct, particular, and full analogies, in the constitution and course of nature.

But it is to be remembered, that, as frivolous as objections of the foregoing sort against revelation are, yet, when a supposed revelation is more consistent with itself, and has a more general and uniform tendency to promote virtue, than, all circumstances considered, could have been expected from enthusiasm and political views; this is a presumptive proof of its not proceeding from them, and so of its truth: because we are competent judges, what might have been expected from enthusiasm and political views.

* Chap. vii.

† Ch. iv. latter part, and v. vi.

CHAP. IV.

OF CHRISTIANITY, CONSIDERED AS A SCHEME OR CONSTITUTION, IMPERFECTLY COMPREHENDED.

It hath been now shown,* that the analogy of nature renders it highly credible beforehand, that, supposing a revelation to be made, it must contain many things very different from what we should have expected, and such as appear open to great objections: and that this observation, in good measure, takes off the force of those objections, or rather precludes them. But it may be alleged, that this is a very partial answer to such objections, or a very unsatisfactory way of obviating them: because it doth not show at all, that the things objected against can be wise, just, and good; much less, that it is credible they are so. It will therefore be proper to show this distinctly; by applying to these objections against the wisdom, justice, and goodness of Christianity, the answer above† given to the like objections against the constitution of Nature: before we consider the particular analogies in the latter, to the particular things objected against in the former. Now that which affords a sufficient answer to objections against the wisdom, justice, and goodness of the constitution of Nature, is its being a constitution, a system, or scheme, imperfectly comprehended; a scheme in which means are made use of to accomplish ends; and which is carried on by general laws. For from these things it has been proved, not only to be possible, but also to be credible, that those things which are objected against may be consistent with wisdom, justice, and goodness; nay, may be instances of them: and even that the constitution and government of Nature may be perfect in the highest possible degree. If Christianity then be a scheme, and of the like kind; it is evident, the like objections against it must admit of the like answer. And,

* In the foregoing Chapter.
† Part I. Ch. vii. to which this all along refers.

I. Christianity is a scheme, quite beyond our comprehension. The moral government of God is exercised, by gradually conducting things so in the course of his providence, that every one, at length and upon the whole, shall receive according to his deserts; and neither fraud nor violence, but truth and right, shall finally prevail. Christianity is a particular scheme under this general plan of Providence, and a part of it, conducive to its completion, with regard to mankind: consisting itself also of various parts, and a mysterious economy, which has been carrying on from the time the world came into its present wretched state, and is still carrying on, for its recovery, by a divine person, the Messiah; who is to *gather together in one the children of God, that are scattered abroad,** and establish *an everlasting kingdom, wherein dwelleth righteousness.*† And in order to it; after various manifestations of things, relating to this great and general scheme of Providence, through a succession of many ages: (For *the Spirit of Christ which was in the prophets, testified beforehand his sufferings, and the glory that should follow: unto whom it was revealed, that not unto themselves, but unto us they did minister the things which are now reported unto us by them that have preached the Gospel; which things the angels desire to look into*:‡)—after various dispensations looking forward and preparatory to, this final salvation: *in the fulness of time*, when infinite wisdom thought fit; He, *being in the form of God,—made himself of no reputation, and took upon him the form of a servant, and was made in the likeness of men: and being found in fashion as a man, he humbled himself, and became obedient to death, even the death of the cross: wherefore God also hath highly exalted him, and given him a name, which is above every name: that at the name of Jesus every knee should bow, of things in heaven, and things in the earth, and things under the earth: and that every tongue should confess, that Jesus Christ is Lord, to the glory of God the Father.*§ Parts likewise of this economy are the miraculous mission of the Holy Ghost, and his ordinary assistances given to good men: the invisible government, which Christ at present exercises over his church: that

* John xi. 52. † 2 Pet. iii. 13. ‡ 1 Pet. i. 11, 12. § Phil. ii.

which he himself refers to in these words; *In my Father's house are many mansions—I go to prepare a place for you:** and his future return to *judge the world in righteousness*, and completely re-establish the kingdom of God. *For the Father judgeth no man; but hath committed all judgment unto the Son: that all men should honour the Son, even as they honour the Father.*† *All power is given unto him in heaven and in earth.*‡ *And he must reign, till he hath put all enemies under his feet. Then cometh the end, when he shall have delivered up the kingdom to God, even the Father; when he shall have put down all rule, and all authority and power. And when all things shall be subdued unto him, then shall the Son also himself be subject unto him that put all things under him, that God may be all in all.*§ Now little, surely, need be said to show, that this system, or scheme of things, is but imperfectly comprehended by us. The Scripture expressly asserts it to be so. And indeed one cannot read a passage relating to this *great mystery of godliness*,‖ but what immediately runs up into something which shows us our ignorance in it; as every thing in nature shows us our ignorance in the constitution of nature. And whoever will seriously consider that part of the Christian scheme, which is revealed in Scripture, will find so much more unrevealed, as will convince him, that, to all the purposes of judging and objecting, we know as little of it, as of the constitution of nature. Our ignorance, therefore, is as much an answer to our objections against the perfection of one, as against the perfection of the other.¶

II. It is obvious too, that in the Christian dispensation, as much as in the natural scheme of things, means are made use of to accomplish ends. And the observation of this furnishes us with the same answer, to objections against the perfection of Christianity, as to objections of the like kind, against the constitution of nature. It shows the credibility, that the things objected against, how *foolish*** soever they appear to men, may be the very best means of accomplishing the very best ends. And their appearing *foolishness* is no pre-

* John xiv. 2. † John v. 22, 23. ‡ Matth. xxviii. 18. ‖ 1 Tim. iii. 16. ¶ P. 153, &c. ** 1 Cor. i

sumption against this, in a scheme so greatly beyond our comprehension.*

III. The credibility, that the Christian dispensation may have been, all along, carried on by general laws,† no less than the course of nature, may require to be more distinctly made out. Consider then, upon what ground it is we say, that the whole common course of nature is carried on according to general fore-ordained laws. We know indeed several of the general laws of matter: and a great part of the natural behaviour of living agents is reducible to general laws. But we know in a manner nothing, by what laws, storms and tempests, earthquakes, famine, pestilence, become the instruments of destruction to mankind. And the laws, by which persons born into the world at such a time and place are of such capacities, geniuses, tempers; the laws, by which thoughts come into our mind, in a multitude of cases; and by which innumerable things happen, of the greatest influence upon the affairs and state of the world; these laws are so wholly unknown to us, that we call the events, which come to pass by them, accidental: though all reasonable men know certainly, that there cannot, in reality, be any such thing as chance; and conclude, that the things which have this appearance are the result of general laws, and may be reduced into them. It is then but an exceeding little way, and in but a very few respects, that we can trace up the natural course of things before us, to general laws. And it is only from analogy, that we conclude the whole of it to be capable of being reduced into them: only from our seeing, that part is so. It is from our finding, that the course of nature, in some respects and so far, goes on by general laws, that we conclude this of the rest. And if that be a just ground for such a conclusion, it is a just ground also, if not to conclude, yet to apprehend, to render it supposable and credible, which is sufficient for answering objections, that God's miraculous interpositions may have been, all along in like manner, by *general* laws of wisdom. Thus, that miraculous powers should be exerted, at such times, upon such occasions,

* P. 156, 157. † P. 158, 159.

in such degrees and manners, and with regard to such persons, rather than others; that the affairs of the world, being permitted to go on in their natural course so far, should, just at such a point, have a new direction given them by miraculous interpositions; that these interpositions should be exactly in such degrees and respects only; all this may have been by general laws. These laws are unknown indeed to us: but no more unknown than the laws from whence it is, that some die as soon as they are born, and others live to extreme old age; that one man is so superior to another in understanding; with innumerable more things, which, as was before observed, we cannot reduce to any laws or rules at all, though it is taken for granted, they are as much reducible to general ones, as gravitation. Now, if the revealed dispensations of Providence, and miraculous interpositions, be by general laws, as well as God's ordinary government in the course of nature, made known by reason and experience; there is no more reason to expect that every exigence, as it arises, should be provided for by these general laws or miraculous interpositions, than that every exigence in nature should, by the general laws of nature: yet there might be wise and good reasons, that miraculous interpositions should be by general laws; and that these laws should not be broken in upon, or deviated from, by other miracles

Upon the whole, then, the appearance of deficiencies and irregularities in nature is owing to its being a scheme but in part made known, and of such a certain particular kind in other respects. Now we see no more reason why the frame and course of nature should be such a scheme, than why Christianity should. And that the former is such a scheme, renders it credible, that the latter, upon supposition of its truth, may be so too. And as it is manifest, that Christianity is a scheme revealed but in part, and a scheme in which means are made use of to accomplish ends, like to that of nature: so the credibility, that it may have been all along carried on by general laws, no less than the course of nature, has been distinctly proved. And from all this it is beforehand credible that there might, I think probable that there would, be the like appearance of deficiencies and irregularities in Christianity, as in nature: *i. e.* that Christianity would be liable to the like objections, as the frame of nature. And these objections are answered by these observations concerning Christianity; as the like objections against the frame of nature are answered by the like observations concerning the frame of nature.

The objections against Christianity, considered as a matter of fact,* having, in general, been obviated in the preceding Chapter; and the same, considered as made against the wisdom and goodness of it, having been obviated in this: the next thing, according to the method proposed, is to show, that the principal objections, in particular, against Christianity, may be answered, by particular and full analogies in nature. And as one of them is made against the whole scheme of it together, as just now described, I choose to consider it here, rather than in a distinct Chapter by itself. The thing objected against this scheme of the Gospel is, "that it seems to suppose God was reduced to the necessity of a long series of intricate means, in order to accomplish his ends, the recovery and salvation of the world: in like sort as men, for want of understanding or power, not being able to come at their ends directly, are forced to go round-about ways, and make use of many perplexed contrivances to arrive at them." Now every thing which we see shows the folly of this, considered as an objection against the truth of Christianity. For, according to our manner of conception, God makes use of variety of means, what we often think tedious ones, in the natural course of providence, for the accomplishment of all his ends. Indeed it is certain there is somewhat in this matter quite beyond our comprehension: but the mystery is as great in nature as in Christianity. We know what we ourselves aim at, as final ends: and what courses we take, merely as means conducing to those ends. But we are greatly ignorant how far things are considered by the Author of Nature, under the single notion of means and ends; so as that it may be said,

* P 149, &c.

this is merely an end, and that merely means, in his regard. And whether there be not some peculiar absurdity in our very manner of conception, concerning this matter, somewhat contradictory arising from our extremely imperfect views of things, it is impossible to say. However, thus much is manifest, that the whole natural world and government of it is a scheme or system; not a fixed, but a progressive one: a scheme in which the operation of various means takes up a great length of time, before the ends they tend to can be attained. The change of seasons, the ripening of the fruits of the earth, the very history of a flower, is an instance of this: and so is human life. Thus vegetable bodies, and those of animals, though possibly formed at once, yet grow up by degrees to a mature state. And thus rational agents, who animate these latter bodies, are naturally directed to form each his own manners and character, by the gradual gaining of knowledge and experience, and by a long course of action. Our existence is not only successive, as it must be of necessity; but one state of our life and being is appointed by God, to be a preparation for another; and that to be the means of attaining to another succeeding one: infancy to childhood; childhood to youth; youth to mature age. Men are impatient, and for precipitating things: but the Author of Nature appears deliberate throughout his operations; accomplishing his natural ends by slow successive steps. And there is a plan of things beforehand laid out, which, from the nature of it, requires various systems of means, as well as length of time, in order to the carrying on its several parts into execution. Thus, in the daily course of natural providence, God operates in the very same manner, as in the dispensation of Christianity; making one thing subservient to another; this, to somewhat further; and soon, through a progressive series of means, which extend, both backward and forward, beyond our utmost view. Of this manner of operation, every thing we see in the course of nature is as much an instance, as any part of the Christian dispensation.

CHAP. V.

OF THE PARTICULAR SYSTEM OF CHRISTIANITY; THE APPOINTMENT OF A MEDIATOR, AND THE REDEMPTION OF THE WORLD BY HIM.

THERE is not, I think, any thing relating to Christianity, which has been more objected against, than the mediation of Christ, in some or other of its parts. Yet upon thorough consideration, there seems nothing less justly liable to it. For,

I. The whole analogy of nature removes all imagined presumption against the general notion of *a Mediator between God and man.** For we find all living creatures are brought into the world, and their life in infancy is preserved, by the instrumentality of others: and every satisfaction of it, some way or other, is bestowed by the like means. So that the visible government, which God exercises over the world, is by the instrumentality and mediation of others. And how far his invisible government be or be not so, it is impossible to determine at all by reason. And the supposition, that part of it is so, appears, to say the least, altogether as credible, as the contrary. There is then no sort of objection, from the light of nature, against the general notion of a mediator between God and man, considered as a doctrine of Christianity, or as an appointment in this dispensation: since we find by experience, that God does appoint mediators, to be the instruments of good and evil to us: the instruments of his justice and his mercy. And the objection here referred to is urged, not against mediation in that high, eminent, and peculiar sense, in which Christ is our mediator; but absolutely against the whole notion itself of a mediator at all.

II. As we must suppose, that the world is under the proper moral government of God, or in a state of religion, before we can enter into consideration of the revealed doctrine, concerning the redemption of it by Christ: so

* 1 Tim. ii. 5.

that supposition is here to be distinctly taken notice of. Now the divine moral government which religion teaches us, implies, that the consequence of vice shall be misery, in some future state, by the righteous judgment of God. That such consequent punishment shall take effect by his appointment, is necessarily implied. But, as it is not in any sort to be supposed, that we are made acquainted with all the ends or reasons, for which it is fit future punishments should be inflicted, or why God has appointed such and such consequent misery should follow vice; and as we are altogether in the dark, how or in what manner it shall follow, by what immediate occasions, or by the instrumentality of what means; there is no absurdity in supposing it may follow in a way analogous to that, in which many miseries follow such and such courses of action at present; poverty, sickness, infamy, untimely death by diseases, death from the hands of civil justice. There is no absurdity in supposing future punishment may follow wickedness of course, as we speak, or in the way of natural consequence from God's original constitution of the world: from the nature he has given us, and from the condition in which he places us; or in a like manner, as a person rashly trifling upon a precipice, in the way of natural consequence, falls down; in the way of natural consequence, breaks his limbs, suppose; in the way of natural consequence of this, without help, perishes.

Some good men may perhaps be offended with hearing it spoken of as a supposable thing that future punishments of wickedness may be in the way of natural consequence: as if this were taking the execution of justice out of the hands of God, and giving it to nature. But they should remember, that when things come to pass according to the course of nature, this does not hinder them from being his doing, who is the God of nature: and that the Scripture ascribes those punishments to divine justice, which are known to be natural; and which must be called so, when distinguished from such as are miraculous. But after all, this supposition, or rather this way of speaking, is here made use of only by way of illustration of the subject before us. For since it must be admitted, that the future punishment of wickedness is not a matter of arbitrary appointment, but of reason, equity, and justice; it comes, for ought I see, to the same thing, whether it is supposed to be inflicted in a way analogous to that, in which the temporal punishments of vice and folly are inflicted, or in any other way. And though there were a difference, it is allowable, in the present case, to make this supposition, plainly not an incredible one; that future punishment may follow wickedness in the way of natural consequence, or according to some general laws of government already established in the universe.

III. Upon this supposition, or even without it, we may observe somewhat, much to the present purpose, in the constitution of nature or appointments of Providence. the provision which is made, that all the bad natural consequences of men's actions should not always actually follow; or that such bad consequences, as, according to the settled course of things, would inevitably have followed if not prevented, should, in certain degrees, be prevented. We are apt presumptuously to imagine, that the world might have been so constituted, as that there would not have been any such thing as misery or evil. On the contrary we find the Author of Nature permits it: but then he has provided reliefs, and in many cases perfect remedies for it, after some pains and difficulties; reliefs and remedies even for that evil, which is the fruit of our own misconduct; and which, in the course of nature, would have continued, and ended in our destruction, but for such remedies. And this is an instance both of severity and of indulgence, in the constitution of nature. Thus all the bad consequences, now mentioned, of a man's trifling upon a precipice, might be prevented. And though all were not, yet some of them might, by proper interposition, if not rejected: by another's coming to the rash man's relief, with his own laying hold on that relief, in such sort as the case required. Persons may do a great deal themselves towards preventing the bad consequences of their follies: and more may be done by themselves, together with the assistance of others their fellow creatures; which assistance nature requires and prompts us to. This is the general constitution of the world. Now suppose it had been so constituted, that after such actions were done, as were foreseen naturally to draw after them misery to the doer, it should have been no more in human power to have prevented that naturally consequent misery, in any instance, than it is in all: no one can say, whether such a more severe constitution of things might not yet have been really good. But, that, on the contrary, provision is made by nature, that we may and do, to so great degree, prevent the bad natural effects of our follies; this may be called mercy or compassion in the original constitution of the world: compassion, as distinguished from goodness in general. And, the whole known constitution and course of things affording us instances of such compassion, it would be according to the analogy of nature, to hope, that, however ruinous the natural consequences of vice might be, from the general laws of God's government over the universe; yet provision might be made, possibly might have been originally made, for preventing those ruinous consequences from inevitably following: at least from following universally, and in all cases.

Many, I am sensible, will wonder at finding this made a question, or spoken of as in any degree doubtful. The generality of mankind are so far from having that awful sense of things, which the present state of vice and misery and darkness seems to make but reasonable, that they have scarce any apprehension or thought at all about this matter, any way: and some serious persons may have spoken unadvisedly concerning it. But let us observe, what we experience to be, and what, from the very constitution of nature, cannot but be, the consequences of irregular and disorderly behaviour: even of such rashness, wilfulness, neglects, as we scarce call vicious. Now it is natural to apprehend, that the bad consequences of irregularity will be greater, in proportion as the irregularity is so. And there is no comparison between these irregularities, and the greater instances of vice, or a dissolute profligate disregard to all religion; if there be any thing at all in religion. For consider what it is for creatures, moral agents, presumptuously to introduce that confusion and misery into the kingdom of God, which mankind have in fact introduced: to blaspheme the Sovereign Lord of all; to contemn his authority; to be injurious, to the degree they are, to their fellow creatures, the creatures of God. Add that the effects of vice in the present world are often extreme misery, irretrievable ruin, and even death: and upon putting all this together, it will appear, that as no one can say, in what degree fatal the unprevented consequences of vice may be, according to the general rule of divine government; so it is by no means intuitively certain, how far these consequences could possibly, in the nature of the thing, be prevented, consistently with the eternal rule of right, or with what is, in fact, the moral constitution of nature. However, there would be large ground to hope, that the universal government was not so severely strict, but that there was room for pardon, or for having those penal consequences prevented. Yet,

IV. There seems no probability, that any thing we could do would alone and of itself prevent them: prevent their following, or being inflicted. But one would think at least, it were impossible that the contrary should be thought certain. For we are not acquainted with the whole of the case. We are not informed of all the reasons, which render it fit that future punishments should be inflicted: and therefore cannot know, whether any thing we could do would make such an alteration, as to render it fit that they should be remitted. We do not know what the whole natural or appointed consequences of vice are; nor in what way they would follow, if not prevented: and therefore can in no sort say, whether we could do any thing which would be sufficient to prevent them. Our ignorance being thus manifest, let us recollect the analogy of Nature or Providence. For, though this may be but a slight ground to raise a positive opinion upon, in this matter; yet it is sufficient to answer a mere arbitrary assertion, without any kind of evidence, urged by way of objection against a doctrine, the proof of which is not reason, but revelation. Consider then: people ruin their fortunes by extravagance; they bring diseases upon themselves by excess; they incur the penalties of civil laws; and surely civil government is natural; will sorrow for these follies past, and behaving well for the future, alone and of itself prevent the natural consequences of them? On the contrary, men's natural abilities of helping themselves are often impaired; or if not, yet they are forced to be beholden to the assistance of others, upon several accounts, and in different ways; assistance which they would have had no occasion for, had it not been for their misconduct; but which, in the disadvantageous condition they had reduced themselves to, is absolutely necessary to their recovery, and retrieving their affairs. Now since this is our case, considering ourselves merely as inhabitants of this world, and as having a temporal interest here, under the natural government of God, which however has a great deal moral in it; why is it not supposable that this may be our case also, in our more important capacity, as under his perfect moral government, and having a more general and future interest depending? If we have misbehaved in this higher capacity, and rendered ourselves obnoxious to the future punishment, which God has annexed to vice: it is plainly credible, that behaving well for the time to come may be—not useless, God forbid—but wholly insufficient, alone and of itself, to prevent that punishment: or to put us in the condition, which we should have been in had we preserved our innocence.

And though we ought to reason with all reverence, whenever we reason concerning the divine conduct: yet it may be added, that it is clearly contrary to all our notions of government, as well as to what is, in fact, the general constitution of nature, to suppose, that doing well for the future should, in all cases, prevent all the judicial bad consequences of having done evil, or all the punishment annexed to disobedience. And we have manifestly nothing from whence to determine, in what degree, and in what cases, reformation would prevent this punishment, even supposing that it would in some. And though the efficacy of repentance itself alone, to prevent what mankind had rendered themselves obnoxious to, and recover what they had forfeited, is now insisted upon, in opposition to Christianity; yet, by the general prevalence of propitiatory sacrifices over the heathen world, this notion of repentance alone being sufficient to expiate guilt, appears to be contrary to the general sense of mankind.

Upon the whole then; had the laws, the general laws of God's government been permitted to operate, without any interposition in our behalf, the future punishment, for ought we know to the contrary, or have any reason to think, must inevitably have followed, notwithstanding any thing we could have done to prevent it. Now,

V. In this darkness, or this light of nature, call it which you please, revelation comes in; confirms every doubting fear, which could enter into the heart of man, concerning the future unprevented consequence of wickedness; supposes the world to be in a state of ruin (a supposition which seems the very ground of the Christian dispensation, and which, if not provable by reason, yet is in no wise contrary to it;) teaches us too, that the rules of divine government are such, as not to admit of pardon immediately and directly upon repentance, or by the sole efficacy of it: but then teaches at the same time, what nature might justly have hoped, that the moral government of the universe was not so rigid, but that there was room for an interposition, to avert the fatal consequences of vice; which therefore, by this means, does admit of pardon. Revelation teaches us, that the unknown laws of God's more general government, no less than the particular laws by which we experience he governs us at present, are compassionate,* as well as good in the more general notion of goodness: and that he hath mercifully provided, that there should be an interposition to prevent the destruction of human kind; whatever that destruction unprevented would have been. *God so loved the world, that he gave his only begotten Son, that whosoever believeth,* not, to be sure, in a speculative, but in a practical sense, *that whosoever believeth in him, should not perish:*† gave his Son in the same way of

* P. 210, &c. † John iii. 16.

goodness to the world, as he affords particular persons the friendly assistance of their fellow creatures: when, without it, their temporal ruin would be the certain consequence of their follies: in the same way of goodness, I say; though in a transcendent and infinitely higher degree. And the Son of God *loved us, and gave himself for us*, with a love, which he himself compares to that of human friendship: though, in this case, all comparisons must fall infinitely short of the thing intended to be illustrated by them. He interposed in such a manner as was necessary and effectual to prevent that execution of justice upon sinners, which God had appointed should otherwise have been executed upon them: or in such a manner, as to prevent that punishment from actually following, which, according to the general laws of divine government, must have followed the sins of the world, had it not been for such interposition.*

If any thing here said should appear, upon first thought, inconsistent with divine goodness; a second, I am persuaded, will entirely remove that appearance. For were we to suppose the constitution of things to be such, as that the whole creation must have perished, had it not been for somewhat, which God had appointed should be, in order to prevent that ruin: even this supposition would not be inconsistent, in any degree, with the most absolutely perfect goodness. But still it may be thought, that this whole manner of treating the subject before us supposes mankind to be naturally in a very strange state. And truly so it does. But it is not Christianity which has put us into this state. Whoever

* It cannot, I suppose, be imagined, even by the most cursory reader, that it is, in any sort, affirmed or implied in any thing said in this chapter, that none can have the benefit of the general redemption, but such as have the advantage of being made acquainted with it in the present life. But it may be needful to mention, that several questions, which have been brought into the subject before us, and determined, are not in the least entered into here: questions which have been, I fear, rashly determined, and perhaps with equal rashness contrary ways. For instance, whether God could have saved the world by other means than the death of Christ, consistently with the general laws of his government. And had not Christ come into the world, what would have been the future condition of the better sort of men; those just persons over the face of the earth, for whom Manasses in his prayer asserts, repentance was not appointed. The meaning of the first of these questions is greatly ambiguous: and neither of them can properly be answered, without going upon that infinitely absurd supposition, that we know the whole of the case. And perhaps the very inquiry, *What would have followed, if God had not done as he has*, may have in it some very great impropriety: and ought not to be carried on any further than is necessary to help our partial and inadequate conceptions of things.

will consider the manifold miseries, and the extreme wickedness of the world; that the best have great wrongnesses within themselves, which they complain of, and endeavour to amend; but that the generality grow more profligate and corrupt with age; that even moralists thought the present state to be a state of punishment: and, what might be added, that the earth our habitation has the appearances of being a ruin: whoever, I say, will consider all these, and some other obvious things, will think he has little reason to object against the Scripture account, that mankind is in a state of degradation; against this being the fact: how difficult soever he may think it to account for, or even to form a distinct conception of the occasions and circumstances of it. But that the crime of our first parents was the occasion of our being placed in a more disadvantageous condition, is a thing throughout and particularly analogous to what we see in the daily course of natural providence; as the recovery of the world by the interposition of Christ has been shown to be so in general.

VI. The particular manner in which Christ interposed in the redemption of the world, or his office as *Mediator*, in the largest sense, *between God and man*, is thus represented to us in the Scripture. *He is the light of the world;** the revealer of the will of God in the most eminent sense. He is a propitiatory sacrifice;† *the Lamb of God:*‡ and, as he voluntarily offered himself up, he is styled our High Priest.§ And, which seems of peculiar weight, he is described beforehand in the Old Testament, under the same characters of a priest, and an expiatory victim.‖ And whereas it is objected, that all this is merely by way of allusion to the sacrifices of the Mosaic law, the Apostle on the contrary affirms, that the *law was a shadow of good things to come, and not the very image of the things:*¶ and that *the priests that offer gifts according to the law—serve unto the example and shadow of heavenly things, as Moses was admonished*

* John i. and viii. 12.
† Rom. iii. 25. v. 11. 1 Cor. v. 7. Eph. v. 2. 1 John ii. 2. Mat. xxvi. 28.
‡ John i. 29, 36, and throughout the book of Revelation.
§ Throughout the epistle to the Hebrews.
‖ Isa. liii. Dan. ix. 24. Ps. cx. 4.
¶ Heb. x. 1.

*of God, when he was about to make the tabernacle. For see, saith he, that thou make all things according to the pattern showed to thee in the mount:** *i. e.* the Levitical priesthood was a shadow of the priesthood of Christ; in like manner as the tabernacle made by Moses was according to that showed him in the mount. The priesthood of Christ, and the tabernacle in the mount, were the originals: of the former of which the Levitical priesthood was a type; and of the latter the tabernacle made by Moses was a copy. The doctrine of this epistle then plainly is, that the legal sacrifices were allusions to the great and final atonement to be made by the blood of Christ; and not that this was an allusion to those. Nor can any thing be more express or determinate than the following passage. *It is not possible that the blood of bulls and of goats should take away sin. Wherefore when he cometh into the world, he saith, Sacrifice and offering,* i. e. of bulls and of goats, *thou wouldest not, but a body hast thou prepared me. Lo, I come to do thy will, O God. By which will we are sanctified, through the offering of the body of Jesus Christ once for all.*† And to add one passage more of the like kind: *Christ was once offered to bear the sins of many; and unto them that look for him shall he appear the second time, without sin;* i. e. without bearing sin, as he did at his first coming, by being an offering for it; without having our *iniquities* again *laid upon him,* without being any more a sin-offering:—*unto them that look for him shall he appear the second time, without sin, unto salvation.*‡ Nor do the inspired writers at all confine themselves to this manner of speaking concerning the satisfaction of Christ; but declare an efficacy in what he did and suffered for us, additional to and beyond mere instruction, example, and government, in great variety of expression: *That Jesus should die for that nation,* the Jews: *and not for that nation only, but that also,* plainly by the efficacy of his death, *he should gather together in one the children of God that were scattered abroad:*§ that *he suffered for sins, the just for the unjust:*‖ that *he gave his life, himself, a ransom:*¶ that *we are bought, bought with a price:*** that

* Heb. viii. 4, 5. † Heb. x. 4, 5, 7, 9, 10. ‡ Heb. ix. 28.
§ John xi. 51, 52. ‖ 1 Pet. iii. 18. ¶ Matt. xx. 28. Mark x. 45. 1 Tim. ii. 6.
** 2 Pet. ii. 1. Rev. xiv. 4. 1 Cor. vi. 20

*he redeemed us with his blood: redeemed us from the curse of the law, being made a curse for us:** that he is our *advocate, intercessor,* and *propitiation:*† that *he was made perfect,* or consummate, *through sufferings; and being* thus *made perfect, he became the author of salvation:*‡ that *God was in Christ reconciling the world to himself; by the death of his Son, by the cross; not imputing their trespasses unto them:*§ and lastly, that *through death he destroyed him that had the power of death.*‖ Christ then having thus *humbled himself, and become obedient to death, even the death of the cross; God also hath highly exalted him, and given him a name, which is above every name: hath given all things into his hands: hath committed all judgment unto him; that all men should honour the Son, even as they honour the Father.*¶ For, *worthy is the Lamb that was slain, to receive power, and riches, and wisdom, and strength, and honour, and glory, and blessing. And every creature which is in heaven, and on the earth, heard I, saying, Blessing, and honour, and glory, and power, be unto him that sitteth upon the throne, and unto the Lamb for ever and ever.***

These passages of Scripture seem to comprehend and express the chief parts of Christ's office, as Mediator between God and man, so far, I mean, as the nature of this his office is revealed; and it is usually treated of by divines under three heads.

First, He was, by way of eminence, the Prophet: *that Prophet that should come into the world,*†† to declare the divine will. He published anew the law of nature, which men had corrupted; and the very knowledge of which, to some degree, was lost among them. He taught mankind, taught us authoritatively, to *live soberly, righteously, and godly in this present world,* in expectation of the future judgment of God. He confirmed the truth of this moral system of nature, and gave us additional evidence of it; the evidence of testimony.‡‡ He distinctly revealed the manner, in which God would be

* 1 Pet. i. 19. Rev. v. 9. Gal. iii. 13.

† Heb. vii. 25. 1 John ii. 1, 2.

‡ Heb. ii. x. v. 9.

§ 2 Cor. v. 19. Rom. v. 10. Eph. ii. 16.

‖ Heb. ii. 14. See also a remarkable passage in the book of Job, xxxiii. 24.

¶ Phil. ii. 8, 9. John iii. 35. v. 22, 23.

** Rev. v. 12, 13.

†† John vi. 14.

‡‡ P. 167, &c.

worshipped, the efficacy of repentance, and the rewards and punishments of a future life. Thus he was a prophet in a sense in which no other ever was. To which is to be added, that he set us a perfect *example, that we should follow his steps.*

Secondly, He has a *kingdom which is not of this world.* He founded a Church, to be to mankind a standing memorial of religion, and invitation to it; which he promised to be with always even to the end. He exercises an invisible government over it, himself, and by his Spirit: over that part of it, which is militant here on earth, a government of discipline, *for the perfecting of the saints, for the edifying his body: till we all come in the unity of the faith, and of the knowledge of the Son of God, unto a perfect man, unto the measure of the stature of the fulness of Christ.** Of this Church, all persons scattered over the world, who live in obedience to his laws, are members. For these he is *gone to prepare a place,* and *will come again to receive them unto himself, that where he is, there they may be also; and reign with him for ever and ever:*† and likewise *to take vengeance on them that know not God, and obey not his Gospel.*‡

Against these parts of Christ's office I find no objections, but what are fully obviated in the beginning of this Chapter.

Lastly, Christ offered himself a propitiatory sacrifice, and made atonement for the sins of the world; which is mentioned last, in regard to what is objected against it. Sacrifices of expiation were commanded the Jews, and obtained amongst most other nations, from tradition, whose original probably was revelation. And they were continually repeated, both occasionally, and at the returns of stated times: and made up great part of the external religion of mankind. *But now once in the end of the world Christ appeared to put away sin by the sacrifice of himself.*§ And this sacrifice was, in the highest degree and with the most extensive influence, of that efficacy for obtaining pardon of sin, which the heathens may be supposed to have thought their sacrifices to have

* Eph. iv. 12, 13. † John xiv. 2, 3. Rev. iii. 21, and xi. 15.
‡ 2 Thess. i. 8. § Heb. ix. 26.

been, and which the Jewish sacrifices really were in some degree, and with regard to some persons.

How and in what particular way it had this efficacy, there are not wanting persons who have endeavoured to explain: but I do not find that the Scripture has explained it. We seem to be very much in the dark concerning the manner in which the ancients understood atonement to be made, *i. e.* pardon to be obtained by sacrifices. And if the Scripture has, as surely it has, left this matter of the satisfaction of Christ mysterious, left somewhat in it unrevealed, all conjectures about it must be, if not evidently absurd, yet at least uncertain. Nor has any one reason to complain for want of further information, unless he can show his claim to it.

Some have endeavoured to explain the efficacy of what Christ has done and suffered for us, beyond what the Scripture has authorized: others, probably because they could not explain it, have been for taking it away, and confining his office as Redeemer of the world to his instruction, example, and government of the church. Whereas the doctrine of the Gospel appears to be, not only that he taught the efficacy of repentance, but rendered it of the efficacy of which it is, by what he did and suffered for us: that he obtained for us the benefit of having our repentance accepted unto eternal life: not only that he revealed to sinners, that they were in a capacity of salvation, and how they might obtain it; but moreover that he put them into this capacity of salvation, by what he did and suffered for them; put us into a capacity of escaping future punishment, and obtaining future happiness. And it is our wisdom thankfully to accept the benefit, by performing the conditions, upon which it is offered, on our part, without disputing how it was procured on his. For,

VII. Since we neither know by what means punishment in a future state would have followed wickedness in this: nor in what manner it would have been inflicted, had it not been prevented; nor all the reasons why its infliction would have been needful, nor the particular nature of that state of happiness, which Christ is gone to prepare for his disciples: and since we are ignorant how far any thing which we could do, would, alone and of itself, have been effectual to prevent that punishment to which we were obnoxious, and recover that happiness, which we had forfeited; it is most evident we are not judges, antecedently to revelation, whether a mediator was or was not necessary, to obtain those ends: to prevent that future punishment, and bring mankind to the final happiness of their nature. And for the very same reasons, upon supposition of the necessity of a mediator, we are no more judges, antecedently to revelation, of the whole nature of his office, or the several parts of which it consists; of what was fit and requisite to be assigned him, in order to accomplish the ends of divine Providence in the appointment. And from hence it follows, that to object against the expediency or usefulness of particular things, revealed to have been done or suffered by him, because we do not see how they were conducive to those ends, is highly absurd. Yet nothing is more common to be met with, than this absurdity. But if it be acknowledged beforehand, that we are not judges in the case, it is evident that no objection can, with any shadow of reason, be urged against any particular part of Christ's mediatorial office revealed in Scripture, till it can be shown positively not to be requisite or conducive to the ends proposed to be accomplished; or that it is in itself unreasonable.

And there is one objection made against the satisfaction of Christ, which looks to be of this positive kind: that the doctrine of his being appointed to suffer for the sins of the world, represents God as being indifferent whether he punished the innocent or the guilty. Now from the foregoing observations we may see the extreme slightness of all such objections; and (though it is most certain all who make them do not see the consequence) that they conclude altogether as much against God's whole original constitution of nature, and the whole daily course of divine Providence in the government of the world, *i. e.* against the whole scheme of Theism and the whole notion of Religion, as against Christianity. For the world is a constitution or system, whose parts have a mutual reference to each other: and there is a scheme of things gradually carrying on, called the course of nature, to the carrying on of which God has appointed us, in various ways, to contribute. And when, in the daily course of natural providence, it is appointed that innocent people should suffer for the faults of the guilty, this is liable to the very same objection, as the instance we are now considering. The infinitely greater importance of that appointment of Christianity, which is objected against, does not hinder but it may be, as it plainly is, an appointment of the very same kind, with what the world affords us daily examples of. Nay, if there were any force at all in the objection, it would be stronger, in one respect, against natural providence, than against Christianity: because under the former we are in many cases commanded, and even necessitated whether we will or no, to suffer for the faults of others; whereas the sufferings of Christ were voluntary. The world's being under the righteous government of God does indeed imply, that finally and upon the whole every one shall receive according to his personal deserts: and the general doctrine of the whole Scripture is, that this shall be the completion of the divine government. But during the progress, and, for ought we know, even in order to the completion of this moral scheme, vicarious punishments may be fit, and absolutely necessary. Men by their follies run themselves into extreme distress; into difficulties which would be absolutely fatal to them, were it not for the interposition and assistance of others. God commands by the law of nature, that we afford them this assistance, in many cases where we cannot do it without very great pains, and labour, and sufferings to ourselves. And we see in what variety of ways one person's sufferings contribute to the relief of another: and how, or by what particular means, this comes to pass, or follows, from the constitution and laws of nature, which came under our notice: and, being familiarized to it, men are not shocked with it. So that the reason of their insisting upon objections of the foregoing kind against the satisfaction of Christ is, either that they do not consider God's settled and uniform appointments as his appointments at all · or else they forget that vicarious punishment is a providential appointment of every day's experience: and then, from their being unacquainted with the more general laws of nature or divine government over the world, and not seeing how the sufferings of Christ could contribute to the redemption of it, unless by arbitrary and tyrannical will; they conclude his sufferings could not contribute to it any other way. And yet, what has been often alleged in justification of this doctrine, even from the apparent natural tendency of this method of our redemption; its tendency to vindicate the authority of God's laws, and deter his creatures from sin; this has never yet been answered, and is I think plainly unanswerable: though I am far from thinking it an account of the whole of the case. But, without taking this into consideration, it abundantly appears, from the observations above made, that this objection is, not an objection against Christianity, but against the whole general constitution of nature. And if it were to be considered as an objection against Christianity, or considering it as it is, an objection against the constitution of nature; it amounts to no more in conclusion than this, that a divine appointment cannot be necessary or expedient, because the objector does not discern it to be so: though he must own that the nature of the case is such, as renders him incapable of judging, whether it be so or not; or of seeing it to be necessary, though it were so.

It is indeed a matter of great patience to reasonable men, to find people arguing in this manner: objecting against the credibility of such particular things revealed in Scripture, that they do not see the necessity or expediency of them. For though it is highly right, and the most pious exercise of our understanding, to inquire with due reverence into the ends and reasons of God's dispensation: yet when those reasons are concealed, to argue from our ignorance, that such dispensations cannot be from God, is infinitely absurd. The presumption of this kind of objections seems almost lost in the folly of them. And the folly of them is yet greater, when they are urged, as usually they are, against things in Christianity analogous or like to those natural dispensations of Providence, which are matter of experience.

Let reason be kept to: and if any part of the Scripture account of the redemption of the world by Christ can be shown to be really contrary to it, let the Scripture, in the name of God, be given up: but let not such poor creatures as we go on objecting against an infinite scheme, that we do not see the necessity or usefulness of all its parts, and call this reasoning; and, which still further heightens the absurdity in the present case, parts which we are not actively concerned in. For it may be worth mentioning,

Lastly, That not only the reason of the thing, but the whole analogy of nature, should teach us, not to expect to have the like information concerning the divine conduct, as concerning our own duty. God instructs us by experience (for it is not reason, but experience which instructs us), what good or bad consequences will follow from our acting in such and such manners: and by this he directs us how we are to behave ourselves. But, though we are sufficiently instructed for the common purposes of life: yet it is but an almost infinitely small part of natural providence, which we are at all let into. The case is the same with regard to revelation. The doctrine of a mediator between God and man, against which it is objected, that the expediency of some things in it is not understood, relates only to what was done on God's part in the appointment, and on the Mediator's in the execution of it. For what is required of us, in consequence of this gracious dispensation, is another subject, in which none can complain for want of information. The constitution of the world, and God's natural government over it, is all mystery, as much as the Christian dispensation. Yet under the first he has given men all things pertaining to life; and under the other all things pertaining unto godliness. And it may be added, that there is nothing hard to be accounted for in any of the common precepts of Christianity: though if there were, surely a divine command is abundantly sufficient to lay us under the strongest obligations to obedience. But the fact is, that the reasons of all the Christian precepts are evident. Positive institutions are manifestly necessary to keep up and propagate religion amongst mankind. And our duty to Christ, the internal and external worship of him; this part of the religion of the Gospel manifestly arises out of what he has done and suffered, his authority and dominion, and the relation which he is revealed to stand in to us.*

CHAP. VI.

OF THE WANT OF UNIVERSALITY IN REVELATION; AND OF THE SUPPOSED DEFICIENCY IN THE PROOF OF IT.

It has been thought by some persons, that if the evidence of revelation appears doubtful, this itself turns into a positive argument against it: because it cannot be supposed, that, if it were true, it would be left to subsist upon doubtful evidence. And the objection against revelation from its not being universal is often insisted upon as of great weight.

Now the weakness of these opinions may be shown, by observing the suppositions on which they are founded: which are really such as these; that it cannot be thought God would have bestowed any favour at all upon us, unless in the degree, which, we think, he might, and which, we imagine, would be most to our particular advantage; and also that it cannot be thought he would bestow a favour upon any, unless he bestowed the same upon all; suppositions, which we find contradicted, not by a few instances in God's natural government of the world, but by the general analogy of nature together.

Persons who speak of the evidence of religion as doubtful, and of this supposed doubtfulness as a positive argument against it, should be put upon considering, what that evidence indeed is, which they act upon with regard to their temporal interests. For, it is not only extremely difficult, but in many cases absolutely impossible, to balance pleasure and pain, satisfaction and uneasiness, so as to be able to say on which side the overplus is. There are the like difficulties and impossibilities in making the due allowances for a change of

* P. 171, &c.

temper and taste, for satiety, disgusts, ill health: any of which render men incapable of enjoying, after they have obtained what they most eagerly desired. Numberless too are the accidents, besides that one of untimely death, which may even probably disappoint the best concerted schemes: and strong objections are often seen to lie against them, not to be removed or answered, but which seem overbalanced by reasons on the other side; so as that the certain difficulties and dangers of the pursuit are, by every one, thought justly disregarded, upon account of the appearing greater advantages in case of success, though there be but little probability of it. Lastly, every one observes our liableness, if we be not upon our guard, to be deceived by the falsehood of men, and the false appearances of things: and this danger must be greatly increased, if there be a strong bias within, suppose from indulged passion, to favour the deceit. Hence arises that great uncertainty and doubtfulness of proof, wherein our temporal interest really consists; what are the most probable means of attaining it; and whether those means will eventually be successful. And numberless instances there are, in the daily course of life, in which all men think it reasonable to engage in pursuits, though the probability is greatly against succeeding; and to make such provision for themselves, as it is supposable they may have occasion for, though the plain acknowledged probability is, that they never shall. Then those who think the objection against revelation, from its light not being universal, to be of weight, should observe, that the Author of Nature, in numberless instances, bestows that upon some, which he does not upon others, who seem equally to stand in need of it. Indeed he appears to bestow all his gifts with the most promiscuous variety among creatures of the same species: health and strength, capacities of prudence and of knowledge, means of improvement, riches, and all external advantages. And as there are not any two men found, of exactly like shape and features; so it is probable there are not any two, of an exactly like constitution, temper, and situation, with regard to the goods and evils of life. Yet, notwithstanding these uncertainties and varieties, God does exercise a natural government over the world; and there is such a thing as a prudent and imprudent institution of life, with regard to our health and our affairs, under that his natural government.

As neither the Jewish nor Christian revelation have been universal; and as they have been afforded to a greater or less part of the world, at different times; so likewise at different times, both revelations have had different degrees of evidence. The Jews who lived during the succession of prophets, that is, from Moses till after the Captivity, had higher evidence of the truth of their religion, than those had, who lived in the interval between the last mentioned period, and the coming of Christ. And the first Christians had higher evidence of the miracles wrought in attestation of Christianity, than what we have now. They had also a strong presumptive proof of the truth of it, perhaps of much greater force, in way of argument, than many think, of which we have very little remaining; I mean the presumptive proof of its truth, from the influence which it had upon the lives of the generality of its professors. And we, or future ages, may possibly have a proof of it, which they could not have, from the conformity between the prophetic history, and the state of the world and of Christianity. And further: if we were to suppose the evidence, which some have of religion, to amount to little more than seeing that it may be true; but that they remain in great doubts and uncertainties about both its evidence and its nature, and great perplexities concerning the rule of life: others to have a full conviction of the truth of religion, with a distinct knowledge of their duty; and others severally to have all the intermediate degrees of religious light and evidence, which lie between these two—if we put the case, that for the present, it was intended, revelation should be no more than a small light, in the midst of a world greatly overspread, notwithstanding it, with ignorance and darkness: that certain glimmerings of this light should extend, and be directed, to remote distances, in such a manner as that those who really partook of it should not discern from whence it originally came: that some in a nearer situation to it should have its light obscured, and, in different ways and degrees, intercepted: and that others should be placed within its clearer influence, and be much more enlivened, cheered, and directed by it; but yet that even to these it should be no more than *a light shining in a dark place:* all this would be perfectly uniform, and of a piece with the conduct of Providence, in the distribution of its other blessings. If the fact of the case really were, that some have received no light at all from the Scripture; as many ages and countries in the heathen world: that others, though they have, by means of it, had essential or natural religion enforced upon their consciences, yet have never had the genuine Scripture revelation, with its real evidence, proposed to their consideration; and the ancient Persians and modern Mahometans may possibly be instances of people in a situation somewhat like to this: that others, though they have had the Scripture laid before them as of divine revelation, yet have had it with the system and evidence of Christianity so interpolated, the system so corrupted, the evidence so blended with false miracles, as to leave the mind in the utmost doubtfulness and uncertainty about the whole; which may be the state of some thoughtful men, in most of those nations who call themselves Christian: and lastly, that others have had Christianity offered to them in its genuine simplicity, and with its proper evidence, as persons in countries and churches of civil and of Christian liberty; but however that even these persons are left in great ignorance in many respects, and have by no means light afforded them enough to satisfy their curiosity, but only to regulate their life, to teach them their duty, and encourage them in the careful discharge of it: I say, if we were to suppose this somewhat of a general true account of the degrees of moral and religious light and evidence, which were intended to be afforded mankind, and of what has actually been and is their situation, in their moral and religious capacity; there would be nothing in all this ignorance, doubtfulness, and uncertainty, in all these varieties, and supposed disadvantages of some in comparison of others, respecting religion, but may be paralleled by manifest analogies in the natural dispensations of Providence at present, and considering ourselves merely in our temporal capacity.

Nor is there any thing shocking in all this, or which would seem to bear hard upon the moral administration in nature, if we would really keep in mind, that every one shall be dealt equitably with: instead of forgetting this, or explaining it away, after it is acknowledged in words. All shadow of injustice, and indeed all harsh appearances, in this various economy of Providence, would be lost; if we would keep in mind, that every merciful allowance shall be made, and no more be required of any one, than what might have been equitably expected of him, from the circumstances in which he was placed; and not what might have been expected, had he been placed in other circumstances: *i. e.* in Scripture language, that every man shall be *accepted according to what he had, not according to what he had not.** This however doth not by any means imply, that all persons' condition here is equally advantageous with respect to futurity. And Providence's designing to place some in greater darkness with respect to religious knowledge, is no more a reason why they should not endeavour to get out of that darkness, and others to bring them out of it; than why ignorant and slow people in matters of other knowledge should not endeavour to learn, or should not be instructed.

It is not unreasonable to suppose, that the same wise and good principle, whatever it was, which disposed the Author of Nature to make different kinds and orders of creatures, disposed him also to place creatures of like kinds in different situations: and that the same principle which disposed him to make creatures of different moral capacities, disposed him also to place creatures of like moral capacities in different religious situations; and even the same creatures, in different periods of their being. And the account or reason of this is also most probably the account why the constitution of things is such, as that creatures of moral natures or capacities, for a considerable part of that duration in which they are living

* 2 Cor. viii. 12.

agents, are not at all subjects of morality and religion; but grow up to be so, and grow up to be so more and more gradually from childhood to mature age.

What, in particular, is the account or reason of these things, we must be greatly in the dark, were it only that we know so very little even of our own case. Our present state may possibly be the consequence of somewhat past, which we are wholly ignorant of: as it has a reference to somewhat to come, of which we know scarce any more than is necessary for practice. A system or constitution, in its notion, implies variety; and so complicated a one as this world, very great variety. So that were revelation universal, yet, from men's different capacities of understanding, from the different lengths of their lives, their different educations and other external circumstances, and from their difference of temper and bodily constitution; their religious situations would be widely different, and the disadvantage of some in comparison of others, perhaps, altogether as much as at present. And the true account, whatever it be, why mankind, or such a part of mankind, are placed in this condition of ignorance, must be supposed also the true account of our further ignorance, in not knowing the reasons why, or whence it is, that they are placed in this condition. But the following practical reflections may deserve the serious consideration of those persons, who think the circumstances of mankind or their own, in the forementioned respects, a ground of complaint.

First, The evidence of religion not appearing obvious, may constitute one particular part of some men's trial in the religious sense: as it gives scope, for a virtuous exercise, or vicious neglect of their understanding, in examining or not examining into that evidence. There seems no possible reason to be given, why we may not be in a state of moral probation, with regard to the exercise of our understanding upon the subject of religion, as we are with regard to our behaviour in common affairs. The former is as much a thing within our power and choice as the latter. And I suppose it is to be laid down for certain, that the same character, the same inward principle, which, after a man is convinced of the truth of religion, renders him obedient to the precepts of it, would, were he not thus convinced, set him about an examination of it, upon its system and evidence being offered to his thoughts: and that in the latter state his examination would be with an impartiality, seriousness, and solicitude, proportionable to what his obedience is in the former. And as inattention, negligence, want of all serious concern, about a matter of such a nature and such importance, when offered to men's consideration, is, before a distinct conviction of its truth, as real immoral depravity and dissoluteness; as neglect of religious practice after such conviction: so active solicitude about it, and fair impartial consideration of its evidence before such conviction, is as really an exercise of a morally right temper; as is religious practice after. Thus, that religion is not intuitively true, but a matter of deduction and inference; that a conviction of its truth is not forced upon every one, but left to be, by some, collected with heedful attention to premises; this as much constitutes religious probation, as much affords sphere, scope, opportunity, for right and wrong behaviour, as any thing whatever does. And their manner of treating this subject, when laid before them, shows what is in their heart, and is an exertion of it.

Secondly, It appears to be a thing as evident, though it is not so much attended to, that if, upon consideration of religion, the evidence of it should seem to any persons doubtful, in the highest supposable degree; even this doubtful evidence will, however, put them into a *general state of probation* in the moral and religious sense. For, suppose a man to be really in doubt, whether such a person had not done him the greatest favour; or, whether his whole temporal interest did not depend upon that person: no one, who had any sense of gratitude and of prudence, could possibly consider himself in the same situation, with regard to such person, as if he had no such doubt. In truth, it is as just to say, that certainty and doubt are the same; as to say the situations now mentioned would leave a man as entirely at liberty in point of gratitude or prudence, as he would be, were he certain he had received no favour from such person, or that he no way depended upon him. And thus, though the evidence of religion which is afforded to some men should be little more than they are given to see, the system of Christianity, or religion in general, to be supposable and credible; this ought in all reason to beget a serious practical apprehension, that it may be true. And even this will afford matter of exercise for religious suspense and deliberation, for moral resolution and self-government; because the apprehension that religion may be true does as really lay men under obligations, as a full conviction that it is true. It gives occasion and motives to consider further the important subject; to preserve attentively upon their minds a general implicit sense that they may be under divine moral government, an awful solicitude about religion, whether natural or revealed. Such apprehension ought to turn men's eyes to every degree of new light which may be had, from whatever side it comes; and induce them to refrain, in the mean time, from all immoralities, and live in the conscientious practice of every common virtue. Especially are they bound to keep at the greatest distance from all dissolute profaneness; for this the very nature of the case forbids; and to treat with highest reverence a matter, upon which their own whole interest and being, and the fate of nature, depend. This behaviour, and an active endeavour to maintain within themselves this temper, is the business, the duty, and the wisdom of those persons, who complain of the doubtfulness of religion: is what they are under the most proper obligations to. And such behaviour is an exertion of, and has a tendency to improve in them, that character, which the practice of all the several duties of religion, from a full conviction of its truth, is an exertion of, and has a tendency to improve in others: others, I say, to whom God has afforded such conviction. Nay, considering the infinite importance of religion, revealed as well as natural, I think it may be said in general, that whoever will weigh the matter thoroughly may see, there is not near so much difference, as is commonly imagined, between what ought in reason to be the rule of life, to those persons who are fully convinced of its truth, and to those who have only a serious doubting apprehension, that it may be true. Their hopes, and fears, and obligations, will be in various degrees: but, as the subject matter of their hopes and fears is the same; so the subject matter of their obligations, what they are bound to do and to refrain from, is not so very unlike.

It is to be observed further, that, from a character of understanding, or a situation of influence in the world, some persons have it in their power to do infinitely more harm or good, by setting an example of profaneness and avowed disregard to all religion, or, on the contrary, of a serious, though perhaps doubting, apprehension of its truth, and of a reverend regard to it under this doubtfulness; than they can do, by acting well or ill in all the common intercourses amongst mankind. And consequently they are most highly accountable for a behaviour, which, they may easily foresee, is of such importance, and in which there is most plainly a right and a wrong; even admitting the evidence of religion to be as doubtful as is pretended.

The ground of these observations, and that which renders them just and true, is, that doubting necessarily implies some degree of evidence for that, of which we doubt. For no person would be in doubt concerning the truth of a number of facts so and so circumstanced, which should accidentally come into his thoughts, and of which he had no evidence at all. And though in the case of an even chance, and where consequently we were in doubt, we should in common language say, that we had no evidence at all for either side; yet that situation of things, which renders it an even chance and no more, that such an event will happen, renders this case equivalent to all others, where there is such evidence on both sides of a question,* as leaves the mind in doubt concerning the truth. Indeed in all these cases, there is no more evidence on one side than on the other; but there is (what is equivalent to) much more for either, than for the truth of a number of facts, which come into one's thoughts at random. And thus, in all these cases, doubt as much presupposes evidence, lower degrees of evidence, as belief presupposes higher, and certainty higher

* Introduction.

still. Any one, who will a little attend to the nature of evidence, will easily carry this observation on, and see, that between no evidence at all, and that degree of it which affords ground of doubt, there are as many intermediate degrees, as there are, between that degree which is the ground of doubt, and demonstration. And though we have not faculties to distinguish these degrees of evidence with any sort of exactness; yet, in proportion as they are discerned, they ought to influence our practice. For it is as real an imperfection in the moral character, not to be influenced in practice by a lower degree of evidence when discerned, as it is in the understanding, not to discern it. And as, in all subjects which men consider, they discern the lower as well as higher degrees of evidence, proportionably to their capacity of understanding; so, in practical subjects, they are influenced in practice, by the lower as well as higher degrees of it, proportionably to their fairness and honesty. And as, in proportion to defects in the understanding, men are unapt to see lower degrees of evidence, are in danger of overlooking evidence when it is not glaring, and are easily imposed upon in such cases; so, in proportion to the corruption of the heart, they seem capable of satisfying themselves with having no regard in practice to evidence acknowledged real, if it be not overbearing. From these things it must follow, that doubting concerning religion implies such a degree of evidence for it, as, joined with the consideration of its importance, unquestionably lays men under the obligations before mentioned, to have a dutiful regard to it in all their behaviour.

Thirdly, The difficulties in which the evidence of religion is involved, which some complain of, is no more a just ground of complaint, than the external circumstances of temptation, which others are placed in; or than difficulties in the practice of it, after a full conviction of its truth. Temptations render our state a more improving state of discipline,* than it would be otherwise: as they give occasion for a more attentive exercise of the virtuous principle, which confirms and strengthens it more, than an easier or less attentive exercise of it could. Now

* Part I. Chap. v.

speculative difficulties are, in this respect, of the very same nature with these external temptations. For the evidence of religion not appearing obvious, is to some persons a temptation to reject it, without any consideration at all; and therefore requires such an attentive exercise of the virtuous principle, seriously to consider that evidence, as there would be no occasion for, but for such temptation. And the supposed doubtfulness of its evidence, after it has been in some sort considered, affords opportunity to an unfair mind of explaining away, and deceitfully hiding from itself, that evidence which it might see; and also for men's encouraging themselves in vice, from hopes of impunity, though they do clearly see thus much at least, that these hopes are uncertain: in like manner as the common temptation to many instances of folly, which end in temporal infamy and ruin, is the ground for hope of not being detected, and of escaping with impunity; *i. e.* the doubtfulness of the proof beforehand, that such foolish behaviour will thus end in infamy and ruin. On the contrary, supposed doubtfulness in the evidence of religion calls for a more careful and attentive exercise of the virtuous principle, in fairly yielding themselves up to the proper influence of any real evidence, though doubtful; and in practising conscientiously all virtue, though under some uncertainty, whether the government in the universe may not possibly be such, as that vice may escape with impunity. And in general, temptation, meaning by this word the lesser allurements to wrong and difficulties in the discharge of our duty, as well as the greater ones; temptation, I say, as such and of every kind and degree, as it calls forth some virtuous efforts, additional to what would otherwise have been wanting, cannot but be an additional discipline and improvement of virtue, as well as probation of it in the other senses of that word.* So that the very same account is to be given, why the evidence of religion should be left in such a manner, as to require, in some, an attentive, solicitous, perhaps painful exercise of their understanding about it; as why others should be placed in such circumstances, as that the practice of its common

* Part I. Chap. iv. and pp. 133, 134.

duties, after a full conviction of the truth of it, should require attention, solicitude, and pains: or, why appearing doubtfulness should be permitted to afford matter of temptation to some; as why external difficulties and allurements should be permitted to afford matter of temptation to others. The same account also is to be given, why some should be exercised with temptations of both these kinds; as why others should be exercised with the latter in such very high degrees, as some have been, particularly as the primitive Christians were.

Nor does there appear any absurdity in supposing, that the speculative difficulties, in which the evidence of religion is involved, may make even the principal part of some persons' trial. For as the chief temptations of the generality of the world are the ordinary motives to injustice or unrestrained pleasure; or to live in the neglect of religion from that frame of mind, which renders many persons almost without feeling as to any thing distant, or which is not the object of their senses: so there are other persons without this shallowness of temper, persons of a deeper sense as to what is invisible and future; who not only see, but have a general practical feeling, that what is to come will be present, and that things are not less real for their not being the objects of sense; and who, from their natural constitution of body and of temper, and from their external condition, may have small temptations to behave ill, small difficulty in behaving well, in the common course of life. Now when these latter persons have a distinct full conviction of the truth of religion, without any possible doubts or difficulties, the practice of it is to them unavoidable, unless they will do a constant violence to their own minds; and religion is scarce any more a discipline to them, than it is to creatures in a state of perfection. Yet these persons may possibly stand in need of moral discipline and exercise in a higher degree, than they would have by such an easy practice of religion. Or it may be requisite, for reasons unknown to us, that they should give some further manifestation* what is their moral character, to the creation of God, than such a practice

* P. 133, 134.

of it would be. Thus in the great variety of religious situations in which men are placed, what constitutes, what chiefly and peculiarly constitutes, the probation, in all senses, of some persons, may be the difficulties in which the evidence of religion is involved: and their principal and distinguished trial may be, how they will behave under and with respect to these difficulties. Circumstances in men's situation in their temporal capacity, analogous in good measure to this respecting religion, are to be observed. We find some persons are placed in such a situation in the world, as that their chief difficulty with regard to conduct, is not the doing what is prudent when it is known; for this, in numberless cases, is as easy as the contrary: but to some the principal exercise is, recollection and being upon their guard against deceits, the deceits suppose of those about them; against false appearances of reason and prudence. To persons in some situations, the principal exercise with respect to conduct is, attention in order to inform themselves what is proper, what is really the reasonable and prudent part to act.

But as I have hitherto gone upon supposition, that men's dissatisfaction with the evidence of religion is not owing to their neglects or prejudices; it must be added, on the other hand, in all common reason, and as what the truth of the case plainly requires should be added, that such dissatisfaction possibly may be owing to those, possibly may be men's own fault. For,

If there are any persons, who never set themselves heartily and in earnest to be informed in religion; if there are any, who secretly wish it may not prove true; and are less attentive to evidence than to difficulties, and more to objections than to what is said in answer to them: these persons will scarce be thought in a likely way of seeing the evidence of religion, though it were most certainly true, and capable of being ever so fully proved. If any accustom themselves to consider this subject usually in the way of mirth and sport: if they attend to forms and representations, and inadequate manners of expression, instead of the real things intended by them: (for signs often can be no more than inadequately expressive of the things signified:) or if they substitute human errors in the room of divine truth; why may not all, or any of these things, hinder some men from seeing that evidence, which really is seen by others; as a like turn of mind, with respect to matters of common speculation and practice, does, we find by experience, hinder them from attaining that knowledge and right understanding, in matters of common speculation and practice, which more fair and attentive minds attain to? And the effect will be the same, whether their neglect of seriously considering the evidence of religion, and their indirect behaviour with regard to it, proceed from mere carelessness, or from the grosser vices; or whether it be owing to this, that forms and figurative manners of expression, as well as errors, administer occasions of ridicule, when the things intended, and the truth itself, would not. Men may indulge a ludicrous turn so far as to lose all sense of conduct and prudence in worldly affairs, and even, as it seems, to impair their faculty of reason. And in general, levity, carelessness, passion, and prejudice *do* hinder us from being rightly informed, with respect to common things: and they *may*, in like manner, and perhaps in some further providential manner, with respect to moral and religious subjects: may hinder evidence from being laid before us, and from being seen when it is. The Scripture* does declare, that every one *shall not understand.* And it makes no difference, by what providential conduct this comes to pass: whether the evidence of Christianity was, originally and with design, put and left so, as that those who are desirous of evading moral obligations should not see it; and that honest-minded persons should: or, whether it comes to pass by any other means.

Further: The general proof of natural religion and of

* Dan. xii. 10. See also Isa. xxix. 13, 14. Matth. vi. 23. and xi. 25. and xiii. 11, 12. John iii. 19. and v. 44. 1 Cor. ii. 14. and 2 Cor. iv. 4. 2 Tim. iii. 13. and that affectionate as well as authoritative admonition, so very many times inculcated, *He that hath ears to hear, let him hear.* Grotius saw so strongly the thing intended in these and other passages of Scripture of the like sense, as to say, that the proof given us of Christianity was less than it might have been, for this very purpose: *Ut ita sermo Evangelii tanquam lapis esset Lydius ad quem ingenia sanabilia explorarentur.* De Ver. R. C. lib. ii. towards the end.

Christianity does, I think, lie level to common men; even those, the greatest part of whose time, from childhood to old age, is taken up with providing for themselves and their families the common conveniences, perhaps necessaries, of life: those I mean, of this rank, who ever think at all of asking after proof, or attending to it. Common men, were they as much in earnest about religion, as about their temporal affairs, are capable of being convinced upon real evidence, that there is a God who governs the world: and they feel themselves to be of a moral nature, and accountable creatures. And as Christianity entirely falls in with this their natural sense of things, so they are capable, not only of being persuaded, but of being made to see, that there is evidence of miracles wrought in attestation of it, and many appearing completions of prophecy. But though this proof is real and conclusive, yet it is liable to objections, and may be run up into difficulties; which however persons who are capable not only of talking of, but of really seeing, are capable also of seeing through: *i. e.* not of clearing up and answering them, so as to satisfy their curiosity, for of such knowledge we are not capable with respect to any one thing in nature; but capable of seeing that the proof is not lost in these difficulties, or destroyed by these objections. But then a thorough examination into religion with regard to these objections, which cannot be the business of every man, is a matter of pretty large compass, and, from the nature of it, requires some knowledge, as well as time and attention; to see, how the evidence comes out, upon balancing one thing with another, and what, upon the whole, is the amount of it. Now if persons who have picked up these objections from others, and take for granted they are of weight, upon the word of those from whom they received them, or, by often retailing of them, come to see or fancy they see them to be of weight; will not prepare themselves for such an examination, with a competent degree of knowledge; or will not give that time and attention to the subject, which, from the nature of it, is necessary for attaining such information: in this case, they must remain in doubtfulness, ignorance, or error: in the same way as they must, with regard to common sciences, and matters of common life, if they neglect the necessary means of being informed in them.

But still perhaps it will be objected, that if a prince or common master were to send directions to a servant, he would take care, that they should always bear the certain marks, who they came from, and that their sense should be always plain: so as that there should be no possible doubt if he could help it, concerning the authority or meaning of them. Now the proper answer to all this kind of objections is, that, wherever the fallacy lies, it is even certain we cannot argue thus with respect to Him, who is the governor of the world: and particularly that he does not afford us such information, with respect to our temporal affairs and interests, as experience abundantly shows. However, there is a full answer to this objection, from the very nature of religion. For, the reason why a prince would give his directions in this plain manner is, that he absolutely desires such an external action should be done, without concerning himself with the motive or principle upon which it is done: *i. e.* he regards only the external event, or the thing's being done; and not at all, properly speaking, the doing of it, or the action. Whereas the whole of morality and religion consisting merely in action itself, there is no sort of parallel between the cases. But if the prince be supposed to regard only the action; *i. e.* only to desire to exercise, or in any sense prove, the understanding or loyalty of a servant; he would not always give his orders in such a plain manner. It may be proper to add, that the will of God, respecting morality and religion, may be considered either as absolute, or as only conditional. If it be absolute, it can only be thus, that we should act virtuously in such given circumstances; not that we should be brought to act so, by his changing of our circumstances. And if God's will be thus absolute, then it is in our power, in the highest and strictest sense, to do or to contradict his will; which is a most weighty consideration. Or his will may be considered only as conditional, that if we act so and so, we shall be rewarded; if otherwise, punished: of which conditional will of the Author of Nature, the whole constitution of it affords most certain instances.

Upon the whole: that we are in a state of religion necessarily implies, that we are in a state of probation: and the credibility of our being at all in such a state being admitted, there seems no peculiar difficulty in supposing our probation to be, just as it is, in those respects which are above objected against. There seems no pretence, from *the reason of the thing*, to say, that the trial cannot equitably be any thing, but whether persons will act suitably to certain information, or such as admits no room for doubt; so as that there can be no danger of miscarriage, but either from their not attending to what they certainly know, or from overbearing passion hurrying them on to act contrary to it. For, since ignorance and doubt afford scope for probation in all senses, as really as intuitive conviction or certainty; and since the two former are to be put to the same account as difficulties in practice; men's moral probation may also be, whether they will take due care to inform themselves by impartial consideration, and afterwards whether they will act as the case requires, upon the evidence which they have, however doubtful. And this, we find by *experience*, is frequently our probation,* in our temporal capacity. For, the information which we want with regard to our worldly interests is by no means always given us of course, without any care of our own. And we are greatly liable to self-deceit from inward secret prejudices, and also to the deceits of others. So that to be able to judge what is the prudent part, often requires much and difficult consideration. Then after we have judged the very best we can, the evidence upon which we must act, if we will live and act at all, is perpetually doubtful to a very high degree. And the constitution and course of the world in fact is such, as that want of impartial consideration what we have to do, and ventur ing upon extravagant courses because it is doubtful what will be the consequence, are often naturally, *i. e.* providentially, altogether as fatal, as misconduct occasioned

* P. 78, 234, &c.

by heedless inattention to what we certainly know, or disregarding it from overbearing passion.

Several of the observations here made may well seem strange, perhaps unintelligible, to many good men. But if the persons for whose sake they are made think so; persons who object as above, and throw off all regard to religion under pretence of want of evidence; I desire them to consider again, whether their thinking so be owing to any thing unintelligible in these observations, or to their own not having such a sense of religion and serious solicitude about it, as even their state of scepticism does in all reason require? It ought to be forced upon the reflection of these persons, that our nature and condition necessarily require us, in the daily course of life, to act upon evidence much lower than what is commonly called probable: to guard, not only against what we fully believe will, but also against what we think it supposable may, happen; and to engage in pursuits when the probability is greatly against success, if it be credible, that possibly we may succeed in them.

CHAP. VII.

OF THE PARTICULAR EVIDENCE FOR CHRISTIANITY.

THE presumptions against revelation, and objections against the general scheme of Christianity, and particular things relating to it, being removed; there remains to be considered, what positive evidence we have for the truth of it; chiefly in order to see, what the analogy of nature suggests with regard to that evidence, and the objections against it: or to see what is, and is allowed to be, the plain natural rule of judgment and of action, in our temporal concerns, in cases where we have the same kind of evidence, and the same kind of objections against it, that we have in the case before us.

Now in the evidence of Christianity there seem to be several things of great weight, not reducible to the head, either of miracles, or the completion of prophecy, in the common acceptation of the words. But these two are its direct and fundamental proofs: and those other things, however considerable they are, yet ought never to be urged apart from its direct proofs, but always to be joined with them. Thus the evidence of Christianity will be a long series of things, reaching, as it seems, from the beginning of the world to the present time, of great variety and compass, taking in both the direct and also the collateral proofs; and making up, all of them together, one argument: the conviction arising from which kind of proof may be compared to what they call *the effect* in architecture or other works of art; a result from a great number of things so and so disposed, and taken into one view. I shall therefore, *first,* make some observations relating to miracles, and the appearing completions of prophecy; and consider what analogy suggests, in answer to the objections brought against this evidence. And, *secondly,* I shall endeavour to give some account of the general argument now mentioned, consisting both of the direct and collateral evidence, considered as making up one argument: this being the kind of proof, upon which we determine most questions of difficulty, concerning common facts, alleged to have happened, or seeming likely to happen; especially questions relating to conduct.

First, I shall make some observations upon the direct proof of Christianity from miracles and prophecy, and upon the objections alleged against it.

I. Now the following observations relating to the historical evidence of miracles wrought in attestation of Christianity appear to be of great weight.

1. The Old Testament affords us the same historical evidence of the miracles of Moses and of the prophets, as of the common civil history of Moses and the kings of Israel; or, as of the affairs of the Jewish nation. And the *Gospels* and *the Acts* afford us the same historical evidence of the miracles of Christ and the Apostles, as of the common matters related in them. This indeed could not have been affirmed by any reasonable man, if the authors of these books, like many other historians, had appeared to make an entertaining manner of writing their aim; though they had interspersed miracles in

their works, at proper distances and upon proper occasions. These might have animated a dull relation, amused the reader, and engaged his attention. And the same account would naturally have been given of them, as of the speeches and descriptions of such authors: the same account, in a manner, as is to be given, why the poets make use of wonders and prodigies. But the facts, both miraculous and natural, in Scripture, are related in plain unadorned narratives: and both of them appear, in all respects, to stand upon the same foot of historical evidence. Further: some parts of Scripture, containing an account of miracles fully sufficient to prove the truth of Christianity, are quoted as genuine, from the age in which they are said to be written, down to the present: and no other parts of them, material in the present question, are omitted to be quoted in such manner, as to afford any sort of proof of their not being genuine. And, as common history, when called in question in any instance, may often be greatly confirmed by contemporary or subsequent events more known and acknowledged; and as the common Scripture history, like many others, is thus confirmed; so likewise is the miraculous history of it, not only in particular instances, but in general. For, the establishment of the Jewish and Christian religions, which were events contemporary with the miracles related to be wrought in attestation of both, or subsequent to them, these events are just what we should have expected, upon supposition such miracles were really wrought to attest the truth of those religions. These miracles are a satisfactory account of those events: of which no other satisfactory account can be given; nor any account at all, but what is imaginary merely, and invented. It is to be added, that the most obvious, the most easy and direct account of this history, how it came to be written and to be received in the world, as a true history, is, that it really is so: nor can any other account of it be easy and direct. Now, though an account, not at all obvious, but very far-fetched and indirect, may indeed be, and often is, the true account of a matter; yet it cannot be admitted on the authority of its being asserted. Mere guess, supposition, and possibility, when opposed to historical evidence, prove nothing, but that historical evidence is not demonstrative.

Now the just consequence from all this, I think, is, that the Scripture-history in general is to be admitted as an authentic genuine history, till somewhat positive be alleged sufficient to invalidate it. But no man will deny the consequence to be, that it cannot be rejected, or thrown by as of no authority, till it can be proved to be of none; even though the evidence now mentioned for its authority were doubtful. This evidence may be confronted by historical evidence on the other side, if there be any: or general incredibility in the things related, or inconsistence in the general turn of the history, would prove it to be of no authority. But since, upon the face of the matter, upon a first and general view, the appearance is, that it is an authentic history; it cannot be determined to be fictitious without some proof that it is so. And the following observations in support of these, and coincident with them, will greatly confirm the historical evidence for the truth of Christianity.

2. The Epistles of St Paul, from the nature of epistolary writing, and moreover from several of them being written, not to particular persons, but to churches, carry in them evidences of their being genuine, beyond what can be in a mere historical narrative, left to the world at large. This evidence, joined with that which they have in common with the rest of the New Testament, seems not to leave so much as any particular pretence for denying their genuineness, considered as an ordinary matter of fact, or of criticism: I say *particular* pretence, for *denying* it; because any single fact, of such a kind and such antiquity, may have *general doubts* raised concerning it, from the very nature of human affairs and human testimony. There is also to be mentioned a distinct and particular evidence of the genuineness of the epistle chiefly referred to here, the first to the Corinthians; from the manner in which it is quoted by Clemens Romanus, in an epistle of his own to that church.* Now these epistles afford a proof of Christianity, detached from all

* Clem. Rom. Ep. 1. c. 47.

others, which is, I think, a thing of weight; and also a proof of a nature and kind peculiar to itself. For,

In them the author declares, that he received the Gospel in general, and the institution of the Communion in particular, not from the rest of the Apostles, or jointly together with them, but alone, from Christ himself; whom he declares likewise, conformably to the history in the Acts, that he saw after his ascension.* So that the testimony of St Paul is to be considered, as detached from that of the rest of the Apostles.

And he declares further, that he was endued with a power of working miracles, as what was publicly known to those very people, speaks of frequent and great variety of miraculous gifts as then subsisting in those very churches, to which he was writing; which he was reproving for several irregularities; and where he had personal opposers: he mentions these gifts incidentally, in the most easy manner, and without effort; by way of reproof to those who had them, for their indecent use of them; and by way of depreciating them, in comparison of moral virtues: in short he speaks to these churches, of these miraculous powers, in the manner, any one would speak to another of a thing, which was as familiar and as much known in common to them both, as any thing in the world.† And this, as hath been observed by several persons, is surely a very considerable thing.

3. It is an acknowledged historical fact, that Christianity offered itself to the world, and demanded to be received, upon the allegation, *i. e.* as unbelievers would speak, upon the pretence, of miracles, publicly wrought to attest the truth of it, in such an age; and that it was actually received by great numbers in that very age, and upon the professed belief of the reality of these miracles. And Christianity, including the dispensation of the Old Testament, seems distinguished by this from all other religions. I mean, that this does not appear to be the case with regard to any other; for surely it will not be supposed to lie upon any person, to prove by positive

* Gal. i. 1 Cor. xi. 23, &c. 1 Cor. xv. 8.

† Rom. xv. 19. 1 Cor. xii. 8, 9, 10—28, &c. and xiii. 1, 2, 8. and the whole xivth chapter. 2 Cor. xii. 12. 13. Gal. iii. 2, 5.

historical evidence, that it was not. It does in no sort appear that Mahometanism was first received in the world upon the foot of supposed miracles,* *i. e.* public ones: for, as revelation is itself miraculous, all pretence to it must necessarily imply some pretence of miracles. And it is a known fact, that it was immediately, at the very first, propagated by other means. And as particular institutions, whether in Paganism or Popery, said to be confirmed by miracles after those institutions had obtained, are not to the purpose: so, were there what might be called historical proof, that any of them were introduced by a supposed divine command, believed to be attested by miracles; these would not be in any wise parallel. For single things of this sort are easy to be accounted for, after parties are formed, and have power in their hands; and the leaders of them are in veneration with the multitude; and political interests are blended with religious claims, and religious distinctions. But before any thing of this kind, for a few persons, and those of the lowest rank, all at once, to bring over such great numbers to a new religion, and get it to be received upon the particular evidence of miracles; this is quite another thing. And I think it will be allowed by any fair adversary, that the fact now mentioned, taking in all the circumstances of it, is peculiar to the Christian religion. However, the fact itself is allowed, that Christianity obtained, *i. e.* was professed to be received in the world, upon the belief of miracles, immediately in the age in which it is said those miracles were wrought: or that this is what its first converts would have alleged, as the reason for their embracing it. Now certainly it is not to be supposed that such numbers of men, in the most distant parts of the world should forsake the religion of their country, in which they had been educated; separate themselves from their friends, particularly in their festival shows and solemnities, to which the common people are so greatly addicted, and which were of a nature to engage them much more, than any thing of that sort amongst us; and embrace a religion, which could not but expose them to many inconveniences, and in-

* See the Koran, c. xiii. and c. xvii.

deed must have been a giving up the world in a great degree, even from the very first, and before the empire engaged in form against them: it cannot be supposed, that such numbers should make so great, and, to say the least, so inconvenient a change in their whole institution of life, unless they were really convinced of the truth of those miracles, upon the knowledge or belief of which they professed to make it. And it will, I suppose, readily be acknowledged, that the generality of the first converts to Christianity must have believed them: that as by becoming Christians they declared to the world, they were satisfied of the truth of those miracles; so this declaration was to be credited. And this their testimony is the same kind of evidence for those miracles, as if they had put it in writing, and these writings had come down to us. And it is real evidence, because it is of facts, which they had capacity and full opportunity to inform themselves of. It is also distinct from the direct or express historical evidence, though it is of the same kind: and it would be allowed to be distinct in all cases. For were a fact expressly related by one or more ancient historians, and disputed in after ages; that this fact is acknowledged to have been believed by great numbers of the age in which the historian says it was done, would be allowed an additional proof of such fact, quite distinct from the express testimony of the historian. The credulity of mankind is acknowledged: and the suspicions of mankind ought to be acknowledged too; and their backwardness even to believe, and greater still to practise, what makes against their interest. And it must particularly be remembered, that education, and prejudice, and authority, were against Christianity, in the age I am speaking of. So that the immediate conversion of such numbers is a real presumption of somewhat more than human in this matter: I say presumption, for it is not alleged as a proof alone and by itself. Nor need any one of the things mentioned in this Chapter be considered as a proof by itself: and yet all of them together may be one of the strongest.*

Upon the whole: as there is large historical evidence,

* P. 273, &c.

both direct and circumstantial, of miracles wrought in attestation of Christianity, collected by those who have writ upon the subject; it lies upon unbelievers to show, why this evidence is not to be credited. This way of speaking is, I think, just; and what persons who write in defence of religion naturally fall into. Yet, in a matter of such unspeakable importance, the proper question is, not whom it lies upon, according to the rules of argument, to maintain or confute objections: but whether there really are any, against this evidence, sufficient, in reason, to destroy the credit of it. However, unbelievers seem to take upon them the part of showing that there are.

They allege, that numberless enthusiastic people, in different ages and countries, expose themselves to the same difficulties which the primitive Christians did; and are ready to give up their lives for the most idle follies imaginable. But it is not very clear, to what purpose this objection is brought. For every one, surely, in every case, must distinguish between opinions and facts. And though testimony is no proof of enthusiastic opinions, or of any opinions at all; yet it is allowed, in all other cases, to be a proof of facts. And a person's laying down his life in attestation of facts or of opinions, is the strongest proof of his believing them. And if the Apostles and their contemporaries did believe the facts, in attestation of which they exposed themselves to sufferings and death; this their belief, or rather knowledge, must be a proof of those facts: for they were such as came under the observation of their senses. And though it is not of equal weight, yet it is of weight, that the martyrs of the next age, notwithstanding they were not eye-witnesses of those facts, as were the Apostles and their contemporaries, had, however, full opportunity to inform themselves, whether they were true or not, and gave equal proof of their believing them to be true.

But enthusiasm, it is said, greatly weakens the evidence of testimony even for facts, in matters relating to religion: some seem to think it totally and absolutely destroys the evidence of testimony upon this subject. And indeed the powers of enthusiasm, and of diseases too, which operate in a like manner, are very wonderful, in particular instances. But if great numbers of men, not appearing in any peculiar degree weak, nor under any peculiar suspicion of negligence, affirm that they saw and heard such things plainly with their eyes and their ears, and are admitted to be in earnest; such testimony is evidence of the strongest kind we can have, for any matter of fact. Yet possibly it may be overcome, strong as it is, by incredibility in the things thus attested, or by contrary testimony. And in an instance where one thought it was so overcome, it might be just to consider, how far such evidence could be accounted for, by enthusiasm; for it seems as if no other imaginable account were to be given of it. But till such incredibility be shown, or contrary testimony produced, it cannot surely be expected, that so far-fetched, so indirect and wonderful an account of such testimony, as that of enthusiasm must be; an account so strange, that the generality of mankind can scarce be made to understand what is meant by it: it cannot, I say, be expected, that such account will be admitted of such evidence; when there is this direct, easy, and obvious account of it, that people really saw and heard a thing not incredible, which they affirm sincerely and with full assurance, they did see and hear. Granting then that enthusiasm is not (strictly speaking) an absurd, but a possible account of such testimony; it is manifest, that the very mention of it goes upon the previous supposition, that the things so attested are incredible: and therefore need not be considered, till they are shown to be so. Much less need it be considered, after the contrary has been proved. And I think it has been proved, to full satisfaction, that there is no incredibility in a revelation, in general; or in such a one as the Christian, in particular. However, as religion is supposed peculiarly liable to enthusiasm, it may just be observed, that prejudices almost without number, and without name, romance, affectation, humour, a desire to engage attention, or to surprise, the party spirit, custom, little competitions, unaccountable likings and dislikings; these influence men strongly in common matters. And as these prejudices are often scarce known or reflected upon by the persons themselves who are influenced by them, they are to be considered as influences of a like kind to enthusiasm. Yet human testimony in common matters is naturally and justly believed notwithstanding.

It is intimated further, in a more refined way of observation, that though it should be proved, that the Apostles and first Christians could not, in some respects, be deceived themselves, and, in other respects, cannot be thought to have intended to impose upon the world; yet it will not follow, that their general testimony is to be believed, though truly handed down to us: because they might still in part, *i. e.* in other respects, be deceived themselves, and in part also designedly impose upon others; which, it is added, is a thing very credible, from that mixture of real enthusiasm, and real knavery, to be met with in the same characters. And, I must confess, I think the matter of fact contained in this observation upon mankind is not to be denied; and that somewhat very much akin to it is often supposed in Scripture as a very common case, and most severely reproved. But it were to have been expected, that persons capable of applying this observation as applied in the objection, might also frequently have met with the like mixed character, in instances where religion was quite out of the case. The thing plainly is, that mankind are naturally endued with reason, or a capacity of distinguishing between truth and falsehood; and as naturally they are endued with veracity, or a regard to truth in what they say: but from many occasions they are liable to be prejudiced and biassed and deceived themselves, and capable of intending to deceive others, in every degree: insomuch that, as we are all liable to be deceived by prejudice, so likewise it seems to be not an uncommon thing, for persons, who, from their regard to truth, would not invent a lie entirely without any foundation at all, to propagate it with heightening circumstances, after it is once invented and set agoing. And others, though they would not *propagate* a lie, yet, which is a lower degree of falsehood, will let it pass without contradiction. But, notwithstanding all this, human testimony remains still a natural ground of assent; and this assent a natural principle of action.

It is objected further, that however it has happened, the *fact* is, that mankind have, in different ages, been strangely deluded with pretences to miracles and wonders. But it is by no means to be admitted, that they have been oftener, or are at all more liable to be deceived by these pretences, than by others.

It is added, that there is a very considerable degree of historical evidence for miracles, which are, on all hands, acknowledged to be fabulous. But suppose there were even *the like* historical evidence for these, to what there is for those alleged in proof of Christianity, which yet is in no wise allowed, but suppose this; the consequence would not be, that the evidence of the latter is not to be admitted. Nor is there a man in the world, who, in common cases, would conclude thus. For what would such a conclusion really amount to but this, that evidence, confuted by contrary evidence, or any way overbalanced, destroys the credibility of other evidence, neither confuted, nor overbalanced? To argue, that because there is, if there were, like evidence from testimony, for miracles acknowledged false, as for those in attestation of Christianity, therefore the evidence in the latter case is not to be credited; this is the same as to argue, that if two men of equally good reputation had given evidence in different cases no way connected, and one of them had been convicted of perjury, this confuted the testimony of the other.

Upon the whole then, the general observation, that human creatures are so liable to be deceived, from enthusiasm in religion, and principles equivalent to enthusiasm in common matters, and in both from negligence; and that they are so capable of dishonestly endeavouring to deceive others; this does indeed weaken the evidence of testimony in all cases, but does not destroy it in any. And these things will appear, to different men, to weaken the evidence of testimony, in different degrees: in degrees proportionable to the observations they have made, or the notions they have any way taken up, concerning the weakness and negligence and dishonesty of man.

kind; or concerning the powers of enthusiasm, and prejudices equivalent to it. But it seems to me, that people do not know what they say, who affirm these things to destroy the evidence from testimony, which we have of the truth of Christianity. Nothing can destroy the evidence of testimony in any case, but a proof or probability, that persons are not competent judges of the facts to which they give testimony; or that they are actually under some indirect influence in giving it, in such particular case. Till this be made out, the *natural* laws of human actions require, that testimony be admitted. It can never be sufficient to overthrow direct historical evidence, indolently to say, that there are so many principles, from whence men are liable to be deceived themselves, and disposed to deceive others, especially in matters of religion, that one knows not what to believe. And it is surprising persons can help reflecting, that this very manner of speaking supposes they are not satisfied that there is nothing in the evidence, of which they speak thus; or that they can avoid observing, if they do make this reflection, that it is on such a subject, a very material one.*

And over against all these objections is to be set the importance of Christianity, as what must have engaged the attention of its first converts, so as to have rendered them less liable to be deceived from carelessness, than they would in common matters; and likewise the strong obligations to veracity, which their religion laid them under: so that the first and most obvious presumption is, that they could not be deceived themselves nor deceive others. And this presumption, in this degree, is peculiar to the testimony we have been considering.

In argument, assertions are nothing in themselves, and have an air of positiveness which sometimes is not very easy: yet they are necessary, and necessary to be repeated; in order to connect a discourse, and distinctly to lay before the view of the reader, what is proposed to be proved, and what is left as proved. Now the conclusion from the foregoing observations is, I think, beyond all doubt, this: that unbelievers must be forced to admit

* See the foregoing Chapter.

the external evidence for Christianity, *i. e.* the proof of miracles wrought to attest it, to be of real weight and very considerable ; though they cannot allow it to be sufficient, to convince them of the reality of those miracles. And as they must, in all reason, admit this ; so it seems to me, that upon consideration they would, in fact, admit it ; those of them, I mean, who know any thing at all of the matter ; in like manner as persons, in many cases, own they see strong evidence from testimony, for the truth of things, which yet they cannot be convinced are true : cases, suppose, where there is contrary testimony ; or things which they think, whether with or without reason, to be incredible. But there is no testimony contrary to that which we have been considering : and it has been fully proved, that there is no incredibility in Christianity in general, or in any part of it.

II. As to the evidence for Christianity from prophecy, I shall only make some few general observations, which are suggested by the Analogy of Nature ; *i. e.* by the acknowledged natural rules of judging in common matters, concerning evidence of a like kind to this from prophecy.

1. The obscurity or unintelligibleness of one part of a prophecy does not, in any degree, invalidate the proof of foresight, arising from the appearing completion of those other parts, which are understood. For the case is evidently the same, as if those parts, which are not understood, were lost, or not written at all, or written in an unknown tongue. Whether this observation be commonly attended to or not, it is so evident, that one can scarce bring oneself to set down an instance in common matters, to exemplify it. However, suppose a writing, partly in cipher, and partly in plain words at length ; and that in the part one understood, there appeared mention of several known facts ; it would never come into any man's thoughts to imagine, that if he understood the whole, perhaps he might find, that those facts were not in reality known by the writer. Indeed, both in this example and the thing intended to be exemplified by it, our not understanding the whole (the whole, suppose, of a sentence or a paragraph) might sometimes occasion a doubt, whether

one understood the literal meaning of such a part: but this comes under another consideration.

For the same reason, though a man should be incapable, for want of learning, or opportunities of inquiry, or from not having turned his studies this way, even so much as to judge whether particular prophecies have been throughout completely fulfilled; yet he may see, in general, that they have been fulfilled to such a degree, as, upon very good ground, to be convinced of foresight more than human in such prophecies, and of such events being intended by them. For the same reason also, though, by means of the deficiencies in civil history, and the different accounts of historians, the most learned should not be able to make out to satisfaction, that such parts of the prophetic history have been minutely and throughout fulfilled; yet a very strong proof of foresight may arise, from that general completion of them, which is made out: as much proof of foresight, perhaps, as the giver of prophecy intended should ever be afforded by such parts of prophecy.

2. A long series of prophecy being applicable to such and such events, is itself a proof that it was intended of them: as the rules by which we naturally judge and determine, in common cases parallel to this, will show. This observation I make in answer to the common objection against the application of the prophecies, that, considering each of them distinctly by itself, it does not at all appear, that they were intended of those particular events, to which they are applied by Christians; and therefore it is to be supposed, that, if they meant any thing, they were intended of other events unknown to us, and not of these at all.

Now there are two kinds of writing, which bear a great resemblance to prophecy, with respect to the matter before us: the mythological, and the satirical, where the satire is, to a certain degree, concealed. And a man might be assured, that he understood what an author intended by a fable or parable related without any application or moral, merely from seeing it to be easily capable of such application, and that such a moral might naturally be deduced from it. And he might be fully assured, that such persons and events were intended in a satirical writing, merely from its being applicable to them. And, agreeable to the last observation, he might be in a good measure satisfied of it, though he were not enough informed in affairs, or in the story of such persons to understand half the satire. For, his satisfaction, that he understood the meaning, the intended meaning, of these writings, would be greater or less in proportion as he saw the general turn of them to be capable of such application; and in proportion to the number of particular things capable of it. And thus, if a long series of prophecy is applicable to the present state of the church, and to the political situations of the kingdoms of the world, some thousand years after these prophecies were delivered, and a long series of prophecy delivered before the coming of Christ is applicable to him; these things are in themselves a proof, that the prophetic history was intended of him, and of those events: in proportion as the general turn of it is capable of such application, and to the number and variety of particular prophecies capable of it. And though, in all just way of consideration, the appearing completion of prophecies is to be allowed to be thus explanatory of, and to determine, their meaning; yet it is to be remembered further, that the ancient Jews applied the prophecies to a Messiah before his coming, in much the same manner as Christians do now: and that the primitive Christians interpreted the prophecies respecting the state of the church and of the world in the last ages, in the sense which the event seems to confirm and verify. And from these things it may be made appear:

3. That the showing even to a high probability, if that could be, that the prophets thought of some other events, in such and such predictions, and not those at all which Christians allege to be completions of those predictions; or that such and such prophecies are capable of being applied to other events than those, to which Christians apply them—that this would not confute or destroy the force of the argument from prophecy, even with regard to those very instances. For, observe how

this matter really is. If one knew such a person to be the sole author of such a book, and was certainly assured, or satisfied to any degree, that one knew the whole of what he intended in it; one should be assured or satisfied to such degree, that one knew the whole meaning of that book: for the meaning of a book is nothing but the meaning of the author. But if one knew a person to have compiled a book out of memoirs, which he received from another, of vastly superior knowledge in the subject of it, especially if it were a book full of great intricacies and difficulties; it would in no wise follow, that one knew the whole meaning of the book, from knowing the whole meaning of the compiler: for the original memoirs, *i. e.* the author of them, might have, and there would be no degree of presumption, in many cases, against supposing him to have, some further meaning than the compiler saw. To say then, that the Scriptures, and the things contained in them, can have no other or further meaning than those persons thought or had, who first recited or wrote them, is evidently saying, that those persons were the original, proper, and sole authors of those books, *i. e.* that they are not inspired: which is absurd, whilst the authority of these books is under examination; *i. e.* till you have determined they are of no divine authority at all. Till this be determined, it must in all reason be supposed, not indeed that they have, for this is taking for granted that they are inspired; but that they may have, some further meaning than what the compilers saw or understood. And, upon this supposition, it is supposable also, that this further meaning may be fulfilled. Now events corresponding to prophecies, interpreted in a different meaning from that, in which the prophets are supposed to have understood them; this affords, in a manner, the same proof, that this different sense was originally intended, as it would have afforded, if the prophets had not understood their predictions in the sense it is supposed they did because there is no presumption of their sense of them being the whole sense of them. And it has been already shown, that the apparent completions of prophecy must be allowed to be explanatory of its meaning. So that the question is, whether a series of prophecy has been fulfilled, in a natural or proper, *i. e.* in any real sense of the words of it. For such completion is equally a proof of foresight more than human, whether the prophets are, or are not, supposed to have understood it in a different sense. I say, supposed: for, though I think it clear, that the prophets did not understand the full meaning of their predictions; it is another question, how far they thought they did, and in what sense they understood them.

Hence may be seen, to how little purpose those persons busy themselves, who endeavour to prove, that the prophetic history is applicable to events of the age in which it was written, or of ages before it. Indeed to have proved this, before there was any appearance of a further completion of it, might have answered some purpose; for it might have prevented the expectation of any such further completion. Thus could Porphyry have shown, that some principal parts of the book of Daniel for instance, the seventh verse of the seventh chapter, which the Christians interpreted of the latter ages, was applicable to events, which happened before or about the age of Antiochus Epiphanes; this might have prevented them from expecting any further completion of it. And, unless there was then, as I think there must have been, external evidence concerning that book, more than is come down to us; such a discovery might have been a stumbling-block in the way of Christianity itself: considering the authority which our Saviour has given to the book of Daniel, and how much the general scheme of Christianity presupposes the truth of it. But even this discovery, had there been any such,* would be of very little weight with reasonable men now; if this passage, thus applicable to events before the age of Porphyry, appears to be applicable also to events, which succeeded the dissolution of the Roman empire. I

* It appears that Porphyry did nothing worth mentioning in this way. For Jerome on the place says: *Duas posteriores bestias—in uno Macedonum regno ponit.* And as to the ten kings; *Decem reges enumerat, qui fuerunt sævissimi: ipsosque reges non unius ponit regni, verbi gratia, Macedoniæ, Syriæ, Asiæ, et Ægypti; sed de diversis regnis unum efficit regum ordinem.* And in this way of interpretation, any thing may be made of any thing.

mention this, not at all as intending to insinuate, that the division of this empire into ten parts, for it plainly was divided into about that number, were, alone and by itself, of any moment in verifying the prophetic history: but only as an example of the thing I am speaking of. And thus upon the whole, the matter of inquiry evidently must be, as above put, Whether the prophecies are applicable to Christ, and to the present state of the world, and of the church; applicable in such a degree, as to imply foresight: not whether they are capable of any other application; though I know no pretence for saying the general turn of them is capable of any other.

These observations are, I think, just; and the evidence referred to in them real: though there may be people who will not accept of such imperfect imformation from Scripture. Some too have not integrity and regard enough to truth, to attend to evidence, which keeps the mind in doubt, perhaps perplexity, and which is much of a different sort from what they expected. And it plainly requires a degree of modesty and fairness, beyond what every one has, for a man to say, not to the world, but to himself, that there is a real appearance of somewhat of great weight in this matter, though he is not able thoroughly to satisfy himself about it; but it shall have its influence upon him, in proportion to its appearing reality and weight. It is much more easy, and more falls in with the negligence, presumption, and wilfulness of the generality, to determine at once, with a decisive air, There is nothing in it. The prejudices arising from that absolute contempt and scorn, with which this evidence is treated in the world, I do not mention. For what indeed can be said to persons, who are weak enough in their understandings to think this any presumption against it; or, if they do not, are yet weak enough in their temper to be influenced by such prejudices, upon such a subject?

I shall now, *Secondly*, endeavour to give some account of the general argument for the truth of Christianity, consisting both of the direct and circumstantial evidence considered as making up one argument. Indeed to state and examine this argument fully, would be a work much beyond the compass of this whole treatise; nor is so much as a proper abridgment of it to be expected here. Yet the present subject requires to have some brief account of it given. For it is the kind of evidence, upon which most questions of difficulty, in common practice, are determined: evidence arising from various coincidences, which support and confirm each other, and in this manner prove, with more or less certainty, the point under consideration. And I choose to do it also: First, because it seems to be of the greatest importance, and not duly attended to by every one, that the proof of revelation is, not some direct and express things only, but a great variety of circumstantial things also; and that though each of these direct and circumstantial things is indeed to be considered separately, yet they are afterwards to be joined together; for that the proper force of the evidence consists in the result of those several things, considered in their respects to each other, and united into one view: and in the next place, because it seems to me, that the matters of fact here set down, which are acknowledged by unbelievers, must be acknowledged by them also to contain together a degree of evidence of great weight, if they could be brought to lay these several things before themselves distinctly, and then with attention consider them together; instead of that cursory thought of them, to which we are familiarized. For being familiarized to the cursory thought of things as really hinders the weight of them from being seen, as from having its due influence upon practice.

The thing asserted, and the truth of which is to be inquired into, is this: That over and above our reason and affections, which God has given us for the information of our judgment and the conduct of our lives, he has also, by external revelation, given us an account of himself and his moral government over the world, implying a future state of rewards and punishments; *i.e.* hath revealed the system of natural religion: for natural religion may be externally* revealed by God, as the ignorant may be taught it by mankind, their fellow creatures—that God, I say, has given us the evidence of revelation, as

* P. 166, &c.

well as the evidence of reason, to ascertain this moral system; together with an account of a particular dispensation of Providence, which reason could no way have discovered, and a particular institution of religion founded on it, for the recovery of mankind out of their present wretched condition, and raising them to the perfection and final happiness of their nature.

This revelation, whether real or supposed, may be considered as wholly historical. For prophecy is nothing but the history of events before they come to pass; doctrines also are matters of fact; and precepts come under the same notion. And the general design of Scripture, which contains in it this revelation, thus considered as historical, may be said to be, to give us an account of the world, in this one single view, as God's world: by which it appears essentially distinguished from all other books, so far as I have found, except such as are copied from it. It begins with an account of God's creation of the world, in order to ascertain, and distinguish from all others, who is the object of our worship, by what he has done: in order to ascertain, who he is, concerning whose providence, commands, promises, and threatenings, this sacred book, all along, treats; the Maker and Proprietor of the world, he whose creatures we are, the God of Nature: in order likewise to distinguish him from the idols of the nations, which are either imaginary beings, *i. e.* no beings at all; or else part of that creation, the historical relation of which is here given. And St John, not improbably, with an eye to this Mosaic account of the creation, begins his Gospel with an account of our Saviour's pre-existence, and that *all things were made by him; and without him was not any thing made that was made:** agreeably to the doctrine of St Paul, that *God created all things by Jesus Christ.*† This being premised, the Scripture, taken together, seems to profess to contain a kind of an abridgment of the history of the world, in the view just now mentioned: that is, a general account of the condition of religion and its professors, during the continuance of that apostasy from God, and state of wickedness, which it every where supposes the world

* John i. 3. † Eph. iii. 9.

to lie in. And this account of the state of religion carries with it some brief account of the political state of things, as religion is affected by it. Revelation indeed considers the common affairs of this world, and what is going on in it, as a mere scene of distraction; and cannot be supposed to concern itself with foretelling at what time Rome, or Babylon, or Greece, or any particular place, should be the most conspicuous seat of that tyranny and dissoluteness, which all places equally aspire to be; cannot, I say, be supposed to give any account of this wild scene for its own sake. But it seems to contain some very general account of the chief governments of the world, as the general state of religion has been, is, or shall be, affected by them, from the first transgression, and during the whole interval of the world's continuing in its present state, to a certain future period, spoken of both in the Old and New Testament, very distinctly, and in great variety of expression: *The times of the restitution of all things:** when *the mystery of God shall be finished, as he hath declared to his servants the prophets:*† when *the God of heaven shall set up a kingdom, which shall never be destroyed: and the kingdom shall not be left to other people,*‡ as it is represented to be during this apostasy, but *judgment shall be given to the saints,*§ and *they shall reign:*‖ *and the kingdom and dominion, and the greatness of the kingdom under the whole heaven, shall be given to the people of the saints of the Most High.*¶

Upon this general view of the Scripture, I would remark, how great a length of time the whole relation takes up, near six thousand years of which are past; and how great a variety of things it treats of; the natural and moral system or history of the world, including the time when it was formed, all contained in the very first book, and evidently written in a rude and unlearned age; and in subsequent books, the various common and prophetic history, and the particular dispensation of Christianity. Now all this together gives the largest scope for criticism; and for confutation of what is capable of being confuted, either from reason, or from common history, or from any

* Acts iii. 21. † Rev. x. 7. ‡ Dan. ii. 44.
§ Dan. vii. 22. ‖ Rev. xi. 17, 18. xx. 6. ¶ Dan. vii. 27.

inconsistence in its several parts. And it is a thing which deserves, I think, to be mentioned, that whereas some imagine the supposed doubtfulness of the evidence for revelation implies a positive argument that it is not true; it appears, on the contrary, to imply a positive argument that it is true. For, could any common relation of such antiquity, extent, and variety (for in these things the stress of what I am now observing lies), be proposed to the examination of the world: that it could not, in an age of knowledge and liberty, be confuted, or shown to have nothing in it, to the satisfaction of reasonable men; this would be thought a strong presumptive proof of its truth. And indeed it must be a proof of it, just in proportion to the probability, that if it were false, it might be shown to be so: and this, I think, is scarce pretended to be shown, but upon principles and in ways of arguing, which have been clearly obviated.* Nor does it at all appear, that any set of men, who believe natural religion, are of the opinion, that Christianity has been thus confuted. But to proceed:

Together with the moral system of the world, the Old Testament contains a chronological account of the beginning of it, and from thence, an unbroken genealogy of mankind for many ages before common history begins; and carried on as much farther as to make up a continued thread of history of the length of between three and four thousand years. It contains an account of God's making a covenant with a particular nation, that they should be his people, and he would be their God, in a peculiar sense; of his often interposing miraculously in their affairs; giving them the promise, and, long after, the possession, of a particular country; assuring them of the greatest national prosperity in it, if they would worship him, in opposition to the idols which the rest of the world worshipped, and obey his commands; and threatening them with unexampled punishments if they disobeyed him, and fell into the general idolatry: insomuch that this one nation should continue to be the observation and the wonder of all the world. It declares particularly, that *God would scatter them among all people,*

* Ch. ii. iii. &c.

from one end of the earth unto the other; but that *when they should return unto the Lord their God, he would have compassion upon them, and gather them from all the nations, whither he had scattered them:* that *Israel should be saved in the Lord, with an everlasting salvation; and not be ashamed or confounded world without end.* And as some of these promises are conditional, others are as absolute, as any thing can be expressed: that the time should come, when *the people should be all righteous, and inherit the land for ever:* that *though God would make a full end of all nations whither he had scattered them, yet would he not make a full end of them:* that *he would bring again the captivity of his people Israel, and plant them upon their land, and they should be no more pulled up out of their land:* that *the seed of Israel should not cease from being a nation for ever.** It foretells, that God would raise them up a particular person, in whom all his promises should finally be fulfilled; the Messiah, who should be, in a high and eminent sense, their anointed Prince and Saviour. This was foretold in such a manner, as raised a general expectation of such a person in the nation, as appears from the New Testament, and is an acknowledged fact; an expectation of his coming at such a particular time, before any one appeared claiming to be that person, and when there was no ground for such an expectation, but from the prophecies: which expectation, therefore, must in all reason be presumed to be explanatory of those prophecies, if there were any doubt about their meaning. It seems moreover to foretell, that this person should be rejected by that nation, to whom he had been so long promised, and though he was so much desired by them.† And it expressly foretells, that he should be the Saviour of the Gentiles; and even that the completion of the scheme contained in this book, and then begun, and in its progress, should be somewhat so great, that in comparison with it, the restoration of the Jews alone would be but of small account. *It is a light thing that thou shouldest be my servant to raise up the*

* Deut. xxviii. 64. xxx. 2, 3. Is. xlv. 17. lx. 21. Jer. xxx. 11. xlvi. 28. Amos ix. 14, 15. Jer. xxxi. 36.

† Is. viii 14, 15. xlix 5 ch. liii. Mal. i. 10, 11. and ch. iii.

tribes of Jacob, and to restore the preserved of Israel: I will also give thee for a light to the Gentiles, that thou mayest be for salvation unto the end of the earth. And, *In the last days, the mountain of the Lord's house shall be established in the top of the mountains, and shall be exalted above the hills; and all nations shall flow into it—for out of Zion shall go forth the law, and the word of the Lord from Jerusalem. And he shall judge among the nations—and the Lord alone shall be exalted in that day, and the idols he shall utterly abolish.** The Scripture further contains an account, that at the time the Messiah was expected, a person rose up in this nation, claiming to be that Messiah, to be the person whom all the prophecies referred to, and in whom they should centre: that he spent some years in a continued course of miraculous works; and endued his immediate disciples and followers with a power of doing the same, as a proof of the truth of that religion, which he commissioned them to publish: that, invested with this authority and power, they made numerous converts in the remotest countries, and settled and established his religion in the world; to the end of which the Scripture professes to give a prophetic account of the state of this religion amongst mankind.

Let us now suppose a person utterly ignorant of history, to have all this related to him out of the Scripture. Or suppose such a one, having the Scripture put into his hands, to remark these things in it, not knowing but that the whole, even its civil history, as well as the other parts of it, might be, from beginning to end, an entire invention; and to ask, What truth was in it, and whether the revelation here related was real, or a fiction? And, instead of a direct answer, suppose him, all at once, to be told the following confessed facts; and then to unite them into one view.

Let him first be told, in how great a degree the profession and establishment of natural religion, the belief that there is one God to be worshipped, that virtue is his law, and that mankind shall be rewarded and punished

* Is. xlix. 6. chap. ii. chap. xi. chap. lvi. 7. Mal. i. 11. To which must be added, the other prophecies of the like kind, several in the New Testament, and very many in the Old: which describe what shall be the completion of the revealed plan of Providence.

hereafter, as they obey and disobey it here; in how very great a degree, I say, the profession and establishment of this moral system in the world is owing to the revelation, whether real or supposed, contained in this book: the establishment of this moral system, even in those countries which do not acknowledge the proper authority of the Scripture.* Let him be told also, what number of nations do acknowledge its proper authority. Let him then take in the consideration, of what importance religion is to mankind. And upon these things he might, I think, truly observe, that this supposed revelation's obtaining and being received in the world, with all the circumstances and effects of it, considered together as one event, is the most conspicuous and important event in the history of mankind: that a book of this nature, and thus promulged and recommended to our consideration, demands, as if by a voice from heaven, to have its claims most seriously examined into: and that, before such examination, to treat it with any kind of scoffing and ridicule, is an offence against natural piety. But it is to be remembered, that how much soever the establishment of natural religion in the world is owing to the Scripture revelation, this does not destroy the proof of religion from reason, any more than the proof of Euclid's Elements is destroyed, by a man's knowing or thinking, that he should never have seen the truth of the several propositions contained in it, nor had those propositions come into his thoughts, but for that mathematician.

Let such a person as we are speaking of be, in the next place, informed of the acknowledged antiquity of the first parts of this book; and that its chronology, its account of the time when the earth, and the several parts of it, were first peopled with human creatures, is no way contradicted, but is really confirmed, by the natural and civil history of the world, collected from common historians, from the state of the earth, and from the late invention of arts and sciences. And as the Scripture contains an unbroken thread of common and civil history, from the creation to the captivity, for between three and four thousand years; let the person we are speaking of

* P. 228

be told, in the next place, that this general history, as it is not contradicted, but is confirmed by profane history as much as there would be reason to expect, upon supposition of its truth; so there is nothing in the whole history *itself*, to give any reasonable ground of suspicion of its not being, in the general, a faithful and literally true genealogy of men, and series of things. I speak here only of the common Scripture-history, or of the course of ordinary events related in it, as distinguished from miracles, and from the prophetic history. In all the Scripture-narrations of this kind, following events arise out of foregoing ones, as in all other histories. There appears nothing related as done in any age, not conformable to the manners of that age: nothing in the account of a succeeding age, which, one would say, could not be true, or was improbable, from the account of things in the preceding one. There is nothing in the characters, which would raise a thought of their being feigned; but all the internal marks imaginable of their being real. It is to be added also, that mere genealogies, bare narratives of the number of years, which persons called by such and such names lived, do not carry the face of fiction; perhaps do carry some presumption of veracity: and all unadorned narratives, which have nothing to surprise, may be thought to carry somewhat of the like presumption too. And the domestic and the political history is plainly credible. There may be incidents in Scripture, which, taken alone in the naked way they are told, may appear strange; especially to persons of other manners, temper, education: but there are also incidents of undoubted truth, in many or most persons' lives, which, in the same circumstances, would appear to the full as strange. There may be mistakes of transcribers, there may be other real or seeming mistakes, not easy to be particularly accounted for: but there are certainly no more things of this kind in the Scripture, than what were to have been expected in books of such antiquity; and nothing, in any wise, sufficient to discredit the general narrative. Now, that a history, claiming to commence from the creation, and extending in one continued series, through so great a length of time, and variety of events, should have such appearances of reality and truth in its whole contexture, is surely a very remarkable circumstance in its favour. And as all this is applicable to the common history of the New Testament, so there is a further credibility, and a very high one, given to it by profane authors: many of these writing of the same times, and confirming the truth of customs and events, which are incidentally as well as more purposely mentioned in it. And this credibility of the common Scripture-history, gives some credibility to its miraculous history: especially as this is interwoven with the common, so as that they imply each other, and both together make up one relation.

Let it then be more particularly observed to this person, that it is an acknowledged matter of fact, which is indeed implied in the foregoing observation, that there was such a nation as the Jews, of the greatest antiquity, whose government and general polity was founded on the law, here related to be given them by Moses as from heaven: that natural religion, though with rites additional yet no way contrary to it, was their established religion, which cannot be said of the Gentile world: and that their very being as a nation, depended upon their acknowledgment of one God, the God of the universe. For, suppose in their captivity in Babylon, they had gone over to the religion of their conquerors, there would have remained no bond of union, to keep them a distinct people. And whilst they were under their own kings, in their own country, a total apostasy from God would have been the dissolution of their whole government. They in such a sense nationally acknowledged and worshipped the Maker of heaven and earth, when the rest of the world were sunk in idolatry, as rendered them, in fact, the peculiar people of God. And this so remarkable an establishment and preservation of natural religion amongst them, seems to add some peculiar credibility to the historical evidence for the miracles of Moses and the Prophets: because these miracles are a full satisfactory account of this event, which plainly wants to be accounted for, and cannot otherwise.

Let this person, supposed wholly ignorant of history,

be acquainted further, that one claiming to be the Messiah, of Jewish extraction, rose up at the time when this nation, from the prophecies above mentioned, expected the Messiah: that he was rejected, as it seemed to have been foretold he should, by the body of the people, under the direction of their rulers: that in the course of a very few years, he was believed on and acknowledged as the promised Messiah, by great numbers among the Gentiles, agreeably to the prophecies of Scripture, yet not upon the evidence of prophecy, but of miracles,* of which miracles we have also strong historical evidence; (by which I mean here no more than must be acknowledged by unbelievers; for let pious frauds and follies be admitted to weaken, it is absurd to say they destroy, our evidence of miracles wrought in proof of Christianity:†) that this religion approving itself to the reason of mankind, and carrying its own evidence with it, so far as reason is a judge of its system, and being no way contrary to reason in those parts of it which require to be believed upon the mere authority of its Author; that this religion, I say, gradually spread and supported itself for some hundred years, not only without any assistance from temporal power, but under constant discouragements, and often the bitterest persecutions from it; and then became the religion of the world: that in the mean time the Jewish nation and government were destroyed in a very remarkable manner, and the people carried away captive and dispersed through the most distant countries; in which state of dispersion they have remained fifteen hundred years: and that they remain a numerous people, united amongst themselves, and distinguished from the rest of the world, as they were in the days of Moses, by the profession of his law; and every where looked upon in a manner, which one scarce knows how distinctly to express, but in the words of the prophetic account of it, given so many ages before it came to pass: *Thou shalt become an astonishment, a proverb, and a by-word, among all nations whither the Lord shall lead thee.*‡

The appearance of a standing miracle, in the Jews

* P. 246, &c. † P. 252, &c. ‡ Deut. xxviii. 37.

remaining a distinct people in their dispersion, and the confirmation which this event appears to give to the truth of revelation, may be thought to be answered, by their religion's forbidding them intermarriages with those of any other, and prescribing them a great many peculiarities in their food, by which they are debarred from the means of incorporating with the people in whose countries they live. This is not, I think, a satisfactory account of that which it pretends to account for. But what does it pretend to account for? The correspondence between this event and the prophecies; or the coincidence of both, with a long dispensation of Providence, of a peculiar nature, towards that people formerly? No. It is only the event itself, which is offered to be thus accounted for; which single event, taken alone, abstracted from all such correspondence and coincidence, perhaps would not have appeared miraculous: but that correspondence and coincidence may be so, though the event itself be supposed not. Thus the concurrence of our Saviour's being born at Bethlehem, with a long foregoing series of prophecy and other coincidences, is doubtless miraculous; the series of prophecy, and other coincidences, and the event, being admitted: though the event itself, his birth at that place, appears to have been brought about in a natural way; of which, however, no one can be certain.

And as several of these events seem, in some degree expressly, to have verified the prophetic history already; so likewise they may be considered further, as having a peculiar aspect towards the full completion of it; as affording some presumption that the whole of it shall, one time or other, be fulfilled. Thus, that the Jews have been so wonderfully preserved in their long and wide dispersion; which is indeed the direct fulfilling of some prophecies, but is now mentioned only as looking forward to somewhat yet to come: that natural religion came forth from Judea, and spread, in the degree it has done over the world, before lost in idolatry; which, together with some other things, have distinguished that very place, in like manner as the people of it are distinguished: that this great change of religion over the earth was brought about under the profession and acknowledgment, that Jesus was the promised Messiah: things of this kind naturally turn the thoughts of serious men towards the full completion of the prophetic history, concerning the final restoration of that people; concerning the establishment of the everlasting kingdom among them, the kingdom of the Messiah; and the future state of the world, under this sacred government. Such circumstances and events, compared with these prophecies, though no completions of them, yet would not, I think, be spoken of as nothing in the argument, by a person upon his first being informed of them. They fall in with the prophetic history of things still future, give it some additional credibility, have the appearance of being somewhat in order to the full completion of it.

Indeed it requires a good degree of knowledge, and great calmness and consideration, to be able to judge thoroughly of the evidence for the truth of Christianity, from that part of the prophetic history which relates to the situation of the kingdoms of the world, and to the state of the church, from the establishment of Christianity to the present time. But it appears from a general view of it, to be very material. And those persons who have thoroughly examined it, and some of them were men of the coolest tempers, greatest capacities, and least liable to imputations of prejudice, insist upon it as determinately conclusive.

Suppose now a person quite ignorant of history, first to recollect the passages above mentioned out of Scripture, without knowing but that the whole was a late fiction, then to be informed of the correspondent facts now mentioned, and to unite them all into one view: that the profession and establishment of natural religion in the world is greatly owing, in different ways, to this book, and the supposed revelation which it contains; that it is acknowledged to be of the earliest antiquity; that its chronology and common history are entirely credible; that this ancient nation, the Jews, of whom it chiefly treats, appear to have been, in fact, the people of God in a distinguished sense; that, as there was a national expectation amongst them, raised from the prophecies, of a Messiah to appear at such a time, so one at this time appeared claiming to be that Messiah; that he was rejected by this nation, but received by the Gentiles, not upon the evidence of prophecy, but of miracles; that the religion he taught supported itself under the greatest difficulties, gained ground, and at length became the religion of the world; that in the mean time the Jewish polity was utterly destroyed, and the nation dispersed over the face of the earth; that notwithstanding this, they have remained a distinct numerous people for so many centuries, even to this day; which not only appears to be the express completion of several prophecies concerning them, but also renders it, as one may speak, a visible and easy possibility that the promises made to them as a nation, may yet be fulfilled. And to these acknowledged truths, let the person we have been supposing add, as I think he ought, whether every one will allow it or no, the obvious appearances which there are, of the state of the world, in other respects besides what relates to the Jews, and of the Christian church, having so long answered, and still answering to the prophetic history. Suppose, I say, these facts set over against the things before mentioned out of the Scripture, and seriously compared with them; the joint view of both together must, I think, appear of very great weight to a considerate reasonable person: of much greater indeed, upon having them first laid before him, than is easy for us, who are so familiarized to them, to conceive, without some particular attention for that purpose.

All these things, and the several particulars contained under them, require to be distinctly and most thoroughly examined into; that the weight of each may be judged of, upon such examination, and such conclusion drawn as results from their united force. But this has not been attempted here. I have gone no further than to show, that the general imperfect view of them now given, the confessed historical evidence for miracles, and the many obvious appearing completions of prophecy, together with the collateral things* here mentioned, and there are

* All the particular things mentioned in this chapter, not reducible to the head of certain miracles, or determinate completions of prophecy. See p. 242

several others of the like sort; that all this together, which, being fact, must be acknowledged by unbelievers, amounts to real evidence of somewhat more than human in this matter: evidence much more important, than careless men, who have been accustomed only to transient and partial views of it, can imagine; and indeed abundantly sufficient to act upon. And these things, I apprehend, must be acknowledged by unbelievers. For though they may say, that the historical evidence of miracles wrought in attestation of Christianity, is not sufficient to convince them, that such miracles were really wrought: they cannot deny, that there is such historical evidence, it being a known matter of fact that there is. They may say, the conformity between the prophecies and events is by accident: but there are many instances in which such conformity itself cannot be denied. They may say, with regard to such kind of collateral things as those above mentioned, that any odd accidental events, without meaning, will have a meaning found in them by fanciful people: and that such as are fanciful in any one certain way, will make out a thousand coincidences, which seem to favour their peculiar follies Men, I say, may talk thus: but no one who is serious, can possibly think these things to be nothing, if he considers the importance of collateral things, and even of lesser circumstances, in the evidence of probability, as distinguished in nature, from the evidence of demonstration. In many cases indeed it seems to require the truest judgment, to determine with exactness the weight of circumstantial evidence: but it is very often altogether as convincing, as that which is the most express and direct.

This general view of the evidence for Christianity, considered as making one argument, may also serve to recommend to serious persons, to set down every thing which they think may be of any real weight at all in proof of it, and particularly the many seeming completions of prophecy: and they will find, that, judging by the natural rules, by which we judge of probable evidence in common matters, they amount to a much higher degree of proof, upon such a joint review, than could be supposed upon considering them separately, at different times; how strong soever the proof might before appear to them, upon such separate views of it. For probable proofs, by being added, not only increase the evidence, but multiply it. Nor should I dissuade any one from setting down, what he thought made for the contrary side. But then it is to be remembered, not in order to influence his judgment, but his practice, that a mistake on one side may be, in its consequences, much more dangerous, than a mistake on the other. And what course is most safe, and what most dangerous, is a consideration thought very material, when we deliberate, not concerning events, but concerning conduct in our temporal affairs. To be influenced by this consideration in our judgment, to believe or disbelieve upon it, is indeed as much prejudice, as any thing whatever. And, like other prejudices, it operates contrary ways, in different men; for some are inclined to believe what they hope, and others what they fear. And it is manifest unreasonableness to apply to men's passions in order to gain their assent. But in deliberations concerning conduct, there is nothing which reason more requires to be taken into the account, than the importance of it. For, suppose it doubtful, what would be the consequence of acting in this, or in a contrary manner: still, that taking one side could be attended with little or no bad consequence, and taking the other might be attended with the greatest, must appear, to unprejudiced reason, of the highest moment towards determining, how we are to act. But the truth of our religion, like the truth of common matters, is to be judged of by all the evidence taken together. And unless the whole series of things which may be alleged in this argument, and every particular thing in it, can reasonably be supposed to have been by accident (for here the stress of the argument for Christianity lies); then is the truth of it proved: in like manner, as if in any common case, numerous events acknowledged, were to be alleged in proof of any other event disputed; the truth of the disputed event would be proved, not only if any one of the acknowledged ones did of itself clearly imply it, but, though no one of them singly did so, if the whole of the acknowledged events taken together could not in reason be supposed to have happened, unless the disputed one were true.

It is obvious, how much advantage the nature of this evidence gives to those persons who attack Christianity, especially in conversation. For it is easy to show, in a short and lively manner, that such and such things are liable to objection, that this and another thing is of little weight in itself; but impossible to show, in like manner, the united force of the whole argument in one view.

However, lastly, as it has been made appear, that there is no presumption against a revelation as miraculous; that the general scheme of Christianity, and the principal parts of it, are conformable to the experienced constitution of things, and the whole perfectly credible: so the account now given of the positive evidence for it, shows, that this evidence is such, as, from the nature of it, cannot be destroyed, though it should be lessened.

CHAP. VIII.

OF THE OBJECTIONS WHICH MAY BE MADE AGAINST ARGUING FROM THE ANALOGY OF NATURE, TO RELIGION.

IF every one would consider, with such attention as they are bound, even in point of morality, to consider, what they judge and give characters of; the occasion of this chapter would be, in some good measure at least, superseded. But since this is not to be expected; for some we find do not concern themselves to understand even what they write against: since this treatise, in common with most others, lies open to objections, which may appear very material to thoughtful men at first sight; and, besides that, seems peculiarly liable to the objections of such as can judge without thinking, and of such as can censure without judging; it may not be amiss to set down the chief of these objections which occur to me, and consider them to their hands. And they are such as these:

"That it is a poor thing to solve difficulties in revelation, by saying, that there are the same in natural religion; when what is wanting is to clear both of them of these their common, as well as other their respective, difficulties: but that it is a strange way indeed of convincing men of the obligations of religion, to show them, that they have as little reason for their worldly pursuits: and a strange way of vindicating the justice and goodness of the Author of Nature, and of removing the objections against both, to which the system of religion lies open, to show, that the like objections lie against natural providence; a way of answering objections against religion, without so much as pretending to make out, that the system of it, or the particular things in it objected against, are reasonable—especially, perhaps some may be inattentive enough to add, Must this be thought strange, when it is confessed that analogy is no answer to such objections: that when this sort of reasoning is carried to the utmost length it can be imagined capable of, it will yet leave the mind in a very unsatisfied state; and that it must be unaccountable ignorance of mankind, to imagine they will be prevailed with to forego their present interests and pleasures, from regard to religion, upon doubtful evidence."

Now, as plausible as this way of talking may appear, that appearance will be found in a great measure owing to half views, which show but part of an object, yet show that indistinctly, and to undeterminate language. By these means weak men are often deceived by others, and ludicrous men, by themselves. And even those, who are serious and considerate, cannot always readily disentangle, and at once clearly see through the perplexities, in which subjects themselves are involved; and which are heightened by the deficiencies and the abuse of words. To this latter sort of persons, the following reply to each part of this objection severally, may be of some assistance; as it may also tend a little to stop and silence others.

First, The thing wanted, *i. e.* what men require, is to have all difficulties cleared. And this is, or, at least for any thing we know to the contrary, it may be, the same, as requiring to comprehend the Divine nature, and the whole plan of Providence from everlasting to everlasting. But it hath always been allowed to argue from what is acknowledged, to what is disputed. And it is in no other sense a poor thing, to argue from natural religion to revealed, in the manner found fault with, than it is to argue in numberless other ways of probable deduction and inference, in matters of conduct, which we are continually reduced to the necessity of doing. Indeed the epithet *poor* may be applied, I fear as properly, to great part or the whole of human life, as it is to the things mentioned in the objection. Is it not a poor thing, for a physician to have so little knowledge in the cure of diseases, as even the most eminent have? To act upon conjecture and guess, where the life of man is concerned? Undoubtedly it is: but not in comparison of having no skill at all in that useful art, and being obliged to act wholly in the dark.

Further: since it is as unreasonable, as it is common, to urge objections against revelation, which are of equal weight against natural religion; and those who do this, if they are not confused themselves, deal unfairly with others, in making it seem, that they are arguing only against revelation, or particular doctrines of it, when in reality they are arguing against moral providence; it is a thing of consequence to show, that such objections are as much levelled against natural religion, as against revealed. And objections, which are equally applicable to both, are properly speaking answered, by its being shown that they are so, provided the former be admitted to be true. And without taking in the consideration how distinctly this is admitted, it is plainly very material to observe, that as the things objected against in natural religion are of the same kind with what is certain matter of experience in the course of providence, and in the information which God affords us concerning our temporal interest under his government; so the objections against the system of Christianity, and the evidence of it, are of the very same kind with those which are made against the system and evidence of natural religion. However, the reader upon review may see, that most of the analogies insisted upon, even in the latter part of this treatise, do not necessarily require to have more taken for granted than is in the former; that there is an Author of nature, or natural Governor of the world: and Christianity is vindicated, not from its analogy to natural religion, but chiefly from its analogy to the experienced constitution of nature.

Secondly, Religion is a practical thing, and consists in such a determinate course of life, as being what, there is reason to think, is commanded by the Author of nature, and will, upon the whole, be our happiness under his government. Now if men can be convinced, that they have the like reason to believe this, as to believe that taking care of their temporal affairs will be to their advantage; such conviction cannot but be an argument to them for the practice of religion. And if there be really any reason for believing one of these, and endeavouring to preserve life, and secure ourselves the necessaries and conveniences of it; then there is reason also for believing the other, and endeavouring to secure the interest it proposes to us. And if the interest, which religion proposes to us, be infinitely greater than our whole temporal interest; then there must be proportionably greater reason for endeavouring to secure one, than the other; since, by the supposition, the probability of our securing one is equal to the probability of our securing the other. This seems plainly unanswerable; and has a tendency to influence fair minds, who consider what our condition really is, or upon what evidence we are naturally appointed to act; and who are disposed to acquiesce in the terms upon which we live, and attend to and follow that practical instruction, whatever it be, which is afforded us.

But the chief and proper force of the argument referred to in the objection, lies in another place. For, it is said that the proof of religion is involved in such inextricable difficulties, as to render it doubtful; and that it cannot be supposed, that, if it were true, it would be left upon doubtful evidence. Here then, over and above the force of each particular difficulty or objection, these difficulties and objections taken together are turned into a positive argument against the truth of religion; which argument would stand thus. If religion were true, it would not be left doubtful, and open to objections to the degree in which it is: therefore that it is thus left, not only renders the evidence of it weak, and lessens its force, in proportion to the weight of such objections; but also shows it to be false, or is a general presumption of its being so. Now the observation, that, from the natural constitution and course of things, we must in our temporal concerns, almost continually, and in matters of great consequence, act upon evidence of a like kind and degree to the evidence of religion, is an answer to this argument; because it shows, that it is according to the conduct and character of the Author of nature to appoint we should act upon evidence like to that which this argument presumes he cannot be supposed to appoint we should act upon: it is an instance, a general one, made up of numerous particular ones, of somewhat in his dealing with us, similar to what is said to be incredible. And as the force of this answer lies merely in the parallel, which there is between the evidence for religion and for our temporal conduct; the answer is equally just and conclusive, whether the parallel be made out, by showing the evidence of the former to be higher, or the evidence of the latter to be lower.

Thirdly, The design of this treatise is not to vindicate the character of God, but to show the obligations of men: it is not to justify his providence, but to show what belongs to us to do. These are two subjects, and ought not to be confounded. And though they may at length run up into each other, yet observations may immediately tend to make out the latter, which do not appear, by any immediate connexion, to the purpose of the former; which is less our concern, than many seem to think. For, first, it is not necessary we should justify the dispensations of Providence against objections, any farther than to show, that the things objected against may, for ought we know, be consistent with justice and goodness. Suppose then, that there are things in the system of this world, and plan of Providence relating to it, which taken alone would be unjust: yet it has been shown unanswerably, that if we could take in the reference, which these things may have to other things present, past, and to come; to the whole scheme, which the things objected against are parts of; these very things might, for ought we know, be found to be, not only consistent with justice, but instances of it. Indeed it has been shown, by the analogy of what we see, not only possible that this may be the case, but credible that it is. And thus objections, drawn from such things, are answered, and Providence is vindicated, as far as religion makes its vindication necessary. Hence it appears, secondly, that objections against the Divine justice and goodness are not endeavoured to be removed, by showing that the like objections, allowed to be really conclusive, lie against natural providence: but those objections being supposed and shown not to be conclusive, the things objected against, considered as matters of fact, are farther shown to be credible, from their conformity to the constitution of nature; for instance, that God will reward and punish men for their actions hereafter, from the observation, that he does reward and punish them for their actions here. And this, I apprehend, is of weight. And I add, thirdly, it would be of weight, even though those objections were not answered. For, there being the proof of religion above set down; and religion implying several facts; for instance again, the fact last mentioned, that God will reward and punish men for their actions hereafter; the observation, that his present method of government is by rewards and punishments, shows that future fact not to be incredible: whatever objections men may think they have against it, as unjust or unmerciful, according to their notions of justice and mercy; or as improbable from their belief of necessity. I say, *as improbable:* for it is evident no objection against it, *as unjust,* can be urged from necessity; since this notion as much destroys injustice, as it does justice. Then, fourthly, Though objections against the reasonableness of the system of religion cannot indeed be answered without entering into consideration of its reasonableness; yet objections against the credibility or truth of it may. Because the system of it is reducible into what is properly matter of fact: and the truth, the probable truth, of facts, may be shown without consideration of their reasonableness. Nor is it necessary, though, in some cases and respects, it is highly useful and proper, yet it is not necessary, to give a proof of the reasonableness of every precept enjoined us, and of every particular dispensation of Providence, which comes into the system of religion. Indeed the more thoroughly a person of a right disposition is convinced of the perfection of the Divine nature and conduct, the farther he will advance towards that perfection of religion, which St John* speaks of. But the general obligations of religion are fully made out, by proving the reasonableness of the practice of it. And that the practice of religion *is* reasonable, may be shown, though no more could be proved, than that the system of it *may be* so, for ought we know to the contrary: and even without entering into the distinct consideration of this. And from hence, fifthly, It is easy to see, that though the analogy of nature is not an immediate answer to objections against the wisdom, the justice, or goodness, of any doctrine or precept of religion; yet it may be, as it is, an immediate and direct answer to what is really intended by such objections; which is, to show that the things objected against are incredible.

Fourthly, It is most readily acknowledged, that the foregoing treatise is by no means satisfactory; very far indeed from it: but so would any natural institution of life appear, if reduced into a system, together with its evidence. Leaving religion out of the case, men are divided in their opinions, whether our pleasures overbalance our pains: and whether it be, or be not, eligible to live in this world. And were all such controversies settled, which perhaps, in speculation, would be found involved in great difficulties; and were it determined upon the evidence of reason, as nature has determined it to our hands, that life is to be preserved: yet still, the rules which God has been pleased to afford us, for escaping the miseries of it, and obtaining its satisfactions, the rules, for instance, of preserving health, and recovering it when lost, are not only fallible and precarious, but

* John iv. 18.

very far from being exact. Nor are we informed by nature, in future contingencies and accidents, so as to render it at all certain, what is the best method of managing our affairs. What will be the success of our temporal pursuits, in the common sense of the word Success, is highly doubtful. And what will be the success of them in the proper sense of the word; *i. e.* what happiness or enjoyment we shall obtain by them, is doubtful in a much higher degree. Indeed the unsatisfactory nature of the evidence, with which we are obliged to take up, in the daily course of life, is scarce to be expressed. Yet men do not throw away life, or disregard the interests of it, upon account of this doubtfulness. The evidence of religion then being admitted real, those who object against it, as not satisfactory, *i. e.* as not being what they wish it, plainly forget the very condition of our being: for satisfaction, in this sense, does not belong to such a creature as man. And, which is more material, they forget also the very nature of religion. For, religion presupposes, in all those who will embrace it, a certain degree of integrity and honesty; which it was intended to try whether men have or not, and to exercise in such as have it, in order to its improvement. Religion presupposes this as much, and in the same sense, as speaking to a man presupposes he understands the language in which you speak; or as warning a man of any danger presupposes that he hath such a regard to himself, as that he will endeavour to avoid it. And therefore the question is not at all, Whether the evidence of religion be satisfactory; but Whether it be, in reason, sufficient to prove and discipline that virtue, which it presupposes. Now the evidence of it is fully sufficient for all those purposes of probation; how far soever it is from being satisfactory, as to the purposes of curiosity, or any other: and indeed it answers the purposes of the former in several respects, which it would not do, if it were as overbearing as is required. One might add farther; that whether the motives or the evidence for any course of action be satisfactory, meaning here, by that word, what satisfies a man, that such a course of action will in event be for his good; this need never be, and I think, strictly speaking, never is, the practical question in common matters. But the practical question in all cases is, Whether the evidence for a course of action be such as, taking in all circumstances, makes the faculty within us, which is the guide and judge of conduct,* determine that course of action to be prudent. Indeed, satisfaction that it will be for our interest or happiness, abundantly determines an action to be prudent: but evidence almost infinitely lower than this, determines actions to be so too; even in the conduct of every day.

Fifthly, As to the objection concerning the influence which this argument, or any part of it, may, or may not be expected to have upon men; I observe, as above, that religion being intended for a trial and exercise of the morality of every person's character, who is a subject of it; and there being, as I have shown, such evidence for it, as is sufficient, in reason, to influence men to embrace it: to object, that it is not to be imagined mankind will be influenced by such evidence, is nothing to the purpose of the foregoing treatise. For the purpose of it is not to inquire, what sort of creatures mankind are; but what the light and knowledge, which is afforded them, requires they should be: to show how, in reason, they ought to behave; not how, in fact, they will behave. This depends upon themselves, and is their own concern; the personal concern of each man in particular. And how little regard the generality have to it, experience indeed does too fully show. But religion, considered as a probation, has had its end upon all persons, to whom it has been proposed with evidence sufficient in reason to influence their practice: for by this means they have been put into a state of probation; let them behave as they will in it. And thus, not only revelation, but reason also, teaches us, that by the evidence of religion being laid before men, the designs of Providence are carrying on, not only with regard to those who will, but likewise with regard to those who will not, be influenced by it. However, lastly, the objection here referred to, allows the things insisted upon in this treatise to be of some weight; and if so, it may be hoped it will

* See Dissert. II.

have some influence. And if there be a probability that it will have any at all, there is the same reason in kind, though not in degree, to lay it before men, as there would be, if it were likely to have a greater influence.

And farther, I desire it may be considered, with respect to the whole of the foregoing objections, that in this treatise I have argued upon the principles of others,* not my own: and have omitted what I think true, and of the utmost importance, because by others thought unintelligible, or not true. Thus I have argued upon the principles of the Fatalists, which I do not believe: and have omitted a thing of the utmost importance which I do believe, the moral fitness and unfitness of actions, prior to all will whatever; which I apprehend as certainly to determine the Divine conduct, as speculative truth and falsehood necessarily determine the Divine judgment. Indeed the principle of liberty, and that of moral fitness, so force themselves upon the mind, that moralists, the ancients as well as moderns, have formed their language upon it. And probably it may appear in mine: though I have endeavoured to avoid it; and, in order to avoid it, have sometimes been obliged to express myself in a manner, which will appear strange to such as do not observe the reason for it: but the general argument here pursued does not at all suppose, or proceed upon these principles. Now, these two abstract principles of liberty and moral fitness being omitted, religion can be considered in no other view, than merely as a question of fact: and in this view it is here considered. It is obvious, that Christianity, and the proof of it, are both historical. And even natural religion is, properly, a matter of fact. For, that there is a righteous Governor of the world, is so: and this proposition contains the general system of natural religion. But then, several abstract truths, and in particular those two principles, are usually taken into consideration in the proof of it: whereas it is here treated of only as a matter of fact. To explain this: that the three angles of a triangle are equal to two right ones,

* By *arguing upon the principles of others*, the reader will observe is meant, not proving any thing *from* those principles, but *notwithstanding* them. Thus religion is proved, not *from* the opinion of necessity; which is absurd: but, *notwithstanding* or *even though* that opinion were admitted to be true.

is an abstract truth: but that they appear so to our mind, is only a matter of fact. And this last must have been admitted, if any thing was, by those ancient sceptics, who would not have admitted the former: but pretended to doubt, Whether there were any such thing as truth, or Whether we could certainly depend upon our faculties of understanding for the knowledge of it in any case. So likewise, that there is, in the nature of things, an original standard of right and wrong in actions, independent upon all will, but which unalterably determines the will of God, to exercise that moral government over the world, which religion teaches, *i. e.* finally and upon the whole to reward and punish men respectively as they act right or wrong; this proposition contains an abstract truth, as well as matter of fact. But suppose, in the present state, every man, without exception, was rewarded and punished, in exact proportion as he followed or transgressed that sense of right and wrong, which God has implanted in the nature of every man: this would not be at all an abstract truth, but only a matter of fact. And though this fact were acknowledged by every one; yet the very same difficulties might be raised as are now, concerning the abstract questions of liberty and moral fitness: and we should have a proof, even the certain one of experience, that the government of the world was perfectly moral, without taking in the consideration of those questions: and this proof would remain, in what way soever they were determined. And thus, God having given mankind a moral faculty, the object of which is actions, and which naturally approves some actions as right, and of good desert, and condemns others as wrong, and of ill desert; that he will, finally and upon the whole, reward the former and punish the latter, is not an assertion of an abstract truth, but of what is as mere a fact, as his doing so at present would be. This future fact I have not, indeed, proved with the force with which it might be proved, from the principles of liberty and moral fitness; but without them have given a really conclusive practical proof of it, which is greatly strengthened by the general analogy of nature: a proof easily cavilled at, easily shown not to be demonstrative, for it is not offered as such; but impossible, I think, to be evaded, or answered. And thus the obligations of religion are made out, exclusively of the questions concerning liberty and moral fitness; which have been perplexed with difficulties and abstruse reasonings, as every thing may.

Hence therefore may be observed distinctly, what is the force of this treatise. It will be, to such as are convinced of religion upon the proof arising out of the two last mentioned principles, an additional proof and a confirmation of it: to such as do not admit those principles, an original proof of it,* and a confirmation of that proof. Those who believe will here find the scheme of Christianity cleared of objections, and the evidence of it in a peculiar manner strengthened: those who do not believe will at least be shown the absurdity of all attempts to prove Christianity false, the plain undoubted credibility of it; and, I hope, a good deal more.

And thus, though some perhaps may seriously think, that analogy, as here urged, has too great stress laid upon it; and ridicule, unanswerable ridicule, may be applied, to show the argument from it in a disadvantageous light; yet there can be no question, but that it is a real one. For religion, both natural and revealed, implying in it numerous facts; analogy, being a confirmation of all facts to which it can be applied, as it is the only proof of most, cannot but be admitted by every one to be a material thing, and truly of weight on the side of religion, both natural and revealed: and it ought to be particularly regarded by such as profess to follow nature, and to be less satisfied with abstract reasonings.

CONCLUSION.

WHATEVER account may be given of the strange inattention and disregard, in some ages and countries, to a matter of such importance as Religion; it would, before experience, be incredible, that there should be the like disregard in those, who have had the moral system of the world laid before them, as it is by Christianity, and

* P. 141, &c.

often inculcated upon them: because this moral system carries in it a good degree of evidence for its truth, upon its being barely proposed to our thoughts. There is no need of abstruse reasonings and distinctions, to convince an unprejudiced understanding, that there is a God who made and governs the world, and will judge it in righteousness; though they may be necessary to answer abstruse difficulties, when once such are raised: when the very meaning of those words, which express most intelligibly the general doctrine of religion, is pretended to be uncertain; and the clear truth of the thing itself is obscured by the intricacies of speculation. But to an unprejudiced mind, ten thousand thousand instances of design cannot but prove a designer. And it is intuitively manifest, that creatures ought to live under a dutiful sense of their Maker; and that justice and charity must be his laws, to creatures whom he has made social, and placed in society. Indeed the truth of revealed religion, peculiarly so called, is not self-evident, but requires external proof, in order to its being received. Yet inattention, among us, to revealed religion, will be found to imply the same dissolute immoral temper of mind, as inattention to natural religion: because, when both are laid before us, in the manner they are in Christian countries of liberty, our obligations to inquire into both, and to embrace both upon supposition of their truth, are obligations of the same nature. For, revelation claims to be the voice of God: and our obligation to attend to his voice is surely moral in all cases. And as it is insisted, that its evidence is conclusive, upon thorough consideration of it; so it offers itself to us with manifest obvious appearances of having something more than human in it, and therefore in all reason requires to have its claims most seriously examined into. It is to be added, that though light and knowledge, in what manner soever afforded us, is equally from God; yet a miraculous revelation has a peculiar tendency, from the first principles of our nature, to awaken mankind, and inspire them with reverence and awe: and this is a peculiar obligation, to attend to what claims to be so with such appearances of truth. It is therefore most certain, that our obligations to inquire seriously into the evidence of Christianity, and, upon supposition of its truth, to embrace it, are of the utmost importance, and moral in the highest and most proper sense. Let us then suppose, that the evidence of religion in general, and of Christianity, has been seriously inquired into, by all reasonable men among us. Yet we find many professedly to reject both, upon speculative principles of infidelity. And all of them do not content themselves with a bare neglect of religion, and enjoying their imaginary freedom from its restraints. Some go much beyond this. They deride God's moral government over the world. They renounce his protection, and defy his justice. They ridicule and vilify Christianity, and blaspheme the author of it; and take all occasions to manifest a scorn and contempt of revelation. This amounts to an active setting themselves against religion; to what may be considered as a positive principle of irreligion; which they cultivate within themselves, and, whether they intend this effect or not, render habitual, as a good man does the contrary principle. And others, who are not chargeable with all this profligateness, yet are in avowed opposition to religion, as if discovered to be groundless. Now admitting, which is the supposition we go upon, that these persons act upon what they think principles of reason, and otherwise they are not to be argued with; it is really inconceivable, that they should imagine they clearly see the whole evidence of it, considered in itself, to be nothing at all: nor do they pretend this. They are far indeed from having a just notion of its evidence: but they would not say its evidence was nothing, if they thought the system of it, with all its circumstances, were credible, like other matters of science or history. So their manner of treating it must proceed, either from such kind of objections against all religion, as have been answered or obviated in the former part of this treatise; or else from objections, and difficulties, supposed more peculiar to Christianity. Thus, they entertain prejudices against the whole notion of a revelation, and miraculous interpositions. They find things in Scripture, whether in incidental passages, or in the general scheme of it, which appear to them unreasonable. They take for granted, that if Christianity were true, the light of it must have been more general, and the evidence of it more satisfactory, or rather overbearing: that it must and would have been, in some way, otherwise put and left, than it is. Now this is not imagining they see the evidence itself to be nothing, or inconsiderable; but quite another thing. It is being fortified against the evidence, in some degree acknowledged, by thinking they see the system of Christianity, or somewhat which appears to them necessarily connected with it, to be incredible or false; fortified against that evidence, which might, otherwise, make great impression upon them. Or, lastly, if any of these persons are, upon the whole, in doubt concerning the truth of Christianity; their behaviour seems owing to their taking for granted, through strange inattention, that such doubting is, in a manner, the same thing as being certain against it.

To these persons, and to this state of opinion concerning religion, the foregoing treatise is adapted. For, all the general objections against the moral system of nature having been obviated, it is shown, that there is not any peculiar presumption at all against Christianity, either considered as not discoverable by reason, or as unlike to what is so discovered; nor any worth mentioning against it as miraculous, if any at all; none, certainly, which can render it in the least incredible. It is shown, that, upon supposition of a divine revelation, the analogy of nature renders it beforehand highly credible, I think probable, that many things in it must appear liable to great objections; and that we must be incompetent judges of it, to a great degree. This observation is, I think, unquestionably true, and of the very utmost importance: but it is urged, as I hope it will be understood, with great caution of not vilifying the faculty of reason, which is *the candle of the Lord within us*;* though it can afford no light, where it does not shine; nor judge, where it has no principles to judge upon. The objections here spoken of, being first answered in the view of objections

* Prov. xx. 27

against Christianity as a matter of fact, are in the next place considered as urged more immediately against the wisdom, justice, and goodness of the Christian dispensation. And it is fully made out, that they admit of exactly the like answer, in every respect, to what the like objections against the constitution of nature admit of: that, as partial views give the appearance of wrong to things, which, upon further consideration and knowledge of their relations to other things, are found just and good; so it is perfectly credible, that the things objected against the wisdom and goodness of the Christian dispensation, may be rendered instances of wisdom and goodness, by their reference to other things beyond our view: because Christianity is a scheme as much above our comprehension, as that of nature; and like that, a scheme in which means are made use of to accomplish ends, and which, as is most credible, may be carried on by general laws. And it ought to be attended to, that this is not an answer taken merely or chiefly from our ignorance; but from somewhat positive, which our observation shows us. For, to like objections, the like answer is experienced to be just, in numberless parallel cases. The objections against the Christian dispensation, and the method by which it is carried on, having been thus obviated, in general and together; the chief of them are considered distinctly, and the particular things objected to are shown credible, by their perfect analogy, each apart, to the constitution of nature. Thus, if man be fallen from his primitive state, and to be restored, and infinite wisdom and power engages in accomplishing our recovery: it were to have been expected, it is said, that this should have been effected at once; and not by such a long series of means, and such a various economy of persons and things; one dispensation preparatory to another, this to a further one, and so on through an indefinite number of ages, before the end of the scheme proposed can be completely accomplished; a scheme conducted by infinite wisdom, and executed by almighty power. But now, on the contrary, our finding that every thing in the constitution and course of nature is thus carried on, shows such expectations concerning revelation to be highly unreasonable; and is a satisfactory answer to them, when urged as objections against the credibility, that the great scheme of Providence in the redemption of the world may be of this kind, and to be accomplished in this manner. As to the particular method of our redemption, the appointment of a Mediator between God and man: this has been shown to be most obviously analogous to the general conduct of nature, *i e.* the God of nature, in appointing others to be the instruments of his mercy, as we experience in the daily course of providence. The condition of this world, which the doctrine of our redemption by Christ presupposes, so much falls in with natural appearances, that heathen moralists inferred it from those appearances: inferred, that human nature was fallen from its original rectitude, and in consequence of this, degraded from its primitive happiness. Or, however this opinion came into the world, these appearances must have kept up the tradition, and confirmed the belief of it. And as it was the general opinion under the light of nature, that repentance and reformation, alone and by itself, was not sufficient to do away sin, and procure a full remission of the penalties annexed to it; and as the reason of the thing does not at all lead to any such conclusion; so every day's experience shows us, that reformation is not, in any sort, sufficient to prevent the present disadvantages and miseries, which, in the natural course of things, God has annexed to folly and extravagance. Yet there may be ground to think, that the punishments, which, by the general laws of divine government, are annexed to vice, may be prevented: that provision may have been, even originally, made, that they should be prevented by some means or other, though they could not by reformation alone. For we have daily instances of *such mercy*, in the general conduct of nature: compassion provided for misery,* medicines for diseases, friends against enemies. There is provision made, in the original constitution of the world, that much of the natural bad consequences of our follies, which persons themselves alone cannot prevent, may be prevented by

* Serm. at the Rolls, p. 106.

he assistance of others; assistance, which nature enables, and disposes, and appoints them to afford. By a method of goodness analogous to this, when the world lay in wickedness, and consequently in ruin, *God so loved the world, that he gave his only begotten Son* to save it: and *he being made perfect by suffering, became the author of eternal salvation to all them that obey him.** Indeed neither reason nor analogy would lead us to think, in particular, that the interposition of Christ, in the manner in which he did interpose, would be of that efficacy for recovery of the world, which the Scripture teaches us it was: but neither would reason nor analogy lead us to think, that other particular means would be of the efficacy, which experience shows they are, in numberless instances. And therefore, as the case before us does not admit of experience; so, that neither reason nor analogy can show how, or in what particular way, the interposition of Christ, as revealed in Scripture, is of that efficacy, which it is there represented to be; this is no kind nor degree of presumption against its being really of that efficacy. Further: the objections against Christianity, from the light of it not being universal, nor its evidence so strong as might possibly be given us, have been answered by the general analogy of nature. That God has made such variety of creatures, is indeed an answer to the former: but that he dispenses his gifts in such variety, both of degrees and kinds, amongst creatures of the same species, and even to the same individuals at different times; is a more obvious and full answer to it And it is so far from being the method of Providence in other cases, to afford us such overbearing evidence, as some require in proof of Christianity; that on the contrary, the evidence upon which we are naturally appointed to act in common matters, throughout a very great part of life, is doubtful in a high degree. And admitting the fact, that God has afforded to some no more than doubtful evidence of religion; the same account may be given of it, as of difficulties and temptations with regard to practice. But as it is not impossible,† surely, that this alleged doubtfulness may be men's own fault; it deserves their

* John iii. 16. Heb. v. 9.

† P. 237, &c.

most serious consideration, whether it be not so. However, it is certain, that doubting implies a degree of evidence for that of which we doubt: and that this degree of evidence as really lays us under obligations as demonstrative evidence.

The whole then of religion is throughout credible: nor is there, I think, any thing relating to the revealed dispensation of things, more different from the experienced constitution and course of nature, than some parts of the constitution of nature are from other parts of it. And if so, the only question which remains is, what positive evidence can be alleged for the truth of Christianity. This too in general has been considered, and the objections against it estimated. Deduct, therefore, what is to be deducted from that evidence, upon account of any weight which may be thought to remain in these objections, after what the analogy of nature has suggested in answer to them: and then consider, what are the practical consequences from all this, upon the most sceptical principles one can argue upon (for I am writing to persons who entertain these principles): and upon such consideration it will be obvious, that immorality, as little excuse as it admits of in itself, is greatly aggravated, in persons who have been made acquainted with Christianity, whether they believe it or not: because the moral system of nature, or natural religion, which Christianity lays before us, approves itself, almost intuitively, to a reasonable mind, upon seeing it proposed. In the next place, with regard to Christianity, it will be observed; that there is a middle between a full satisfaction of the truth of it, and a satisfaction of the contrary. The middle state of mind between these two consists in a serious apprehension, that it may be true, joined with doubt whether it be so. And this, upon the best judgment I am able to make, is as far towards speculative infidelity, as any sceptic can at all be supposed to go, who has had true Christianity, with the proper evidences of it, laid before him, and has in any tolerable measure considered them. For I would not be mistaken to comprehend all who have ever heard of it: because it seems evident, that in many countries called Christian, neither

Christianity, nor its evidence, are fairly laid before men And in places where both are, there appear to be some who have very little attended to either, and who reject Christianity with a scorn proportionate to their inattention; and yet are by no means without understanding in other matters. Now it has been shown, that a serious apprehension that Christianity may be true, lays persons under the strictest obligations of a serious regard to it, throughout the whole of their life; a regard not the same exactly, but in many respects nearly the same with what a full conviction of its truth would lay them under *Lastly*, it will appear, that blasphemy and profaneness, I mean with regard to Christianity, are absolutely without excuse. For there is no temptation to it, but from the wantonness of vanity or mirth; and these, considering the infinite importance of the subject, are no such temptations as to afford any excuse for it. If this be a just account of things, and yet men can go on to vilify or disregard Christianity, which is to talk and act as if they had a demonstration of its falsehood; there is no reason to think they would alter their behaviour to any purpose, though there were a demonstration of its truth.

DISSERTATION I.

OF PERSONAL IDENTITY.

WHETHER we are to live in a future state, as it is the most important question which can possibly be asked, so it is the most intelligible one which can be expressed in language. Yet strange perplexities have been raised about the meaning of that identity or sameness of person, which is implied in the notion of our living now and hereafter, or in any two successive moments. And the solution of these difficulties hath been stranger than the difficulties themselves. For, personal identity has been explained so by some, as to render the inquiry concerning a future life of no consequence at all to us the persons who are making it. And though few men can be misled by such subtleties; yet it may be proper a little to consider them.

Now, when it is asked wherein personal identity consists, the answer should be the same, as if it were asked wherein consists similitude, or equality; that all attempts to define would but perplex it. Yet there is no difficulty at all in ascertaining the idea. For as, upon two triangles being compared or viewed together, there arises to the mind the idea of similitude; or upon twice two and four, the idea of equality: so likewise, upon comparing the consciousness of one's self, or one's own existence, in any two moments, there as immediately arises to the mind the idea of personal identity. And as the two former comparisons not only give us the ideas of similitude and equality; but also show us, that two triangles are alike, and twice two and four are equal: so the latter comparison not only gives us the idea of personal identity, but also shows us the identity of ourselves in those two moments; the present, suppose, and that immediately past; or the present, and that a month, a year, or twenty years past. Or in other words, by reflecting upon that which is myself now, and that which was myself twenty years ago, I discern they are not two, but one and the same self.

But though consciousness of what is past does thus ascertain our personal identity to ourselves, yet to say, that it makes personal identity, or is necessary to our being the same persons, is to say, that a person has not existed a single moment, nor done one action, but what he can remember; indeed none but what he reflects upon. And one should really think it self-evident, that consciousness of personal identity presupposes, and therefore cannot constitute, personal identity; any more than knowledge, in any other case, can constitute truth, which it presupposes.

This wonderful mistake may possibly have arisen from hence; that to be endued with consciousness is inseparable from the idea of a person, or intelligent being. For, this might be expressed inaccurately thus, that consciousness makes personality: and from hence it might be concluded to make personal identity. But though present consciousness of what we at present do and feel is necessary to our being the persons we now are; yet present consciousness of past actions or feelings is not necessary to our being the same persons who performed those actions, or had those feelings.

The inquiry, what makes vegetables the same in the common acceptation of the word, does not appear to have any relation to this of personal identity: because, the word *same*, when applied to them and to person, is not only applied to different subjects, but it is also used in different senses. For when a man swears to the same tree, as having stood fifty years in the same place, he means only the same as to all the purposes of property and uses of common life, and not that the tree has been all that time the same in the strict philosophical sense of the word. For he does not know, whether any one particle of the present tree be the same with any one particle of the tree which stood in the same place fifty years ago. And if they have not one common particle of matter, they cannot be the same tree in the proper philosophic sense of the word *same:* it being evidently a contradiction in terms, to say they are, when no part of their substance, and no one of their properties is the same: no part of their substance, by the supposition; no one of their properties, because it is allowed, that the same property cannot be transferred from one substance to another. And therefore when we say the identity or sameness of a plant consists in a continuation of the same life, communicated under the same organization, to a number of particles of matter, whether the same or not; the word *same*, when applied to life and to organization, cannot possibly be understood to signify, what it signifies in this very sentence, when applied to matter. In a loose and popular sense then, the life and the organization and the plant are justly said to be the same, notwithstanding the perpetual change of the parts. But in a strict and philosophical manner of speech, no man, no being, no mode of being, no anything, can be the same with that, with which it has indeed nothing the same. Now sameness is used in this latter sense, when applied to persons. The identity of these, therefore, cannot subsist with diversity of substance.

The thing here considered, and demonstratively, as I think, determined, is proposed by Mr Locke in these words, *Whether it*, i. e. the same self or person, *be the same identical substance?* And he has suggested what is a much better answer to the question, than that which he gives it in form. For he defines Person, *a thinking intelligent being*, &c., and personal identity, *the sameness of a rational Being*.* The question then is, whether the same rational being is the same substance: which needs no answer, because Being and Substance, in this place, stand for the same idea. The ground of the doubt, whether the same person be the same substance, is said to be this; that the consciousness of our own existence, in youth and in old age, or in any two joint successive moments, is not the *same individual action*,† i. e. not the same consciousness, but different successive consciousnesses. Now it is strange that this should have occasioned such perplexities. For it is surely conceivable, that a person may have a capacity of knowing some object or other to be the same now, which it was when he

* Locke's Works, vol. i. p. 146. † Locke, p. 146, 147.

contemplated it formerly: yet in this case, where, by the supposition, the object is perceived to be the same, the perception of it in any two moments cannot be one and the same perception. And thus, though the successive consciousnesses, which we have of our own existence, are not the same, yet are they consciousnesses of one and the same thing or object; of the same person, self, or living agent. The person, of whose existence the consciousness is felt now, and was felt an hour or a year ago, is discerned to be, not two persons, but one and the same person; and therefore is one and the same.

Mr Locke's observations upon this subject appear hasty: and he seems to profess himself dissatisfied with suppositions, which he has made relating to it.* But some of those hasty observations have been carried to a strange length by others; whose notion, when traced and examined to the bottom, amounts, I think, to this:† "That Personality is not a permanent, but a transient thing: that it lives and dies, begins and ends continually: that no one can any more remain one and the same person two moments together, than two successive moments can be one and the same moment: that our substance is indeed continually changing; but whether this be so or not, is, it seems, nothing to the purpose; since it is not substance, but consciousness alone, which constitutes personality: which consciousness, being successive, cannot be the same in any two moments, nor consequently the personality constituted by it." And from hence it must follow, that it is a fallacy upon ourselves, to charge our present selves with any thing we did, or to imagine our present selves interested in any thing which befell us yesterday; or that our present self will be interested in what will befall us to-morrow: since our present self is not, in reality, the same with the self of yesterday, but another like self or person coming in its room, and mistaken for it; to which another self will succeed to-morrow. This, I say, must follow: for if the self or person of to-day, and that of to-morrow, are not the same, but

* Locke, p. 152.

† See an Answer to Dr Clarke's Third Defence of his Letter to Mr Dodwell, 2d edit. p. 44, 56, &c.

only like persons; the person of to-day is really no more interested in what will befall the person of to-morrow, than in what will befall any other person. It may be thought, perhaps, that this is not a just representation of the opinion we are speaking of: because those who maintain it allow, that a person is the same as far back as his remembrance reaches. And indeed they do use the words, *identity*, and *same person*. Nor will language permit these words to be laid aside; since if they were, there must be I know not what ridiculous periphrasis substituted in the room of them. But they cannot consistently with themselves, mean, that the person is really the same. For it is self-evident, that the personality cannot be really the same, if, as they expressly assert, that in which it consists is not the same. And as, consistently with themselves, they cannot, so, I think it appears, they do not, mean, that the person is *really* the same, but only that he is so in a fictitious sense: in such a sense only as they assert, for this they do assert, that any number of persons whatever may be the same person. The bare unfolding this notion, and laying it thus naked and open, seems the best confutation of it. However, since great stress is said to be put upon it, I add the following things.

First, This notion is absolutely contradictory to that certain conviction, which necessarily and every moment rises within us, when we turn our thoughts upon ourselves, when we reflect upon what is past, and look forward upon what is to come. All imagination of a daily change of that living agent which each man calls himself, for another, or of any such change throughout our whole present life, is entirely borne down by our natural sense of things. Nor is it possible for a person in his wits to alter his conduct, with regard to his health or affairs, from a suspicion, that, though he should live to-morrow, he should not, however, be the same person he is to-day. And yet, if it be reasonable to act, with respect to a future life, upon this notion, that personality is transient; it is reasonable to act upon it, with respect to the present. Here then is a notion equally applicable to religion and to our temporal concerns; and every one sees and feels the inexpressible absurdity of it in the latter case ; if, therefore, any can take up with it in the former, this cannot proceed from the reason of the thing, but must be owing to an inward unfairness, and secret corruption of heart.

Secondly, It is not an idea, or abstract notion, or quality, but a being only, which is capable of life and action, of happiness and misery. Now all beings confessedly continue the same, during the whole time of their existence. Consider then a living being now existing, and which has existed for any time alive : this living being must have done and suffered and enjoyed, what it has done and suffered and enjoyed formerly (this living being, I say, and not another), as really as it does and suffers and enjoys, what it does and suffers and enjoys this instant. All these successive actions, enjoyments, and sufferings, are actions, enjoyments, and sufferings, of the same living being. And they are so, prior to all consideration of its remembering or forgetting : since remembering or forgetting can make no alteration in the truth of past matter of fact. And suppose this being endued with limited powers of knowledge and memory, there is no more difficulty in conceiving it to have a power of knowing itself to be the same living being which it was some time ago, of remembering some of its actions, sufferings, and enjoyments, and forgetting others, than in conceiving it to know or remember or forget any thing else.

Thirdly, Every person is conscious, that he is now the same person or self he was as far back as his remembrance reaches : since when any one reflects upon a past action of his own, he is just as certain of the person who did that action, namely, himself, the person who now reflects upon it, as he is certain that the action was at all done. Nay, very often a person's assurance of an action having been done, of which he is absolutely assured, arises wholly from the consciousness that he himself did it. And this he, person, or self, must either be a substance, or the property of some substance. If he, if person, be a substance ; then consciousness that he is the same person is consciousness that he is the same substance. If the person, or he, be the property of a substance, still consciousness that he is the same property is as certain a proof that his substance remains the same, as consciousness that he remains the same substance would be: since the same property cannot be transferred from one substance to another.

But though we are thus certain, that we are the same agents, living beings, or substances, now, which we were as far back as our remembrance reaches; yet it is asked, whether we may not possibly be deceived in it? And this question may be asked at the end of any demonstration whatever: because it is a question concerning the truth of perception by memory. And he who can doubt, whether perception by memory can in this case be depended upon, may doubt also, whether perception by deduction and reasoning, which also include memory, or indeed whether intuitive perception can. Here then we can go no further. For it is ridiculous to attempt to prove the truth of those perceptions, whose truth we can no otherwise prove, than by other perceptions of exactly the same kind with them, and which there is just the same ground to suspect; or to attempt to prove the truth of our faculties, which can no otherwise be proved, than by the use or means of those very suspected faculties themselves.

DISSERTATION II.

OF THE NATURE OF VIRTUE.

THAT which renders beings capable of moral government, is their having a moral nature, and moral faculties of perception and of action. Brute creatures are impressed and actuated by various instincts and propensions: so also are we. But additional to this, we have a capacity of reflecting upon actions and characters, and making them an object to our thought: and on doing this, we naturally and unavoidably approve some actions, under the peculiar view of their being virtuous and of good desert;

and disapprove others, as vicious and of ill desert. That we have this moral approving and disapproving* faculty, is certain from our experiencing it in ourselves, and recognizing it in each other. It appears from our exercising it unavoidably, in the approbation and disapprobation even of feigned characters: from the words right and wrong, odious and amiable, base and worthy, with many others of like signification in all languages applied to actions and characters: from the many written systems of morals which suppose it; since it cannot be imagined, that all these authors, throughout all these treatises, had absolutely no meaning at all to their words, or a meaning merely chimerical: from our natural sense of gratitude, which implies a distinction between merely being the instrument of good, and intending it: from the like distinction every one makes between injury and mere harm, which, Hobbes says, is peculiar to mankind; and between injury and just punishment, a distinction plainly natural, prior to the consideration of human laws. It is manifest great part† of common language, and of common behaviour over the world, is formed upon supposition of such a moral faculty; whether called conscience, moral reason, moral sense, or divine reason; whether considered as a sentiment of the understanding, or as a perception of the heart; or, which seems the truth, as including both. Nor is it at all doubtful in the general, what course of action this faculty, or practical discerning power within us, approves and what it disapproves. For, as much as it has been disputed wherein virtue consists, or whatever ground for doubt there may be about particulars; yet, in general, there is in reality a universally acknowledged standard of it. It is that, which all ages and all countries have made profession of in public: it is that, which every man you meet puts on the show of: it is that

* This way of speaking is taken from Epictetus,† and is made use of as seeming the most full, and least liable to cavil. And the moral faculty may be understood to have these two epithets, δοκιμαστικὴ and ἀποδοκιμαστικὴ, upon a double account; because, upon a survey of actions, whether before or after they are done, it determines them to be good or evil; and also because it determines itself to be the guide of action and of life, in contradistinction from all other faculties, or natural principles of action; in the very same manner as speculative reason *directly* and naturally judges of speculative truth and falsehood: and at the same time is attended with a consciousness upon *reflection*, that the natural right to judge of them belongs to it.

† Arr. Epict. lib. i. cap I.

which the primary and fundamental laws of all civil constitutions over the face of the earth make it their business and endeavour to enforce the practice of upon mankind: namely justice, veracity, and regard to common good. It being manifest then, in general, that we have such a faculty or discernment as this, it may be of use to remark some things more distinctly concerning it.

First, It ought to be observed, that the object of this faculty is actions,* comprehending under that name active or practical principles: those principles from which men would act, if occasions and circumstances gave them power; and which, when fixed and habitual in any person, we call his character. It does not appear, that brutes have the least reflex sense of actions, as distinguished from events: or that will and design, which constitute the very nature of actions as such, are at all an object to their perception. But to ours they are: and they are the object, and the only one, of the approving and disapproving faculty. Acting conduct, behaviour, abstracted from all regard to what is in fact and event, the consequence of it, is itself the natural object of the moral discernment; as speculative truth and falsehood is of speculative reason. Intention of such and such consequences, indeed, is always included; for it is part of the action itself: but though the intended good or bad consequences do not follow, we have exactly the same sense of the action as if they did. In like manner we think well or ill of characters, abstracted from all consideration of the good or the evil, which persons of such characters have it actually in their power to do. We never, in the moral way, applaud or blame either ourselves or others, for what we enjoy or what we suffer, or for having impressions made upon us which we consider as altogether out of our power: but only for what we do, or would have done, had it been in our power: or for what we leave undone, which we might have done, or would have left undone, though we could have done it.

Secondly, Our sense or discernment of actions as

* Οὐδὲ ἡ ἀρετὴ καὶ κακία — ἐν πείσει, ἀλλὰ ἐνεργείᾳ, M. Anton. lib. ix. 16. Virtutis laus omnis in actione consistit. Cic. Off. lib. i. cap. 6.

morally good or evil, implies in it a sense or discernment of them as of good or ill discernment. It may be difficult to explain this perception, so as to answer all the questions which may be asked concerning it: but every one speaks of such and such actions as deserving punishment; and it is not, I suppose, pretended, that they have absolutely no meaning at all to the expression. Now the meaning plainly is not, that we conceive it for the good of society, that the doer of such actions should be made to suffer. For if, unhappily, it were resolved, that a man, who, by some innocent action, was infected with the plague, should be left to perish, lest, by other people's coming near him, the infection should spread; no one would say he deserved this treatment. Innocence and ill desert are inconsistent ideas. Ill desert always supposes guilt: and if one be no part of the other, yet they are evidently and naturally connected in our mind. The sight of a man in misery raises our compassion towards him; and, if this misery be inflicted on him by another, our indignation against the author of it. But when we are informed, that the sufferer is a villain, and is punished only for his treachery or cruelty; our compassion exceedingly lessens, and in many instances our indignation wholly subsides. Now what produces this effect is the conception of that in the sufferer, which we call ill desert. Upon considering then, or viewing together, our notion of vice and that of misery, there results a third, that of ill desert. And thus there is in human creatures an association of the two ideas, natural and moral evil, wickedness and punishment. If this association were merely artificial or accidental, it were nothing: but being most unquestionably natural, it greatly concerns us to attend to it, instead of endeavouring to explain it away.

It may be observed further, concerning our perception of good and of ill desert, that the former is very weak with respect to common instances of virtue. One reason of which may be, that it does not appear to a spectator, how far such instances of virtue proceed from a virtuous principle, or in what degree this principle is prevalent: since a very weak regard to virtue may be sufficient to make men act well in many common instances. And on the other hand, our perception of ill desert in vicious actions lessens, in proportion to the temptations men are thought to have had to such vices. For, vice in human creatures consisting chiefly in the absence or want of the virtuous principle; though a man be overcome, suppose, by tortures, it does not from thence appear to what degree the virtuous principle was wanting. All that appears is, that he had it not in such a degree, as to prevail over the temptation; but possibly he had it in a degree, which would have rendered him proof against common temptations.

Thirdly, Our perception of vice and ill desert arises from, and is the result of, a comparison of actions with the nature and capacities of the agent. For the mere neglect of doing what we ought to do, would, in many cases, be determined by all men to be in the highest degree vicious. And this determination must arise from such comparison, and be the result of it; because such neglect would not be vicious in creatures of other natures and capacities, as brutes. And it is the same also with respect to positive vices, or such as consist in doing what we ought not. For, every one has a different sense of harm done by an idiot, madman, or child, and by one of mature and common understanding; though the action of both, including the intention, which is part of the action, be the same: as it may be, since idiots and madmen, as well as children, are capable not only of doing mischief, but also of intending it. Now this difference must arise from somewhat discerned in the nature or capacities of one, which renders the action vicious; and the want of which, in the other, renders the same action innocent or less vicious: and this plainly supposes a comparison, whether reflected upon or not, between the action and capacities of the agent, previous to our determining an action to be vicious. And hence arises a proper application of the epithets, incongruous, unsuitable, disproportionate, unfit, to actions which our moral faculty determines to be vicious.

Fourthly, It deserves to be considered, whether men are more at liberty, in point of morals, to make themselves miserable without reason, than to make other people so: or dissolutely to neglect their own greater good, for the sake of a present lesser gratification, than they are to neglect the good of others, whom nature has committed to their care. It should seem, that a due concern about our own interest or happiness, and a reasonable endeavour to secure and promote it, which is, I think, very much the meaning of the word prudence, in our language; it should seem, that this is virtue, and the contrary behaviour faulty and blamable; since, in the calmest way of reflection, we approve of the first, and condemn the other conduct, both in ourselves and others. This approbation and disapprobation are altogether different from mere desire of our own, or of their happiness, and from sorrow upon missing it. For the object or occasion of this last kind of perception is satisfaction or uneasiness: whereas the object of the first is active behaviour. In one case, what our thoughts fix upon is our condition: in the other, our conduct. It is true indeed, that nature has not given us so sensible a disapprobation of imprudence and folly, either in *ourselves* or *others*, as of falsehood, injustice, and cruelty: I suppose, because that constant habitual sense of private interest and good, which we always carry about with us, renders such sensible disapprobation less necessary, less wanting, to keep us from imprudently neglecting our own happiness, and foolishly injuring ourselves, than it is necessary and wanting to keep us from injuring others, to whose good we cannot have so strong and constant a regard: and also because imprudence and folly, appearing to bring its own punishment more immediately and constantly than injurious behaviour, it less needs the additional punishment, which would be inflicted upon it by others, had they the same sensible indignation against it, as against injustice, and fraud, and cruelty. Besides, unhappiness being in itself the natural object of compassion; the unhappiness which people bring upon themselves, though it be wilfully, excites in us some pity for them: and this of course lessens our displeasure against them. But still it is matter of experience, that we are formed so as to reflect very severely upon the greater instances of imprudent neglect and foolish rashness, both in ourselves and others. In instances of this kind, men often say of themselves with remorse, and of others with some indignation, that they deserved to suffer such calamities, because they brought them upon themselves, and would not take warning. Particularly when persons come to poverty and distress by a long course of extravagance, and after frequent admonitions, though without falsehood or injustice; we plainly, do not regard such people as alike objects of compassion with those, who are brought into the same condition by unavoidable accidents. From these things it appears, that prudence is a species of virtue, and folly of vice: meaning by *folly*, somewhat quite different from mere incapacity; a thoughtless want of that regard and attention to our own happiness, which we had capacity for. And this the word properly includes; and, as it seems, in its usual acceptation: for we scarcely apply it to brute creatures.

However, if any person be disposed to dispute the matter, I shall very willingly give him up the words Virtue and Vice, as not applicable to prudence and folly: but must beg leave to insist, that the faculty within us, which is the judge of actions, approves of prudent actions, and disapproves imprudent ones: I say prudent and imprudent *actions* as such, and considered distinctly from the happiness or misery which they occasion. And, by the way, this observation may help to determine what justness there is in that objection against religion, that it teaches us to be interested and selfish.

Fifthly, Without inquiring how far, and in what sense, virtue is resolvable into benevolence, and vice into the want of it; it may be proper to observe, that benevolence, and the want of it, singly considered, are in no sort the whole of virtue and vice. For if this were the case, in the review of one's own character, or that of others, our moral understanding and moral sense would be indifferent to every thing, but the degrees in which benevolence prevailed, and the degrees in which it was wanting. That is, we should neither approve of benevolence to some persons rather than to others, nor disapprove injustice and falsehood upon any other account, than merely as an overbalance of happiness was foreseen likely to be produced by the first, and of misery by the second. But now, on the contrary, suppose two men competitors for any thing whatever, which would be of equal advantage to each of them; though nothing indeed would be more impertinent, than for a stranger to busy himself to get one of them preferred to the other; yet such endeavour would be virtue, in behalf of a friend or benefactor, abstracted from all consideration of distant consequence: as that examples of gratitude, and the cultivation of friendship, would be of general good to the world. Again, suppose one man should, by fraud or violence, take from another the fruit of his labour, with intent to give it to a third, who he thought would have as much pleasure from it as would balance the pleasure which the first possessor would have had in the enjoyment, and his vexation in the loss of it; suppose also that no bad consequences would follow: yet such an action would surely be vicious. Nay, further, were treachery, violence, and injustice, no otherwise vicious, than as foreseen likely to produce an overbalance of misery to society; then, if in any case a man could procure to himself as great advantage by an act of injustice, as the whole foreseen inconvenience, likely to be brought upon others by it, would amount to; such a piece of injustice would not be faulty or vicious at all: because it would be no more than, in any other case, for a man to prefer his own satisfaction to another's in equal degrees. The fact, then, appears to be, that we are constituted so as to condemn falsehood, unprovoked violence, injustice, and to approve of benevolence to some preferably to others, abstracted from all consideration, which conduct is likeliest to produce an overbalance of happiness or misery. And therefore, were the Author of nature to propose nothing to himself as an end but the production of happiness, were his moral character merely that of benevolence; yet ours is not so. Upon that supposition indeed, the only reason of his giving us the above mentioned approbation of benevolence to some persons rather than others, and disapprobation of falsehood, unprovoked violence, and injustice, must be, that he foresaw this constitution of our nature would produce more happiness, than forming us with a temper of mere general benevolence. But still, since this is our constitution; falsehood, violence, injustice, must be vice in us, and benevolence to some, preferably to others, virtue; abstracted from all consideration of the overbalance of evil or good, which they may appear likely to produce.

Now if human creatures are endued with such a moral nature as we have been explaining, or with a moral faculty, the natural object of which is actions: moral government must consist in rendering them happy and unhappy, in rewarding and punishing them, as they follow, neglect, or depart from, the moral rule of action interwoven in their nature, or suggested and enforced by this moral faculty;* in rewarding and punishing them upon account of their so doing.

I am not sensible that I have, in this fifth observation, contradicted what any author designed to assert. But some of great and distinguished merit, have, I think, expressed themselves in a manner, which may occasion some danger, to careless readers, of imagining the whole of virtue to consist in singly aiming, according to the best of their judgment, at promoting the happiness of mankind in the present state; and the whole of vice, in doing what they foresee, or might foresee, is likely to produce an overbalance of unhappiness in it: than which mistakes, none can be conceived more terrible. For it is certain, that some of the most shocking instances of injustice, adultery, murder, perjury, and even of persecution, may, in many supposable cases, not have the appearance of being likely to produce an overbalance of misery in the present state; perhaps sometimes may have the contrary appearance. For this reflection might easily be carried on, but I forbear.—The happiness of the world is the concern of him who is the lord and the proprietor of it: nor do we know what we are about, when we endeavour to promote the good of mankind in any ways, but those which he has directed; that is

* P. 145.

indeed in all ways not contrary to veracity and justice. I speak thus upon supposition of persons really endeavouring, in some sort, to do good without regard to these. But the truth seems to be, that such supposed endeavours proceed, almost always, from ambition, the spirit of party, or some indirect principle, concealed perhaps in great measure from persons themselves. And though it is our business and our duty to endeavour, within the bounds of veracity and justice, to contribute to the ease, convenience, and even cheerfulness and diversion of our fellow creatures: yet, from our short views, it is greatly uncertain, whether this endeavour will, in particular instances, produce an overbalance of happiness upon the whole; since so many and distant things must come into the account. And that which makes it our duty is, that there is some appearance that it will, and no positive appearance sufficient to balance this, on the contrary side; and also, that such benevolent endeavour is a cultivation of that most excellent of all virtuous principles, the active principle of benevolence.

However, though veracity, as well as justice, is to be our rule of life; it must be added, otherwise a snare will be laid in the way of some plain men, that the use of common forms of speech, generally understood, cannot be falsehood; and, in general, that there can be no designed falsehood without designing to deceive. It must likewise be observed, that in numberless cases, a man may be under the strictest obligations to what he foresees will deceive, without his intending it. For it is impossible not to foresee, that the words and actions of men, in different ranks and employments, and of different educations, will perpetually be mistaken by each other: and it cannot but be so, whilst they will judge with the utmost carelessness, as they daily do, of what they are not, perhaps, enough informed to be competent judges of, even though they considered it with great attention.

END OF ANALOGY.

SERMONS

BY THE

RIGHT REVEREND FATHER IN GOD

JOSEPH BUTLER, D.C.L.,

LATE

LORD BISHOP OF DURHAM.

NEW YORK:
ROBERT CARTER & BROTHERS
No. 530 BROADWAY.
1873.

PREFACE.

THOUGH it is scarce possible to avoid judging, in some way or other, of almost every thing which offers itself to one's thoughts; yet it is certain, that many persons, from different causes, never exercise their judgment, upon what comes before them, in the way of determining whether it be conclusive, and holds. They are perhaps entertained with some things, not so with others; they like, and they dislike: but whether that which is proposed to be made out be really made out or not; whether a matter be stated according to the real truth of the case, seems to the generality of people merely a circumstance of no consideration at all. Arguments are often wanted for some accidental purpose: but proof, as such, is what they never want for themselves; for their own satisfaction of mind, or conduct in life. Not to mention the multitudes who read merely for the sake of talking, or to qualify themselves for the world, or some such kind of reasons; there are, even of the few who read for their own entertainment, and have a real curiosity to see what is said, several, which is prodigious, who have no sort of curiosity to see what is true: I say, curiosity; because it is too obvious to be mentioned, how much that religious and sacred attention, which is due to truth, and to the important question, What is the rule of life? is lost out of the world.

For the sake of this whole class of readers, for they are of different capacities, different kinds, and get into this way from different occasions, I have often wished that it had been the custom to lay before people nothing in matters of argument but premises, and leave them to draw conclusions themselves; which, though it could not be done in all cases, might in many.

The great number of books and papers of amusement,

which, of one kind or another, daily come in one's way, have in part occasioned, and most perfectly fall in with and humour, this idle way of reading and considering things. By this means, time even in solitude is happily got rid of, without the pain of attention: neither is any part of it more put to the account of idleness, one can scarce forbear saying, is spent with less thought, than great part of that which is spent in reading.

Thus people habituate themselves to let things pass through their minds, as one may speak, rather than to think of them. Thus by use they become satisfied merely with seeing what is said, without going any further. Review and attention, and even forming a judgment, becomes fatigue; and to lay any thing before them that requires it, is putting them quite out of their way.

There are also persons, and there are at least more of them than have a right to claim such superiority, who take for granted, that they are acquainted with every thing; and that no subject, if treated in the manner it should be, can be treated in any manner but what is familiar and easy to them.

It is true indeed, that few persons have a right to demand attention; but it is also true, that nothing can be understood without that degree of it, which the very nature of the thing requires. Now morals, considered as a science, concerning which speculative difficulties are daily raised, and treated with regard to those difficulties, plainly require a very peculiar attention. For here ideas never are in themselves determinate, but become so by the train of reasoning and the place they stand in; since it is impossible that words can always stand for the same ideas, even in the same author, much less in different ones. Hence an argument may not readily be apprehended, which is different from its being mistaken; and even caution to avoid being mistaken may, in some cases, render it less readily apprehended. It is very unallowable for a work of imagination or entertainment not to be of easy comprehension, but may be unavoidable in a work of another kind, where a man is not to form or accommodate, but to state things as he finds them.

It must be acknowledged, that some of the following Discourses are very abstruse and difficult; or, if you please, obscure; but I must take leave to add, that those alone are judges, whether or no and how far this is a fault, who are judges, whether or no and how far it might have been avoided—those only who will be at the trouble to understand what is here said, and to see how far the things here insisted upon, and not other things, might have been put in a plainer manner; which yet I am very far from asserting that they could not.

Thus much however will be allowed, that general criticisms concerning obscurity considered as a distinct thing from confusion and perplexity of thought, as in some cases there may be ground for them; so in others, they may be nothing more at the bottom than complaints, that every thing is not to be understood with the same ease that some things are. Confusion and perplexity in writing is indeed without excuse, because any one may, if he pleases, know whether he understands and sees through what he is about: and it is unpardonable for a man to lay his thoughts before others, when he is conscious that he himself does not know whereabouts he is, or how the matter before him stands. It is coming abroad in disorder, which he ought to be dissatisfied to find himself in at home.

But even obscurities arising from other causes than the abstruseness of the argument may not be always inexcusable. Thus a subject may be treated in a manner, which all along supposes the reader acquainted with what has been said upon it, both by ancient and modern writers; and with what is the present state of opinion in the world concerning such subject. This will create a difficulty of a very peculiar kind, and even throw an obscurity over the whole before those who are not thus informed; but those who are will be disposed to excuse such a manner, and other things of the like kind, as a saving of their patience.

However upon the whole, as the title of Sermons gives some right to expect what is plain and of easy comprehension, and as the best auditories are mixed, I shall not set about to justify the propriety of preaching, or under that title publishing, Discourses so abstruse as some of these are: neither is it worth while to trouble the reader with the account of my doing either. He must not however impute to me, as a repetition of the impropriety, this second edition,* but to the demand for it.

Whether he will think he has any amends made him by the following illustrations of what seemed most to require them, I myself am by no means a proper judge.

There are two ways in which the subject of morals may be treated. One begins from inquiring into the abstract relations of things: the other from a matter of fact, namely, what the particular nature of man is, its several parts, their economy or constitution; from whence it proceeds to determine what course of life it is, which is correspondent to this whole nature. In the former method the conclusion is expressed thus, that vice is contrary to the nature and reason of things: in the latter, that it is a violation or breaking in upon our own nature. Thus they both lead us to the same thing, our obligations to the practice of virtue; and thus they exceedingly strengthen and enforce each other. The first seems the most direct formal proof, and in some respects the least liable to cavil and dispute: the latter is in a peculiar manner adapted to satisfy a fair mind; and is more easily applicable to the several particular relations and circumstances in life.

The following Discourses proceed chiefly in this latter method. The three first wholly. They were intended to explain what is meant by the nature of man, when it is said that virtue consists in following, and vice in deviating from it; and by explaining to show that the assertion is true. That the ancient moralists had some inward feeling or other, which they chose to express in this manner, that man is born to virtue, that it consists in following nature, and that vice is more contrary to this nature than tortures or death, their works in our hands are instances. Now a person who found no mystery in this way of speaking of the ancients; who, without being very explicit with himself, kept to his natural feeling, went along with them, and found within

* The preface stands exactly as it did before the second edition of the Sermons.

himself a full conviction, that what they laid down was just and true; such a one would probably wonder to see a point, in which he never perceived any difficulty, so laboured as this is, in the second and third Sermons; insomuch perhaps as to be at a loss for the occasion, scope, and drift of them. But it need not be thought strange that this manner of expression, though familiar with them, and, if not usually carried so far, yet not uncommon amongst ourselves, should want explaining; since there are several perceptions daily felt and spoken of, which yet it may not be very easy at first view to explicate, to distinguish from all others, and ascertain exactly what the idea or perception is. The many treatises upon the passions are a proof of this; since so many would never have undertaken to unfold their several complications, and trace and resolve them into their principles, if they had thought, what they were endeavouring to show was obvious to every one, who felt and talked of those passions. Thus, though there seems no ground to doubt, but that the generality of mankind have the inward perception expressed so commonly in that manner by the ancient moralists, more than to doubt whether they have those passions; yet it appeared of use to unfold that inward conviction, and lay it open in a more explicit manner, than I had seen done; especially when there were not wanting persons, who manifestly mistook the whole thing, and so had great reason to express themselves dissatisfied with it. A late author of great and deserved reputation says, that to place virtue in following nature, is at best a loose way of talk. And he has reason to say this, if what I think he intends to express, though with great decency, be true, that scarce any other sense can be put upon those words, but acting as any of the several parts, without distinction, of a man's nature happened most to incline him.*

Whoever thinks it worth while to consider this matter thoroughly, should begin with stating to himself exactly the idea of a system, economy, or constitution of any particular nature, or particular any thing: and he will,

* Rel. of Nature Delin. ed. 1724. pp. 22, 23.

I suppose, find, that it is a one or a whole, made up of several parts; but yet, that the several parts even considered as a whole do not complete the idea, unless in the notion of a whole you include the relations and respects which those parts have to each other. Every work both of nature and of art is a system: and as every particular thing, both natural and artificial, is for some use or purpose out of and beyond itself, one may add, to what has been already brought into the idea of a system, its conduciveness to this one or more ends. Let us instance in a watch—Suppose the several parts of it taken to pieces, and placed apart from each other; let a man have ever so exact a notion of these several parts, unless he considers the respects and relations which they have to each other, he will not have any thing like the idea of a watch. Suppose these several parts brought together and any how united: neither will he yet, be the union ever so close, have an idea which will bear any resemblance to that of a watch. But let him view those several parts put together, or consider them as to be put together in the manner of a watch; let him form a notion of the relations which those several parts have to each other—all conducive in their respective ways to this purpose, showing the hour of the day; and then he has the idea of a watch. Thus it is with regard to the inward frame of man. Appetites, passions, affections, and the principle of reflection, considered merely as the several parts of our inward nature, do not at all give us an idea of the system or constitution of this nature; because the constitution is formed by somewhat not yet taken into consideration, namely, by the relations which these several parts have to each other; the chief of which is the authority of reflection or conscience. It is from considering the relations which the several appetites and passions in the inward frame have to each other, and, above all, the supremacy of reflection or conscience, that we get the idea of the system or constitution of human nature. And from the idea itself it will as fully appear, that this our nature, *i.e.* constitution, is adapted to virtue, as from the idea of a watch it appears, that its nature, *i.e.* constitution or system, is adapted to measure time.

What in fact or event commonly happens is nothing to this question. Every work of art is apt to be out of order: but this is so far from being according to its system, that let the disorder increase, and it will totally destroy it. This is merely by way of explanation, what an economy, system, or constitution is. And thus far the cases are perfectly parallel. If we go further, there is indeed a difference, nothing to the present purpose, but too important a one ever to be omitted. A machine is inanimate and passive: but we are agents. Our constitution is put in our own power. We are charged with it; and therefore are accountable for any disorder or violation of it.

Thus nothing can possibly be more contrary to nature than vice; meaning by nature not only the *several parts* of our internal frame, but also the *constitution* of it. Poverty and disgrace, tortures and death, are not so contrary to it. Misery and injustice are indeed equally contrary to some different parts of our nature taken singly: but injustice is moreover contrary to the whole constitution of the nature.

If it be asked, whether this constitution be really what those philosophers meant, and whether they would have explained themselves in this manner; the answer is the same, as if it should be asked, whether a person, who had often used the word *resentment*, and felt the thing, would have explained this passion exactly in the same manner, in which it is done in one of these Discourses. As I have no doubt, but that this is a true account of that passion, which he referred to and intended to express by the word *resentment;* so I have no doubt, but that this is the true account of the ground of that conviction which they referred to, when they said, vice was contrary to nature. And though it should be thought that they meant no more than that vice was contrary to the higher and better part of our nature; even this implies such a constitution as I have endeavoured to explain. For the very terms, higher and better, imply a relation or respect of parts to each other; and these relative parts, being in one and the same nature, form a constitution, and are the very idea of it.

They had a perception that injustice was contrary to their nature, and that pain was so also. They observed these two perceptions totally different, not in degree, but in kind: and the reflecting upon each of them, as they thus stood in their nature, wrought a full intuitive conviction, that more was due and of right belonged to one of these inward perceptions, than to the other; that it demanded in all cases to govern such a creature as man. So that, upon the whole, this is a fair and true account of what was the ground of their conviction; of what they intended to refer to, when they said, virtue consisted in following nature: a manner of speaking not loose and undeterminate, but clear and distinct, strictly just and true.

Though I am persuaded the force of this conviction is felt by almost every one; yet since, considered as an argument and put in words, it appears somewhat abstruse, and since the connexion of it is broken in the three first Sermons, it may not be amiss to give the reader the whole argument here in one view.

Mankind has various instincts and principles of action, as brute creatures have; some leading most directly and immediately to the good of the community, and some most directly to private good.

Man has several which brutes have not; particularly reflection or conscience, an approbation of some principles or actions, and disapprobation of others.

Brutes obey their instincts or principles of action, according to certain rules; suppose the constitution of their body, and the objects around them.

The generality of mankind also obey their instincts and principles, all of them; those propensions we call good, as well as the bad, according to the same rules; namely, the constitution of their body, and the external circumstances which they are in. [Therefore it is not a true representation of mankind to affirm, that they are wholly governed by self-love, the love of power, and sensual appetites: since, as on the one hand they are often actuated by these, without any regard to right or wrong; so on the other it is manifest fact, that the same persons, the generality, are frequently influenced by friendship, compassion, gratitude; and even a general abhorrence of what is base, and liking of what is fair and just, takes its turn amongst the other motives of action. This is the partial inadequate notion of human nature treated of in the first Discourse: and it is by this nature, if one may speak so, that the world is in fact influenced, and kept in that tolerable order, in which it is.]

Brutes in acting according to the rules before mentioned, their bodily constitution and circumstances, act suitably to their whole nature. [It is however to be distinctly noted, that the reason why we affirm this is not merely that brutes in fact act so; for this alone, however universal, does not at all determine, whether such course of action be correspondent to their whole nature: but the reason of the assertion is, that as in acting thus they plainly act conformably to somewhat in their nature, so, from all observations we are able to make upon them, there does not appear the least ground to imagine them to have any thing else in their nature, which requires a different rule or course of action.]

Mankind also in acting thus would act suitably to their whole nature, if no more were to be said of man's nature than what has been now said; if that, as it is a true, were also a complete, adequate account of our nature.

But that is not a complete account of man's nature. Somewhat further must be brought in to give us an adequate notion of it; namely, that one of those principles of action, conscience or reflection, compared with the rest as they all stand together in the nature of man, plainly bears upon it marks of authority over all the rest, and claims the absolute direction of them all, to allow or forbid their gratification: a disapprobation of reflection being in itself a principle manifestly superior to a mere propension. And the conclusion is, that to allow no more to this superior principle or part of our nature, than to other parts; to let it govern and guide only occasionally in common with the rest, as its turn happens to come, from the temper and circumstances one happens to be in; this is not to act conformably to the constitution of man: neither can any human creature be said to act conformably to his constitution of nature, unless he allows to that superior principle the absolute authority which is due to it. And this conclusion is abundantly confirmed from hence, that one may determine what course of action the economy of man's nature requires, without so much as knowing in what degrees of *strength* the several principles prevail, or which of them have actually the greatest influence.

The practical reason of insisting so much upon this natural authority of the principle of reflection or conscience is, that it seems in great measure overlooked by many, who are by no means the worst sort of men. It is thought sufficient to abstain from gross wickedness, and to be humane and kind to such as happen to come in their way. Whereas in reality the very constitution of our nature requires, that we bring our whole conduct before this superior faculty; wait its determination; enforce upon ourselves its authority, and make it the business of our lives, as it is absolutely the whole business of a moral agent, to conform ourselves to it. This is the true meaning of that ancient precept, *Reverence thyself.*

The not taking into consideration this authority, which is implied in the idea of reflex approbation or disapprobation, seems a material deficiency or omission in lord Shaftesbury's Inquiry concerning Virtue. He has shown beyond all contradiction, that virtue is naturally the interest or happiness, and vice the misery, of such a creature as man, placed in the circumstances which we are in this world. But suppose there are particular exceptions: a case which this author was unwilling to put, and yet surely it is to be put: or suppose a case which he has put and determined, that of a sceptic not convinced of this happy tendency of virtue, or being of a contrary opinion. His determination is, that it would be *without remedy.** One may say more explicitly, that leaving out the authority of reflex approbation or disapprobation, such a one would be under an obligation to act viciously; since interest, one's own happiness, is a manifest obligation, and there is not supposed to be any other

* Characteristics, vol. ii. p. 69.

obligation in the case. "But does it much mend the matter, to take in that natural authority of reflection? There indeed would be an obligation to virtue; but would not the obligation from supposed interest on the side of vice remain?" If it should, yet to be under two contrary obligations, *i. e.* under none at all, would not be exactly the same, as to be under a formal obligation to be vicious, or to be in circumstances in which the constitution of man's nature plainly required that vice should be preferred. But the obligation on the side of interest really does not remain. For the natural authority of the principle of reflection is an obligation the most near and intimate, the most certain and known: whereas the contrary obligation can at the utmost appear no more than probable; since no man can be *certain* in any circumstances that vice is his interest in the present world, much less can he be certain against another: and thus the certain obligation would entirely supersede and destroy the uncertain one; which yet would have been of real force without the former.

In truth, the taking in this consideration totally changes the whole state of the case; and shows, what this author does not seem to have been aware of, that the greatest degree of scepticism which he thought possible will still leave men under the strictest moral obligations, whatever their opinion be concerning the happiness of virtue. For that mankind upon reflection felt an approbation of what was good, and disapprobation of the contrary, he thought a plain matter of fact, as it undoubtedly is, which none could deny, but from mere affectation. Take in then that authority and obligation, which is a constituent part of this reflex approbation, and it will undeniably follow, though a man should doubt of every thing else, yet, that he would still remain under the nearest and most certain obligation to the practice of virtue; an obligation implied in the very idea of virtue, in the very idea of reflex approbation.

And how little influence soever this obligation alone can be expected to have in fact upon mankind, yet one may appeal even to interest and self-love, and ask, since from man's nature, condition, and the shortness of life, so little, so very little indeed, can possibly in any case be gained by vice; whether it be so prodigious a thing to sacrifice that little to the most intimate of all obligations; and which a man cannot transgress without being self-condemned, and, unless he has corrupted his nature, without real self-dislike: this question, I say, may be asked, even upon supposition that the prospect of a future life were ever so uncertain.

The observation, that man is thus by his very nature a law to himself, pursued to its just consequences, is of the utmost importance; because from it it will follow, that though men should, through stupidity or speculative scepticism, be ignorant of, or disbelieve, any authority in the universe to punish the violation of this law; yet, if there should be such authority, they would be as really liable to punishment, as though they had been beforehand convinced, that such punishment would follow. For in whatever sense we understand justice, even supposing, what I think would be very presumptuous to assert, that the end of divine punishment is no other than that of civil punishment, namely, to prevent future mischief; upon this bold supposition, ignorance or disbelief of the sanction would by no means exempt even from this justice: because it is not foreknowledge of the punishment which renders us obnoxious to it; but merely violating a known obligation.

And here it comes in one's way to take notice of a manifest error or mistake in the author now cited, unless perhaps he has incautiously expressed himself so as to be misunderstood; namely, that *it is malice only, and not goodness, which can make us afraid.** Whereas in reality, goodness is the natural and just object of the greatest fear to an ill man. Malice may be appeased or satiated; humour may change, but goodness is a fixed, steady, immovable principle of action. If either of the former holds the sword of justice, there is plainly ground for the greatest of crimes to hope for impunity: but if it be goodness, there can be no possible hope, whilst the reasons of things, or the ends of government, call for punishment. Thus every one sees how much

* Characteristics, vol. i. p. 86.

greater chance of impunity an ill man has in a partial administration, than in a just and upright one. It is said, that *the interest or good of the whole must be the interest of the universal Being, and that he can have no other.* Be it so. This author has proved, that vice is naturally the misery of mankind in this world. Consequently it was for the good of the whole that it should be so. What shadow of reason then is there to assert, that this may not be the case hereafter? Danger of future punishment (and if there be danger, there is ground of fear) no more supposes malice, than the present feeling of punishment does.

The Sermon *upon the character of Balaam,* and that *upon Self-deceit,* both relate to one subject. I am persuaded, that a very great part of the wickedness of the world is, one way or other, owing to the self-partiality, self-flattery, and self-deceit, endeavoured there to be laid open and explained. It is to be observed amongst persons of the lowest rank, in proportion to their compass of thought, as much as amongst men of education and improvement. It seems, that people are capable of being thus artful with themselves, in proportion as they are capable of being so with others. Those who have taken notice that there is really such a thing, namely, plain falseness and insincerity in men with regard to themselves, will readily see the drift and design of these Discourses: and nothing that I can add will explain the design of them to him, who has not beforehand remarked, at least, somewhat of the character. And yet the admonitions they contain may be as much wanted by such a person, as by others; for it is to be noted, that a man may be entirely possessed by this unfairness of mind, without having the least speculative notion what the thing is.

The account given of *Resentment* in the eighth Sermon is introductory to the following one *upon Forgiveness of Injuries.* It may possibly have appeared to some, at first sight, a strange assertion, that injury is the only natural object of settled resentment, or that men do not in fact resent deliberately any thing but under this appearance of injury. But I must desire the reader not to take any assertion alone by itself, but to consider the whole of what is said upon it: because this is necessary, not only in order to judge of the truth of it, but often, such is the nature of language, to see the very meaning of the assertion. Particularly as to this, injury and injustice is, in the Sermon itself, explained to mean, not only the more gross and shocking instances of wickedness, but also contempt, scorn, neglect, any sort of disagreeable behaviour towards a person, which he thinks other than what is due to him. And the general notion of injury or wrong plainly comprehends this, though the words are mostly confined to the higher degrees of it.

Forgiveness of injuries is one of the very few moral obligations which has been disputed. But the proof, that it is really an obligation, what our nature and condition require, seems very obvious, were it only from the consideration, that revenge is doing harm merely for harm's sake. And as to the love of our enemies: resentment cannot supersede the obligation to universal benevolence, unless they are in the nature of the thing inconsistent, which they plainly are not.*

This divine precept, to forgive injuries and love our enemies, though to be met with in Gentile moralists, yet is in a peculiar sense a precept of Christianity; as our Saviour has insisted more upon it than upon any other single virtue. One reason of this doubtless is, that it so peculiarly becomes an imperfect, faulty creature. But it may be observed also, that a virtuous temper of mind, consciousness of innocence, and good meaning towards every body, and a strong feeling of injustice and injury, may itself, such is the imperfection of our virtue, lead a person to violate this obligation, if he be not upon his guard. And it may well be supposed, that this is another reason why it is so much insisted upon by him, who *knew what was in man.*

The chief design of the eleventh Discourse is to state the notion of self-love and disinterestedness, in order to show that benevolence is not more unfriendly to self-love, than any other particular affection whatever

* Page 108

There is a strange affectation in many people of explaining away all particular affections, and representing the whole of life as nothing but one continued exercise of self-love. Hence arises that surprising confusion and perplexity in the Epicureans* of old, Hobbes, the author of *Reflections, Sentences, et Maximes Morales*, and this whole set of writers; the confusion of calling actions interested which are done in contradiction to the most manifest known interest, merely for the gratification of a present passion. Now all this confusion might easily be avoided, by stating to ourselves wherein the idea of self-love in general consists, as distinguished from all particular movements towards particular external objects; the appetites of sense, resentment, compassion, curiosity, ambition, and the rest.† When this is done, if the words *selfish* and *interested* cannot be parted with, but must be applied to every thing; yet, to avoid such total confusion of all language, let the distinction be made by epithets: and the first may be called cool or settled selfishness, and the other passionate or sensual selfishness. But the most natural way of speaking plainly is, to call the first only, self-love, and the actions proceeding from it, interested: and to say of the latter, that they are not love to ourselves, but movements towards somewhat external: honour, power, the harm or good of another: and that the pursuit of these external objects, so far as it proceeds from these movements (for it may proceed from self-love‡), is no otherwise interested, than as every action of every creature must, from the nature of the thing, be; for no one can act but from a desire, or choice, or preference of his own.

Self-love and any particular passion may be joined together; and from this complication, it becomes impos-

* One need only look into Torquatus's account of the Epicurean system, in Cicero's first book *De Finibus*, to see in what a surprising manner this was done by them. Thus the desire of praise, and of being beloved, he explains to be no other than desire of safety: regard to our country, even in the most virtuous character, to be nothing but regard to ourselves. The author of *Reflections, &c. Morales*, says, Curiosity proceeds from interest or pride; which pride also would doubtless have been explained to be self-love. Page 85, ed. 1725. As if there were no such passions in mankind as desire of esteem, or of being beloved, or of knowledge. Hobbes's account of the affections of good-will and pity are instances of the same kind.

† Page 126, &c. ‡ See the note, page 29.

sible in numberless instances to determine precisely, how far an action, perhaps even of one's own, has for its principle general self-love, or some particular passion. But this need create no confusion in the ideas themselves of self-love and particular passions. We distinctly discern what one is, and what the other are: though we may be uncertain how far one or the other influences us. And though, from this uncertainty, it cannot but be that there will be different opinions concerning mankind, as more or less governed by interest; and some will ascribe actions to self-love, which others will ascribe to particular passions: yet it is absurd to say that mankind are wholly actuated by either; since it is manifest that both have their influence. For as, on the one hand, men form a general notion of interest, some placing it in one thing, and some in another, and have a considerable regard to it throughout the course of their life, which is owing to self-love; so, on the other hand, they are often set on work by the particular passions themselves, and a considerable part of life is spent in the actual gratification of them, *i. e.* is employed, not by self-love, but by the passions.

Besides, the very idea of an interested pursuit necessarily presupposes particular passions or appetites; since the very idea of interest or happiness consists in this, that an appetite or affection enjoys its object. It is not because we love ourselves that we find delight in such and such objects, but because we have particular affections towards them. Take away these affections, and you leave self-love absolutely nothing at all to employ itself about;* no end or object for it to pursue, excepting only that of avoiding pain. Indeed the Epicureans, who maintained that absence of pain was the highest happiness, might, consistently with themselves, deny all affection, and, if they had so pleased, every sensual appetite too: but the very idea of interest or happiness other than absence of pain implies particular appetites or passions; these being necessary to constitute that interest or happiness.

The observation, that benevolence is no more disin-

* Page 128.

terested than any of the common particular passions,* seems in itself worth being taken notice of; but is insisted upon to obviate that scorn, which one sees rising upon the faces of people who are said to know the world, when mention is made of a disinterested, generous, or public-spirited action. The truth of that observation might be made appear in a more formal manner of proof: for whoever will consider all the possible respects and relations which any particular affection can have to self-love and private interest, will, I think, see demonstrably, that benevolence is not in any respect more at variance with self-love, than any other particular affection whatever, but that it is in every respect, at least, as friendly to it.

If the observation be true, it follows, that self-love and benevolence, virtue and interest, are not to be opposed, but only to be distinguished from each other; in the same way as virtue and any other particular affection, love of arts, suppose, are to be distinguished. Every thing is what it is, and not another thing. The goodness or badness of actions does not arise from hence, that the epithet, interested or disinterested, may be applied to them, any more than that any other indifferent epithet, suppose inquisitive or jealous, may or may not be applied to them; not from their being attended with present or future pleasure or pain; but from their being what they are; namely, what becomes such creatures as we are, what the state of the case requires, or the contrary. Or in other words, we may judge and determine, that an action is morally good or evil, before we so much as consider, whether it be interested or disinterested. This consideration no more comes in to determine whether an action be virtuous, than to determine whether it be resentful. Self-love in its due degree is as just and morally good, as any affection whatever. Benevolence towards particular persons may be to a degree of weakness, and so be blameable: and disinterestedness is so far from being in itself commendable, that the utmost possible depravity which we can in imagination conceive, is that of disinterested cruelty.

* Page 130, &c.

Neither does there appear any reason to wish self-love were weaker in the generality of the world than it is. The influence which it has seems plainly owing to its being constant and habitual, which it cannot but be, and not to the degree or strength of it. Every caprice of the imagination, every curiosity of the understanding, every affection of the heart, is perpetually showing its weakness, by prevailing over it. Men daily, hourly sacrifice the greatest known interest, to fancy, inquisitiveness, love, or hatred, any vagrant inclination. The thing to be lamented is, not that men have so great regard to their own good or interest in the present world, for they have not enough;* but that they have so little to the good of others. And this seems plainly owing to their being so much engaged in the gratification of particular passions unfriendly to benevolence, and which happen to be most prevalent in them, much more than to self-love. As a proof of this may be observed, that there is no character more void of friendship, gratitude, natural affection, love to their country, common justice, or more equally and uniformly hard-hearted, than the *abandoned* in, what is called, the way of pleasure——hard-hearted and totally without feeling in behalf of others; except when they cannot escape the sight of distress, and so are interrupted by it in their pleasures. And yet it is ridiculous to call such an abandoned course of pleasure interested, when the person engaged in it knows beforehand, goes on under the feeling and apprehension, that it will be as ruinous to himself, as to those who depend upon him.

Upon the whole, if the generality of mankind were to cultivate within themselves the principle of self-love; if they were to accustom themselves often to set down and consider, what was the greatest happiness they were capable of attaining for themselves in this life, and if self-love were so strong and prevalent, as that they would uniformly pursue this their supposed chief temporal good, without being diverted from it by any particular passion; it would manifestly prevent numberless follies and vices. This was in a great measure the Epicurean system of philosophy. It is indeed by no means the religious or

* Page 34.

even moral institution of life. Yet, with all the mistakes men would fall into about interest, it would be less mischievous than the extravagances of mere appetite, will, and pleasure: for certainly self-love, though confined to the interest of this life, is, of the two, a much better guide than passion,* which has absolutely no bound nor measure, but what is set to it by this self-love, or moral considerations.

From the distinction above made between self-love, and the several particular principles or affections in our nature, we may see how good ground there was for that assertion, maintained by the several ancient schools of philosophy against the Epicureans, namely, that virtue is to be pursued as an end, eligible in and for itself. For, if there be any principles or affections in the mind of man distinct from self-love, that the things those principles tend towards, or that the objects of those affections are, each of them, in themselves eligible, to be pursued upon its own account, and to be rested in as an end, is implied in the very idea of such principle or affection.† They indeed asserted much higher things of virtue, and with very good reason; but to say thus much of it, that it is to be pursued for itself, is to say no more of it, than may truly be said of the object of every natural affection whatever.

The question, which was a few years ago disputed in France, concerning *the love of God*, which was there called enthusiasm, as it will every where by the generality of the world; this question, I say, answers in religion to that old one in morals now mentioned. And both of them are, I think, fully determined by the same observation, namely, that the very nature of affection, the idea itself, necessarily implies resting in its object as an end.

I shall not here add any thing further to what I have said in the two Discourses upon that most important subject, but only this: that if we are constituted such sort of creatures, as from our very nature to feel certain affections or movements of mind, upon the sight or contemplation of the meanest inanimate part of the creation,

* P. 44. † P. 155.

for the flowers of the field have their beauty; certainly there must be somewhat due to him himself, who is the Author and Cause of all things; who is more intimately present to us than any thing else can be, and with whom we have a nearer and more constant intercourse, than we can have with any creature: there must be some movements of mind and heart which correspond to his perfections, or of which those perfections are the natural object: and that when we are commanded to *love the Lord our God with all our heart, and with all our mind, and with all our soul;* somewhat more must be meant than merely that we live in hope of rewards or fear of punishments from him; somewhat more than this must be intended: though these regards themselves are most just and reasonable, and absolutely necessary to be often recollected in such a world as this.

It may be proper just to advertise the reader, that he is not to look for any particular reason for the choice of the greatest part of these Discourses; their being taken from amongst many others, preached in the same place, through a course of eight years, being in great measure accidental. Neither is he to expect to find any other connexion between them, than that uniformity of thought and design, which will always be found in the writings of the same person, when he writes with simplicity and in earnest.

Stanhope, Sept. 16, 1729.

CONTENTS.

UPON HUMAN NATURE, OR MAN CONSIDERED AS A MORAL AGENT.

SIX SERMONS

PREACHED UPON PUBLIC OCCASIONS.

SERMON I.

UPON HUMAN NATURE.

For as we have many members in one body, and all members have not the same office: so we being many are one body in Christ, and every one members one of another.—Rom. xii. 4, 5.

THE Epistles in the New Testament have all of them a particular reference to the condition and usages of the Christian world at the time they were written. Therefore as they cannot be thoroughly understood, unless that condition and those usages are known and attended to: so further, though they be known, yet if they be discontinued or changed; exhortations, precepts, and illustrations of things, which refer to such circumstances now ceased or altered, cannot at this time be urged in that manner, and with that force which they were to the primitive Christians. Thus the text now before us, in its first intent and design, relates to the decent management of those extraordinary gifts which were then in the church,* but which are now totally ceased. And even as to the allusion that *we are one body in Christ;* though what the Apostle here intends is equally true of Christians in all circumstances; and the consideration of it is plainly still an additional motive, over and above moral considerations, to the discharge of the several duties and offices of a Christian: yet it is manifest this allusion must have appeared with much greater force to those, who, by the many difficulties they went through for the sake of their religion, were led to keep always in view the relation they stood in to their Saviour, who had undergone the same; to those, who, from the idolatries of all around them, and their ill-treatment, were taught

* 1 Cor. xii.

to consider themselves as not of the world in which they lived, but as a distinct society of themselves; with laws and ends, and principles of life and action, quite contrary to those which the world professed themselves at that time influenced by. Hence the relation of a Christian was by them considered as nearer than that of affinity and blood; and they almost literally esteemed themselves as members one of another.

It cannot indeed possibly be denied, that our being God's creatures, and virtue being the natural law we are born under, and the whole constitution of man being plainly adapted to it, are prior obligations to piety and virtue, than the consideration that God sent his Son into the world to save it, and the motives which arise from the peculiar relation of Christians, as members one of another under Christ our head. However, though all this be allowed, as it expressly is by the inspired writers; yet it is manifest that Christians at the time of the revelation, and immediately after, could not but insist mostly upon considerations of this latter kind.

These observations show the original particular reference of the text; and the peculiar force with which the thing intended by the allusion in it, must have been felt by the primitive Christian world. They likewise afford a reason for treating it at this time in a more general way.

The relation which the several parts or members of the natural body have to each other and to the whole body, is here compared to the relation which each particular person in society has to other particular persons and to the whole society; and the latter is intended to be illustrated by the former. And if there be a likeness between these two relations, the consequence is obvious: that the latter shows us we were intended to do good to others, as the former shows us that the several members of the natural body were intended to be instruments of good to each other and to the whole body. [But as there is scarce any ground for a comparison between society and the mere material body, this without the mind being a dead unactive thing; much less can the comparison be carried to any length.] And since the apostle speaks of the several members as having distinct offices, which implies the mind; it cannot be thought an unallowable liberty, instead of the *body* and *its members*, to substitute the *whole nature of man*, and *all the variety of internal principles which belong to it.* And then the comparison will be between the nature of man as respecting self, and tending to private good, his own preservation and happiness; and the nature of man as having respect to society, and tending to promote public good, the happiness of that society. These ends do indeed perfectly coincide; and to aim at public and private good are so far from being inconsistent, that they mutually promote each other: yet in the following discourse they must be considered as entirely distinct; otherwise the nature of man as tending to one, or as tending to the other, cannot be compared. There can no comparison be made, without considering the things compared as distinct and different.

From this review and comparison of the nature of man as respecting self, and as respecting society, it will plainly appear, that *there are as real and the same kind of indications in human nature, that we were made for society and to do good to our fellow creatures; as that we were intended to take care of our own life and health and private good: and that the same objections lie against one of these assertions, as against the other.* For,

First, There is a natural principle of *benevolence** in

* Suppose a man of learning to be writing a grave book upon *human nature*, and to show in several parts of it that he had an insight into the subject he was considering; amongst other things, the following one would require to be accounted for; the appearance of benevolence or good-will in men towards each other in the instances of natural relation, and in others.* Cautious of being deceived with outward show, he retires within himself to see exactly, what that is in the mind of man from whence this appearance proceeds; and, upon deep reflection, asserts the principle in the mind to be only the love of power, and delight in the exercise of it. Would not every body think here was a mistake of one word for another? that the philosopher was contemplating and accounting for some other *human actions*, some other behaviour of man to man? And could any one be thoroughly satisfied, that what is commonly called benevolence or good will was really the affection meant, but only by being made to understand that this learned person had a general hypothesis, to which the appearance of good-will could no otherwise be reconciled? That what has this appearance is often nothing but ambition; that delight in superiority often (suppose always) mixes itself with benevolence, only makes it more specious to call it ambition than hunger, of the two: but in reality that passion does no more account for the whole appearances of good-will than this appetite does Is there not often the appearance of one man's wishing that good to another, which he knows himself unable to procure him; and rejoicing in it, though bestowed by a third person? And can love of power any way possibly come in to account for this desire or delight?

* Hobbes of Human Nature, c. ix. § 7

man; which is in some degree to *society*, what *self-love* is to the *individual*. And if there be in mankind any disposition to friendship; if there be any such thing as compassion, for compassion is momentary love; if there be any such thing as the paternal or filial affections; if there be any affection in human nature, the object and end of which is the good of another; this is itself benevolence, or the love of another. Be it ever so short, be it in ever so low a degree, or ever so unhappily confined; it proves the assertion, and points out what we were designed for, as really as though it were in a higher degree and more extensive. I must however remind you that though benevolence and self-love are different; though the former tends most directly to public good, and the latter to private: yet they are so perfectly coin-

Is there not often the appearance of men's distinguishing between two or more persons, preferring one before another, to do good to, in cases where love of power cannot in the least account for the distinction and preference? For this principle can no otherwise distinguish between objects, than as it is a greater instance and exertion of power to do good to one rather than to another. Again, suppose good-will in the mind of man to be nothing but delight in the exercise of power: men might indeed be restrained by distant and accidental consideration; but these restraints being removed, they would have a disposition to, and delight in mischief as an exercise and proof of power: and this disposition and delight would arise from, or be the same principle in the mind, as a disposition to, and delight in charity. Thus cruelty, as distinct from envy and resentment, would be exactly the same in the mind of man as good-will: that one tends to the happiness, the other to the misery of our fellow creatures, is, it seems, merely an accidental circumstance, which the mind has not the least regard to. These are the absurdities which even men of capacity run into, when they have occasion to belie their nature, and will perversely disclaim that image of God which was originally stamped upon it, the traces of which, however faint, are plainly discernible upon the mind of man.

If any person can in earnest doubt, whether there be such a thing as good-will in one man towards another; (for the question is not concerning either the degree or extensiveness of it, but concerning the affection itself:) let it be observed, that *whether man be thus, or otherwise constituted, what is the inward frame in this particular*, is a mere question of fact or natural history, not proveable immediately by reason. It is therefore to be judged of and determined in the same way other facts or matters of natural history are: by appealing to the external senses, or inward perceptions, respectively, as the matter under consideration is cognizable by one or the other: by arguing from acknowledged facts and actions; for a great number of actions in the same kind, in different circumstances, and respecting different objects will prove to a certainty, what principles they do not, and, to the greatest probability, what principles they do proceed from: and lastly, by the testimony of mankind. Now that there is some degree of benevolence amongst men, may be as strongly and plainly proved in all these ways, as it could possibly be proved, supposing there was this affection in our nature. And should any one think fit to assert, that resentment in the mind of man was absolutely nothing but reasonable concern for our own safety, the falsity of this, and what is the real nature of that passion, could be shown in no other way than those in which it may be shown, that there is such a thing in *some degree* as *real* good-will in man towards man. It is sufficient that the seeds of it be implanted in our nature by God. There is, it is owned, much left for us to do upon our own heart and temper; to cultivate, to improve, to call it forth, to exercise it in a steady, uniform manner. This is our work; this is virtue and religion.

cident, that the greatest satisfactions to ourselves depend upon our having benevolence in a due degree; and that self-love is one chief security of our right behaviour towards society. It may be added, that their mutual coinciding, so that we can scarce promote one without the other, is equally a proof that we were made for both.

Secondly, This will further appear, from observing that the *several passions* and *affections*, which are distinct* both from benevolence and self-love, do in general contribute and lead us to *public* good as really as to *private.* It might be thought too minute and particular, and would carry us too great a length, to distinguish between and compare together the several passions or appetites distinct from benevolence, whose primary use and intention is the security and good of society; and the passions distinct from self-love, whose primary intention and design is the security and good of the individual.† It is enough to the present argument, that

* Every body makes a distinction between self-love, and the several particular passions, appetites, and affections; and yet they are often confounded again. That they are totally different, will be seen by any one who will distinguish between the passions and appetites *themselves*, and *endeavouring* after the means of their gratification. Consider the appetite of hunger, and the desire of esteem: these being the occasion both of pleasure and pain, the coolest *self-love*, as well as the appetites and passions themselves, may put us upon making use of the *proper methods of obtaining* that pleasure, and avoiding that pain; but the *feelings themselves*, the pain of hunger and shame, and the delight from esteem, are no more self-love than they are any thing in the world. Though a man hated himself, he would as much feel the pain of hunger as he would that of the gout: and it is plainly supposable there may be creatures with self-love in them to the highest degree, who may be quite insensible and indifferent (as men in some cases are) to the contempt and esteem of those, upon whom their happiness does not in some further respects depend. And as self-love and the several particular passions and appetites are in themselves totally different; so, that some actions proceed from one, and some from the other, will be manifest to any who will observe the two following very supposable cases. One man rushes upon certain ruin for the gratification of a present desire: nobody will call the principle of this action self-love. Suppose another man to go through some laborious work upon promise of a great reward, without any distinct knowledge what the reward will be: this course of action cannot be ascribed to any particular passion. The former of these actions is plainly to be imputed to some particular passion or affection, the latter as plainly to the general affection or principle of self-love. That there are some particular pursuits or actions concerning which we cannot determine how far they are owing to one, and how far to the other, proceeds from this that the two principles are frequently mixed together, and run up into each other. This distinction is further explained in the eleventh sermon.

† If any desire to see this distinction and comparison made in a particular instance, the appetite and passion now mentioned may serve for one. Hunger is to be considered as a private appetite; because the end for which it was given us is the preservation of the individual. Desire of esteem is a public passion; because the end for which it was given us is to regulate our behaviour towards society. The respect which this has to private good is as remote as the respect that has to public good: and the appetite is no more self-love, than the passion is benevolence. The object and end of the former is merely food; the object and end of the latter is

desire of esteem from others, contempt and esteem of them, love of society as distinct from affection to the good of it, indignation against successful vice, that these are public affections or passions; have an immediate respect to others, naturally lead us to regulate our behaviour in such a manner as will be of service to our fellow creatures. If any or all of these may be considered likewise as private affections, as tending to private good; this does not hinder them from being public affections too, or destroy the good influence of them upon society, and their tendency to public good. It may be added, that as persons without any conviction from reason of the desirableness of life, would yet of course preserve it merely from the appetite of hunger; so by acting merely from regard (suppose) to reputation, without any consideration of the good of others, men often contribute to public good. In both these instances they are plainly instruments in the hands of another, in the hands of Providence, to carry on ends, the preservation of the individual and good of society, which they themselves have not in their view or intention. The sum is, men have various appetites, passions, and particular affections, quite distinct both from self-love and from benevolence: all of these have a tendency to promote both public and private good, and may be considered as respecting others and ourselves equally and in common: but some of them seem most immediately to respect others, or tend to public good; others of them most immediately to respect self, or tend to private good: as the former are not benevolence, so the latter are not self-love: neither sort are instances of our love either to ourselves or others; but only instances of our Maker's care and love both of the individual and the species, and proofs that he intended we should be instruments of good to each other, as well as that we should be so to ourselves.

Thirdly, There is a principle of reflection in men, by which they distinguish between, approve and disapprove

merely esteem: but the latter can no more be gratified, without contributing to the good of society; than the former can be gratified, without contributing to the preservation of the individual.

their own actions. We are plainly constituted such sort of creatures as to reflect upon our own nature. The mind can take a view of what passes within itself, its propensions, aversions, passions, affections, as respecting such objects, and in such degrees; and of the several actions consequent thereupon. In this survey it approves of one, disapproves of another, and towards a third is affected in neither of these ways, but is quite indifferent. This principle in man, by which he approves or disapproves his heart, temper, and actions, is conscience; for this is the strict sense of the word, though sometimes it is used so as to take in more. And that this faculty tends to restrain men from doing mischief to each other, and leads them to do good, is too manifest to need being insisted upon. Thus a parent has the affection of love to his children: this leads him to take care of, to educate, to make due provision for them; the natural affection leads to this: but the reflection that it is his proper business, what belongs to him, that it is right and commendable so to do; this added to the affection becomes a much more settled principle, and carries him on through more labour and difficulties for the sake of his children, than he would undergo from that affection alone, if he thought it, and the course of action it led to, either indifferent or criminal. This indeed is impossible, to do that which is good and not to approve of it; for which reason they are frequently not considered as distinct, though they really are: for men often approve of the actions of others, which they will not imitate, and likewise do that which they approve not. It cannot possibly be denied, that there is this principle of reflection or conscience in human nature. Suppose a man to relieve an innocent person in great distress; suppose the same man afterwards, in the fury of anger, to do the greatest mischief to a person who had given no just cause of offence; to aggravate the injury, add the circumstances of former friendship, and obligation from the injured person; let the man who is supposed to have done these two different actions, coolly reflect upon them afterwards, without regard to their consequences to himself: to assert that any common man would be affected in the same way towards these different actions, that he would make no distinction between them, but approve or disapprove them equally, is too glaring a falsity to need being confuted. There is therefore this principle of reflection or conscience in mankind. It is needless to compare the respect it has to private good, with the respect it has to public; since it plainly tends as much to the latter as to the former, and is commonly thought to tend chiefly to the latter. This faculty is now mentioned merely as another part in the inward frame of man, pointing out to us in some degree what we are intended for, and as what will naturally and of course have some influence. The particular place assigned to it by nature, what authority it has, and how great influence it ought have, shall be hereafter considered.

From this comparison of benevolence and self-love, of our public and private affections, of the courses of life they lead to, and of the principle of reflection or conscience as respecting each of them, it is as manifest, that *we were made for society, and to promote the happiness of it; as that we were intended to take care of our own life, and health, and private good.*

And from this whole review must be given a different draught of human nature from what we are often presented with. Mankind are by nature so closely united, there is such a correspondence between the inward sensations of one man and those of another, that disgrace is as much avoided as bodily pain, and to be the object of esteem and love as much desired as any external goods: and in many particular cases, persons are carried on to do good to others, as the end their affection tends to and rests in; and manifest that they find real satisfaction and enjoyment in this course of behaviour. There is such a natural principle of attraction in man towards man, that having trod the same tract of land, having breathed in the same climate, barely having been in the same artificial district or division, becomes the occasion of contracting acquaintances and familiarities many years after: for any thing may serve the purpose. Thus relations merely nominal are sought and invented, not by governors, but by the lowest of the people; which are found sufficient to hold mankind together in little fraternities and copartnerships: weak ties indeed, and what may afford fund enough for ridicule, if they are absurdly considered as the real principles of that union: but they are in truth merely the occasions, as any thing may be of any thing, upon which our nature carries us on according to its own previous bent and bias; which occasions therefore would be nothing at all, were there not this prior disposition and bias of nature. Men are so much one body, that in a peculiar manner they feel for each other, shame, sudden danger, resentment, honour, prosperity, distress; one or another, or all of these, from the social nature in general, from benevolence, upon the occasion of natural relation, acquaintance, protection, dependence; each of these being distinct cements of society. And therefore to have no restraint from, no regard to others in our behaviour, is the speculative absurdity of considering ourselves as single and independent, as having nothing in our nature which has respect to our fellow creatures, reduced to action and practice. And this is the same absurdity, as to suppose a hand, or any part, to have no natural respect to any other, or to the whole body.

But allowing all this, it may be asked, "Has not man dispositions and principles within, which lead him to do evil to others, as well as to do good? Whence come the many miseries else, which men are the authors and instruments of to each other?" These questions, so far as they relate to the foregoing discourse, may be answered by asking, Has not man also dispositions and principles within, which lead him to do evil to himself as well as good? Whence come the many miseries else, sickness, pain, and death, which men are instruments and authors of to themselves?

It may be thought more easy to answer one of these questions than the other, but the answer to both is really the same; that mankind have ungoverned passions which they will gratify at any rate, as well to the injury of others, as in contradiction to known private interest: but that as there is no such thing as self-hatred, so neither is there any such thing as ill-will in one man towards another, emulation and resentment being away; whereas there is plainly benevolence or good-will: there is no such thing as love of injustice, oppression, treachery, ingratitude; but only eager desires after such and such external goods; which, according to a very ancient observation, the most abandoned would choose to obtain by innocent means, if they were as easy, and as effectual to their end: that even emulation and resentment, by any one who will consider what these passions really are in nature,* will be found nothing to the purpose of this objection: and that the principles and passions in the mind of man, which are distinct both from self-love and benevolence, primarily and most directly lead to right behaviour with regard to others as well as himself, and only secondarily and accidentally to what is evil. Thus, though men, to avoid the shame of one villany, are sometimes guilty of a greater, yet it is easy to see, that the original tendency of shame is to prevent the doing of shameful actions; and its leading men to conceal such actions when done, is only in consequence of their being done; *i. e.* of the passion's not having answered its first end.

If it be said, that there are persons in the world, who are in great measure without the natural affections towards their fellow creatures: there are likewise instances of persons without the common natural affections to themselves: but the nature of man is not to be judged of by either of these, but by what appears in the common world, in the bulk of mankind.

I am afraid it would be thought very strange, if to confirm the truth of this account of human nature, and make out the justness of the foregoing comparison, it should be added, that, from what appears, men in fact as much and as often contradict that *part* of their nature which respects *self*, and which leads them to their *own private*

* Emulation is merely the desire and hope of equality with, or superiority over others, with whom we compare ourselves. There does not appear to be any *other grief* in the natural passion, but only *that want* which is implied in desire. However this may be so strong as to be the occasion of great *grief*. To desire the attainment of this equality or superiority by the *particular means* of others being brought down to our own level, or below it, is, I think, the distinct notion of envy. From whence it is easy to see, that the real end, which the natural passion emulation, and which the unlawful one envy aims at, is exactly the same; namely, that equality or superiority: and consequently, that to do mischief is not the end of envy, but merely the means it makes use of to attain its end. As to resentment, see the eighth sermon.

good and happiness; as they contradict that *part* of it which respects *society*, and tends to *public* good: that there are as few persons, who attain the greatest satisfaction and enjoyment which they might attain in the present world; as who do the greatest good to others which they might do; nay, that there are as few who can be said really and in earnest to aim at one, as at the other. Take a survey of mankind: the world in general, the good and bad, almost without exception, equally are agreed, that were religion out of the case, the happiness of the present life would consist in a manner wholly in riches, honours, sensual gratifications; insomuch that one scarce hears a reflection made upon prudence, life, conduct, but upon this supposition. Yet on the contrary, that persons in the greatest affluence of fortune are no happier than such as have only a competency; that the cares and disappointments of ambition for the most part far exceed the satisfactions of it; as also the miserable intervals of intemperance and excess, and the many untimely deaths occasioned by a dissolute course of life: these things are all seen, acknowledged, by every one acknowledged; but are thought no objections against, though they expressly contradict, this universal principle, that the happiness of the present life consists in one or other of them. Whence is all this absurdity and contradiction? Is not the middle way obvious? Can any thing be more manifest, than that the happiness of life consists in these possessed and enjoyed only to a certain degree; that to pursue them beyond this degree, is always attended with more inconvenience than advantage to a man's self, and often with extreme misery and unhappiness. Whence then, I say, is all this absurdity and contradiction? Is it really the result of consideration in mankind, how they may become most easy to themselves, most free from care, and enjoy the chief happiness attainable in this world? Or is it not manifestly owing either to this, that they have not cool and reasonable concern enough for themselves to consider wherein their chief happiness in the present life consists; or else, if they do consider it, that they will not act conformably to what is the result of that consideration: *i. e.* reasonable concern for themselves, or cool self-love is prevailed over by passion and appetite. So that from what appears, there is no ground to assert that those principles in the nature of man, which most directly lead to promote the good of our fellow creatures, are more generally or in a greater degree violated, than those, which most directly lead us to promote our own private good and happiness.

The sum of the whole is plainly this. The nature of man, considered in his single capacity, and with respect only to the present world, is adapted and leads him to attain the greatest happiness he can for himself in the present world. The nature of man, considered in his public or social capacity, leads him to a right behaviour in society to that course of life which we call virtue. Men follow or obey their nature in both these capacities and respects to a certain degree, but not entirely: their actions do not come up to the whole of what their nature leads them to in either of these capacities or respects: and they often violate their nature in both, *i. e.* as they neglect the duties they owe to their fellow creatures, to which their nature leads them; and are injurious, to which their nature is abhorrent; so there is a manifest negligence in men of their real happiness or interest in the present world, when that interest is inconsistent with a present gratification; for the sake of which they negligently, nay, even knowingly, are the authors and instruments of their own misery and ruin. Thus they are as often unjust to themselves as to others, and for the most part are equally so to both by the same actions.

SERMON II. III.

UPON HUMAN NATURE.

For when the Gentiles, which have not the law, do by nature the things contained in the law, these, having not the law, are a law unto themselves.—Rom. ii. 14.

As speculative truth admits of different kinds of proof, so likewise moral obligations may be shown by different methods. If the real nature of any creature leads him and is adapted to such and such purposes only, or more than to any other; this is a reason to believe the author of that nature intended it for those purposes. Thus there is no doubt the eye was intended for us to see with. And the more complex any constitution is, and the greater variety of parts there are which thus tend to some one end, the stronger is the proof that such end was designed. However, when the inward frame of man is considered as any guide in morals, the utmost caution must be used that none make peculiarities in their own temper, or any thing which is the effect of particular customs, though observable in several, the standard of what is common to the species; and above all, that the highest principle be not forgot or excluded, that to which belongs the adjustment and correction of all other inward movements and affections: which principle will of course have some influence, but which being in nature supreme, as shall now be shown, ought to preside over and govern all the rest. The difficulty of rightly observing the two former cautions; the appearance there is of some small diversity amongst mankind with respect to this faculty, with respect to their natural sense of moral good and evil; and the attention necessary to survey with any exactness what passes within, have occasioned that it is not so much agreed what is the standard of the internal nature of man, as of his external form. Neither is this last exactly settled. Yet we understand one another when we speak of the shape of a human body: so likewise we do when we speak of the heart and inward principles, how far soever the standard is from being exact or precisely fixed. There is therefore ground for an attempt of showing men to themselves, of showing them what course of life and behaviour their real nature points out and would lead them to. Now obligations of virtue shown, and motives to the practice of it enforced, from a review of the nature of man, are to be considered as an appeal to each particular person's heart and natural conscience: as the external senses are appealed to for the proof of things cognizable by them. Since then our inward feelings, and the perceptions we receive from our external senses, are equally real; to argue from the former to life and conduct is as little liable to exception, as to argue from the latter to absolute speculative truth. A man can as little doubt whether his eyes were given him to see with, as he can doubt of the truth of the science of *optics*, deduced from ocular experiments. And allowing the inward feeling, shame; a man can as little doubt whether it was given him to prevent his doing shameful actions, as he can doubt whether his eyes were given him to guide his steps. And as to these inward feelings themselves; that they are real, that man has in his nature passions and affections, can no more be questioned, than that he has external senses. Neither can the former be wholly mistaken; though to a certain degree liable to greater mistakes than the latter.

There can be no doubt but that several propensions or instincts, several principles in the heart of man, carry him to society, and to contribute to the happiness of it, in a sense and a manner in which no inward principle leads him to evil. These principles, propensions, or instincts which lead him to do good, are approved of by a certain faculty within, quite distinct from these propensions themselves. All this hath been fully made out in the foregoing discourse.

But it may be said, "What is all this, though true, to the purpose of virtue and religion? these require, not only that we do good to others when we are led this way, by benevolence or reflection, happening to be stronger than other principles, passions, or appetites; but likewise that the *whole* character be formed upon thought and reflection; that *every* action be directed by some determinate rule, some other rule than the strength and prevalency of any principle or passion. What sign is there in our nature (for the inquiry is only about what is to be collected from thence) that this was intended by its Author? Or how does so various and fickle a temper as that of man appear adapted thereto? It may indeed be absurd and unnatural for men to act without any reflection; nay, without regard to that particular kind of reflection which you call conscience; because this does belong to our nature. For as there never was a man but who approved one place, prospect, building, before another: so it does not appear that there ever was a man who would not have approved an action of humanity rather than of cruelty; interest and passion being quite out of the case. But interest and passion do come in, and are often too strong for and prevail over reflection and conscience. Now as brutes have various instincts, by which they are carried on to the end the Author of their nature intended them for: is not man in the same condition; with this difference only, that to his instincts (*i. e.* appetites and passions) is added the principle of reflection or conscience? And as brutes act agreeably to their nature, in following that principle or particular instinct which for the present is strongest in them: does not man likewise act agreeably to his nature, or obey the law of his creation, by following that principle, be it passion or conscience, which for the present happens to be strongest in him? Thus different men are by their particular nature hurried on to pursue honour, or riches, or pleasure: there are also persons whose temper leads them in an uncommon degree to kindness, compassion, doing good to their fellow creatures: as there are others who are given to suspend their judgment, to weigh and consider things, and to act upon thought and reflection. Let every one then quietly follow his nature; as passion, reflection, appetite, the several parts of it, happen to be strongest: but let not the man of virtue take upon him to blame the ambitious, the covetous, the dissolute; since these equally with him obey and follow their nature. Thus, as in some cases we follow our nature in doing the works *contained in the law,* so in other cases we follow nature in doing contrary."

Now all this licentious talk entirely goes upon a supposition, that men follow their nature in the same sense, in violating the known rules of justice and honesty for the sake of a present gratification, as they do in following those rules when they have no temptation to the contrary. And if this were true, that could not be so which St Paul asserts, that men are *by nature a law to themselves.* If by following nature were meant only acting as we please, it would indeed be ridiculous to speak of nature as any guide in morals: nay the very mention of deviating from nature would be absurd; and the mention of following it, when spoken by way of distinction, would absolutely have no meaning. For did ever any one act otherwise than as he pleased? And yet the ancients speak of deviating from nature as vice; and of following nature so much as a distinction, that according to them the perfection of virtue consists therein. So that language itself should teach people another sense to the words *following nature,* than barely acting as we please. Let it however be observed, that though the words *human nature* are to be explained, yet the real question of this discourse is not concerning the meaning of words, any other than as the explanation of them may be needful to make out and explain the assertion, that *every man is naturally a law to himself,* that *every one may find within himself the rule of right, and obligations to follow it.* This St Paul affirms in the words of the text, and this the foregoing objection really denies by seeming to allow it. And the objection will be fully answered, and the text before us explained, by observing that *nature* is considered in different views, and the word used in different senses; and by showing in what view it is considered, and in what sense the word is used, when intended to express and signify that which is the guide of life, that by which men are a law to themselves. I say, the explanation of the term will be sufficient, because from thence it will appear, that in some senses of the word *nature* cannot be, but that in another sense it manifestly is, a law to us.

I. By nature is often meant no more than some prin

ciple in man, without regard either to the kind or degree of it. Thus the passion of anger, and the affection of parents to their children, would be called equally *natural.* And as the same person hath often contrary principles, which at the same time draw contrary ways, he may by the same action both follow and contradict his nature in this sense of the word; he may follow one passion and contradict another.

II. *Nature* is frequently spoken of as consisting in those passions which are strongest, and most influence the actions; which being vicious ones, mankind is in this sense naturally vicious, or vicious by nature. Thus St Paul says of the Gentiles, *who were dead in trespasses and sins, and walked according to the spirit of disobedience, that they were by nature the children of wrath.** They could be no otherwise *children of wrath* by nature, than they were vicious by nature.

Here then are two different senses of the word *nature,* in neither of which men can at all be said to be a law to themselves. They are mentioned only to be excluded; to prevent their being confounded, as the latter is in the objection, with another sense of it, which is now to be inquired after and explained.

III. The apostle asserts, that the Gentiles *do by nature the things contained in the law.* Nature is indeed here put by way of distinction from revelation, but yet it is not a mere negative. He intends to express more than that by which they *did not,* that by which they *did* the works of the law; namely, by *nature.* It is plain the meaning of the word is not the same in this passage as in the former, where it is spoken of as evil; for in this latter it is spoken of as good; as that by which they acted, or might have acted virtuously. What that is in man by which he is *naturally a law to himself,* is explained in the following words: *Which shew the work of the law written in their hearts, their consciences also bearing witness, and their thoughts the mean while accusing or else excusing one another.* If there be a distinction to be made between the *works written in their hearts,* and the *witness of conscience;* by the former must be meant the

* Ephes. ii. 3.

natural disposition to kindness and compassion, to do what is of good report, to which this apostle often refers: that part of the nature of man, treated of in the foregoing discourse, which with very little reflection and of course leads him to society, and by means of which he naturally acts a just and good part in it, unless other passions or interests lead him astray. Yet since other passions, and regards to private interest, which lead us (though indirectly, yet they lead us) astray, are themselves in a degree equally natural, and often most prevalent; and since we have no method of seeing the particular degrees in which one or the other is placed in us by nature; it is plain the former, considered merely as natural, good and right as they are, can no more be a law to us than the latter. But there is a superior principle of reflection or conscience in every man, which distinguishes between the internal principles of his heart, as well as his external actions: which passes judgment upon himself and them; pronounces determinately some actions to be in themselves just, right, good; others to be in themselves evil, wrong, unjust: which, without being consulted, without being advised with, magisterially exerts itself, and approves or condemns him the doer of them accordingly: and which, if not forcibly stopped, naturally and always of course goes on to anticipate a higher and more effectual sentence, which shall hereafter second and affirm its own. But this part of the office of conscience is beyond my present design explicitly to consider. It is by this faculty, natural to man, that he is a moral agent, that he is a law to himself: but this faculty, I say, not to be considered merely as a principle in his heart, which is to have some influence as well as others; but considered as a faculty in kind and in nature supreme over all others, and which bears its own authority of being so.

This *prerogative*, this *natural supremacy*, of the faculty which surveys, approves or disapproves the several affections of our mind and actions of our lives, being that by which men *are a law to themselves*, their conformity or disobedience to which law of our nature renders their actions, in the highest and most proper sense, natural or unnatural; it is fit it be further explained to you: and I hope it will be so, if you will attend to the following reflections.

Man may act according to that principle or inclination which for the present happens to be strongest, and yet act in a way disproportionate to, and violate his real proper nature. Suppose a brute creature by any bait to be allured into a snare, by which he is destroyed. He plainly followed the bent of his nature, leading him to gratify his appetite: there is an entire correspondence between his whole nature and such an action: such action therefore is natural. But suppose a man, foreseeing the same danger of certain ruin, should rush into it for the sake of a present gratification; he in this instance would follow his strongest desire, as did the brute creature: but there would be as manifest a disproportion, between the nature of a man and such an action, as between the meanest work of art and the skill of the greatest master in that art: which disproportion arises, not from considering the action singly in *itself*, or in its *consequences;* but from *comparison* of it with the nature of the agent. And since such an action is utterly disproportionate to the nature of man, it is in the strictest and most proper sense unnatural; this word expressing that disproportion. Therefore instead of the words *disproportionate to his nature*, the word *unnatural* may now be put; this being more familiar to us: but let it be observed, that it stands for the same thing precisely.

Now what is it which renders such a rash action unnatural? Is it that he went against the principle of reasonable and cool self-love, considered *merely* as a part of his nature? No: for if he had acted the contrary way, he would equally have gone against a principle, or part of his nature, namely, passion or appetite. But to deny a present appetite, from foresight that the gratification of it would end in immediate ruin or extreme misery, is by no means an unnatural action; whereas to contradict or go against cool self-love for the sake of such gratification, is so in the instance before us. Such an action then being unnatural; and its being so not arising from a man's going against a principle or desire barely, nor in going against that principle or desire which happens for the present to be strongest; it necessarily follows, that there must be some other difference or distinction to be made between these two principles, passion and cool self-love, than what I have yet taken notice of. And this difference, not being a difference in strength or degree, I call a difference in *nature* and in *kind.* And since, in the instance still before us, if passion prevails over self-love, the consequent action is unnatural; but if self-love prevails over passion, the action is natural: it is manifest that self-love is in human nature a superior principle to passion. This may be contradicted without violating that nature; but the former cannot. So that, if we will act conformably to the economy of man's nature, reasonable self-love must govern. Thus, without particular consideration of conscience, we may have a clear conception of the *superior nature* of one inward principle to another; and see that there really is this natural superiority, quite distinct from degrees of strength and prevalency.

Let us now take a view of the nature of man, as consisting partly of various appetites, passions, affections, and partly of the principle of reflection or conscience; leaving quite out all consideration of the different degrees of strength, in which either of them prevail, and it will further appear that there is this natural superiority of one inward principle to another, and that it is even part of the idea of reflection or conscience.

Passion or appetite implies a direct simple tendency towards such and such objects, without distinction of the means by which they are to be obtained. Consequently it will often happen there will be a desire of particular objects, in cases where they cannot be obtained without manifest injury to others. Reflection or conscience comes in, and disapproves the pursuit of them in these circumstances; but the desire remains. Which is to be obeyed, appetite or reflection? Cannot this question be answered, from the economy and constitution of human nature merely, without saying which is strongest? Or need this at all come into consideration? Would not the question be *intelligibly* and fully answered by saying, that the principle of reflection or conscience being compared with the various appetites, passions, and affections in men, the former is manifestly superior and chief, without regard to strength? And how often soever the latter happens to prevail, it is mere *usurpation:* the former remains in nature and in kind its superior; and every instance of such prevalence of the latter is an instance of breaking in upon and violation of the constitution of man.

All this is no more than the distinction, which every body is acquainted with, between *mere power* and *authority:* only instead of being intended to express the difference between what is possible, and what is lawful in civil government; here it has been shown applicable to the several principles in the mind of man. Thus that principle, by which we survey, and either approve or disapprove our own heart, temper, and actions, is not only to be considered as what is in its turn to have some influence; which may be said of every passion, of the lowest appetites: but likewise as being superior; as from its very nature manifestly claiming superiority over all others; insomuch that you cannot form a notion of this faculty, conscience, without taking in judgment, direction, superintendency. This is a constituent part of the idea, that is, of the faculty itself: and, to preside and govern, from the very economy and constitution of man, belongs to it. Had it strength, as it had right: had it power, as it had manifest authority, it would absolutely govern the world.

This gives us a further view of the nature of man; shows us what course of life we were made for: not only that our real nature leads us to be influenced in some degree by reflection and conscience; but likewise in what degree we are to be influenced by it, if we will fall in with, and act agreeably to the constitution of our nature: that this faculty was placed within to be our proper governor; to direct and regulate all under principles, passions, and motives of action. This is its right and office: thus sacred is its authority. And how often soever men violate and rebelliously refuse to submit to it, for supposed interest which they cannot otherwise obtain, or for the sake of passion which they cannot otherwise gratify; this makes no alteration as to the *natural right* and *office* of conscience.

Let us now turn this whole matter another way, and suppose there was no such thing at all as this natural supremacy of conscience; that there was no distinction to be made between one inward principle and another, but only that of strength; and see what would be the consequence.

Consider then what is the latitude and compass of the actions of man with regard to himself, his fellow creatures, and the Supreme Being? What are their bounds, besides that of our natural power? With respect to the two first, they are plainly no other than these: no man seeks misery as such for himself; and no one unprovoked does mischief to another for its own sake. For in every degree within these bounds, mankind knowingly from passion or wantonness bring ruin and misery upon themselves and others. And impiety and profaneness, I mean, what every one would call so who believes the being of God, have absolutely no bounds at all. Men blaspheme the Author of nature, formally and in words renounce their allegiance to their Creator. Put an instance then with respect to any one of these three. Though we should suppose profane swearing, and in general that kind of impiety now mentioned, to mean nothing, yet it implies wanton disregard and irreverence towards an infinite Being, our Creator; and is this as suitable to the nature of man, as reverence and dutiful submission of heart towards that Almighty Being? Or suppose a man guilty of parricide, with all the circumstances of cruelty which such an action can admit of. This action is done in consequence of its principle being for the present strongest: and if there be no difference between inward principles, but only that of strength; the strength being given, you have the whole nature of the man given, so far as it relates to this matter. The action plainly corresponds to the principle, the principle being in that degree of strength it was: it therefore corresponds to the whole nature of the man. Upon comparing the action and the whole nature, there arises no disproportion, there appears no unsuitableness between them. Thus the *murder of a father* and the *nature of man* correspond to each other, as the same nature and an act of filial duty. If there be no difference between inward principles, but only that of strength; we can make no distinction between these two actions, considered as the actions of such a creature; but in our coolest hours must approve or disapprove them equally: than which nothing can be reduced to a greater absurdity.

SERMON III.

THE natural supremacy of reflection or conscience being thus established; we may from it form a distinct notion of what is meant by *human nature,* when virtue is said to consist in following it, and vice in deviating from it.

As the idea of a civil constitution implies in it united strength, various subordinations, under one direction, that of the supreme authority; the different strength of each particular member of the society not coming into the idea; whereas, if you leave out the subordination, the union, and the one direction, you destroy and lose it: so reason, several appetites, passions, and affections, prevailing in different degrees of strength, is not *that* idea or notion of *human nature;* but *that nature* consists in these several principles considered as having a natural respect to each other, in the several passions being naturally subordinate to the one superior principle of reflection or conscience. Every bias, instinct, propension within, is a natural part of our nature, but not the whole: add to these the superior faculty, whose office it is to adjust, manage, and preside over them, and take in this its natural superiority, and you complete the idea of human nature. And as in civil government the constitution is broken in upon, and violated by power and strength prevailing over authority; so the constitution of man is broken in upon and violated by the lower faculties or principles within prevailing over that which is in its nature supreme over them all. Thus, when it is said by ancient writers, that tortures and death are not so contrary to human nature as injustice; by this to be sure is not meant, that the aversion to the former in mankind is less strong and prevalent than their aversion to the latter: but that the former is only contrary to our nature considered in a partial view, and which takes in only the lowest part of it, that which we have in common with the brutes; whereas the latter is contrary to our nature, considered in a higher sense, as a system and constitution contrary to the whole economy of man.*

And from all these things put together, nothing can be more evident, than that, exclusive of revelation, man cannot be considered as a creature left by his Maker to act at random, and live at large up to the extent of his natural power, as passion, humour, wilfulness, happen to carry him; which is the condition brute creatures are in: but that *from his make, constitution, or nature, he is in the strictest and most proper sense a law to himself*. He hath the rule of right within: what is wanting is only that he honestly attend to it.

The inquiries which have been made by men of lei-

* Every man in his physical nature is one individual single agent. He has likewise properties and principles, each of which may be considered separately, and without regard to the respects which they have to each other. Neither of these are the nature we are taking a view of. But it is the inward frame of man considered as a *system* or *constitution:* whose several parts are united, not by a physical principle of individuation, but by the respects they have to each other; the chief of which is the subjection which the appetites, passions, and particular affections have to the one supreme principle of reflection or conscience. The system or constitution is formed by and consists in these respects and this subjection. Thus the body is a *system* or *constitution:* so is a tree: so is every machine. Consider all the several parts of a tree without the natural respects they have to each other, and you have not at all the idea of a tree; but add these respects, and this gives you the idea. The body may be impaired by sickness, a tree may decay, a machine be out of order, and yet the system and constitution of them not totally dissolved. There is plainly somewhat which answers to all this in the moral constitution of man. Whoever will consider his own nature, will see that the several appetites, passions, and particular affections, have different respects amongst themselves. They are restraints upon, and are in a proportion to each other. This proportion is just and perfect, when all those under principles are perfectly coincident with conscience, so far as their nature permits, and in all cases under its absolute and entire direction. The least excess or defect, the least alteration of the due proportions amongst themselves, or of their coincidence with conscience, though not proceeding into action, is some degree of disorder in the moral constitution. But perfection, though plainly intelligible and unsupposable, was never attained by any man. If the higher principle of reflection maintains its place, and as much as it can corrects that disorder, and hinders it from breaking out into action, this is all that can be expected from such a creature as man. And though the appetites and passions have not their exact due proportion to each other; though they often strive for mastery with judgment or reflection: yet, since the superiority of this principle to all others is the chief respect which forms the constitution, so far as this superiority is maintained. the character, the man, is good, worthy, virtuous.

sure after some general rule, the conformity to, or disagreement from which, should denominate our actions good or evil, are in many respects of great service. Yet let any plain honest man, before he engages in any course of action, ask himself, Is this I am going about right, or is it wrong? Is it good, or is it evil? I do not in the least doubt, but that this question would be answered agreeably to truth and virtue, by almost any fair man in almost any circumstance. Neither do there appear any cases which look like exceptions to this; but those of superstition, and of partiality to ourselves. Superstition may perhaps be somewhat of an exception: but partiality to ourselves is not; this being itself dishonesty. For a man to judge that to be the equitable, the moderate, the right part for him to act, which he would see to be hard, unjust, oppressive in another; this is plain vice, and can proceed only from great unfairness of mind.

But allowing that mankind hath the rule of right within himself, yet it may be asked, "What obligations are we under to attend to and follow it?" I answer: it has been proved that man by his nature is a law to himself, without the particular distinct consideration of the positive sanctions of that law; the rewards and punishments which we feel, and those which from the light of reason we have ground to believe, are annexed to it. The question then carries its own answer along with it. Your obligation to obey this law, is its being the law of your nature. That your conscience approves of and attests to such a course of action, is itself alone an obligation. Conscience does not only offer itself to show us the way we should walk in, but it likewise carries its own authority with it, that it is our natural guide; the guide assigned us by the Author of our nature: it therefore belongs to our condition of being, it is our duty to walk in that path, and follow this guide, without looking about to see whether we may not possibly forsake them with impunity.

However, let us hear what is to be said against obeying this law of our nature. And the sum is no more than this. "Why should we be concerned about any thing out of and beyond ourselves? If we do find within ourselves regards to others, and restraints of we know not how many different kinds; yet these being embarrassments, and hindering us from going the nearest way to our own good, why should we not endeavour to suppress and get over them?"

Thus people go on with words, which, when applied to human nature, and the condition in which it is placed in this world, have really no meaning. For does not all this kind of talk go upon supposition, that our happiness in this world consists in somewhat quite distinct from regard to others; and that it is the privilege of vice to be without restraint or confinement? Whereas, on the contrary, the enjoyments, in a manner all the common enjoyments of life, even the pleasures of vice, depend upon these regards of one kind or another to our fellow creatures. Throw off all regards to others, and we should be quite indifferent to infamy and to honour; there could be no such thing at all as ambition; and scarce any such thing as covetousness; for we should likewise be equally indifferent to the disgrace of poverty, the several neglects and kinds of contempt which accompany this state; and to the reputation of riches, the regard and respect they usually procure. Neither is restraint by any means peculiar to one course of life: but our very nature, exclusive of conscience and our condition, lays us under an absolute necessity of it. We cannot gain any end whatever without being confined to the proper means, which is often the most painful and uneasy confinement. And in numberless instances a present appetite cannot be gratified without such apparent and immediate ruin and misery, that the most dissolute man in the world chooses to forego the pleasure, rather than endure the pain.

Is the meaning then, to indulge those regards to our fellow creatures, and submit to those restraints, which upon the whole are attended with more satisfaction than uneasiness, and get over only those which bring more uneasiness and inconvenience than satisfaction? "Doubtless this was our meaning." You have changed sides then. Keep to this; be consistent with yourselves; and you and the men of virtue are *in general* perfectly agreed. But let us take care and avoid mistakes. Let it not be taken for granted that the temper of envy, rage, resentment, yields greater delight than meekness, forgiveness, compassion, and good-will: especially when it is acknowledged that rage, envy, resentment, are in themselves mere misery; and the satisfaction arising from the indulgence of them is little more than relief from that misery; whereas the temper of compassion and benevolence is itself delightful; and the indulgence of it, by doing good, affords new positive delight and enjoyment. Let it not be taken for granted, that the satisfaction arising from the reputation of riches and power, however obtained, and from the respect paid to them, is greater than the satisfaction arising from the reputation of justice, honesty, charity, and the esteem which is universally acknowledged to be their due. And if it be doubtful which of these satisfactions is the greatest, as there are persons who think neither of them very considerable, yet there can be no doubt concerning ambition and covetousness, virtue and a good mind, considered in themselves, and as leading to different courses of life; there can, I say, be no doubt, which temper and which course is attended with most peace and tranquillity of mind, which with most perplexity, vexation, and inconvenience. And both the virtues and vices which have been now mentioned, do in a manner equally imply in them regards of one kind or another to our fellow creatures. And with respect to restraint and confinement: whoever will consider the restraints from fear and shame, the dissimulation, mean arts of concealment, servile compliances, one or other of which belong to almost every course of vice, will soon be convinced that the man of virtue is by no means upon a disadvantage in this respect. How many instances are there in which men feel and own and cry aloud under the chains of vice with which they are enthralled, and which yet they will not shake off! How many instances, in which persons manifestly go through more pains and self-denial to gratify a vicious passion, than would have been necessary to the conquest of it! To this is to be added, that when virtue is become habitual, when the temper of it is acquired, what was before confinement ceases to be so, by becoming choice and delight. Whatever restraint and guard upon ourselves may be needful to unlearn any unnatural distortion or odd gesture; yet, in all propriety of speech, natural behaviour must be the most easy and unrestrained. It is manifest that, in the common course of life, there is seldom any inconsistency between our duty and what is *called* interest: it is much seldomer that there is an inconsistency between duty and what is really our present interest; meaning by interest, happiness and satisfaction. Self-love then, though confined to the interest of the present world, does in general perfectly coincide with virtue; and leads us to one and the same course of life. But, whatever exceptions there are to this, which are much fewer than they are commonly thought, all shall be set right at the final distribution of things. It is a manifest absurdity to suppose evil prevailing finally over good, under the conduct and administration of a perfect mind.

The whole argument, which I have been now insisting upon, may be thus summed up, and given you in one view. The nature of man, is adapted to some course of action or other. Upon comparing some actions with this nature, they appear suitable and correspondent to it: from comparison of other actions with the same nature, there arises to our view some unsuitableness or disproportion. The correspondence of actions to the nature of the agent renders them natural: their disproportion to it, unnatural. That an action is correspondent to the nature of the agent, does not arise from its being agreeable to the principle which happens to be the strongest: for it may be so, and yet be quite disproportionate to the nature of the agent. The correspondence therefore, or disproportion, arises from somewhat else. This can be nothing but a difference in nature and kind, altogether distinct from strength, between the inward principles. Some then are in nature and kind superior to others. And the correspondence arises from the action being conformable to the higher principle; and the unsuitableness from its being contrary to it.

Reasonable self-love and conscience are the chief or superior principles in the nature of man: because an action may be suitable to this nature, though all other principles be violated; but becomes unsuitable, if either of those are. Conscience and self-love, if we understand our true happiness, always lead us the same way. Duty and interest are perfectly coincident: for the most part in this world, but entirely and in every instance if we take in the future, and the whole; this being implied in the notion of a good and perfect administration of things. Thus they who have been so wise in their generation as to regard only their own supposed interest, at the expense and to the injury of others, shall at last find, that he who has given up all the advantages of the present world, rather than violate his conscience and the relations of life, has infinitely better provided for himself, and secured his own interest and happiness.

SERMON IV.

UPON THE GOVERNMENT OF THE TONGUE.

If any man among you seem to be religious, and bridleth not his tongue, but deceiveth his own heart, this man's religion is vain.—James i. 26.

THE translation of this text would be more determinate by being more literal, thus: *If any man among you seemeth to be religious. not bridling his tongue, but deceiving his own heart, this man's religion is vain.* This determines, that the words, *but deceiveth his own heart,* are not put in opposition to, *seemeth to be religious,* but to, *bridleth not his tongue.* The certain determinate meaning of the text then being, that he who seemeth to be religious, and bridleth not his tongue, but in that particular deceiveth his own heart, this man's religion is vain; we may observe somewhat very forcible and expressive in these words of St James. As if the apostle had said, No man surely can make any pretences to religion, who does not at least believe that he bridleth his tongue: if he puts on any appearance or face of religion, and yet does not govern his tongue, he must surely deceive himself in that particular, and think he does: and whoever is so unhappy as to deceive himself in this, to imagine he keeps that unruly faculty in due subjection, when indeed he does not, whatever the other part of his life be, his religion is vain; the government of the tongue being a most material restraint which virtue lays us under: without it no man can be truly religious.

In treating upon this subject, I will consider,

First, What is the general vice or fault here referred to: or what disposition in men is supposed in moral reflections and precepts concerning *bridling the tongue.*

Secondly, When it may be said of any one, that he has a due government over himself in this respect.

I. Now the fault referred to, and the disposition supposed, in precepts and reflections concerning the government of the tongue, is not evil-speaking from malice, nor lying or bearing false witness from indirect selfish designs. The disposition to these, and the actual vices themselves, all come under other subjects. The tongue may be employed about, and made to serve all the purposes of vice, in tempting and deceiving, in perjury and injustice. But the thing here supposed and referred to, is talkativeness: a disposition to be talking, abstracted from the consideration of what is to be said; with very little or no regard to, or thought of doing, either good or harm. And let not any imagine this to be a slight matter, and that it deserves not to have so great weight laid upon it; till he has considered, what evil is implied in it, and the bad effects which follow from it. It is perhaps true, that they who are addicted to this folly would choose to confine themselves to trifles and indifferent subjects, and so intend only to be guilty of being impertinent: but as they cannot go on for ever talking of nothing, as common matters will not afford a sufficient fund for perpetual continued discourse: when subjects of this kind are exhausted, they will go on to defamation, scandal, divulging of secrets, their own secrets as well as those of others, any thing rather than be silent. They are plainly hurried on in the heat of their talk to say quite different things from what they first intended, and which they afterwards wish unsaid: or improper things, which they had no end in saying, but only to afford employment to their tongue. And if these people expect to be heard and regarded, for there are some content merely with talking, they will invent to engage your attention: and, when they have heard the least imperfect hint of an affair, they will out of their own head add the circumstances of time and place, and other matters to make out their story, and give the appearance of probability to it: not that they have any concern about being believed, otherwise than as a means of being heard. The thing is, to engage your attention; to take you up wholly for the present time: what reflections will be made afterwards, is in truth the least of their thoughts. And further, when persons, who indulge themselves in these liberties of the tongue, are in any degree offended with another, as little disgusts and misunderstandings will be, they allow themselves to defame and revile such a one without any moderation or bounds; though the offence is so very slight, that they themselves would not do, nor perhaps wish him an injury in any other way. And in this case the scandal and revilings are chiefly owing to talkativeness, and not bridling their tongue; and so come under our present subject. The least occasion in the world will make the humour break out in this particular way, or in another. It is like a torrent, which must and will flow; but the least thing imaginable will first of all give it either this or another direction, turn it into this or that channel: or like a fire; the nature of which, when in a heap of combustible matter, is to spread and lay waste all around; but any one of a thousand little accidents will occasion it to break out first either in this or another particular part.

The subject then before us, though it does run up into, and can scarce be treated as entirely distinct from all others; yet it needs not to be so much mixed or blended with them as it often is. Every faculty and power may be used as the instrument of premeditated vice and wickedness, merely as the most proper and effectual means of executing such designs. But if a man, from deep malice and desire of revenge, should meditate a falsehood with a settled design to ruin his neighbour's reputation, and should with great coolness and deliberation spread it; nobody would choose to say of such a one, that he had no government of his tongue. A man may use the faculty of speech as an instrument of false witness, who yet has so entire a command over that faculty, as never to speak but from forethought and cool design. Here the crime is injustice and perjury: and, strictly speaking, no more belongs to the present subject, than perjury and injustice in any other way. But there is such a thing as a disposition to be talking for its own sake; from which persons often say any thing, good or bad, of others, merely as a subject of discourse, according to the particular temper they themselves happen to be in, and to pass away the present time. There is likewise to be observed in persons such a strong and eager desire of engaging attention to what they say, that they will speak good or evil, truth or otherwise, merely as one or the other seems to be most hearkened to: and this, though it is sometimes joined, is not the same with the desire of being thought important and men of consequence. There is in some such a disposition to be talking, that an offence of the slightest kind, and such as would not raise any other resentment, yet raises, if I may so speak, the resentment of the tongue, puts it into a flame, into the most ungovernable motions. This outrage, when the person it respects is present, we distinguish in the lower rank of people by a peculiar term: and let it be observed, that though the decencies of behaviour are a little kept, the same outrage and virulence, indulged when he is absent, is an offence of the same kind. But not to distinguish any farther in this manner: men run into faults and follies, which cannot so properly be referred to any one general head as this, that they have not a due government over their tongue.

And this unrestrained volubility and wantonness of speech is the occasion of numberless evils and vexations in life. It begets resentment in him who is the subject of it; sows the seed of strife and dissension amongst others: and inflames little disgusts and offences, which if let alone would wear away of themselves: it is often of as bad effect upon the good name of others, as deep envy or malice: and, to say the least of it in this respect, it destroys and perverts a certain equity of the utmost importance to society to be observed; namely, that praise and dispraise, a good or bad character, should always be bestowed according to desert. The tongue used in such a licentious manner is like a sword in the hand of a madman; it is employed at random, it can scarce possibly do any good, and for the most part does a world of mischief; and implies not only great folly and a trifling spirit, but great viciousness of mind, great indifference to truth and falsity, and to the reputation, welfare, and good of others. So much reason is there for what St James says of the tongue.* *It is a fire, a world of iniquity, it defileth the whole body, setteth on fire the course of nature, and is itself set on fire of hell.* This is the faculty or disposition which we are required to keep a guard upon: these are the vices and follies it runs into, when not kept under due restraint.

II. Wherein the due government of the tongue consists, or when it may be said of any one in a moral and religious sense that he *bridleth his tongue*, I come now to consider.

The due and proper use of any natural faculty or power, is to be judged of by the end and design for which it was given us. The chief purpose, for which the faculty of speech was given to man, is plainly that we might communicate our thoughts to each other, in order to carry on the affairs of the world; for business, and for our improvement in knowledge and learning. But the good Author of our nature designed us not only necessaries, but likewise enjoyment and satisfaction, in that being he hath graciously given, and in that condition of life he hath placed us in. There are secondary uses of our faculties: they administer to delight, as well as to necessity: and as they are equally adapted to both, there is no doubt but he intended them for our gratification, as well as for the support and continuance of our being. The secondary use of speech is to please and be enter-

* Chap. iii. ver. 6.

taining to each other in conversation. This is in every respect allowable and right: it unites men closer in alliances and friendships; gives us a fellow feeling of the prosperity and unhappiness of each other; and is in several respects serviceable to virtue, and to promote good behaviour in the world. And provided there be not too much time spent in it, if it were considered only in the way of gratification and delight, men must have strange notions of God and of religion, to think that he can be offended with it, or that it is any way inconsistent with the strictest virtue. But the truth is, such sort of conversation, though it has no particular good tendency, yet it has a general good one: it is social and friendly, and tends to promote humanity, good-nature, and civility.

As the end and use, so likewise the abuse of speech, relates to the one or other of these; either to business, or to conversation. As to the former; deceit in the management of business and affairs does not properly belong to the subject now before us: though one may just mention that multitude, that endless number of words, with which business is perplexed; when a much fewer would, as it should seem, better serve the purpose: but this must be left to those who understand the matter. The government of the tongue, considered as a subject of itself, relates chiefly to conversation; to that kind of discourse which usually fills up the time spent in friendly meetings, and visits of civility. And the danger is, lest persons entertain themselves and others at the expense of their wisdom and their virtue, and to the injury or offence of their neighbour. If they will observe and keep clear of these, they may be as free, and easy, and unreserved, as they can desire.

The cautions to be given for avoiding these dangers, and to render conversation innocent and agreeable, fall under the following particulars: silence; talking of indifferent things; and which makes up too great a part of conversation, giving of characters, speaking well or evil of others.

The Wise Man observes, that *there is a time to speak, and a time to keep silence.* One meets with people in the world, who seem never to have made the last of these observations. And yet these great talkers do not at all speak from their having any thing to say, as every sentence shows, but only from their inclination to be talking. Their conversation is merely an exercise of the tongue: no other human faculty has any share in it. It is strange these persons can help reflecting, that unless they have in truth a superior capacity, and are in an extraordinary manner furnished for conversation; if they are entertaining, it is at their own expense. Is it possible, that it should never come into people's thoughts to suspect, whether or no it be to their advantage to show so very much of themselves? *Oh that you would altogether hold your peace, and it should be your wisdom.** Remember likewise there are persons who love fewer words, an inoffensive sort of people, and who deserve some regard, though of too still and composed tempers for you. Of this number was the son of Sirach: for he plainly speaks from experience, when he says, *As hills of sands are to the steps of the aged, so is one of many words to a quiet man.* But one would think it should be obvious to every one, that when they are in company with their superiors of any kind, in years, knowledge, and experience: when proper and useful subjects are discoursed of, which they cannot bear a part in; that these are times for silence: when they should learn to hear, and be attentive; at least in their turn. It is indeed a very unhappy way these people are in: they in a manner cut themselves out from all advantage of conversation, except that of being entertained with their own talk: their business in coming into company not being at all to be informed, to hear, to learn; but to display themselves; or rather to exert their faculty, and talk without any design at all. And if we consider conversation as an entertainment, as somewhat to unbend the mind; as a diversion from the cares, the business, and the sorrows of life; it is of the very nature of it, that the discourse be mutual. This, I say is implied in the very notion of what we distinguish by conversation, or being in company. Attention to the continued discourse of one alone grows more painful often, than the cares and business we come to be diverted from.

* Job xiii.

He therefore who imposes this upon us is guilty of a double offence; arbitrarily enjoining silence upon all the rest, and likewise obliging them to this painful attention.

I am sensible these things are apt to be passed over, as too little to come into a serious discourse: but in reality men are obliged, even in point of morality and virtue, to observe all the decencies of behaviour. The greatest evils in life have had their rise from somewhat, which was thought of too little importance to be attended to. And as to the matter we are now upon, it is absolutely necessary to be considered. For if people will not maintain a due government over themselves, in regarding proper times and seasons for silence, but *will* be talking; they certainly, whether they design it or not at first, will go on to scandal and evil-speaking, and divulging secrets.

If it were needful to say any thing further, to persuade men to learn this lesson of silence; one might put them in mind, how insignificant they render themselves by this excessive talkativeness: insomuch that, if they do chance to say any thing which deserves to be attended to and regarded, it is lost in the variety and abundance which they utter of another sort.

The occasions of silence then are obvious, and one would think should be easily distinguished by every body: namely, when a man has nothing to say; or nothing but what is better unsaid: better, either in regard to particular persons he is present with; or from its being an interruption to conversation itself; or to conversation of a more agreeable kind; or better, lastly, with regard to himself. I will end this particular with two reflections of the Wise Man: one of which, in the strongest manner, exposes the ridiculous part of this licentiousness of the tongue; and the other, the great danger and viciousness of it. *When he that is a fool walketh by the way side, his wisdom faileth him, and he saith to every one that he is a fool.** The other is, *In the multitude of words there wanteth not sin.*†

As to the government of the tongue in respect to talking upon indifferent subjects: after what has been said

* Eccles. x. 3. † Prov. x. 19.

concerning the due government of it in respect to the occasions and times for silence, there is little more necessary, than only to caution men to be fully satisfied, that the subjects are indeed of an indifferent nature; and not to spend too much time in conversation of this kind. But persons must be sure to take heed, that the subject of their discourse be at least of an indifferent nature: that it be no way offensive to virtue, religion, or good manners; that it be not of a licentious dissolute sort, this leaving always ill impressions upon the mind; that it be no way injurious or vexatious to others; and that too much time be not spent this way, to the neglect of those duties and offices of life which belong to their station and condition in the world. However, though there is not any necessity that men should aim at being important and weighty in every sentence they speak: yet since useful subjects, at least of some kinds, are as entertaining as others; a wise man, even when he desires to unbend his mind from business, would choose that the conversation might turn upon somewhat instructive.

The last thing is, the government of the tongue as relating to discourse of the affairs of others, and giving of characters. These are in a manner the same: and one can scarce call it an indifferent subject, because discourse upon it almost perpetually runs into somewhat criminal.

And first of all, it were very much to be wished that this did not take up so great a part of conversation; because it is indeed a subject of a dangerous nature. Let any one consider the various interests, competitions, and little misunderstandings which arise amongst men; and he will soon see, that he is not unprejudiced and impartial; that he is not, as I may speak, neutral enough, to trust himself with talking of the character and concerns of his neighbour, in a free, careless, and unreserved manner. There is perpetually, and often it is not attended to, a rivalship amongst people of one kind or another, in respect to wit, beauty, learning, fortune, and that one thing will insensibly influence them to speak to the disadvantage of others, even where there is no formed malice or ill design. Since therefore it is so hard to enter into this subject without offending, the first thing to be observed is, that people should learn to decline it; to get over that strong inclination most have to be talking of the concerns and behaviour of their neighbour.

But since it is impossible that this subject should be wholly excluded conversation; and since it is necessary that the characters of men should be known: the next thing is, that it is a matter of importance what is said; and therefore, that we should be religiously scrupulous and exact to say nothing, either good or bad, but what is true. I put it thus, because it is in reality of as great importance to the good of society, that the characters of bad men should be known, as that the characters of good men should. People, who are given to scandal and detraction, may indeed make an ill use of this observation; but truths which are of service towards regulating our conduct, are not to be disowned, or even concealed because a bad use may be made of them. This however would be effectually prevented, if these two things were attended to. First, That, though it is equally of bad consequence to society, that men should have either good or ill characters which they do not deserve; yet, when you say somewhat good of a man which he does not deserve, there is no wrong done him in particular; whereas, when you say evil of a man which he does not deserve, here is a direct formal injury, a real piece of injustice done him. This therefore makes a wide difference; and gives us, in point of virtue, much greater latitude in speaking well than ill of others. Secondly, A good man is friendly to his fellow creatures, and a lover of mankind; and so will, upon every occasion, and often without any, say all the good he can of every body: but so far as he is a good man, will never be disposed to speak evil of any, unless there be some other reason for it, besides barely that it is true. If he be charged with having given an ill character, he will scarce think it a sufficient justification of himself to say it was a true one, unless he can also give some further account how he came to do so: a just indignation against particular instances of villany, where they are great and scandalous; or to prevent an innocent man from being deceived and betrayed, when he has great trust and confidence in one who does not deserve it. Justice must be done to every part of a subject when we are considering it. If there be a man, who bears a fair character in the world, whom yet we know to be without faith or honesty, to be really an ill man; it must be allowed in general, that we shall do a piece of service to society, by letting such a one's true character be known. This is no more than what we have an instance of in our Saviour himself; though he was mild and gentle beyond example.* However, no words can express too strongly the caution which should be used in such a case as this.

Upon the whole matter: If people would observe the obvious occasions of silence, if they would subdue the inclinations to tale-bearing, and that eager desire to engage attention, which is an original disease in some minds; they would be in little danger of offending with their tongue; and would, in a moral and religious sense, have due government over it.

I will conclude with some precepts and reflections of the Son of Sirach upon this subject. *Be swift to hear; and, if thou hast understanding, answer thy neighbour; if not, lay thy hand upon thy mouth. Honour and shame is in talk. A man of an ill tongue is dangerous in his city, and he that is rash in his talk shall be hated. A wise man will hold his tongue till he see opportunity; but a babbler and a fool will regard no time. He that useth many words shall be abhorred; and he that taketh to himself authority therein, shall be hated. A backbiting tongue hath disquieted many; strong cities hath it pulled down, and overthrown the houses of great men. The tongue of a man is his fall; but if thou love to hear, thou shalt receive understanding.*

* Mark xii. 38, 40.

SERMON V.

UPON COMPASSION.

Rejoice with them that do rejoice, and weep with them that weep.
Rom. xii. 15.

EVERY man is to be considered in two capacities, the private and public; as designed to pursue his own interest, and likewise to contribute to the good of others. Whoever will consider, may see, that in general there is no contrariety between these; but that from the original constitution of man, and the circumstances he is placed in, they perfectly coincide, and mutually carry on each other. But, amongst the great variety of affections or principles of action in our nature, some in their primary intention and design seem to belong to the single or private, others to the public or social capacity. The affections required in the text are of the latter sort. When we rejoice in the prosperity of others, and compassionate their distresses, we, as it were, substitute them for ourselves, their interest for our own; and have the same kind of pleasure in their prosperity, and sorrow in their distress, as we have from reflection upon our own. Now there is nothing strange or unaccountable in our being thus carried out, and affected towards the interests of others. For, if there be any appetite, or any inward principle besides self-love; why may there not be an affection to the good of our fellow creatures, and delight from that affection's being gratified, and uneasiness from things going contrary to it?*

* There being manifestly this appearance of men's substituting others for themselves, and being carried out and affected towards them as towards themselves; some persons, who have a system which excludes every affection of this sort, have taken a pleasant method to solve it; and tell you it is *not another* you are at all concerned about, but your *self only*, when you feel the affection called compassion, i. e. Here is a plain matter of fact, which men cannot reconcile with the general account they think fit to give of things: they therefore, instead of *that* manifest fact, substitute *another*, which is reconcileable to their own scheme. For does not every body by compassion mean an affection, the object of which is another in distress? Instead of this, but designing to have it mistaken for this, they speak of an affection or passion, the object of which is ourselves, or danger to ourselves. Hobbes defines *pity, imagination, or fiction of future calamity to ourselves, proceeding from the sense* (he means

Of these two, delight in the prosperity of others, and compassion for their distresses, the last is felt much more generally than the former. Though men do not universally rejoice with all whom they see rejoice, yet, acci-

sight or knowledge) *of another man's calamity*. Thus fear and compassion would be the same idea, and a fearful and a compassionate man the same character, which every man immediately sees are totally different. Further, to those who give any scope to their affections, there is no perception or inward feeling more universal than this: that one who has been merciful and compassionate throughout the course of his behaviour, should himself be treated with kindness, if he happens to fall into circumstances of distress. Is fear, then, or cowardice, so great a recommendation to the favour of the bulk of mankind? Or is it not plain, that mere fearlessness (and therefore not the contrary) is one of the most popular qualifications? This shows that mankind are not affected towards compassion as fear, but as somewhat totally different.

Nothing would more expose such accounts as these of the affections which are favourable and friendly to our fellow creatures, than to substitute the definitions, which this author, and others who follow his steps, give of such affections, instead of the words by which they are commonly expressed. Hobbes, after having laid down, that pity or compassion is only fear for ourselves, goes on to explain the reason why we pity our friends in distress more than others. Now substitute the *definition* instead of the word *pity* in this place, and the inquiry will be, why we fear our friends, &c., which words (since he really does not mean why we are afraid of them) make no question or sentence at all. So that common language, the words *to compassionate, to pity*, cannot be accommodated to his account of compassion. The very joining of the words to *pity our friends*, is a direct contradiction to his definition of pity: because these words, so joined, necessarily express that our friends are the objects of the passion: whereas his definition of it asserts, that ourselves (or danger to ourselves) are the only objects of it. He might indeed have avoided this absurdity, by plainly saying what he is going to account for; namely, why the sight of the innocent, or of our friends in distress, raises greater fear for ourselves than the sight of other persons in distress. But had he put the thing thus plainly, the fact itself would have been doubted; that *the sight of our friends in distress raises in us greater fear for ourselves, than the sight of others in distress*. And in the next place it would immediately have occurred to every one, that the fact now mentioned, which at least is *doubtful*, whether true or false, was not the same with this fact, which nobody ever doubted, that *the sight of our friends in distress raises in us greater compassion than the sight of others in distress*: every one, I say, would have seen that these are not the *same*, but *two different* inquiries; and consequently, that fear and compassion are not the same. Suppose a person to be in real danger, and by some means or other to have forgot it; any trifling accident, any sound might alarm him, recall the danger to his remembrance, and renew his fear: but it is almost too grossly ridiculous (though it is to show an absurdity) to speak of that sound or accident as an object of compassion; and yet, according to Mr Hobbes, our greatest friend in distress is no more to us, no more the object of compassion, or of any affection in our heart: neither the one nor the other raises any emotion in our mind, but only the thoughts of our liableness to calamity, and the fear of it; and both equally do this. It is fit such sort of accounts of human nature should be shown to be what they really are, because there is raised upon them a general scheme which undermines the whole foundation of common justice and honesty. See *Hobbes of Human Nature*, c. 9. § 10.

There are often three distinct perceptions or inward feelings upon sight of persons in distress: real sorrow and concern for the misery of our fellow creatures; some degree of satisfaction from a consciousness of our freedom from that misery; and as the mind passes on from one thing to another, it is not unnatural from such an occasion to reflect upon our liableness to the same or other calamities. The two last frequently accompany the first, but it is the first *only* which is proper compassion, of which the distressed are objects, and which directly carries us with calmness and thought to their assistance. Any one of these, from various and complicated reasons may in particular cases prevail over the other two; and there are, I suppose, instances, where the bare *sight* of distress, without our feeling any compassion for it,

dental obstacles removed, they naturally compassionate all, in some degree, whom they see in distress; so far as they have any real perception or sense of that distress: insomuch that words expressing this latter, pity, compassion, frequently occur; whereas we have scarce any single one, by which the former is distinctly expressed. Congratulation indeed answers condolence: but both these words are intended to signify certain forms of civility, rather than any inward sensation or feeling. This difference or inequality is so remarkable, that we plainly consider compassion as itself an original, distinct, particular affection in human nature; whereas to rejoice in the good of others, is only a consequence of the general affection of love and good-will to them. The reason and account of which matter is this: when a man has obtained any particular advantage or felicity, his end is gained; and he does not in that particular want the assistance of another: there was therefore no need of a distinct affection towards that felicity of another already obtained: neither would such affection directly carry him on to do good to that person: whereas men in distress want assistance; and compassion leads us directly to assist them. The object of the former is the present felicity of another; the object of the latter is the present misery of another. It is easy to see that the latter wants a particular affection for its relief, and that the former does not want one, because it does not want assistance. And upon supposition of a distinct affection in both cases, the one must rest in the exercise of itself, having nothing further to gain; the other does not rest in itself, but carries us on to assist the distressed.

But, supposing these affections natural to the mind,

may be the occasion of either or both of the two latter perceptions. One might add that if there be really any such thing as the fiction or imagination of danger to our selves from the sight of the misery of others, which Hobbes speaks of, and which he has absurdly mistaken for the whole of compassion; if there be any thing of this sort common to mankind, distinct from the reflection of reason, it would be a most remarkable instance of what was furthest from the thoughts, namely, of a mutual sympathy between each particular of the species, a fellow feeling common to mankind. It would not indeed be an example of our substituting others for ourselves, but it would be an example of substituting ourselves for others. And as it would not be an instance of benevolence, so neither would it be an instance of self-love: for this phantom of danger to ourselves, naturally rising to view upon sight of the distresses of others would be no more an instance of love to ourselves, than the pain of hunger is.

particularly the last; "Has not each man troubles enough of his own? must he indulge an affection which appropriates to himself those of others? which leads him to contract the least desirable of all friendships, friendships with the unfortunate? Must we invert the known rule of prudence, and choose to associate ourselves with the distressed? or, allowing that we ought, so far as it is in our power to relieve them, yet is it not better to do this from reason and duty? Does not passion and affection of every kind perpetually mislead us? Nay, is not passion and affection itself a weakness, and what a perfect being must be entirely free from?" Perhaps so: but it is mankind I am speaking of; imperfect creatures, and who naturally, and, from the condition we are placed in, necessarily depend upon each other. With respect to such creatures, it would be found of as bad consequence to eradicate all natural affections, as to be entirely governed by them. This would almost sink us to the condition of brutes; and that would leave us without a sufficient principle of action. [Reason alone, whatever any one may wish, is not in reality a sufficient motive of virtue in such a creature as man; but this reason joined with those affections which God has impressed upon his heart: and when these are allowed scope to exercise themselves, but under strict government and direction of reason; then it is we act suitably to our nature, and to the circumstances God has placed us in. Neither is affection itself at all a weakness; nor does it argue defect, any otherwise than as our senses and appetites do; they belong to our condition of nature, and are what we cannot do without. God Almighty is, to be sure, unmoved by passion or appetite, unchanged by affection: but then it is to be added, that he neither sees, nor hears, nor perceives things by any senses like ours; but in a manner infinitely more perfect. Now, as it is an absurdity almost too gross to be mentioned, for a man to endeavour to get rid of his senses, because the Supreme Being discerns things more perfectly without them; it is a real, though not so obvious an absurdity, to endeavour to eradicate the passions he has given us, because he is without them. For, since our passions are as really a part of our constitution as our senses; since the former as really belong to our condition of nature as the latter to get rid of either is equally a violation of, and breaking in upon, that nature and constitution he has given us. Both our senses and our passions are a supply to the imperfection of our nature: thus they show that we are such sort of creatures, as to stand in need of those helps which higher orders of creatures do not. But it is not the supply, but the deficiency; as it is not a remedy, but a disease, which is the imperfection. However, our appetites, passions, senses, no way imply disease: nor indeed do they imply deficiency or imperfection of any sort; but only this, that the constitution of nature, according to which God has made us, is such as to require them. And it is far from being true, that a wise man must entirely suppress compassion, and all fellow feeling for others, as a weakness; and trust to reason alone to teach and enforce upon him the practice of the several charities we owe to our kind; that, on the contrary, even the bare exercise of such affections would itself be for the good and happiness of the world; and the imperfection of the higher principles of reason and religion in man, the little influence they have upon our practice, and the strength and prevalency of contrary ones, plainly require these affections to be a restraint upon these latter, and a supply to the deficiencies of the former.

First, The very exercise itself of these affections in a just and reasonable manner and degree, would upon the whole increase the satisfactions, and lessen the miseries of life.

It is the tendency and business of virtue and religion to procure, as much as may be, universal good-will, trust, and friendship amongst mankind. If this could be brought to obtain; and each man enjoyed the happiness of others, as every one does that of a friend; and looked upon the success and prosperity of his neighbour, as every one does upon that of his children and family; it is too manifest to be insisted upon, how much the enjoyments of life would be increased. There would be so much happiness introduced into the world, without any deduction or inconvenience from it, in proportion as the precept of *rejoicing with those who rejoice* was universally obeyed. Our Saviour has owned this good affection as belonging to our nature, in the parable of the *lost sheep*, and does not think it to the disadvantage of a perfect state, to represent its happiness as capable of increase, from reflection upon that of others.

But since in such a creature as man, compassion or sorrow for the distress of others seems so far necessarily connected with joy in their prosperity, as that whoever rejoices in one must unavoidably compassionate the other; there cannot be that delight or satisfaction, which appears to be so considerable, without the inconveniences, whatever they are, of compassion.

However, without considering this connexion, there is no doubt but that more good than evil, more delight than sorrow, arises from compassion itself; there being so many things which balance the sorrow of it. There is first the relief which the distressed feel from this affection in others towards them. There is likewise the additional misery which they would feel from the reflection, that no one commiserated their case. It is indeed true, that any disposition, prevailing beyond a certain degree, becomes somewhat wrong; and we have ways of speaking, which, though they do not directly express that excess, yet, always lead our thoughts to it, and give us the notion of it. Thus, when mention is made of delight in being pitied, this always conveys to our mind the notion of somewhat which is really a weakness: the manner of speaking, I say, implies a certain weakness and feebleness of mind, which is and ought to be disapproved. But men of the greatest fortitude would in distress feel uneasiness, from knowing that no person in the world had any sort of compassion or real concern for them; and in some cases, especially when the temper is enfeebled by sickness, or any long and great distress, doubtless, would feel a kind of relief even from the helpless good-will and ineffectual assistances of those about them. Over against the sorrow of compassion is likewise to be set a peculiar calm kind of satisfaction, which accompanies it, unless in cases where the distress of another is by some means so brought home to ourselves, as to become in a manner our own; or when from weakness of mind the affection rises too high, which ought to be corrected. This tranquillity or calm satisfaction proceeds partly from consciousness of a right affection and temper of mind, and partly from a sense of our own freedom from the misery we compassionate. This last may possibly appear to some at first sight faulty; but it really is not so. It is the same with that positive enjoyment, which sudden ease from pain for the present affords, arising from a real sense of misery, joined with a sense of our freedom from it; which in all cases must afford some degree of satisfaction.

To these things must be added the observation, which respects both the affections we are considering; that they who have got over all fellow feeling for others, have withal contracted a certain callousness of heart, which renders them insensible to most other satisfactions, but those of the grossest kind.

Secondly, Without the exercise of these affections, men would certainly be much more wanting in the offices of charity they owe to each other, and likewise more cruel and injurious, than they are at present.

The private interest of the individual would not be sufficiently provided for by reasonable and cool self-love alone; therefore the appetites and passions are placed within as a guard and further security, without which it would not be taken due care of. It is manifest our life would be neglected, were it not for the calls of hunger, and thirst, and weariness; notwithstanding that without them reason would assure us, that the recruits of food and sleep are the necessary means of our preservation. It is therefore absurd to imagine, that without affection, the same reason alone would be more effectual to engage us to perform the duties we owe to our fellow creatures. One of this make would be as defective, as much wanting, considered with respect to society, as one of the former make would be defective, or wanting, considered as an individual, or in his private capacity. Is it possible any can in earnest think, that a public spirit, i. e. a settled reasonable principle of benevolence to mankind, is so prevalent and strong in the species, as that we may venture to throw off the under affections, which are its assistants, carry it forward and mark out particular courses for it; family, friends, neighbourhood, the distressed, our country? The common joys and the common sorrows, which belong to these relations and circumstances, are as plainly useful to society, as the pain and pleasure belonging to hunger, thirst, and weariness, are of service to the individual. In defect of that higher principle of reason, compassion is often the only way by which the indigent can have access to us: and therefore, to eradicate this, though it is not indeed formally to deny them that assistance which is their due; yet it is to cut them off from that which is too frequently their only way of obtaining it. And as for those who have shut up this door against the complaints of the miserable, and conquered this affection in themselves; even these persons will be under great restraints from the same affection in others. Thus a man who has himself no sense of injustice, cruelty, oppression, will be kept from running the utmost lengths of wickedness, by fear of that detestation, and even resentment of inhumanity, in many particular instances of it, which compassion for the object towards whom such inhumanity is exercised, excites in the bulk of mankind. And this is frequently the chief danger, and the chief restraint, which tyrants and the great oppressors of the world feel.

In general, experience will show, that as want of natural appetite to food supposes and proceeds from some bodily disease; so the apathy the Stoics talk of, as much supposes, or is accompanied with, somewhat amiss in the moral character, in that which is the health of the mind. Those who formerly aimed at this upon the foot of philosophy, appear to have had better success in eradicating the affections of tenderness and compassion, than they had with the passions of envy, pride, and resentment: these latter, at best, were but concealed, and that imperfectly too. How far this observation may be extended to such as endeavour to suppress the natural impulses of their affections, in order to form themselves for business and the world, I shall not determine. But there does not appear any capacity or relation to be named, in which men ought to be entirely deaf to the calls of affection, unless the judicial one is to be excepted.

And as to those who are commonly called the men of pleasure, it is manifest, that the reason they set up for hardness of heart, is to avoid being interrupted in their course, by the ruin and misery they are the authors of: neither are persons of this character always the most free from the impotencies of envy and resentment. What may men at last bring themselves to, by suppressing their passions and affections of one kind, and leaving those of the other in their full strength? But surely it might be expected that persons who make pleasure their study and their business, if they understood what they profess, would reflect, how many of the entertainments of life, how many of those kind of amusements which seem peculiarly to belong to men of leisure and education, they become insensible to by this acquired hardness of heart.

I shall close these reflections with barely mentioning the behaviour of that divine Person, who was the example of all perfection in human nature, as represented in the Gospels mourning, and even, in a literal sense, weeping over the distresses of his creatures.

The observation already made, that, of the two affections mentioned in the text, the latter exerts itself much more than the former; that, from the original constitution of human nature, we much more generally and sensibly compassionate the distressed, than rejoice with the prosperous, requires to be particularly considered. This observation, therefore, with the reflections which arise out of it, and which it leads our thoughts to, shall be the subject of another discourse.

For the conclusion of this, let me just take notice of the danger of over-great refinements; of going besides or beyond the plain, obvious, first appearances of things, upon the subject of morals and religion. The least observation will show, how little the generality of men are capable of speculations. Therefore morality and religion must be somewhat plain and easy to be understood: it must appeal to what we call plain common sense, as distinguished from superior capacity and improvement; because it appeals to mankind. Persons of superior capacity and improvement have often fallen into errors, which no one of mere common understanding could. Is it possible that one of this latter character could ever of himself have thought, that there was absolutely no such thing in mankind as affection to the good of others? Suppose of parents to their children; or that what he felt upon seeing a friend in distress was only fear for himself; or, upon supposition of the affections of kindness and compassion, that it was the business of wisdom and virtue to set him about extirpating them as fast as he could? And yet each of these manifest contradictions to nature has been laid down by men of speculation, as a discovery in moral philosophy; which they, it seems, have found out through all the specious appearances to the contrary. This reflection may be extended further. The extravagancies of enthusiasm and superstition do not at all lie in the road of common sense; and therefore, so far as they are *original mistakes*, must be owing to going beside or beyond it. Now, since inquiry and examination can relate only to things so obscure and uncertain as to stand in need of it, and to persons who are capable of it; the proper advice to be given to plain honest men, to secure them from the extremes both of superstition and irreligion, is that of the son of Sirach: *In every good work trust thy own soul; for this is the keeping of the commandment.**

* Eccles. xxxii. 23.

SERMON VI.

UPON COMPASSION.

PREACHED THE FIRST SUNDAY IN LENT.

Rejoice with them that do rejoice, and weep with them that weep.—Rom. xii. 15.

There is a much more exact correspondence between the natural and moral world, than we are apt to take notice of. The inward frame of man does in a peculiar manner answer to the external condition and circumstances of life, in which he is placed. This is a particular instance of that general observation of the son of Sirach: *All things are double one against another, and God hath made nothing imperfect.** The several passions and affections in the heart of man, compared with the circumstances of life in which he is placed, afford, to such as will attend to them, as certain instances of final causes, as any whatever, which are more commonly alleged for such: since those affections lead him to a certain determinate course of action suitable to those circumstances, as (for instance) compassion, to relieve the distressed. And as all observations of final causes, drawn from the principles of action in the heart of man, compared with the condition he is placed in, serve all the good uses which instances of final causes in the material world about us do; and both these are equally proofs of wisdom and design in the Author of nature: so the former serve to further good purposes; they show us what course of life we are made for, what is our duty, and in a peculiar manner enforce upon us the practice of it.

Suppose we are capable of happiness and of misery in degrees equally intense and extreme, yet, we are capable of the latter for a much longer time, beyond all comparison. We see men in the tortures of pain for hours, days, and, excepting the short suspensions of sleep, for months together, without intermission; to which no enjoyments of life do, in degree and continuance, bear any

* Ecclus. xlii. 24.

sort of proportion. And such is our make and that of the world about us, that any thing may become the instrument of pain and sorrow to us. Thus almost any one man is capable of doing mischief to any other, though he may not be capable of doing him good: and if he be capable of doing him some good, he is capable of doing him more evil. And it is, in numberless cases, much more in our power to lessen the miseries of others, than to promote their positive happiness, any otherwise than as the former often includes the latter; ease from misery occasioning for some time the greatest positive enjoyment. This constitution of nature, namely, that it is so much more in our power to occasion and likewise to lessen misery, than to promote positive happiness, plainly required a particular affection, to hinder us from abusing, and to incline us to make a right use of the former powers, i. e. the powers both to occasion and to lessen misery; over and above what was necessary to induce us to make a right use of the latter power, that of promoting positive happiness. The power we have over the misery of our fellow creatures, to occasion or lessen it, being a more important trust than the power we have of promoting their positive happiness; the former requires and has a further, an additional security and guard against its being violated, beyond and over and above what the latter has. The social nature of man, and general good-will to his species, equally prevent him from doing evil, incline him to relieve the distressed, and to promote the positive happiness of his fellow creatures: but compassion only restrains him from the first, and carries him to the second; it hath nothing to do with the third.

The final causes then of compassion are to prevent and to relieve misery.

As to the former: this affection may plainly be a restraint upon resentment, envy, unreasonable self-love; that is, upon all the principles from which men do evil to one another. Let us instance only in resentment. It seldom happens, in regulated societies, that men have an enemy so entirely in their power, as to be able to satiate their resentment with safety. But if we were to put this case, it is plainly supposable, that a person might bring his enemy into such a condition, as from being the object of anger and rage, to become an object of compassion, even to himself, though the most malicious man in the world: and in this case compassion would stop him, if he could stop with safety, from pursuing his revenge any further. But since nature has placed within us more powerful restraints to prevent mischief, and since the final cause of compassion is much more to relieve misery, let us go on to the consideration of it in this view.

As this world was not intended to be a state of any great satisfaction or high enjoyment; so neither was it intended to be a mere scene of unhappiness and sorrow. Mitigations and reliefs are provided by the merciful Author of nature, for most of the afflictions in human life. There is kind provision made even against our frailties; as we are so constituted, that time abundantly abates our sorrows, and begets in us that resignment of temper, which ought to have been produced by a better cause; a due sense of the authority of God, and our state of dependence. This holds in respect to far the greatest part of the evils of life; I suppose, in some degree as to pain and sickness. Now this part of the constitution or make of man, considered as some relief to misery, and not as provision for positive happiness, is, if I may so speak, an instance of nature's compassion for us: and every natural remedy or relief to misery may be considered in the same view.

But since in many cases it is very much in our power to alleviate the miseries of each other; and benevolence, though natural in man to man, yet is in a very low degree kept down by interest and competitions; and men, for the most part, are so engaged in the business and pleasures of the world, as to overlook and turn away from objects of misery; which are plainly considered as interruptions to them in their way, as intruders upon their business, their gaiety and mirth; compassion is an advocate within us in their behalf, to gain the unhappy admittance and access, to make their case attended to. If it sometimes serves a contrary purpose, and makes men industriously turn away from the miserable, these are only instances of abuse and perversion: for the end, for which the affection was given us, most certainly is not to make us avoid, but to make us attend to, the objects of it. And if men would only resolve to allow thus much to it; let it bring before their view, the view of their mind, the miseries of their fellow creatures; let it gain for them that their case be considered; I am persuaded it would not fail of gaining more, and that very few real objects of charity would pass unrelieved. Pain and sorrow and misery have a right to our assistance: compassion puts us in mind of the debt, and that we owe it to ourselves as well as to the distressed. For, to endeavour to get rid of the sorrow of compassion by turning from the wretched, when yet it is in our power to relieve them, is as unnatural, as to endeavour to get rid of the pain of hunger by keeping from the sight of food. That we can do one with greater success than we can the other, is no proof that one is less a violation of nature than the other. Compassion is a call, a demand of nature, to relieve the unhappy; as hunger is a natural call for food. This affection plainly gives the objects of it an additional claim to relief and mercy, over and above what our fellow creatures in common have to our good-will. Liberality and bounty are exceedingly commendable; and a particular distinction in such a world as this, where men set themselves to contract their heart, and close it to all interests but their own. It is by no means to be opposed to mercy, but always accompanies it: the distinction between them is only, that the former leads our thoughts to a more promiscuous and undistinguished distribution of favours; to those who are not, as well as those who are necessitous; whereas the object of compassion is misery. But in the comparison, and where there is not a possibility of both, mercy is to have the preference: the affection of compassion manifestly leads us to this preference. Thus, to relieve the indigent and distressed, to single out the unhappy, from whom can be expected no returns either of present entertainment or future service, for the objects of our favours; to esteem a man's being friendless as a recommendation; dejection, and incapacity of struggling through the world, as a motive for assisting him; in a word, to consider these circumstances of disadvantage, which are usually thought a sufficient reason for neglect and overlooking a person, as a motive for helping him forward: this is the course of benevolence which compassion marks out and directs us to: this is that humanity, which is so peculiarly becoming our nature and circumstances in this world.

To these considerations, drawn from the nature of man, must be added the reason of the thing itself we are recommending, which accords to and shows the same. For since it is so much more in our power to lessen the misery of our fellow creatures, than to promote their positive happiness; in cases where there is an inconsistency, we shall be likely to do much more good by setting ourselves to mitigate the former, than by endeavouring to promote the latter. Let the competition be between the poor and the rich. It is easy, you will say, to see which will have the preference. True: but the question is, which ought to have the preference? What proportion is there between the happiness produced by doing a favour to the indigent, and that produced by doing the same favour to one in easy circumstances? It is manifest, that the addition of a very large estate to one who before had an affluence, will in many instances yield him less new enjoyment or satisfaction, than an ordinary charity would yield to a necessitous person. So that it is not only true, that our nature, i. e. the voice of God within us, carries us to the exercise of charity and benevolence in the way of compassion or mercy, preferably to any other way; but we also manifestly discern much more good done by the former; or, if you will allow me the expressions, more misery annihilated, and happiness created. If charity and benevolence, and endeavouring to do good to our fellow creatures, be any thing, this observation deserves to be most seriously considered by all who have to bestow. And it holds with great exactness, when applied to the several degrees of greater and less indigency throughout the various ranks in human life: the happiness or good produced not being in proportion to what is bestowed, but in proportion to this joined with the need there was of it.

It may perhaps be expected, that upon this subject notice should be taken of occasions, circumstances, and characters, which seem at once to call forth affections of different sorts. Thus vice may be thought the object both of pity and indignation: folly, of pity and of laughter. How far this is strictly true, I shall not inquire; but only observe upon the appearance, how much more humane it is to yield and give scope to affections, which are most directly in favour of, and friendly towards, our fellow creatures; and that there is plainly much less danger of being led wrong by these, than by the other.

But, notwithstanding all that has been said in recommendation of compassion, that it is most amiable, most becoming human nature, and most useful to the world; yet it must be owned, that every affection, as distinct from a principle of reason, may rise too high, and be beyond its just proportion. And by means of this one carried too far, a man throughout his life is subject to much more uneasiness than belongs to his share: and in particular instances, it may be in such a degree as to incapacitate him from assisting the very person who is the object of it. But as there are some who upon principle set up for suppressing this affection itself as weakness, there is also I know not what of fashion on this side; and, by some means or other, the whole world almost is run into the extremes of insensibility towards the distresses of their fellow creatures: so that general rules and exhortations must always be on the other side.

And now to go on to the uses we should make of the foregoing reflections, the further ones they lead to, and the general temper they have a tendency to beget in us. There being that distinct affection implanted in the nature of man, tending to lessen the miseries of life, that particular provision made for abating its sorrows, more than for increasing its positive happiness, as before explained; this may suggest to us what should be our general aim respecting ourselves, in our passage through this world: namely, to endeavour chiefly to escape misery, keep free from uneasiness, pain, and sorrow, or to get relief and mitigation of them; to propose to ourselves peace and tranquillity of mind, rather than pursue after high enjoyments. This is what the constitution of nature before explained marks out as the course we should follow, and the end we should aim at. To make pleasure and mirth and jollity our business, and be constantly hurrying about after some gay amusement, some new gratification of sense or appetite, to those who will consider the nature of man and our condition in this world, will appear the most romantic scheme of life that ever entered into thought. And yet how many are there who go on in this course, without learning better from the daily, the hourly disappointments, listlessness, and satiety, which accompany this fashionable method of wasting away their days!

The subject we have been insisting upon would lead us into the same kind of reflections, by a different connexion. The miseries of life brought home to ourselves by compassion, viewed through this affection considered as the sense by which they are perceived, would beget in us that moderation, humility, and soberness of mind, which has been now recommended; and which peculiarly belongs to a season of recollection, the only purpose of which is to bring us to a just sense of things, to recover us out of that forgetfulness of ourselves, and our true state, which it is manifest far the greatest part of men pass their whole life in. Upon this account Solomon says, that *it is better to go to the house of mourning, than to go to the house of feasting;* i. e. it is more to a man's advantage to turn his eyes towards objects of distress, to recall sometimes to his remembrance the occasions of sorrow, than to pass all his days in thoughtless mirth and gaiety. And he represents the wise as choosing to frequent the former of these places; to be sure not for its own sake, but because *by the sadness of the countenance the heart is made better.* Every one observes how temperate and reasonable men are when humbled and brought low by afflictions, in comparison of what they are in high prosperity. By this voluntary resort to the house of mourning, which is here recommended, we might learn all those useful instructions which calamities teach, without undergoing them ourselves; and grow wiser and better at a more easy rate than men commonly do. The objects themselves, which in that place of sorrow lie before our view, naturally give us a seriousness and attention, check that wantonness which is the growth of prosperity and ease, and lead us to reflect upon the deficiencies of human life itself; that *every man, at his best estate, is altogether vanity*. This would correct the florid and gaudy prospects and expectations which we are too apt to indulge, teach us to lower our notions of happiness and enjoyment, bring them down to the reality of things, to what is attainable, to what the frailty of our condition will admit of, which, for any continuance, is only tranquillity, ease, and moderate satisfactions. Thus we might at once become proof against the temptations with which the whole world almost is carried away; since it is plain, that not only what is called a life of pleasure, but also vicious pursuits in general, aim at somewhat besides and beyond these moderate satisfactions.

And as to that obstinacy and wilfulness, which renders men so insensible to the motives of religion; this right sense of ourselves and of the world about us would bend the stubborn mind, soften the heart, and make it more apt to receive impression: and this is the proper temper in which to call our ways to remembrance, to review and set home upon ourselves the miscarriages of our past life. In such a compliant state of mind, reason and conscience will have a fair hearing; which is the preparation for, or rather the beginning of, that repentance, the outward show of which we all put on at this season.

Lastly, The various miseries of life which lie before us wherever we turn our eyes, the frailty of this mortal state we are passing through, may put us in mind that the present world is not our home; that we are merely strangers and travellers in it, as all our fathers were. It is therefore to be considered as a foreign country; in which our poverty and wants, and the insufficient supplies of them, were designed to turn our views to that higher and better state we are heirs to: a state where will be no follies to be overlooked, no miseries to be pitied, no wants to be relieved; where the affection we have been now treating of will happily be lost, as there will be no objects to exercise it upon: for *God shall wipe away all tears from their eyes, and there shall be no more death, neither sorrow, nor crying: neither shall there be any more pain; for the former things are passed away.*

SERMON VII.

UPON THE CHARACTER OF BALAAM.

PREACHED THE SECOND SUNDAY AFTER EASTER.

Let me die the death of the righteous, and let my last end be like his. Numb. xxiii. 10.

THESE words, taken alone, and without respect to him who spoke them, lead our thoughts immediately to the different ends of good and bad men. For though the comparison is not expressed, yet it is manifestly implied; as is also the preference of one of these characters to the other in that last circumstance, death. And, since dying the death of the righteous or of the wicked necessarily implies men's being righteous or wicked, *i. e.* having lived righteously or wickedly; a comparison of them in their lives also might come into consideration, from such a single view of the words themselves. But my present design is to consider them with a particular reference or respect to him who spoke them; which reference, if you please to attend, you will see. And if what shall be offered to your consideration at this time be thought a discourse upon the whole history of this man, rather than upon the particular words I have read, this is of no consequence; it is sufficient, if it afford reflection of use and service to ourselves.

But, in order to avoid cavils respecting this remarkable relation in Scripture, either that part of it which you have heard in the first lesson for the day, or any others; let me just observe, that as this is not a place for answering them, so they no way affect the following discourse; since the character there given is plainly a real one in life, and such as there are parallels to.

The occasion of Balaam's coming out of his own country into the land of Moab, where he pronounced this solemn prayer or wish, he himself relates in the first parable or prophetic speech, of which it is the conclusion. In which is a custom referred to, proper to be taken notice of: that of devoting enemies to destruction, before the entrance upon a war with them. This custom appears to have prevailed over a great part of the world; for we find it amongst the most distant nations. The Romans had public officers, to whom it belonged as a stated part of their office. But there was somewhat more particular in the case now before us; Balaam being looked upon as an extraordinary person, whose blessing or curse was thought to be always effectual.

In order to engage the reader's attention to this passage, the sacred historian has enumerated the preparatory circumstances, which are these. Balaam requires the king of Moab to build him seven altars, and to prepare him the same number of oxen and of rams. The sacrifice being over, he retires alone to a solitude sacred to these occasions, there to wait the divine inspiration or answer, for which the foregoing rites were the preparation. *And God met Balaam, and put a word in his mouth;** upon receiving which, he returns back to the altars, where was the king, who had all this while attended the sacrifice, as appointed; he and all the princes of Moab standing, big with expectation of the prophet's reply. *And he took up his parable, and said, Balak the king of Moab hath brought me from Aram, out of the mountains of the east, saying, Come, curse me Jacob, and come, defy Israel. How shall I curse, whom God hath not cursed? Or how shall I defy, whom the Lord hath not defied? For from the top of the rocks I see him, and from the hills I behold him: lo, the people shall dwell alone, and shall not be reckoned among the nations. Who can count the dust of Jacob, and the number of the fourth part of Israel? Let me die the death of the righteous, and let my last end be like his.*†

It is necessary, as you will see in the progress of this discourse, particularly to observe what he understood

* Ver. 4, 5. † Ver. 6

by *righteous.* And he himself is introduced in the book of Micah* explaining it; if by *righteous* is meant *good,* as to be sure it is. *O my people, remember now what Balak king of Moab consulted, and what Balaam the son of Beor answered him from Shittim unto Gilgal.* From the mention of Shittim, it is manifest, that it is this very story which is here referred to, though another part of it, the account of which is not now extant; as there are many quotations in Scripture out of books which are not come down to us. *Remember what Balaam answered, that ye may know the righteousness of the Lord;* i. e. the righteousness which God will accept. Balak demands, *Wherewith shall I come before the Lord, and bow myself before the high God? Shall I come before him with burnt-offerings, with calves of a year old? Will the Lord be pleased with thousands of rams, or with ten thousands of rivers of oil? Shall I give my first-born for my transgression, the fruit of my body for the sin of my soul?* Balaam answers him, *He hath showed thee, O man, what is good: and what doth the Lord require of thee, but to do justly, and to love mercy, and to walk humbly with thy God?* Here is a good man expressly characterized, as distinct from a dishonest and a superstitious man. No words can more strongly exclude dishonesty and falseness of heart, than *doing justice,* and *loving mercy:* and both these, as well as *walking humbly with God,* are put in opposition to those ceremonial methods of recommendation, which Balak hoped might have served the turn. From hence appears what he meant by the *righteous* whose *death* he desires to die.

Whether it was his own character shall now be inquired: and in order to determine it, we must take a view of his whole behaviour upon this occasion. When the elders of Moab came to him, though he appears to have been much allured with the rewards offered, yet he had such regard to the authority of God, as to keep the messengers in suspense until he had consulted his will. *And God said to him, Thou shalt not go with them, thou shalt not curse the people, for they are blessed.*† Upon this he dismisses the ambassadors, with an absolute re-

* Micah vi. † Chap. xxii. 12.

fusal of accompanying them back to their king. Thus far his regards to duty prevailed, neither does there any thing appear as yet amiss in his conduct. His answer being reported to the king of Moab, a more honourable embassy is immediately despatched, and greater rewards proposed. Then the iniquity of his heart began to disclose itself. A thorough honest man would without hesitation have repeated his former answer, that he could not be guilty of so infamous a prostitution of the sacred character with which he was invested, as in the name of a prophet to curse those whom he knew to be blessed. But instead of this, which was the only honest part in these circumstances that lay before him, he desires the princes of Moab to tarry that night with him also; and for the sake of the reward deliberates, whether by some means or other he might not be able to obtain leave to curse Israel; to do that, which had been before revealed to him to be contrary to the will of God, which yet he resolves not to do without that permission. Upon which, as when this nation afterward rejected God from reigning over them, he gave them a king in his anger; in the same way, as appears from other parts of the narration, he gives Balaam the permission he desired: for this is the most natural sense of the words. Arriving in the territories of Moab, and being received with particular distinction by the king, and he repeating in person the promise of the rewards he had before made to him by his ambassadors: he seeks, the text says, by *sacrifices* and *enchantments* (what these were is not to our purpose), to obtain leave of God to curse the people; keeping still his resolution, not to do it without that permission: which not being able to obtain, he had such regard to the command of God, as to keep this resolution to the last. The supposition of his being under a supernatural restraint is a mere fiction of Philo: he is plainly represented to be under no other force or restraint, than the fear of God. However, he goes on persevering in that endeavour, after he had declared, that *God had not beheld iniquity in Jacob, neither had he seen perverseness in Israel;** i. e. they were a people of virtue and piety, so

* Ver. 21.

far as not to have drawn down, by their iniquity, that curse which he was soliciting leave to pronounce upon them. So that the state of Balaam's mind was this: he wanted to do what he knew to be very wicked, and contrary to the express command of God; he had inward checks and restraints, which he could not entirely get over; he therefore casts about for ways to reconcile this wickedness with his duty. How great a paradox soever this may appear, as it is indeed a contradiction in terms, it is the very account which the scripture gives us of him.

But there is a more surprising piece of iniquity yet behind. Not daring in his religious character, as a prophet, to assist the king of Moab, he considers whether there might not be found some other means of assisting him against that very people, whom he himself by the fear of God was restrained from cursing in words. One would not think it possible, that the weakness, even of religious self-deceit in its utmost excess, could have so poor a distinction, so fond an evasion, to serve itself of. But so it was: and he could think of no other method, than to betray the children of Israel to provoke his wrath, who was their only strength and defence. The temptation which he pitched upon, was that concerning which Solomon afterward observed, that it had *cast down many wounded; yea, many strong men had been slain by it:* and of which he himself was a sad example, when *his wives turned away his heart after other gods.* This succeeded: the people sin against God; and thus the prophet's counsel brought on that destruction, which he could by no means be prevailed upon to assist with the religious ceremony of execration, which the king of Moab thought would itself have effected it. Their crime and punishment are related in Deuteronomy,* and Numbers.† And from the relation repeated in Numbers,‡ it appears, that Balaam was the contriver of the whole matter. It is also ascribed to him in the Revelation,§ where he is said to have *taught Balak to cast a stumbling-block before the children of Israel.*

This was the man, this Balaam, I say, was the man who desired to *die the death of the righteous,* and that his

* Chap. iv. † Chap. xxv ‡ Chap. xxxi. § Chap. ii.

last end might be like his: and this was the state of his mind, when he pronounced these words.

So that the object we have now before us is the most astonishing in the world: a very wicked man, under a deep sense of God and religion, persisting still in his wickedness, and preferring the wages of unrighteousness, even when he had before him a lively view of death, and that approaching period of his days, which should deprive him of all those advantages for which he was prostituting himself; and likewise a prospect, whether certain or uncertain, of a future state of retribution: all this joined with an explicit ardent wish, that, when he was to leave this world, he might be in the condition of a righteous man. Good God, what inconsistency, what perplexity is here! With what different views of things, with what contradictory principles of action, must such a mind be torn and distracted! It was not unthinking carelessness, by which he ran on headlong in vice and folly, without ever making a stand to ask himself what he was doing: no; he acted upon the cool motives of interest and advantage. Neither was he totally hard and callous to impressions of religion, what we call abandoned; for he absolutely denied to curse Israel. When reason assumes her place, when convinced of his duty, when he owns and feels, and is actually under the influence of the divine authority; whilst he is carrying on his views to the grave, the end of all temporal greatness; under this sense of things, with the better character and more desirable state present—full before him—in his thoughts, in his wishes, voluntarily to choose the worse—what fatality is here! Or how otherwise can such a character be explained? And yet strange as it may appear, it is not altogether an uncommon one: nay, with some small alterations, and put a little lower, it is applicable to a very considerable part of the world. For if the reasonable choice be seen and acknowledged, and yet men make the unreasonable one, is not this the same contradiction; that very inconsistency, which appeared so unaccountable?

To give some little opening to such characters and behaviour, it is to be observed in general, that there is no account to be given in the way of reason, of men's so strong attachments to the present world: our hopes and fears and pursuits are in degrees beyond all proportion to the known value of the things they respect. This may be said without taking into consideration religion and a future state; and when these are considered, the disproportion is infinitely heightened. Now when men go against their reason, and contradict a more important interest at a distance, for one nearer, though of less consideration; if this be the whole of the case, all that can be said is, that strong passions, some kind of brute force within, prevails over the principle of rationality. However, if this be with a clear, full, and distinct view of the truth of things, then it is doing the utmost violence to themselves, acting in the most palpable contradiction to their very nature. But if there be any such thing in mankind as putting half-deceits upon themselves; which there plainly is, either by avoiding reflection, or (if they do reflect) by religious equivocation, subterfuges, and palliating matters to themselves; by these means conscience may be laid asleep, and they may go on in a course of wickedness with less disturbance. All the various turns, doubles, and intricacies in a dishonest heart, cannot be unfolded or laid open; but that there is somewhat of that kind is manifest, be it to be called self-deceit, or by any other name. Balaam had before his eyes the authority of God, absolutely forbidding him what he, for the sake of a reward, had the strongest inclination to: he was likewise in a state of mind sober enough to consider death and his last end: by these considerations he was restrained, first from going to the king of Moab; and after he did go, from cursing Israel. But notwithstanding this, there was great wickedness in his heart. He could not forego the rewards of unrighteousness: he therefore first seeks for indulgences; and when these could not be obtained, he sins against the whole meaning, end, and design of the prohibition, which no consideration in the world could prevail with him to go against the letter of. And surely that impious counsel he gave to Balak against the children of Israel, was, considered in itself, a greater piece of wickedness, than if he had cursed them in words.

If it be inquired what his situation, his hopes, and fears were, in respect to this his wish; the answer must be, that consciousness of the wickedness of his heart must necessarily have destroyed all settled hopes of dying the death of the righteous: he could have no calm satisfaction in this view of his last end: yet, on the other hand, it is possible that those partial regards to his duty, now mentioned, might keep him from perfect despair.

Upon the whole, it is manifest, that Balaam had the most just and true notions of God and religion; as appears, partly from the original story itself, and more plainly from the passage in Micah; where he explains religion to consist in real virtue and real piety, expressly distinguished from superstition, and in terms which most strongly exclude dishonesty and falseness of heart. Yet you see his behaviour: he seeks indulgences for plain wickedness; which not being able to obtain, he glosses over the same wickedness, dresses it up in a new form, in order to make it pass off more easily with himself. That is, he deliberately contrives to deceive and impose upon himself, in a matter which he knew to be of the utmost importance.

To bring these observations home to ourselves: it is too evident, that many persons allow themselves in very unjustifiable courses, who yet make great pretences to religion; not to deceive the world, none can be so weak as to think this will pass in our age; but from principles, hopes, and fears, respecting God and a future state; and go on thus with a sort of tranquillity and quiet of mind. This cannot be upon a thorough consideration, and full resolution, that the pleasures and advantages they propose are to be pursued at all hazards, against reason, against the law of God, and though everlasting destruction is to be the consequence. This would be doing too great violence upon themselves. No, they are for making a composition with the Almighty. These of his commands they will obey: but as to others—why they will make all the atonements in their power; the ambitious, the covetous, the dissolute man, each in a way which shall not contradict his respective pursuit. Indulgences before, which was Balaam's fir though he was not so successful in it as to deceive himself, or atonements afterwards, are all the same. And here perhaps come in faint hopes that they may, and half-resolves that they will, one time or other, make a change.

Besides these, there are also persons, who, from a more just way of considering things, see the infinite absurdity of this, of substituting sacrifice instead of obedience; there are persons far enough from superstition, and not without some real sense of God and religion upon their minds; who yet are guilty of most unjustifiable practices, and go on with great coolness and command over themselves. The same dishonesty and unsoundness of heart discovers itself in these another way. In all common ordinary cases we see intuitively at first view what is our duty, what is the honest part. This is the ground of the observation, that the first thought is often the best. In these cases doubt and deliberation is itself dishonesty; as it was in Balaam upon the second message. That which is called considering what is our duty in a particular case, is very often nothing but endeavouring to explain it away. Thus those courses, which, if men would fairly attend to the dictates of their own consciences, they would see to be corruption, excess, oppression, uncharitableness; these are refined upon—things were so and so circumstantiated — great difficulties are raised about fixing bounds and degrees: and thus every moral obligation whatever may be evaded. Here is scope, I say, for an unfair mind to explain away every moral obligation to itself. Whether men reflect again upon this internal management and artifice, and how explicit they are with themselves, is another question. There are many operations of the mind, many things pass within, which we never reflect upon again; which a bystander, from having frequent opportunities of observing us and our conduct, may make shrewd guesses at.

That great numbers are in this way of deceiving themselves is certain. There is scarce a man in the world, who has entirely got over all regards, hopes, and fears, concerning God and a future state; and these apprehensions in the generality, bad as we are, prevail in considerable degrees: yet men will and can be wicked, with calmness and thought; we see they are. There must therefore be some method of making it sit a little easy upon their minds; which, in the superstitious, is those indulgences and atonements before mentioned, and this self-deceit of another kind in persons of another character. And both these proceed from a certain unfairness of mind, a peculiar inward dishonesty; the direct contrary to that simplicity which our Saviour recommends, under the notion of *becoming little children,* as a necessary qualification for our entering into the kingdom of heaven.

But to conclude: How much soever men differ in the course of life they prefer, and in their ways of palliating and excusing their vices to themselves; yet all agree in the one thing, desiring to *die the death of the righteous.* This is surely remarkable. The observation may be extended further, and put thus: Even without determining what that is which we call guilt or innocence, there is no man but would choose, after having had the pleasure or advantage of a vicious action, to be free of the guilt of it, to be in the state of an innocent man. This shows at least the disturbance and implicit dissatisfaction in vice. If we inquire into the grounds of it, we shall find it proceeds partly from an immediate sense of having done evil, and partly from an apprehension, that this inward sense shall one time or another be seconded by a higher judgment, upon which our whole being depends. Now to suspend and drown this sense, and these apprehensions, be it by the hurry of business or of pleasure, or by superstition, or moral equivocations, this is in a manner one and the same, and makes no alteration at all in the nature of our case. Things and actions are what they are, and the consequences of them will be what they will be: why then should we desire to be deceived? As we are reasonable creatures, and have any regard to ourselves, we ought to lay these things plainly and honestly before our mind, and upon this, act as you please, as you think most fit; make that choice, and prefer that course of life, which you can justify to yourselves, and which sits more easy upon your own mind. It will immediately appear, that vice cannot be the happiness, but must upon the whole be the misery, of such a creature as man; a moral, an accountable agent. Superstitious observances, self-deceit, though of a more refined sort, will not in reality at all mend matters with us. And the result of the whole can be nothing else, but that with simplicity and fairness we *keep innocency, and take heed unto the thing that is right; for this alone shall bring a man peace at the last.*

SERMON VIII.

UPON RESENTMENT.

Ye have heard that it hath been said, Thou shalt love thy neighbour, and hate thine enemy: but I say unto you, Love your enemies, bless them that curse you, do good to them that hate you, and pray for them which despitefully use you and persecute you.—Matth. v. 43, 44.

SINCE perfect goodness in the Deity is the principle from whence the universe was brought into being, and by which it is preserved; and since general benevolence is the great law of the whole moral creation; it is a question which immediately occurs, *Why had man implanted in him a principle, which appears the direct contrary to benevolence?* Now the foot upon which inquiries of this kind should be treated is this: to take human nature as it is, and the circumstances in which it is placed as they are; and then consider the correspondence between that nature and those circumstances, or what course of action and behaviour, respecting those circumstances, any particular affection or passion leads us to. This I mention to distinguish the matter now before us from disquisitions of quite another kind; namely, *Why we are not made more perfect creatures, or placed in better circumstances?* these being questions which we have not, that I know of, any thing at all to do with. God Almighty undoubtedly foresaw the disorders, both natural and moral, which would happen in this state of things. If upon this we set ourselves to search and examine why he did not prevent them; we shall, I am afraid, be in danger of running into somewhat worse than impertinent curiosity. But upon this to examine how far the nature which he hath given us hath a respect to those circumstances, such as they are; how far it leads us to act a proper part in them; plainly belongs to us: and such inquiries are in many ways of excellent use. Thus the thing to be considered is, not, *Why we were not made of such a nature, and placed in such circumstances, as to have no need of so harsh and turbulent a passion as resentment:* but, taking our nature and condition as being what they are, *Why, or for what end such a passion was given us:* and this chiefly in order to show what are the abuses of it.

The persons who laid down for a rule, *Thou shalt love thy neighbour, and hate thine enemy,* made short work with this matter. They did not, it seems, perceive any thing to be disapproved in hatred, more than in good-will: and, according to their system of morals, our enemy was the proper natural object of one of these passions, as our neighbour was of the other of them.

This was all they had to say, and all they thought needful to be said, upon the subject. But this cannot be satisfactory; because hatred, malice, and revenge, are directly contrary to the religion we profess, and to the nature and reason of the thing itself. Therefore, since no passion God hath endued us with can be in itself evil; and yet since men frequently indulge a passion in such ways and degrees that at length it becomes quite another thing from what it was originally in our nature; and those vices of malice and revenge in particular take their occasion from the natural passion of resentment: it will be needful to trace this up to its original, that we may see *what it is in itself, as placed in our nature by its Author;* from which it will plainly appear, *for what ends it was placed there.* And when we know what the passion is in itself, and the ends of it, we shall easily see, *what are the abuses of it, in which malice and revenge consist;* and which are so strongly forbidden in the text, by the direct contrary being commanded.

Resentment is of two kinds: *hasty and sudden, or settled and deliberate.* The former is called anger, and often *passion;* which, though a general word, is frequently appropriated and confined to the particular feeling, sudden anger, as distinct from deliberate resentment, malice, and revenge. In all these words is usually implied somewhat vicious; somewhat unreasonable as to the occasion of the passion, or immoderate as to the degree or duration of it. But that the natural passion itself is indifferent, St Paul has asserted in that precept, *Be ye angry, and sin not:** which though it is by no means to be understood as an encouragement to indulge ourselves in anger, the sense being certainly this, *Though ye be angry, sin not;* yet here is evidently a distinction made between anger and sin; between the natural passion, and sinful anger.

Sudden anger, upon certain occasions, is mere instinct: as merely so, as the disposition to close our eyes upon the apprehension of somewhat falling into them; and no more necessarily implies any degree of reason. I say, *necessarily:* for to be sure *hasty,* as well as *deliberate,* anger may be occasioned by injury or contempt; in which cases reason suggests to our thoughts that injury and contempt, which is the occasion of the passion: but I am speaking of the former only so far as it is to be distinguished from the latter. The only way in which our reason and understanding can raise anger, is by representing to our mind injustice or injury of some kind or other. Now momentary anger is frequently raised, not only without any real, but without any apparent reason; that is, without any appearance of injury, as distinct from hurt or pain. It cannot, I suppose, be thought, that this passion in infants; in the lower species of animals; and which is often seen, in men towards them; it cannot, I say, be imagined, that these instances of this passion are the effect of reason: no, they are occasioned by mere sensation and feeling. It is opposition, sudden hurt, violence, which naturally excites the passion; and the real demerit or fault of him who offers that violence, or is the cause of that opposition or hurt, does not, in many cases, so much as come into thought.

* Ephes. iv. 26

The reason and end, for which man was made thus liable to this passion, is, that he might be better qualified to prevent, and likewise (or perhaps chiefly) to resist and defeat, sudden force, violence, and opposition, considered merely as such, and without regard to the fault or demerit of him who is the author of them. Yet, since violence may be considered in this other and further view, as implying fault; and since injury, as distinct from harm, may raise sudden anger; sudden anger may likewise accidentally serve to prevent, or remedy, such fault and injury. But, considered as distinct from settled anger, it stands in our nature for self-defence, and not for the administration of justice. There are plainly cases, and in the uncultivated parts of the world, and, where regular governments are not formed, they frequently happen, in which there is no time for consideration, and yet to be passive is certain destruction; in which sudden resistance is the only security.

But from *this*, *deliberate anger or resentment* is essentially distinguished, as the latter is not naturally excited by, or intended to prevent mere harm without appearance of wrong or injustice. Now, in order to see, as exactly as we can, what is the natural object and occasion of such resentment; let us reflect upon the manner in which we are touched with reading, suppose, a feigned story of baseness and villany, properly worked up to move our passions. This immediately raises indignation, somewhat of a desire that it should be punished. And though the designed injury be prevented, yet that it was designed is sufficient to raise this inward feeling. Suppose the story true, this inward feeling would be as natural and as just: and one may venture to affirm, that there is scarce a man in the world, but would have it upon some occasions. It seems *in us* plainly connected with a sense of virtue and vice, of moral good and evil. Suppose further, we knew both the person who did and who suffered the injury: neither would this make any alteration, only that it would probably affect us more. The indignation raised by cruelty and injustice, and the desire of having it punished, which persons unconcerned would feel, is by no means malice. No, it is resentment against vice and wickedness: it is one of the common bonds, by which society is held together; a fellow feeling, which each individual has in behalf of the whole species, as well as of himself. And it does not appear that this, generally speaking, is at all too high amongst mankind. Suppose now the injury I have been speaking of to be done against ourselves; or those whom we consider as ourselves. It is plain, the way in which we should be affected would be exactly the same in kind: but it would certainly be in a higher degree, and less transient; because a sense of our own happiness and misery is most intimately and always present to us; and from the very constitution of our nature, we cannot but have a greater sensibility to, and be more deeply interested in, what concerns ourselves. And this seems to be the whole of this passion, which is, properly speaking, natural to mankind: namely, a resentment against injury and wickedness in general; and in a higher degree when towards ourselves, in proportion to the greater regard which men naturally have for themselves, than for others. From hence it appears, that it is not natural, but moral evil; it is not suffering, but injury, which raises that anger or resentment, which is of any continuance. The natural object of it is not one, who appears to the suffering person to have been only the innocent occasion of his pain or loss; but one, who has been in a moral sense injurious either to ourselves or others. This is abundantly confirmed by observing what it is which heightens or lessens resentment; namely, the same which aggravates or lessens the fault: friendship, and former obligations, on one hand; or inadvertency, strong temptations, and mistake, on the other. All this is so much understood by mankind, how little soever it be reflected upon, that a person would be reckoned quite distracted, who should coolly resent a harm, which had not to himself the appearance of injury or wrong. Men do indeed resent what is occasioned through carelessness: but then they expect observance as their due, and so that carelessness is considered as faulty. It is likewise true, that they resent more strongly an injury done, than one which, though designed, was prevented, in cases where the guilt is perhaps the same: the reason however is, not that bare pain or loss raises resentment, but, that it gives a new, and, as I may speak, additional sense of the injury or injustice. According to the natural course of the passions, the degrees of resentment are in proportion, not only to the degree of design and deliberation in the injurious person; but in proportion to this, joined with the degree of the evil designed or premeditated; since this likewise comes in to make the injustice greater or less. And the evil or harm will appear greater when they feel it, than when they only reflect upon it: so therefore will the injury: and consequently the resentment will be greater.

The natural object or occasion of settled resentment then being injury, as distinct from pain or loss; it is easy to see, that to prevent and to remedy such injury, and the miseries arising from it, is the end for which this passion was implanted in man. It is to be considered as a weapon, put into our hands by nature, against injury, injustice, and cruelty: how it may be innocently employed and made use of, shall presently be mentioned.

The account which has been now given of this passion is, in brief, that sudden anger is raised by, and was chiefly intended to prevent or remedy, mere harm distinct from injury; but that it *may* be raised by injury, and *may* serve to prevent or to remedy it; and then the occasions and effects of it are the same with the occasions and effects of deliberate anger. But they are essentially distinguished in this, that the latter is never occasioned by harm, distinct from injury; and its natural proper end is to remedy or prevent only that harm, which implies, or is supposed to imply, injury or moral wrong. Every one sees that these observations do not relate to those, who have habitually suppressed the course of their passions and affections, out of regard either to interest or virtue; or who, from habits of vice and folly, have changed their nature. But, I suppose, there can be no doubt but this, now described, is the general course of resentment, considered as a natural passion, neither increased by indulgence, nor corrected by virtue, nor prevailed over by other passions, or particular habits of life.

As to the abuses of anger, which it is to be observed may be in all different degrees, the first which occurs is what is commonly called *passion;* to which some men are liable, in the same way as others are to the *epilepsy,* or any sudden particular disorder. This distemper of the mind seizes them upon the least occasion in the world, and perpetually without any real reason at all: and by means of it they are plainly, every day, every waking hour of their lives, liable and in danger of running into the most extravagant outrages. Of a less boisterous, but not of a less innocent kind, is *peevishness;* which I mention with pity, with real pity to the unhappy creatures, who, from their inferior station, or other circumstances and relations, are obliged to be in the way of, and to serve for a supply to it. Both these, for ought that I can see, are one and the same principle: but as it takes root in minds of different makes, it appears differently, and so is come to be distinguished by different names. That which in a more feeble temper is peevishness, and languidly discharges itself upon every thing which comes in its way; the same principle in a temper of greater force and stronger passions, becomes rage and fury. In one, the humour discharges itself at once; in the other, it is continually discharging. This is the account of *passion* and *peevishness,* as distinct from each other, and appearing in different persons. It is no objection against the truth of it, that they are both to be seen sometimes in one and the same person.

With respect to deliberate resentment, the chief instances of abuse are: when, from partiality to ourselves, we imagine an injury done us, when there is none: when this partiality represents it to us greater than it really is: when we fall into that extravagant and monstrous kind of resentment, towards one who has innocently been the occasion of evil to us; that is, resentment upon account of pain or inconvenience, without injury; which is the same absurdity, as settled anger at a thing that is inanimate: when the indignation against injury and injustice rises too high, and is beyond proportion to the particular ill action it is exercised upon: or, lastly, when pain or harm of any kind is inflicted merely in consequence of, and to gratify, that resentment, though naturally raised.

It would be endless to descend into and explain all the peculiarities of perverseness and wayward humour which might be traced up to this passion. But there is one thing, which so generally belongs to and accompanies all excess and abuse of it, as to require being mentioned: a certain determination, and resolute bent of mind not to be convinced or set right; though it be ever so plain, that there is no reason for the displeasure, that it was raised merely by error or misunderstanding. In this there is doubtless a great mixture of pride; but there is somewhat more, which I cannot otherwise express, than that resentment has taken possession of the temper and of the mind, and will not quit its hold. It would be too minute to inquire whether this be any thing more than bare obstinacy: it is sufficient to observe, that it, in a very particular manner and degree, belongs to the abuses of this passion.

But, notwithstanding all these abuses, "Is not just indignation against cruelty and wrong one of the *instruments of death*, which the Author of our nature hath provided? Are not cruelty, injustice, and wrong, the natural objects of that indignation? Surely then it may one way or other be innocently employed against them." True. Since therefore it is necessary for the very subsistence of the world, that injury, injustice, and cruelty, should be punished; and since compassion, which is so natural to mankind, would render that execution of justice exceedingly difficult and uneasy; indignation against vice and wickedness is, and may be allowed to be, a balance to that weakness of pity, and also to any thing else which would prevent the necessary methods of severity. Those who have never thought upon these subjects, may perhaps not see the weight of this: but let us suppose a person guilty of murder, or any other action of cruelty, and that mankind had naturally no indignation against such wickedness and the authors of it; but that every body was affected towards such a criminal in the same way as towards an innocent man: compassion, amongst other things, would render the execution of justice exceedingly painful and difficult, and would often quite prevent it. And notwithstanding that the principle of benevolence is denied by some and is really in a very low degree, that men are in great measure insensible to the happiness of their fellow creatures; yet they are not insensible to their misery, but are very strongly moved with it: insomuch that there plainly is occasion for that feeling, which is raised by guilt and demerit, as a balance to that of compassion. Thus much may, I think, justly be allowed to resentment, in the strictest way of moral consideration.

The good influence which this passion has in fact upon the affairs of the world, is obvious to every one's notice. Men are plainly restrained from injuring their fellow creatures by fear of their resentment; and it is very happy that they are so, when they would not be restrained by a principle of virtue. And after an injury is done, and there is a necessity that the offender should be brought to justice; the cool consideration of reason, that the security and peace of society requires examples of justice should be made, might indeed be sufficient to procure laws to be enacted, and sentence passed: but is it that cool reflection in the injured person, which, for the most part, brings the offender to justice? Or is it not resentment and indignation against the injury and the author of it? I am afraid there is no doubt, which is commonly the case. This however is to be considered as a good effect, notwithstanding it were much to be wished that men would act from a better principle, reason and cool reflection.

The account now given of the passion of resentment, as distinct from all the abuses of it, may suggest to our thoughts the following reflections.

First, That vice is indeed of ill desert, and must finally be punished. Why should men dispute concerning the reality of virtue, and whether it be founded in the nature of things, which yet surely is not matter of question; but why should this, I say, be disputed, when every man carries about him this passion, which affords him demonstration, that the rules of justice and equity are to be the guide of his actions? For every man naturally feels an indignation upon seeing instances of villany and baseness, and therefore cannot commit the same without being self-condemned.

Secondly, That we should learn to be cautious, lest we *charge God foolishly*, by ascribing that to him, or the nature he has given us, which is owing wholly to our own abuse of it. Men may speak of the degeneracy and corruption of the world, according to the experience they have had of it; but human nature, considered as the divine workmanship, should methinks be treated as sacred: for *in the image of God made he man.* That passion, from whence men take occasion to run into the dreadful vices of malice and revenge; even that passion, as implanted in our nature by God, is not only innocent, but a generous movement of mind. It is in itself, and in its original, no more than indignation against injury and wickedness: that which is the only deformity in the creation, and the only reasonable object of abhorrence and dislike. How manifold evidence have we of the divine wisdom and goodness, when even pain in the natural world, and the passion we have been now considering in the moral, come out instances of it!

SERMON IX.

UPON FORGIVENESS OF INJURIES.

Ye have heard that it hath been said, Thou shalt love thy neighbour, and hate thine enemy: but I say unto you, Love your enemies, bless them that curse you, do good to them that hate you, and pray for them which despitefully use you and persecute you. — Matt. v 43, 44.

As God Almighty foresaw the irregularities and disorders, both natural and moral, which would happen in this state of things; he hath graciously made some provision against them, by giving us several passions and affections, which arise from, or whose objects are, those disorders. Of this sort are fear, resentment, compassion, and others; of which there could be no occasion or use in a perfect state: but in the present we should be exposed to greater inconveniences without them; though there are very considerable ones, which they themselves are the occasions of. They are encumbrances indeed, but such as we are obliged to carry about with us, through this various journey of life: some of them as a guard against the violent assaults of others, and in our own defence; some in behalf of others; and all of them to put us upon, and help to carry us through a course of behaviour suitable to our condition, in default of that perfection of wisdom and virtue, which would be in all respects our better security.

The passion of anger or resentment hath already been largely treated of. It hath been shown, that mankind naturally feel some emotion of mind against injury and injustice, whoever are the sufferers by it; and even though the injurious design be prevented from taking effect. Let this be called anger, indignation, resentment, or by whatever name any one shall choose; the thing itself is understood, and is plainly natural. It has likewise been observed, that this natural indignation is generally moderate and low enough in mankind, in each particular man, when the injury which excites it doth not affect himself, or one whom he considers as himself. Therefore the precepts to *forgive*, and to *love our enemies*, do not relate to that general indignation against injury and the authors of it, but to this feeling, or resentment when raised by private or personal injury. But no man could be thought in earnest, who should assert, that, though indignation against injury, when others are the sufferers, is innocent and just; yet the same indignation against it, when we ourselves are the sufferers, becomes faulty and blameable. These precepts therefore cannot be understood to forbid this in the latter case, more than in the former. Nay they cannot be understood to forbid this feeling in the latter case, though raised to a higher degree than in the former: because, as was also observed further, from the very constitution of our nature, we cannot but have a greater sensibility to what concerns ourselves. Therefore the precepts in the text, and others of the like import with them, must be understood to forbid only the excess and abuse of this natural feeling, in cases of personal and private injury: the chief instances of which excess and abuse have likewise been already remarked; and all of them, excepting that of retaliation, do so plainly in the very terms express somewhat unreasonable, disproportionate, and absurd, as to admit of no pretence or shadow of justification.

But since custom and false honour are on the side of retaliation and revenge, when the resentment is natural and just; and reasons are sometimes offered in justification of revenge in these cases; and since love of our enemies is thought *too hard a saying* to be obeyed: I will show *the absolute unlawfulness of the former; the obligations we are under to the latter;* and then proceed to *some reflections, which may have a more direct and immediate tendency to beget in us a right temper of mind towards those who have offended us.*

In showing the unlawfulness of revenge, it is not my present design to examine what is alleged in favour of it, from the tyranny of custom and false honour, but only to consider the nature and reason of the thing itself; which ought to have prevented, and ought now to extirpate, every thing of that kind.

First, Let us begin with the supposition of that being innocent, which is pleaded for, and which shall be shown to be altogether vicious, the supposition that we were allowed to *render evil for evil,* and see what would be the consequence. Malice or resentment towards any man hath plainly a tendency to beget the same passion in him who is the object of it; and this again increases it in the other. It is of the very nature of this vice to propagate itself, not only by way of example, which it does in common with other vices, but in a peculiar way of its own; for resentment itself, as well as what is done in consequence of it, is the object of resentment: hence it comes to pass, that the first offence, even when so slight as presently to be dropped and forgotten, becomes the occasion of entering into a long intercourse of ill offices: neither is it at all uncommon to see persons, in this progress of strife and variance, change parts: and him, who was at first the injured person, become more injurious and blameable than the aggressor. Put the case then, that the law of retaliation was universally received, and allowed, as an innocent rule of life, by all; and the observance of it thought by many (and then it would soon come to be thought by all) a point of honour: this supposes every man in private cases to pass sentence in his own cause; and likewise, that anger or resentment is to be the judge. Thus, from the numberless partialities which we all have for ourselves, every one would often think himself injured when he was not: and in most cases would represent an injury as much greater than it really is; the imagined dignity of the person offended would scarce ever fail to magnify the offence. And, if bare retaliation, or returning just the mischief received, always begets resentment in the person upon whom we retaliate, what would that excess do? Add to this, that he likewise has his partialities—there is no going on to represent this scene of rage and madness: it is manifest there would be no bounds, nor any end. *If the beginning of strife is as when one letteth out water*, what would it come to when allowed this free and unrestrained course? *As coals are to burning coals, or wood to fire;* so would these *contentious men be to kindle strife.* And, since the indulgence of revenge hath manifestly this tendency, and does actually produce these effects in proportion as it is allowed; a passion of so dangerous a nature ought not to be indulged, were there no other reason against it.

Secondly, It hath been shown that the passion of resentment was placed in man, upon supposition of, and as a prevention or remedy to, irregularity and disorder. Now whether it be allowed or not, that the passion itself and the gratification of it joined together are painful to the malicious person; it must however be so with respect to the person towards whom it is exercised, and upon whom the revenge is taken. Now, if we consider mankind, according to that fine allusion of St Paul, as *one body, and every one members one of another;* it must be allowed that resentment is, with respect to society, a painful remedy. Thus then the very notion or idea of this passion, as a remedy or prevention of evil, and as in itself a painful means, plainly shows that it ought never to be made use of, but only in order to produce some greater good.

It is to be observed, that this argument is not founded upon an allusion or simile; but that it is drawn from the very nature of the passion itself, and the end for which it was given us. We are obliged to make use of words taken from sensible things, to explain what is the most remote from them: and every one sees from whence the words Prevention and Remedy are taken. But, if you please, let these words be dropped: the thing itself, I suppose, may be expressed without them.

That mankind is a community, that we all stand in a relation to each other, that there is a public end and interest of society which each particular is obliged to promote, is the sum of morals. Consider then the passion of resentment, as given to this one body, as given to society. Nothing can be more manifest, than that resentment is to be considered as a secondary passion, placed in us upon supposition, upon account of, and with regard to, injury; not, to be sure, to promote and further it, but to render it, and the inconveniences and miseries arising from it, less and fewer than they would be without this passion. It is as manifest, that the indulgence of it is, with regard to society, a painful means of obtaining these ends. Considered in itself, it is very undesirable, and what society must very much wish to be without. It is in every instance absolutely an evil in itself, because it implies producing misery: and consequently must never be indulged or gratified for itself, by any one who considers mankind as a community or family, and himself as a member of it.

Let us now take this in another view. Every natural appetite, passion, and affection, may be gratified in particular instances, without being subservient to the particular chief end, for which these several principles were respectively implanted in our nature. And, if neither this end, nor any other moral obligation, be contradicted, such gratification is innocent. Thus, I suppose, there are cases in which each of these principles, this one of resentment excepted, may innocently be gratified, without being subservient to what is the main end of it: that is, though it does not conduce to, yet it may be gratified without contradicting, that end, or any other obligation. But the gratification of resentment, if it be not conducive to the end for which it was given us, must necessarily contradict, not only the general obligation to benevolence, but likewise that particular end itself. The end, for which it was given, is to prevent or remedy injury, *i. e.* the misery occasioned by injury; *i. e.* misery itself; and the gratification of it consists in producing misery; *i. e.* in contradicting the end for which it was implanted in our nature.

This whole reasoning is built upon the difference there is between this passion and all others. No other principle, or passion, hath for its end the misery of our fellow creatures. But malice and revenge meditates evil itself; and to do mischief, to be the author of misery, is the very thing which gratifies the passion: this is what it directly tends towards, as its proper design. Other vices eventually do mischief: this alone aims at it as an end.

Nothing can with reason be urged in justification of revenge, from the good effects which the indulgence of it were before mentioned * to have upon the affairs of the world; because, though it be a remarkable instance of the wisdom of Providence to bring good out of evil, yet vice is vice to him who is guilty of it. "But suppose these good effects are foreseen:" that is, suppose reason in a particular case leads a man the same way as passion? Why then, to be sure, he should follow his reason, in this as well as in all other cases. So that, turn the matter which way ever you will, no more can be allowed to this passion, than what hath been already.†

As to that love of our enemies, which is commanded; this supposes the general obligation to benevolence or good-will towards mankind: and this being supposed, that precept is no more than to forgive injuries; that is, to keep clear of those abuses before mentioned: because that we have the habitual temper of benevolence is taken for granted.

Resentment is not inconsistent with good-will; for we

* Serm. VIII. p. 100. † Ibid p. 99.

often see both together in very high degrees; not only in parents towards their children, but in cases of friendship and dependence, where there is no natural relation. These contrary passions, though they may lessen, do not necessarily destroy each other. We may therefore love our enemy, and yet have resentment against him for his injurious behaviour towards us. But when this resentment entirely destroys our natural benevolence towards him, it is excessive, and becomes malice or revenge. The command to prevent its having this effect, *i. e.* to forgive injuries, is the same as to love our enemies; because that love is always supposed, unless destroyed by resentment.

"But though mankind is the natural object of benevolence, yet may it not be lessened upon vice, *i. e.* injury?" Allowed: but if every degree of vice or injury must destroy that benevolence, then no man is the object of our love; for no man is without faults.

"But if lower instances of injury may lessen our benevolence, why may not higher, or the highest, destroy it?" The answer is obvious. It is not man's being a social creature, much less his being a moral agent, from whence *alone* our obligations to good-will towards him arise. There is an obligation to it prior to either of these, arising from his being a sensible creature; that is, capable of happiness or misery. Now this obligation cannot be superseded by his moral character. What justifies public executions is, not that the guilt, or demerit of the criminal dispenses with the obligation of good-will, neither would this justify any severity; but, that his life is inconsistent with the quiet and happiness of the world: that is, a general and more enlarged obligation necessarily destroys a particular and more confined one of the same kind inconsistent with it. Guilt or injury then does not dispense with or supersede the duty of love and good-will.

Neither does that peculiar regard to ourselves, which was before allowed to be natural* to mankind, dispense with it: because that can no way innocently heighten our resentment against those who have been injurious

* Serm. VIII. p. 96.

to ourselves in particular, any otherwise than as it heightens our sense of the injury or guilt; and guilt, though in the highest degree, does not, as hath been shown, dispense with or supersede the duty of love and good-will.

If all this be true, what can a man say, who will dispute the reasonableness, or the possibility, of obeying the divine precept we are now considering? Let him speak out, and it must be thus he will speak. "Mankind, *i. e.* a creature defective and faulty, is the proper object of good-will, whatever his faults are, when they respect others; but not when they respect me myself." That men should be *affected* in this manner, and *act* accordingly, is to be accounted for like other vices; but to *assert* that it *ought*, and *must* be thus, is self-partiality possessed of the very understanding.

Thus love to our enemies, and those who have been injurious to us, is so far from being a *rant*, as it has been profanely called, that it is in truth the law of our nature, and what every one must see and own, who is not quite blinded with self-love.

From hence it is easy to see, what is the degree in which we are commanded to love our enemies, or those who have been injurious to us. It were well if it could as easily be reduced to practice. It cannot be imagined, that we are required to love them with any peculiar kind of affection. But suppose the person injured to have a due natural sense of the injury, and no more; he ought to be affected towards the injurious person in the same way any good men, uninterested in the case, would be; if they had the same just sense, which we have supposed the injured person to have, of the fault: after which there will yet remain real good-will towards the offender.

Now what is there in all this, which should be thought impracticable? I am sure there is nothing in it unreasonable. It is indeed no more than that we should not indulge a passion, which, if generally indulged, would propagate itself so as almost to lay waste the world: that we should suppress that partial, that false self-love, which is the weakness of our nature: that uneasiness and misery should not be produced, without any good purpose to be served by it: and that we should not be affected towards persons differently from what their nature and character require.

But since to be convinced that any temper of mind, and course of behaviour, is our duty, and the contrary vicious, hath but a distant influence upon our temper and actions; let me add some few reflections, which may have a more direct tendency to subdue those vices in the heart, to beget in us this right temper, and lead us to a right behaviour towards those who have offended us: which reflections however shall be such as will further show the obligations we are under to it.

No one, I suppose, would choose to have an indignity put upon him, or to be injuriously treated. If then there be any probability of a misunderstanding in the case, either from our imagining we are injured when we are not, or representing the injury to ourselves as greater than it really is; one would hope an intimation of this sort might be kindly received, and that people would be glad to find the injury not so great as they imagined. Therefore, without knowing particulars, I take upon me to assure all persons who think they have received indignities or injurious treatment, that they may depend upon it, as in a manner certain, that the offence is not so great as they themselves imagine. We are in such a peculiar situation, with respect to injuries done to ourselves, that we can scarce any more see them as they really are, than our eye can see itself. If we could place ourselves at a due distance, *i. e.* be really unprejudiced, we should frequently discern that to be in reality inadvertence and mistake in our enemy, which we now fancy we see to be malice or scorn. From this proper point of view, we should likewise in all probability see something of these latter in ourselves, and most certainly a great deal of the former. Thus the indignity or injury would almost infinitely lessen, and perhaps at last come out to be nothing at all. Self-love is a medium of a peculiar kind; in these cases it magnifies every thing which is amiss in others, at the same time that it lessens every thing amiss in ourselves.

Anger also or hatred may be considered as another

false medium of viewing things, which always represents characters and actions much worse than they really are. Ill-will not only never speaks, but never thinks well, of the person towards whom it is exercised. Thus in cases of offence and enmity, the whole character and behaviour is considered with an eye to that particular part which has offended us, and the whole man appears monstrous, without any thing right or human in him: whereas the resentment should surely at least be confined to that particular part of the behaviour which gave offence: since the other parts of a man's life and character stand just the same as they did before.

In general, there are very few instances of enmity carried to any length, but inadvertency, misunderstanding, some real mistake of the case, on one side however, if not on both, has a great share in it.

If these things were attended to, these ill-humours could not be carried to any length amongst good men, and they would be exceedingly abated amongst all. And one would hope they might be attended to: for all that these cautions come to is really no more than desiring, that things may be considered and judged of as they are in themselves, that we should have an eye to, and beware of, what would otherwise lead us into mistakes. So that to make allowances for inadvertence, misunderstanding, for the partialities of self-love, and the false light which anger sets things in; I say, to make allowances for these, is not to be spoken of as an instance of humbleness of mind, or meekness and moderation of temper; but as what common sense should suggest, to avoid judging wrong of a matter before us, though virtue and morals were out of the case. And therefore it as much belongs to ill men, who will indulge the vice I have been arguing against, as to good men, who endeavour to subdue it in themselves. In a word, all these cautions, concerning anger and self-love, are no more than desiring a man, who was looking through a glass, which either magnified or lessened, to take notice, that the objects are not in themselves what they appear through that medium.

To all these things one might add, that, resentment

being out of the case, there is not, properly speaking, any such thing as direct ill-will in one man towards another: therefore the first indignity or injury, if it be not owing to inadvertence or misunderstanding, may however be resolved into other particular passions or self-love: principles quite distinct from ill-will, and which we ought all to be disposed to excuse in others, from experiencing so much of them in ourselves. A great man of antiquity is reported to have said, that, as he never was indulgent to any one fault in himself, he could not excuse those of others. This sentence could scarce with decency come out of the mouth of any human creature. But if we invert the former part, and put it thus: that he was indulgent to many faults in himself, as it is to be feared the best of us are, and yet was implacable; how monstrous would such an assertion appear! And this is the case in respect to every human creature, in proportion as he is without the forgiving spirit I have been recommending.

Further, though injury, injustice, oppression, the baseness of ingratitude, are the natural objects of indignation, or if you please of resentment, as before explained; yet they are likewise the objects of compassion, as they are their own punishment, and without repentance will for ever be so. No one ever did a designed injury to another, but at the same time he did a much greater to himself. If therefore we would consider things justly, such a one is, according to the natural course of our affections, an object of compassion, as well as of displeasure: and to be affected really in this manner, I say really, in opposition to show and pretence, argues the true greatness of mind. We have an example of forgiveness in this way in its utmost perfection, and which indeed includes in it all that is good, in that prayer of our blessed Saviour on the cross: *Father, forgive them; for they know not what they do.*

But lastly, The offences which we are all guilty of against God, and the injuries which men do to each other, are often mentioned together: and, making allowances for the infinite distance between the Majesty of Heaven, and a frail mortal, and likewise for this, that he cannot possibly be affected or moved as we are; offences committed by others against ourselves, and the manner in which we are apt to be affected with them, give a real occasion for calling to mind our own sins against God. Now there is an apprehension and presentiment, natural to mankind, that we ourselves shall one time or other be dealt with as we deal with others; and a peculiar acquiescence in, and feeling of, the equity and justice of this equal distribution. This natural notion of equity the son of Sirach has put in the strongest way. *He that revengeth shall find vengeance from the Lord, and he will surely keep his sins in remembrance. Forgive thy neighbour the hurt he hath done unto thee, so shall thy sins be forgiven when thou prayest. One man beareth hatred against another; and doth he seek pardon from the Lord? He sheweth no mercy to a man which is like himself; and doth he ask forgiveness of his own sins?** Let any one read our Saviour's parable of *the king who took account of his servants;*† and the equity and rightness of the sentence which was passed upon him who was unmerciful to his fellow servant, will be felt. There is somewhat in human nature, which accords to and falls in with that method of determination. Let us then place before our eyes the time which is represented in the parable; that of our own death, or the final judgment. Suppose yourselves under the apprehensions of approaching death; that you were just going to appear naked and without disguise before the Judge of all the earth, to give an account of your behaviour towards your fellow creatures: could any thing raise more dreadful apprehensions of that judgment, than the reflection that you had been implacable, and without mercy towards those who had offended you: without that forgiving spirit towards others, which that it may now be exercised towards yourselves, is your only hope? And these natural apprehensions are authorized by our Saviour's application of the parable: *So likewise shall my heavenly Father do also unto you, if ye from your hearts forgive not every one his brother their trespasses.* On the other hand, suppose a good man in the same circumstance, in the last part and close of life; conscious of many frailties,

* Ecclus. xxviii. 1—4. † Matt. xviii.

as the best are, but conscious too that he had been meek, forgiving, and merciful; that he had in simplicity of heart been ready to pass over offences against himself: the having felt this good spirit will give him, not only a full view of the amiableness of it, but the surest hope that he shall meet with it in his Judge. This likewise is confirmed by his own declaration: *If ye forgive men their trespasses, your heavenly Father will likewise forgive you.* And that we might have a constant sense of it upon our mind, the condition is expressed in our daily prayer. A forgiving spirit is therefore absolutely necessary, as ever we hope for pardon of our own sins, as ever we hope for peace of mind in our dying moments, or for the divine mercy at that day when we shall most stand in need of it.

SERMON X

UPON SELF-DECEIT.

And Nathan said to David, Thou art the man.—2 Sam. xii. 7

These words are the application of Nathan's parable to David, upon occasion of his adultery with Bathsheba, and the murder of Uriah her husband. The parable, which is related in the most beautiful simplicity, is this: **There were two men in one city; the one rich and the other poor. The rich man had exceeding many flocks and herds: but the poor man had nothing, save one little ewe-lamb, which he had bought and nourished up: and it grew up together with him, and with his children; it did eat of his own meat, and drank of his own cup, and lay in his bosom, and was unto him as a daughter. And there came a traveller unto the rich man, and he spared to take of his own flock, and of his own herd, to dress for the way-faring man that was come unto him, but took the poor man's lamb, and dressed it for the man that was come to him. And David's anger was greatly kindled against the man, and he*

* Ver. 1.

said to Nathan, As the Lord liveth, the man that hath done this thing shall surely die. And he shall restore the lamb four-fold, because he did this thing, and because he had no pity. David passes sentence, not only that there should be a fourfold restitution made; but he proceeds to the rigour of justice, *the man that hath done this thing shall die:* and this judgment is pronounced with the utmost indignation against such an act of inhumanity; *As the Lord liveth, he shall surely die; and his anger was greatly kindled against the man.* And the prophet answered, *Thou art the man.* He had been guilty of much greater inhumanity, with the utmost deliberation, thought, and contrivance. Near a year must have passed, between the time of the commission of his crimes, and the time of the prophet's coming to him; and it does not appear from the story, that he had in all this while the least remorse or contrition.

There is not any thing, relating to men and characters, more surprising and unaccountable, than this partiality to themselves, which is observable in many; as there is nothing of more melancholy reflection, respecting morality, virtue, and religion. Hence it is that many men seem perfect strangers to their own characters. They think, and reason, and judge quite differently upon any matter relating to themselves, from what they do in cases of others where they are not interested. Hence it is one hears people exposing follies, which they themselves are eminent for; and talking with great severity against particular vices, which, if all the world be not mistaken, they themselves are notoriously guilty of. This self-ignorance and self-partiality may be in all different degrees. It is a lower degree of it which David himself refers to in these words, *Who can tell how oft he offendeth? O cleanse thou me from my secret faults.* This is the ground of that advice of Elihu to Job: *Surely it is meet to be said unto God,—That which I see not, teach thou me; if I have done iniquity, I will do no more.* And Solomon saw this thing in a very strong light, when he said, *He that trusteth his own heart is a fool.* This likewise was the reason why that precept, *Know thyself*, was so frequently inculcated by the philosophers of old. For if it were not for that partial and fond regard to ourselves, it would certainly be no great difficulty to know our own character, what passes within the bent and bias of our mind; much less would there be any difficulty in judging rightly of our own actions. But from this partiality it frequently comes to pass, that the observation of many men's being themselves last of all acquainted with what falls out in their own families, may be applied to a nearer home, to what passes within their own breasts.

There is plainly, in the generality of mankind, an absence of doubt or distrust, in a very great measure, as to their moral character and behaviour; and likewise a disposition to take for granted, that all is right and well with them in these respects. The former is owing to their not reflecting, not exercising their judgment upon themselves; the latter, to self-love. I am not speaking of that extravagance, which is sometimes to be met with; instances of persons declaring in words at length, that they never were in the wrong, nor had ever any diffidence of the justness of their conduct, in their whole lives. No, these people are too far gone to have any thing said to them. The thing before us is indeed of this kind, but in a lower degree, and confined to the moral character; somewhat of which we almost all of us have, without reflecting upon it. Now consider, how long and how grossly, a person of the best understanding might be imposed upon by one of whom he had not any suspicion, and in whom he placed an entire confidence; especially if there were friendship and real kindness in the case: surely this holds even stronger with respect to that self we are all so fond of. Hence arises in men a disregard of reproof and instruction, rules of conduct and moral discipline, which occasionally come in their way: a disregard, I say, of these; not in every respect, but in this single one, namely, as what may be of service to them in particular towards mending their own hearts and tempers, and making them better men. It never in earnest comes into their thoughts, whether such admonitions may not relate, and be of service to themselves, and this quite distinct from a positive persuasion to the contrary, a persuasion from reflection that they are innocent and blameless in those respects. Thus we may invert the observation which is somewhere made upon Brutus, that he never read, but in order to make himself a better man. It scarce comes into the thoughts of the generality of mankind, that this use is to be made of moral reflections which they meet with; that this use, I say, is to be made of them by themselves, for every body observes and wonders that it is not done by others.

Further, there are instances of persons having so fixed and steady an eye upon their own interest, whatever they place it in, and the interest of those whom they consider as themselves, as in a manner to regard nothing else; their views are almost confined to this alone. Now we cannot be acquainted with, or in any propriety of speech be said to know any thing, but what we attend to. If therefore they attend only to one side, they really will not, cannot see or know what is to be alleged on the other. Though a man hath the best eyes in the world, he cannot see any way but that which he turns them. Thus these persons, without passing over the least, the most minute thing, which can possibly be urged in favour of themselves, shall overlook entirely the plainest and most obvious things on the other side. And whilst they are under the power of this temper, thought and consideration upon the matter before them has scarce any tendency to set them right: because they are engaged; and their deliberation concerning an action to be done, or reflection upon it afterwards, is not to see whether it be right, but to find out reasons to justify or palliate it; palliate it, not to others, but to themselves.

In some there is to be observed a general ignorance of themselves, and wrong way of thinking and judging in every thing relating to themselves; their fortune, reputation, every thing in which self can come in: and this perhaps attended with the rightest judgment in all other matters. In others this partiality is not so general, has not taken hold of the whole man, but is confined to some particular favourite passion, interest, or pursuit; suppose ambition, covetousness, or any other. And these persons may probably judge and determine what is perfectly just and proper, even in things in which they themselves are concerned, if these things have no relation to their particular favourite passion or pursuit. Hence arises that amazing incongruity, and seeming inconsistency of character, from whence slight observers take it for granted, that the whole is hypocritical and false; not being able otherwise to reconcile the several parts: whereas in truth there is real honesty, so far as it goes. There is such a thing as men's being honest to such a degree, and in such respects, but no further. And this, as it is true, so it is absolutely necessary to be taken notice of, and allowed them; such general and undistinguishing censure of their whole character, as designing and false, being one main thing which confirms them in their self-deceit. They know that the whole censure is not true; and so take for granted that no part of it is.

But to go on with the explanation of the thing itself: Vice in general consists in having an unreasonable and too great regard to ourselves, in comparison of others. Robbery and murder is never from the love of injustice or cruelty, but to gratify some other passion, to gain some supposed advantage: and it is false selfishness alone, whether cool or passionate, which makes a man resolutely pursue that end, be it ever so much to the injury of another. But whereas, in common and ordinary wickedness, this unreasonableness, this partiality and selfishness, relates only, or chiefly, to the temper and passions, in the characters we are now considering, it reaches to the understanding, and influences the very judgment.* And, besides that general want of distrust and diffidence concerning our own character, there are,

* That peculiar regard for ourselves which frequently produces this partiality of judgment in our own favour, may have a quite contrary effect, and occasion the utmost diffidence and distrust of ourselves; were it only, as it may set us upon a more frequent and strict survey and review of our own character and behaviour. This search or recollection itself implies somewhat of diffidence; and the discoveries we make, what is brought to our view, may possibly increase it. Good-will to another may either blind our judgment, so as to make us overlook his faults; or it may put us upon exercising that judgment with greater strictness, to see whether he is so faultless and perfect as we wish him. If that peculiar regard to ourselves leads us to examine our own character with this greater severity, in order really to improve and grow better, it is the most commendable turn of mind possible, and can scarce be to excess. But if, as every thing hath its counterfeit, we are so much employed about ourselves in order to disguise what is amiss, and to make a better appearance; or if our attention to ourselves has chiefly this effect; it is liable to run up into the greatest weakness and excess, and is like all other excesses its own disappointment: for scarce any show themselves to advantage, who are over solicitous of doing so.

you see, two things, which may thus prejudice and darken the understanding itself: that over-fondness for ourselves, which we are all so liable to; and also being under the power of any particular passion or appetite, or engaged in any particular pursuit. And these, especially the last of the two, may be in so great a degree, as to influence our judgment, even of other persons and their behaviour. Thus a man, whose temper is formed to ambition or covetousness, shall even approve of them sometimes in others.

This seems to be in a good measure the account of self-partiality and self-deceit, when traced up to its original. Whether it be, or be not thought satisfactory, that there is such a thing is manifest; and that it is the occasion of great part of the unreasonable behaviour of men towards each other: that by means of it they palliate their vices and follies to themselves: and that it prevents their applying to themselves those reproofs and instructions, which they meet with either in scripture or in moral and religious discourses, though exactly suitable to the state of their own mind, and the course of their behaviour. There is one thing further to be added here, that the temper we distinguish by hardness of heart with respect to others, joined with this self-partiality, will carry a man almost any lengths of wickedness, in the way of oppression, hard usage of others, and even to plain injustice; without his having, from what appears, any real sense at all of it. This indeed was not the general character of David: for he plainly gave scope to the affections of compassion and good-will, as well as to his passions of another kind.

But as some occasions and circumstances lie more open to this self-deceit, and give it greater scope and opportunities than others, these require to be particularly mentioned.

It is to be observed then, that as there are express determinate acts of wickedness, such as murder, adultery, theft: so, on the other hand, there are numberless cases in which the vice and wickedness cannot be exactly defined; but consists in a certain general temper and course of action, or in the neglect of some duty, suppose charity or any other, whose bounds and degrees are not fixed. This is the very province of self-deceit and self-partiality: here it governs without check or control. "For what commandment is there broken? Is there a transgression where there is no law? a vice which cannot be defined?"

Whoever will consider the whole commerce of human life, will see that a great part, perhaps the greatest part, of the intercourse amongst mankind, cannot be reduced to fixed determinate rules. Yet in these cases there is a right and a wrong: a merciful, a liberal, a kind and compassionate behaviour, which surely is our duty; and an unmerciful contracted spirit, a hard and oppressive course of behaviour, which is most certainly immoral and vicious. But who can define precisely, wherein that contracted spirit and hard usage of others consist, as murder and theft may be defined? There is not a word in our language, which expresses more detestable wickedness than *oppression;* yet the nature of this vice cannot be so exactly stated, nor the bounds of it so determinately marked, as that we shall be able to say in all instances, where rigid right and justice ends, and oppression begins. In these cases there is great latitude left, for every one to determine for, and consequently to deceive himself. It is chiefly in these cases that self-deceit comes in; as every one must see that there is much larger scope for it here, than in express, single, determinate acts of wickedness. However it comes in with respect to the *circumstances* attending the most gross and determinate acts of wickedness. Of this, the story of David, now before us, affords the most astonishing instance. It is really prodigious, to see a man, before so remarkable for virtue and piety, going on deliberately from adultery to murder, with the same cool contrivance, and, from what appears, with as little disturbance, as a man would endeavour to prevent the ill consequences of a mistake he had made in any common matter. That total insensibility of mind with respect to those horrid crimes, after the commission of them, manifestly shows that he did some way or other delude himself: and this could not be with respect to the crimes themselves, they were so manifestly of the grossest kind. What the particular circumstances were, with which he extenuated them, and quieted and deceived himself, is not related.

Having thus explained the nature of internal hypocrisy and self-deceit, and remarked the occasions upon which it exerts itself; there are several things further to be observed concerning it: that all of the sources, to which it was traced up, are sometimes observable together in one and the same person: but that one of them is more remarkable, and to a higher degree, in some, and others of them are so in others: that in general it is a complicated thing; and may be in all different degrees and kinds: that the temper itself is essentially in its own nature vicious and immoral. It is unfairness: it is dishonesty; it is falseness of heart: and is therefore so far from extenuating guilt, that it is itself the greatest of all guilt in proportion to the degree it prevails; for it is a corruption of the whole moral character in its principle. Our understanding, and sense of good and evil, is the light and guide of life: *If therefore this light that is in thee be darkness, how great is that darkness!** For this reason our Saviour puts an *evil eye* as the direct opposite to a *single eye;* the absence of that simplicity, which these last words imply, being itself evil and vicious. And whilst men are under the power of this temper, in proportion still to the degree they are so, they are fortified on every side against conviction: and when they hear the vice and folly of what is in truth their own course of life, exposed in the justest and strongest manner, they will often assent to it, and even carry the matter further; persuading themselves, one does not know how, but some way or other persuading themselves, that they are out of these, and that it hath no relation to them. Yet, notwithstanding this, there *frequently appears* a suspicion, that all is not right, or as it should be; and perhaps there *is always* at bottom somewhat of this sort. There are doubtless many instances of the ambitious, the revengeful, the covetous, and those whom with too great indulgence we only call the men of pleasure, who will not allow themselves to think how guilty they are, who explain and

* Matt. vi. 23.

argue away their guilt to themselves: and though they do really impose upon themselves in some measure, yet there are none of them but have, if not a proper knowledge, yet at least an implicit suspicion, where the weakness lies, and what part of their behaviour they have reason to wish unknown or forgotten for ever. Truth, and real good sense, and thorough integrity, carry along with them a peculiar consciousness of their own genuineness: there is a feeling belonging to them, which does not accompany their counterfeits, error, folly, half-honesty, partial and slight regards to virtue and right, so far only as they are consistent with that course of gratification which men happen to be set upon. And, if this be the case, it is much the same as if we should suppose a man to have had a general view of some scene, enough to satisfy him that it was very disagreeable, and then to shut his eyes, that he might not have a particular or distinct view of its several deformities. It is as easy to close the eyes of the mind, as those of the body: and the former is more frequently done with wilfulness, and yet not attended to, than the latter; the actions of the mind being more quick and transient, than those of the senses. This may be further illustrated by another thing observable in ordinary life. It is not uncommon for persons, who run out their fortunes, entirely to neglect looking into the state of their affairs, and this from a general knowledge, that the condition of them is bad. These extravagant people are perpetually ruined before they themselves expected it: and they tell you for an excuse, and tell you truly, that they did not think they were so much in debt, or that their expenses so far exceeded their income. And yet no one will take this for an excuse, who is sensible that their ignorance of their particular circumstances was owing to their general knowledge of them; that is, their general knowledge, that matters were not well with them, prevented their looking into particulars. There is somewhat of the like kind with this in respect to morals, virtue, and religion. Men find that the survey of themselves, their own heart and temper, their own life and behaviour, doth not afford them satisfaction: things are not as they should be.

therefore they turn away, will not go over particulars, or look deeper, lest they should find more amiss. For who would choose to be put out of humour with himself? No one, surely, if it were not in order to mend, and to be more thoroughly and better pleased with himself for the future.

If this sincere self-enjoyment and home-satisfaction be thought desirable, and worth some pains and diligence; the following reflections will, I suppose, deserve your attention; as what may be of service and assistance to all who are in any measure honestly disposed, for avoiding that fatal self-deceit, and towards getting acquainted with themselves.

The first is, that those who have never had any suspicion of, who have never made allowances for, this weakness in themselves, who have never (if I may be allowed such a manner of speaking) caught themselves in it, may almost take for granted that they have been very much misled by it. For consider: nothing is more manifest, than that affection and passion of all kinds influence the judgment. Now as we have naturally a greater regard to ourselves than to others, as the private affection is more prevalent than the public; the former will have proportionally a greater influence upon the judgment, upon our way of considering things. People are not backward in owning this partiality of judgment, in cases of friendship and natural relation. The reason is obvious, why it is not so readily acknowledged, when the interest which misleads us is more confined, confined to ourselves: but we all take notice of it in each other in these cases. There is not any observation more common, than that there is no judging of a matter from hearing only one side. This is not founded upon supposition, at least it is not always, of a formed design in the relater to deceive: for it holds in cases, where he expects that the whole will be told over again by the other side. But the supposition, which this observation is founded upon, is the very thing now before us; namely, that men are exceedingly prone to deceive themselves, and judge too favourably in every respect, where themselves and their own interest are concerned. Thus, though we have not the least reason to suspect that such an interested person hath any intention to deceive us, yet we of course make great allowances for his having deceived himself. If this be general, almost universal, it is prodigious that every man can think himself an exception, and that he is free from this self-partiality. The direct contrary is the truth. Every man may take for granted that he has a great deal of it, till, from the strictest observation upon himself, he finds particular reason to think otherwise.

Secondly, There is one easy and almost sure way to avoid being misled by this self-partiality, and to get acquainted with our real character: to have regard to the suspicious part of it, and keep a steady eye over ourselves in that respect. Suppose then a man fully satisfied with himself, and his own behaviour; such a one, if you please, as the Pharisee in the Gospel, or a better man.—Well; but allowing this good opinion you have of yourself to be true, yet every one is liable to be misrepresented. Suppose then an enemy were to set about defaming you, what part of your character would he single out? What particular scandal, think you, would he be most likely to fix upon you? And what would the world be most ready to believe? There is scarce a man living but could, from the most transient superficial view of himself, answer this question. What is that ill thing, that faulty behaviour, which I am apprehensive an enemy, who was thoroughly acquainted with me, would be most likely to lay to my charge, and which the world would be most apt to believe? It is indeed possible that a man may not be guilty in that respect. All that I say is, let him in plainness and honesty fix upon that part of his character for a particular survey and reflection; and by this he will come to be acquainted, whether he be guilty or innocent in that respect, and how far he is one or the other.

Thirdly, It would very much prevent our being misled by this self-partiality, to reduce that practical rule of our Saviour, *Whatsoever ye would that men should do to you, even so do unto them,* to our judgment and way of thinking. This rule, you see, consists of two parts

One is, to substitute another for yourself, when you take a survey of any part of your behaviour, or consider what is proper and fit and reasonable for you to do upon any occasion: the other part is, that you substitute yourself in the room of another; consider yourself as the person affected by such a behaviour, or towards whom such an action is done: and then you would not only see, but likewise feel, the reasonableness or unreasonableness of such an action or behaviour. But, alas! the rule itself may be dishonestly applied: there are persons who have not impartiality enough with respect to themselves, nor regard enough for others, to be able to make a just application of it. This just application, if men would honestly make it, is in effect all that I have been recommending; is the whole thing, the direct contrary to that inward dishonesty as r ecting our intercourse with our fellow creatures. And even the bearing this rule in their thoughts may be of some service; the attempt thus to apply it, is an attempt towards being fair and impartial, and may chance unawares to show them to themselves, to show them the truth of the case they are considering.

Upon the whole it is manifest, that there is such a thing as this self-partiality and self-deceit: that in some persons it is to a degree which would be thought incredible, were not the instances before our eyes; of which the behaviour of David is perhaps the highest possible one, in a single particular case; for there is not the least appearance, that it reached his general character: that we are almost all of us influenced by it in some degree, and in some respects: that therefore every one ought to have an eye to and beware of it. And all that I have further to add upon this subject is, that either there is a difference between right and wrong, or there is not: religion is true, or it is not. If it be not, there is no reason for any concern about it: but if it be true, it requires real fairness of mind and honesty of heart. And, if people will be wicked, they had better of the two be so from the common vicious passions without such refinements, than from this deep and calm source of delusion; which undermines the whole principle of good;

darkens that light, that *candle of the Lord within*, which is to direct our steps; and corrupts conscience, which is the guide of life.

SERMON XI.

UPON THE LOVE OF OUR NEIGHBOUR.

PREACHED ON ADVENT SUNDAY.

And if there be any other commandment, it is briefly comprehended in this saying, namely, Thou shalt love thy neighbour as thyself.— Rom. xiii. 9.

It is commonly observed, that there is a disposition in men to complain of the viciousness and corruption of the age in which they live, as greater than that of former ones; which is usually followed with this further observation, that mankind has been in that respect much the same in all times. Now, not to determine whether this last be not contradicted by the accounts of history; thus much can scarce be doubted, that vice and folly takes different turns, and some particular kinds of it are more open and avowed in some ages than in others: and, I suppose, it may be spoken of as very much the distinction of the present to profess a contracted spirit, and greater regards to self-interest, than appears to have been done formerly. Upon this account it seems worth while to inquire, whether private interest is likely to be promoted in proportion to the degree in which self-love engrosses us, and prevails over all other principles; *or whether the contracted affection may not possibly be so prevalent as to disappoint itself, and even contradict its own end, private good.*

And since, further, there is generally thought to be some peculiar kind of contrariety between self-love and the love of our neighbour, between the pursuit of public and of private good; insomuch that when you are recommending one of these, you are supposed to be speaking against the other; and from hence arises a secret prejudice against, and frequently open scorn of all talk of public spirit, and real good-will to our fellow creatures; it will be necessary to *inquire what respect benevolence hath to self-love, and the pursuit of private interest to the pursuit of public:* or whether there be any thing of that peculiar inconsistence and contrariety between them, over and above what there is between self-love and other passions and particular affections, and their respective pursuits.

These inquiries, it is hoped, may be favourably attended to: for there shall be all possible concessions made to the favourite passion, which hath so much allowed to it, and whose cause is so universally pleaded: it shall be treated with the utmost tenderness and concern for its interests.

In order to this, as well as to determine the forementioned questions, it will be necessary to *consider the nature, the object, and end of that self-love, as distinguished from other principles or affections in the mind, and their respective objects.*

Every man hath a general desire of his own happiness; and likewise a variety of particular affections, passions, and appetites to particular external objects. The former proceeds from, or is self-love; and seems inseparable from all sensible creatures, who can reflect upon themselves and their own interest or happiness, so as to have that interest an object to their minds: what is to be said of the latter is, that they proceed from, or together make up that particular nature, according to which man is made. The object the former pursues is somewhat internal, our own happiness, enjoyment, satisfaction; whether we have, or have not, a distinct particular perception what it is, or wherein it consists: the objects of the latter are this or that particular external thing, which the affections tend towards, and of which it hath always a particular idea or perception. The principle we call self-love never seeks any thing external for the sake of the thing, but only as a means of happiness or good: particular affections rest in the external things themselves. One belongs to man as a reasonable creature reflecting upon his own interest or happiness. The other, though quite distinct from reason, are as much a part of human nature.

That all particular appetites and passions are towards *external things themselves,* distinct from the *pleasure arising from them,* is manifested from hence; that there could not be this pleasure, were it not for that prior suitableness between the object and the passion: there could be no enjoyment or delight from one thing more than another, from eating food more than from swallowing a stone, if there were not an affection or appetite to one thing more than another.

Every particular affection, even the love of our neighbour, is as really our own affection, as self-love; and the pleasure arising from its gratification is as much my own pleasure, as the pleasure self-love would have, from knowing I myself should be happy some time hence, would be my own pleasure. And if, because every particular affection is a man's own, and the pleasure arising from its gratification his own pleasure, or pleasure to himself, such particular affection must be called self-love; according to this way of speaking, no creature whatever can possibly act but merely from self-love; and every action and every affection whatever is to be resolved up into this one principle. But then this is not the language of mankind: or if it were, we should want words to express the difference, between the principle of an action, proceeding from cool consideration that it will be to my own advantage; and an action, suppose of revenge, or of friendship, by which a man runs upon certain ruin, to do evil or good to another. It is manifest the principles of these actions are totally different, and so want different words to be distinguished by: all that they agree in is, that they both proceed from, and are done to gratify an inclination in a man's self. But the principle or inclination in one case is self-love: in the other, hatred or love of another. There is then a distinction between the cool principle of self-love, or general desire of our own happiness, as one part of our nature, and one principle of action; and the particular affections towards particular external objects, as another part of our nature, and another principle of action. How much soever therefore is to be allowed to self-love, yet it cannot be allowed to be the whole of our inward constitution; because, you see, there are other parts or principles which come into it.

Further, private happiness or good is all which self-love can make us desire, or be concerned about: in having this consists its gratification; it is an affection to ourselves; a regard to our own interest, happiness, and private good: and in the proportion a man hath this, he is interested, or a lover of himself. Let this be kept in mind; because there is commonly, as I shall presently have occasion to observe, another sense put upon these words. On the other hand, particular affections tend towards particular external things: these are their objects: having these is their end: in this consists their gratification: no matter whether it be, or be not, upon the whole, our interest or happiness. An action done from the former of these principles is called an interested action. An action proceeding from any of the latter has its denomination of passionate, ambitious, friendly, revengeful, or any other, from the particular appetite or affection from which it proceeds. Thus self-love as one part of human nature, and the several particular principles as the other part, are, themselves, their objects and ends, stated and shown.

From hence it will be easy to see, how far, and in what ways, each of these can contribute and be subservient to the private good of the individual. Happiness does not consist in self-love. The desire of happiness is no more the thing itself, than the desire of riches is the possession or enjoyment of them. People may love themselves with the most entire and unbounded affection, and yet be extremely miserable. Neither can self-love any way help them out, but by setting them on work to get rid of the causes of their misery, to gain or make use of those objects which are by nature adapted to afford satisfaction. Happiness or satisfaction consists only in the enjoyment of those objects, which are by nature suited to our several particular appetites, passions, and affections. So that if self-love wholly engrosses us and leaves no room for any other principle, there can be absolutely no such thing at all as happiness, or enjoyment of any kind whatever; since happiness consists in the gratification of particular passions, which supposes the having of them. Self-love then does not constitute *this* or *that* to be our interest or good; but, our interest or good being constituted by nature and supposed, self-love only puts us upon obtaining and securing it. Therefore, if it be possible, that self-love may prevail and exert itself in a degree or manner which is not subservient to this end; then it will not follow, that our interest will be promoted in proportion to the degree in which that principle engrosses us, and prevails over others. Nay further, the private and contracted affection, when it is not subservient to this end, private good, may, for any thing that appears, have a direct contrary tendency and effect. And if we will consider the matter, we shall see that it often really has. *Disengagement* is absolutely necessary to enjoyment: and a person may have so steady and fixed an eye upon his own interest, whatever he places it in, as may hinder him from *attending* to many gratifications within his reach, which others have their minds *free* and *open* to. Over-fondness for a child is not generally thought to be for its advantage: and, if there be any guess to be made from appearances, surely that character we call selfish is not the most promising for happiness. Such a temper may plainly be, and exert itself in a degree and manner which may give unnecessary and useless solicitude and anxiety, in a degree and manner which may prevent obtaining the means and materials of enjoyment, as well as the making use of them. Immoderate self-love does very ill consult its own interest: and how much soever a paradox it may appear, it is certainly true, that even from self-love we should endeavour to get over all inordinate regard to, and consideration of ourselves. Every one of our passions and affections hath its natural stint and bound, which may easily be exceeded; whereas our enjoyments can possibly be but in a determinate measure and degree. Therefore such excess of the affection, since it cannot procure any enjoyment, must in all cases be useless; but is generally attended with inconveniences, and often is downright pain and misery. This holds as much with regard to self-love as to all other affections. The natural degree of it, so far as it sets us on work to gain and make use of the materials of satisfaction, may be to our real advantage; but beyond or besides this, it is in several respects an inconvenience and disadvantage. Thus it appears, that private interest is so far from being likely to be promoted in proportion to the degree in which self-love engrosses us, and prevails over all other principles; that *the contracted affection may be so prevalent as to disappoint itself, and even contradict its own end, private good.*

"But who, except the most sordidly covetous, ever thought there was any rivalship between the love of greatness, honour, power, or between sensual appetites, and self-love? No, there is a perfect harmony between them. It is by means of these particular appetites and affections that self-love is gratified in enjoyment, happiness, and satisfaction. The competition and rivalship is between self-love and the love of our neighbour: that affection which leads us out of ourselves, makes us regardless of our own interest, and substitute that of another in its stead." Whether then there be any peculiar competition and contrariety in this case, shall now be considered.

Self-love and interestedness was stated to consist in or be an affection to ourselves, a regard to our own private good: it is therefore distinct from benevolence, which is an affection to the good of our fellow creatures. But that benevolence is distinct from, that is, not the same thing with self-love, is no reason for it being looked upon with any peculiar suspicion; because every principle whatever, by means of which self-love is gratified, is distinct from it: and all things which are distinct from each other are equally so. A man has an affection or aversion to another: that one of these tends to, and is gratified by doing good, that the other tends to, and is gratified by doing harm, does not in the least alter the respect which either one or the other of these inward feelings has to self-love. We use the word *property* so as to exclude any other persons having an interest in that of which we say a particular man has the property. And we often use the word *selfish* so as to exclude in the same manner all regards to the good of others. But the cases are not parallel: for though that exclusion is really part of the idea of property; yet such positive exclusion, or bringing this peculiar disregard to the good of others into the idea of self-love, is in reality adding to the idea, or changing it from what it was before stated to consist in, namely, in an affection to ourselves.* This being the whole idea of self-love, it can no otherwise exclude good-will or love of others, than merely by not including it, no otherwise, than it excludes love of arts or of reputation, or of any thing else. Neither on the other hand does benevolence, any more than love of arts or of reputation, exclude self-love. Love of our neighbour then has just the same respect to, is no more distant from self-love, than hatred of our neighbour, or than love or hatred of any thing else. Thus the principles, from which men rush upon certain ruin for the destruction of an enemy, and for the preservation of a friend, have the same respect to the private affection, and are equally interested, or equally disinterested: and it is of no avail, whether they are said to be one or the other. Therefore to those who are shocked to hear virtue spoken of as disinterested, it may be allowed that it is indeed absurd to speak thus of it; unless hatred, several particular instances of vice, and all the common affections and aversions in mankind, are acknowledged to be disinterested too. Is there any less inconsistence, between the love of inanimate things, or of creatures merely sensitive, and self-love; than between self-love and the love of our neighbour? Is desire of and delight in the happiness of another any more a diminution of self-love, than desire of and delight in the esteem of another? They are both equally desire of and delight in somewhat external to ourselves: either both or neither are so. The object of self-love is expressed in the term self: and every appetite of sense, and every particular affection of the heart, are equally interested or disinterested, because the objects of them all are equally self or somewhat else. Whatever ridicule therefore the mention of a disinterested principle or action may be supposed to lie open to, must, upon the matter being

* P. 127.

thus stated, relate to ambition, and every appetite and particular affection, as much as to benevolence. And indeed all the ridicule, and all the grave perplexity, of which this subject hath had its full share, is merely from words. The most intelligible way of speaking of it seems to be this: that self-love and the actions done in consequence of it (for these will presently appear to be the same as to this question) are interested; that particular affections towards external objects, and the actions done in consequence of those affections, are not so. But every one is at liberty to use words as he pleases. All that is here insisted upon is, that ambition, revenge, benevolence, all particular passions whatever, and the actions they produce, are equally interested or disinterested.

Thus it appears that there is no peculiar contrariety between self-love and benevolence; no greater competition between these, than between any other particular affections and self-love. This relates to the affections themselves. Let us now see whether there be any peculiar contrariety between the respective courses of life which these affections lead to; whether there be any greater competition between the pursuit of private and of public good, than between any other particular pursuits and that of private good.

There seems no other reason to suspect that there is any such peculiar contrariety, but only that the courses of action which benevolence leads to, has a more direct tendency to promote the good of others, than that course of action which love of reputation suppose, or any other particular affection leads to. But that any affection tends to the happiness of another, does not hinder its tending to one's own happiness too. That others enjoy the benefit of the air and the light of the sun, does not hinder but that these are as much one's own private advantage now, as they would be if we had the property of them exclusive of all others. So a pursuit which tends to promote the good of another, yet may have as great tendency to promote private interest, as a pursuit which does not tend to the good of another at all, or which is mischievous to him. All particular affections whatever, resentment, benevolence, love of arts, equally lead to a course of action for their own gratification, *i.e.* the gratification of ourselves; and the gratification of each gives delight: so far then it is manifest they have all the same respect to private interest. Now take into consideration further, concerning these three pursuits, that the end of the first is the harm, of the second, the good of another, of the last, somewhat indifferent; and is there any necessity, that these additional considerations should alter the respect, which we before saw these three pursuits, had to private interest; or render any one of them less conducive to it, than any other? Thus one man's affection is to honour as his end; in order to obtain which he thinks no pains too great. Suppose another, with such a singularity of mind, as to have the same affection to public good as his end, which he endeavours with the same labour to obtain. In case of success, surely the man of benevolence hath as great enjoyment as the man of ambition; they both equally having the end of their affections, in the same degree, tended to: but in case of disappointment, the benevolent man has clearly the advantage; since endeavouring to do good considered as a virtuous pursuit, is gratified by its own consciousness, *i.e.* is in a degree its own reward.

And as to these two, or benevolence and any other particular passions whatever, considered in a further view, as forming a general temper, which more or less disposes us for enjoyment of all the common blessings of life, distinct from their own gratification: is benevolence less the temper of tranquillity and freedom than ambition or covetousness? Does the benevolent man appear less easy with himself, from his love to his neighbour? Does he less relish his being? Is there any peculiar gloom seated on his face? Is his mind less open to entertainment, to any particular gratification? Nothing is more manifest, than that being in good humour, which is benevolence whilst it lasts, is itself the temper of satisfaction and enjoyment.

Suppose then a man sitting down to consider how he might become most easy to himself, and attain the greatest pleasure he could; all that which is his real natural happiness. This can only consist in the enjoyment of those objects, which are by nature adapted to our several faculties. These particular enjoyments make up the sum total of our happiness: and they are supposed to arise from riches, honours, and the gratification of sensual appetites: be it so: yet none profess themselves so completely happy in these enjoyments, but that there is room left in the mind of others, if they were presented to them: nay, these, as much as they engage us, are not thought so high, but that human nature is capable even of greater. Now there have been persons in all ages, who have professed that they found satisfaction in the exercise of charity, in the love of their neighbour, in endeavouring to promote the happiness of all they had to do with, and in the pursuit of what is just, and right, and good, as the general bent of their mind, and end of their life; and that doing an action of baseness or cruelty would be as great violence to *their* self, as much breaking in upon their nature, as any external force. Persons of this character would add, if they might be heard, that they consider themselves as acting in the view of an infinite Being, who is in a much higher sense the object of reverence and of love, than all the world besides; and therefore they could have no more enjoyment from a wicked action done under his eye, than the persons to whom they are making their apology could, if all mankind were the spectators of it; and that the satisfaction of approving themselves to his unerring judgment, to whom they thus refer all their actions, is a more continued settled satisfaction than any this world can afford; as also that they have, no less than others, a mind free and open to all the common innocent gratifications of it such as they are. And if we go no further, does there appear any absurdity in this? Will any one take upon him to say, that a man cannot find his account in this general course of life, as much as in the most unbounded ambition, and the excesses of pleasure? Or that such a person has not consulted so well for himself, for the satisfaction and peace of his own mind, as the ambitious or dissolute man? And though the consideration, that God himself will in the end justify their taste, and support their cause, is not formally to be insisted upon here·

yet thus much comes in, that all enjoyments whatever are much more clear and unmixed from the assurance that they will end well. Is it certain then that there is nothing in these pretensions to happiness? especially when there are not wanting persons, who have supported themselves with satisfactions of this kind in sickness, poverty, disgrace, and in the very pangs of death; whereas it is manifest all other enjoyments fail in these circumstances. This surely looks suspicious of having somewhat in it. Self-love methinks should be alarmed. May she not possibly pass over greater pleasures, than those she is so wholly taken up with?

The short of the matter is no more than this. Happiness consists in the gratification of certain affections, appetites, passions, with objects which are by nature adapted to them. Self-love may indeed set us on work to gratify these; but happiness or enjoyment has no immediate connexion with self-love, but arises from such gratification alone. Love of our neighbour is one of those affections. This, considered as a *virtuous principle*, is gratified by a consciousness of *endeavouring* to promote the good of others; but considered as natural affection, its gratification consists in the actual accomplishment of this endeavour. Now indulgence or gratification of this affection, whether in that consciousness, or this accomplishment, has the same respect to interest, as indulgence of any other affection; they equally proceed from or do not proceed from self-love, they equally include or equally exclude this principle. Thus it appears, that *benevolence and the pursuits of public good hath at least as great respect to self-love and the pursuits of private good, as any other particular passions, and their respective pursuits.*

Neither is covetousness, whether as a temper or pursuit, any exception to this. For if by covetousness is meant the desire and pursuit of riches for their own sake, without any regard to, or consideration of, the uses of them; this hath as little to do with self-love, as benevolence hath. But by this word is usually meant, not such madness and total distraction of mind, but immoderate affection to and pursuit of riches as possessions in order to some further end; namely, satisfaction, interest, or good. This therefore is not a particular affection, or particular pursuit, but it is the general principle of self-love, and the general pursuit of our own interest; for which reason, the word selfish is by every one appropriated to this temper and pursuit. Now as it is ridiculous to assert, that self-love and the love of our neighbour are the same: so neither is it asserted, that following these different affections hath the same tendency and respect to our own interest. The comparison is not between self-love and the love of our neighbour; between pursuit of our own interest, and the interest of others: but between the several particular affections in human nature towards external objects, as one part of the comparison; and the one particular affection to the good of our neighbour, as the other part of it: and it has been shown, that all these have the same respect to self-love and private interest.

There is indeed frequently an inconsistence or interfering between self-love or private interest, and the several particular appetites, passions, affections, or the pursuits they lead to. But this competition or interfering is merely accidental; and happens much oftener between pride, revenge, sensual gratifications, and private interest, than between private interest and benevolence. For nothing is more common, than to see men give themselves up to a passion or an affection to their known prejudice and ruin, and in direct contradiction to manifest and real interest, and the loudest calls of self-love: whereas the seeming competitions and interfering, between benevolence and private interest, relate much more to the materials or means of enjoyment, than to enjoyment itself. There is often an interfering in the former, when there is none in the latter. Thus as to riches: so much money as a man gives away, so much less will remain in his possession. Here is a real interfering. But though a man cannot possibly give without lessening his fortune, yet there are multitudes might give without lessening their own enjoyment; because they may have more than they can turn to any real use or advantage to themselves. Thus, the more thought and time any one employs about the interests and good of others, he must necessarily have less to attend his own; but he may have so ready and large a supply of his own wants, that such thought might be really useless to himself, though of great service and assistance to others.

The general mistake, that there is some greater inconsistence between endeavouring to promote the good of another and self-interest, than between self-interest and pursuing any thing else, seems, as hath already been hinted, to arise from our notions of property; and to be carried on by this property's being supposed to be itself our happiness or good. People are so very much taken up with this one subject, that they seem from it to have formed a general way of thinking, which they apply to other things that they have nothing to do with. Hence, in a confused and slight way, it might well be taken for granted, that another's having no interest in an affection, (*i. e.* his good not being the object of it,) renders, as one may speak, the proprietor's interest in it greater; and that if another had an interest in it, this would render his less, or occasion that such affection could not be so friendly to self-love, or conducive to private good, as an affection or pursuit which has not a regard to the good of another. This, I say, might be taken for granted, whilst it was not attended to, that the object of every particular affection is equally somewhat external to ourselves; and whether it be the good of another person, or whether it be any other external thing, makes no alteration with regard to its being one's own affection, and the gratification of it one's own private enjoyment. And so far as it is taken for granted, that barely having the means and materials of enjoyment is what constitutes interest and happiness; that our interest or good consists in possessions themselves, in having the property of riches, houses, lands, gardens, not in the enjoyment of them; so far it will even more strongly be taken for granted, in the way already explained, that an affection's conducing to the good of another, must even necessarily occasion it to conduce less to private good, if not to be positively detrimental to it. For, if property and happiness are one and the same thing, as by increasing the property of another, you lessen your own property, so by promoting the happiness of another, you must lessen your own happiness. But whatever occasion the mistake, I hope it has been fully proved to be one; as it has been proved, that there is no peculiar rivalship or competition between self-love and benevolence; that as there may be a competition between these two, so there may also between any particular affection whatever and self-love; that every particular affection, benevolence among the rest, is subservient to self-love, by being the instrument of private enjoyment; and that in one respect benevolence contributes more to private interest, *i. e.* enjoyment or satisfaction, than any other of the particular common affections, as it is in a degree its own gratification.

And to all these things may be added, that religion, from whence arises our strongest obligation to benevolence, is so far from disowning the principle of self-love, that it often addresses itself to that very principle, and always to the mind in that state when reason presides: and there can no access be had to the understanding, but by convincing men, that the course of life we would persuade them to is not contrary to their interest. It may be allowed, without any prejudice to the cause of virtue and religion, that our ideas of happiness and misery are of all our ideas the nearest and most important to us; that they will, nay, if you please, that they ought to prevail over those of order, and beauty, and harmony, and proportion, if there should ever be, as it is impossible there ever should be, any inconsistence between them: though these last, too, as expressing the fitness of actions, are real as truth itself. Let it be allowed, though virtue or moral rectitude does indeed consist in affection to and pursuit of what is right and good, as such; yet, that when we sit down in a cool hour, we can neither justify to ourselves this or any other pursuit, till we are convinced that it will be for our happiness, or at least not contrary to it.

Common reason and humanity, will have some influence upon mankind, whatever becomes of speculations: but, so far as the interests of virtue depend upon the theory of it being secured from open scorn, so far its very being in the world depends upon its appearing to have no contrariety to private interest and self-love. The foregoing observations, therefore, it is hoped, may have gained a little ground in favour of the precept before us; the particular explanation of which shall be the subject of the next discourse.

I will conclude at present, with observing the peculiar obligation which we are under to virtue and religion, as enforced in the verses following the text, in the epistle for the day, from our Saviour's coming into the world. *The night is far spent, the day is at hand; let us therefore cast off the works of darkness, and let us put on the armour of light*, &c. The meaning and force of which exhortation is, that Christianity lays us under new obligations to a good life, as by it the will of God is more clearly revealed, and as it affords additional motives to the practice of it, over and above those which arise out of the nature of virtue and vice; I might add, as our Saviour has set us a perfect example of goodness in our own nature. Now love and charity is plainly the thing in which he hath placed his religion; in which, therefore, as we have any pretence to the name of Christians, we must place ours. He hath at once enjoined it upon us by way of command with peculiar force; and by his example, as having undertaken the work of our salvation out of pure love and good-will to mankind. The endeavour to set home this example upon our minds is a very proper employment of this season, which is bringing on the festival of his birth: which as it may teach us many excellent lessons of humility, resignation, and obedience to the will of God; so there is none it recommends with greater authority, force, and advantage, than this of love and charity; since it was *for us men, and for our salvation*, that *he came down from heaven, and was incarnate, and was made man;* that he might teach us our duty, and more especially that he might enforce the practice of it, reform mankind, and finally bring us to that *eternal salvation*, of which *he is the Author to all those that obey him.*

SERMON XII.

UPON THE LOVE OF OUR NEIGHBOUR.

And if there be any other commandment, it is briefly comprehended in this saying, namely, Thou shalt love thy neighbour as thyself.—Rom. xiii. 9.

HAVING already removed the prejudices against public spirit, or the love of our neighbour, on the side of private interest and self-love; I proceed to the particular explanation of the precept before us, by showing, *Who is our neighbour: In what sense we are required to love him as ourselves: The influence such love would have upon our behaviour in life:* and lastly, *How this commandment comprehends in it all others.*

I. The objects and due extent of this affection will be understood by attending to the nature of it, and to the nature and circumstances of mankind in this world. The love of our neighbour is the same with charity, benevolence, or good-will: it is an affection to the good and happiness of our fellow creatures. This implies in it a disposition to produce happiness: and this is the simple notion of goodness, which appears so amiable wherever we meet with it. From hence it is easy to see, that the perfection of goodness consists in love to the whole universe. This is the perfection of Almighty God.

But as man is so much limited in his capacity, as so small a part of the creation comes under his notice and influence, and as we are not used to consider things in so general a way; it is not to be thought of, that the universe should be the object of benevolence to such creatures as we are. Thus in that precept of our Saviour, *Be ye perfect, even as your Father which is in heaven is perfect,** the perfection of the divine goodness is proposed to our imitation as it is promiscuous, and extends to the evil as well as the good; not as it is absolutely universal, imitation of it in this respect being plainly beyond us. The object is too vast. For this reason

* Matt. v. 48.

moral writers also have substituted a less general object for our benevolence, mankind. But this likewise is an object too general, and very much out of our view. Therefore persons more practical have, instead of mankind, put our country; and this is what we call a public spirit; which in men of public stations is the character of a patriot. But this is speaking to the upper part of the world. Kingdoms and governments are large; and the sphere of action of far the greatest part of mankind is much narrower than the government they live under: or, however, common men do not consider their actions as affecting the whole community of which they are members. There plainly is wanting a less general and nearer object of benevolence for the bulk of men, than that of their country. Therefore the scripture, not being a book of theory and speculation, but a plain rule of life for mankind, has with the utmost possible propriety put the principle of virtue upon the love of our neighbour; which is that part of the universe, that part of mankind, that part of our country, which comes under our immediate notice, acquaintance, and influence, and with which we have to do.

This is plainly the true account or reason, why our Saviour places the principle of virtue in the love of our *neighbour;* and the account itself shows who are comprehended under that relation.

II. Let us now consider in what sense we are commanded to love our neighbour *as ourselves.*

This precept, in its first delivery by our Saviour, is thus introduced: *Thou shalt love the Lord thy God with all thine heart, with all thy soul, and with all thy strength; and thy neighbour as thyself.* These very different manners of expression do not lead our thoughts to the same measure or degree of love, common to both objects; but to one, peculiar to each. Supposing then, which is to be supposed, a distinct meaning and propriety in the words, *as thyself;* the precept we are considering will admit of any of these senses: that we bear the *same kind* of affection to our neighbour, as we do to ourselves: or, that the love we bear to our neighbour should have *some certain proportion or other* to self-love: or, lastly, that it should bear the particular proportion of *equality*, that *it be in the same degree*.

First, The precept may be understood as requiring only, that we have the *same kind* of affection to our fellow creatures, as to ourselves: that, as every man has the principle of self-love, which disposes him to avoid misery, and consult his own happiness; so we should cultivate the affection of good-will to our neighbour, and that it should influence us to have the same kind of regard to him. This at least must be commanded: and this will not only prevent our being injurious to him, but will also put us upon promoting his good. There are blessings in life, which we share in common with others; peace, plenty, freedom, healthful seasons. But real benevolence to our fellow creatures would give us the notion of a common interest in a stricter sense: for in the degree we love another, his interest, his joys and sorrows, are our own. It is from self-love that we form the notion of private good, and consider it as our own: love of our neighbour would teach us thus to appropriate to ourselves his good and welfare, to consider ourselves as having a real share in his happiness. Thus the principle of benevolence would be an advocate within our own breasts, to take care of the interests of our fellow creatures in all the interfering and competitions which cannot but be, from the imperfection of our nature, and the state we are in. It would likewise, in some measure, lessen that interfering; and hinder men from forming so strong a notion of private good, exclusive of the good of others, as we commonly do. Thus, as the private affection makes us in a peculiar manner sensible of humanity, justice or injustice, when exercised towards ourselves; love of our neighbour would give us the same kind of sensibility in his behalf. This would be the greatest security of our uniform obedience to that most equitable rule; *Whatsoever ye would that men should do unto you, do ye even so unto them.*

All this is indeed no more than that we should have a real love to our neighbour: but then, which is to be observed, the words, *as thyself*, express this in the most distinct manner, and determine the precept to relate to the affection itself. The advantage, which this principle of benevolence has over other remote considerations, is that it is itself the temper of virtue: and likewise, that it is the chief, nay the only effectual security of our performing the several offices of kindness we owe to our fellow creatures. When from distant considerations men resolve upon any thing to which they have no liking, or perhaps an averseness, they are perpetually finding out evasions and excuses; which need never be wanting, if people look for them: and they equivocate with themselves in the plainest cases in the world. This may be in respect to single determinate acts of virtue: but it comes in much more, where the obligation is to a general course of behaviour; and most of all, if it be such as cannot be reduced to fixed determinate rules. This observation may account for the diversity of the expression, in that known passage of the prophet Micah: *to do justly, and to love mercy.* A man's heart must be formed to humanity and benevolence, he must *love mercy*, otherwise he will not act mercifully in any settled course of behaviour. As consideration of the future sanctions of religion is our only security of persevering in our duty, in cases of great temptations: so to get our heart and temper formed to a love and liking of what is good, is absolutely necessary in order to our behaving rightly in the familiar and daily intercourses amongst mankind.

Secondly, The precept before us may be understood to require, that we love our neighbour in some certain *proportion* or other, *according as* we love ourselves. And indeed a man's character cannot be determined by the love he bears to his neighbour, considered absolutely: but the proportion which this bears to self-love, whether it be attended to or not, is the chief thing which forms the character, and influences the actions. For, as the form of the body is a composition of various parts; so likewise our inward structure is not simple or uniform, but a composition of various passions, appetites, affections, together with rationality; including in this last both the discernment of what is right, and a disposition to regulate ourselves by it. There is greater variety of parts in what we call a character, than there are features in a face: and the morality of that is no more determined by one part, than the beauty or deformity of this is by one single feature: each is to be judged of by all the parts or features, not taken singly, but together. In the inward frame the various passions, appetites, affections, stand in different respects to each other. The principles in our mind may be contradictory, or checks and allays only, or incentives and assistants to each other. And principles, which in their nature have no kind of contrariety or affinity, may yet accidentally be each other's allays or incentives.

From hence it comes to pass, that though we were able to look into the inward contexture of the heart, and see with the greatest exactness in what degree any one principle is in a particular man; we could not from thence determine, how far that principle would go towards forming the character, or what influence it would have upon the actions, unless we could likewise discern what other principles prevailed in him, and see the proportion which that one bears to the others. Thus, though two men should have the affection of compassion in the same degree exactly: yet one may have the principle of resentment, or of ambition so strong in him, as to prevail over that of compassion, and prevent its having any influence upon his actions; so that he may deserve the character of an hard or cruel man: whereas the other having compassion in just the same degree only, yet having resentment or ambition in a lower degree, his compassion may prevail over them, so as to influence his actions, and to denominate his temper compassionate. So that, how strange soever it may appear to people who do not attend to the thing, yet it is quite manifest, that, when we say one man is more resenting or compassionate than another, this does not necessarily imply that one has the principle of resentment or of compassion stronger than the other. For if the proportion, which resentment or compassion bears to other inward principles, is greater in one than in the other; this is itself sufficient to denominate one more resenting or compassionate than the other.

Further, the whole system, as I may speak, of affections (including rationality), which constitute the heart, as this word is used in Scripture and on moral subjects, are each and all of them stronger in some than in others. Now the proportion which the two general affections, benevolence and self-love, bear to each other, according to this interpretation of the text, denominates men's character as to virtue. Suppose then one man to have the principle of benevolence in an higher degree than another: it will not follow from hence, that his general temper, or character, or actions, will be more benevolent than the other's. For he may have self-love in such a degree as quite to prevail over benevolence; so that it may have no influence at all upon his actions; whereas benevolence in the other person, though in a lower degree, may yet be the strongest principle in his heart; and strong enough to be the guide of his actions, so as to denominate him a good and virtuous man. The case is here as in scales: it is not one weight, considered in itself, which determines whether the scale shall ascend or descend; but this depends upon the proportion which that one weight hath to the other.

It being thus manifest that the influence which benevolence has upon our actions, and how far it goes towards forming our character, is not determined by the degree itself of this principle in our mind; but by the proportion it has to self-love and other principles: a comparison also being made in the text between self-love and the love of our neighbour; these joint considerations afforded sufficient occasion for treating here of that proportion: it plainly is implied in the precept, though it should be questioned, whether it be the exact meaning of the words, *as thyself.*

Love of our neighbour then must bear some proportion to self-love, and virtue to be sure consists in the due proportion. What this due proportion is, whether as a principle in the mind, or as exerted in actions, can be judged of only from our nature and condition in this world. Of the degree in which affections and the principles of action, considered in themselves, prevail, we have no measure: let us then proceed to the course of behaviour. the actions they produce.

Both our nature and condition require, that each particular man should make particular provision for himself: and the inquiry, what proportion benevolence should have to self-love, when brought down to practice, will be, what is a competent care and provision for ourselves. And how certain soever it be, that each man must determine this for himself; and how ridiculous soever it would be, for any to attempt to determine it for another: yet it is to be observed, that the proportion is real; and that a competent provision has a bound; and that it cannot be all which we can possibly get and keep within our grasp, without legal injustice. Mankind almost universally bring in vanity, supplies for what is called a life of pleasure, covetousness, or imaginary notions of superiority over others, to determine this question: but every one who desires to act a proper part in society, would do well to consider, how far any of them come in to determine it, in the way of moral consideration. All that can be said is, supposing, what, as the world goes, is so much to be supposed that is scarce to be mentioned, that persons do not neglect what they really owe to themselves; the more of their care and thought, and of their fortune, they employ in doing good to their fellow creatures, the nearer they come up to the law of perfection, *Thou shalt love thy neighbour as thyself.*

Thirdly, if the words, *as thyself,* were to be understood of an equality of affection; it would not be attended with those consequences, which perhaps may be thought to follow from it. Suppose a person to have the same settled regard to others, as to himself; that in every deliberate scheme or pursuit he took their interest into the account in the same degree as his own, so far as an equality of affection would produce this: yet he would in fact, and ought to be, much more taken up and employed about himself, and his own concerns, than about others, and their interests. For, besides the one common affection toward himself and his neighbour, he would have several other particular affections, passions, appetites, which he could not possibly feel in common both for himself and others: now these sensations themselves very much employ us; and have perhaps as great influence as self-love. So far indeed as self-love, and cool reflection upon what is for our interest, would set us on work to gain a supply of our own several wants; so far the love of our neighbour would make us do the same for him: but the degree in which we are put upon seeking and making use of the means of gratification, by the feeling of those affections, appetites, and passions, must necessarily be peculiar to ourselves.

That there are particular passions (suppose shame, resentment,) which men seem to have, and feel in common, both for themselves and others, makes no alteration in respect to those passions and appetites which cannot possibly be thus felt in common. From hence (and perhaps more things of the like kind might be mentioned) it follows, that though there were an equality of affection to both, yet regard to ourselves, would be more prevalent than attention to the concerns of others.

And from moral considerations it ought to be so, supposing still the equality of affection commanded: because we are in a peculiar manner, as I may speak, intrusted with ourselves; and therefore care of our own interests, as well as of our conduct, particularly belongs to us.

To these things must be added, that moral obligations can extend no further than to natural possibilities. Now we have a perception of our own interests, like consciousness of our own existence, which we always carry about with us; and which, in its continuation, kind, and degree, seems impossible to be felt in respect to the interests of others.

From all these things it fully appears, that though we were to love our neighbour in the same degree as we love ourselves, so far as this is possible; yet the care of ourselves, of the individual, would not be neglected; the apprehended danger of which seems to be the only objection against understanding the precept in this strict sense.

III. The general temper of mind which the due love of our neighbour would form us to, and the influence it would have upon our behaviour in life, is now to be considered.

The temper and behaviour of charity is explained at

large, in that known passage of St Paul:* *Charity suffereth long, and is kind; charity envieth not, doth not behave itself unseemly, seeketh not her own, thinketh no evil, beareth all things, believeth all things, hopeth all things.* As to the meaning of the expressions, *seeketh not her own, thinketh no evil, believeth all things;* however those expressions may be explained away, this meekness, and in some degree easiness of temper, readiness to forego our right for the sake of peace, as well as in the way of compassion, freedom from mistrust, and disposition to believe well of our neighbour, this general temper, I say, accompanies, and is plainly the effect of love and good-will. And, though such is the world in which we live, that experience and knowledge of it not only may, but must beget in us greater regard to ourselves, and doubtfulness of the characters of others, than is natural to mankind; yet these ought not to be carried further than the nature and course of things make necessary. It is still true, even in the present state of things, bad as it is, that a real good man had rather be deceived, than be suspicious; had rather forego his known right, than run the venture of doing even a hard thing. This is the general temper of that charity, of which the apostle asserts, that if he had it not, giving his *body to be burned would avail him nothing;* and which he says *shall never fail.*

The happy influence of this temper extends to every different relation and circumstance in human life. It plainly renders a man better, more to be desired, as to all the respects and relations we can stand in to each other. The benevolent man is disposed to make use of all external advantages in such a manner as shall contribute to the good of others, as well as to his own satisfaction. His own satisfaction consists in this. He will be easy and kind to his dependents, compassionate to the poor and distressed, friendly to all with whom he has to do. This includes the good neighbour, parent, master, magistrate: and such a behaviour would plainly make dependence, inferiority, and even servitude, easy. So that a good or charitable man of superior rank

* 1 Cor. xiii.

in wisdom, fortune, authority, is a common blessing to the place he lives in: happiness grows under his influence. This good principle in inferiors would discover itself in paying respect, gratitude, obedience, as due. It were therefore, methinks, one just way of trying one's own character, to ask ourselves, am I in reality a better master or servant, a better friend, a better neighbour, than such and such persons; whom, perhaps, I may think not to deserve the character of virtue and religion so much as myself?

And as to the spirit of party, which unhappily prevails amongst mankind, whatever are the distinctions which serve for a supply to it, some or other of which have obtained in all ages and countries: one who is thus friendly to his kind will immediately make due allowances for it, as what cannot but be amongst such creatures as men, in such a world as this. And as wrath and fury and overbearing upon these occasions proceed, as I may speak, from men's feeling only on their own side: so a common feeling, for others as well as for ourselves, would render us sensible to this truth, which it is strange can have so little influence; that we ourselves differ from others, just as much as they do from us. I put the matter in this way, because it can scarce be expected that the generality of men should see, that those things which are made the occasions of dissension and fomenting the party-spirit, are really nothing at all: but it may be expected from all people, how much soever they are in earnest about their respective peculiarities, that humanity, and common good-will to their fellow creatures, should moderate and restrain that wretched spirit.

This good temper of charity likewise would prevent strife and enmity arising from other occasions: it would prevent our giving just cause of offence, and our taking it without cause. And in cases of real injury, a good man will make all the allowances which are to be made; and, without any attempts of retaliation, he will only consult his own and other men's security for the future, against injustice and wrong.

IV. I proceed to consider lastly, what is affirmed of

the precept now explained, that it comprehends in it all others; *i.e.* that to love our neighbour as ourselves includes in it all virtues.

Now the way in which every maxim of conduct, or general speculative assertion, when it is to be explained at large, should be treated, is, to show what are the particular truths which were designed to be comprehended under such a general observation, how far it is strictly true; and then the limitations, restrictions, and exceptions, if there be exceptions, with which it is to be understood. But it is only the former of these; namely, how far the assertion in the text holds, and the ground of the pre-eminence assigned to the precept of it, which in strictness comes into our present consideration.

However, in almost every thing that is said, there is somewhat to be understood beyond what is explicitly laid down, and which we of course supply; somewhat, I mean, which would not be commonly called a restriction, or limitation. Thus, when benevolence is said to be the sum of virtue, it is not spoken of as a blind propension, but as a principle in reasonable creatures, and so to be directed by their reason: for reason and reflection come into our notion of a moral agent. And that will lead us to consider distant consequences, as well as the immediate tendency of an action: it will teach us, that the care of some persons, suppose children and families, is particularly committed to our charge by Nature and Providence; as also that there are other circumstances, suppose friendship or former obligations, which require that we do good to some preferably to others. Reason, considered merely as subservient to benevolence, as assisting to produce the greatest good, will teach us to have particular regard to these relations and circumstances; because it is plainly for the good of the world that they should be regarded. And as there are numberless cases, in which, notwithstanding appearances, we are not competent judges, whether a particular action will upon the whole do good or harm; reason in the same way will teach us to be cautious how we act in these cases of uncertainty. It will suggest to our consideration, which is the safer side; how liable we are to be led wrong by passion and private interest; and what regard is due to laws, and the judgment of mankind. All these things must come into consideration, were it only in order to determine which way of acting is likely to produce the greatest good. Thus, upon supposition that it were in the strictest sense true, without limitation, that benevolence includes in it all virtues; yet reason must come in as its guide and director, in order to attain its own end, the end of benevolence, the greatest public good. Reason then being thus included, let us now consider the truth of the assertion itself.

First, It is manifest that nothing can be of consequence to mankind or any creature, but happiness. This then is all which any person can, in strictness of speaking, be said to have a right to. We can therefore *owe no man any thing*, but only to further and promote his happiness, according to our abilities. And therefore a disposition and endeavour to do good to all with whom we have to do, in the degree and manner which the different relations we stand in to them require, is a discharge of all the obligations we are under to them.

As human nature is not one simple uniform thing, but a composition of various parts, body, spirit, appetites, particular passions, and affections; for each of which reasonable self-love would lead men to have due regard, and make suitable provision: so society consists of various parts, to which we stand in different respects and relations; and just benevolence would as surely lead us to have due regard to each of these, and behave as the respective relations require. Reasonable good-will, and right behaviour towards our fellow creatures, are in a manner the same: only that the former expresseth the principle as it is in the mind; the latter, the principle as it were become external, *i. e.* exerted in actions.

And so far as temperance, sobriety, and moderation in sensual pleasures, and the contrary vices, have any respect to our fellow creatures, any influence upon their quiet, welfare, and happiness; as they always have a real, and often a near influence upon it; so far it is manifest those virtues may be produced by the love of our neighbour, and that the contrary vices would be prevented by it. Indeed if men's regard to themselves will not restrain them from excess; it may be thought little probable, that their love to others will be sufficient: but the reason is, that their love to others is not, any more than their regard to themselves, just, and in its due degree. There are however manifest instances of persons kept sober and temperate from regard to their affairs, and the welfare of those who depend upon them. And it is obvious to every one, that habitual excess, a dissolute course of life, implies a general neglect of the duties we owe towards our friends, our families, and our country.

From hence it is manifest that the common virtues, and the common vices of mankind, may be traced up to benevolence, or the want of it. And this entitles the precept, *Thou shalt love thy neighbour as thyself*, to the pre-eminence given to it; and is a justification of the Apostle's assertion, that all other commandments are comprehended in it; whatever cautions and restrictions* there are, which might require to be considered, if we were to state particularly and at length, what is virtue and right behaviour in mankind. But,

Secondly, It might be added, that in a higher and more general way of consideration, leaving out the par-

* For instance: as we are not competent judges, what is upon the whole for the good of the world, there may be other immediate ends appointed us to pursue, besides that one of doing good, or producing happiness. Though the good of the creation be the only end of the Author of it, yet he may have laid us under particular obligations, which we may discern and feel ourselves under, quite distinct from a perception, that the observance or violation of them is for the happiness or misery of our fellow creatures. And this is in fact the case. For there are certain dispositions of mind, and certain actions, which are in themselves approved or disapproved by mankind, abstracted from the consideration of their tendency to the happiness or misery of the world; approved or disapproved by reflection, by that principle within, which is the guide of life, the judge of right and wrong. Numberless instances of this kind might be mentioned. There are pieces of treachery, which in themselves appear base and detestable to every one. There are actions, which perhaps can scarce have any other general name given them, than indecencies, which yet are odious and shocking to human nature. There is such a thing as meanness, a little mind; which, as it is quite distinct from incapacity, so it raises a dislike and disapprobation quite different from that contempt, which men are too apt to have, of mere folly. On the other hand; what we call greatness of mind is the object of another sort of approbation, than superior understanding. Fidelity, honour, strict justice, are themselves approved in the highest degree, abstracted from the consideration of their tendency. Now, whether it be thought that each of these are connected with benevolence in our nature, and so may be considered as the same thing with it; or whether some of them be thought an inferior kind of virtues and vices, somewhat like natural beauties and deformities; or lastly, plain exceptions to the general rule; thus much however is certain, that the things now instanced in, and numberless others, are approved or disapproved by mankind in general, in quite another view than as conducive to the happiness or misery of the world.

ticular nature of creatures, and the particular circumstances in which they are placed, benevolence seems in the strictest sense to include in it all that is good and worthy; all that is good, which we have any distinct particular notion of. We have no clear conception of any positive moral attribute in the supreme Being, but what may be resolved up into goodness. And, if we consider a reasonable creature or moral agent, without regard to the particular relations and circumstances in which he is placed; we cannot conceive any thing else to come in towards determining whether he is to be ranked in a higher or lower class of virtuous beings, but the higher or lower degree in which that principle, and what is manifestly connected with it, prevail in him.

That which we more strictly call piety, or the love of God, and which is an essential part of a right temper, some may perhaps imagine no way connected with benevolence: yet surely they must be connected, if there be indeed in being an object infinitely good. Human nature is so constituted, that every good affection implies the love of itself; *i. e.* becomes the object of a new affection in the same person. Thus, to be righteous, implies in it the love of righteousness; to be benevolent, the love of benevolence; to be good, the love of goodness; whether this righteousness, benevolence, or goodness, be viewed as in our own mind, or in another's: and the love of God as a being perfectly good, is the love of perfect goodness contemplated in a being or person. Thus morality and religion, virtue and piety, will at last necessarily coincide, run up into one and the same point, and *love* will be in all senses *the end of the commandment.*

O Almighty God, inspire us with this divine principle; kill in us all the seeds of envy and ill-will; and help us, by cultivating within ourselves the love of our neighbour, to improve in the love of thee. Thou hast placed in us various kindreds, friendships, and relations, as the school of discipline for our affections: help us, by the due exercise of them, to improve to perfection; till all partial affection be lost in that entire universal one, and thou, O God, shalt be all in all.

SERMON XIII. XIV.

UPON THE LOVE OF GOD.

Thou shalt love the Lord thy God with all thy heart, and with all thy soul, and with all thy mind.—Matt. xxii. 37.

EVERY body knows, you therefore need only just be put in mind, that there is such a thing, as having so great horror of one extreme, as to run insensibly and of course into the contrary; and that a doctrine's having been a shelter for enthusiasm, or made to serve the purposes of superstition, is no proof of the falsity of it: truth or right being somewhat real in itself, and so not to be judged of by its liableness to abuse, or by its supposed distance from or nearness to error. It may be sufficient to have mentioned this in general, without taking notice of the particular extravagancies, which have been vented under the pretence or endeavour of explaining the love of God; or how manifestly we are got into the contrary extreme, under the notion of a reasonable religion; so very reasonable, as to have nothing to do with the heart and affections, if these words signify any thing but the faculty by which we discern speculative truth.

By the love of God, I would understand all those regards, all those affections of mind which are due immediately to him from such a creature as man, and which rest in him as their end. As this does not include servile fear; so neither will any other regards, how reasonable soever, which respect any thing out of or besides the perfection of divine nature, come into consideration here. But all fear is not excluded, because, his displeasure is itself the natural proper object of fear. Reverence, ambition of his love and approbation, delight in the hope or consciousness of it, come likewise into this definition of the love of God; because he is the natural object of all those affections or movements of mind, as really as he is the object of the affection, which is in the strictest sense called love; and all of them equally rest in him, as their end. And they may all be understood to be implied in these words of our Saviour, without putting any force upon them: for he is speaking of the love of God and our neighbour, as containing the whole of piety and virtue.

It is plain that the nature of man is so constituted, as to feel certain affections upon the sight or contemplation of certain objects. Now the very notion of affection implies resting in its object as an end. And the particular affection to good characters, reverence and moral love of them, is natural to all those who have any degree of real goodness in themselves. This will be illustrated by the description of a perfect character in a creature; and by considering the manner, in which a good man in his presence would be affected towards such a character. He would of course feel the affections of love, reverence, desire of his approbation, delight in the hope or consciousness of it. And surely all this is applicable, and may be brought up to that Being, who is infinitely more than an adequate object of all those affections: whom we are commanded to *love with all our heart, with all our soul, and with all our mind.* And of these regards towards Almighty God, some are more particularly suitable to and becoming so imperfect a creature as man, in this mortal state we are passing through; and some of them, and perhaps other exercises of the mind, will be the employment and happiness of good men in a state of perfection.

This is a general view of what the following discourse will contain. And it is manifest the subject is a real one: there is nothing in it enthusiastical or unreasonable. And if it be indeed at all a subject, it is one of the utmost importance.

As mankind have a faculty by which they discern speculative truth; so we have various affections towards external objects. Understanding and temper, reason and affection, are as distinct ideas, as reason and hunger; and one would think could no more be confounded. It is by reason that we get the ideas of several objects of our affections: but in these cases reason and affection are no more the same, than sight of a particular object, and the pleasure or uneasiness consequent thereupon, are the same. Now, as reason tends to and rests in the discernment of truth, the object of it; so the very nature of affection consists in tending towards, and resting in, its objects as an end. We do indeed often in common language say, that things are loved, desired, esteemed, not for themselves, but for somewhat further, somewhat out of and beyond them: yet, in these cases, whoever will attend, will see, that these things are not in reality the objects of the affections, *i. e.* are not loved, desired, esteemed, but the somewhat further and beyond them. If we have no affections which rest in what are called their objects, then what is called affection, love, desire, hope, in human nature, is only an uneasiness in being at rest; an unquiet disposition to action, progress, pursuit, without end or meaning. But if there be any such thing as delight in the company of one person, rather than of another; whether in the way of friendship, or mirth and entertainment, it is all one, if it be without respect to fortune, honour, or increasing our stores of knowledge, or any thing beyond the present time; here is an instance of an affection absolutely resting in its objects as its end, and being gratified in the same way as the appetite of hunger is satisfied with food. Yet nothing is more common than to hear it asked, what advantage a man hath in such a course, suppose of study, particular friendships, or in any other: nothing, I say, is more common than to hear such a question put in a way which supposes no gain, advantage, or interest, but as a means to somewhat further: and if so, then there is no such thing at all as real interest, gain, or advantage. This is the same absurdity with respect to life, as infinite series of effects without a cause is in speculation. The gain, advantage, or interest, consists in the delight itself, arising from such a faculty's having its object: neither is there any such thing as happiness or enjoyment, but what arises from hence. The pleasures of hope and of reflection are not exceptions: the former being only this happiness anticipated; the latter, the same happiness enjoyed over again after its time. And even the general expectation of future happiness can afford satisfaction, only as it is a present object to the principle of self-love.

It was doubtless intended, that life should be very much a pursuit to the gross of mankind. But this is carried so much further than is reasonable, that what gives immediate satisfaction, *i. e.* our present interest, is scarce considered as our interest at all. It is inventions which have only a remote tendency towards enjoyment, perhaps but a remote tendency towards gaining the means only of enjoyment, which are chiefly spoken of as useful to the world. And though this way of thinking were just with respect to the imperfect state we are now in, where we know so little of satisfaction without satiety; yet it must be guarded against, when we are considering the happiness of a state of perfection; which happiness being enjoyment and not hope, must necessarily consist in this, that our affections have their objects, and rest in those objects as an end, *i. e.* be satisfied with them. This will further appear in the sequel of this discourse.

Of the several affections, or inward sensations, which particular objects excite in man, there are some, the having of which implies the love of them, when they are reflected upon.* This cannot be said of all our affections, principles, and motives of action. It were ridiculous to assert, that a man upon reflection hath the same kind of approbation of the appetite of hunger, or the passion of fear, as he hath of good-will to his fellow creatures. To be a just, a good, a righteous man, plainly carries with it a peculiar affection to or love of justice, goodness, righteousness, when these principles are the objects of contemplation. Now if a man approves of, or hath an affection to, any principle in and for itself, incidental things allowed for, it will be the same whether he views it in his own mind, or in another; in himself, or in his neighbour. This is the account of our approbation of, our moral love and affection to good characters; which cannot but be in those who have any degrees

* St Austin observes, Amor ipse ordinate amandus est, quo bene amatur quod amandum est, ut sit in nobis virtus qui vivitur bene, i. e. *The affection which we rightly have for what is lovely, must* ordinate *justly, in due manner and proportion, become the object of a new affection, or be itself beloved, in order to our being endued with that virtue which is the principle of a good life.* Civ. Dei. l. xv. c. 22.

of real goodness in themselves, and who discern and take notice of the same principle in others.

From observation of what passes within ourselves, our own actions, and the behaviour of others, the mind may carry on its reflections as far as it pleases; much beyond what we experience in ourselves, or discern in our fellow creatures. It may go on, and consider goodness as become a uniform continued principle of action, as conducted by reason, and forming a temper and character absolutely good and perfect, which is in a higher sense excellent, and proportionably the object of love and approbation.

Let us then suppose a creature perfect according to his created nature; let his form be human, and his capacities no more than equal to those of the chief of men: goodness shall be his proper character; with wisdom to direct it, and power within some certain determined sphere of action to exert it; but goodness must be the simple actuating principle within him; this being the moral quality which is amiable, or the immediate object of love as distinct from other affections of approbation. Here then is a finite object for our mind to tend towards, to exercise itself upon: a creature, perfect according to his capacity, fixed, steady, equally unmoved by weak pity or more weak fury and resentment; forming the justest scheme of conduct; going on undisturbed in the execution of it, through the several methods of severity and reward, towards his end, namely, the general happiness of all with whom he hath to do, as in itself right and valuable. This character, though uniform in itself, in its principle, yet exerting itself in different ways, or considered in different views, may by its appearing variety move different affections. Thus, the severity of justice would not affect us in the same way as an act of mercy: the adventitious qualities of wisdom and power may be considered in themselves: and even the strength of mind, which this immoveable goodness supposes, may likewise be viewed as an object of contemplation, distinct from the goodness itself. Superior excellence of any kind, as well as superior wisdom and power, is the object of awe and reverence to all creatures, whatever their moral character be: but so far as creatures of the lowest rank were good, so far the view of this character, as simply good, must appear amiable to them, be the object of, or beget love. Further, suppose we were conscious, that this superior person so far approved of us, that we had nothing servilely to fear from him; that he was really our friend, and kind and good to us in particular, as he had occasionally intercourse with us: we must be other creatures than we are, or we could not but feel the same kind of satisfaction and enjoyment (whatever would be the degree of it) from this higher acquaintance and friendship, as we feel from common ones; the intercourse being real, and the persons equally present, in both cases. We should have a more ardent desire to be approved by his better judgment, and a satisfaction in that approbation of the same sort with what would be felt in respect to common persons, or be wrought in us by their presence.

Let us now raise the character, and suppose this creature, for we are still going on with the supposition of a creature, our proper guardian and governor; that we were in a progress of being towards somewhat further; and that his scheme of government was too vast for our capacities to comprehend: remembering still that he is perfectly good, and our friend as well as our governor. Wisdom, power, goodness, accidentally viewed any where, would inspire reverence, awe, love: and as these affections would be raised in higher or lower degrees, in proportion as we had occasionally more or less intercourse with the creature endued with those qualities; so this further consideration and knowledge, that he was our proper guardian and governor, would much more bring these objects and qualities home to ourselves; teach us they had a greater respect to us in particular, that we had a higher interest in that wisdom and power and goodness. We should, with joy, gratitude, reverence, love, trust, and dependence, appropriate the character, as what we had a right in; and make our boast in such our relation to it. And the conclusion of the whole would be, that we should refer ourselves implicitly to him, and cast ourselves entirely upon him. As the whole attention of life should be to obey his commands; so the highest enjoyment of it must arise from the contemplation of this character, and our relation to it, from a consciousness of his favour and approbation, and from the exercise of those affections towards him which could not but be raised from his presence. A Being who hath these attributes, who stands in this relation, and is thus sensibly present to the mind, must necessarily be the object of these affections: there is as real a correspondence between them, as between the lowest appetite of sense and its object.

That this being is not a creature, but the Almighty God; that he is of infinite power and wisdom and goodness, does not render him less the object of reverence and love, than he would be if he had those attributes only in a limited degree. The being who made us, and upon whom we entirely depend, is the object of some regards. He hath given us certain affections of mind, which correspond to wisdom, power, goodness; *i. e.* which are raised upon view of those qualities. If then he be really wise, powerful, good; he is the natural object of those affections, which he has endued us with, and which correspond to those attributes. That he is infinite in power, perfect in wisdom and goodness, makes no alteration, but only that he is the object of those affections raised to the highest pitch. He is not indeed to be discerned by any of our senses. *I go forward, but he is not there; and backward, but I cannot perceive him: on the left hand where he doth work, but I cannot behold him: he hideth himself on the right hand, that I cannot see him. O that I knew where I might find him! that I might come even to his seat!** But is he then afar off? does he not fill heaven and earth with his presence? The presence of our fellow creatures affects our senses, and our senses give us the knowledge of their presence; which hath different kinds of influence upon us; love, joy, sorrow, restraint, encouragement, reverence. However this influence is not immediately from our senses, but from that knowledge. Thus suppose a person neither to see nor hear another, not to know by any of his senses, but yet certainly to know, that another was with him; this knowledge might, and in many cases would, have one or more of the effects before mentioned. It is therefore not only

* Job. xxiii

reasonable, but also natural, to be affected with a presence, though it be not the object of our senses: whether it be, or be not, is merely an accidental circumstance, which needs not come into consideration: it is the certainty that he is with us, and we with him, which hath the influence. We consider persons then as present, not only when they are within reach of our senses, but also when we are assured by any other means that they are within such a nearness; nay, if they are not, we can recall them to our mind, and be moved towards them as present: and must He, who is so much more intimately with us, that *in him we live and move and have our being*, be thought too distant to be the object of our affections? We own and feel the force of amiable and worthy qualities in our fellow creatures: and can we be insensible to the contemplation of perfect goodness? Do we reverence the shadows of greatness here below, are we solicitous about honour and esteem and the opinion of the world: and shall we not feel the same with respect to him, whose are wisdom and power in their original, who *is the God of judgment by whom actions are weighed?* Thus love, reverence, desire of esteem, every faculty, every affection, tends towards, and is employed about its respective object in common cases: and must the exercise of them be suspended with regard to him alone, who is an object, an infinitely more than adequate object, to our most exalted faculties; him, *of whom, and through whom, and to whom are all things?*

As we cannot remove from this earth, or change our general business on it, so neither can we alter our real nature. Therefore no exercise of the mind can be recommended, but only the exercise of those faculties you are conscious of. Religion does not demand new affections, but only claims the direction of those you already have, those affections you daily feel; though unhappily confined to objects, not altogether unsuitable, but altogether unequal to them. We only represent to you the higher, the adequate objects of those very faculties and affections. Let the man of ambition go on still to consider disgrace as the greatest evil; honour, as his chief good. But disgrace, in whose estimation? Honour, in whose judgment? This is the only question. If shame and delight in esteem, be spoken of as real, as any settled ground of pain or pleasure; both these must be in proportion to the supposed wisdom and worth of him, by whom we are contemned or esteemed. Must it then be thought enthusiastical to speak of a sensibility of this sort, which shall have respect to an unerring judgment, to infinite wisdom; when we are assured this unerring judgment, this infinite wisdom, does observe upon our actions?

It is the same with respect to the love of God in the strictest and most confined sense. We only offer and represent the highest object of an affection, supposed already in your mind. Some degree of goodness must be previously supposed: this always implies the love of itself, an affection to goodness: the highest, the adequate object of this affection, is perfect goodness; which therefore we are to *love with all our heart, with all our soul, and with all our strength.* "Must we, then, forgetting our own interest, as it were go out of ourselves, and love God for his own sake?" No more forget your own interest, no more go out of yourselves, than when you prefer one place, one prospect, the conversation of one man to that of another. Does not every affection necessarily imply, that the object of it be itself loved? If it be not, it is not the object of the affection. You may and ought if you can, but it is a great mistake to think you can love or fear or hate any thing, from consideration that such love or fear or hatred may be a means of obtaining good or avoiding evil. But the question, whether we ought to love God for his sake or for our own, being a mere mistake in language; the real question, which this is mistaken for, will, I suppose, be answered by observing, that the goodness of God already exercised towards us, our present dependence upon him, and our expectation of future benefits, ought, and have a natural tendency, to beget in us the affection of gratitude, and greater love towards him, than the same goodness exercised towards others: were it only for this reason, that every affection is moved in proportion to the sense we have of the object of it; and we cannot but have a more lively sense of goodness, when exercised towards ourselves, than when exercised towards others. I added expectation of future benefits, because the ground of that expectation is present goodness.

Thus Almighty God is the natural object of the several affections, love, reverence, fear, desire of approbation. For though he is simply one, yet we cannot but consider him in partial and different views. He is in himself one uniform being, and for ever the same without *variableness or shadow of turning:* but his infinite greatness, his goodness, his wisdom, are different objects to our mind. To which is to be added, that from the changes in our characters, together with his unchangeableness, we cannot but consider ourselves as more or less the objects of his approbation, and really be so. For if he approves what is good, he cannot, merely from the unchangeableness of his nature, approve what is evil. Hence must arise more various movements of mind, more different kinds of affections. And this greater variety also is just and reasonable in such creatures as we are, though it respects a Being simply one, good and perfect. As some of these affections are most particularly suitable to so imperfect a creature as man, in this mortal state we are passing through; so there may be other exercises of mind, or some of these in higher degrees, our employment and happiness in a state of perfection.

SERMON XIV

CONSIDER then our ignorance, the imperfection of our nature, our virtue and our condition in this world, with respect to an infinitely good and just Being, our Creator and Governor; and you will see what religious affections of mind are most particularly suitable to this mortal state we are passing through.

Though we are not affected with any thing so strongly, as what we discern with our senses; and though our nature and condition require, that we be much taken up about sensible things; yet our reason convinces us that

God is present with us, and we see and feel the effects of his goodness: he is therefore the object of some regards. The imperfection of our virtue, joined with the consideration of his absolute rectitude or holiness, will scarce permit that perfection of love, which entirely casts out all fear: yet goodness is the object of love to all creatures who have any degree of it themselves; and consciousness of a real endeavour to approve ourselves to him, joined with the consideration of his goodness, as it quite excludes servile dread and horror, so it is plainly a reasonable ground for hope of his favour. Neither fear, nor hope, nor love then are excluded: and one or another of these will prevail, according to the different views we have of God; and ought to prevail, according to the changes we find in our own character. There is a temper of mind made up of, or which follows from all three, fear, hope, love; namely, resignation to the divine will, which is the general temper belonging to this state; which ought to be the habitual frame of our mind and heart, and to be exercised at proper seasons more distinctly, in acts of devotion.

Resignation to the will of God is the whole of piety: it includes in it all that is good, and is a source of the most settled quiet and composure of mind. There is the general principle of submission in our nature. Man is not so constituted as to desire things, and be uneasy in the want of them, in proportion to their known value: many other considerations come in to determine the degrees of desire; particularly whether the advantage we take a view of be within the sphere of our rank. Who ever felt uneasiness, upon observing any of the advantages brute creatures have over us? And yet it is plain they have several. It is the same with respect to advantages belonging to creatures of a superior order. Thus though we see a thing to be highly valuable, yet that it does not belong to our condition of being, is sufficient to suspend our desires after it, to make us rest satisfied without such advantage. Now there is just the same reason for quiet resignation in the want of every thing equally unattainable, and out of our reach in particular, though others of our species be possessed of it. All this may be applied to the whole of life; to positive inconveniences as well as wants; not indeed to the sensations of pain and sorrow, but to all the uneasinesses of reflection, murmuring, and discontent. Thus is human nature formed to compliance, yielding, submission of temper. We find the principles of it within us; and every one exercises it towards some objects or other; *i. e.* feels it with regard to some persons, and some circumstances. Now this is an excellent foundation of a reasonable and religious resignation. Nature teaches and inclines us to take up with our lot: the consideration, that the course of things is unalterable, hath a tendency to quiet the mind under it, to beget a submission of temper to it. But when we can add, that this unalterable course is appointed and continued by infinite wisdom and goodness; how absolute should be our submission, how entire our trust and dependence!

This would reconcile us to our condition; prevent all the supernumerary troubles arising from imagination, distant fears, impatience; all uneasiness, except that which necessarily arises from the calamities themselves we may be under. How many of our cares should we by this means be disburdened of! Cares not properly our own, how apt soever they may be to intrude upon us, and we to admit them; the anxieties of expectation, solicitude about success and disappointment, which in truth are none of our concern. How open to every gratification would that mind be, which was clear of these encumbrances!

Our resignation to the will of God may be said to be perfect, when our will is lost and resolved up into his; when we rest in his will as our end, as being itself most just, and right, and good. And where is the impossibility of such an affection to what is just, and right, and good. such a loyalty of heart to the Governor of the universe, as shall prevail over all sinister indirect desires of our own? Neither is this at bottom any thing more than faith, and honesty, and fairness of mind; in a more enlarged sense indeed, than those words are commonly used. And as in common cases, fear and hope and other passions are raised in us by their respective objects: so this submission of heart and soul and mind, this religious resignation, would be as naturally produced by our having just conceptions of Almighty God, and a real sense of his presence with us. In how low a degree soever this temper usually prevails amongst men, yet it is a temper right in itself: it is what we owe to our Creator: it is particularly suitable to our mortal condition, and what we should endeavour after for our own sakes in our passage through such a world as this; where is nothing upon which we can rest or depend; nothing but what we are liable to be deceived and disappointed in. Thus we might *acquaint ourselves with God, and be at peace.* This is piety and religion in the strictest sense, considered as an habit of mind; an habitual sense of God's presence with us; being affected towards him, as present, in the manner his superior nature requires from such a creature as man: this is to *walk with God.*

Little more need be said of devotion or religious worship, than that it is this temper exerted into act. The nature of it consists in the actual exercise of those affections towards God, which are supposed habitual in good men. He is always equally present with us: but we are so much taken up with sensible things, that *Lo, he goeth by us, and we see him not: he passeth on also, but we perceive him not.** Devotion is retirement, from the world he has made, to him alone: it is to withdraw from the avocations of sense, to employ our attention wholly upon him as upon an object actually present, to yield ourselves up to the influence of the divine presence, and to give full scope to the affections of gratitude, love, reverence, trust, and dependence; of which infinite power, wisdom, and goodness, is the natural and only adequate object. We may apply to the whole of devotion those words of the son of Sirach, *When you glorify the Lord, exalt him as much as you can; for even yet will he far exceed; and when you exalt him, put forth all your strength, and be not weary; for you can never go far enough.*† Our most raised affections of every kind cannot but fall short and be disproportionate, when an infinite Being is the object of them. This is the highest exercise and employment of

* Job ix. 11. † Ecclus. xliii. 30.

mind that a creature is capable of. As this divine service and worship is itself absolutely due to God, so also is it necessary in order to a further end, to keep alive upon our minds a sense of his authority, a sense that in our ordinary behaviour amongst men we act under him as our governor and judge.

Thus you see the temper of mind respecting God, which is particularly suitable to a state of imperfection; to creatures in a progress of being towards somewhat further.

Suppose now this something further attained; that we were arrived at it: what a perception will it be, to see and know and feel that our trust was not vain, our dependence not groundless? that the issue, event, and consummation came out such as fully to justify and answer that resignation? If the obscure view of the divine perfection, which we have in this world, ought in just consequence to beget an entire resignation; what will this resignation be exalted into, when *we shall see face to face, and know as we are known?* If we cannot form any distinct notion of that perfection of the love of God, which *casts out all fear;* of that enjoyment of him, which will be the happiness of good men hereafter; the consideration of our wants and capacities of happiness, and that he will be an adequate supply to them, must serve us instead of such distinct conception of the particular happiness itself.

Let us then suppose a man entirely disengaged from business and pleasure, sitting down alone and at leisure, to reflect upon himself and his own condition of being. He would immediately feel that he was by no means complete of himself, but totally insufficient for his own happiness. One may venture to affirm, that every man hath felt this, whether he hath again reflected upon it or not. It is feeling this deficiency, that they are unsatisfied with themselves, which makes men look out for assistance from abroad; and which has given rise to various kinds of amusements, altogether needless any otherwise than as they serve to fill up the blank spaces of time, and so hinder their feeling this deficiency, and being uneasy with themselves. Now, if these external things we take up with were really an adequate supply to this deficiency of human nature, if by their means our capacities and desires were all satisfied and filled up; then it might be truly said, that we had found out the proper happiness of man; and so might sit down satisfied, and be at rest in the enjoyment of it. But if it appears, that the amusements, which men usually pass their time in, are so far from coming up to or answering our notions and desires of happiness, or good, that they are really no more than what they are commonly called, somewhat to pass away the time; *i. e.* somewhat which serves to turn us aside from, and prevent our attending to, this our internal poverty and want; if they serve only, or chiefly, to suspend, instead of satisfying our conceptions and desires of happiness; if the want remains, and we have found out little more than barely the means of making it less sensible; then are we still to seek for somewhat to be an adequate supply to it. It is plain that there is a capacity in the nature of man, which neither riches, nor honours, nor sensual gratifications, nor any thing in this world can perfectly fill up, or satisfy: there is a deeper and more essential want, than any of these things can be the supply of. Yet surely there is a possibility of somewhat, which may fill up all our capacities of happiness; somewhat, in which our souls may find rest; somewhat, which may be to us that satisfactory good we are inquiring after. But it cannot be any thing which is valuable only as it tends to some further end. Those therefore who have got this world so much into their hearts, as not to be able to consider happiness as consisting in any thing but property and possessions, which are only valuable as the means to somewhat else, cannot have the least glimpse of the subject before us; which is the end, not the means; the thing itself, not somewhat in order to it. But if you can lay aside that general, confused, undeterminate notion of happiness, as consisting in such possessions; and fix in your thoughts, that it really can consist in nothing but in a faculty's having its proper object; you will clearly see, that in the coolest way of consideration, without either the heat of fanciful enthusiasm, or the warmth of real devotion, nothing is more certain, than that an infinite Being may himself be, if he pleases, the supply to all the capacities of our nature. All the common enjoyments of life are from the faculties he hath endued us with, and the objects he hath made suitable to them. He may himself be to us infinitely more than all these: he may be to us all that we want. As our understanding can contemplate itself, and our affections be exercised upon themselves by reflection, so may each be employed in the same manner upon any other mind: and since the supreme Mind, the Author and Cause of all things, is the highest possible object to himself, he may be an adequate supply to all the faculties of our souls; a subject to our understanding, and an object to our affections.

Consider then: when we shall have put off this mortal body, when we shall be divested of sensual appetites. and those possessions which are now the means of gratification shall be of no avail; when this restless scene of business and vain pleasures, which now diverts us from ourselves, shall be all over; we, our proper self, shall still remain: we shall still continue the same creatures we are, with wants to be supplied, and capacities of happiness. We must have faculties of perception, though not sensitive ones; and pleasure or uneasiness from our perceptions, as now we have.

There are certain ideas, which we express by the words, order, harmony, proportion, beauty, the furthest removed from any thing sensual. Now what is there in those intellectual images, forms, or ideas, which begets that approbation, love, delight, and even rapture, which is seen in some persons' faces upon having those objects present to their minds?—"Mere enthusiasm!"—Be it what it will: there are objects, works of nature and of art, which all mankind have delight from, quite distinct from their affording gratification to sensual appetites; and from quite another view of them, than as being for their interest and further advantage. The faculties from which we are capable of these pleasures, and the pleasures themselves, are as natural, and as much to be accounted for, as any sensual appetite whatever, and the pleasure from its gratification. Words to be sure are wanting upon this subject: to say, that every thing of grace and beauty, throughout the whole of nature, every thing excellent and amiable shared in differently lower degrees by the whole creation, meet in the Author and Cause of all things; this is an inadequate, and perhaps improper way of speaking of the divine nature: but it is manifest that absolute rectitude, the perfection of being, must be in all senses, and in every respect, the highest object to the mind.

In this world it is only the effects of wisdom, and power, and greatness, which we discern: it is not impossible, that hereafter the qualities themselves in the supreme Being may be the immediate object of contemplation. What amazing wonders are opened to view by late improvements! What an object is the universe to a creature, if there be a creature who can comprehend its system! But it must be an infinitely higher exercise of the understanding, to view the scheme of it in that mind, which projected it, before its foundations were laid. And surely we have meaning to the words, when we speak of going further; and viewing, not only this system in his mind, but the wisdom and intelligence itself from whence it proceeded. The same may be said of power. But since wisdom and power are not God, he is a wise, a powerful Being; the divine nature may therefore be a further object to the understanding. It is nothing to observe that our senses give us but an imperfect knowledge of things: effects themselves, if we knew them thoroughly, would give us but imperfect notions of wisdom and power; much less of his Being, in whom they reside. I am not speaking of any fanciful notion of seeing all things in God; but only representing to you, how much an higher object to the understanding an infinite Being himself is, than the things which he has made: and this is no more than saying, that the Creator is superior to the works of his hands.

This may be illustrated by a low example. Suppose a machine, the sight of which would raise, and discoveries in its contrivance gratify, our curiosity: the real delight, in this case, would arise from its being the effect of skill and contrivance. This skill in the mind of the artificer would be an higher object, if we had any senses or ways to discern it. For, observe, the contemplation of that principle, faculty, or power which produced any effect, must be an higher exercise of the understanding, than the contemplation of the effect itself. The cause must be an higher object to the mind than the effect.

But whoever considers distinctly what the light of knowledge is, will see reason to be satisfied that it cannot be the chief good of man: all this, as it is applicable, so it was mentioned with regard to the attribute of goodness. I say, goodness. Our being and all our enjoyments are the effects of it: just men bear its resemblance: but how little do we know of the original, of what it is in itself? Recall what was before observed concerning the affection to moral characters; which, in how low a degree soever, yet is plainly natural to man, and the most excellent part of his nature: suppose this improved, as it may be improved, to any degree whatever, in the *spirits of just men made perfect;* and then suppose that they had a real view of that *righteousness, which is an everlasting righteousness;* of the conformity of the divine will to the *law of truth*, in which the moral attributes of God consist; of that goodness in the sovereign Mind, which gave birth to the universe: add, what will be true of all good men hereafter, a consciousness of having an interest in what they are contemplating; suppose them able to say, *This God is our God for ever and ever:* would they be any longer to seek for what was their chief happiness, their final good? Could the utmost stretch of their capacities look further? Would not infinite perfect goodness be their very end, the last end and object of their affections; beyond which they could neither have, nor desire; beyond which they could not form a wish or thought?

Consider wherein that presence of a friend consists, which has often so strong an effect, as wholly to possess the mind, and entirely suspend all other affections and regards; and which itself affords the highest satisfaction and enjoyment. He is within reach of the senses. Now, as our capacities of perception improve, we shall have, perhaps by some faculty entirely new, a perception of

God s presence with us in a nearer and stricter way, since it is certain he is more intimately present with us than any thing else can be. Proof of the existence and presence of any being is quite different from the immediate perception, the consciousness of it. What then will be the joy of heart, which his presence, and *the light of his countenance*, who is the life of the universe, will inspire good men with, when they shall have a sensation, that he is the sustainer of their being, that they exist in him; when they shall feel his influence to cheer and enliven and support their frame, in a manner of which we have now no conception? He will be in a literal sense *their strength and their portion for ever.*

When we speak of things so much above our comprehension, as the employment and happiness of a future state, doubtless it behoves us to speak with all modesty and distrust of ourselves. But the Scripture represents the happiness of that state under the notions of *seeing God, seeing him as he is, knowing as we are known, and seeing face to face.* These words are not general or undetermined, but express a particular determinate happiness. And I will be bold to say, that nothing can account for, or come up to these expressions, but only this, that God himself will be an object to our faculties, that he himself will be our happiness; as distinguished from the enjoyments of the present state, which seem to arise, not immediately from him, but from the objects he has adapted to give us delight.

To conclude: Let us suppose a person tired with care and sorrow and the repetition of vain delights which fill up the round of life; sensible that every thing here below in its best estate is altogether vanity. Suppose him to feel that deficiency of human nature, before taken notice of; and to be convinced that God alone was the adequate supply to it. What could be more applicable to a good man in this state of mind; or better express his present wants and distant hopes, his passage through this world as a progress towards a state of perfection, than the following passages in the devotions of the royal prophet? They are plainly in an higher and more proper sense applicable to this, than they could be to any thing else.

I have seen an end of all perfection. Whom have I in heaven but thee? And there is none upon earth that I desire in comparison of thee. My flesh and my heart faileth: but God is the strength of my heart, and my portion for ever. Like as the hart desireth the water-brooks, so longeth my soul after thee, O God. My soul is athirst for God, yea, even for the living God: when shall I come to appear before him? How excellent is thy loving-kindness, O God! and the children of men shall put their trust under the shadow of thy wings. They shall be satisfied with the plenteousness of thy house: and thou shalt give them drink of thy pleasures, as out of the river. For with thee is the well of life: and in thy light shall we see light. Blessed is the man whom thou choosest, and receivest unto thee: he shall dwell in thy court, and shall be satisfied with the pleasures of thy house, even of thy holy temple. Blessed is the people, O Lord, that can rejoice in thee: they shall walk in the light of thy countenance. Their delight shall be daily in thy name, and in thy righteousness shall they make their boast. For thou art the glory of their strength: and in thy loving-kindness they shall be exalted. As for me, I will behold thy presence in righteousness: and when I awake up after thy likeness, I shall be satisfied with it. Thou shalt shew me the path of life; in thy presence is the fulness of joy, and at thy right hand there is pleasure for evermore.

SERMON XV.

UPON THE IGNORANCE OF MAN.

When I applied mine heart to know wisdom, and to see the business that is done upon the earth: then I beheld all the work of God, that a man cannot find out the work that is done under the sun: because though a man labour to seek it out, yet he shall not find it; yea further, though a wise man think to know it, yet shall he not be able to find it.—Eccles. viii. 16, 17.

THE writings of Solomon are very much taken up with reflections upon human nature and human life; to which he hath added, in this book, reflections upon the constitution of things. And it is not improbable, that the little satisfaction and the great difficulties he met with in his researches into the general constitution of nature, might be the occasion of his confining himself, so much as he hath done, to life and conduct. However, upon that joint review he expresses great ignorance of the works of God, and the method of his providence in the government of the world; great labour and weariness in the search and observation he had employed himself about; and great disappointment, pain, and even vexation of mind, upon that which he had remarked of the appearances of things, and of what was going forward upon this earth. This whole review and inspection, and the result of it, sorrow, perplexity, a sense of his necessary ignorance, suggests various reflections to his mind. But, notwithstanding all this ignorance and dissatisfaction, there is somewhat upon which he assuredly rests and depends; somewhat, which is the conclusion of the whole matter, and the only concern of man. Following this his method and train of reflection, let us consider,

I. The assertion of the text, the ignorance of man; that the wisest and most knowing cannot comprehend the ways and works of God: and then,

II. What are the just consequences of this observation and knowledge of our own ignorance, and the reflections which it leads us to.

I. The wisest and most knowing cannot comprehend the works of God, the methods and designs of his providence in the creation and government of the world.

Creation is absolutely and entirely out of our depth, and beyond the extent of our utmost reach. And yet it is as certain that God made the world, as it is certain that effects must have a cause. It is indeed in general no more than effects, that the most knowing are acquainted with: for as to causes, they are as entirely in the dark as the most ignorant. What are the laws by which matter acts upon matter, but certain effects; which some, having observed to be frequently repeated, have reduced to general rules? The real nature and essence of beings likewise is what we are altogether ignorant of. All these things are so entirely out of our reach, that we have not the least glimpse of them. And we know little more of ourselves, than we do of the world about us: how we were made, how our being is continued and preserved, what the faculties of our minds are, and upon what the power of exercising them depends. *I am fearfully and wonderfully made: marvellous are thy works, and that my soul knoweth right well.* Our own nature, and the objects we are surrounded with, serve to raise our curiosity; but we are quite out of a condition of satisfying it. Every secret which is disclosed, every discovery which is made, every new effect which is brought to view, serves to convince us of numberless more which remain concealed, and which we had before no suspicion of. And what if we were acquainted with the whole creation, in the same way and as thoroughly as we are with any single object in it? What would all this natural knowledge amount to? It must be a low curiosity indeed which such superficial knowledge could satisfy. On the contrary, would it not serve to convince us of our ignorance still; and to raise our desire of knowing the nature of things themselves, the author, the cause, and the end of them?

As to the government of the world: though from consideration of the final causes which come within our knowledge; of characters, personal merit and demerit; of the favour and disapprobation, which respectively are due and belong to the righteous and the wicked, and which therefore must necessarily be in a mind which sees things as they really are; though, I say, from hence we may know somewhat concerning the designs of Providence in the government of the world, enough to enforce upon us religion and the practice of virtue: yet, since the monarchy of the universe is a dominion unlimited in extent, and everlasting in duration; the general system of it must necessarily be quite beyond our comprehension. And, since there appears such a subordination and reference of the several parts to each other, as to constitute it properly one administration or government; we cannot have a thorough knowledge of any part, without knowing the whole. This surely should convince us, that we are much less competent judges of the very small part which comes under our notice in this world, than we are apt to imagine. *No heart can think upon these things worthily: and who is able to conceive his way? It is a tempest which no man can see: for the most part of his works are hid. Who can declare the works of his justice? for his covenant is afar off, and the trial of all things is in the end:* i. e. The dealings of God with the children of men are not yet completed, and cannot be judged of by that part which is before us. *So that a man cannot say, This is worse than that: for in time they shall be well approved. Thy faithfulness, O Lord, reacheth unto the clouds: thy righteousness standeth like the strong mountains: thy judgments are like the great deep. He hath made every thing beautiful in his time: also he hath set the world in their heart; so that no man can find out the work that God maketh from the beginning to the end.* And thus St Paul concludes a long argument upon the various dispensations of Providence: *O the depth of the riches, both of the wisdom and knowledge of God! How unsearchable are his judgments, and his ways past finding out! For who hath known the mind of the Lord?*

Thus the scheme of Providence, the ways and works of God, are too vast, of too large extent for our capacities. There is, as I may speak, such an expense of power, and wisdom, and goodness, in the formation and government of the world, as is too much for us to take in, or comprehend. Power, and wisdom, and goodness, are manifest to us in all those works of God, which come within our view: but there are likewise infinite stores of each poured forth throughout the immensity of the creation; no part of which can be thoroughly understood, without taking in its reference and respect to the whole: and this is what we have not faculties for.

And as the works of God, and his scheme of government, are above our capacities thoroughly to comprehend: so there possibly may be reasons which originally made it fit that many things should be concealed from us, which we have perhaps natural capacities of understanding; many things concerning the designs, methods, and ends of divine Providence in the government of the world. There is no manner of absurdity in supposing a veil on purpose drawn over some scenes of infinite power, wisdom, and goodness, the sight of which might some way or other strike us too strongly; or that better ends are designed and served by their being concealed, than could be by their being exposed to our knowledge. The Almighty may cast clouds and darkness round about him, for reasons and purposes of which we have not the least glimpse or conception.

However, it is surely reasonable, and what might have been expected, that creatures in some stage of their being, suppose in the infancy of it, should be placed in a state of discipline and improvement, where their patience and submission is to be tried by afflictions, where temptations are to be resisted, and difficulties gone through in the discharge of their duty. Now if the greatest pleasures and pains of the present life may be overcome and suspended, as they manifestly may, by hope and fear, and other passions and affections; then the evidence of religion, and the sense of the consequences of virtue and vice, might have been such, as entirely in all cases to prevail over those afflictions, difficulties, and temptations; prevail over them so, as to render them absolutely none at all. But the very notion itself now mentioned, of a state of discipline and improvement, necessarily excludes such sensible evidence and conviction of religion, and of the consequences of virtue and vice. Religion consists in submission and resignation to the divine will. Our condition in this world is a school of exercise for this temper: and our ignorance, the shallowness of our reason, the temptations, difficulties, afflictions, which we are exposed to, all equally contribute to make it so. The general observation may be carried on; and whoever will attend to the thing will plainly see, that less sensible evidence, with less difficulty in practice, is the same, as more sensible evidence, with greater difficulty in practice. Therefore difficulties in speculation as much come into the notion of a state of discipline, as difficulties in practice: and so the same reason or account is to be given of both Thus, though it is indeed absurd to talk of the greater merit of assent, upon little or no evidence, than upon demonstration; yet the strict discharge of our duty, with less sensible evidence, does imply in it a better character, than the same diligence in the discharge of it upon more sensible evidence. This fully accounts for and explains that assertion of our Saviour, *Blessed are they that have not seen, and yet have believed;** have become Christians and obeyed the gospel upon less sensible evidence than that which Thomas, to whom he is speaking, insisted upon.

But after all, the same account is to be given, why we were placed in these circumstances of ignorance, as why nature has not furnished us with wings; namely, that we were designed to be inhabitants of this earth. I am afraid we think too highly of ourselves; of our rank in the creation, and of what is due to us. What sphere of action, what business is assigned to man, that he has not capacities and knowledge fully equal to? It is manifest he has reason, and knowledge, and faculties superior to the business of the present world: faculties which appear superfluous, if we do not take in the respect which they have to somewhat further, and beyond it. If to acquire knowledge were our proper end, we should indeed be but poorly provided: but if somewhat else be our business and duty, we may, notwithstanding our ignorance, be well enough furnished for it; and the observation of our ignorance may be of assistance to us in the discharge of it.

II. Let us then consider, what are the consequences of this knowledge and observation of our own ignorance, and the reflection it leads us to.

First, We may learn from it, with what temper of mind a man ought to inquire into the subject of religion; namely, with expectation of finding difficulties, and with a disposition to take up and rest satisfied with any evidence whatever, which is real.

He should beforehand expect things mysterious, and such as he will not be able thoroughly to comprehend, or go to the bottom of. To expect a distinct comprehensive view of the whole subject, clear of difficulties and objections, is to forget our nature and condition; neither of which admit of such knowledge, with respect

* John xx. 29.

to any science whatever. And to inquire with this expectation, is not to inquire as a man, but as one of another order of creatures.

Due sense of the general ignorance of man would also beget in us a disposition to take up and rest satisfied with any evidence whatever, which is real. I mention this as the contrary to a disposition, of which there are not wanting instances, to find fault with and reject evidence, because it is not such as was desired. If a man were to walk by twilight, must he not follow his eyes as much as if it were broad day and clear sunshine? Or if he were obliged to take a journey by night, would he not *give heed to* any *light shining in the darkness, till the day should break and the day-star arise?* It would not be altogether unnatural for him to reflect how much better it were to have daylight; he might perhaps have great curiosity to see the country round about him; he might lament that the darkness concealed many extended prospects from his eyes, and wish for the sun to draw away the veil: but how ridiculous would it be to reject with scorn and disdain the guidance and direction which that lesser light might afford him, because it was not the sun itself! If the make and constitution of man, the circumstances he is placed in, or the reason of things affords the least hint or intimation, that virtue is the law he is born under; scepticism itself should lead him to the most strict and inviolable practice of it; that he may not make the dreadful experiment, of leaving the course of life marked out for him by nature, whatever that nature be, and entering paths of his own, of which he can know neither the dangers, nor the end. For though no danger be seen, yet darkness, ignorance, and blindness are no manner of security.

Secondly, Our ignorance is the proper answer to many things, which are called objections against religion; particularly, to those which arise from the appearances of evil and irregularity in the constitution of nature and the government of the world. In all other cases it is thought necessary to be thoroughly acquainted with the whole of a scheme, even one of so narrow a compass as those which are formed by men, in order to judge of the goodness or badness of it: and the most slight and superficial view of any human contrivance comes abundantly nearer to a thorough knowledge of it, than that part, which we know of the government of the world, does to the general scheme and system of it; to the whole set of laws by which it is governed. From our ignorance of the constitution of things, and the scheme of Providence in the government of the world; from the reference the several parts have to each other, and to the whole; and from our not being able to see the end and the whole; it follows, that however perfect things are, they must even necessarily appear to us otherwise less perfect than they are.*

Thirdly, Since the constitution of nature, and the methods and designs of Providence in the government of the world, are above our comprehension, we should acquiesce in, and rest satisfied with, our ignorance, turn our thoughts from that which is above and beyond us, and apply ourselves to that which is level to our capacities, and which is our real business and concern. Knowledge is not our proper happiness. Whoever will in the least attend to the thing will see, that it is the

* Suppose some very *complicated piece of work*, some *system* or *constitution*, formed for some *general end*, to which each of the *parts* had a *reference*. The perfection or justness of this work or constitution would consist in the reference and respect, which the several parts have to the general design. This reference of parts to the general design may be infinitely various, both in degree and kind. Thus one part may only contribute and be subservient to another; this to a third; and so on through a long series, the last part of which alone may contribute immediately and directly to the general design. Or a part may have this distant reference to the general design, and may also contribute immediately to it. For instance: if the general design or end, for which the complicated frame of nature was brought into being, is happiness; whatever affords present satisfaction, and likewise tends to carry on the course of things, hath this double respect to the general design. Now suppose a spectator of that work or constitution was in a great measure ignorant of such various reference to the general end, whatever that end be; and that, upon a very slight and partial view which he had of the work, several things appeared to his eye disproportionate and wrong; others, just and beautiful; what would he gather from these appearances? He would immediately conclude there was a probability, if he could see the whole reference of the parts appearing wrong to the general design, that this would destroy the appearance of wrongness and disproportion: but there is no probability, that the reference would destroy the particular right appearances, though that reference might show the things already appearing just, to be so likewise in a higher degree or another manner. There is a probability, that the right appearances were intended: there is no probability, that the wrong appearances were. We cannot suspect irregularity and disorder to be designed. The pillars of a building appear beautiful; but their being likewise its support does not destroy that beauty: there still remains a reason to believe that the architect intended the beautiful appearance, after we have found out the reference, support. It would be reasonable for a man of himself to think thus, upon the first piece of architecture he ever saw.

gaining, not the having of it, which is the entertainment of the mind. Indeed, if the proper happiness of man consisted in knowledge considered as a possession or treasure, men who are possessed of the largest share would have a very ill time of it; as they would be infinitely more sensible than others of their poverty in this respect. Thus *he who increases knowledge would* eminently *increase sorrow*. Men of deep research and curious inquiry should just be put in mind, not to mistake what they are doing. If their discoveries serve the cause of virtue and religion, in the way of proof, motive to practice, or assistance in it; or if they tend to render life less unhappy, and promote its satisfactions; then they are most usefully employed: but bringing things to light, alone and of itself, is of no manner of use, any otherwise than as entertainment or diversion. Neither is this at all amiss, if it does not take up the time which should be employed in better work. But it is evident that there is another mark set up for us to aim at; another end appointed us to direct our lives to: another end, which the most knowing may fail of, and the most ignorant arrive at. *The secret things belong unto the Lord our God; but those things which are revealed belong unto us, and to our children for ever, that we may do all the words of this law.* Which reflection of Moses, put in general terms, is, that the only knowledge, which is of any avail to us, is that which teaches us our duty, or assists us in the discharge of it. The economy of the universe, the course of nature, almighty power exerted in the creation and government of the world, is out of our reach. What would be the consequence, if we could really get an insight into these things, is very uncertain; whether it would assist us in, or divert us from, what we have to do in this present state. If then there be a sphere of knowledge, of contemplation and employment, level to our capacities, and of the utmost importance to us; we ought surely to apply ourselves with all diligence to this our proper business, and esteem every thing else nothing, nothing as to us, in comparison of it. Thus Job, discoursing of natural knowledge, how much it is above us, and of wisdom in general, says, *God understandeth the way thereof, and he knoweth the place thereof. And unto man he said, Behold, the fear of the Lord, that is wisdom, and to depart from evil is understanding.* Other orders of creatures may perhaps be let into the secret counsels of heaven; and have the designs and methods of Providence, in the creation and government of the world, communicated to them: but this does not belong to our rank or condition. *The fear of the Lord, and to depart from evil,* is the only wisdom which man should aspire after, as his work and business. The same is said, and with the same connexion and context, in the conclusion of the book of Ecclesiastes. Our ignorance, and the little we can know of other things, affords a reason why we should not perplex ourselves about them; but no way invalidates that which is the *conclusion of the whole matter, Fear God, and keep his commandments; for this is the whole concern of man.* So that Socrates was not the first who endeavoured to draw men off from labouring after, and laying stress upon other knowledge, in comparison of that which related to morals. Our province is virtue and religion, life and manners; the science of improving the temper, and making the heart better. This is the field assigned us to cultivate: how much it has lain neglected is indeed astonishing. Virtue is demonstrably the happiness of man: it consists in good actions, proceeding from a good principle, temper, or heart. Overt-acts are entirely in our power. What remains is, that we learn to *keep our heart;* to govern and regulate our passions, mind, affections: that so we may be free from the impotencies of fear, envy, malice, covetousness, ambition: that we may be clear of these, considered as vices seated in the heart, considered as constituting a general wrong temper; from which general wrong frame of mind, all the mistaken pursuits, and far the greatest part of the unhappiness of life, proceed. He, who should find out one rule to assist us in this work, would deserve infinitely better of mankind, than all the improvers of other knowledge put together.

Lastly, Let us adore that infinite wisdom and power and goodness, which is above our comprehension. *To whom hath the root of wisdom been revealed? Or who hath known her wise counsels? There is one wise and greatly to be feared; the Lord sitting upon his throne. He created her, and saw her, and numbered her, and poured her out upon all his works.* If it be thought a considerable thing to be acquainted with a few, a very few, of the effects of infinite power and wisdom; the situation, bigness, and revolution of some of the heavenly bodies; what sentiments should our minds be filled with concerning Him, who appointed to each its place and measure and sphere of motion, all which are kept with the most uniform constancy! *Who stretched out the heavens, and telleth the number of the stars, and calleth them all by their names. Who laid the foundations of the earth, who comprehendeth the dust of it in a measure, and weigheth the mountains in scales, and the hills in a balance.* And, when we have recounted all the appearances which come within our view, we must add, *Lo, these are part of his ways: but how little a portion is heard of him! Canst thou by searching find out God? Canst thou find out the Almighty unto perfection? It is as high as heaven; what canst thou do? deeper than hell; what canst thou know?*

The conclusion is, that in all lowliness of mind we set lightly by ourselves: that we form our temper to an implicit submission to the divine Majesty; beget within ourselves an absolute resignation to all the methods of his providence, in his dealings with the children of men: that, in the deepest humility of our souls, we prostrate ourselves before him, and join in that celestial song; *Great and marvellous are thy works, Lord God Almighty! just and true are thy ways, thou King of saints! Who shall not fear thee, O Lord, and glorify thy name!*

SIX SERMONS

PREACHED UPON

PUBLIC OCCASIONS.

SERMON I.

PREACHED BEFORE THE INCORPORATED SOCIETY FOR THE PROPAGATION OF THE GOSPEL IN FOREIGN PARTS, AT THEIR ANNIVERSARY MEETING IN THE PARISH CHURCH OF ST MARY-LE-BOW, ON FRIDAY, FEB. 16, 1738-9.

And this gospel of the kingdom shall be preached in all the world, for a witness unto all nations.—Matt. xxiv. 14.

THE general doctrine of religion, that all things are under the direction of one righteous Governor, having been established by repeated revelations in the first ages of the world, was left with the bulk of mankind, to be honestly preserved pure and entire, or carelessly forgotten, or wilfully corrupted. And though reason, almost intuitively, bare witness to the truth of this moral system of nature, yet it soon appeared, that *they did not like to retain God in their knowledge,** as to any purposes of real piety. Natural religion became gradually more and more darkened with superstition, little understood, less regarded in practice; and the face of it scarce discernible at all, in the religious establishments of the most learned, polite nations. And how much soever could have been done towards the revival of it by the light of reason, yet this light could not have discovered, what so nearly concerned us, that important part in the scheme of this world, which regards a Mediator; nor how far the settled constitution of its government admitted repentance to be accepted for remission of sins; after the obscure intimations of these things, from tradition, were corrupted or forgotten. One

* Rom. i. 28.

people indeed had clearer notices of them, together with the genuine scheme of natural religion, preserved in the primitive and subsequent revelations committed to their trust; and were designed to be a witness of God, and a providence to the nations around them: but this people also had corrupted themselves and their religion to the highest degree, that was consistent with keeping up the form of it.

In this state of things, when infinite Wisdom saw proper, the general doctrine of religion was authoritatively republished in its purity; and the particular dispensation of Providence, which this world is under, manifested to all men, even, *the dispensation of the grace of God** towards us, as sinful, lost creatures, to be recovered by repentance through a Mediator; who was *to make reconciliation for iniquity, and to bring in everlasting righteousness,*† and at length establish that new state of things foretold by the prophet Daniel, under the character of *a kingdom, which the God of heaven would set up, and which should never be destroyed.*‡ This, including a more distinct account of the instituted means, whereby Christ the Mediator would *gather together in one the children of God, that were scattered abroad,*§ and conduct them to *the place he is gone to prepare for them;*‖ is *the Gospel of the kingdom,* which he here foretels, and elsewhere commands, should *be preached in all the world, for a witness unto all nations.* And it *first began to be spoken by the Lord, and was confirmed unto us by them that heard him; God also bearing them witness, both with signs and wonders, and with divers miracles, and gifts of the Holy Ghost, according to his own will:*¶ by which means it was spread very widely among the nations of the world, and became *a witness unto them.*

When thus much was accomplished, as there is a wonderful uniformity in the conduct of Providence, Christianity was left with Christians, to be transmitted down pure and genuine, or to be corrupted and sunk; in like manner as the religion of nature had been before left with mankind in general. There was however this

* Eph. iii. 2. † Dan. ix. 24. ‡ Dan. ii. 44.
§ John xi. 52. ‖ John xiv. 2, 3. ¶ Heb. ii. 3, 4.

difference, that by an institution of external religion fitted for all men (consisting in a common form of Christian worship, together with a standing ministry of instruction and discipline), it pleased God to unite Christians in communities or visible churches, and all along to preserve them, over a great part of the world; and thus perpetuate a general publication of the gospel. For these communities, which together make up the catholic visible church, are, first, the repositories of the written oracles of God; and, in every age, have preserved and published them, in every country, where the profession of Christianity has obtained. Hence it has come to pass, and it is a thing very much to be observed in the appointment of Providence, that even such of these communities, as, in a long succession of years, have corrupted Christianity the most, have yet continually carried, together with their corruptions, the confutation of them: for they have every where preserved the pure original standard of it, the Scripture, to which recourse might have been had, both by the deceivers and the deceived, in every successive age. Secondly, any particular church, in whatever place established, is like *a city that is set on a hill, which cannot be hid*,* inviting all who pass by, to enter into it. All persons, to whom any notices of it come, have, in Scripture language, the *kingdom of God come nigh unto them*. They are reminded of that religion, which natural conscience attests the truth of: and they may, if they will, be instructed in it more distinctly, and likewise in the gracious means, whereby sinful creatures may obtain eternal life; that chief and final good, which all men, in proportion to their understanding and integrity, even in all ages and countries of the heathen world, were ever in pursuit of. And, lastly, out of these churches have all along gone forth persons, who have preached the gospel in remote places, with greater or less good effect: for the establishment of any profession of Christianity, however corrupt, I call a good effect, whilst accompanied with a continued publication of the Scripture, notwithstanding it may for some time lie quite neglected.

From these things, it may be worth observing by the way, appears the weakness of all pleas for neglecting the public service of the church. For though a man prays with as much devotion and less interruption at home, and reads better sermons there, yet that will by no means excuse the neglect of his appointed part in keeping up the profession of Christianity amongst mankind. And this neglect, were it universal, must be the dissolution of the whole visible church, *i.e.* of all Christian communities; and so must prevent those good purposes, which were intended to be answered by them, and which they have, all along, answered over the world. For we see that by their means the event foretold in the text, which began in the preaching of Christ and the apostles, has been carried on, more or less ever since, and is still carrying on; these being the providential means of its progress. And it is, I suppose, the completion of this event, which St John had a representation of, under the figure of *an angel flying in the midst of heaven, having the everlasting gospel to preach unto them that dwell on the earth, and to every nation, and kindred, and tongue, and people.**

Our Lord adds in the text, that this should be *for a witness unto them;* for an evidence of their duty, and an admonition to perform it. But what would be the effect, or success of the general preaching of the gospel, is not here mentioned. And therefore the prophecy of the text is not parallel to those others in Scripture, which seem to foretel the glorious establishment of Christianity in the last days: nor does it appear that they are coincident; otherwise than as the former of these events must be supposed preparatory to the latter. Nay, it is not said here, that *God willeth all men should be saved, and come unto the knowledge of the truth:* † though this is the language of Scripture elsewhere. The text declares no more, than that it was the appointment of God, in his righteous government over the world, that *the gospel of the kingdom should be preached for a witness unto it.*

The visible constitution and course of nature, the moral law written in our hearts, the positive institutions of religion, and even any memorial of it, are all spoken of

* Rev. xiv. 6. † 1 Tim. ii. 4.

in Scripture under this, or the like denomination: so are the prophets, apostles, and our Lord himself. They are all *witnesses*, for the most part unregarded witnesses, in behalf of God, to mankind. They inform us of his being and providence, and of the particular dispensation of religion which we are under; and continually remind us of them. And they are equally witnesses of these things, whether we regard them or not. Thus after a declaration, that Ezekiel should be sent with a divine message to the children of Israel, it is added, *and they, whether they will hear, or whether they will forbear (for they are a rebellious house), yet shall know that there hath been a prophet among them.** And our Lord directs the seventy disciples, upon their departure from any city, which refused to receive them, to declare, *Notwithstanding, be ye sure of this, that the kingdom of God is come nigh unto you.*† The thing intended in both these passages is that which is expressed in the text by the word *witness.* And all of them together evidently suggest thus much, that the purposes of Providence are carried on, by the preaching of the gospel, to those who reject it, as well as to those who embrace it. It is indeed true, *God willeth that all men should be saved:* yet, from the unalterable constitution of his government, the salvation of every man cannot but depend upon his behaviour, and therefore cannot but depend upon himself; and is necessarily his own concern, in a sense, in which it cannot be another's. All this the Scripture declares, in a manner the most forcible and alarming: *Can a man be profitable unto God, as he that is wise may be profitable unto himself? Is it any pleasure to the Almighty, that thou art righteous? or is it gain to Him, that thou makest thy way perfect?*‡ *If thou be wise, thou shalt be wise for thyself: but if thou scornest, thou alone shalt bear it.*§ *He that heareth, let him hear; and he that forbeareth, let him forbear.*|| And again, *He that hath ears to hear, let him hear: but if any man be ignorant,* i. e. wilfully, *let him be ignorant.*¶ To the same purpose are those awful words of the angel, in the person of Him, to whom *all judgment is committed:***

* Ezek. ii. 5, 7. † Luke x. 11. ‡ Job xxii. 2, 3. § Prov. ix. 12.
|| Ezek. iii. 27. ¶ 1 Cor. xiv. 38. ** John v. 22.

*He that is unjust, let him be unjust still: and he which is filthy, let him be filthy still: and he that is righteous, let him be righteous still: and he that is holy, let him be holy still. And behold, I come quickly; and my reward is with me, to give every man according as his work shall be.** The righteous government of the world must be carried on; and, of necessity, men shall remain the subjects of it, by being examples of its mercy, or of its justice. *Life and death are set before them, and whether they like shall be given them.*† They are to make their choice, and abide by it: but which soever their choice be, the gospel is equally a *witness* to them; and the purposes of Providence are answered by this *witness* of the gospel.

From the foregoing view of things we should be reminded, that the same reasons which make it our duty to instruct the ignorant in the relation, which the light of nature shows they stand in to God their maker, and in the obligations of obedience, resignation, and love to him, which arise out of that relation; make it our duty likewise to instruct them in all those other relations, which revelation informs us of, and in the obligations of duty, which arise out of them. And the reasons for instructing men in both these are of the very same kind, as for communicating any useful knowledge whatever. God, if he had so pleased, could indeed miraculously have revealed every religious truth which concerns mankind, to every individual man; and so he could have every common truth; and thus have superseded all use of human teaching in either. Yet he has not done this: but has appointed, that men should be instructed by the assistance of their fellow creatures in both. Further: though all knowledge from reason is as really from God, as revelation is: yet this last is a distinguished favour to us, and naturally strikes us with the greatest awe, and carries in it an assurance, that those things which we are informed of by it are of the utmost importance to us to be informed of. Revelation therefore, as it demands to be received with a regard and reverence peculiar to itself; so it lays us under obligations of a like peculiar sort, to communicate the light of it. Further still: it being an

* Rev. xxii. 11, 12. † Ecclus. xv. 17.

indispensable law of the gospel, that Christians should unite in religious communities, and these being intended for repositories* of the written *oracles of God*, for standing memorials of religion to unthinking men, and for the propagation of it in the world; Christianity is very particularly to be considered as a trust, deposited with us in behalf of others, in behalf of mankind, as well as for our own instruction. No one has a right to be called a Christian, who doth not do somewhat in his station, towards the discharge of this trust; who doth not, for instance, assist in keeping up the profession of Christianity where he lives. And it is an obligation but little more remote, to assist in doing it in our factories abroad; and in the colonies to which we are related, by their being peopled from our own mother-country, and subjects, indeed very necessary ones, to the same government with ourselves: and nearer yet is the obligation upon such persons in particular, as have the intercourse of an advantageous commerce with them.

Of these our colonies, the slaves ought to be considered as inferior members, and therefore to be treated as members of them; and not merely as cattle or goods, the property of their masters. Nor can the highest property, possible to be acquired in these servants, cancel the obligation to take care of their religious instruction. Despicable as they may appear in our eyes, they are the creatures of God, and of the race of mankind, for whom Christ died: and it is inexcusable to keep them in ignorance of the end for which they were made, and the means whereby they may become partakers of the general redemption. On the contrary, if the necessity of the case requires, that they may be treated with the very utmost rigour, that humanity will at all permit, as they certainly are; and, for our advantage, made as miserable as they well can be in the present world; this surely heightens our obligation to put them into as advantageous a situation as we are able, with regard to another.

The like charity we owe to the natives; owe to them in a much stricter sense than we are apt to consider, were it only from neighbourhood, and our having gotten possessions in their country. For incidental circumstances

* P. 185.

of this kind appropriate all the general obligations of charity to particular persons; and make such and such instances of it the duty of one man rather than another. We are most strictly bound to consider these poor uninformed creatures, as being in all respects, of one family with ourselves, the family of mankind; and instruct them in our *common salvation:** that they may not pass through this stage of their being like brute beasts; but be put into a capacity of moral improvements, how low soever they must remain as to others, and so into a capacity of qualifying themselves for a higher state of life hereafter.

All our affairs should be carried on in the fear of God, in subserviency to his honour, and the good of mankind. And thus navigation and commerce should be consecrated to the service of religion, by being made the means of propagating it in every country, with which we have any intercourse. And the more widely we endeavour to spread its light and influence, as the forementioned circumstances, and others of a like kind, open and direct our way, the more faithful shall we be judged in the discharge of that trust,† which is committed to us as Christians, when our Lord shall require an account of it.

And it may be some encouragement to cheerful perseverance in these endeavours to observe, not only that they are our duty, but also that they seem the means of carrying on a great scheme of Providence, which shall certainly be accomplished. For *the everlasting gospel shall be preached to every nation.*‡ and *the kingdoms of this world shall become the kingdoms of our Lord, and of his Christ.*§

However, we ought not to be discouraged in this good work, though its future success were less clearly foretold; and though its effect now in reforming mankind appeared to be as little as our adversaries pretend. They, indeed, and perhaps some others, seem to require more than either experience or Scripture give ground to hope for, in the present course of the world. But the bare establishment of Christianity in any place, even the external form and profession of it, is a very important and valuable effect. It is a serious call upon men to attend to the

* Jude 3. † P. 190. ‡ Rev. xiv. 6. § Rev. xi. 15.

natural and the revealed doctrine of religion. It is a standing publication of the gospel, and renders it a *witness* to them: and by this means the purposes of Providence are carrying on, with regard to remote ages, as well as to the present. *Cast thy bread upon the waters; for thou shalt find it after many days. In the morning sow thy seed, and in the evening withhold not thine hand; for thou knowest not whether shall prosper, either this or that, or whether they both shall be alike good.** We can look but a very little way into the connexions and consequences of things: our duty is to spread the *incorruptible seed* as widely as we can, and leave it to *God to give the increase.*† Yet thus much we may be almost assured of, that the gospel, wherever it is planted, will have its genuine effect upon some few; upon more perhaps than are taken notice of in the hurry of the world. There are, at least, a few persons in every country and successive age, scattered up and down, and mixed among the rest of mankind; who, not being corrupted past amendment, but having within them the principles of recovery, will be brought to a moral and religious sense of things, by the establishment of Christianity where they live; and then will be influenced by the peculiar doctrines of it, in proportion to the integrity of their minds, and to the clearness, purity, and evidence, with which it is offered them. Of these our Lord speaks in the parable of the sower, as *understanding the word; and bearing fruit, and bringing forth, some an hundred fold, some sixty, some thirty.*‡ One might add, that these persons, in proportion to their influence, do at present better the state of things: better it even in the civil sense, by giving some check to that avowed profligateness, which is a contradiction to all order and government; and, if not checked, must be the subversion of it.

These important purposes, which are certainly to be expected from the good work before us, may serve to show, how little weight there is in that objection against it, from the want of those miraculous assistances, with which the first preachers of Christianity proved its truth. The plain state of the case is, that the gospel, though it

* Eccles. xi. 1, 6. † 1 Cor. iii. 6. ‡ Matt. xiii. 23.

be not in the same degree a *witness* to all, who have it made known to them; yet in some degree is so to all. Miracles to the spectators of them are intuitive proofs of its truth: but the bare preaching of it is a serious admonition to all who hear it, to attend to the notices which God has given of himself by the light of nature; and, if Christianity be preached with its proper evidence, to submit to its peculiar discipline and laws; if not, to inquire honestly after its evidence, in proportion to their capacities. And there are persons of small capacities for inquiry and examination, who yet are wrought upon by it, to *deny ungodliness and worldly lusts, and live soberly, righteously, and godly in this present world,** in expectation of a future judgment by Jesus Christ. Nor can any Christian, who understands his religion, object, that these persons are Christians without evidence: for he cannot be ignorant who has declared, that *if any man will do his will, he shall know of the doctrine, whether it be of God.*† And, since the whole end of Christianity is to influence the heart and actions, were an unbeliever to object in that manner, he should be asked, whether he would think it to the purpose to object against persons of like capacities, that they are prudent without evidence, when, as is often the case, they are observed to manage their worldly affairs with discretion.

The design before us being therefore in general unexceptionably good, it were much to be wished, that serious men of all denominations would join in it. And let me add, that the foregoing view of things affords distinct reasons why they should. For, first, by so doing, they assist in a work of the most useful importance, that of spreading over the world the Scripture itself, as a divine revelation: and it cannot be spread under this character, for a continuance, in any country, unless Christian churches be supported there; but will always more or less, so long as such churches subsist: and therefore their subsistence ought to be provided for. In the next place, they should remember, that if Christianity is to be propagated at all, which they acknowledge it should, it must be in some particular form of profession. And

* Titus ii. 12, 13. † John vii. 17.

though they think ours liable to objections, yet it is possible they themselves may be mistaken; and whether they are or no, the very nature of society requires some compliance with others. And whilst, together with our particular form of Christianity, the confessed standard of Christian religion, the Scripture, is spread; and especially whilst every one is freely allowed to study it, and worship God according to his conscience: the evident tendency is, that genuine Christianity will be understood and prevail. Upon the whole therefore, these persons would do well to consider, how far they can with reason satisfy themselves in neglecting what is certainly right, on account of what is doubtful, whether it be wrong; and when the right is of so much greater consequence one way, than the supposed wrong can be to the other.

To conclude: Atheistical immorality and profaneness, surely, is not better in itself, nor less contrary to the design of revelation, than superstition. Nor is superstition the distinguishing vice of the present age, either at home or abroad. But if our colonies abroad are left without a public religion, and the means of instruction, what can be expected, but that, from living in a continued forgetfulness of God, they will at length cease to believe in him; and so sink into stupid atheism? And there is too apparent danger of the like horrible depravity at home, without the like excuse for it. Indeed amongst creatures naturally formed for religion, yet so much under the powers of imagination, so apt to deceive themselves, and so liable to be deceived by others, as men are; superstition is an evil, which can never be out of sight. But even against this, true religion is a great security; and the only one. True religion takes up that place in the mind, which superstition would usurp, and so leaves little room for it; and likewise lays us under the strongest obligations to oppose it. On the contrary, the danger of superstition cannot but be increased by the prevalence of irreligion: and by its general prevalence, the evil will be unavoidable. For the common people, wanting a religion, will of course take up with almost any superstition, which is thrown in their way: and, in process of time, amidst the infinite vicissitudes of the political world, the leaders of parties will certainly be able to serve themselves of that superstition, whatever it be, which is getting ground: and will not fail to carry it on to the utmost length their occasions require. The general nature of the thing shows this; and history and fact confirm it. But what brings the observation home to ourselves is, that the great superstition of which this nation, in particular, has reason to be afraid, is imminent; and the ways in which we may, very supposably, be overwhelmed by it, obvious. It is therefore wonderful, those people who seem to think there is but one evil in life, that of superstition, should not see, that atheism and profaneness must be the introduction of it. So that in every view of things, and upon all accounts, irreligion is at present our chief danger. Now the several religious associations among us, in which many good men have of late united, appear to be providentially adapted to this present state of the world. And as all good men are equally concerned in promoting the end of them; to do it more effectually, they ought to unite in promoting it: which yet is scarce practicable upon any new models, and quite impossible upon such as every one would think unexceptionable. They ought therefore to come into those already formed to their hands; and even take advantage of any occasion of union, to add mutual force to each other's endeavours in furthering their common end; however they may differ as to the best means, or any thing else subordinate to it. Indeed there are well-disposed persons, who much want to be admonished, how dangerous a thing it is, to discountenance what is good, because it is not better; and hinder what they approve, by raising prejudices against some under-part of it. Nor can they assist in rectifying what they think capable of amendment, in the manner of carrying on these designs, unless they will join in the designs themselves; which they must acknowledge to be good and necessary ones. For what can be called good and necessary by Christians, if it be not so, to support Christianity where it must otherwise sink, and propagate it where it must otherwise be unknown; to restrain abandoned, barefaced vice, by making useful examples, at least of shame, perhaps of repentance; and to take care of the education of such children, as otherwise must be, even educated in wickedness, and trained up to destruction? Yet good men separately can do nothing, proportionable to what is wanting, in any of these ways; but their common, united endeavours may do a great deal in all of them.

And besides the particular purposes, which these several religious associations serve, the more general ones, which they all serve, ought not to be passed over. Every thing of this kind is, in some degree, a safeguard to religion; an obstacle, more or less, in the way of those who want to have it extirpated out of the world. Such societies also contribute more especially towards keeping up the face of Christianity among ourselves; and by their obtaining here, the gospel is rendered more and more a *witness* to us.

And if it were duly attended to, and had its genuine influence upon our minds, there would be no need of persuasions to impart the blessing: nor would the means of doing it be wanting. Indeed the present income of this Society, which depends upon voluntary contributions, with the most frugal management of it, can in no wise sufficiently answer the bare purposes of our charter: but the nation, or even this opulent city itself, has it in its power to do so very much more, that I fear the mention of it may be thought too severe a reproof, since so little is done. But if the gospel had its proper influence upon the Christian world in general, as it is the centre of trade and seat of learning, a very few ages, in all probability, would settle Christianity in every country, without miraculous assistances. For scarce any thing else, I am persuaded, would be wanting to effect this, but laying it before men in its divine simplicity, together with an exemplification of it in the lives of Christian nations. *The unlearned and unbelievers, falling down on their faces, would worship God, and report that God is in us of a truth.**

* 1 Cor. xiv. 24

SERMON II.

PREACHED BEFORE THE RIGHT HON. THE LORD MAYOR, THE COURT OF ALDERMEN, THE SHERIFFS, AND THE GOVERNORS OF THE SEVERAL HOSPITALS OF THE CITY OF LONDON, AT THE PARISH CHURCH OF ST BRIDGET, ON MONDAY IN EASTER-WEEK, 1740.

The rich and poor meet together: the Lord is the maker of them all.—Prov. xxii. 2.

THE constitution of things being such, that the labour of one man, or the united labour of several, is sufficient to procure more *necessaries* than he or they stand in need of, which it may be supposed was, in some degree, the case, even in the first ages; this immediately gave room for riches to arise in the world, and for men's acquiring them by honest means; by diligence, frugality, and prudent management. Thus some would very soon acquire greater plenty of *necessaries* than they had occasion for; and others by contrary means, or by cross accidents, would be in want of them: and he who should supply their wants would have the property in a proportionable labour of their hands; which he would scarce fail to make use of, instead of his own, or perhaps together with them, to provide future *necessaries* in greater plenty. Riches then were first bestowed upon the world, as they are still continued in it, by the blessing of God upon the industry of men, in the use of their understanding and strength. Riches themselves have always this source; though the possession of them is conveyed to particular persons by different channels. Yet still, *the hand of the diligent maketh rich,** and, other circumstances being equal, in proportion to its diligence.

But to return to the first rich man; whom we left in possession of dependants, and plenty of *necessaries* for himself and them. A family would not be long in this state, before *conveniences*, somewhat *ornamental*, and for *entertainment*, would be wanted, looked for, and found out. And, by degrees, these secondary wants, and inventions for the supply of them, the fruits of leisure

* Prov. x. 4.

seemed to be endless. The best remedies too, when unskilfully, much more if dishonestly applied, may produce new diseases; and with the rightest application the success of them is often doubtful. In many cases they are not at all effectual: where they are, it is often very slowly: and the application of them, and the necessary regimen accompanying it, is, not uncommonly, so disagreeable, that some will not submit to them; and satisfy themselves with the excuse, that, if they would, it is not certain whether it would be successful. And many persons, who labour under diseases, for which there are known natural remedies, are not so happy as to be always, if ever, in the way of them. In a word, the remedies which nature has provided for diseases are neither certain, perfect, nor universal. And indeed the same principles of arguing, which would lead us to conclude, that they must be so, would lead us likewise to conclude, that there could be no occasion for them; *i. e.* that there could be no diseases at all. And therefore our experience that there are diseases shows, that it is credible beforehand, upon supposition nature has provided remedies for them, that these remedies may be, as by experience we find they are, not certain, nor perfect, nor universal; because it shows, that the principles upon which we should expect the contrary are fallacious.

And now, what is the just consequence from all these things? Not that reason is no judge of what is offered to us as being of divine revelation. For this would be to infer that we are unable to judge of any thing, because we are unable to judge of all things. Reason can, and it ought to judge, not only of the meaning, but also of the morality and the evidence of revelation. *First,* It is the province of reason to judge of the morality of the Scripture; *i. e.* not whether it contains things different from what we should have expected from a wise, just, and good Being; for objections from hence have been now obviated: but whether it contains things plainly contradictory to wisdom, justice, or goodness; to what the light of nature teaches us of God. And I know nothing of this sort objected against Scripture, excepting such ob-

things, together with some other improvements, gave full scope for riches to increase in the hands of particular persons, and likewise to circulate into more hands. Now this, though it was not the first origin of covetousness, yet it gives greater scope, encouragement, and temptation to covetousness than it had before. And there is moreover the appearance, that this artificial kind of riches, money, has begot an artificial kind of passion for them: both which follies well-disposed persons must, by all means, endeavour to keep clear of. For indeed *the love of riches is the root of all evil:** though riches themselves may be made instrumental in promoting every thing that is good.

The improvement of trade and commerce has made another change, just hinted at, and I think a very happy one, in the state of the world, as it has enlarged the middle rank of people: many of which are, in good measure, free from the vices of the highest and the lowest part of mankind. Now these persons must remember, that whether, in common language, they do or do not pass under the denomination of rich, yet they really are so, with regard to the indigent and necessitous; and that considering the great numbers which make up this middle rank among us, and how much they mix with the poor, they are able to contribute very largely to their relief, and have in all respects a very great influence over them.

You have heard now the origin and progress of what this great city so much abounds with, riches; as far as I had occasion to speak of these things. For this brief account of them has been laid before you for the sake of the good admonitions it afforded. Nor will the admonitions be thought foreign to the charities, which we are endeavouring to promote. For these must necessarily be less, and the occasions for them greater, in proportion as industry should abate, or luxury increase. And the temper of covetousness is, we all know, directly contrary to that of charity, and eats out the very heart of it. Then, lastly, there are good sort of people who really want to be told, that they are included in the admonitions to be

* Tim. vi. 10.

given to the rich, though they do see others richer than themselves.

The ranks of rich and poor being thus formed, they *meet together;* they continue to make up one society. The mutual want, which they still have of each other, still unites them inseparably. But they *meet* upon a foot of great inequality. For, as Solomon expresses it in brief, and with much force, *the rich ruleth over the poor.** And this their general intercourse, with the superiority on one hand, and dependence on the other, are in no sort accidental, but arise necessarily from a settled providential disposition of things, for their common good. Here then is a real, standing relation between the rich and the poor. And the former must take care to perform the duties belonging to their part of it, for these chiefly the present occasion leads me to speak to, from regard to Him, who placed them in that relation to the poor, from whence those duties arise, and who *is the Maker of them all.*

What these duties are, will easily be seen, and the obligations to them strongly enforced, by a little further reflection upon both these ranks, and the natural situation which they are in with respect to each other.

The lower rank of mankind go on, for the most part, in some tract of living, into which they got by direction or example; and to this their understanding and discourse, as well as labour, are greatly confined. Their opinions of persons and things they take upon trust. Their behaviour has very little in it original or of home-growth; very little which may not be traced up to the influence of others, and less which is not capable of being changed by such influence. Then as God has made plentiful provision for all his creatures, the wants of all, even of the poorest, might be supplied, so far as it is fit they should, by a proper distribution of it. This being the condition of the lower part of mankind, consider now what influence, as well as power, their superiors must, from the nature of the case, have over them. For they can instil instruction, and recommend it in a peculiar manner by their example, and enforce it still further with

* Prov. xxii. 7.

favour and discouragement of various kinds. And experience shows, that they do direct and change the course of the world as they please. Not only the civil welfare, but the morals and religion of their fellow creatures, greatly depend upon them; much more indeed than they would, if the common people were not greatly wanting to their duty. All this is evidently true of superiors in general; superiors in riches, authority, and understanding, taken together. And need I say how much of this whole superiority goes along with riches? It is no small part of it, which arises out of riches themselves. In all governments, particularly in our own, a good share of civil authority accompanies them. Superior natural understanding may, or may not: but when it does not, yet riches afford great opportunities for improvement, and may command information; which things together are equivalent to natural superiority of understanding.

But I am sure you will not think I have been reminding you of these advantages of riches in order to beget in you that complacency and trust in them, which you find the Scripture every where warning you against. No: the importance of riches, this their power and influence, affords the most serious admonition in the world to those who are possessed of them. For it shows, how very blameable even their carelessness in the use of that power and influence must be: since it must be blameable in a degree proportionate to the importance of what they are thus careless about.

But it is not only true, that the rich have the power of doing a great deal of good, and must be highly blameable for neglecting to do it: but it is moreover true, that this power is given them by way of trust, in order to their keeping down that vice and misery, with which the lower people would otherwise be quite overrun. For without instruction and good influence they, of course, grow rude and vicious, and reduce themselves to the utmost distresses; often to very terrible ones without deserving much blame. And to these must be added their unavoidable distresses, which yet admit of relief. This their case plainly requires, that some natural provision should be made for it: as the case of children does, who, if left to their own ways, would almost infallibly ruin themselves. Accordingly Providence has made provision for this case of the poor: not only by forming their minds peculiarly apt to be influenced by their superiors, and giving those superiors abilities to direct and relieve them; but also by putting the latter under the care and protection of the former: for this is plainly done, by means of that intercourse of various kinds between them, which in the natural course of things, is unavoidably necessary. In the primitive ages of the world, the manner in which *the rich and the poor met together*, was in families. Rich men had the poor for their servants: not only a few for the offices about their persons, and for the care of what we now call domestic affairs; but great numbers also for the keeping of their cattle, the tillage of their fields, for working up their wool into furniture and vestments of necessary use as well as ornament, and for preparing them those many things at home, which now pass through a multitude of unknown poor hands successively, and are by them prepared, at a distance, for the use of the rich. The instruction of these large families, and the oversight of their morals and religion, plainly belonged to the heads of them. And that obvious humanity, which every one feels, must have induced them to be kind to all whom they found under their roof, in sickness and old age. In this state of the world, the relation between the rich and the poor could not but be universally seen and acknowledged. Now indeed it is less in sight, by means of artificial methods of carrying on business, which yet are not blameable. But the relation still subsists, and the obligations arising out of it; and cannot but remain the same, whilst the rich have the same want of the poor, and make the same use of them, though not so immediately under their eye; and whilst the instruction, and manners, and good or bad state of the poor, really depend in so great a degree upon the rich, as all these things evidently do; partly in their capacity of magistrates, but very much also in their private capacity. In short, he who has distributed men into these different ranks, and at the same time united them into one society, in such sort as men are united, has, by this constitution of things, formally put the poor under the superintendency and patronage of the rich. The rich then are charged, by natural providence, as much as by revealed appointment, with the care of the poor: not to maintain them idle; which, were it possible they could be so maintained, would produce greater mischiefs than those which charity is to prevent; but to take care, that they maintain themselves by their labour, or in case they cannot, then to relieve them; to restrain their vices, and form their minds to virtue and religion. This is a trust, yet it is not a burden, but a privilege, annexed to riches. And if every one discharged his share of the trust faithfully, whatever be his share of it, the world would be quite another place from what it is. But that cannot be, till covetousness, debauchery, and every vice, be unknown among the rich. Then, and not before, will the manners of the poor be, in all respects, what they ought to be, and their distresses find the full relief, which they ought to find. And, as far as things of this sort can be calculated, in proportion to the right behaviour of persons whom God has placed in the former of these ranks, will be the right behaviour and good condition of those who are cast into the latter. Every one of ability then is to be persuaded to do somewhat towards this, keeping up a sense of virtue and religion among the poor, and relieving their wants; each as much as he can be persuaded to. Since the generality will not part with their vices, it were greatly to be wished, they would bethink themselves, and do what good they are able, so far only as is consistent with them. A vicious rich man cannot pass through life without doing an incredible deal of mischief, were it only by his example and influence; besides neglecting the most important obligations, which arise from his superior fortune. Yet still, the fewer of them he neglects, and the less mischief he does, the less share of the vices and miseries of his inferiors will lie at his door: the less will be his guilt and punishment. But conscientious persons of this rank must revolve again and again in their minds, how great the trust is, which God has annexed to it. They must each of them consider impartially, what is his own particular share of that trust; which is determined by his situation, character, and fortune together: and then set himself to be as useful as he can in those particular ways, which he finds thus marked out for him. This is exactly the precept of St Peter: *As every man hath received the gift, even so minister the same one to another, as good stewards of the manifold grace of God.** And as rich men, by a right direction of their greater capacity, may entitle themselves to a greater reward; so by a wrong direction of it, or even by great negligence, they may become *partakers of other men's sins,*† and chargeable with other men's miseries. For if there be at all any measures of proportion, any sort of regularity and order in the administration of things, it is self-evident, that *unto whomsover much is given, of him shall much be required: and to whom much is committed, of him shall more be demanded.*‡

But still it is to be remembered, that every man's behaviour is his own concern, for every one must give account of his own works; and that the lower people are very greatly to blame in yielding to any ill influence, particularly following the ill example of their superiors; though these are more to blame in setting them such an example. For, as our Lord declares, in the words immediately preceding those just mentioned, *that servant which knew his Lord's will, and prepared not himself, neither did according to his will, shall be beaten with many stripes. But he that knew not, and did commit things worthy of stripes, shall be beaten with few stripes.*§ Vice is itself of ill desert, and therefore shall be punished in all, though its ill desert is greater or less, and so shall be its punishment, in proportion to men's knowledge of God and religion: but it is in the most literal sense true, that *he who knew not his Lord's will, and committed things worthy of stripes, shall be beaten,* though *with few stripes.* For it being the discernment, that such and such actions are evil, which renders them vicious in him who does them, ignorance of other things, though it may lessen,

* 1 Pet. iv. 10. † 1 Tim. v. 22. ‡ Luke xii. 48. § Luke xii. 47, 48.

yet it cannot remit the punishment of such actions in a just administration, because it cannot destroy the guilt of them: much less can corrupt deference and regard to the example of superiors in matters of plain duty and sin have this effect. Indeed the lowest people know very well, that such ill example affords no reason why they should do ill; but they hope it will be an excuse for them, and thus deceive themselves to their ruin: which is a forcible reason why their superiors should not lay this snare in their way.

All this approves itself to our natural understanding; though it is by means of Christianity chiefly, that it is thus enforced upon our consciences. And Christianity, as it is more than a dispensation of goodness, in the general notion of goodness, even a dispensation of forgiveness, of mercy and favour on God's part, does in a peculiar manner heighten our obligations to charity among ourselves. *In this was manifested the love of God towards us,*—that *he sent his Son to be the propitiation for our sins. Beloved, if God so loved us, we ought also to love one another.** With what unanswerable force is that question of our Lord to be applied to every branch of this duty, *Shouldest not thou also have compassion on thy fellow-servant, even as I had pity on thee?*† And can there be a stronger inducement to endeavour the reformation of the world, and bringing it to a sense of virtue and religion, than the assurance given us, *that he which converteth a sinner from the error of his way,* and, in like manner, he also who preventeth a person's being corrupted, by taking care of his education, *shall save a soul from death, and hide a multitude of sins?*‡

These things lead us to the following observations on the several charities, which are the occasion of these annual solemnities.

1. What we have to bestow in charity being a trust, we cannot discharge it faithfully, without taking some care to satisfy ourselves in some degree, that we bestow it upon the proper objects of charity. One hears persons complaining, that it is difficult to distinguish who are such; yet often seeming to forget, that this is a reason

* 1 John iv. 9, 10, 11. † Matt. xviii. 33. ‡ James v 20.

for using their best endeavours to do it. And others make a custom of giving to idle vagabonds: a kind of charity, very improperly so called, which one really wonders people can allow themselves in; merely to be relieved from importunity, or at best to gratify a false good nature. For they cannot but know, that it is, at least, very doubtful, whether what they thus give will not immediately be spent in riot and debauchery. Or suppose it be not, yet still they know, they do a great deal of certain mischief, by encouraging this shameful trade of begging in the streets, and all the disorders which accompany it. But the charities towards which I now ask your assistance, as they are always open, so every one may contribute to them with full assurance, that he bestows upon proper objects, and in general that he does vastly more good, than by equal sums given separately to particular persons. For that these charities really have these advantages, has been fully made out, by some who have gone before me in the duty I am discharging, and by the reports annually published at this time.

Here the Report annexed was read.

Let us thank God for these charities, in behalf of the poor; and also on our own behalf, as they give us such clear opportunities of doing good. Indeed without them, vice and misery, of which there is still so much, would abound so much more in this populous city, as to render it scarce an habitable place.

2. Amongst the peculiar advantages of public charities above private ones, is also to be mentioned, that they are examples of great influence. They serve for perpetual memorials of what I have been observing, of the relation which subsists between the rich and the poor, and the duties which arise out of it. They are standing admonitions to all within sight or hearing of them, to *go and do likewise.** Educating poor children in virtue and religion, relieving the sick, and correcting offenders in order to their amendment, are, in themselves, some of the very best of good works. These charities would indeed be the glory of your city, though their influence were

* Luke x. 37.

confined to it. But important as they are in themselves, their importance still increases, by their being examples to the rest of the nation; which, in process of time, of course copies after the metropolis. It has indeed already imitated every one of these charities; for of late, the most difficult and expensive of them, hospitals for the sick and wounded, have been established; some within your sight, others in remote parts of the kingdom. You will give me leave to mention particularly that* in its second trading city; which is conducted with such disinterested fidelity and prudence, as I dare venture to compare with yours. Again, there are particular persons very blameably unactive and careless, yet not without good dispositions, who, by these charities, are reminded of their duty, and *provoked to love and to good works.*† And let me add, though one is sorry any should want so slight a reason for contributing to the most excellent designs, yet if any are supposed to do so merely of course, because they see others do it, still they help to support these monuments of charity, which are a continued admonition to the rich, and relief to the poor: and herein all good men *rejoice*, as St Paul speaks of himself in a like case, *yea, and will rejoice.*‡

3. As all human schemes admit of improvement, all public charities, methinks, should be considered as standing open to proposals for it; that the whole plan of them, in all its parts, may be brought to as great perfection as is possible. Now it should seem, that employing some share of the children's time in easy labour, suitable to their age, which is done in some of our charity schools, might be done in most others of them, with very good effect; as it is in all those of a neighbouring kingdom. Then as the only purposes of punishments less than

* As it is of very particular benefit to those, who ought always to be looked upon with particular favour by us, I mean our seamen; so likewise it is of very extensive benefit to the large tracts of country west and north of it. Then the medicinal waters near the city render it a still more proper situation for an infirmary. And so likewise does its neighbourhood to the Bath hospital. For it may well be supposed, that some poor objects will be sent thither in hopes of relief from the Bath waters, whose case may afterwards be found to require the assistance of physic or surgery: and on the other hand, that some may be sent to our infirmary for help from those arts, whose case may be found to require the Bath waters. So that if I am not greatly partial, the Bristol infirmary as much deserves encouragement as any charitable foundation in the kingdom.

† Heb. x. 24.

‡ Phil. i. 18.

capital are to reform the offenders themselves, and warn the innocent by their example, every thing which should contribute to make this kind of punishments answer these purposes better than it does, would be a great improvement. And whether it be not a thing practicable, and what would contribute somewhat towards it, to exclude utterly all sorts of revel-mirth from places where offenders are confined, to separate the young from the old, and force them both, in solitude, with labour and low diet, to make the experiment, how far their natural strength of mind can support them under guilt and shame and poverty; this may deserve consideration. Then again, some religious instruction particularly adapted to their condition would as properly accompany those punishments which are intended to reform, as it does capital ones. God forbid that I should be understood to discourage the provision which is made for it in this latter case: I heartily wish it were better than it is; especially since it may well be supposed, as the state of religion is at present among us, that some condemned malefactors may have never had the doctrine of the gospel enforced upon their consciences. But since it must be acknowledged of greater consequence, in a religious as well as civil respect, how persons live, than how they die; it cannot but be even more incumbent on us to endeavour, in all ways, to reclaim those offenders who are to return again into the world, than those who are to be removed out of it: and the only effectual means of reclaiming them, is to instil into them a principle of religion. If persons of authority and influence would take things of this and a like kind under their consideration, they might perhaps still improve those charities; which are already, I truly believe, under a better management than any other of so large a compass in the world. But,

4. With regard to the two particular branches of them last mentioned, I would observe, that our laws and whole constitution, civil and ecclesiastical, go more upon supposition of an equality amongst mankind, than the constitution and laws of other countries. Now this plainly requires that more particular regard should be had to the education of the lower people here, than in

places, where they are born slaves of power, and to be made slaves of superstition. It is, I suppose, acknowledged, that they have greater liberty here, than they have any where else in the world. But unless care be taken for giving them some inward principle, to prevent their abusing this greater liberty which is their birthright, can we expect it will prove a blessing to them? or will they not in all probability become more dissolute, or more wild and extravagant, whatever wrong turn they happen to take, than people of the same rank in other countries?

5. Let me again remind you of the additional reason, which persons of fortune have to take particular care of their whole behaviour, that it be in all respects good and exemplary, upon account of the influence which it will have upon the manners of their inferiors. And pray observe how strictly this is connected with the occasion of our present meeting; how much your good behaviour in private life will contribute to promote the good design of all these charities; and how much the contrary would tend to defeat it, and even to produce the evils which they are intended to prevent or to remedy. Whatever care be taken in the education of these poor children at school, there is always danger of their being corrupted, when they come from it. And this danger is greater, in proportion to the greater wickedness of the age they are to pass through. But if, upon their coming abroad into the world, they find the principles of virtue and religion recommended by the example of their superiors, and vice and irreligion really discountenanced, this will confirm them in the good principles in which they have been brought up, and give the best ground to hope they will never depart from them. And the like is to be said of offenders, who may have had a sense of virtue and religion wrought in them, under the discipline of labour and confinement. Again; dissolute and debauched persons of fortune greatly increase the general corruption of manners; and this is what increases want and misery of all kinds. So that they may contribute largely to any or all of these charities, and yet undo but a very small part of the mischief which they do, by their example, as well as in other ways. But still this mischief which they

do, suppose by their example, is an additional reason why they should contribute to them; even in justice to particular persons, in whose ruin they may have an unknown share of guilt; or however in justice to society in general; for which they will deserve commendation, how blameable soever they are for the other. And indeed amidst the dark prospect before us, from that profligateness of manners, and scorn of religion, which so generally abound, this good spirit of charity to the poor discovering itself in so great a degree, upon these occasions, and likewise in the late necessitous time, even amongst persons far from being blameless in other respects; this cannot but afford hopes, that we are not given over by Providence, and also that they themselves will at length consider, and not go on contributing, by the example of their vices, to the introduction of that distress, which they so commendably relieve by their liberality.

To conclude: Let our charity towards men be exalted into piety towards God, from the serious consideration, that we are all his creatures; a consideration which enforces that duty upon our consciences, as we have any regard to him. This kind of adjuration, and a most solemn one it is, one often hears profaned by a very unworthy sort of people, when they ask relief *for God's sake.* But surely the principle itself, which contains in it every thing great, and just, and good, is grievously forgotten among us. To relieve the poor *for God's sake*, is to do it in conformity to the order of nature, and to his will, and his example, who is the Author and Governor of it; and in thankful remembrance, that all we have is from his bounty. It is to do it in his behalf, and as to him. For *he that hath pity upon the poor lendeth unto the Lord:** and our Saviour has declared, that he will take as given to himself, what is given in a well-chosen charity.† Lastly, it is to do it under a sense of the account which will be required of what is committed to our trust, when *the rich and poor*, who *meet* here upon terms of so great inequality, shall *meet* hereafter upon a level, before him who *is the Maker of them all.*

* Prov. xix. 17. † Matt. xxv. 40.

SERMON III.

PREACHED BEFORE THE HOUSE OF LORDS, IN THE ABBEY-CHURCH OF WESTMINSTER, ON FRIDAY, JANUARY 30, 1740-41, BEING THE DAY APPOINTED TO BE OBSERVED AS THE DAY OF THE MARTYRDOM OF KING CHARLES I.

And not using your liberty for a cloak of maliciousness, but as the servants of God.—1 Peter ii. 16.

A HISTORY so full of important and interesting events as that which this day recalls annually to our thoughts, cannot but afford them very different subjects for their most serious and useful employment. But there seems none which it more naturally leads us to consider than that of hypocrisy, as it sets before us so many examples of it; or which will yield us more practical instruction, as these examples so forcibly admonish us, not only to be upon our guard against the pernicious effects of this vice in others, but also to watch over our own hearts, against every thing of the like kind in ourselves: for hypocrisy, in the moral and religious consideration of things, is of much larger extent than every one may imagine.

In common language, which is formed upon the common intercourses amongst men, hypocrisy signifies little more than their pretending what they really do not mean, in order to delude one another. But in Scripture, which treats chiefly of our behaviour towards God and our own consciences, it signifies, not only the endeavour to delude our fellow creatures, but likewise insincerity towards him, and towards ourselves. And therefore, according to the whole analogy of Scripture language, *to use liberty as a cloak of maliciousness,** must be under-

* The hypocrisy laid to the charge of the Pharisees and Sadducees, in Matt. xvi. at the beginning, and in Luke xii. 54, is determinately this, that their vicious passions blinded them so as to prevent their discerning the evidence of our Saviour's mission; though no more understanding was necessary to discern it, than what they had, and made use of in common matters. Here they are called hypocrites merely upon account of their insincerity towards God and their own consciences, and not at all upon account of any insincerity towards men. This last indeed is included in that general hypocrisy, which, throughout the gospels, is represented as their distinguished character; but the former is as much included. For they were not men, who, without any belief at all of religion, put on the appearance of it only in order to deceive the world: on the contrary, they believed their religion, and were zealous in it. But their

stood to mean, not only endeavouring to impose upon others, by indulging wayward passions, or carrying on indirect designs, under pretences of it; but also excusing and palliating such things to ourselves; serving ourselves of such pretences to quiet our own minds in any thing which is wrong.

Liberty in the writings of the New Testament, for the most part, signifies, being delivered from the bondage of the ceremonial law; or of sin and the devil, which St Paul calls *the glorious liberty of the children of God.** This last is a progressive state: and the perfection of it, whether attainable in this world or not, consists in that *perfect love,*† which St John speaks of; and which, as it implies an entire coincidence of our wills with the will of God, must be a state of the most absolute freedom, in the most literal and proper sense. But whatever St Peter distinctly meant by this word, *liberty*, the text gives occasion to consider any kind of it, which is liable to the abuse he here warns us against. However, it appears that he meant to comprehend that liberty, were it more

religion, which they believed, and were zealous in, was in its nature hypocritical: for it was the form, not the reality; it allowed them in immoral practices; and indeed was itself in some respects immoral, as they indulged their pride and uncharitableness under the notion of zeal for it. See Jer. ix. 6, Psalm lxxviii. 36. Job iii. 19. and Matt. xv. 7—14. and xxiii. 13, 16, 19, 24, 26. where *hypocrite* and *blind* are used promiscuously. Again, the Scripture speaks of the *deceitfulness of sin;* and its deceiving those who are guilty of it: Heb. iii. 13. Eph. iv. 22. Rom. vii. 11. of men's acting as if they could *deceive and mock God:* Is. xxix. 15. Acts v. 3. Gal. vi. 7. of their *blinding their own eyes:* Matt. iii. 15. Acts xxviii. 27. and *deceiving themselves;* which is quite a different thing from being deceived. 1 Cor. iii. 18. 1 John i. 8. Galatians vi. 3. James i. 22, 26. Many more coincident passages might be mentioned: but I will add only one. In 2 Thess. ii. it is foretold that by means of some *force*, some *energy of delusion*, men should believe *the lie* which is there treated of: this *force of delusion* is not any thing without them, but somewhat within them, which it is expressly said they should bring upon themselves, by *not receiving the love of the truth, but having pleasure in unrighteousness*. Answering to all this is that very remarkable passage of our Lord, Matt. vi. 22, 23. Luke xi. 34, 35. and that admonition repeated fourteen times in the New Testament; *He that hath ears to hear, let him hear*. And the ground of this whole manner of considering things; for it is not to be spoken of as only a peculiar kind of phraseology, but is a most accurate and strictly just manner of considering characters and moral conduct; the ground of it I say, is, that when persons will not be influenced by such evidence in religion as they act upon in the daily course of life, or when their notions of religion (and I might add of virtue) are in any sort reconcileable with what is vicious, it is some faulty negligence or prejudice which thus deludes them; in very different ways, perhaps, and very different degrees. But when any one is thus deluded through his own fault, in whatever way or degree it is, he deludes himself. And this is as properly hypocrisy towards himself, as deluding the world is hypocrisy towards the world: and he who is guilty of it acts as if he could deceive and mock God: and therefore is an hypocrite towards him, in as strict and literal a sense as the nature of the subject will admit.

* Rom. viii. 21. † 1 John iv. 18.

or less, which they to whom he was writing enjoyed under civil government: for of civil government he is speaking just before and afterwards: *Submit yourselves to every ordinance of man for the Lord's sake: whether it be to the king, as supreme; or unto governors, as unto them that are sent by him. For so is the will of God, that with well-doing,* of which dutiful behaviour towards authority is a very material instance, *ye may put to silence the ignorance of foolish men:** *as free,* perhaps in distinction from the servile state, of which he speaks afterwards, *and not using your liberty for a cloak of maliciousness,*† of any thing wrong, for so the word signifies; and therefore comprehends petulance, affection of popularity, with any other like frivolous turn of mind, as well as the more hateful and dangerous passions, such as malice, or ambition; for all of which *liberty* may equally be *used as a cloak.* The apostle adds, *but as the servants of God: as free—but as his servants,* who requires dutiful submission to *every ordinance of man,* to magistracy; and to whom we are accountable for our manner of using the liberty we enjoy under it; as well as for all other parts of our behaviour. *Not using your liberty as a cloak of maliciousness, but as the servants of God.*

Here are three things offered to our consideration:

First, A general supposition, that what is wrong cannot be avowed in its proper colours, but stands in need of some *cloak* to be thrown over it: Secondly, A particular one, that there is danger, some singular danger, of liberty's being made use of for this purpose: Lastly, An admonition not to make this ill use of our liberty, *but* to use it *as the servants of God.*

I. Here is a general supposition, that what is wrong cannot be avowed in its proper colours, but stands in need of some *cloak* to be thrown over it. God has constituted our nature, and the nature of society, after such a manner, that generally speaking, men cannot encourage or support themselves in wickedness upon the foot of there being no difference between right and wrong, or by a direct avowal of wrong; but by disguising it, and endeavouring to spread over it some colours of right.

* 1 Pet. ii. 13—15. † Ver. 16.

And they do this in every capacity and every respect, in which there is a right or a wrong. They do it, not only as social creatures under civil government, but also as moral agents under the government of God; in one case to make a proper figure in the world, and delude their fellow creatures; in the other to keep peace within themselves, and delude their own consciences. And the delusion in both cases being voluntary, is, in Scripture, called by one name, and spoken against in the same manner: though doubtless they are much more explicit with themselves, and more distinctly conscious of what they are about, in one case than in the other.

The fundamental laws of all governments are virtuous ones, prohibiting treachery, injustice, cruelty: and the law of reputation enforces those civil laws, by rendering these vices everywhere infamous, and the contrary virtues honourable and of good report. Thus far the constitution of society is visibly moral: and hence it is, that men cannot live in it without taking care to cover those vices when they have them, and make some profession of the opposite virtues, fidelity, justice, kind regard to others, when they have them not: but especially is this necessary in order to disguise and colour over indirect purposes, which require the concurrence of several persons.

Now all false pretences of this kind are to be called hypocritical, as being contrary to simplicity; though not always designed, properly speaking, to beget a false belief. For it is to be observed, that they are often made without any formal intention to have them believed, or to have it thought that there is any reality under these pretences. Many examples occur of verbal professions of fidelity, justice, public regards, in cases where there could be no imagination of their being believed. And what other account can be given of these merely verbal professions, but that they were thought the proper language for the public ear; and made in business for the very same kind of reasons as civility is kept up in conversation?

These false professions of virtue, which men have, in all ages, found it necessary to make their appearance with abroad, must have been originally taken up in order to deceive in the proper sense: then they became habitual, and often intended merely by way of form: yet often still, to serve their original purpose of deceiving.

There is doubtless amongst mankind a great deal of this hypocrisy towards each other: but not so much as may sometimes be supposed. For part which has, at first sight, this appearance, is in reality that other hypocrisy before mentioned; that self-deceit, of which the Scripture so remarkably takes notice. There are indeed persons who *live without God in the world:** and some appear so hardened as to keep no measures with themselves. But as very ill men may have a real and strong sense of virtue and religion, in proportion as this is the case with any, they cannot be easy within themselves but by deluding their consciences. And though they should, in great measure, get over their religion, yet this will not do. For as long as they carry about with them any such sense of things, as makes them condemn what is wrong in others, they could not but condemn the same in themselves, and dislike and be disgusted with their own character and conduct, if they would consider them distinctly, and in a full light. But this sometimes they carelessly neglect to do, and sometimes carefully avoid doing. And as *the integrity of the upright guides him,*† guides even a man's judgment so wickedness may distort it to such a degree, as that he may *call evil good, and good evil; put darkness for light, and light for darkness;*‡ and *think wickedly, that God is such an one as himself.*§ Even the better sort of men are, in some degree, liable to disguise and palliate their failings to themselves: but perhaps there are few men who go on calmly in a course of very bad things, without somewhat of the kind now described in a very high degree. They try appearances upon themselves as well as upon the world, and with at least as much success; and choose to manage so as to make their own minds easy with their faults, which can scarce be without management, rather than to mend them.

* Eph. ii. 12. † Prov xi. 3. ‡ Isa. v. 20. § Psalm l. 21.

But whether from men's deluding themselves, or from their intending to delude the world, it is evident scarce any thing wrong in public has ever been accomplished, or even attempted, but under false colours: either by pretending one thing, which was right, to be designed, when it was really another thing, which was wrong; or if that which was wrong was avowed, by endeavouring to give it some appearance of right. For tyranny, and faction so friendly to it, and which is indeed tyranny out of power, and unjust wars, and persecution, by which the earth has been laid waste; all this has all along been carried on with pretences of truth, right, general good. So it is, men cannot find in their heart to join in such things, without such honest words to be the bond of the union, though they know among themselves, that they are only words, and often though they know, that every body else knows it too.

These observations might be exemplified by numerous instances in the history which led to them: and without them it is impossible to understand in any sort the general character of the chief actors in it, who were engaged in the black design of subverting the constitution of their country. This they completed with the most enormous act of mere power, in defiance of all laws of God and man, and in express contradiction to the real design and public votes of that assembly, whose commission, they professed, was their only warrant for any thing they did throughout the whole rebellion. Yet with unheard-of hypocrisy towards men, towards God and their own consciences, for without such a complication of it their conduct is inexplicable; even this action, which so little admitted of any cloak, was, we know, contrived and carried into execution, under pretences of authority, religion, liberty, and by profaning the forms of justice in an arraignment and trial, like to what is used in regular legal procedures. No age indeed can show an example of hypocrisy parallel to this. But the history of all ages and all countries will show, what has been really going forward over the face of the earth, to be very different from what has been always pretended; and that virtue has been every where professed much more than it has been any where practised; nor could society, from the very nature of its constitution, subsist without some general public profession of it. Thus the face and appearance which the world has in all times put on, for the ease and ornament of life, and in pursuit of further ends, is the justest satire upon what has in all times been carrying on under it: and ill men are destined, by the condition of their being as social creatures, always to bear about with them, and, in different degrees, to profess, that law of virtue, by which they shall finally be judged and condemned.

II. As fair pretences, of one sort or other, have thus always been made use of by mankind to colour over indirect and wrong designs from the world, and to palliate and excuse them to their own minds; liberty, in common with all other good things, is liable to be made this use of, and is also liable to it in a way more peculiar to itself: which was the second thing to be considered.

In the history which this day refers us to, we find our constitution, in Church and State, destroyed under pretences, not only of religion, but of securing liberty, and carrying it to a greater height. The destruction of the former was with zeal of such a kind, as would not have been warrantable, though it had been employed in the destruction of heathenism. And the confusions, the persecuting spirit, and incredible fanaticism, which grew up upon its ruins, cannot but teach sober-minded men to reverence so mild and reasonable an establishment, now it is restored; for the preservation of Christianity, and keeping up a sense of it amongst us, and for the instruction and guide of the ignorant; nay were it only for guarding religion from such extravagances: especially as these important purposes are served by it without being hard in the least upon any.

And the concurrent course of things, which brought on the ruin of our civil constitution, and what followed upon it, are no less instructive. The opposition, by legal and parliamentary methods, to prerogatives unknown to the constitution, was doubtless formed upon the justest fears in behalf of it. But new distrusts arose: new causes were given for them: these were most unreasonably aggravated. The better part gradually gave way to the more violent: and the better part themselves seem to have insisted upon impracticable securities against that one danger to liberty, of which they had too great cause to be apprehensive; and wonderfully overlooked all dangers to it, which yet were, and ever will be, many and great. Thus they joined in the current measures, till they were utterly unable to stop the mischiefs, to which, with too much distrust on one side, and too little on the other, they had contributed. Never was a more remarkable example of the Wise Man's observation, that *the beginning of strife is as when one letteth out water.** For this opposition, thus begun, surely without intent of proceeding to violence; yet, as it went on, like an overflowing stream in its progress, it collected all sort of impurities, and grew more outrageous as it grew more corrupted; 'till at length it bore down every thing good before it. This naturally brought on arbitrary power in one shape, which was odious to every body, and which could not be accommodated to the forms of our constitution; and put us in the utmost danger of having it entailed upon us under another, which might. For at the king's return, such was the just indignation of the public at what it had seen, and fear of feeling again what it had felt, from the popular side; such the depression and compliance, not only of the more guilty, but also of those, who with better meaning had gone on with them; and a great deal too far many of this character had gone; and such the undistinguishing distrust the people had of them all, that the chief security of our liberties seems to have been, their not being attempted at that time.

But though persons contributed to all this mischief and danger with different degrees of guilt, none could contribute to them with innocence, who at all knew what they were about. Indeed the destruction of a free constitution of government, though men see or fancy many defects in it, and whatever they design or pretend, ought not to be thought of without horror. For the design is in itself unjust, since it is romantic to suppose it legal: it cannot be prosecuted without the most wicked

* Prov. xvii. 14.

means; nor accomplished but with the present ruin of liberty, religious as well as civil; for it must be the ruin of its present security. Whereas the restoration of it must depend upon a thousand future contingencies, the integrity, understanding, power of the persons, into whose hands anarchy and confusion should throw things; and who they will be, the history before us may surely serve to show, no human foresight can determine; even though such a terrible crisis were to happen in an age, not distinguished for the want of principle and public spirit, and when nothing particular were to be apprehended from abroad. It would be partiality to say, that no constitution of government can possibly be imagined more perfect than our own. And ingenuous youth may be warmed with the idea of one, against which nothing can be objected. But it is the strongest objection against attempting to put in practice the most perfect theory, that it is impracticable, or too dangerous to be attempted. And whoever will thoroughly consider, in what degree mankind are really influenced by reason, and in what degree by custom, may, I think, be convinced, that the state of human affairs does not even admit of an equivalent for the mischief of setting things afloat; and the danger of parting with those securities of liberty, which arise from regulations of long prescription and ancient usage; especially at a time when the directors are so very numerous, and the obedient so few. Reasonable men therefore will look upon the general plan of our constitution, transmitted down to us by our ancestors, as sacred; and content themselves with calmly doing what their station requires, towards rectifying the particular things which they think amiss, and supplying the particular things which they think deficient in it, so far as is practicable without endangering the whole.

But liberty is in many other dangers from itself, besides those which arise from formed designs of destroying it, under hypocritical pretences, or romantic schemes of restoring it upon a more perfect plan. It is particularly liable to become excessive, and to degenerate insensibly into licentiousness; in the same manner as liberality, for example, is apt to degenerate into extravagance.

And as men cloak their extravagance to themselves under the notion of liberality, and to the world under the name of it, so licentiousness passes under the name and notion of liberty. Now it is to be observed, that there is, in some respects or other, a very peculiar contrariety between those vices which consist in excess, and the virtues of which they are said to be the excess, and the resemblance, and whose names they affect to bear; the excess of any thing being always to its hurt, and tending to its destruction. In this manner licentiousness is, in its very nature, a present infringement upon liberty, and dangerous to it for the future. Yet it is treated by many persons with peculiar indulgence under this very notion, as being an excess of liberty. And an excess of liberty it is to the licentious themselves: but what is it to those who suffer by them, and who do not think, that amends is at all made them by having it left in their power to retaliate safely? When by popular insurrections, or defamatory libels, or in any like way, the needy and the turbulent securely injure quiet people in their fortune or good name, so far quiet people are no more free than if a single tyrant used them thus. A particular man may be licentious without being less free: but a community cannot; since the licentiousness of one will unavoidably break in upon the liberty of another. Civil liberty, the liberty of a community, is a severe and a restrained thing; implies in the notion of it, authority, settled subordinations, subjection, and obedience; and is altogether as much hurt by too little of this kind, as by too much of it. And the love of liberty, when it is indeed the love of liberty, which carries us to withstand tyranny, will as much carry us to reverence authority, and support it; for this most obvious reason, that one is as necessary to the very being of liberty, as the other is destructive of it. And therefore the love of liberty, which does not produce this effect; the love of liberty, which is not a real principle of dutiful behaviour towards authority; is as hypocritical, as the religion which is not productive of a good life. Licentiousness is, in truth, such an excess of liberty as is of the same nature with tyranny. For what is the difference between them, but that one is lawless power exercised under pretence of authority, or by persons invested with it; the other lawless power exercised under pretence of liberty, or without any pretence at all? A people then must always be less free in proportion as they are more licentious; licentiousness being not only different from liberty, but directly contrary to it; a direct breach upon it.

It is moreover of a growing nature; and of speedy growth too; and, with the culture which it has amongst us, needs no great length of time to get to such a height as no legal government will be able to restrain, or subsist under: which is the condition the historian describes in saying, they could neither bear their vices, nor the remedies of them.* I said legal government: for, in the present state of the world, there is no danger of our becoming savages. Had licentiousness finished its work, and destroyed our constitution, power would not be wanting, from one quarter or another, sufficient to subdue us, and keep us in subjection. But government, as distinguished from mere power, free government, necessarily implies reverence in the subjects of it, for authority, or power regulated by laws; and an habit of submission to the subordinations in civil life, throughout its several ranks: nor is a people capable of liberty without somewhat of this kind. But it must be observed, and less surely cannot be observed, this reverence and submission will at best be very precarious, if it be not founded upon a sense of authority being God's ordinance, and the subordinations in life a providential appointment of things. Now let it be considered, for surely it is not duly considered, what is really the short amount of those representations, which persons of superior rank give, and encourage to be given of each other, and which are spread over the nation? Is it not somewhat, in itself, and in its circumstances, beyond any thing in any other age or country of the world? And what effect must the continuance of this extravagant licentiousness in them, not to mention other kinds of it, have upon the people in those respects just mentioned? Must it not necessarily tend to wear out of their minds all reverence

* Nec vitia nostra, nec remedia pati possumus.—Liv. lib. i. c. 1.

for authority, and respect for superiors of every sort, and, joined with the irreligious principles we find so industriously propagated, to introduce a total profligateness amongst them; since, let them be as bad as they will, it is scarce possible they can be so bad as they are instructed they may be, or worse than they are told their superiors are? And is there no danger that all this, to mention only one supposable course of it, may raise somewhat like that levelling spirit, upon atheistical principles, which, in the last age, prevailed upon enthusiastic ones? not to speak of the possibility, that different sorts of people may unite in it upon these contrary principles. And may not this spirit, together with a concurrence of ill humours, and of persons who hope to find their account in confusion, soon prevail to such a degree, as will require more of the good old principles of loyalty and of religion to withstand it, than appear to be left amongst us?

What legal remedies can be provided against these mischiefs, or whether any at all, are considerations the farthest from my thoughts. No government can be free, which is not administered by general stated laws: and these cannot comprehend every case, which wants to be provided against: nor can new ones be made for every particular case, as it arises: and more particular laws, as well as more general ones, admit of infinite evasions: and legal government forbids any but legal methods of redress; which cannot but be liable to the same sort of imperfections: besides the additional one of delay; and whilst redress is delayed, however unavoidably, wrong subsists. Then there are very bad things, which human authority can scarce provide against at all, but by methods dangerous to liberty; nor fully, but by such as would be fatal to it. These things show, that liberty, in the very nature of it, absolutely requires, and even supposes, that people be able to govern themselves in those respects in which they are free; otherwise their wickedness will be in proportion to their liberty, and this greatest of blessings will become a curse.

III. These things show likewise, that there is but one adequate remedy to the forementioned evils, even that which the apostle prescribes in the last words of the text, to consider ourselves *as the servants of God*, who enjoins dutiful submission to civil authority, as his ordinance; and to whom we are accountable for the use we make of the liberty which we enjoy under it. Since men cannot live out of society, nor in it without government, government is plainly a divine appointment; and consequently submission to it, a most evident duty of the law of nature. And we all know in how forcible a manner it is put upon our consciences in Scripture. Nor can this obligation be denied formally upon any principles, but such as subvert all other obligations. Yet many amongst us seem not to consider it as any obligation at all. This doubtless is, in a great measure, owing to dissoluteness and corruption of manners: but I think it is partly owing to their having reduced it to nothing in theory. Whereas this obligation ought to be put upon the same foot with all other general ones, which are not absolute and without exception: and our submission is due in all cases but those, which we really discern to be exceptions to the general rule. And they who are perpetually displaying the exceptions, though they do not indeed contradict the meaning of any particular texts of Scripture, which surely intended to make no alteration in men's civil rights; yet they go against the general tenor of Scripture. For the Scripture, throughout the whole of it, commands submission; supposing men apt enough of themselves to make the exceptions, and not to need being continually reminded of them. Now if we are really under any obligations of duty at all to magistrates, honour and respect, in our behaviour towards them, must doubtless be their due. And they who refuse to pay them this small and easy regard, who *despise dominion, and speak evil of dignities*,* should seriously ask themselves, what restrains them from any other instance whatever of undutifulness? And if it be principle, why not from this? Indeed free government supposes, that the conduct of affairs may be inquired into, and spoken of with freedom. Yet surely this should be done with decency, for the sake of liberty

* Jude 8.

itself; for its honour and its security. But be it done as it will, it is a very different thing from libelling, and endeavouring to vilify the persons of such as are in authority. It will be hard to find an instance, in which a serious man could calmly satisfy himself in doing this It is in no case necessary, and in every case of very pernicious tendency. But the immorality of it increases in proportion to the integrity and superior rank of the persons thus treated. It is therefore in the highest degree immoral, when it extends to the supreme authority in the person of a prince, from whom our liberties are in no imaginable danger, whatever they may be from ourselves; and whose mild and strictly legal government could not but make any virtuous people happy.

A free government, which the good providence of God has preserved to us through innumerable dangers, is an invaluable blessing. And our ingratitude to him in abusing of it must be great in proportion to the greatness of the blessing, and the providential deliverances by which it has been preserved to us. Yet the crime of abusing this blessing receives further aggravation from hence, that such abuse always is to the reproach, and tends to the ruin of it. The abuse of liberty has directly overturned many free governments, as well as our own, on the popular side; and has, in various ways, contributed to the ruin of many, which have been overturned on the side of authority. Heavy therefore must be their guilt, who shall be found to have given such advantages against it, as well as theirs who have taken them.

Lastly, The consideration, that we are the servants of God, reminds us, that we are accountable to him for our behaviour in those respects, in which it is out of the reach of all human authority; and is the strongest enforcement of sincerity, as *all things are naked and open unto the eyes of him with whom we have to do.** Artificial behaviour might perhaps avail much towards quieting our consciences, and making our part good in the short competitions of this world: but what will it avail us considered as under the government of God? Under

* Heb. iv. 13.

his government, *there is no darkness, nor shadow of death, where the workers of iniquity may hide themselves.** He has indeed instituted civil government over the face of the earth, *for the punishment of evil-doers, and for the praise*, the apostle does not say the rewarding, but, *for the praise of them that do well.*† Yet as the worst answer these ends in some measure, the best can do it very imperfectly. Civil government can by no means take cognizance of *every work*, which is good or evil; many *things* are done in *secret;* the authors unknown to it, and often the things themselves: then it cannot so much consider actions, under the view of their being morally *good*, or *evil*, as under the view of their being mischievous, or beneficial to society: nor can it in any wise execute *judgment* in rewarding what is *good*, as it can, and ought, and does, in punishing what is *evil*. But *God shall bring every work into judgment, with every secret thing, whether it be good, or whether it be evil.*‡

SERMON IV.

PREACHED IN THE PARISH CHURCH OF CHRIST-CHURCH, LONDON, ON THURSDAY, MAY 9, 1745, BEING THE TIME OF THE YEARLY MEETING OF THE CHILDREN EDUCATED IN THE CHARITY-SCHOOLS IN AND ABOUT THE CITIES OF LONDON AND WESTMINSTER.

Train up a child in the way he should go: and when he is old, he will not depart from it.—Prov. xxii. 6.

HUMAN creatures, from the constitution of their nature and the circumstances in which they are placed, cannot but acquire habits during their childhood, by the impressions which are given them, and their own customary actions. And long before they arrive at mature age, these habits form a general settled character. And the observation of the text, that the most early habits are usually the most lasting, is likewise every one's observation. Now whenever children are left to themselves, and to the guides and companions which they choose, or by hazard light upon, we find by experience, that the first

* Job xxxiv. 22. † 1 Pet. ii. 14. ‡ Eccles. xii. 14.

impressions they take, and course of action they get into, are very bad; and so consequently must be their habits, and character, and future behaviour. Thus if they are not trained up in the way they *should go*, they will certainly be trained up in the way they *should not go*, and in all probability will persevere in it, and become miserable themselves, and mischievous to society: which, in event, is worse, upon account of both, than if they had been exposed to perish in their infancy. On the other hand, the ingenuous docility of children before they have been deceived, their distrust of themselves, and natural deference to grown people, whom they find here settled in a world where they themselves are strangers; and to whom they have recourse for advice, as readily as for protection; which deference is still greater towards those who are placed over them: these things give the justest grounds to expect that they may receive such impressions, and be influenced to such a course of behaviour, as will produce lasting good habits; and, together with the dangers before mentioned, are as truly a natural demand upon us to *train them up in the way they should go*, as their bodily wants are a demand to provide them bodily nourishment. Brute creatures are appointed to do no more than this last for their offspring, nature forming them by instincts to the particular manner of life appointed them; from which they never deviate. But this is so far from being the case of men, that, on the contrary, considering communities collectively, every successive generation is left, in the ordinary course of Providence, to be formed by the preceding one; and becomes good or bad, though not without its own merit or demerit, as this trust is discharged or violated, chiefly in the management of youth.

We ought, doubtless, to instruct and admonish grown persons; to restrain them from what is evil, and encourage them in what is good, as we are able: but this care of youth, abstracted from all consideration of the parental affection, I say, this care of youth, which is the general notion of *education*, becomes a distinct subject, and a distinct duty, from the particular danger of their ruin, if left to themselves, and the particular reason we have to expect they will do well, if due care be taken of them. And from hence it follows, that children have as much right to some proper education, as to have their lives preserved; and that when this is not given them by their parents, the care of it devolves upon all persons, it becomes the duty of all, who are capable of contributing to it, and whose help is wanted.

These trite, but most important things, implied indeed in the text, being thus premised as briefly as I could express them, I proceed to consider distinctly the general manner in which the duty of education is there laid before us: which will further show its extent, and further obviate the idle objections which have been made against it. And all this together will naturally lead us to consider the occasion and necessity of schools for the education of poor children, and in what light the objections against them are to be regarded.

Solomon might probably intend the text for a particular admonition to educate children in a manner suitable to their respective ranks, and future employments: but certainly he intended it for a general admonition to educate them in virtue and religion, and good conduct of themselves in their temporal concerns. And all this together, in which they are to be educated, he calls *the way they should go*, i. e. he mentions it not as a matter of speculation, but of practice. And conformably to this description of the things in which children are to be educated, he describes education itself: for he calls it *training them up;* which is a very different thing from merely teaching them some truths, necessary to be known or believed. It is endeavouring to form such truths into practical principles in the mind, so as to render them of habitual good influence upon the temper and actions, in all the various occurrences of life. And this is not done by bare instruction; but by that, together with admonishing them frequently as occasion offers; restraining them from what is evil, and exercising them in what is good. Thus the precept of the apostle concerning this matter is to *bring up children in the nurture and admonition of the Lord;** as it were

* Eph. vi. 4.

by way of distinction from acquainting them merely with the principles of Christianity, as you would with any common theory. Though education were nothing more than informing children of some truths of importance to them, relating to religion and common life, yet there would be great reason for it, notwithstanding the frivolous objections concerning the danger of giving them prejudices. But when we consider that such information itself is really the least part of it; and that it consists in endeavouring to put them into right dispositions of mind, and right habits of living, in every relation and every capacity; this consideration shows such objections to be quite absurd: since it shows them to be objections against doing a thing of the utmost importance at the natural opportunity of our doing it, childhood and youth; and which is indeed, properly speaking, our only one. For when they are grown up to maturity, they are out of our hands, and must be left to themselves. The natural authority on one side ceases, and the deference on the other. God forbid, that it should be impossible for men to recollect themselves, and reform at an advanced age: but it is in no sort in the power of others to gain upon them; to turn them away from what is wrong, and enforce upon them what is right, at that season of their lives, in the manner we might have done in their childhood.

Doubtless religion requires instruction, for it is founded in knowledge and belief of some truths. And so is common prudence in the management of our temporal affairs Yet neither of them consist in the knowledge or belief even of these fundamental truths; but in our being brought by such knowledge or belief to a correspondent temper and behaviour. Religion, as it stood under the Old Testament, is perpetually styled *the fear of God:* under the New, *faith in Christ.* But as that fear of God does not signify literally being afraid of him, but having a good heart, and leading a good life, in consequence of such fear; so this faith in Christ does not signify literally *believing* in him in the sense that word is used in common language, but becoming his real disciples, in consequence of such belief.

Our religion being then thus practical, consisting in a frame of mind and course of behaviour, suitable to the dispensation we are under, and which will bring us to our final good; children ought, by education, to be habituated to this course of behaviour, and formed into this frame of mind. And it must ever be remembered, that if no care be taken to do it, they will grow up in a direct contrary behaviour, and be hardened in direct contrary habits. They will more and more corrupt themselves, and spoil their proper nature. They will alienate themselves further from God; and not only neglect, but *trample under foot*, the means which he in his infinite mercy has appointed for our recovery. And upon the whole, the same reasons, which show, that they ought to be instructed and exercised in what will render them useful to society, secure them from the present evils they are in danger of incurring, and procure them that satisfaction which lies within the reach of human prudence, show likewise, that they ought to be instructed and exercised in what is suitable to the highest relations in which we stand, and the most important capacity in which we can be considered; in that temper of mind and course of behaviour, which will secure them from their chief evil, and bring them to their chief good. Besides that religion is the principal security of men's acting a right part in society, and even in respect to their own temporal happiness, all things duly considered.

It is true indeed, children may be taught superstition, under the notion of religion; and it is true also, that, under the notion of prudence, they may be educated in great mistakes as to the nature of real interest and good, respecting the present world. But this is no more a reason for not educating them according to the best of our judgment, than our knowing how very liable we all are to err in other cases, is a reason why we should not, in those other cases, act according to the best of our judgment.

It being then of the greatest importance, that children should be thus educated, the providing schools to give this education to such of them as would not otherwise have it, has the appearance, at least at first sight, of deserving a place amongst the very best of good works. One would be backward, methinks, in entertaining prejudices against it; and very forward, if one had any, to lay them aside, upon being shown that they were groundless. Let us consider the whole state of the case. For though this will lead us some little compass, yet I choose to do it; and the rather, because there are people who speak of charity-schools as a new invented scheme, and therefore to be looked upon with I know not what suspicion. Whereas it will appear, that the scheme of charity-schools, even the part of it which is most looked upon in this light, teaching the children letters and accounts, is no otherwise new, than as the occasion for it is so.

Formerly not only the education of poor children, but also their maintenance, with that of the other poor, were left to voluntary charities. But great changes of different sorts happening over the nation, and charity becoming more cold, or the poor more numerous, it was found necessary to make some legal provision for them. This might, much more properly than charity-schools, be called a new scheme. For, without question, the education of poor children was all along taken care of by voluntary charities, more or less: but obliging us by law to maintain the poor, was new in the reign of queen Elizabeth. Yet, because a change of circumstances made it necessary, its novelty was no reason against it. Now in that legal provision for the maintenance of the poor, poor children must doubtless have had a part in common with grown people. But this could never be sufficient for children, because their case always requires more than mere maintenance; it requires that they be educated in some proper manner. Wherever there are poor who want to be maintained by charity, there must be poor children who, besides this, want to be educated by charity. And whenever there began to be need of *legal* provision for the *maintenance* of the poor, there must immediately have been need also of some *particular* legal provision in behalf of poor children for their *education;* this not being included in what we call their maintenance. And many whose parents are able to maintain them, and do so, may yet be utterly neglected as to their education. But possibly it might not at first be attended to, that the case of poor children was thus a case by itself, which required its own particular provision. Certainly it would not appear, to the generality, so urgent a one as the want of food and raiment. And it might be necessary, that a burden so entirely new as that of a poor-tax was at the time I am speaking of, should be as light as possible. Thus the legal provision for the poor was first settled; without any particular consideration of that additional want in the case of children; as it still remains, with scarce any alteration in this respect. In the mean time, as the poor still increased, or charity still lessened, many poor children were left exposed, not to perish for want of food, but to grow up in society, and learn every thing that is evil and nothing that is good in it; and when they were grown up, greatly at a loss in what honest way to provide for themselves, if they could be supposed inclined to it. And larger numbers, whose case was not so bad as this, yet were very far from having due care taken of their education. And the evil went on increasing, till it was grown to such a degree, as to be quite out of the compass of separate charities to remedy. At length some excellent persons, who were united in a Society* for carrying on almost every good work, took into consideration the neglected case I have been representing; and first of all, as I understand it, set up charity-schools; or however promoted them, as far as their abilities and influence could extend. Their design was not in any sort to remove poor children out of the rank in which they were born, but, keeping them in it, to give them the assistance which their circumstances plainly called for; by educating them in the principles of religion, as well as civil life; and likewise making some sort of provision for their maintenance: under which last I include clothing them, giving them such learning, if it is to be called by that name, as may qualify them for some common employment, and placing them out to it as they grow up. These two general designs coincide in many respects,

* Society for promoting Christian Knowledge.

and cannot be separated. For teaching the children to read, though I have ranked it under the latter, equally belongs to both: and without some advantages of the latter sort, poor people would not send their children to our charity-schools: nor could the poorest of all be admitted into any schools, without some charitable provision of clothing. And care is taken, that it be such as cannot but be a restraint upon the children. And if this, or any part of their education, gives them any little vanity, as has been poorly objected, whilst they are children, it is scarce possible but that it will have even a quite contrary effect when they are grown up, and ever after remind them of their rank. Yet still we find it is apprehended that what they here learn may set them above it.

But why should people be so extremely apprehensive of the danger, that poor persons will make a perverse use of every the least advantage, even the being able to read, whilst they do not appear at all apprehensive of the like danger for themselves or their own children, in respect of riches or power, how much soever; though the danger of perverting these advantages is surely as great, and the perversion itself of much greater and worse consequence? And by what odd reverse of things has it happened, that such as pretend to be distinguished for the love of liberty should be the only persons who plead for keeping down the poor, as one may speak; for keeping them more inferior in this respect, and which must be the consequence, in other respects, than they were in times past? For till within a century or two all ranks were nearly upon a level as to the learning in question. The art of printing appears to have been providentially reserved till these latter ages, and then providentially brought into use, as what was to be instrumental for the future in carrying on the appointed course of things. The alterations which this art has even already made in the face of the world are not inconsiderable. By means of it, whether immediately or remotely, the methods of carrying on business are, in several respects, improved, *knowledge has been increased,**

* Dan. xii. 4.

and some sort of literature is become general. And if this be a blessing, we ought to let the poor, in their degree, share it with us. The present state of things and course of providence plainly leads us to do so.

And if we do not, it is certain, how little soever it be attended to, that they will be upon a greater disadvantage, on many accounts, especially in populous places, than they were in the dark ages: for they will be more ignorant, comparatively with the people about them, than they were then; and the ordinary affairs of the world are now put in a way which requires that they should have some knowledge of letters, which was not the case then. And therefore to bring up the poor in their former ignorance, now this knowledge is so much more common and wanted, would be, not to keep them in the same, but to put them into a lower condition of life than what they were in formerly. Nor let people of rank flatter themselves, that ignorance will keep their inferiors more dutiful and in greater subjection to them: for surely there must be danger that it will have a contrary effect under a free government such as ours, and in a dissolute age. Indeed the principles and manners of the poor, as to virtue and religion, will always be greatly influenced, as they always have been, by the *example* of their superiors, if that would mend the matter. And this influence will, I suppose, be greater, if they are kept more inferior than formerly in all knowledge and improvement. But unless their superiors of the present age, superiors, I mean of the middle, as well as higher ranks in society, are greater examples of public spirit, of dutiful submission to authority, human and divine, of moderation in diversions, and proper care of their families and domestic affairs; unless, I say, superiors of the present age are greater examples of decency, virtue, and religion, than those of former times; for what reason in the world is it desirable that their example should have this greater influence over the poor? On the contrary, why should not the poor, by being taught to read, be put into a capacity of making some improvement in moral and religious knowledge, and confirming themselves in those good principles, which will be a great security for their following the example of their superiors if it be good, and some sort of preservative against their following it if it be bad? And serious persons will further observe very singular reasons for this amongst us; from the discontinuance of that religious intercourse between pastors and people in private, which remain in Protestant churches abroad, as well as in the church of Rome, and from our small public care and provision for keeping up a sense of religion in the lower rank, except by distributing religious books. For in this way they have been assisted; and any well-disposed person may do much good amongst them, and at a very trifling expense, since the worthy Society before mentioned has so greatly lessened the price of such books. But this pious charity is an additional reason why the poor should be taught to read, that they may be in a capacity of receiving the benefit of it. Vain indeed would be the hope, that any thing in this world can be fully secured from abuse. For as it is the general scheme of divine Providence to bring good out of evil; so the wickedness of men will, if it be possible, bring evil out of good. But upon the whole, incapacity and ignorance must be favourable to error and vice; and knowledge and improvement contribute, in due time, to the destruction of impiety as well as superstition, and to the general prevalence of true religion. But some of these observations may perhaps be thought too remote from the present occasion. It is more obviously to the purpose of it to obsérve, that reading, writing, and accounts, are useful, and, whatever cause it is owing to, would really now be wanted in the very lowest stations: and that the trustees of our charity-schools are fully convinced of the great fitness of joining to instruction easy labour, of some sort or other, as fast as it is practicable; which they have already been able to do in some of them.

Then as to placing out the poor children, as soon as they are arrived at a fit age for it; this must be approved by every one, as it is putting them in a way of industry under domestic government, at a time of life, in some respects, more dangerous than even childhood. And it is a known thing, that care is taken to do it in a manner which does not set them above their rank: though it is not possible always to do it exactly as one would wish. Yet, I hope it may be observed without offence, if any of them happen to be of a very weakly constitution, or of a very distinguished capacity, there can be no impropriety in placing these in employments adapted to their particular cases; though such as would be very improper for the generality.

But the principal design of this charity is to educate poor children in such a manner, as has a tendency to make them good, and useful, and contented, whatever their particular station be. The care of this is greatly neglected by the poor: nor truly is it more regarded by the rich, considering what might be expected from them. And if it were as practicable to provide charity-schools, which should supply this shameful neglect in the rich, as it is to supply the like, though more excusable, neglect in the poor, I should think certainly, that both ought to be done for the same reasons. And most people, I hope, will think so too, if they attend to the thing I am speaking of; which is the moral and religious part of education; what is equally necessary for all ranks, and grievously wanting in all. Yet in this respect the poor must be greatly upon a disadvantage, from the nature of the case; as will appear to any one who will consider it.

For if poor children are not sent to school, several years of their childhood of course pass away in idleness and loitering. This has a tendency to give them perhaps a feeble listlessness, perhaps a headstrong profligateness of mind; certainly an indisposition to proper application as they grow up, and an aversion afterward, not only to the restraints of religion, but to those which any particular calling, and even the nature of society, require. Whereas children kept to stated orders, and who many hours of the day are in employment, are by this means habituated both to submit to those who are placed over them, and to govern themselves; and they are also by this means prepared for industry, in any way of life in which they may be placed. And all this holds abstracted from the consideration of their being taught to read without which, however, it will be impracticable to employ their time: not to repeat the unanswerable reasons for it before mentioned. Now several poor people cannot, others will not be at the expense of sending their children to school. And let me add, that such as can and are willing, yet if it be very inconvenient to them, ought to be eased of it, and the burden of children made as light as may be to their poor parents.

Consider next the manner in which the children of the poor, who have vicious parents, are brought up, in comparison with other children whose parents are of the same character. The children of dissolute men of fortune may have the happiness of not seeing much of their parents. And this, even though they are educated at home, is often the case, by means of a customary distance between them, which cannot be kept amongst the poor. Nor is it impossible that a rich man of this character, desiring to have his children better than himself, may provide them such an education as may make them so, without his having any restraint or trouble in the matter. And the education which children of better rank must have, for their improvement in the common accomplishments belonging to it, is of course, as yet, for the most part, attended with some sort of religious education. But the poor, as they cannot provide persons to educate their children; so, from the way in which they live together in poor families, a child must be an eye and ear witness of the worst part of his parents' talk and behaviour. And it cannot but be expected, that his own will be formed upon it. For as example in general has very great influence upon all persons, especially children, the example of their parents is of authority with them, when there is nothing to balance it on the other side. Now take in the supposition, that these parents are dissolute, profligate people; then, over and above giving their children no sort of good instruction, and a very bad example, there are more crimes than one in which, it may be feared, they will directly instruct and encourage them; besides letting them ramble abroad wherever they will, by which, of course, they learn the very same principles and manners they do at home. And from all these things together, such poor children will have their characters formed to vice, by those whose business it is to restrain them from it. They will be disciplined and trained up in it. This surely is a case which ought to have some public provision made for it. If it cannot have an adequate one, yet such a one as it can: unless it be thought so rare as not to deserve our attention. But in reality, though there should be no more parents of this character amongst the poor, in proportion, than amongst the rich, the case which I have been putting will be far from being uncommon. Now notwithstanding the danger to which the children of such wretched parents cannot but be exposed, from what they see at home; yet by instilling into them the principles of virtue and religion at school, and placing them soon out in sober families, there is ground to hope they may avoid those ill courses, and escape that ruin, into which, without this care, they would almost certainly run. I need not add how much greater ground there is to expect, that those of the children who have religious parents will do well. For such parents, besides setting their children a good example, will likewise repeat and enforce upon them at home the good instructions they receive at school.

After all, we find the world continues very corrupt. And it would be miraculous indeed, if charity-schools alone should make it otherwise: or if they should make even all who are brought up in them proof against its corruptions. The truth is, every method that can be made use of to prevent or reform the bad manners of the age, will appear to be of less effect, in proportion to the greater occasion there is for it; as cultivation, though the most proper that can be, will produce less fruit, or of a worse sort, in a bad climate than in a good one. And thus the character of the common people, with whom these children are to live, in the ordinary intercourse of business and company when they come out into the world, may more or less defeat the good effects of their education. And so likewise may the character of men of rank, under whose influence they are to live. But whatever danger may be apprehended from either or both of these, it can be no reason why we should not endeavour, by the likeliest methods we can, to better the world, or keep it from growing worse. The good tendency of the method before us is unquestionable. And I think myself obliged to add, that upon a comparison of parishes where charity-schools have been for a considerable time established, with neighbouring ones, in like situations, which have had none, the good effects of them, as I am very credibly informed, are most manifest. Notwithstanding I freely own, that it is extremely difficult to make the necessary comparisons in this case, and form a judgment upon them. And a multitude of circumstances must come in to determine, from appearances only, concerning the positive good which is produced by this charity, and the evil which is prevented by it; which last is full as material as the former, and can scarce be estimated at all. But surely there can be no doubt whether it be useful or not, to educate children in order, virtue, and religion.

However, suppose, which is yet far from being the case, but suppose it should seem, that this undertaking did not answer the expense and trouble of it, in the civil or political way of considering things. What is this to persons who profess to be engaged in it, not only upon mere civil views, but upon moral and Christian ones? We are to do our endeavours to promote virtue and religion amongst men, and leave the success to God: the designs of his providence are answered by these endeavours, *whether they will hear, or whether they will forbear; i. e.* whatever be the success of them: and the least success in such endeavours is a great and valuable effect.*

From these foregoing observations, duly considered, it will appear that the objections, which have been made against charity-schools, are to be regarded in the same light with those which are made against any other necessary things; for instance, against providing for the sick and the aged poor. Objections in this latter case could be considered no otherwise than merely as warnings of some inconvenience which might accompany such charity, and might, more or less, be guarded against, the charity itself being still kept up; or as proposals for

* See the Sermon before the Society for the Propagation of the Gospel.

placing it upon some better foot. For though, amidst the disorder and imperfection in all human things, these objections were not obviated, they could not however possibly be understood as reasons for discontinuing such charity; because, thus understood, they would be reasons for leaving necessitous people to perish. Well-disposed persons therefore will take care, that they be not deluded with objections against this before us, any more than against other necessary charities; as though such objections were reasons for suppressing them, or not contributing to their support, unless we can procure an alteration of that to which we object. There can be no possible reasons for leaving poor children in that imminent danger of ruin, in which many of these must be left, were it not for this charity. Therefore objections against it cannot, from the nature of the case, amount to more than reasons for endeavouring, whether with or without success, to put it upon a right and unexceptionable foot, in the particular respects objected against. And if this be the intention of the objectors, the managers of it have shown themselves remarkably ready to second them: for they have shown even a docility in receiving admonitions of any thing thought amiss in it, and proposals for rendering it more complete: and, under the influence of this good spirit, the management of it is really improving; particularly in greater endeavours to introduce manufactures into these schools; and in more particular care to place the children out to employments in which they are most wanted, and may be most serviceable, and which are most suitable to their ranks. But if there be any thing in the management of them, which some particular persons think should be altered, and others are of a contrary opinion, these things must be referred to the judgment of the public, and the determination of the public complied with. Such compliance is an essential principle of all charitable associations; for without it they could not subsist at all: and by charitable associations, multitudes are put in mind to do good, who otherwise would not have thought of it; and infinitely more good may be done, than possibly can by the separate endeavours of the same number of charitable persons. Now he who refuses to help forward the good work before us, because it is not conducted exactly in his own way, breaks in upon that general principle of union, which those who are friends to the indigent and distressed part of our fellow creatures will be very cautious how they do in any case: but more especially will they beware, how they break in upon that necessary principle in a case of so great importance as is the present. For the public is as much interested in the education of poor children, as in the preservation of their lives.

This last, I observed, is legally provided for. The former is left amongst other works of charity, neglected by many who care for none of these things, and to be carried on by such only as think it their concern to be doing good. Some of you are able, and in a situation, to assist in it in an eminent degree, by being trustees, and overlooking the management of these schools; or in different ways countenancing and recommending them; as well as by contributing to their maintenance: others can assist only in this latter way. In what manner and degree then it belongs to you, and to me, and to any particular person, to help it forward, let us all consider seriously, not for one another, but each of us for himself.

And may the blessing of Almighty God accompany this work of charity, which he has put into the hearts of his servants, in behalf of these poor children; that being now *trained up in the way they should go, when they are old they may not depart from it.* May he, of his mercy keep them safe amidst the innumerable dangers of this bad world, through which they are to pass, and preserve them unto his heavenly kingdom.

SERMON V.

PREACHED BEFORE THE HOUSE OF LORDS, IN THE ABBEY-CHURCH OF WESTMINSTER, ON THURSDAY, JUNE 11, 1747, BEING THE ANNIVERSARY OF HIS MAJESTY'S HAPPY ACCESSION TO THE THRONE.

I exhort, that, first of all, supplications, prayers, intercessions, and giving of thanks, be made for all men; for kings, and for all that are in authority; that we may lead a quiet and peaceable life, in all godliness and honesty.—1 Tim. ii. 1, 2.

It is impossible to describe the general end which Providence has appointed us to aim at in our passage through the present world, in more expressive words than these very plain ones of the apostle, *to lead a quiet and peaceable life, in all godliness and honesty: a quiet and peaceable life*, by way of distinction, surely, from eager tumultuary pursuits in our private capacity, as well as in opposition both to our making insurrections in the state, and to our suffering oppression from it. *To lead a quiet and peaceable life in all godliness and honesty*, is the whole that we have any reason to be concerned for. To this the constitution of our nature carries us; and our external condition is adapted to it.

Now in aid to this general appointment of Providence, civil government has been instituted over the world, both by the light of nature and by revelation, to instruct men in the duties of fidelity, justice, and regard to common good, and enforce the practice of these virtues, without which there could have been no peace or quiet amongst mankind; and to preserve, in different ways, a sense of religion as well as virtue, and of God's authority over us For if we could suppose men to have lived out of government, they must have run wild, and all knowledge of divine things must have been lost from among them. But by means of their uniting under it, they have been preserved in some tolerable security from the fraud and violence of each other; order, a sense of virtue, and the practice of it, has been in some measure kept up; and religion, more or less pure, has been all along spread and propagated. So that I make no scruple to affirm, that civil government has been, in all ages, a standing publication of the law of nature, and an enforcement of it; though never in its perfection, for the most part greatly corrupted, and I suppose always so in some degree.

And considering that civil government is that part of God's government over the world, which he exercises by the instrumentality of men, wherein that which is oppression, injustice, cruelty, as coming from them, is under his direction, necessary discipline, and just punishment; considering that *all power is of God*,* all authority is properly of divine appointment; men's very living under magistracy might naturally have led them to the contemplation of authority in its source and origin; the one, supreme, absolute authority of Almighty God; by which he *doeth according to his will in the army of heaven, and among the inhabitants of the earth:*† which he now exerts, visibly and invisibly, by different instruments, in different forms of administration, different methods of discipline and punishment; and which he will continue to exert hereafter, not only over mankind when this mortal life shall be ended, but throughout his universal kingdom; till, by having rendered to all according to their works, he shall have completely executed that just scheme of government, which he has already begun to execute in this world, by their hands, whom he has appointed, for the present *punishment of evil-doers, and for the praise of them that do well.*‡

And though that perfection of justice cannot in any sort take place in this world, even under the very best governments; yet under the worst, men have been enabled to lead much more quiet and peaceable lives, as well as attend to and keep up a sense of religion much more, than they could possibly have done without any government at all. But a free Christian government is adapted to answer these purposes in a higher degree, in proportion to its just liberty, and the purity of its religious establishment. And as we enjoy these advantages, civil and religious, in a very eminent degree, under a good prince, and those he has placed in authority over us, we are eminently obliged to offer up supplications

* Rom. xiii. 1. † Dan. iv. 35. ‡ 1 Pet. ii. 14.

and thanksgivings in their behalf; to pay them all that duty which these prayers imply; and *to lead,* as those advantages enable and have a tendency to dispose us to do, *quiet and peaceable lives in all godliness and honesty.*

Of the former of these advantages, our free constitution of civil government, we seem to have a very high value. And if we would keep clear from abuses of it, it could not be overvalued; otherwise than as every thing may, when considered as respecting this world only. We seem, I say, sufficiently sensible of the value of our civil liberty. It is our daily boast, and we are in the highest degree jealous of it. Would to God we were somewhat more judicious in our jealousy of it, so as to guard against its chief enemy, one might say, the only enemy of it, we have at present to fear; I mean licentiousness; which has undermined so many free governments, and without whose treacherous help no free government, perhaps, ever was undermined. This licentiousness indeed is not only dangerous to liberty, but it is actually a present infringement of it in many instances.—But I must not turn this good day into a day of reproach. Dropping then the encroachments which are made upon our liberty, peace, and quiet by licentiousness, we are certainly a freer nation than any other we have an account of; and as free, it seems, as the very nature of government will permit. Every man is equally under the protection of the laws; may have equal justice against the most rich and powerful; and securely enjoy all the common blessings of life, with which the industry of his ancestors, or his own, has furnished him. In some other countries the upper part of the world is free, but in Great Britain the whole body of the people is free. For we have at length, to the distinguished honour of those who began, and have more particularly laboured in it, emancipated our northern provinces from most of their *legal* remains of slavery: for *voluntary* slavery cannot be abolished, at least not directly, by law. I take leave to speak of this long-desired work as done; since it wants only his concurrence, who, as we have found by many years' experience, considers the good of his people as his own. And I cannot but look upon these acts of the legislature in a further view, as instances of regard to posterity; and declarations of its readiness to put every subject upon an equal foot of security and freedom, if any of them are not so, in any other respects, which come into its view; and as a precedent and example for doing it.

Liberty, which is the very genius of our civil constitution, and runs through every branch of it, extends its influence to the ecclesiastical part of it. A religious establishment without a toleration of such as think they cannot in conscience conform to it, is itself a general tyranny; because it claims absolute authority over conscience; and would soon beget particular kinds of tyranny of the worse sort, tyranny over the mind, and various superstitions; after the way should be paved for them, as it soon must, by ignorance. On the other hand, a constitution of civil government without any religious establishment is a chimerical project, of which there is no example: and which, leaving the generality without guide and instruction, must leave religion to be sunk and forgotten amongst them; and at the same time give full scope to superstition, and the gloom of enthusiasm; which last, especially, ought surely to be diverted and checked, as far as it can be done without force. Now a reasonable establishment provides instruction for the ignorant, withdraws them, not in the way of force, but of guidance, from running after those kinds of conceits. It doubtless has a tendency likewise to keep up a sense of real religion and real Christianity in a nation; and is moreover necessary for the encouragement of learning; some parts of which the scripture revelation absolutely requires should be cultivated.

It is to be remarked further, that the value of any particular religious establishment is not to be estimated merely by what it is in itself, but also by what it is in comparison with those of other nations; a comparison which will sufficiently teach us not to expect perfection in human things. And what is still more material, the value of our own ought to be very much heightened in our esteem, by considering what it is a security from; I mean that great corruption of Christianity, popery, which is ever hard at work to bring us again under its yoke.

Whoever will consider the popish claims, to the disposal of the whole earth, as of divine right, to dispense with the most sacred engagements, the claims to supreme absolute authority in religion; in short, the general claims which the canonists express by the words *plenitude of power*—whoever, I say, will consider popery as it is professed at Rome, may see, that it is manifest, open usurpation of all human and divine authority. But even in those Roman Catholic countries where these monstrous claims are not admitted, and the civil power does, in many respects, restrain the papal; yet persecution is professed, as it is absolutely enjoined by what is acknowledged to be their highest authority, a general council, so called, with the pope at the head of it; and is practised in all of them, I think without exception, where it can be done safely. Thus they go on to substitute force instead of argument; and external profession made by force instead of reasonable conviction. And thus corruptions of the grossest sort have been in vogue, for many generations, in parts many of Christendom; and are so still, even where popery obtains in its least absurd form: and their antiquity and wide extent are insisted upon as proofs of their truth; a kind of proof, which at best can be only presumptive, but which loses all its little weight, in proportion as the long and large prevalence of such corruptions have been obtained by force.

Indeed it is said in the book of Job, that the worship of *the sun and moon was an iniquity to be punished by the judge.** And this, though it is not so much as a precept, much less a general one, is, I think, the only passage of scripture which can with any colour be alleged in favour of persecution of any sort: for what the Jews did, and what they were commanded to do, under their theocracy, are both quite out of the case. But whenever that book was written, the scene of it is laid at a time when idolatry was in its infancy, an acknowledged novelty, essentially destructive of true religion, arising perhaps from mere wantonness of imagination. In these circumstances, this greatest of evils, which afterwards laid waste true religion over the face of the earth, might have been

* Job xxxi. 26, 27, 28.

suppressed at once, without danger of mistake or abuse. And one might go on to add, that if those to whom the care of this belonged, instead of serving themselves of prevailing superstitions, had in all ages and countries opposed them in their rise, and adhered faithfully to that primitive religion, which was received *of old, since man was placed upon earth;** there could not possibly have been any such difference of opinion concerning the Almighty Governor of the world, as could have given any pretence for tolerating the idolatries which overspread it. On the contrary, his universal monarchy must have been universally recognised, and the general laws of it more ascertained and known, than the municipal ones of any particular country can be. In such a state of religion, as it could not but have been acknowledged by all mankind, that immorality of every sort was disloyalty to him, *the high and lofty One that inhabiteth eternity, whose name is holy;*† so it could not but have been manifest, that idolatry, in those determinate instances of it, was plain rebellion against him; and therefore might have been punished as an offence, of the highest kind, against the Supreme Authority in nature. But this is in no sort applicable to the present state of religion in the world. For if the principle of punishing idolatry were now admitted amongst the several different parties in religion, the weakest in every place would run a great risk of being convicted of it; or however heresy and schism would soon be found crimes of the same nature, and equally deserving punishment. Thus the spirit of persecution would range without any stop or control, but what should arise from its want of power. But our religious establishment disclaims all principles of this kind, and desires not to keep persons in its communion, or gain proselytes to it, by any other methods than the Christian ones of argument and conviction.

These hints may serve to remind us of the value we ought to set upon our constitution in Church and State, the advantages of which are the proper subjects of our commemoration on this day, as his majesty has shown himself, not in words, but in the whole course of his reign,

* Job xx. 4. † Isaiah lvii. 15.

the guardian and protector of both. And the blessings of his reign are not only rendered more sensible, but are really heightened, by its securing us from that pretender to his crown, whom we had almost forgot, till our late danger renewed our apprehensions; who, we know, is a professed enemy to our church; and grown old in resentments and maxims of government directly contrary to our civil constitution; nay his very claim is founded in principles destructive of it. Our deliverance and our security from this danger, with all the other blessings of the king's government, are so many reasons, for *supplications, prayers, intercessions, and giving of thanks,* to which we are exhorted; as well as for all other dutiful behaviour towards it; and should also remind us to take care and make due improvement of those blessings, by *leading,* in the enjoyment of them, *quiet and peaceable lives, in all godliness and honesty.*

The Jewish church offered sacrifices even for heathen princes to whom they were in subjection: and the primitive Christian church, the Christian sacrifices of supplications and prayers for the prosperity of the emperor and the state; though they were falsely accused of being enemies to both, because they would not join in their idolatries. In conformity to these examples of the church of God in all ages, prayers for the king and those in authority under him are part of the daily service of our own. And for the day of his inauguration a particular service is appointed, which we are here assembled in the house of God to celebrate. This is the first duty we owe to kings, and those who are in authority under them, that we make prayers and thanksgivings for them. And in it is comprehended, what yet may be considered as another, paying them honour and reverence. Praying for them is itself an instance and expression of this, as it gives them a part in our highest solemnities. It also reminds us of that further honour and reverence which we are to pay them, as occasions offer, throughout the whole course of our behaviour. *Fear God, honour the king,** are apostolic precepts; and *despising government, and speaking evil of*

* 1 Pet. ii. 17.

dignities, apostolic descriptions of such as *are reserved unto the day of judgment to be punished.*† And if these *evil speeches* are so highly criminal, it cannot be a thing very innocent to make a custom of entertaining ourselves with them.

Further, if we are to pray, *that we may*, that it may be permitted us, to *lead a quiet and peaceable life*, we ought surely to live so, when, by means of a mild, equal government, it is permitted us; and be very thankful, first to God, and then to those whom he makes the instruments of so great good to us, and pay them all obedience and duty; though every thing be not conducted according to our judgment, nor every person in employment whom we may think deserving of it. Indeed opposition, in a legal, regular way, to measures which a person thinks wrong, cannot but be allowed in a free government. It is in itself just, and also keeps up the spirit of liberty. But opposition, from indirect motives, to measures which he sees to be necessary, is itself immoral: it keeps up the spirit of licentiousness; is the greatest reproach of liberty, and in many ways most dangerous to it; and has been a principal means of overturning free governments. It is well too if the *legal subjection* to the government we live under, which may accompany such behaviour, be not the reverse of *Christian subjection; subjection for wrath only*, and *not for conscience' sake.*‡ And one who wishes well to his country will beware how he inflames the common people against measures, whether right or wrong, which they are not judges of. For no one can foresee how far such disaffection will extend; but every one sees, that it diminishes the reverence which is certainly owing to authority. Our due regards to these things are indeed instances of our loyalty, but they are in reality as much instances of our patriotism too. Happy the people who live under a prince, the justice of whose government renders them coincident.

Lastly, As by the good providence of God we were born under a free government, and are members of a pure reformed church, both of which he has wonderfully

* 2 Pet. i. 10. † 2 Pet ii. 9. ‡ Rom. xiii. 5.

preserved through infinite dangers; if we do not take heed to live like Christians, nor to govern ourselves with decency in those respects in which we are free, we shall be a dishonour to both. Both are most justly to be valued: but they may be valued in the wrong place. It 's no more a recommendation of civil, than it is of natural liberty,* that it must put us into a capacity of behaving ill. Let us then value our civil constitution, not because it leaves us the power of acting as mere humour and passion carry us, in those respects, in which governments less free lay men under restraints; but for its equal laws, by which the great are disabled from oppressing those below them. Let us transfer, each of us, the equity of this our civil constitution to our whole personal character; and be sure to be as much afraid of subjection to mere arbitrary will and pleasure in ourselves, as to the arbitrary will of others. For the tyranny of our own lawless passions is the nearest and most dangerous of all tyrannies.

Then as to the other part of our constitution; let us value it, not because it leaves us at liberty to have as little religion as we please, without being accountable to human judicatories; but because it affords us the means and assistances to worship God according to his word; because it exhibits to our view, and enforces upon our conscience, genuine Christianity, free from the superstitions with which it is defiled in other countries. These superstitions naturally tend to *abate* its force: our profession of it in its purity is a particular call upon us to yield ourselves up to its *full* influence; *to be pure in heart;*† *to be holy in all manner of conversation.*‡ Much of *the form of godliness* is laid aside amongst us: this itself should admonish us to attend more to *the power thereof.*§ We have discarded many burdensome ceremonies: let us be the more careful to cultivate inward religion. We have thrown off a multitude of superstitious practices, which were called good works: let us the more abound in all moral virtues, these being unquestionably such. Thus our lives will justify and recommend the reformation; and we shall *adorn the doctrine of God our Saviour in all things.*‖

* Natural liberty as opposed to necessity, or fate

† Matt. v. 8. ‡ 1 Pet. i. 15. § 2 Tim. iii. 5. ‖ Titus ii. 10.

SERMON VI.

PREACHED BEFORE HIS GRACE CHARLES DUKE OF RICHMOND, PRESIDENT AND THE GOVERNORS OF THE LONDON INFIRMARY, FOR THE RELIEF OF SICK AND DISEASED PERSONS, ESPECIALLY MANUFACTURERS, AND SEAMEN IN MERCHANT-SERVICE, &c. AT THE PARISH CHURCH OF ST LAWRENCE-JEWRY ON THURSDAY, MARCH 31, 1748.

And, above all things, have fervent charity among yourselves: for charity shall cover the multitude of sins.—1 Pet. iv. 8.

As we owe our being, and all our faculties, and the very opportunities of exerting them, to Almighty God, and are plainly his and not our own, we are admonished, even though we should *have done all those things which are commanded us, to say, We are unprofitable servants.** And with much deeper humility must we make this acknowledgment, when we consider in how *many things we have all offended.*† But still the behaviour of such creatures as men, highly criminal in some respects, may yet in others be such as to render them the proper objects of mercy, and, our Saviour does not decline saying, *thought worthy of it.*‡ And, conformably to our natural sense of things, the Scripture is very express, that mercy, forgiveness, and, in general, charity to our fellow creatures, has this efficacy in a very high degree.

Several copious and remote reasons have been alleged, why such pre-eminence is given to this grace or virtue; some of great importance, and none of them perhaps without its weight. But the proper one seems to be very short and obvious, that by fervent charity, with a course of beneficence proceeding from it, a person may make amends for the good he has blamably omitted, and the injuries he has done, so far, as that society would have no demand upon him for such his misbehaviour; nor consequently would justice have any in behalf of society, whatever it might have upon other accounts. Thus by fervent charity he may even merit forgiveness of men: and this seems to afford a very singular reason why it may be graciously granted him

* Luke xvii. 10. † James iii. 2. ‡ Luke xx. 35.

by God; a very singular reason, the Christian covenant of pardon always supposed, why divine justice should permit, and divine mercy appoint, that such his charity should be allowed to *cover the multitude of sins.*

And this reason leads me to observe, what Scripture and the whole nature of the thing shows, that the charity here meant must be such hearty love to our fellow creatures, as produceth a settled endeavour to promote, according to the best of our judgment, their real lasting good, both present and future; and not that easiness of temper, which with peculiar propriety is expressed by the word good-humour, and is a sort of benevolent instinct left to itself, without the direction of our judgment. For this kind of good-humour is so far from making the amends before mentioned, that, though it be agreeable in conversation, it is often most mischievous in every other intercourse of life; and always puts men out of a capacity of doing the good they might, if they could withstand importunity, and the sight of distress, when the case requires they should be withstood; many instances of which cases daily occur, both in public and private. Nor is it to be supposed, that we can any more promote the lasting good of our fellow creatures, by acting from mere kind inclinations, without *considering* what are the proper means of promoting it, than that we can attain our own personal good, by a *thoughtless* pursuit of every thing which pleases us. For the love of our neighbour, as much as self-love, the social affections, as much as the private ones, from their very nature, require to be under the direction of our judgment. Yet it is to be remembered, that it does in no sort become such a creature as man to harden himself against the distresses of his neighbour, except where it is really necessary; and that even well-disposed persons may run into great perplexities, and great mistakes too, by being over-solicitous in distinguishing what are the most proper occasions for their charity, or who the greatest objects of it. And therefore, as on the one side we are obliged to take some care not to squander that which, one may say, belongs to the poor, as we shall do, unless we competently satisfy ourselves beforehand, that what we put to our account of charity will answer some good purpose; so on the other side, when we are competently satisfied of this, in any particular instance before us, we ought by no means to neglect such present opportunity of doing good, under the notion of making further inquiries: for of these delays there will be no end.

Having thus briefly laid before you the ground of that singular efficacy, which the text ascribes to charity in general; obviated the objection against its having this efficacy; and distinguished the virtue itself from its counterfeits; let us now proceed to observe the genuineness and excellency of the particular charity, which we are here met together to promote.

Medicine and every other relief, *under the calamity of bodily diseases and casualties*, no less than the daily necessaries of life, are natural provisions, which God has made for our present indigent state; and which he has granted in common to the children of men, whether they be poor or rich: to the rich by inheritance, or acquisition; and by their hands to the disabled poor.

Nor can there be any doubt, but that public infirmaries are the most effectual means of administering such relief besides that they are attended with incidental advantages of great importance: both which things have been fully shown, and excellently enforced, in the annual sermons upon this and the like occasions.

But indeed public infirmaries are not only the best they are the only possible means by which the poor, especially in this city, can be provided, in any competent measure, with the several kinds of assistance, which *bodily diseases and casualties* require. Not to mention poor foreigners; it is obvious no other provision can be made for poor strangers out of the country, when they are overtaken by these calamities, as they often must be, whilst they are occasionally attending their affairs in this centre of business. But even the poor who are settled here are in a manner strangers to the people amongst whom they live; and, were it not for this provision, must unavoidably be neglected, in the hurry and concourse around them, and be left unobserved to languish in sickness, and suffer extremely, much more than they could in less populous places; where every one is known to every one; and any great distress presently becomes the common talk; and where also poor families are often under the particular protection of some or other of their rich neighbours, in a very different way from what is commonly the case here. Observations of this kind show, that there is a peculiar occasion, and even a necessity, in such a city as this, for public infirmaries, to which easy admittance may be had: and here in ours no security is required, nor any sort of gratification allowed; and that they ought to be multiplied, or enlarged, proportionably to the increase of our inhabitants: for to this the increase of the poor will always bear proportion; though less in ages of sobriety and diligence, and greater in ages of profusion and debauchery.

Now though nothing, to be called an objection in the way of argument, can be alleged against thus providing for poor sick people, in the properest, indeed the only way in which they can be provided for; yet persons of too severe tempers can, even upon this occasion, talk in a manner, which, contrary surely to their intention, has a very malignant influence upon the spirit of charity—talk of the ill deserts of the poor, the good uses they might make of being let to suffer more than they do, under distresses which they bring upon themselves, or however might, by diligence and frugality, provide against; and the idle uses they may make of knowing beforehand that they shall be relieved in case of those distresses. Indeed there is such a thing as a prejudice against them, arising from their very state of poverty, which ought greatly to be guarded against; a kind of prejudice, to which perhaps most of us, upon some occasions, and in some degree, may inattentively be liable, but which pride and interest may easily work up to a settled hatred of them; the utter reverse of that amiable part of the character of Job, that *he was a father to the poor.** But it is undoubtedly fit, that such of them as are good and industrious should have the satisfaction of knowing beforehand, that they shall be relieved under *diseases and casualties:* and those, it is

* Job xxix. 16.

most obvious, ought to be relieved preferably to others. But these others, who are not of that good character, might possibly have the apprehension of those calamities in so great a degree, as would be very mischievous, and of no service, if they thought they must be left to perish under them. And though their idleness and extravagance are very inexcusable, and ought by all reasonable methods to be restrained; and they are highly to be blamed for not making some provision against age and supposable disasters, when it is in their power; yet it is not to be desired, that the anxieties of avarice should be added to the natural inconveniences of poverty.

It is said, that our common fault towards the poor is not harshness, but too great lenity and indulgence. And if allowing them in debauchery, idleness, and open beggary; in drunkenness, profane cursing and swearing in our streets, nay in our houses of correction; if this be lenity, there is doubtless a great deal too much of it. And such lenity towards the poor is very consistent with the most cruel neglects of them, in the extreme misery to which those vices reduce them. Now though this last certainly is not our general fault; yet it cannot be said every one is free from it. For this reason, and that nothing, which has so much as the shadow of an objection against our public charities, may be entirely passed over, you will give me leave to consider a little the supposed case above mentioned, though possibly some may think it unnecessary, that of persons reduced to poverty and distress by their own faults.

Instances of this there certainly are. But it ought to be very distinctly observed, that in judging which are such, we are liable to be mistaken: and more liable to it, in judging to what degree those are faulty, who really are so in some degree. However, we should always look with mildness upon the behaviour of the poor; and be sure not to expect more from them than can be expected, in a moderate way of considering things. We should be forward not only to admit and encourage the good deserts of such as do well, but likewise as to those of them who do not, be ever ready to make due allowances for their bad education, or, which is the same, their having had none; for what may be owing to the ill example of their superiors, as well as companions, and for temptations of all kinds. And remember always, that be men's vices what they will, they have not forfeited their claim to relief under necessities, till they have forfeited their lives to justice.

*Our heavenly Father is kind to the unthankful and to the evil; and sendeth his rain on the just and on the unjust.** And, in imitation of him, our Saviour expressly requires, that our beneficence be promiscuous. But we have moreover the divine example for relieving those distresses which are brought upon persons by their own faults; and this is exactly the case we are considering. Indeed the general dispensation of Christianity is an example of this; for its general design is to save us from our sins, and the punishments which would have been the just consequence of them. But the divine example in the daily course of nature is a more obvious and sensible one. And though the natural miseries which are foreseen to be annexed to a vicious course of life are providentially intended to prevent it, in the same manner as civil penalties are intended to prevent civil crimes; yet those miseries, those natural penalties admit of and receive natural reliefs, no less than any other miseries, which could not have been foreseen or prevented. Charitable providence then, thus manifested in the course of nature, which is the example of our heavenly Father, most evidently leads us to relieve, not only such distresses as were unavoidable, but also such as people by their own faults have brought upon themselves. The case is, that we cannot judge in what degree it was intended they should suffer, by considering what, in the natural course of things, would be the whole bad consequences of their faults, if those consequences were not prevented, when nature has provided means to prevent great part of them. We cannot, for instance, estimate what degree of present sufferings God has annexed to drunkenness, by considering the diseases which follow from this vice, as they would be if they admitted of no reliefs or remedies; but by considering the remaining misery of those diseases,

* Matt. v. 45. Luke vi. 35.

after the application of such remedies as nature has provided. For as it is certain on the one side, that those diseases are providential corrections of intemperance, it is as certain on the other, that the remedies are providential mitigations of those corrections; and altogether as much providential, when administered by the good hand of charity in the case of our neighbour, as when administered by self-love in our own. Thus the pain, and danger, and other distresses of sickness and poverty remaining, after all the charitable relief which can be procured; and the many uneasy circumstances which cannot but accompany that relief, though distributed with all supposable humanity; these are the natural corrections of idleness and debauchery, supposing these vices brought on those miseries. And very severe corrections they are: and they ought not to be increased by withholding that relief, or by harshness in the distribution of it. Corrections of all kinds, even the most necessary ones, may easily exceed their proper bound: and when they do so, they become mischievous; and mischievous in the measure they exceed it. And the natural corrections which we have been speaking of would be excessive, if the natural mitigations provided for them were not administered.

Then persons who are so scrupulously apprehensive of every thing which can possibly, in the most indirect manner, encourage idleness and vice (which, by the way, any thing may accidentally do), ought to turn their thoughts to the moral and religious tendency of infirmaries. The religious manner in which they are carried on has itself a direct tendency to bring the subject of religion into the consideration of those whom they relieve; and, in some degree, to recommend it to their love and practice, as it is productive of so much good to them, as restored ease and health, and a capacity of resuming their several employments. It is to virtue and religion, they may mildly be admonished, that they are indebted for their relief. And this, amongst other admonitions of their spiritual guide, and the quiet and order of their house, out of the way of bad examples, together with a regular course of devotion.

which it were greatly to be wished might be daily; these means, it is to be hoped, with the common grace of God, may enforce deeply upon their consciences those serious considerations, to which a state of affliction naturally renders the mind attentive, and that they will return, as from a religious retreat, to their several employments in the world, with lasting impressions of piety in their hearts. By such united advantages, which these poor creatures can in no sort have any other way, very remarkable reformations have been wrought. Persons of the strictest characters therefore would give a more satisfactory proof, not to the world, but to their own consciences, of their desire to suppress vice and idleness, by setting themselves to cultivate the religious part of the institution of infirmaries, which, I think, would admit of great improvements; than by allowing themselves to talk in a manner which tends to discountenance either the institution itself, or any particular branch of it.

Admitting then the usefulness and necessity of these kinds of charity, which indeed cannot be denied; *yet every thing has its bounds.* And, in the spirit of severity before mentioned, it is imagined, that *people are enough disposed,* such, it seems, is the present turn, *to contribute largely to them.* And some, whether from dislike of the charities themselves, or from mere profligateness, think *these formal recommendations of them at church every year might very well be spared.*

But surely it is desirable, that a customary way should be kept open for removing prejudices as they may arise against these institutions; for rectifying any misrepresentations which may, at any time, be made of them; and informing the public of any new emergencies; as well as for repeatedly enforcing the known obligations of charity, and the excellency of this particular kind of it. Then sermons, you know, amongst Protestants, always of course accompany these more solemn appearances in the house of God: nor will these latter be kept up without the other. Now public devotions should ever attend and consecrate public charities. And it would be a sad presage of the decay of these charities, if ever they should cease to be professedly carried on in the fear of God, and upon the principles of religion. It may be added, that real charitable persons will approve of these frequent exhortations to charity, even though they should be conscious that they do not themselves stand in need of them, upon account of such as do. And such can possibly have no right to complain of being too often admonished of their duty, till they are pleased to practise it. It is true indeed, we have the satisfaction of seeing a spirit of beneficence prevail, in a very commendable degree, amongst all ranks of people, and in a very distinguished manner in some persons amongst the highest; yet it is evident, too many of all ranks are very deficient in it, who are of great ability, and of whom much might be expected. Though every thing therefore were done in behalf of the poor which is wanted, yet these persons ought repeatedly to be told, how highly blamable they are for letting it be done without them; and done by persons, of whom great numbers must have much less ability than they.

But whoever can really think, that the necessities of the disabled poor are sufficiently provided for already, must be strangely prejudiced. If one were to send you to them themselves to be better informed, you would readily answer, that their demands would be very extravagant; that persons are not to be their own judges in claims of justice, much less in those of charity. You then, I am speaking to the hard people above mentioned, you are to judge, what provision is to be made for the necessitous, so far as it depends upon your contributions. But ought you not to remember that you are interested, that you are parties in the affair as well as they. For is not the giver as really so as the receiver? And as there is danger that the receiver will err one way, is there not danger that the giver may err the other? since it is not matter of arbitrary choice, which has no rule, but matter of real equity, to be considered as in the presence of God, what provision shall be made for the poor? And therefore, though you are yourselves the only judges, what you will do in their behalf, for the case admits no other; yet let me tell you, you will not be impartial, you will not be equitable judges, until you have guarded against the influence which interest is apt to have upon your judgment, and cultivated within you the spirit of charity to balance it. Then you will see the various remaining necessities which call for relief. But that there are many such must be evident at first sight to the most careless observer, were it only from hence, that both this and the other hospitals are often obliged to reject poor objects which offer, even for want of room, or wards to contain them.

Notwithstanding many persons have need of these admonitions, yet there is a good spirit of beneficence, as I observed, pretty generally prevailing. And I must congratulate you upon the great success it has given to the particular good work before us; great, I think, beyond all example for the time it has subsisted. Nor would it be unsuitable to the present occasion to recount the particulars of this success. For the necessary accommodations which have been provided, and the numbers who have been relieved, in so short a time, cannot but give high reputation to the London Infirmary. And the reputation of any particular charity, like credit in trade, is so much real advantage, without the inconveniences to which that is sometimes liable. It will bring in contributions for its support; and men of character, as they shall be wanted, to assist in the management of it; men of skill in the professions, men of conduct in business, to perpetuate, improve, and bring it to perfection. So that you, the contributors to this charity, and more especially those of you by whose immediate care and economy it is in so high repute, are encouraged to go on with *your labour of love*,* not only by the present good, which you see is here done, but likewise by the prospect of what will probably be done, by your means, in future times, when this infirmary shall become, as I hope it will, no less renowned than the city in which it is established.

But to see how far it is from being yet complete, for want of contributions, one need only look upon the settled rules of the house for *admission of patients*. See there the limitations which necessity prescribes, as to

* Heb. vi. 10.

the persons to be admitted. Read but that one order, though others might be mentioned, that *none who are judged to be in an asthmatic, consumptive, or dying condition, be admitted on any account whatsoever.* Harsh as these words sound, they proceed out of the mouth of Charity herself. Charity pronounces it to be better, that poor creatures, who might receive much ease and relief, should be denied it, if their case does not admit of recovery, rather than that others, whose case does admit of it, be left to perish. But it shocks humanity to hear such an alternative mentioned; and to think, that there should be a necessity, as there is at present, for such restrictions, in one of the most beneficent and best managed schemes in the world. May more numerous or larger contributions, at length, open a door to such as these; that what renders their case in the highest degree compassionable, their languishing under incurable diseases, may no longer exclude them from the house of mercy.

But besides the persons to whom I have been now more particularly speaking, there are others, who do not cast about for excuses for not contributing to the relief of the necessitous; perhaps are rather disposed to relieve them; who yet are not so careful as they ought to be, to put themselves into a capacity of doing it. For we are as really accountable for not doing the good which we might have in our power to do, if we would manage our affairs with prudence, as we are for not doing the good which is in our power now at present. And hence arise the obligations of economy upon people in the highest, as well as in the lower stations of life, in order to enable themselves to do that good, which, without economy, both of them must be incapable of; even though without it they could answer the strict demands of justice; which yet we find neither of them can. *A good man sheweth favour, and lendeth; and,* to enable himself to do so, *he will guide his affairs with discretion.** For want of this, many a one has reduced his family to the necessity of asking relief from those public charities, to which he might have left them in a condition of largely contributing.

As economy is the duty of all persons, without excep-

* Psalm cxii. 5.

tion, frugality and diligence are duties which particularly belong to the middle as well as lower ranks of men, and more particularly still to persons in trade and commerce, whatever their fortunes be. For trade and commerce cannot otherwise be carried on, but is plainly inconsistent with idleness and profusion: though indeed were it only from regard to propriety, and to avoid being absurd, every one should conform his behaviour to what his situation in life requires, without which the order of society must be broken in upon. And considering how inherited riches and a life of leisure are often employed, the generality of mankind have cause to be thankful that their station exempts them from so great temptations; that it engages them in a sober care of their expenses, and in a course of application to business: especially as these virtues, moreover, tend to give them, what is an excellent groundwork for all others, a stayed equality of temper and command of their passions. But when a man is diligent and frugal, in order to have it in his power to do good; when he is more industrious, or more sparing perhaps than his circumstances necessarily require, that he may *have to give to him that needeth;** when he *labours in order to support the weak;*† such care of his affairs is itself charity, and the actual beneficence which it enables him to practise is additional charity.

You will easily see why I insist thus upon these things, because I would particularly recommend the good work before us to all ranks of people in this great city. And I think I have reason to do so, from the consideration, that it very particularly belongs to them to promote it. The gospel indeed teaches us to look upon every one in distress as our neighbour, yet neighbourhood in the literal sense, and likewise several other circumstances, are providential recommendations of such and such charities, and excitements to them; without which the necessitous would suffer much more than they do at present. For our general disposition to beneficence would not be sufficiently directed, and in other respects would be very ineffectual, if it were not called forth into action

* Ephes. iv. 28. † Acts xx. 35.

by some or other of those providential circumstances, which form particular relations between the rich and the poor, and are of course regarded by every one in some degree. But though many persons among you, both in the way of contributions, and in other ways no less useful, have done even more than was to be expected, yet I must be allowed to say, that I do not think the relation the inhabitants of this city bear to the persons for whom our infirmary was principally designed, is sufficiently attended to by the generality; which may be owing to its late establishment. It is, you know, designed principally for *diseased manufacturers, seamen in merchant-service, and their wives and children:* and *poor manufacturers* comprehend all who are employed in any labour whatever belonging to trade and commerce. The description of these objects shows their relation, and a very near one it is, to you, my neighbours, the inhabitants of this city. If any of your domestic servants were disabled by sickness, there is none of you but would think himself bound to do somewhat for their relief Now these seamen and manufacturers are employed in your immediate business. They are servants of merchants, and other principal traders; as much your servants as if they lived under your roof: though by their not doing so, the relation is less in sight. And supposing they do not all depend upon traders of lower rank in exactly the same manner, yet many of them do; and they have all connexions with you, which give them a claim to your charity preferably to strangers. They are indeed servants of the public; and so are all industrious poor people as well as they. But that does not hinder the latter from being more immediately yours. And as their being servants to the public is a general recommendation of this charity to all other persons, so their being more immediately yours is, surely, a particular recommendation of it to you. Notwithstanding all this, I will not take upon me to say, that every one of you is blamable who does not contribute to your infirmary, for yours it is in a peculiar sense, but I will say, that those of you who do are highly commendable. I will say more, that you promote a very excellent work, which your particular station is a providential call upon you to promote. And there can be no stronger reason than this for doing any thing, except the one reason, that it would be criminal to omit it.

These considerations, methinks, might induce every trader of higher rank in this city to become a subscriber to the infirmary which is named from it; and others of you to contribute somewhat yearly to it, in the way in which smaller contributions are given. This would be a most proper offering out of your increase to him, whose *blessing maketh rich.** Let it be more or less, *every man according as he purposeth in his heart; not grudgingly, or of necessity: for God loveth a cheerful giver.*†

The large benefactions of some persons of ability may be necessary in the first establishment of a public charity, and are greatly useful afterwards in maintaining it: but the expenses of this before us, in the extent and degree of perfection to which one would hope it might be brought, cannot be effectually supported, any more than the expenses of civil government, without the contribution of great numbers. You have already the assistance of persons of highest rank and fortune, of which the list of our governors, and the present appearance, are illustrious examples. And their assistance would be far from lessening by a general contribution to it amongst yourselves. On the contrary, the general contribution to it amongst yourselves, which I have been proposing, would give it still higher repute, and more invite such persons to continue their assistance, and accept the honour of being in its direction. For the greatest persons receive honour from taking the direction of a good work, as they likewise give honour to it. And by these concurrent endeavours, our infirmary might at length be brought to answer, in some competent measure, to the occasions of our city.

Blessed are they who employ their riches in promoting so excellent a design. The temporal advantages of them are far from coming up, in enjoyment, to what they promise at a distance. But the distinguished

* Prov. x. 22. † 2 Cor. ix. 7.

privilege, the prerogative of riches, is, that they increase our power of doing good. This is their proper use. In proportion as men make this use of them, they imitate Almighty God; and co-operate together with him in promoting the happiness of the world; and may expect the most favourable judgment, which their case will admit of, at the last day, upon the general, repeated maxim of the gospel, that we shall then be treated ourselves as we now treat others. They have moreover the prayers of all good men, those of them particularly whom they have befriended; and, by such exercise of charity, they improve within themselves the temper of it, which is the very temper of heaven. Consider next the peculiar force with which this branch of charity, almsgiving, is recommended to us in these words; *He that hath pity upon the poor lendeth unto the Lord:** and in these of our Saviour, *Verily I say unto you, Inasmuch as ye have done it*, relieved the sick and needy, *unto one of the least of these my brethren, ye have done it unto me.*† Beware you do not explain away these passages of Scripture, under the notion, that they have been made to serve superstitious purposes: but ponder them fairly in your heart; and you will feel them to be of irresistible weight. Lastly, let us remember, in how many instances we have all left undone those things which we ought to have done, and done those things which we ought not to have done. Now whoever has a serious sense of this will most earnestly desire to supply the good, which he was obliged to have done, but has not, and undo the evil which he has done, or neglected to prevent; and when that is impracticable, to make amends, in some other way, for his offences—I *can* mean only to our fellow creatures. To make amends, in some way or other, to a particular person, against whom we have offended, either by positive injury, or by neglect; is an express condition of our obtaining forgiveness of God, when it is in our power to make it. And when it is not, surely the next best thing is to make amends to society by fervent charity, in a course of doing good: which riches, as I observed, put very much within our power.

* Prov. xix. 17. † Matt. xxv. 40.

How unhappy a choice then do those rich men make, who sacrifice all these high prerogatives of their state, to the wretched purposes of dissoluteness and vanity, or to the sordid itch of heaping up, to no purpose at all; whilst in the mean time they stand charged with the important trust, in which they are thus unfaithful, and of which a strict account remains to be given!

A

CHARGE

DELIVERED TO

THE CLERGY

AT THE

PRIMARY VISITATION OF THE DIOCESS OF DURHAM,

IN THE YEAR MDCCLI.*

It is impossible for me, my brethren, upon our first meeting of this kind, to forbear lamenting with you the general decay of religion in this nation; which is now observed by every one, and has been for some time the complaint of all serious persons. The influence of it is more and more wearing out of the minds of men, even of those who do not pretend to enter into speculations upon the subject: but the number of those who do, and who profess themselves unbelievers, increases, and with their numbers their zeal. Zeal, it is natural to ask—for what? Why truly *for* nothing, but *against* every thing that is good and sacred amongst us.

Indeed, whatever efforts are made against our religion, no Christian can possibly despair of it. For he, who has *all power in heaven and earth*, has promised, that *he will be with us to the end of the world.* Nor can the present decline of it be any stumbling-block to such as are considerate; since he himself has so strongly expressed what is as remarkably predicted in other passages of Scripture, the great defection from his religion which should be in the latter days, by that prophetic question, *When the Son of man cometh, shall he find faith upon the*

* The publication of Bishop Butler's Charge, in the year 1751, was followed by a pamphlet, printed in 1752, entitled, " A Serious Inquiry into the Use and Importance of External Religion, occasioned by some passages in the Right Reverend the Lord Bishop of Durham's Charge to the Clergy of that Diocess, &c., humbly addressed to his Lordship." This pamphlet has been reprinted in a miscellaneous work: such part of it as seemed most worthy of observation, the reader will find in the following note upon those passages of the Charge to which the pamphlet refers.

earth? How near this time is, God only knows; but this kind of Scripture signs of it is too apparent. For as different ages have been distinguished by different sorts of particular errors and vices, the deplorable distinction of ours is an avowed scorn of religion in some, and a growing disregard to it in the generality.

As to the professed enemies of religion, I know not how often they may come in your way; but often enough, I fear, in the way of some at least amongst you, to require consideration, what is the proper behaviour towards them. One would, to be sure, avoid great familiarities with these persons; especially if they affect to be licentious and profane in their common talk. Yet if you fall into their company, treat them with the regards which belong to their rank; for so we must people who are vicious in any other respect. We should study what St James, with wonderful elegance and expressiveness, calls *meekness of wisdom,* in our behaviour towards all men; but more especially towards these men; not so much as being what we owe to them, but to ourselves and our religion; that we may *adorn the doctrine of God our Saviour,* in our carriage towards those who labour to vilify it.

For discourse with them; the caution commonly given, not to attempt answering objections which we have not considered, is certainly just. Nor need any one in a particular case be ashamed frankly to acknowledge his ignorance, provided it be not general. And though it were, to talk of what he is not acquainted with, is a dangerous method of endeavouring to conceal it. But a considerate person, however qualified he be to defend his religion, and answer the objections he hears made against it, may sometimes see cause to decline that office. Sceptical and profane men are extremely apt to bring up this subject at meetings of entertainment, and such as are of the freer sort: innocent ones I mean, otherwise I should not suppose you would be present at them. Now religion is by far too serious a matter to be the hackney subject upon these occasions. And by preventing its being made so, you will better secure the reverence which is due to it, than by entering into its defence

Every one observes, that men's having examples of vice often before their eyes, familiarizes it to the mind, and has a tendency to take off that just abhorrence of it which the innocent at first felt, even though it should not alter their *judgment* of vice, or make them really *believe* it to be less evil or dangerous. In like manner, the hearing religion often disputed about in light familiar conversation, has a tendency to lessen that sacred regard to it, which a good man would endeavour always to keep up, both in himself and others. But this is not all: people are too apt inconsiderately to take for granted, that things are really questionable, because they hear them often disputed. This indeed is so far from being a consequence, that we know demonstrated truths have been disputed, and even matters of fact, the objects of our senses. But were it a consequence, were the evidence of religion no more than doubtful, then it ought not to be concluded false any more than true, nor denied any more than affirmed; for suspense would be the reasonable state of mind with regard to it. And then it ought in all reason, considering its infinite importance, to have nearly the same influence upon practice, as if it were thoroughly believed. For would it not be madness for a man to forsake a safe road, and prefer to it one in which he acknowledges there is an even chance he should lose his life, though there were an even chance likewise of his getting safe through it? Yet there are people absurd enough, to take the supposed doubtfulness of religion for the same thing as a proof of its falsehood, after they have concluded it doubtful from hearing it often called in question. This shows how infinitely unreasonable sceptical men are, with regard to religion, and that they really lay aside their reason upon this subject as much as the most extravagant enthusiasts. But further, cavilling and objecting upon any subject is much easier than clearing up difficulties: and this last part will always be put upon the defenders of religion. Now a man may be fully convinced of the truth of a matter, and upon the strongest reasons, and yet not be able to answer all the difficulties which may be raised upon it.

Then again, the general evidence of religion is complex and various. It consists of a long series of things, one preparatory to and confirming another, from the very beginning of the world to the present time. And it is easy to see how impossible it must be, in a cursory conversation, to unite all this into one argument, and represent it as it ought; and, could it be done, how utterly indisposed people would be to attend to it—I say in a cursory conversation: whereas unconnected objections are thrown out in a few words, and are easily apprehended, without more attention than is usual in common talk. So that, notwithstanding we have the best cause in the world, and though a man were very capable of defending it, yet I know not why he should be forward to undertake it upon so great a disadvantage, and to so little good effect, as it must be done amidst the gaiety and carelessness of common conversation.

But then it will be necessary to be very particularly upon your guard, that you may not *seem*, by way of compliance, to join in with any levity of discourse respecting religion. Nor would one let any pretended argument against it pass entirely without notice; nor any gross ribaldry upon it, without expressing our thorough disapprobation. This last may sometimes be done by silence: for silence sometimes is very expressive; as was that of our blessed Saviour before the Sanhedrim and before Pilate. Or it may be done by observing mildly, that religion deserves another sort of treatment, or a more thorough consideration, than such a time, or such circumstances admit. However, as it is absolutely necessary, that we take care, by diligent reading and study, to be always prepared, to be *ready always to give an answer to every man that asketh a reason of the hope that is in us;* so there may be occasions when it will highly become us to do it. And then we must take care to do it in the spirit which the apostle requires, *with meekness and fear:** *meekness* towards those who give occasions for entering into the defence of our religion; and with *fear*, not of them, but of God; with that reverential fear, which the nature of religion requires,

* 1 Pet. iii. 15.

and which is so far from being inconsistent with, that it will inspire proper courage towards men. Now this reverential fear will lead us to insist strongly upon the infinite greatness of God's scheme of government, both in extent and duration, together with the wise connexion of its parts, and the impossibility of accounting fully for the several parts, without seeing the whole plan of Providence to which they relate; which is beyond the utmost stretch of our understanding. And to all this must be added the necessary deficiency of human language, when things divine are the subject of it. These observations are a proper full answer to many objections and very material with regard to all.

But your standing business, and which requires constant attention, is with the body of the people; to revive in them the spirit of religion, which is so much declining. And it may seem, that whatever reason there be for caution as to entering into an argumentative defence of religion *in common conversation*, yet that it is necessary to do this *from the pulpit*, in order to guard the people against being corrupted, however in some places. But then surely it should be done in a manner as little controversial as possible. For though such as are capable of seeing the force of objections are capable also of seeing the force of the answers which are given to them; yet the truth is, the people will not competently attend to either. But it is easy to see which they will attend to most. And to hear religion treated of as what many deny, and which has much said against it as well as for it; this cannot but have a tendency to give them ill impressions at any time; and seems particularly improper for all persons at a time of devotion; even for such as are arrived at the most settled state of piety: I say at a time of devotion, when we are assembled to yield ourselves up to the full influence of the Divine Presence, and to call forth into actual exercise every pious affection of heart. For it is to be repeated, that the heart and course of affections may be disturbed when there is no alteration of judgment. Now the evidence of religion may be laid before men without any air of controversy. The proof of the being of God, from final causes, or the design and wisdom which appears in every part of nature; together with the law of virtue written upon our hearts:* the proof of Christianity from miracles, and the accomplishment of prophecies; and the confirmation which the natural and civil history of the world give to the Scripture account of things: these evidences of religion might properly be insisted on, in a way to affect and influence the heart, though there were no professed unbelievers in the world; and therefore may be insisted on, without taking much notice that there are such. And even their

* The author of the Inquiry, mentioned above, informs us, in his postscript, that "the certain consequence of referring mankind to a *law of nature, or virtue, written upon their hearts*, is their having recourse to *their own sense of things* on all occasions; which being, in a great majority, no better than family superstition, party-prejudice, or self-interested artifice (perhaps a compound of all), will be too apt to overrule the plain precepts of the gospel." And he declares, he has "no better opinion of the *clearness, certainty, uniformity, universality*, &c., of this law, than" he has "of the *importance of external religion.*" What then must we say to St Paul, who not only asserts, in the strongest terms, the reality of such a law, but speaks of its obligation as extending to all mankind? blaming some among the Gentiles as *without excuse*, for not adverting to and obeying it: and commending others for *doing by nature* (in contradistinction to revelation) *the things contained in the law*, thus *showing the work of the law written in their hearts.* If, because "natural religion is liable to be mistaken, it is high time to have done with it in the pulpit;" how comes it that the same apostle refers the Philippians to the study of this religion, to *whatsoever things are true, honest, just, lovely, and of good report?* And yet, without such a study, our knowledge of the moral law must always remain imperfect; for a complete system of morality is certainly no where to be found either in the Old or New Testament.† When a Christian minister is enforcing the duties or doctrines of revealed religion, he may perhaps do well to "tell his people he has *no other* proof of the original, truth, obligations, present benefits and future rewards of religion, to lay before them, than what is contained in the Scriptures." But what if his purpose be to inculcate some moral virtue? Will it not be useful here, besides observing that the practice of that virtue is enjoined by a divine command, to recommend it still further to his hearers, by showing that it approves itself to our inward sense and perception, and accords with the native sentiments and suggestions of our minds? Metaphysicians may say what they will of our feelings of this sort being all illusive. liable to be perverted by education and habit, and judged of by men's *own sense of things;* they, whose understandings are yet *unspoiled by philosophy and vain deceit*, will be little disposed to listen to such assertions. Nor are there wanting arguments which prove, and, as should seem, to the satisfaction of every reasonable inquirer, that the great and leading principles of moral duties have in all ages been the same; that such virtues as benevolence, justice, compassion, gratitude, accidental obstacles removed, and when the precise meaning of the words has been once explained, are instinctively known and approved by all men; and that our approbation of these is as much a part of our nature implanted in us by God, and as little liable to caprice and fashion, as the sense of seeing, given us also by him, by which all bodies appear to us in an erect, and not an inverted position.‡ Mr Locke's authority has been generally looked up to as decisive on such questions; and his sentiments have been embraced implicitly, and without examination. That great and good man, however, is not to be charged with the pernicious consequences which others have drawn from his opinions: consequences which have been carried to such a length, as to destroy all moral difference of human actions; making virtue and vice altogether arbitrary; *calling evil good, and good evil; putting darkness for light, and light for darkness; putting bitter for sweet, and sweet for bitter.*

† See the second of Dr Balguy's Charges. ‡ See the third of Bishop Hurd's Sermons, vol. i.

particular objections may be obviated without a formal mention of them. Besides, as to religion in general, it is a practical thing, and no otherwise a matter of speculation, than common prudence in the management of our worldly affairs is so. And if one were endeavouring to bring a plain man to be more careful with regard to this last, it would be thought a strange method of doing it, to perplex him with stating formally the several objections which men of gaiety or speculation have made against prudence, and the advantages which they pleasantly tell us folly has over it; though one could answer those objections ever so fully.

Nor does the want of religion in the generality of the common people appear owing to a speculative disbelief or denial of it, but chiefly to thoughtlessness and the common temptations of life. Your chief business therefore is to endeavour to beget a practical sense of it upon their hearts, as what they acknowledge their belief of, and profess they ought to conform themselves to. And this is to be done by keeping up, as we are able, the form and face of religion with decency and reverence, and in such a degree as to bring the thoughts of religion often to their minds;* and then endeavouring to make this form more and more subservient to promote the reality and power of it. The form of religion may indeed be where there is little of the thing itself; but the thing itself cannot be preserved amongst mankind without the form.† And this form frequently occurring

* To this it is said by our *inquirer*, that "the clergy of the church of England have no way of keeping up the *form* and *face* of religion, any *oftener*, or in *any other degree*, than is directed by the prescribed order of the church." As if the whole duty of a parish priest consisted in reading prayers and a sermon on Sundays, and performing the occasional offices appointed in the liturgy! One would think the writer who made this objection had never read more of the Charge than the *four pages* he has particularly selected for the subject of his animadversions. Had he looked further, he would have found other methods recommended to the clergy, of introducing a sense of religion into the minds of their parishioners which occur *much oftener* than the times allotted for the public services of the church: such as family prayers; acknowledging the divine bounty at our meals; personal applications from ministers of parishes to individuals under their care, on particular occasions and circumstances: as at the time of confirmation, at first receiving the holy communion, on recovery from sickness, and the like; none of which are prescribed in our established ritual, any more than those others so ludicrously mentioned by this writer, "bowing to the east, turning the face to that quarter in repeating the creeds, dipping the finger in water, and therewith crossing the child's forehead in baptism."

† The quakers reject all forms, even the two of Christ's own institution: will it be said, that "these men have no religion preserved among them?" It will neither

in some instance or other of it will be a frequent admonition to bad men to repent, and to good men to grow better; and also be the means of their doing so.*

That which men have accounted religion in the several countries of the world, generally speaking, has had a great and conspicuous part in all public appearances, and the face of it been kept up with great reverence throughout all ranks, from the highest to the lowest; not only upon occasional solemnities, but also in the daily course of behaviour. In the heathen world, their superstition was the chief subject of statuary, sculpture, painting, and poetry. It mixed itself with business, civil forms, diversions, domestic entertainments, and every part of common life. The Mahometans are obliged to short devotions five times between morning and evening. In Roman Catholic countries, people cannot pass a day without having religion recalled to their thoughts, by some or other memorial of it; by some ceremony or public religious form occurring in their way:† besides

be said nor insinuated. The quakers, though they have not the *form*, are careful to keep up the *face* of religion; as appears not only from the custom of assembling themselves for the purposes of public worship on the Lord's day, but from their silent meetings on other days of the week. And that they are equally sensible of the importance of maintaining the influence of religion on their minds, is manifest from the practice of what they call *inward prayer*, in conformity to the direction of Scripture to *pray continually*: "which," saith Robert Barclay, "cannot be understood of *outward* prayer, because it were impossible that men should be always upon their knees, expressing the *words* of prayer; which would hinder them from the exercise of those duties no less positively commanded."—*Apology for the Quakers*, Prop. xi. *Of Worship.*

* Here it has been objected, that "the *number*, *variety*, and *frequent* occurrence of forms in religion, are too apt to be considered by *the generality* as *commutations* for their vices, as something *substituted* in lieu of repentance, as loads and encumbrances upon true Christian edification." This way of arguing against the use of a thing from the abuse of it, instead of arguing from the nature of the thing itself, is the master sophism that pervades the whole performance we are here examining. What reasonable man ever denied, that the pomp of outward worship has been sometimes mistaken for inward piety? that positive institutions, when rested in as ends, instead of being applied as means, are hurtful to the interests of true religion? Not Bishop Butler certainly, who blames the observances of the papists on this account, some of them as being "in themselves wrong and superstitious;" and others, as being "made subservient to the purposes of superstition," and for this reason "abolished by our reformers." In the mean while, it will still be true, that bodily worship is by no means to be discarded, as unuseful in exciting spiritual devotion; on the contrary, that they mutually assist and strengthen each other; and that a mere mental intercourse with God, and a religious service purely intellectual, is altogether unsuitable to such a creature as man, during his present state on earth.

† "What in the former period" (when speaking of the heathen world) "was called *superstition*, becomes in this" (when speaking of Roman Catholics) "*religion, and religious forms*; which the papists pretending to connect with Christianity, and the Charge giving no hint that this is no more than a pretence, a plain reader must needs take this as spoken of the *means and memorials* of true religion, and will accordingly

their frequent holydays, the short prayers they are daily called to, and the occasional devotion enjoined by confessors. By these means their superstition sinks deep into the minds of the people, and their religion also into the minds of such among them as are serious and well-disposed. Our reformers, considering that some of these observances were in themselves wrong and superstitious, and others of them made subservient to the purposes of superstition, abolished them, reduced the form of religion to great simplicity, and enjoined no more particular rules, nor left any thing more of what was external in religion, than was in a manner necessary to preserve a sense of religion itself upon the minds of the people. But a great part of this is neglected by the generality amongst us; for instance, the service of the church, not only upon common days, but also upon saints' days; and several other things might be mentioned. Thus they have no customary admonition, no public call to recollect the thoughts of God and religion from one Sunday to another.

It was far otherwise under the law. *These words,** says Moses to the children of Israel, *which I command thee, shall be in thine heart: and thou shalt teach them*

consider these as recommended to his practice and imitation." If a plain reader, at first view of the passage alluded to, should inadvertently fall into such a mistake, he would find that mistake immediately corrected by the very next sentence that follows, where the religion of the Roman Catholics, and their superstition, are distinguished from each other in express words But the terms in question are used with the strictest propriety. The design of the bishop, in this part of his Charge, is to consider religion, not under the notion of its being true, but as it affects the senses and imaginations of the multitude. For so the paragraph begins: "That which men *have accounted* religion in the several countries of the world" (whether the religion be true or false is beside his present argument), "generally speaking, has had a great and conspicuous part in all public appearances." This position he illustrates by three examples, the Heathen, the Mahometan, and the Roman Catholic religions. The two first of these, having little or nothing of true religion belonging to them, may well enough be characterized under the common name of superstition: the last contains a mixture of both; which therefore the bishop, like a good writer, as well as a just reasoner, is careful to distinguish. In Roman Catholic countries, a man can hardly travel a mile without passing a crucifix erected on the road side: he may either stop to worship the image represented on the cross, or he may simply be reminded by it of his own relation to Christ crucified; thus by one and the same outward sign, "religion may be recalled to his thoughts," or superstition may take possession of his mind. In the celebration of the eucharist, the elements of bread and wine are regarded by a papist as the very body and blood of Christ; to a protestant, they appear only as symbols and memorials of that body and blood: what in one is an act of rational devotion, becomes in the other an instance of the grossest superstition, if not idolatry.

* Deut. vi. 6, 7.

*diligently unto thy children, and shalt talk of them when thou sittest in thine house, and when thou walkest by the way, and when thou liest down, and when thou risest up.** And as they were commanded this, so it is obvious how much the constitution of that law was adapted to effect it, and keep religion ever in view. And without somewhat of this nature, piety will grow languid even among the better sort of men; and the worst will go on quietly in an abandoned course, with fewer interruptions from within than they would have, were religious reflections forced oftener upon their minds,† and consequently with

* Allowing that "what Moses in this passage wanted to have effected was obedience to the *moral* law," nothing, sure, could be of greater use in securing that obedience than the practice here enjoined. Our *inquirer*, however, is of a different opinion, and "very much questions whether his lordship could have fallen upon any passage in the Old Testament, which relates at all to his subject, that would have been less favourable to his argument." *Who shall decide*, &c.?—The bishop goes on, "As they (the Jews) were commanded this, so it is obvious how much the constitution of their law was adapted to effect it, and keep religion ever in view." Upon which the *inquirer* remarks, "It was then very ill, or at least very unwisely done, to abrogate that law, whose constitution was adapted to so excellent a purpose." Let us first see what may be offered in defence of the bishop, and then consider what is to be said in answer to his opponent. The purpose for which the Mosaic constitution was established was this: to preserve, amidst a world universally addicted to polytheism and idolatry, the great doctrine of the Unity of the Divine Nature, *till the seed should come to whom the promise was made.* As a means to this end, the Israelites were not only to be kept separate from every other nation; but, the better to ensure such separation, they were to be constantly employed in a multifarious ritual, which left them neither time nor opportunity for deviating into the superstitious observances of their pagan neighbours. And this, I suppose, may suffice for vindicating the bishop's assertion, that "the constitution of the Jewish law was adapted to keep religion ever in view." But the Jewish law was not only adapted to this end; we are next to observe, that the end itself was actually gained. For though it be too notorious to be denied, that the Jews did not always confine their religious homage to the God of Israel, but polluted the service, due to him alone, with foreign worship; yet, even in their worst defection, it should be remembered, they never totally rejected the true Jehovah; and after their return from captivity, they were so thoroughly cured of all remaining propensity to the idolatrous rites of heathenism, as never again to violate their allegiance to the God of their fathers. It appears then, that, in consequence of the Jewish separation, the principle of the Unity was in fact preserved inviolate among that people till the coming of Christ. When the Mosaic constitution had thus attained its end, and mankind were now prepared for the reception of a *better covenant*, the law expired of course; the partition wall that had divided the Jew from the Gentile was taken down, and all distinction between them lost, under the common name of Christians. And this may suffice to show, in opposition to our *inquirer*, that it was both very *well* and very *wisely* done to abrogate a law, when the purpose for which the law had been enacted was accomplished.

† "According to the bishop's doctrine," then, says the *inquirer*, "it should be not only good policy, but wholesome discipline, to *force* men in *England* to come to church, and in *France* to go to mass." And again, "If externals have this virtue to *enforce* religious reflections, it must be right to *compel* those who are indisposed to such reflections, to attend these memorials." Yes; granting that the sense of the passage in the Charge is not shamefully perverted, and that we are to understand the bishop here to speak of *external* force and compulsion. Whereas, by "religious reflections *forced*," is plainly meant no more than religious reflections oftener *thrown*

less probability of their amendment. Indeed in most ages of the church, the care of reasonable men has been, as there has been for the most part occasion, to draw the people off from laying too great weight upon external things; upon formal acts of piety. But the state of matters is quite changed now with us. These things are neglected to a degree, which is, and cannot but be attended with a decay of all that is good. It is highly seasonable now to instruct the people in the importance of external religion.*

And doubtless under this head must come into consideration a proper regard to the structures which are consecrated to the service of God. In the present turn of the age, one may observe a wonderful frugality in every thing which has respect to religion, and extravagance in every thing else. But amidst the appearances of opulence and improvement in all common things, which are now seen in most places, it would be hard to find a reason why these monuments of ancient piety should not be preserved in their original beauty and magnificence. But in the least opulent places they must be preserved in becoming repair; and every thing relating to the divine service be, however, decent and clean; otherwise we shall vilify the face of religion whilst we keep it up. All this is indeed principally the duty of others. Yours is to press strongly upon them what is their duty in this respect, and admonish them of it often, if they are negligent.

in men s way, *brought* more frequently *into their thoughts*, so as to produce an habitual recollection that they are always in the divine presence.

* "The importance of external religion," the *inquirer* remarks, "is the grand engine of the papists, which they play with the greatest effect upon our common people, who are always soonest taken and ensnared by *form* and *show*; and, so far as we concur with them in the principle, we are doing their work; since, if externals, as such, are important, the plain natural consequence is, *the more of them the better.*" He had the same reflection once before: "If true religion cannot be preserved among men without *forms*, the consequence must be, that the *Romish* religion, having ——*more frequent* occurrences of forms, is better than other religions which have *fewer* of these——occurrences." To this argument I reply, *Nego consequentiam.* There may be too much of form in religion, as well as too little: the one leads to enthusiasm, the other degenerates into superstition; one is puritanism, the other popery; whereas the rational worship of God is equally removed from either extreme. Did the *inquirer* never hear of the possibility of having too much of a good thing? Or does he suppose, with the late historian of Great Britain, that all religion is divided into two species, the superstitious and the fanatical; and that whatever is not one of these, must of necessity be the other?

But then you must be sure to take care and not neglect that part of the sacred fabric which belongs to you to maintain in repair and decency. Such neglect would be great impiety in you, and of most pernicious example to others. Nor could you, with any success, or any propriety, urge upon them their duty in a regard in which you yourselves should be openly neglectful of it.

Bishop Fleetwood has observed,* that *unless the good public spirit of building, repairing, and adorning* churches *prevails a great deal more among us, and be more encouraged, a hundred years will bring to the ground a huge number of our churches.* This excellent prelate made this observation forty years ago: and no one, I believe, will imagine, that the good spirit he has recommended prevails more at present than it did then.

But if these appendages of the divine service are to be regarded, doubtless the divine service itself is more to be regarded; and the conscientious attendance upon it ought often to be inculcated upon the people, as a plain precept of the gospel, as the means of grace, and what has peculiar promises annexed to it. But external acts of piety and devotion, and the frequent returns of them, are, moreover, necessary to keep up a sense of religion, which the affairs of the world will otherwise wear out of men's hearts. And the frequent returns, whether of public devotions, or of any thing else, to introduce religion into men's serious thoughts, will have an influence upon them, in proportion as they are susceptible of religion, and not given over to a reprobate mind. For this reason, besides others, the service of the church ought to be celebrated as often as you can have a congregation to attend it.

But since the body of the people, especially in country places, cannot be brought to attend it oftener than one day in a week; and since this is in no sort enough to keep up in them a due sense of religion; it were greatly to be wished they could be persuaded to any thing which might, in some measure, supply the want of more frequent public devotions, or serve the like purposes.

* Charge to the Clergy of St Asaph, 1710.

Family prayers, regularly kept up in every house, would have a great and good effect.

Secret prayer, as expressly as it is commanded by our Saviour, and as evidently as it is implied in the notion of piety, will yet, I fear, be grievously forgotten by the generality, till they can be brought to fix for themselves certain times of the day for it; since this is not done to their hands, as it was in the Jewish church by custom or authority. Indeed custom, as well as the manifest propriety of the thing, and examples of good men in Scripture, justify us in insisting, that none omit their prayers morning or evening, who have not thrown off all regards to piety. But secret prayer comprehends not only devotions before men begin and after they have ended the business of the day, but such also as may be performed while they are employed in it, or even in company. And truly, if, besides our more set devotions, morning and evening, all of us would fix upon certain times of the day, so that the return of the hour should remind us, to say short prayers, or exercise our thoughts in a way equivalent to this; perhaps there are few persons in so high and habitual a state of piety, as not to find the benefit of it. If it took up no more than a minute or two, or even less time than that, it would serve the end I am proposing; it would be a recollection, that we are in the Divine presence, and contribute to our *being in the fear of the Lord all the day long.*

A duty of the like kind, and serving to the same purpose, is the particular acknowledgment of God when we are partaking of his bounty at our meals. The neglect of this is said to have been scandalous to a proverb in the heathen world;* but it is without shame laid aside at the tables of the highest and the lowest rank among us.

And as parents should be admonished, and it should be pressed upon their consciences, to teach their children their prayers and catechism, it being what they are obliged to upon all accounts; so it is proper to be mentioned here, as a means by which they will bring the

* Cudworth on the Lord's Supper, p. 8. Casaub. in Athenæum, l. i. c. xi. p. 22. Dupert. Præl. in Theophrastum, ed. Needham, c. ix. p. 335, &c.

principles of Christianity often to their own minds, instead of laying aside all thoughts of it from week's-end to week's-end.

General exhortations to piety, abstracted from the particular circumstances of it, are of great use to such as are already got into a religious course of life; but, such as are not, though they be touched with them, yet when they go away from church, they scarce know where to begin, or how to set about what they are exhorted to. And it is with respect to religion, as in the common affairs of life, in which many things of great consequence intended, are yet never done at all, because they may be done at any time, and in any manner; which would not be, were some determinate time and manner voluntarily fixed upon for the doing of them. Particular rules and directions then concerning the times and circumstances of performing acknowledged duties, bring religion nearer to practice; and such as are really proper, and cannot well be mistaken, and are easily observed.—Such particular rules in religion, prudently recommended, would have an influence upon the people.

All this indeed may be called form: as every thing external in religion may be merely so. And therefore whilst we endeavour, in these and other like instances, to keep up the *form of godliness** amongst those who are our care, and over whom we have any influence, we must endeavour also that this form be made more and more subservient to promote the *power* of it.* Admonish them to take heed that they mean what they say in their prayers, that their thoughts and intentions go along with their words, that they really in their hearts exert and exercise before God the affections they express with their mouth. Teach them, not that external religion is nothing, for this is not true in any sense; it being scarce possible, but that it will lay some sort of restraint upon a man's morals; and it is moreover of good effect with respect to the world about him. But teach them that regard to one duty will in no sort atone for the neglect of any other. Endeavour to raise in their hearts such a sense of God as shall be an habitual, ready principle of reverence

* 2 Tim. iii. 5.

love, gratitude, hope, trust, resignation, and obedience. Exhort them to make use of every circumstance, which brings the subject of religion at all before them; to turn their hearts habitually to him; to recollect seriously the thoughts of his presence *in whom they live and move and have their being*, and by a short act of their mind devote themselves to his service. — If, for instance, persons would accustom themselves to be thus admonished by the very sight of a church, could it be called superstition? Enforce upon them the necessity of making religion their principal concern, as what is the express condition of the gospel covenant, and what the very nature of the thing requires. Explain to them the terms of that covenant of mercy, founded in the incarnation, sacrifice, and intercession of Christ, together with the promised assistance of the Holy Ghost, not to supersede our own endeavours, but to render them effectual. The greater festivals of the church, being instituted for commemorating the several parts of the gospel history, of course lead you to explain these its several doctrines, and show the Christian practice which arises out of them. And the more occasional solemnities of religion, as well as these festivals, will often afford you the fairest opportunities of enforcing all these things in familiar conversation. Indeed all *affectation* of talking piously is quite nauseous: and though there be nothing of this, yet men will easily be disgusted at the too great frequency or length of these occasional admonitions. But a word of God and religion dropped sometimes in conversation, gently, and without any thing severe or forbidding in the manner of it, this is not unacceptable. It leaves an impression, is repeated again by the hearers, and often remembered by plain well-disposed persons longer than one would think. Particular circumstances too, which render men more apt to receive instruction, should be laid hold of to talk seriously to their consciences. For instance, after a man's recovery from a dangerous sickness, how proper is it to advise him to recollect and ever bear in mind, what were his hopes or fears, his wishes and resolutions, when under the apprehension of death; in order to bring him to repentance, or confirm him in a course of piety, according as his life and character has been. So likewise the terrible accidents which often happen from riot and debauchery, and indeed almost every vice, are occasions providentially thrown in your way, to discourse against these vices in common conversation, as well as from the pulpit, upon any such accidents happening in your parish, or in a neighbouring one. Occasions and circumstances of a like kind to some or other of these occur often, and ought, if I may so speak, to be catched at, as opportunities of conveying instruction, both public and private, with great force and advantage.

Public instruction is absolutely necessary, and can in no sort be dispensed with. But as it is common to all who are present, many persons strangely neglect to appropriate what they hear to themselves, to their own heart and life. Now the only remedy for this in our power is a particular personal application. And a personal application makes a very different impression from a common, general one. It were therefore greatly to be wished, that every man should have the principles of Christianity, and his own particular duty enforced upon his conscience, in a manner suited to his capacity, in private. And besides the occasional opportunities of doing this, some of which have been intimated, there are stated opportunities of doing it. Such, for instance, is confirmation: and the usual age for confirmation is that time of life, from which youth must become more and more their own masters, when they are often leaving their father's house, going out into the wide world and all its numerous temptations; against which they particularly want to be fortified, by having strong and lively impressions of religion made upon their minds. Now the 61st canon expressly requires, that every minister that hath care of souls shall use his best endeavour to prepare and make able as many as he can to be confirmed; which cannot be done as it ought without such personal application to each candidate in particular as I am recommending. Another opportunity for doing this is, when any one of your parishioners signifies his name as intending for the first time to be partaker of the communion. The rubric requires, that all persons, whenever they intend to receive, shall signify their names beforehand to the minister; which, if it be not insisted upon in all cases, ought absolutely to be insisted upon for the first time. Now this even lays it in your way to discourse with them in private upon the nature and benefits of this sacrament, and enforce upon them the importance and necessity of religion. However I do not mean to put this upon the same foot with catechising youth, and preparing them for confirmation; these being indispensable obligations, and expressly commanded by our canons. This private intercourse with your parishioners preparatory to their first communion, let it, if you please, be considered as a voluntary service to religion on your part, and a voluntary instance of docility on theirs. I will only add as to this practice, that it is regularly kept up by some persons, and particularly by one, whose exemplary behaviour in every part of the pastoral office is enforced upon you by his station of authority and influence in (this part* especially of) the diocess.

I am very sensible, my brethren, that some of these things in places where they are greatly wanted are impracticable, from the largeness of parishes, suppose. And where there is no impediment of this sort, yet the performance of them will depend upon others, as well as upon you. People cannot be admonished or instructed in private, unless they will permit it. And little will you be able to do in forming the minds of children to a sense of religion, if their parents will not assist you in it; and yet much less, if they will frustrate your endeavours, by their bad example, and giving encouragement to their children to be dissolute. The like is to be said also of your influence in reforming the common people in general, in proportion as their superiors act in like manner to such parents; and whilst they, the lower people I mean, must have such numerous temptations to drunkenness and riot every where placed in their way. And it is cruel usage we often meet with, in being censured for not doing what we cannot do, without what he cannot have, the concurrence of our censurers. Doubtless very much reproach which now lights upon

* The archdeaconry of Northumberland.

the clergy would be found to fall elsewhere, if due allowances were made for things of this kind. But then we, my brethren, must take care and not make more than due allowances for them. If others deal uncharitably with us, we must deal impartially with ourselves, as in a matter of conscience, in determining what good is in our power to do: and not let indolence keep us from setting about what really is in our power; nor any heat of temper create obstacles in the prosecution of it, or render insuperable such as we find, when perhaps gentleness and patience would prevent or overcome them.

Indeed all this diligence to which I have been exhorting you and myself, for God forbid I should not consider myself as included in all the general admonitions you receive from me; all this diligence in these things does indeed suppose, that we *give ourselves wholly to them.* It supposes, not only that we have a real sense of religion upon our own minds, but also, that to promote the practice of it in others is habitually uppermost in our thought and intention, as the business of our lives. And this, my brethren, is the business of our lives, in every sense, and upon every account. It is the general business of all Christians as they have opportunity: it is our particular business. It is so, as we have devoted ourselves to it by the most solemn engagements; as, according to our *Lord's appointment,* we *live of the gospel;** and as the preservation and advancement of religion, in such and such districts, are, in some respects, our appropriated trust.

By being faithful in the discharge of this our trust, by thus *taking heed to the ministry we have received in the Lord that we fulfil it,*† we shall do our part towards reviving a practical sense of religion amongst the people committed to our care. And this will be the securest barrier against the efforts of infidelity; a great source of which plainly is, the endeavour to get rid of religious restraints. But whatever be our success with regard to others, we shall have the approbation of our consciences, and may rest assured, that, as to ourselves at least, *our labour is not in vain in the Lord.*‡

* 1 Cor. ix. 14. † Col. iv. 17. ‡ 1 Cor. xv. 58.

CORRESPONDENCE

BETWEEN

DR BUTLER AND DR CLARKE.

THE FIRST LETTER.

REVEREND SIR,

I SUPPOSE you will wonder at the present trouble from one who is a perfect stranger to you, though you are not so to him; but I hope the occasion will excuse my boldness. I have made it, sir, my business, ever since I thought myself capable of such sort of reasoning, to prove to myself the being and attributes of God. And being sensible that it is a matter of the last consequence, I endeavoured after a demonstrative proof; not only more fully to satisfy my own mind, but also in order to defend the great truths of natural religion, and those of the Christian revelation which follow from them, against all opposers: but must own with concern, that hitherto I have been unsuccessful; and though I have got very probable arguments, yet I can go but a very little way with demonstration in the proof of those things. When first your book on those subjects (which by all, whom I have discoursed with, is so justly esteemed) was recommended to me, I was in great hopes of having all my inquiries answered. But since in some places, either through my not understanding your meaning, or what else I know not, even that has failed me, I almost despair of ever arriving to such a satisfaction as I aim at, unless by the method I now use. You cannot but know, sir, that of two different expressions of the same thing, though equally clear to some persons, yet to others one of them is sometimes very obscure, though the other be perfectly intelligible. Perhaps this may be my case here; and could I see those of your arguments, of which I doubt, differently proposed, possibly I might yield a ready assent to them. This, sir, I cannot but think a sufficient excuse for the present trouble; it being such a one as I hope may prevail for an answer, with one who seems to aim at nothing more than that good work of instructing others.

In your Demonstration of the Being and Attributes of God, Prop. VI.* [edit. 2d. pp. 69, 70,] you propose to prove the infinity or omnipresence of the self-existent Being. The former part of the proof seems highly probable; but the latter part, which seems to aim at demonstration, is not to me convincing. The latter part of the paragraph is, if I mistake not, an entire argument of itself, which runs thus: "To suppose a finite being to be self-existent, is to say that it is a contradiction for that being not to exist, the absence of which may yet be conceived without a contradiction; which is the greatest absurdity in the world." The sense of these words ["the absence of which"] seems plainly to be determined by the following sentence, to mean its absence from any particular place. Which sentence is to prove it to be an absurdity; and is this: "For if a being can, without a contradiction, be absent from one place, it may, without a contradiction, be absent from another place, and from all places." Now supposing this to be a consequence, all that it proves is, that if a being can, without a contradiction, be absent from one place at one time, it may, without a contradiction, be absent from another place, and so from all places, at different times; (for I cannot see, that if a being can be absent from one place at one time, therefore it may, without a contradiction, be absent from all places at the same time, *i. e.* may cease to exist.) Now, if it proves no more than this, I cannot see that it reduces the supposition to any absurdity. Suppose I could demonstrate, that any particular man should live a thousand years; this man might, without a contradiction, be absent from one and from all places at different times; but it would not from thence follow, that he might be absent from all places at the same time, *i. e.* that he might cease to exist. No; this would be a contradiction, because I am supposed to have demonstrated that he should live a

* P. 45, edit. 4; p. 41, edit. 6; p. 43, edit. 7; p. 44, edit. 8.

thousand years. It would be exactly the same, if, instead of a thousand years, I should say, for ever; and the proof seems the same, whether it be applied to a self-existent or a dependent being.

What else I have to offer is in relation to your proof, that the self-existent being must of necessity be but one. Which proof is as follows, in Prop. VII.* [edit. 2d. p. 74.] "To suppose two or more different natures existing of themselves, necessarily, and independent from each other, implies this plain contradiction; that, each of them being independent from the other, they may either of them be supposed to exist alone; so that it will be no contradiction to imagine the other not to exist, and consequently neither of them will be necessarily existing." The supposition indeed implies, that since each of these beings is independent from the other, they may either of them exist alone, *i. e.* without any relation to, or dependence on, the other: but where is the third idea, to connect this proposition and the following one, viz., "so that it will be no contradiction to imagine the other not to exist?" Were this a consequence of the former proposition, I allow it would be demonstration, by the first corollary of Prop. III.† [2d edit. p. 26.] but since these two propositions, ["they may either of them be supposed to exist alone,"] and, ["so that it will be no contradiction to imagine the other not to exist,"] are very widely different; since likewise it is no immediate consequence, that because either may be supposed to exist independent from the other, therefore the other may be supposed not to exist at all; how is what was proposed, proved? That the propositions are different, I think is plain; and whether there be an immediate connexion, every body that reads your book must judge for themselves. I must say, for my own part, the absurdity does not appear at first sight, any more than the absurdity of saying that the angles below the base in an isosceles triangle are unequal; which though it is absolutely false, yet I suppose no one will lay down the contrary for an axiom; because, though it is true, yet there is need of a proof to make it appear so.

* P. 48. edit. 4; p. 44. edit. 6; p. 46. edit. 7; p. 47 edit. 8.

† P. 16, 17. edit. 4, 6, 7, and 8.

Perhaps it may be answered, that I have not rightly explained the words, "to exist alone;" and that they do not mean only, to exist independent from the other; but that "existing alone" means that nothing exists with it. Whether this or the other was meant, I cannot determine: but, which ever it was, what I have said will hold. For if this last be the sense of those words, ["they either of them may be supposed to exist alone;"] it indeed implies that it will be no contradiction to suppose the other not to exist: but then I ask, how come these two propositions to be connected; that, to suppose two different natures existing of themselves necessarily and independent from each other, implies that each of them may be supposed to exist alone in this sense? Which is exactly the same as I said before, only applied to different sentences. So that if "existing alone" be understood as I first took it, I allow it is implied in the supposition; but cannot see that the consequence is, that it will be no contradiction to suppose the other not to exist. But if the words, "existing alone," are meant in the latter sense, I grant, that if either of them be supposed thus to exist alone, it will be no contradiction to suppose the other not to exist: but then I cannot see, that to suppose two different natures existing, of themselves, necessarily and independent from each other, implies that either of them may be supposed to exist alone in this sense of the words; but, only, that either of them may be supposed to exist without having any relation to the other, and that there will be no need of the existence of the one in order to the existence of the other. But though upon this account, were there no other principle of its existence, it might cease to exist; yet on the account of the necessity of its own nature, which is quite distinct from the other, it is an absolute absurdity to suppose it not to exist.

Thus, sir, I have proposed my doubts, with the reasons of them. In which if I have wrested your words to another sense than you designed them, or in any respect argued unfairly, I assure you it was without design. So I hope you will impute it to mistake. And, if it will not be too great a trouble, let me once more beg the favour of a line from you, by which you will lay me under a particular obligation to be, what, with the rest of the world, I now am,

Reverend Sir, your most obliged servant, &c.

Nov. 4, 1713.

THE ANSWER TO THE FIRST LETTER.

Sir,

Did men who publish controversial papers accustom themselves to write with that candour and ingenuity, with which you propose your difficulties, I am persuaded almost all disputes might be very amicably terminated, either by men's coming at last to agree in opinion, or at least finding reason to suffer each other friendly to differ.

Your two objections are very ingenious, and urged with great strength and acuteness Yet I am not without hopes of being able to give you satisfaction in both of them. To your first, therefore, I answer: Whatever may, without a contradiction, be absent from any one place, at any one time, may also, without a contradiction, be absent from all places at all times. For, whatever is absolutely necessary at all, is absolutely necessary in every part of space, and in every point of duration. Whatever can at any time be conceived possible to be absent from any one part of space, may for the same reason [viz. the implying no contradiction in the nature of things] be conceived possible to be absent from every other part of space at the same time; either by ceasing to be, or by supposing it never to have begun to be. Your instance about demonstrating a man to live a thousand years, is what, I think, led you into the mistake; and is a good instance to lead you out of it again. You may suppose a man shall live a thousand years, or God may reveal and promise he shall live a thousand years; and upon that supposition, it shall not be possible for the man to be absent from all places in any part of that time. Very true: but why shall it not be possible? only because it is contrary to the supposition, or to the promise of God; but not contrary to the absolute nature of things; which would be the case, if the man existed necessarily, as every part of space does.

In supposing you could demonstrate, a man should live a thousand years, or one year; you make an impossible and contradictory supposition. For though you may know certainly (by revelation suppose) that he will live so long; yet this is only the certainty of a thing true in fact, not in itself necessary: and demonstration is applicable to nothing but what is necessary in itself, necessary in all places and at all times equally.

To your second difficulty, I answer: What exists necessarily, not only must so exist alone, as to be independent of any thing else; but, (being self-sufficient) may also so exist alone, as that every thing else may possibly (or without any contradiction in the nature of things) be supposed not to exist at all: and consequently (since that which may possibly be supposed not to exist at all, is not necessarily existent), no other thing can be necessarily existent. Whatever is necessarily existing, there is need of its existence in order to the supposal of the existence of any other thing; so that nothing can possibly be supposed to exist, without presupposing and including antecedently the existence of that which is necessary. For instance; the supposal of the existence of any thing whatever includes necessarily a presupposition of the existence of space and time; and if any thing could exist without space or time, it would follow that space and time were not necessarily existing. Therefore, the supposing any thing possibly to exist alone, so as not necessarily to include the presupposal of some other thing, proves demonstrably that that other thing is not necessarily existing; because, whatever has necessity of existence cannot possibly, in any conception whatsoever, be supposed away. There cannot possibly be any notion of the existence of any thing, there cannot possibly be any notion of existence at all, but what shall necessarily preinclude the notion of that which has necessary existence. And consequently the two propositions, which you judged independent, are really necessarily connected. These sorts of things are indeed very difficult to express, and not easy to be conceived but by very attentive minds: but to such as can and will attend, nothing, I think, is more demonstrably convictive.

If any thing still sticks with you in this or any other part of my books, I shall be very willing to be informed of it; who am, Sir, Your assured friend and servant,

S. C.

Nov. 10, 1713.

P. S. Many readers, I observe, have misunderstood my second general proposition; as if the words [" some one unchangeable and independent being,"] meant [one only—being;] whereas the true meaning, and all that the argument there requires, is, [some one at least.] That there can be but one, is the thing proved afterwards in the seventh proposition.

THE SECOND LETTER.

Reverend Sir,

I have often thought that the chief occasions of men s differing so much in their opinions, were, either their not understanding each other; or else, that, instead of ingenuously searching after truth, they have made it their business to find out arguments for the proof of what they have once asserted. However, it is certain there may be other reasons for persons not agreeing in their opinions: and where it is so, I cannot but think with you, that they will find reason to suffer each other to differ friendly; every man having a way of thinking, in some respects, peculiarly his own.

I am sorry I must tell you, your answers to my objections are not satisfactory. The reasons why I think them not so are as follow.

You say, " Whatever is absolutely necessary at all is absolutely necessary in every part of space, and in every point of duration." Were this evident, it would certainly prove what you bring it for; viz. that " whatever may, without a contradiction, be absent from one place at one time, may also be absent from all places at all times." But I do not conceive, that the idea of ubiquity is contained in the idea of self-existence, or directly follows from it; any otherwise than as, whatever exists must exist somewhere. You add, "Whatever can at any time be conceived possible to be absent from any one part of space, may for the same reason [viz. the implying no contradiction in the nature of things] be conceived possible to be absent from every other part of space, at the same time." Now I cannot see, that I can make these two suppositions for the same reason, or upon the same account. The reason why I conceive this being may be absent from one place, is because it doth not contradict the former proof [drawn from the nature of things], in which I proved only that it must necessarily exist. But the other supposition, viz. that I can conceive it possible to be absent from every part of space at one and the same time, directly contradicts the proof that it must exist somewhere; and so is an express contradiction. Unless it be said, that as, when we have proved the three angles of a triangle equal to two right ones, that relation of the equality of its angles to two right ones will be wherever a triangle exists; so, when we have proved the necessary existence of a being, this being must exist every where. But there is a great difference between these two things: the one being the proof of a certain relation, upon supposition of such a being's existence with such particular properties; and consequently, wherever this being and these properties exist, this relation must exist too: but from the proof of the necessary existence of a being, it is no evident consequence that it exists every where. My using the word *demonstration*, instead of *proof which leaves no room for doubt*, was through negligence, for I never heard of strict demonstration of matter of fact.

In your answer to my second difficulty, you say, "Whatsoever is necessarily existing, there is need of its existence, in order to the supposal of the existence of any other thing." All the consequences you draw from this proposition, I see proved demonstrably; and consequently, that the two propositions I thought independent are closely connected. But how, or upon what account, is there need of the existence of whatever is necessarily existing, in order to the existence of any other thing? Is it as there is need of space and duration, in order to the existence of any thing; or is it needful only as the cause of the existence of all other things? If the former be said, as your instance seems to intimate: I answer; space and duration are very abstruse in their natures, and, I think, cannot properly be called things, but are considered rather as affections which belong, and in the order of our thoughts are antecedently necessary, to the existence of all things. And I can no more conceive how a necessarily existent being can, on the same account, or in the same manner as space and duration are, be needful in order to the existence of any other being, than I can conceive extension attributed to a thought; that idea no more belonging to a thing existing, than extension belongs to thought. But if the latter be said, that there is need of the existence of whatever is a necessary being, in order to the existence of any other thing; only as this necessary being must be the cause of the existence of all other things: I think this is plainly begging the question; for it supposes that there is no other being exists, but what is casual, and so not necessary. And on what other account, or in what other manner than one of these two, there can be need of the existence of a necessary being in order to the existence of any thing else, I cannot conceive.

Thus, sir, you see I entirely agree with you in all the consequences you have drawn from your suppositions, but cannot see the truth of the suppositions themselves.

I have aimed at nothing in my style, but only to be intelligible; being sensible that it is very difficult (as you observe) to express one's self on these sorts of subjects, especially for one who is altogether unaccustomed to write upon them.

I have nothing at present more to add, but my sincerest thanks for your trouble in answering my letter, and for your professed readiness to be acquainted with any other difficulty that I may meet with in any of your writings I am willing to interpret this, as somewhat like a promise of an answer to what I have now written, if there be any thing in it which deserves one. I am, Reverend Sir,

Your most obliged humble servant.

Nov. 23, 1713.

THE ANSWER TO THE SECOND LETTER.

SIR,

IT seems to me, that the reason why you do not apprehend ubiquity to be necessarily connected with self-existence, is because, in the order of your ideas, you first conceive a being (a finite being, suppose), and then conceive self-existence to be a property of that being; as the angles are properties of a triangle, when a triangle exists: whereas, on the contrary, necessity of existence, not being a property consequent upon the supposition of the things existing, but antecedently the cause or ground of that existence; it is evident this necessity, being not limited to any antecedent subject, as angles are to a triangle; but being itself original, absolute, and (in order of nature) antecedent to all existence; cannot but be every where, for the same reason that it is any where. By applying this reasoning to the instance of space, you will find, that by consequence it belongs truly to that substance, whereof space is a property,* as duration also is. What you say about a necessary being existing somewhere, supposes it to be finite; and being finite, supposes some cause which determined that such a certain quantity of that being should exist, neither more nor less: and that cause must either be a voluntary cause; or else such a necessary cause, the quantity of whose power must be determined and limited by some other cause. But in original absolute necessity, antecedent (in order of nature) to the existence of any thing, nothing of all this can have place; but the necessity is necessarily every where alike.

Concerning the second difficulty, I answer: That which exists necessarily, is needful to the existence of any other thing; not considered now as a cause (for that indeed is begging the question), but as a *sine quo non;* in the sense as space is necessary to every thing, and nothing can possibly be conceived to exist, without thereby presupposing space: which therefore I apprehend to be a property or mode of the self-existent substance;

* Or, mode of existence.

and that, by being evidently necessary itself, it proves that the substance, of which it is a property, must also be necessary; necessary both in itself, and needful to the existence of any thing else whatsoever. Extension indeed does not belong to thought, because thought is not a being; but there is need of extension to the existence of every being, to a being which has or has not thought, or any other quality whatsoever. I am, Sir,

Your real friend and servant.

London, Nov. 28, 1713.

THE THIRD LETTER.

Reverend Sir,

I do not very well understand your meaning, when you say that you think, "in the order of my ideas I first conceive a being (finite suppose) to exist, and then conceive self-existence to be a property of that being." If you mean that I first suppose a finite being to exist I know not why; affirming necessity of existence to be only a consequent of its existence; and that, when I have supposed it finite, I very safely conclude it is not infinite; I am utterly at a loss, upon what expressions in my letter this conjecture can be founded. But if you mean, that I first of all prove a being to exist from eternity, and then, from the reasons of things, prove that such a being must be eternally necessary; I freely own it. Neither do I conceive it to be irregular or absurd; for there is a great difference between the order in which things exist, and the order in which I prove to myself that they exist. Neither do I think my saying a necessary being exists somewhere, suppose it to be finite; it only supposes that this being exists in space, without determining whether here, or there, or every where.

To my second objection, you say, "That which exists necessarily, is needful to the existence of any other thing, as a *sine qua non;* in the sense space is necessary to every thing: which is proved (you say) by this consideration, that space is a property of the self-existent substance; and being both necessary in itself, and needful to the existence of every thing else; consequently the substance, of which it is a property, must be so too." Space, I own, is in one sense a property of the self-existent substance; but, in the same sense, it is also a property of all other substances. The only difference is in respect to the quantity. And since every part of space, as well as the whole, is necessary; every substance consequently must be self-existent, because it hath this self-existent property. Which since you will not admit for true; if it directly follows from your arguments, they cannot be conclusive.

What you say under the first head proves, I think, to a very great probability, though not to me with the evidence of demonstration: but your arguments under the second I am not able to see the force of.

I am so far from being pleased that I can form objections to your arguments, that, besides the satisfaction it would have given me in my own mind, I should have thought it an honour to have entered into your reasonings, and seen the force of them. I cannot desire to trespass any more upon your better employed time; so shall only add my hearty thanks for your trouble on my account, and that I am with the greatest respect,

Reverend Sir,

Your most obliged humble servant.

Dec. 5, 1713.

THE ANSWER TO THE THIRD LETTER.

SIR,

THOUGH, when I turn my thoughts every way, I fully persuade myself there is no defect in the argument itself; yet in my manner of expression I am satisfied there must be some want of clearness, when there remains any difficulty to a person of your abilities and sagacity. I did not mean that your saying a necessary being exists somewhere, does necessarily suppose it to be finite; but that the manner of expression is apt to excite in the mind an idea of a finite being, at the same time that you are thinking of a necessary being, without accurately attending to the nature of that necessity by which it exists. Necessity absolute, and antecedent (in order of nature) to the existence of any subject, has nothing to limit it; but, if it operates at all (as it must needs do), it must operate (if I may so speak) every where and at all times alike. Determination of a particular quantity, or particular time or place of existence of any thing, cannot arise but from somewhat external to the thing itself. For example: why there should exist just such a small determinate quantity of matter, neither more nor less, interspersed in the immense vacuities of space, no reason can be given. Nor can there be any thing in nature, which could have determined a thing so indifferent in itself, as is the measure of that quantity; but only the will of an intelligent and free agent. To suppose matter, or any other substance, necessarily existing in a finite determinate quantity; in an inch-cube, for instance; or in any certain number of cube-inches, and no more; is exactly the same absurdity, as supposing it to exist necessarily, and yet for a finite duration only: which every one sees to be a plain contradiction. The argument is likewise the same, in the question about the original of motion. Motion cannot be necessarily existing; because, it being evident that all determinations of motion are equally possible in themselves, the original determination of the motion of any particular body this way rather than the contrary way, could not be necessarily in itself, but was either caused by the will of an intelligent and free agent, or else was an effect produced and determined without any cause at all; which is an express contradiction: as I have shown in my *Demonstration of the Being and Attributes of God.* [Page 14, edit. 4th and 5th; page 12, edit. 6th and 7th.]

To the second head of argument, I answer: Space is a property [or mode] of the self-existent substance; but not of any other substances. All other substances are in space, and are penetrated by it; but the self-existent substance is not in space, nor penetrated by it, but is itself (if I may so speak) the substratum of space, the ground of the existence of space and duration itself. Which [space and duration] being evidently necessary, and yet themselves not substances, but properties or modes, show evidently that the substance, without which these properties could not subsist, is itself much more (if that were possible) necessary. And as space and duration are needful (i. e. *sine qua non*) to the existence of every thing else; so consequently is the substance, to which these properties belong in that peculiar manner which I before mentioned. I am, Sir,

Your affectionate friend and servant.

Dec. 10, 1713.

THE FOURTH LETTER.

REVEREND SIR,

WHATEVER is the occasion of my not seeing the force of your reasonings, I cannot impute it to [what you do] the want of clearness in your expression. I am too well acquainted with myself, to think my not understanding an argument, a sufficient reason to conclude that it is either improperly expressed, or not conclusive; unless I can clearly show the defect of it. It is with the greatest satisfaction I must tell you, that the more I reflect on your first argument, the more I am convinced of the truth of it; and it now seems to me altogether unreasonable to suppose absolute necessity can have any relation to one part of space more than to another; and if so, an absolutely necessary being must exist every where.

I wish I was as well satisfied in respect to the other. You say, "All substances, except the self-existent one, are in space, and are penetrated by it." All substances doubtless, whether body or spirit, exist in space: but when I say that a spirit exists in space, were I put upon telling my meaning, I know not how I could do it any other way than by saying, such a particular quantity of space terminates the capacity of acting in finite spirits at one and the same time; so that they cannot act beyond that determined quantity. Not but that I think there is somewhat in the manner of existence of spirits in respect of space, that more directly answers to the manner of the existence of body; but what that is, or of the manner of their existence, I cannot possibly form an idea. And it seems (if possible) much more difficult to determine what relation the self-existent Being hath to space. To say he exists in space, after the same manner that other substances do (somewhat like which I too rashly asserted in my last), perhaps would be placing the Creator too much on a level with the creature; or however, it is not plainly and evidently true: and to say the self-existent substance is the substratum of space, in the common sense of the word, is scarce intelligible, or at least is not evident. Now though there may be a hundred relations distinct from either of these; yet how we should come by ideas of them, I cannot conceive. We may indeed have ideas to the words, and not altogether depart from the common sense of them, when we say the self-existent substance is the substratum of space, or the ground of its existence: but I see no reason to think it true, because space seems to me to be as absolutely self-existent, as it is possible any thing can be: so that, make what other supposition you please, yet we cannot help supposing immense space; because there must be either an infinity of being, or (if you will allow the expression) an infinite vacuity of being. Perhaps it may be objected to this, that though space is really necessary, yet the reason of its being necessary is its being a property of the self-existent substance; and that it being so evidently necessary, and its dependence on the self-existent substance not so evident, we are ready to conclude it absolutely self-existent, as well as necessary; and that this is the reason why the idea of space forces itself on our minds, antecedent to, and exclusive of (as to the ground of its existence) all other things. Now this, though it is really an objection, yet is no direct answer to what I have said: because it supposes the only thing to be proved, viz. that the reason why space is necessary is its being a property of a self-existent substance. And supposing it not to be evident, that space is absolutely self-existent; yet, while it is doubtful, we cannot argue as though the contrary were certain, and we were sure that space was only a property of the se'f-existent substance. But now, if space be not absolutely independent, I do not see what we can conclude is so: for it is manifestly necessary itself, as well as antecedently needful to the existence of all other things, not excepting (as I think) even the self-existent substance.

All your consequences, I see, follow demonstrably from your supposition; and, were that evident, I believe it would serve to prove several other things as well as what you bring it for. Upon which account, I should be extremely pleased to see it proved by any one. For, as I design the search after truth as the business of my life, I shall not be ashamed to learn from any person; though, at the same time, I cannot but be sensible, that instruction from some men is like the gift of a prince, it reflects an honour on the person on whom it lays an obligation. I am, Reverend Sir,

Your obliged servant.

Dec. 16, 1713.

THE ANSWER TO THE FOURTH LETTER.

SIR,

MY being out of town most part of the month of January, and some other accidental avocations, hindered me from answering your letter sooner. The sum of the difficulties it contains is, I think, this: that "it is difficult to determine what relation the self-existent substance has to space:" that "to say it is the substratum of space, in the common sense of the word, is scarce intelligible, or, at least, is not evident:" that "space seems to be as absolutely self-existent, as it is possible any thing can be:" and that "its being a property of the self-existent substance is supposing the thing that was to be proved." This is entering indeed into the very bottom of the matter; and I will endeavour to give you as brief and clear an answer as I can.

That the self-existent substance is the substratum of space, or space a property of the self-existent substance, are not perhaps very proper expressions; nor is it easy to find such. But what I mean is this: The idea of space (as also of time or duration) is an abstract or partial idea; an idea of a certain quality or relation, which we evidently see to be necessarily existing; and yet which (not being itself a substance) at the same time necessarily presupposes a substance, without which it could not exist; which substance consequently must be itself (much more, if possible) necessarily existing. I know not how to explain this so well as by the following similitude. A blind man, when he tries to frame to himself the idea of body, his idea is nothing but that of hardness. A man that had eyes, but no power of motion, or sense of feeling at all; when he tried to frame to himself the idea of body, his idea would be nothing but that of colour. Now as, in these cases, hardness is not body, and colour is not body; but yet, to the understanding of these persons, those properties necessarily infer the being of a substance, of which substance itself the persons have no idea: so space to us is not itself substance, but it necessarily infers the being of a substance, which affects none of our present senses; and, being itself necessary, it follows, that the substance, which it infers, is (much more) necessary. I am, Sir,

Your affectionate friend and servant.

Jan. 29, 1713.

THE FIFTH LETTER.

REVEREND SIR,

YOU have very comprehensively expressed, in six or seven lines, all the difficulties of my letter; which I should have endeavoured to have made shorter, had I not been afraid an improper expression might possibly occasion a mistake of my meaning. I am very glad the debate is come into so narrow a compass; for I think now it entirely turns upon this, whether our ideas of space and duration are partial, so as to presuppose the existence of some other thing. Your similitude of the blind man is very apt, to explain your meaning (which I think I fully understand), but does not seem to come entirely up to the matter. For what is the reason that the blind man concludes there must be somewhat external, to give him that idea of hardness? It is because he supposes it impossible for him to be thus affected, unless there were some cause of it; which cause, should it be removed, the effect would immediately cease too; and he would no more have the idea of hardness, but by remembrance. Now to apply this to the instance of space and duration: Since a man, from his having these ideas, very justly concludes there must be somewhat external, which is the cause of them; consequently, should this cause (whatever it is) be taken away, his ideas would be so too: therefore, if what is supposed to be the cause be removed, and yet the idea remains, that supposed cause cannot be the real one. Now, granting the self-existent substance to be the substratum of these ideas, could we make the supposition of its ceasing to be, yet space and duration would still remain unaltered: which seems to show, that the self-existent substance is not the substratum of space and duration. Nor would it be an answer to the difficulty, to say that every property of the self-existent substance is as necessary as the substance itself; since that will only hold, while the substance itself exists; for there is implied, in the idea of a property, an impossibility of subsisting without its substratum. I grant, the supposition is absurd: but how otherwise can we know whether any thing be a property of such a substance, but by examining whether it should cease to be, if its supposed substance should do so? Notwithstanding what I have now said, I cannot say that I believe your argument not conclusive; for I must own my ignorance, that I am really at a loss about the nature of space and duration. But did it plainly appear that they were properties of a substance, we should have an easy way with the atheists: for it would at once prove demonstrably an eternal, necessary, self-existent Being; that there is but one such; and that he is needful in order to the existence of all other things. Which makes me think, that though it may be true, yet it is not obvious to every capacity: otherwise it would have been generally used, as a fundamental argument to prove the being of God.

I must add one thing more; that your argument for

the omnipresence of God seemed always to me very probable. But being very desirous to have it appear demonstrably conclusive, I was sometimes forced to say what was not altogether my opinion: not that I did this for the sake of disputing, (for, besides the particular disagreeableness of this to my own temper, I should surely have chosen another person to have trifled with;) but I did it to set off the objection to advantage, that it might be more fully answered. I heartily wish you as fair treatment from your opponents in print, as I have had from you; though, I must own, I cannot see, in those that I have read, that unprejudiced search after truth, which I would have hoped for.

I am, Reverend Sir,
Your most humble servant.

Feb 3, 1713.

THE ANSWER TO THE FIFTH LETTER.

Sir,

In a multitude of business, I mislaid your last letter, and could not answer it, till it came again to my hands by chance. We seem to have pushed the matter in question between us as far as it will go; and, upon the whole, I cannot but take notice, I have very seldom met with persons so reasonable and unprejudiced as yourself, in such debates as these.

I think all I need say, in answer to the reasoning in your letter, is, that your granting the absurdity of the supposition you were endeavouring to make, is consequently granting the necessary truth of my argument. If* space and duration necessarily remain, even after they are supposed to be taken away; and be not (as it is plain they are not) themselves substances; that the† substance,

* Ut partium temporis ordo est immutabilis, sic etiam ordo partium spatii. Moventur hæ de locis suis, et movebuntur (ut ita dicam) de seipsis. *Newton. Princip. Mathemat. schol. ad definit.* 8.

† Deus non est æternitas vel infinitas, sed æternus et infinitus; non est duratio vel spatium, sed durat et adest. Durat semper, et adest ubique; et existendo semper et ubique, durationem et spatium, æternitatem et infinitatem, constituit. Cum unaquæque spatii particula sit semper; et unumquodque durationis indivisibile momentum ubique; certe rerum omnium Fabricator ac Dominus non erit nunquam nusquam. Omnipræsens est, non per virtutem solam, sed etiam per substantiam: nam virtus sine substantia subsistere non potest. In ipso continentur et moventur universa &c. *Newton. Princip. Mathemat. Schol. general. sub finem.*

on whose existence they depend, will necessarily remain likewise, even after it is supposed to be taken away: which shows that supposition to be impossible and contradictory.

As to your observation at the end of your letter; that the argument I have insisted on, if it were obvious to every capacity, should have more frequently been used as a fundamental argument for a proof of the being of God: the true cause why it has been seldom urged, is, I think, this; that the universal prevalency of Cartes's absurd notions (teaching that* matter is necessarily infinite and necessarily eternal, and ascribing all things to mere mechanic laws of motion, exclusive of final causes, and of all will and intelligence and divine Providence from the government of the world) hath incredibly blinded the eyes of common reason, and prevented men from discerning *him in whom they live, and move, and have their being*. The like has happened in some other instances. How universally have men for many ages believed, that eternity is no duration at all, and infinity no amplitude! Something of the like kind has happened in the matter of transubstantiation, and, I think, in the scholastic notion of the Trinity, &c.

I am, Sir,
Your affectionate friend and servant.

April 8, 1713.

* Puto implicare contradictionem, ut mundus [meaning the material world] sit finitus *Cartes. Epist.* 69. *Partis primæ.*

THE END.

www.ingramcontent.com/pod-product-compliance
Lightning Source LLC
LaVergne TN
LVHW021105110826
845150LV00001B/171